193—227

# The First Amendment

ASPEN CASEBOOK SERIES

# The First Amendment

**Fifth Edition**

## Geoffrey R. Stone
Edward H. Levi, Distinguished Service Professor
University of Chicago Law School

## Louis M. Seidman
Carmack Waterhouse Professor of Constitutional Law
Georgetown University Law Center

## Cass R. Sunstein
Robert Walmsley University Professor
Harvard Law School

## Mark V. Tushnet
William Nelson Cromwell Professor of Law
Harvard Law School

## Pamela S. Karlan
Kenneth and Harle Montgomery Professor of Public Interest Law
Stanford Law School

Published by Wolters Kluwer in New York.

Wolters Kluwer Legal & Regulatory Solutions U.S. serves customers worldwide with CCH, Aspen Publishers, and Kluwer Law International products. (www.WKLegaledu.com)

To contact Customer Service, e-mail customer.service@wolterskluwer.com, call 1-800-234-1660, fax 1-800-901-9075, or mail correspondence to:

Wolters Kluwer
Attn: Order Department
PO Box 990
Frederick, MD 21705

Printed in the United States of America.

2 3 4 5 6 7 8 9 0

ISBN 978-1-4548-6824-8

**Library of Congress Cataloging-in-Publication Data**

Names: Stone, Geoffrey R., author. | Seidman, Louis Michael, author. | Sunstein, Cass R., author. | Tushnet, Mark V., 1945- author. | Karlan, Pamela S., author.
Title: The First Amendment / Geoffrey R. Stone, Louis M. Seidman, Cass R.Sunstein, Mark V. Tushnet, Pamela S. Karlan.
Description: Fifth edition. | New York : Wolters Kluwer, 2016. | Series: Aspen casebook series | Includes bibliographical references and index.
Identifiers: LCCN 2015040253 | ISBN 9781454868248 (alk. paper)
 Subjects: LCSH: Freedom of speech — United States. | Freedom of the press — United States. | Freedom of religion — United States. | United States. Constitution. 1st Amendment.
Classification: LCC KF4770 .F558 2016 | DDC 342.7308/53 — dc23 LC record available at http://lccn.loc.gov/2015040253

# About Wolters Kluwer Legal & Regulatory Solutions U.S.

Wolters Kluwer Legal & Regulatory Solutions U.S. delivers expert content and solutions in the areas of law, corporate compliance, health compliance, reimbursement, and legal education. Its practical solutions help customers successfully navigate the demands of a changing environment to drive their daily activities, enhance decision quality and inspire confident outcomes.

Serving customers worldwide, its legal and regulatory solutions portfolio includes products under the Aspen Publishers, CCH Incorporated, Kluwer Law International, ftwilliam.com and MediRegs names. They are regarded as exceptional and trusted resources for general legal and practice-specific knowledge, compliance and risk management, dynamic workflow solutions, and expert commentary.

For our families

For our families

# Summary of Contents

## PART I

## Freedom of Expression                                          1

## I

### The History and Philosophy of Free Expression                3

## II

### Content-Based Restrictions: Dangerous Ideas and Information    17

## III

### Overbreadth, Vagueness, and Prior Restraint                    111

## IV

### Content-Based Restrictions: "Low" Value Speech                 133

## V

### Content-Neutral Restrictions: Limitations on the Means of Communication and the Problem of Content-Neutrality    287

# Contents

## PART I

## I

## II

# III

## Overbreadth, Vagueness, and Prior Restraint       111

# IV

## Content-Based Restrictions: "Low" Value Speech                           133

# V

Content-Neutral Restrictions: Limitations on the
Means of Communication and the Problem of
Content-Neutrality                                                      287

Contents

# VI

## Freedom of the Press                                          497

# PART II

## The Constitution and Religion                                            537

# VII

## Historical and Analytical Overview                                       539

# VIII

## The Establishment Clause                                                 561

# Preface

This work is derived from Stone, Seidman, Sunstein, Tushnet, and Karlan, *Constitutional Law* (7th ed. 2013). It incorporates the material in chapters VII and VIII of that book and its most recent Supplement, with only modest revisions. It presents the most recent developments in the area.

The first amendment is a suitable subject for treatment apart from the rest of constitutional law. First amendment cases and issues raise questions both about constitutional law generally and about the specific domains of free expression and religious liberty. Although this book generally assumes that students have had an introduction in which they have already considered the justifications offered for judicial review, the cases and materials allow students to explore questions about the appropriate roles of courts and legislatures in developing fundamental law. The free expression materials show how such important considerations as democratic theory and the claim that individuals are self-directing, autonomous beings might influence the development of constitutional doctrine. The materials on the first amendment's religion clauses pose questions, among others, about the ability of constitutional law to foster or support religious liberty in a society characterized by religious pluralism. These characteristics of the first amendment materials intersect with characteristics of constitutional law and theory in other substantive areas of constitutional law, and students might be encouraged to think about the connections.

The goals we pursue are to introduce students to the main lines of first amendment doctrine, to place that doctrine in its historical setting (particularly emphasized in Chapter II of Part I) and its social setting (an important theme in Part II), and to ensure that students connect particular doctrines and lines of doctrinal development with more general approaches to constitutional interpretation such as originalism, natural law/natural rights thinking, and the like. Although the materials assume a general familiarity with controversies over the justifications for judicial review, the book can be used in a free-standing course on the first amendment. At some points the materials present information about constitutional practices in other democratic societies, in an effort to combat the parochialism of United States constitutional thinking. As noted in *Constitutional Law*, "we offer no systematic survey; but we do hope to shed light on our own problems by exploring how other nations operate."

January 2016                                                                      G.R.S.
                                                                                  L.M.S.
                                                                                  C.R.S.
                                                                                  M.V.T.
                                                                                  P.S.K.

# Acknowledgments

Excerpts from the following books and articles appear with the kind permission of the copyright holders:

Alfange, Dean. The Draft-Card Burning Case. 1968 Supreme Court Review 1, 15, 16, 23, 26, 27. Copyright © 1969 by The University of Chicago. Reprinted with permission.

Anderson, David. Libel and Press Self-Censorship. Published originally in 53 Texas Law Review 422 (1975). Copyright © 1975 by the Texas Law Review Association. Reprinted with permission of the Texas Law Review Association and the author.

Baker, C. Edwin. Advertising and a Democratic Press. 140 University of Pennsylvania Law Review 2097, 2139, 2178, 2180-2181 (1992). Reprinted with permission of the University of Pennsylvania Law Review, Fred B. Rothman & Company, and the author.

_____. Scope of the First Amendment Freedom of Speech. 25 UCLA Law Review 964, 974-978 (1978). Reprinted with permission of Fred B. Rothman Company.

_____. Turner Broadcasting: Content-Based Regulation of Persons and Presses. 1994 Supreme Court Review 57, 61, 66, 72, 85-86, 91. Copyright © 1995 by The University of Chicago. Reprinted with permission.

Barnett, Stephen. The Puzzle of Prior Restraint. Copyright © 1977 by the Board of Trustees of the Leland Stanford University. Reprinted with permission of the Stanford Law Review and the Fred B. Rothman Company.

Bat-Ada, Judith. Freedom of Speech as Mythology, or Quill Pen and Parchment Thinking in an Electronic Environment. 8 N.Y.U. Review of Law and Social Change 271, 275, 278-279 (1978-1979). Reprinted with permission.

Berman, Jerry and Daniel Weitzner. Abundance and User Control: Renewing the Democratic Heart of the First Amendment in the Age of Interactive

Yale Law Journal Company, the author, and Fred B. Rothman & Company from The Yale Law Journal, Vol. 104, pp. 1652-1653.

Brownstein, Rules of Engagement for Culture Wars: Regulating Conduct, Unprotected Speech, and Protected Expression in Anti-Abortion Protests, 29 U.C. Davis Law Rev. 553, 586-588, 628 (1996). Copyright © 1996 Regents of The University of California. Reprinted with permission.

Cantor, Norman. Forced Payments to Service Institutions and Constitutional Interests in Ideological Non-Association. 36 Rutgers Law Review 3, 16, 26 (1984). Reprinted with permissions.

Chaffee, Zechariah. Book Review. 62 Harvard Law Review 891, 899-900 (1949). Copyright © 1949 by the Harvard Law Review Association. Reprinted with permission of the Harvard Law Review Association.

_____. Free Speech in the United States. Copyright © 1941 by the President and Fellows of Harvard College. Reprinted with permission of Harvard University Press.

Clark, Lorene. "Liberalism and Pornography," originally appearing in In Search of the Feminist Perspective: The Changing Potency of Women (Resources for Feminist Research Special Publication #5, Toronto, Spring 1975).

Clor, Harry. Obscenity and Public Morality. Copyright © 1969 by The University of Chicago. Reprinted with permission.

Coase, Ronald. Advertising and Free Speech. 6 Journal of Legal Studies 1, 2, 14 (1977). Copyright © 1977 by The University of Chicago. Reprinted with permission.

_____. The Federal Communications Commission. 2 Journal of Law & Economics 1, 14-18 (1959). Copyright © 1959 by The University of Chicago. Reprinted with permission.

Collins, Ronald and David Skover. The Death of Discourse (1996). Copyright © 1996 by WestviewPress. Reprinted by permission of WestviewPress.

Comment. *Snepp v. United States:* The CIA Secrecy Agreement and the First Amendment. This article originally appeared at 81 Columbia Law Review 662 (1981). Reprinted with permission of the Columbia Law Review and the author.

Cox, Archibald. Foreword, Freedom of Expression in the Burger Court. Copyright © 1980 by the Harvard Law Review Association. Reprinted with permission of the Harvard Law Review Association and the author.

Developments Note. The National Security Interest and Civil Liberties. Copyright © 1972 by the Harvard Law Review Association. Reprinted with permission of the Harvard Law Review Association.

Diamond, David. The First Amendment and Public Schools. Published originally in 59 Texas Law Review 477 (1981). Copyright © 1981 by the Texas Law Review Association. Reprinted with permission of the Texas Law Review Association and the author.

Easterbrook, Frank. Insider Trading, Secret Agents, Evidentiary Privileges, and the Production of Information. 1981 Supreme Court Review 309, 345-347. Copyright © 1982 by The University of Chicago. Reprinted with permission.

Ely, John Hart. Democracy and Distrust. Copyright © 1980 by the President and Fellows of Harvard College. Reprinted with permission of Harvard University Press.

_____. Flag Desecration: A Case Study in the Roles of Categorization and Balancing in First Amendment Analysis. Copyright © 1975 by the Harvard Law Review Association. Reprinted with permission of the Harvard Law Review Association and the author.

Emerson, Thomas. The Affirmative Side of the First Amendment. This article was originally published at 15 Georgia Law Review 795 (1981) and is reprinted with permission.

_____. The Doctrine of Prior Restraint. 20 Law & Contemporary Problems 648, 656-660 (1955). Reprinted with permission.

Epstein, Richard. Was *New York Times v. Sullivan* Wrong? 53 University of Chicago Law Review 782, 797, 804 (1986). Reprinted with permission.

Fairman, Christopher M. FUCK: Word Taboo and Protecting Our First Amendment Liberties 27-29, 44-45, 55, 60 (2009). Used by permission of Sourcebooks.

Farber, Daniel. Commercial Speech and First Amendment Theory. 74 Northwestern University Law Review 372, 385-386 (1979). Reprinted with permission of Daniel Farber.

Farber, Daniel and John Nowak. The Misleading Nature of Public Forum Analysis: Content and Context in First Amendment Adjudication. 70 Virginia Law Review 1219, 1234 (1984). Reprinted with permission.

Fiss, Owen. In Search of a New Paradigm. Reprinted with permission of the Yale Law Journal Company, the author, and Fred B. Rothman & Company from The Yale Law Journal, Vol. 104, pp. 1614-1615.

Freund, Paul. The Supreme Court and Civil Liberties. 4 Vanderbilt Law Review 533, 539 (1951). Reprinted with permission.

Goldberger, David. Judicial Scrutiny in Public Forum Cases: Misplaced Trust in the Judgment of Public Officials. 32 Buffalo Law Review 175, 206-207, 217-218 (1983). Copyright © 1983 by the Buffalo Law Review. Reprinted with permission.

_____. A Reconsideration of *Cox v. New Hampshire*. Published originally in 62 Texas Law Review 403 (1983). Copyright © 1983 by the Texas Law Review Association. Reprinted with permission of the Texas Law Review Association and the author.

Goldstein, Robert. Political Repression in Modern America (1978). Reprinted with permission of Schenkman Books and the author.

Graber, Mark. Old Wine in New Bottles: The Constitutional Status of Unconstitutional Speech. 48 Vanderbilt Law Review 349, 352, 364, 367-368, 371-372 (1995). Reprinted with permission.

Greenawalt, Kent. Free Speech Justifications. This article originally appeared at 89 Columbia Law Review 119 (1989). Reprinted with permission of the Columbia Law Review and the author.

Greene, Abner. The Political Balance of the Religion Clauses. Reprinted with permission of the Yale Law Journal Company, the author, and Fred B. Rothman & Company from The Yale Law Journal, Vol. 102, p. 1611.

Gunther, Gerald. Learned Hand and the Origins of Modern First Amendment Doctrine: Some Fragments of History. Copyright © 1975 by the Board of Trustees of the Leland Stanford University. Reprinted with the author's permission.

Harper, Michael. The Consumer's Emerging Right to Boycott. Reprinted with permission of the Yale Law Journal Company, the author, and Fred B. Rothman & Company from The Yale Law Journal, Vol. 93, p. 425.

Henkin, Louis. Foreword: On Drawing Lines. Copyright © 1968 by the Harvard Law Review Association. Reprinted with permission of the Harvard Law Review Association and the author.

Howe, Mark DeWolfe. The Garden and the Wilderness (1965). Reprinted by permission of the Frank L. Weil Institute for Studies in Religion and Humanities, Hebrew Union College-Jewish Institute of Religion.

Imwinkelried, Edward and Donald Zillman. An Evolution in the First Amendment: Overbreadth Analysis and Free Speech Within the Military Community. Published originally in 54 Texas Law Review 42 (1975). Copyright © 1975 by the Texas Law Review Association. Reprinted with permission of the Texas Law Review Association and the authors.

Ingber, Stanley. The Marketplace of Ideas: A Legitimizing Myth. 1984 Duke Law Journal 1, 4-5. Reprinted with permission.

Israel, Jerrold. *Elfbrandt v. Russell*: The Demise of the Oath? 1966 Supreme Court Review 193, 219. Copyright © 1967 by The University of Chicago. Reprinted with permission.

Jackson, Thomas and John Jeffries. Commercial Speech: Economic Due Process and the First Amendment. 65 Virginia Law Review 1, 17-18, 30-31 (1979). Reprinted with permission.

Kagan, Elena. The Changing Faces of First Amendment Neutrality. 1992 Supreme Court Review 29, 31-32, 38-40. Copyright © 1993 by The University of Chicago. Reprinted with permission.

_____. Private Speech, Public Purpose: The Role of Governmental Motive in First Amendment Doctrine, 63 U. Chi. L. Rev. 415, 467-475 (1996). Copyright © 1996 by University of Chicago Law Review. Reprinted with permission.

Kalven, Harry. The Concept of the Public Forum: *Cox v. Louisiana.* 1965 Supreme Court Review 1, 18-21. Copyright © 1966 by The University of Chicago. Reprinted with permission.

_____. The Metaphysics of the Law of Obscenity. 1960 Supreme Court Review 1, 15-16. Copyright © 1961 by The University of Chicago. Reprinted with permission.

_____. The Negro and the First Amendment (1965). Reprinted with permission of Betty Kalven.

_____. The *New York Times* Case: A Note on "The Central Meaning of the First Amendment." 1964 Supreme Court Review 191, 208-209. Copyright © 1965 by The University of Chicago. Reprinted with permission.

_____. A Worthy Tradition: Freedom of Speech in America (1988). Copyright © 1988 by The Harry Kalven, Jr. Trust. Reprinted by permission of Harper-Collins Publishers, Inc.

Krattenmaker, Thomas and L. Scot Powe. Converging First Amendment Principles for Converging Communications Media. Reprinted with permission of the Yale Law Journal Company, the authors, and Fred B. Rothman & Company from The Yale Law Journal, Vol. 104, pp. 1721-1740.

Kurland, Philip. The Religion Clauses and the Burger Court. 34 Catholic University Law Review 1, 13-14 (1984). Reprinted with permission.

LeBel, Paul. Reforming the Tort of Defamation: An Accommodation of the Competing Interests Within the Current Constitutional Framework. 66 Nebraska Law Review 249, 293 (1987). Copyright © 1987 by the University of Nebraska. Reprinted with permission.

Lessig, Lawrence. The Path of Cyberlaw. Reprinted with permission of the Yale Law Journal Company, the author, and Fred B. Rothman & Company from The Yale Law Journal, Vol. 104, pp. 1750-1752.

Lockhart, William and Robert McClure. Literature, the Law of Obscenity, and the Constitution. 38 Minnesota Law Review 295, 374-375 (1954). Reprinted with permission of the University of Minnesota Law School.

MacKinnon, Catherine. Feminism Unmodified: Discourses on Life and Law. Copyright © 1987 by the President and Fellows of Harvard College. Reprinted with permission of Harvard University Press.

Matsuda, Mari. Public Response to Racist Speech: Considering the Victim's Story. 87 Michigan Law Review 2320, 2332, 2336-2337, 2357, 2359 (1982). Reprinted with permission of the Michigan Law Review Association and the author.

McConnell, Michael. Accommodation of Religion. 1985 Supreme Court Review 1, 1-3. Copyright © 1986 by The University of Chicago. Reprinted with permission.

_____. The Proper Role of the Prior Restraint Doctrine in First Amendment Theory. 70 Virginia Law Review 53, 55, 58 (1984). Reprinted with permission.

_____. The Value of Free Speech. 130 University of Pennsylvania Law Review 591, 633 (1982). Reprinted with permission of the University of Pennsylvania Law Review. Fred B. Rothman & Company, and the author.

Richards, David. Free Speech and Obscenity Law: Toward a Moral Theory of the First Amendment. 123 University of Pennsylvania Law Review 45, 62, 82 (1974). Reprinted with the author's permission.

Rubenfeld, Jed. The First Amendment's Purpose, 53 Stan. L. Rev. 767, 768-769 (2001). Copyright © 2001 by Stanford Law Review. Reproduced with permission of Stanford Law Review in the format textbook via Copyright Clearance Center.

Scanlon, Thomas. Freedom of Expression and Categories of Expression. 40 University of Pittsburgh Law Review 519, 532-533, 547 (1979). Reprinted with permission of the University of Pittsburgh Law Review and the author.

Schauer, Frederick. Speech and "Speech" — Obscenity and "Obscenity": An Exercise in the Interpretation of Constitutional Language. 67 Georgetown Law Journal 899, 906, 922, 923, 926 (1979). Reprinted with permission of the publisher © 1979 and Georgetown University.

Shiffrin, Stephen. The First Amendment, Democracy, and Romance. Copyright © 1990 by the President and Fellows of Harvard College. Reprinted with permission of Harvard University Press.

Smolla, Rodney. Let the Author Beware: The Rejuvenation of the American Law of Libel. 132 University of Pennsylvania Law Review 1, 4-7, 12, 91-93 (1984). Reprinted with permission of the University of Pennsylvania Law Review, Fred B. Rothman & Company, and the author.

Solove, Daniel J. Reprinted by permission of the publisher from "Speech, Privacy, and Reputation on the Internet" by Daniel J. Solove in The Offensive Internet: Speech, Privacy, and Reputation, edited by Saul Levmore and Martha C. Nussbaum, pp. 16, 17, 18, 20, 21, 28, Cambridge, Mass.: Harvard University Press, Copyright © 2010 by the President and Fellows of Harvard College.

Stewart, Potter. "Or of the Press." Reprinted from 26 Hastings Law Journal 631, 633-634 (1975) by permission.

Stone, Geoffrey. Content Regulation and the First Amendment. 25 William & Mary Law Review 189, 217, 222-223, 225-226, 243-244, 280 (1983). Reprinted with permission.

_____. The Equal Access Controversy: The Religion Clauses and the Meaning of "Neutrality." Reprinted by special permission of Northwestern University School of Law, Northwestern University Law Review, Volume 81, Issue 1, pp. 168, 169-170 (1986).

_____. Fora Americana: Speech in Public Places. 1974 Supreme Court Review 233, 237, 238, 251-252. Copyright © 1975 by The University of Chicago. Reprinted with permission.

_____. Reflections on the First Amendment: The Evolution of the American Jurisprudence of Free Expression. 131 Proceedings 251, 253 (1987). Reprinted with permission.

_____. Restrictions of Speech Because of Its Content: The Peculiar Case of Subject Matter Restrictions. 46 University of Chicago Law Review 81, 83, 108 (1978). Reprinted with permission.

Strauss, David. Corruption, Equality, and Campaign Finance Reform. This article originally appeared at 94 Columbia Law Review 1369 (1994). Reprinted with permission of the Columbia Law Review and the author.

_____. Persuasion, Autonomy, and Freedom of Expression. This article originally appeared at 91 Columbia Law Review 334 (1991). Reprinted with permission of the Columbia Law Review and the author.

Sullivan, Kathleen. Cheap Spirits, Cigarettes, and Free Speech: The Implications of _44 Liquormart_, 1996 Supreme Court Review 123, 126-128, 148-149, 152, 157. Copyright © 1997 by The University of Chicago. Reprinted with permission.

Sunstein, Cass. The First Amendment in Cyberspace. Reprinted with permission of the Yale Law Journal Company, the author, and Fred B. Rothman & Company from The Yale Law Journal, Vol. 104, pp. 1767-1768.

_____. Free Speech Now. 59 University of Chicago Law Review 255, 263-267, 272, 291-292, 301, 304-306 (1992). Reprinted with permission.

_____. Government Control of Information. Copyright © 1986 by California Law Review Inc. Reprinted from California Law Review, Vol. 74, No. 3 (May 1986), pp. 889-921, by permission.

_____. Neutrality in Constitutional Law (with Special Reference to Pornography, Abortion, and Surrogacy). This article originally appeared at 92 Columbia Law Review 1 (1992). Reprinted with permission of the Columbia Law Review and the author.

_____. The Partial Constitution. Copyright © 1993 by the President and Fellows of Harvard College. Reprinted with permission of Harvard University Press.

_____. Pornography and the First Amendment. 1986 Duke Law Journal 589, 603-604, 612. Reprinted with permission.

_____. republic.com. Copyright © 2001 by Princeton University Press. Reprinted by permission of Princeton University Press.

Tribe, Laurence. American Constitutional Law (First Edition) (1978). Reprinted with permission of Foundation Press.

_____. American Constitutional Law (Second Edition) (1988). Reprinted with permission of West and the Author.

Van Alstyne, William. The Demise of the Right-Privilege Distinction in Constitutional Law. Copyright © 1968 by the Harvard Law Review

Association. Reprinted with permission of the Harvard Law Review Association and the author.

_____. The First Amendment and the Free Press: A Comment on Some New Trends and Some Old Theories. 9 Hofstra Law Review 1, 19-23 (1980). Reprinted with permission.

_____. The Mobius Strip of the First Amendment: Perspectives on *Red Lion*. 29 South Carolina Law Review 539, 562 (1978). Reprinted with the author's permission.

Wellington, Harry. On Freedom of Expression. Reprinted with permission of the Yale Law Journal Company, the author, and Fred B. Rothman & Company from The Yale Law Journal, Vol. 88, pp. 1106-1132.

West, Robin. The Feminist-Conservative Anti-Pornography Alliance and the 1986 Attorney General's Commission on Pornography Report. 1987 American Bar Foundation Research Journal 681, 686, 691-692. Copyright © 1987 by the American Bar Foundation. Reprinted with permission.

Wigmore, John H. *Abrams v. United States:* Freedom of Speech and Freedom of Thuggery in War-Time and Peace-Time. Reprinted by special permission of Northwestern University School of Law, Illinois Law Review, Volume 14, pp. 539, 549-550 (1920).

Wright, J. Skelly. Politics and the Constitution: Is Money Speech? Reprinted with permission of the Yale Law Journal Company and Fred B. Rothman & Company from The Yale Law Journal, Vol. 85, pp. 1005-1019.

Zimmerman, Diane. Requiem for a Heavyweight: A Farewell to Warren and Brandeis's Privacy Tort. 68 Cornell Law Review 291, 332-334 (1983). Copyright © 1983 by Cornell University. All Rights Reserved. Reprinted with permission.

# Editorial Notice

Throughout this book additions to quoted material are indicated by brackets, and deletions are indicated either by brackets or ellipses. Citations and footnotes are sometimes omitted without notice.

# The First Amendment

AMENDMENT I [1791]

Congress shall make no law respecting an establishment of religion, or prohibiting the free exercise thereof; or abridging the freedom of speech, or of the press; or the right of the people peaceably to assemble, and to petition the Government for a redress of grievances.

# The Constitution of
# the United States

We the People of the United States, in Order to form a more perfect Union, establish Justice, insure domestic Tranquility, provide for the common defence, promote the general Welfare, and secure the Blessings of Liberty to ourselves and our Posterity, do ordain and establish this Constitution for the United States of America.

ARTICLE I

*Section 1.* All legislative Powers herein granted shall be vested in a Congress of the United States which shall consist of a Senate and House of Representatives.

*Section 2.* [1] The House of Representatives shall be composed of Members chosen every second Year by the People of the several States, and the Electors in each State shall have the Qualifications requisite for Electors of the most numerous Branch of the State Legislature.

[2] No Person shall be a Representative who shall not have attained to the Age of twenty five Years, and been seven Years a Citizen of the United States, and who shall not, when elected, be an Inhabitant of that State in which he shall be chosen.

[3] Representatives and direct Taxes shall be apportioned among the several States which may be included within this Union, according to their respective Numbers, which shall be determined by adding to the whole Number of free Persons, including those bound to Service for a Term of Years, and excluding Indians not taxed, three fifths of all other Persons. The actual Enumeration shall be made within three Years after the first Meeting of the Congress of the United States, and within every subsequent Term of ten Years, in such Manner as they shall by Law direct. The Number of Representatives shall not exceed one for every thirty Thousand, but each State shall have at Least One Representative; and until such enumeration shall be made, the State of

New Hampshire shall be entitled to chuse three, Massachusetts eight, Rhode Island and Providence Plantations one, Connecticut five, New York six, New Jersey four, Pennsylvania eight, Delaware one, Maryland six, Virginia ten, North Carolina five, South Carolina five, and Georgia three.

[4] When vacancies happen in the Representation from any State, the Executive Authority thereof shall issue Writs of Election to fill such Vacancies.

[5] The House of Representatives shall chuse their Speaker and other Officers; and shall have the sole Power of Impeachment.

*Section 3.* [1] The Senate of the United States shall be composed of two Senators from each State, chosen by the Legislature thereof, for six Years; and each Senator shall have one Vote.

[2] Immediately after they shall be assembled in Consequence of the first Election, they shall be divided as equally as may be into three Classes. The Seats of the Senators of the first Class shall be vacated at the Expiration of the second Year, of the second Class at the Expiration of the fourth Year, and of the third Class at the Expiration of the sixth Year, so that one third may be chosen every second Year; and if Vacancies happen by Resignation, or otherwise, during the Recess of the Legislature of any State, the Executive thereof may make temporary Appointments until the next Meeting of the Legislature, which shall then fill such Vacancies.

[3] No Person shall be a Senator who shall not have attained to the Age of thirty Years, and been nine Years a Citizen of the United States, and who shall not, when elected, be an Inhabitant of that State for which he shall be chosen.

[4] The Vice President of the United States shall be President of the Senate, but shall have no Vote, unless they be equally divided.

[5] The Senate shall chuse their other Officers, and also a President pro tempore, in the absence of the Vice President, or when he shall exercise the Office of President of the United States.

[6] The Senate shall have the sole Power to try all Impeachments. When sitting for that Purpose, they shall be on Oath or Affirmation. When the President of the United States is tried, the Chief Justice shall preside: And no Person shall be convicted without the Concurrence of two thirds of the Members present.

[7] Judgment in Cases of Impeachment shall not extend further than to removal from Office, and disqualification to hold and enjoy any Office of honor, Trust or Profit under the United States: but the Party convicted shall nevertheless be liable and subject to Indictment, Trial, Judgment and Punishment, according to Law.

*Section 4.* [1] The Times, Places and Manner of holding Elections for Senators and Representatives, shall be prescribed in each State by the Legislature thereof; but the Congress may at any time by Law make or alter such Regulations, except as to the Places of chusing Senators.

[2] The Congress shall assemble at least once in every Year, and such Meeting shall be on the first Monday in December, unless they shall by Law appoint a different Day.

*Section* 5. [1] Each House shall be the Judge of the Elections, Returns and Qualifications of its own Members, and a Majority of each shall constitute a Quorum to do Business; but a smaller Number may adjourn from day to day, and may be authorized to compel the Attendance of absent Members, in such Manner, and under such Penalties as each House may provide.

[2] Each House may determine the Rules of its Proceedings, punish its Members for disorderly Behavior, and, with the Concurrence of two thirds, expel a Member.

[3] Each House shall keep a Journal of its Proceedings, and from time to time publish the same, excepting such Parts as may in their Judgment require Secrecy; and the Yeas and Nays of the Members of either House on any question shall, at the Desire of one fifth of those Present, be entered on the Journal.

[4] Neither House, during the Session of Congress, shall, without the Consent of the other, adjourn for more than three days, nor to any other Place than that in which the two Houses shall be sitting.

*Section* 6. [1] The Senators and Representatives shall receive a Compensation for their Services, to be ascertained by Law, and paid out of the Treasury of the United States. They shall in all Cases, except Treason, Felony and Breach of the Peace, be privileged from Arrest during their Attendance at the Session of their respective Houses, and in going to and returning from the same; and for any Speech or Debate in either House, they shall not be questioned in any other Place.

[2] No Senator or Representative shall, during the Time for which he was elected, be appointed to any civil Office under the Authority of the United States, which shall have been created, or the Emoluments whereof shall have been encreased during such time; and no Person holding any Office under the United States, shall be a Member of either House during his Continuance in Office.

*Section* 7. [1] All Bills for raising Revenue shall originate in the House of Representatives; but the Senate may propose or concur with Amendments as on other Bills.

[2] Every Bill which shall have passed the House of Representatives and the Senate, shall, before it becomes a Law, be presented to the President of the United States; If he approve he shall sign it, but if not he shall return it, with his Objections to the House in which it shall have originated, who shall enter the Objections at large on their Journal, and proceed to reconsider it. If after such Reconsideration two thirds of that House shall agree to pass the Bill, it shall be sent, together with the Objections, to the other House, by which it shall likewise be reconsidered, and if approved by two thirds of that House, it shall become a Law. But in all such Cases the Votes of both Houses shall be determined by yeas and Nays, and the Names of the Persons voting for and against the Bill shall be entered on the Journal of each House respectively. If any Bill shall not be returned by the President within ten Days (Sundays excepted) after it shall have been presented to him, the Same shall be a Law, in like Manner as if he had signed it, unless the Congress by their Adjournment prevents its Return, in which Case it shall not be a Law.

[3] Every Order, Resolution, or Vote to Which the Concurrence of the Senate and House of Representatives may be necessary (except on a question of Adjournment) shall be presented to the President of the United States; and before the Same shall take Effect, shall be approved by him, or being disapproved by him, shall be repassed by two thirds of the Senate and House of Representatives, according to the Rules and Limitations prescribed in the Case of a Bill.

*Section* 8. [1] The Congress shall have Power To lay and collect Taxes, Duties, Imposts and Excises, to pay the Debts and provide for the common Defence and general Welfare of the United States; but all Duties, Imposts and Excises shall be uniform throughout the United States;

[2] To borrow money on the credit of the United States;

[3] To regulate Commerce with foreign Nations, and among the several States, and with the Indian Tribes;

[4] To establish an uniform Rule of Naturalization, and uniform Laws on the subject of Bankruptcies throughout the United States;

[5] To coin Money, regulate the value thereof, and of foreign Coin, and fix the Standard of Weights and Measures;

[6] To provide the Punishment of counterfeiting the Securities and current Coin of the United States;

[7] To establish Post Offices and post Roads;

[8] To promote the Progress of Science and useful Arts, by securing for limited Times to Authors and Inventors the exclusive Right to their respective Writings and Discoveries;

[9] To constitute Tribunals inferior to the supreme Court;

[10] To define and punish Piracies and Felonies committed on the high Seas, and Offenses against the Law of Nations;

[11] To declare War, grant Letters of Marque and Reprisal, and make Rules concerning Captures on Land and Water;

[12] To raise and support Armies, but no Appropriation of Money to that Use shall be for a longer Term than two Years;

[13] To provide and maintain a Navy;

[14] To make Rules for the Government and Regulation of the land and naval Forces;

[15] To provide for calling forth the Militia to execute the Laws of the Union, suppress Insurrections and repel Invasions;

[16] To provide for organizing, arming, and disciplining, the Militia, and for governing such Part of them as may be employed in the Service of the United States, reserving to the States respectively, the Appointment of the Officers, and the Authority of training the Militia according to the discipline prescribed by Congress;

[17] To exercise exclusive Legislation in all Cases whatsoever, over such District (not exceeding ten Miles square) as may, by Cession of particular States, and the Acceptance of Congress, become the Seat of the Government of the United States, and to exercise like Authority over all Places purchased by

the Consent of the Legislature of the State in which the Same shall be, for the Erection of Forts, Magazines, Arsenals, dock-Yards, and other needful Buildings; — And

[18] To make all Laws which shall be necessary and proper for carrying into Execution the foregoing Powers, and all other Powers vested by this Constitution in the Government of the United States, or in any Department or Officer thereof.

*Section 9.* [1] The Migration or Importation of such Persons as any of the States now existing shall think proper to admit, shall not be prohibited by the Congress prior to the Year one thousand eight hundred and eight, but a Tax or duty may be imposed on such Importation, not exceeding ten dollars for each Person.

[2] The privilege of the Writ of Habeas Corpus shall not be suspended, unless when in Cases of Rebellion or Invasion the public Safety may require it.

[3] No Bill of Attainder or ex post facto Law shall be passed.

[4] No Capitation, or other direct, Tax shall be laid, unless in Proportion to the Census or Enumeration herein before directed to be taken.

[5] No Tax or Duty shall be laid on Articles exported from any State.

[6] No Preference shall be given by any Regulation of Commerce or Revenue to the Ports of one State over those of another: nor shall Vessels bound to, or from, one State, be obliged to enter, clear, or pay Duties in another.

[7] No Money shall be drawn from the Treasury, but in Consequence of Appropriations made by Law; and a regular Statement and Account of the Receipts and Expenditures of all public Money shall be published from time to time.

[8] No Title of Nobility shall be granted by the United States: And no Person holding any Office of Profit or Trust under them, shall, without the Consent of the Congress, accept of any present, Emolument, Office, or Title, of any kind whatever, from any King, Prince, or foreign State.

*Section 10.* [1] No State shall enter into any Treaty, Alliance, or Confederation; grant Letters of Marque and Reprisal; coin Money; emit Bills of Credit; make any Thing but gold and silver Coin a Tender in Payment of Debts; pass any Bill of Attainder, ex post facto Law, or Law impairing the Obligation of Contracts, or grant any Title of Nobility.

[2] No State shall, without the Consent of the Congress, lay any Imposts or Duties on Imports or Exports, except what may be absolutely necessary for executing its inspection Laws: and the net Produce of all Duties and Imposts, laid by any State on Imports or Exports, shall be for the Use of the Treasury of the United States; and all such Laws shall be subject to the Revision and Controul of the Congress.

[3] No State shall, without the Consent of Congress, lay any Duty of Tonnage, keep Troops, or Ships of War in time of Peace, enter into any Agreement or Compact with another State, or with a foreign Power, or engage in War, unless actually invaded, or in such imminent Danger as will not admit of delay.

ARTICLE II

*Section 1*. [1] The executive Power shall be vested in a President of the United States of America. He shall hold his Office during the Term of four Years, and, together with the Vice President, chosen for the same Term, be elected, as follows:

[2] Each State shall appoint, in such Manner as the Legislature thereof may direct, a Number of Electors, equal to the whole Number of Senators and Representatives to which the State may be entitled in the Congress: but no Senator or Representative, or Person holding an Office of Trust or Profit under the United States, shall be appointed an Elector.

[3] The Electors shall meet in their respective States, and vote by Ballot for two Persons, of whom one at least shall not be an Inhabitant of the same State with themselves. And they shall make a List of all the Persons voted for, and of the Number of Votes for each; which List they shall sign and certify, and transmit sealed to the Seat of the Government of the United States, directed to the President of the Senate. The President of the Senate shall, in the Presence of the Senate and House of Representatives, open all the Certificates, and the Votes shall then be counted. The Person having the greatest Number of Votes shall be the President, if such Number be a Majority of the whole Number of Electors appointed; and if there be more than one who have such Majority, and have an equal Number of Votes, then the House of Representatives shall immediately chuse by Ballot one of them for President; and if no Person have a Majority, then from the five highest on the List the said House shall in like Manner chuse the President. But in chusing the President, the Votes shall be taken by States, the Representation from each State having one Vote; a quorum for this Purpose shall consist of a Member or Members from two thirds of the States, and a Majority of all the States shall be necessary to a Choice. In every Case, after the Choice of the President, the Person having the greatest Number of Votes of the Electors shall be the Vice President. But if there should remain two or more who have equal Votes, the Senate shall chuse from them by Ballot the Vice President.

[4] The Congress may determine the Time of chusing the Electors, and the Day on which they shall give their Votes; which Day shall be the same throughout the United States.

[5] No person except a natural born Citizen, or a Citizen of the United States, at the time of the Adoption of this Constitution, shall be eligible to the Office of President; neither shall any Person be eligible to that Office who shall not have attained to the Age of thirty five Years, and been fourteen Years a Resident within the United States.

[6] In case of the removal of the President from Office, or of his Death, Resignation or Inability to discharge the Powers and Duties of the said Office, the Same shall devolve on the Vice President, and the Congress may by Law

provide for the Case of Removal, Death, Resignation or Inability, both of the President and Vice President, declaring what Officer shall then act as President, and such Officer shall act accordingly, until the Disability be removed, or a President shall be elected.

[7] The President shall, at stated Times, receive for his Services, a Compensation, which shall neither be increased nor diminished during the Period for which he shall have been elected, and he shall not receive within that Period any other Emolument from the United States, or any of them.

[8] Before he enter on the Execution of his Office, he shall take the following Oath or Affirmation: "I do solemnly swear (or affirm) that I will faithfully execute the Office of President of the United States, and will to the best of my Ability, preserve, protect and defend the Constitution of the United States."

*Section 2.* [1] The President shall be Commander in Chief of the Army and Navy of the United States, and of the Militia of the several States, when called into the actual Service of the United States; he may require the Opinion, in writing, of the principal Officer in each of the executive Departments, upon any subject relating to the Duties of their respective Offices, and he shall have Power to grant Reprieves and Pardons for Offenses against the United States, except in Cases of Impeachment.

[2] He shall have Power, by and with the Advice and Consent of the Senate, to make Treaties, provided two thirds of the Senators present concur; and he shall nominate, and by and with the Advice and Consent of the Senate, shall appoint Ambassadors, other public Ministers and Consuls, Judges of the supreme Court, and all other Officers of the United States, whose Appointments are not herein otherwise provided for, and which shall be established by Law: but the Congress may by Law vest the Appointment of such inferior Officers, as they think proper, in the President alone, to the Courts of Law, or in the Heads of Departments.

[3] The President shall have Power to fill up all Vacancies that may happen during the Recess of the Senate, by granting Commissions which shall expire at the End of their next Session.

*Section 3.* He shall from time to time give to the Congress Information of the State of the Union, and recommend to their Consideration such Measures as he shall judge necessary and expedient; he may, on extraordinary occasions, convene both Houses, or either of them, and in Case of Disagreement between them, with Respect to the time of Adjournment, he may adjourn them to such Time as he shall think proper; he shall receive Ambassadors and other public Ministers; he shall take Care that the Laws be faithfully executed, and shall Commission all the Officers of the United States.

*Section 4.* The President, Vice President and all civil Officers of the United States, shall be removed from Office on Impeachment for, and Conviction of, Treason, Bribery, or other high Crimes and Misdemeanors.

## Article III

*Section 1.* The judicial Power of the United States, shall be vested in one supreme Court, and in such inferior Courts as the Congress may from time to time ordain and establish. The Judges, both of the supreme and inferior Courts, shall hold their Offices during good Behaviour, and shall, at stated Times, receive for their Services, a Compensation, which shall not be diminished during their Continuance in Office.

*Section 2.* [1] The Judicial Power shall extend to all Cases, in Law and Equity, arising under this Constitution, the Laws of the United States, and Treaties made, or which shall be made, under their Authority; — to all Cases affecting Ambassadors, other public Ministers and Consuls; — to all Cases of admiralty and maritime Jurisdiction; — to Controversies to which the United States shall be a Party; — to Controversies between two or more States; — between a State and Citizens of another State; — between Citizens of different States; — between Citizens of the same State claiming Lands under Grants of different States, and between a State, or the Citizens thereof, and foreign States, Citizens or Subjects.

[2] In all Cases affecting Ambassadors, other public Ministers and Consuls, and those in which a State shall be a Party, the supreme Court shall have original Jurisdiction. In all the other Cases before mentioned, the supreme Court shall have appellate Jurisdiction, both as to Law and Fact, with such Exceptions, and under such Regulations as the Congress shall make.

[3] The trial of all Crimes, except in Cases of Impeachment, shall be by Jury; and such Trial shall be held in the State where the said Crimes shall have been committed; but when not committed within any State, the Trial shall be at such Place or Places as the Congress may by Law have directed.

*Section 3.* [1] Treason against the United States, shall consist only in levying War against them, or in adhering to their Enemies, giving them Aid and Comfort. No person shall be convicted of Treason unless on the Testimony of two Witnesses to the same overt Act, or on Confession in open Court.

[2] The Congress shall have Power to declare the Punishment of Treason, but no Attainder of Treason shall work Corruption of Blood, or Forfeiture except during the Life of the Person attainted.

## Article IV

*Section 1.* Full Faith and Credit shall be given in each State to the public Acts, Records, and judicial Proceedings of every other State. And the Congress may by general Laws prescribe the Manner in which such Acts, Records and Proceedings shall be proved, and the Effect thereof.

*Section 2.* [1] The Citizens of each State shall be entitled to all Privileges and Immunities of Citizens in the several States.

[2] A Person charged in any State with Treason, Felony, or other Crime, who shall flee from Justice, and be found in another State, shall on demand of the executive Authority of the State from which he fled, be delivered up, to be removed to the State having Jurisdiction of the Crime.

[3] No Person held to Service or Labour in one State, under the Laws thereof, escaping into another, shall, in Consequence of any Law or Regulation therein, be discharged from such Service or Labour, but shall be delivered up on Claim of the Party to whom such Service or Labour may be due.

*Section 3.* [1] New States may be admitted by the Congress into this Union; but no new State shall be formed or erected within the Jurisdiction of any other State; nor any State be formed by the Junction of two or more States, or Parts of States, without the Consent of the Legislatures of the States concerned as well as of the Congress.

[2] The Congress shall have Power to dispose of and make all needful Rules and Regulations respecting the Territory or other Property belonging to the United States; and nothing in this Constitution shall be so construed as to Prejudice any Claims of the United States, or of any particular State.

*Section 4.* The United States shall guarantee to every State in this Union a Republican Form of Government, and shall protect each of them against Invasion; and on Application of the Legislature, or of the Executive (when the Legislature cannot be convened) against domestic Violence.

## ARTICLE V

The Congress, whenever two thirds of both Houses shall deem it necessary, shall propose Amendments to this Constitution, or, on the Application of the Legislatures of two thirds of the several States, shall call a Convention for proposing Amendments, which, in either Case, shall be valid to all Intents and Purposes, as part of this Constitution, when ratified by the Legislatures of three fourths of the several States, or by Conventions in three fourths thereof, as the one or the other Mode of Ratification may be proposed by the Congress; Provided that no Amendment which may be made prior to the Year One thousand eight hundred and eight shall in any Manner affect the first and fourth Clauses in the Ninth Section of the first Article; and that no State, without its Consent, shall be deprived of its equal Suffrage in the Senate.

## ARTICLE VI

[1] All Debts contracted and Engagements entered into, before the Adoption of this Constitution, shall be as valid against the United States under this Constitution, as under the Confederation.

[2] This Constitution, and the Laws of the United States which shall be made in Pursuance thereof; and all Treaties made, or which shall be made, under the Authority of the United States, shall be the supreme Law of the

Land; and the Judges in every State shall be bound thereby, any Thing in the Constitution or Laws of any State to the Contrary notwithstanding.

[3] The Senators and Representatives before mentioned, and the Members of the several State Legislatures, and all executive and judicial Officers, both of the United States and of the several States, shall be bound by Oath or Affirmation, to support this Constitution; but no religious Test shall ever be required as a Qualification to any Office or public Trust under the United States.

## Article VII

The Ratification of the Conventions of nine States shall be sufficient for the Establishment of this Constitution between the States so ratifying the Same.

Done in Convention by the Unanimous Consent of the States present the Seventeenth Day of September in the Year of our Lord one thousand seven hundred and Eighty seven and of the Independence of the United States of America the Twelfth.

ARTICLES IN ADDITION TO, AND AMENDMENT OF, THE CONSTITUTION OF THE UNITED STATES OF AMERICA, PROPOSED BY CONGRESS, AND RATIFIED BY THE LEGISLATURES OF THE SEVERAL STATES, PURSUANT TO THE FIFTH ARTICLE OF THE ORIGINAL CONSTITUTION

## Amendment I [1791]

Congress shall make no law respecting an establishment of religion, or prohibiting the free exercise thereof; or abridging the freedom of speech, or of the press; or the right of the people peaceably to assemble, and to petition the Government for a redress of grievances.

## Amendment II [1791]

A well regulated Militia, being necessary to the security of a free State, the right of the people to keep and bear Arms, shall not be infringed.

## Amendment III [1791]

No Soldier shall, in time of peace be quartered in any house, without the consent of the Owner, nor in time of war, but in a manner to be prescribed by law.

## Amendment IV [1791]

The right of the people to be secure in their persons, houses, papers, and effects, against unreasonable searches and seizures, shall not be violated, and no Warrants shall issue, but upon probable cause, supported by Oath or affirmation, and particularly describing the place to be searched, and the persons or things to be seized.

### Amendment V [1791]

No person shall be held to answer for a capital, or otherwise infamous crime, unless on a presentment or indictment of a Grand Jury, except in cases arising in the land or naval forces, or in the Militia, when in actual service in time of War or public danger; nor shall any person be subject for the same offence to be twice put in jeopardy of life or limb; nor shall be compelled in any criminal case to be a witness against himself, nor be deprived of life, liberty, or property, without due process of law; nor shall private property be taken for public use, without just compensation.

### Amendment VI [1791]

In all criminal prosecutions, the accused shall enjoy the right to a speedy and public trial, by an impartial jury of the State and district wherein the crime shall have been committed, which district shall have been previously ascertained by law, and to be informed of the nature and cause of the accusation; to be confronted with the witnesses against him; to have compulsory process for obtaining witnesses in his favor, and to have the Assistance of Counsel for his defence.

### Amendment VII [1791]

In Suits at common law, where the value in controversy shall exceed twenty dollars, the right of trial by jury shall be preserved, and no fact tried by a jury, shall be otherwise re-examined in any Court of the United States, than according to the rules of the common law.

### Amendment VIII [1791]

Excessive bail shall not be required, nor excessive fines imposed, nor cruel and unusual punishments inflicted.

### Amendment IX [1791]

The enumeration in the Constitution, of certain rights, shall not be construed to deny or disparage others retained by the people.

### Amendment X [1791]

The powers not delegated to the United States by the Constitution, nor prohibited by it to the States, are reserved to the States respectively, or to the people.

### AMENDMENT XI [1798]

The Judicial power of the United States shall not be construed to extend to any suit in law or equity, commenced or prosecuted against one of the United States by Citizens of another State, or by Citizens or Subjects of any Foreign State.

### AMENDMENT XII [1804]

The Electors shall meet in their respective states and vote by ballot for President and Vice-President, one of whom, at least, shall not be an inhabitant of the same state with themselves; they shall name in their ballots the person voted for as President, and in distinct ballots the person voted for as President, and they shall make distinct lists of all persons voted for as Vice-President, and of all persons voted for each, which lists they shall sign and certify, and transmit sealed to the seat of the government of the United States, directed to the President of the Senate; — The President of the Senate shall, in the presence of the Senate and House of Representatives, open all the certificates and the votes shall then be counted; — The person having the greatest number of votes for President, shall be the President, if such number be a majority of the whole number of Electors appointed; and if no person have such majority, then from the persons having the highest numbers not exceeding three on the list of those voted for as President, the House of Representatives shall choose immediately, by ballot, the President. But in choosing the President, the votes shall be taken by states, the representation from each state having one vote; a quorum for this purpose shall consist of a member or members from two-thirds of the states, and a majority of all the states shall be necessary to a choice. And if the House of Representatives shall not choose a President whenever the right of choice shall devolve upon them, before the fourth day of March next following, then the Vice-President shall act as President, as in the case of the death or other constitutional disability of the President. — The person having the greatest number of votes as Vice-President, shall be the Vice-President, if such number be a majority of the whole number of Electors appointed, and if no person have a majority, then from the two highest numbers on the list, the Senate shall choose the Vice-President; a quorum for the purpose shall consist of two-thirds of the whole number of Senators, and a majority of the whole number shall be necessary to a choice. But no person constitutionally ineligible to the office of President shall be eligible to that of Vice-President of the United States.

### AMENDMENT XIII [1865]

*Section 1.* Neither slavery nor involuntary servitude, except as a punishment for crime whereof the party shall have been duly convicted, shall exist within the United States, or any place subject to their jurisdiction.

*Section 2.* Congress shall have power to enforce this article by appropriate legislation.

## AMENDMENT XIV [1868]

*Section 1.* All persons born or naturalized in the United States, and subject to the jurisdiction thereof, are citizens of the United States and of the State wherein they reside. No State shall make or enforce any law which shall abridge the privileges or immunities of citizens of the United States; nor shall any State deprive any person of life, liberty, or property, without due process of law; nor deny to any person within its jurisdiction the equal protection of the laws.

*Section 2.* Representatives shall be apportioned among the several States according to their respective numbers, counting the whole number of persons in each State, excluding Indians not taxed. But when the right to vote at any election for the choice of electors for President and Vice President of the United States, Representatives in Congress, the Executive and Judicial officers of a State, or the members of the Legislature thereof, is denied to any of the male inhabitants of such State, being twenty-one years of age, and citizens of the United States, or in any way abridged, except for participation in rebellion, or other crime, the basis of representation therein shall be reduced in the proportion which the number of such male citizens shall bear to the whole number of male citizens twenty-one years of age in such State.

*Section 3.* No person shall be a Senator or Representative in Congress, or elector of President and Vice President, or hold any office, civil or military, under the United States, or under any State, who, having previously taken an oath, as a member of Congress, or as an officer of the United States, or as a member of any State legislature, or as an executive or judicial officer of any State, to support the Constitution of the United States, shall have engaged in insurrection or rebellion against the same, or given aid or comfort to the enemies thereof. But Congress may by a vote of two-thirds of each House, remove such disability.

*Section 4.* The validity of the public debt of the United States; authorized by law, including debts incurred for payment of pensions and bounties for services in suppressing insurrection or rebellion, shall not be questioned. But neither the United States nor any State shall assume or pay any debt or obligation incurred in aid of insurrection or rebellion against the United States, or any claim for the loss of emancipation of any slave; but all such debts, obligations and claims shall be held illegal and void.

*Section 5.* The Congress shall have power to enforce, by appropriate legislation, the provisions of this article.

AMENDMENT **XV** [1870]

*Section 1*. The right of citizens of the United States to vote shall not be denied or abridged by the United States or by any State on account of race, color, or previous condition of servitude.

*Section 2*. The Congress shall have power to enforce this article by appropriate legislation.

AMENDMENT **XVI** [1913]

The Congress shall have power to lay and collect taxes on incomes, from whatever source derived, without apportionment among the several States, and without regard to any census or enumeration.

AMENDMENT **XVII** [1913]

[1] The Senate of the United States shall be composed of two Senators from each State, elected by the people thereof, for six years, and each Senator shall have one vote. The electors in each State shall have the qualifications requisite for electors of the most numerous branch of the State legislatures.

[2] When vacancies happen in the representation of any State in the Senate, the executive authority of such State shall issue writs of election to fill such vacancies: *Provided,* That the legislature of any State may empower the executive thereof to make temporary appointments until the people fill the vacancies by election as the legislature may direct.

[3] This amendment shall not be so construed as to affect the election or term of any Senator chosen before it becomes valid as part of the Constitution.

AMENDMENT **XVIII** [1919]

*Section 1*. After one year from the ratification of this article the manufacture, sale, or transportation of intoxicating liquors within, the importation thereof into, or the exportation thereof from the United States and all territory subject to the jurisdiction thereof for beverage purposes is hereby prohibited.

*Section 2*. The Congress and the several States shall have concurrent power to enforce this article by appropriate legislation.

*Section 3*. This article shall be inoperative unless it shall have been ratified as an amendment to the Constitution by the legislatures of the several States, as provided in the Constitution, within seven years from the date of the submission hereof to the States by the Congress.

## AMENDMENT XIX [1920]

[1] The right of citizens of the United States to vote shall not be denied or abridged by the United States or by any State on account of sex.

[2] Congress shall have power to enforce this article by appropriate legislation.

## AMENDMENT XX [1933]

*Section 1.* The terms of the President and Vice President shall end at noon on the 20th day of January, and the terms of Senators and Representatives at noon on the 3d day of January, of the years in which such terms would have ended if this article had not been ratified; and the terms of their successors shall then begin.

*Section 2.* The Congress shall assemble at least once in every year, and such meeting shall begin at noon on the 3d day of January, unless they shall by law appoint a different day.

*Section 3.* If, at the time fixed for the beginning of the term of the President, the President elect shall have died, the Vice President elect shall become President. If a President shall not have been chosen before the time fixed for the beginning of his term, or if the President elect shall have failed to qualify, then the Vice President elect shall act as President until a President shall have qualified; and the Congress may by law provide for the case wherein neither a President elect nor a Vice President elect shall have qualified, declaring who shall then act as President, or the manner in which one who is to act shall be selected, and such person shall act accordingly until a President or Vice President shall have qualified.

*Section 4.* The Congress may by law provide for the case of the death of any of the persons from whom the House of Representatives may choose a President whenever the right of choice shall have devolved upon them, and for the case of the death of any of the persons from whom the Senate may choose a Vice President whenever the right of choice shall have devolved upon them.

*Section 5.* Sections 1 and 2 shall take effect on the 15th day of October following the ratification of this article.

*Section 6.* This article shall be inoperative unless it shall have been ratified as an amendment to the Constitution by the legislatures of three-fourths of the several States within seven years from the date of its submission.

## AMENDMENT XXI [1933]

*Section 1.* The eighteenth article of amendment to the Constitution of the United States is hereby repealed.

*Section* 2. The transportation or importation into any State, Territory, or possession of the United States for delivery or use therein of intoxicating liquors, in violation of the laws thereof, is hereby prohibited.

*Section* 3. This article shall be inoperative unless it shall have been ratified as an amendment to the Constitution by conventions in the several States, as provided in the Constitution, within seven years from the date of the submission hereof to the States by the Congress.

## AMENDMENT **XXII** [1951]

*Section* 1. No person shall be elected to the office of the President more than twice, and no person who has held the office of President, or acted as President, for more than two years of a term to which some other person was elected President shall be elected to the office of the President more than once. But this Article shall not apply to any person holding the office of President when this Article was proposed by the Congress, and shall not prevent any person who may be holding the office of President, or acting as President, during the term within which the Article becomes operative from holding the office of President, or acting as President during the remainder of such term.

*Section* 2. This article shall be inoperative unless it shall have been ratified as an amendment to the Constitution by the legislatures of three-fourths of the several States within seven years from the date of its submission to the States by the Congress.

## AMENDMENT **XXIII** [1961]

*Section* 1. The District constituting the seat of Government of the United States shall appoint in such manner as the Congress may direct:

A number of electors of President and Vice President equal to the whole number of Senators and Representatives in Congress to which the District would be entitled if it were a State, but in no event more than the least populous State; they shall be in addition to those appointed by the States, but they shall be considered, for the purposes of the election of President and Vice President, to be electors appointed by a State; and they shall meet in the District and perform such duties as provided by the twelfth article of amendment.

*Section* 2. The Congress shall have power to enforce this article by appropriate legislation.

## AMENDMENT **XXIV** [1964]

*Section* 1. The right of citizens of the United States to vote in any primary or other election for President or Vice President, for electors for President or Vice President, or for Senator or Representative in Congress, shall not be denied or abridged by the United States or any State by reason of failure to pay any poll tax or other tax.

*Section 2.* The Congress shall have power to enforce this article by appropriate legislation.

## AMENDMENT XXV [1967]

*Section 1.* In case of the removal of the President from office or of his death or resignation, the Vice President shall become President.

*Section 2.* Whenever there is a vacancy in the office of the Vice President, the President shall nominate a Vice President who shall take office upon confirmation by a majority vote of both Houses of Congress.

*Section 3.* Whenever the President transmits to the President pro tempore of the Senate and the Speaker of the House of Representatives his written declaration that he is unable to discharge the powers and duties of his office, and until he transmits to them a written declaration to the contrary, such powers and duties shall be discharged by the Vice President as Acting President.

*Section 4.* Whenever the Vice President and a Majority of either the principal officers of the executive departments or of such other body as Congress may by law provide, transmit to the President pro tempore of the Senate and the Speaker of the House of Representatives their written declaration that the President is unable to discharge the powers and duties of his office, the Vice President shall immediately assume the powers and duties of the office as Acting President.

Thereafter, when the President transmits to the President pro tempore of the Senate and the Speaker of the House of Representatives his written declaration that no inability exists, he shall resume the powers and duties of his office unless the Vice President and a majority of either the principal officers of the executive department or of such other body as Congress may by law provide, transmit within four days to the President pro tempore of the Senate and the Speaker of the House of Representatives their written declaration that the President is unable to discharge the powers and duties of his office. Thereupon Congress shall decide the issue, assembling within forty-eight hours for that purpose if not in session. If the Congress, within twenty-one days after receipt of the latter written declaration, or, if Congress is not in session, within twenty-one days after Congress is required to assemble, determines by two-thirds vote of both Houses that the President is unable to discharge the powers and duties of his office, the Vice President shall continue to discharge the same as Acting President; otherwise, the President shall resume the powers and duties of his office.

## AMENDMENT XXVI [1971]

*Section 1.* The right of citizens of the United States, who are eighteen years of age or older, to vote shall not be denied or abridged by the United States or by any State on account of age.

*Section 2.* The Congress shall have power to enforce this article by appropriate legislation.

## Amendment XXVII [1992]

No law varying the Compensation for the services of the Senators and Representatives shall take effect, unless an election of Representatives shall have intervened.

# Biographical Notes on Selected
# U.S. Supreme Court Justices

The brief sketches that follow are designed to offer at least some sense of the background, personality, and intellectual style of the justices who have had the greatest impact on first amendment jurisprudence. Because they are no substitute for serious biography, we have frequently suggested additional sources for further investigation. On less significant justices, see Currie, The Most Insignificant Justice: A Preliminary Inquiry, 50 U. Chi. L. Rev. 466 (1983); Easterbrook, The Most Insignificant Justice: Further Evidence, 50 U. Chi. L. Rev. 481 (1983).

**SAMUEL ALITO (1950- ):** Samuel Alito was born in 1950 in Trenton, New Jersey. He received his bachelor's degree from Princeton and his law degree from Yale, where he served as an editor of the Yale Law Journal. After serving as a law clerk to Judge Leonard Garth of the U.S. Court of Appeals for the Third Circuit, Alito worked as an Assistant U.S. Attorney and specialized in appellate litigation. From 1981 to 1985, he served as Assistant to the Solicitor General in the Reagan administration, and argued a dozen cases on behalf of the federal government in the U.S. Supreme Court. From 1985 to 1987, he served as Deputy Assistant Attorney General in the Office of Legal Counsel, where he provided constitutional advice to the Executive Branch. From 1987 to 1989, Alito served as U.S. Attorney for the District of New Jersey, where he focused on prosecuting white collar and organized crime. In 1990, President George H. W. Bush nominated Alito to the U.S. Court of Appeals for the Third Circuit. Fifteen years later, after the failed nomination of Harriet Miers, President George W. Bush nominated Alito to succeed Justice O'Connor on the Supreme Court of the United States. Although a number of civil liberties organizations opposed Alito's nomination because, in the words of the ACLU, his record revealed "a willingness to support government actions that abridge individual freedoms," Alito's nomination was confirmed by the Senate by a vote of 58-42 on January 31, 2006.

**HUGO L. BLACK** (1886-1971): In 1937, President Roosevelt chose Hugo Black to fill the first available vacancy on the Court. A southern progressive who had defended the rights of labor organizers and investigated police brutality before coming to Washington, Black served in the U.S. Senate for ten years prior to his appointment. As a senator, he strongly defended New Deal programs, including Roosevelt's "Court-packing" plan. Shortly after his confirmation he became the subject of controversy when it was revealed that he had belonged to the Ku Klux Klan for two years in the 1920s. The controversy subsided after Black in a dramatic radio address, admitted his prior membership, but added that he had resigned many years before and would comment no further. As a justice, Black was known for his insistence on what he claimed to be literal enforcement of constitutional guarantees, especially the first amendment guarantee of free speech. Although frequently characterized as an "activist" because of his willingness to subject to intensive review legislation that arguably violated express constitutional provisions, Black himself thought that literalism was necessary to confine judicial power. Thus, his insistence that the fourteenth amendment incorporated and made applicable to the states the guarantees of the first eight amendments was premised in part on his belief that any other approach would leave justices free to read their own values into the Constitution. See Adamson v. California, 332 U.S. 46 (1947). Consistent with this view, in cases such as Griswold v. Connecticut, 381 U.S. 479 (1965), Black rejected the notion that the Constitution contained general guarantees of "privacy" or "natural rights" beyond those expressly articulated in the text. See G. Dunne, Hugo Black and the Judicial Revolution (1977).

**HARRY A. BLACKMUN** (1908-1999): Harry Blackmun was President Nixon's third choice to fill the seat vacated when Abe Fortas resigned in 1970. After failing to secure confirmation of Clement Haynsworth of South Carolina and G. Harrold Carswell of Florida, Nixon announced that the Senate "as it is presently constituted" would not confirm a southerner and turned to Blackmun, a judge on the Eighth Circuit Court of Appeals. A boyhood friend of Chief Justice Burger, Blackmun was quickly dubbed "the Minnesota Twin" by the press. During his early years on the Court, he regularly voted with the chief justice. Later he distanced himself from the Court's conservative bloc and increasingly joined Justices Marshall and Brennan in dissent. Blackmun is best known for his majority opinion in Roe v. Wade, 410 U.S. 113 (1973), upholding the constitutional right of women to decide for themselves whether to have an abortion. It has been suggested that the opinion was influenced by Blackmun's pre-judicial experience as house counsel for the Mayo Clinic, where he frequently advised doctors and defended their right to make medical judgments.

**LOUIS D. BRANDEIS** (1856-1941): The son of Jewish immigrants from Bohemia, Louis Brandeis successfully practiced law in Boston for forty years before his nomination to the Court. Although he became wealthy from his practice, Brandeis preferred to live simply and set a ceiling on personal expenditures of one-fifth of his income. Even after his appointment to the Court, he provided financial support for the work of his proteges, one of whom was Felix Frankfurter. He devoted himself to a host of public causes. He defended municipal control of Boston's subway system, opposed monopolistic practices of the New Haven Railroad, arbitrated labor disputes in New York's garment industry, and argued in support of the constitutionality of state maximum hour and minimum wage statutes. His nomination to the Court by President Wilson in 1916 sparked heated opposition, including protests from seven ex-presidents of the American Bar Association. During his long tenure on the Court, Brandeis insisted on respect for jurisdictional and procedural limitations on the Court's power. His distrust of large and powerful institutions, and of dogmatic adherence to the received wisdom, led him to support the constitutional authority of the states to experiment with unconventional social and economic theories. He also frequently dissented from the Court's conservative majority when it blocked efforts of the federal government to intervene in the economy. Some of his most eloquent opinions, however, were written in defense of limits on governmental power when civil liberties were at issue. His famous concurring opinion in Whitney v. California, 274 U.S. 357 (1927), argued for freedom of expression on the ground that "it is hazardous to discourage thought, hope and imagination; that fear breeds repression; that repression breeds hate; that hate menaces stable government; that the path of safety lies in the opportunity to discuss freely supposed grievances and proposed remedies; and that the fitting remedy for evil counsels is good ones." And in Olmstead v. United States, 277 U.S. 438 (1928), Brandeis dissented from the Court's refusal to condemn wiretapping, noting that "[O]ur Government is the potent, the omnipresent teacher. For good or for ill, it teaches the whole people by its example." See L. Paper, Brandeis (1983); M. Urofsky, A Mind of One Piece: Brandeis and American Reform (1971).

**WILLIAM J. BRENNAN, JR.** (1906-1997): After graduating from Harvard Law School, William Brennan returned to his native Newark, where he joined a prominent law firm and specialized in labor law. As his practice grew, Brennan, a devoted family man, resented the demands it made on his time and accepted an appointment on the New Jersey Superior Court in order to lessen his workload. Brennan attracted attention as an efficient and fair-minded judge and was elevated to the New Jersey Supreme Court in 1952. President Eisenhower appointed him to the Supreme Court in 1956. The appointment was criticized at the time as "political" on the ground that the nomination of a Catholic Democrat on the eve of the 1956 presidential election was intended to win votes. Once on the Court, Justice Brennan firmly established himself as a leader of the "liberal" wing. He authored important opinions in the areas of free expression, criminal procedure, and reapportionment. Often credited with providing critical behind-the-scenes leadership

during the Warren Court years, Brennan continued to play a significant role —
although more often as a dissenter lamenting what he believed to be the
evisceration of Warren Court precedents — as the ideological complexion
of the Court shifted in the 1970s and 1980s. Brennan's own spirit is perhaps
best captured in his celebration in New York Times v. Sullivan, 376 U.S. 255
(1964), of "our profound national commitment to the principle that debate on
public issues should be uninhibited, robust, and wide-open."

**STEPHEN G. BREYER (1938- ):** Prior to his appointment to the Supreme
Court, Stephen Breyer had compiled a distinguished record as a legal
academic and in all three branches of the federal government. Educated at
Oxford and Harvard Law School, he served as law clerk to Justice Arthur
Goldberg and in the Justice Department before returning to Harvard to
teach. During leaves of absence, he worked for Watergate Special Counsel
Archibald Cox and served as chief counsel to the Senate Judiciary Committee.
In 1980, President Carter named him to the U.S. Court of Appeals. As chief
judge of the First Circuit, Breyer gained a reputation for his ability to forge
consensus and to write opinions that were clear, concise, and trenchant. An
expert on administrative law and an author of important works about risk
assessment, Breyer is a cautious and thoughtful moderate who is known for
his pragmatism, his erudition, and his willingness to rethink old ideas.

**WARREN E. BURGER (1907-1995):** The son of financially hard-pressed
parents, Warren Burger attended college and law school at night while selling
life insurance during the day. After graduation, he entered private practice and
assisted Harold Stassen in his unsuccessful bid for the Republican presidential
nomination in 1948. In 1953, he came to Washington to serve as assistant
attorney general for the Civil Division of the Justice Department. While in that
post, he attracted public attention by defending the government's dismissal of
John F. Peters for disloyalty after Solicitor General Sobeloff refused to argue
the case on grounds of conscience. Shortly thereafter President Eisenhower
appointed him to the U.S. Court of Appeals for the District of Columbia
Circuit. His tenure on that court was marked by sharp clashes with the court's
liberal majority, especially over criminal justice issues. In 1969, President
Nixon named Burger chief justice to replace Earl Warren. A strong advocate
of "strict construction" and a "plain meaning" approach to statutory and
constitutional interpretation, Burger firmly identified himself with the Court's
conservative wing and often voted to limit Warren Court decisions. But he also
authored important opinions upholding the right of trial judges to order busing
as a remedy for school segregation, interpreting federal civil rights statutes as
imposing an "effects" test for employment discrimination, and upholding the
right of the press to remain free of prior restraints in covering criminal trials.
Burger wrote for a unanimous Court in United States v. Nixon, 418 U.S. 683
(1974), upholding the subpoena for the Watergate tapes, which a few days later

resulted in President Nixon's resignation. The Court's legacy under his leadership is much disputed, with some seeing continuity with the Warren Court years and others claiming that he began a period of substantial retrenchment.

**BENJAMIN N. CARDOZO (1870-1938):** The son of a Tammany Hall judge who was implicated in the Boss Tweed scandal and resigned, rather than face impeachment, Benjamin Cardozo began his judicial career by narrowly defeating a Tammany candidate for a position on the New York Supreme Court. Shortly thereafter he was appointed to the New York Court of Appeals, where he served for eighteen years, during the last six of which he was chief judge. Cardozo is probably best remembered for his skills as a state common law judge. He was responsible for making the New York Court of Appeals the most respected state court in the country, and his judicial writings and lectures were immensely influential. Upon Justice Holmes's retirement, President Hoover was inundated with requests that Cardozo be elevated to the Supreme Court. But there were already two New Yorkers and one Jew serving on the Court, and Hoover resisted. Only when Justice Stone offered to resign to make way for Cardozo did the President relent. Cardozo was a bachelor who had very few friends and lived for most of his life with his unmarried sister. Called "the hermit philosopher" by some, Cardozo was remembered by others for "the strangely compelling power of [his] reticent, sensitive almost mystical personality." See R. Posner, Cardozo, A Study in Reputation (1990); Andrew L. Kaufman, Cardozo (1998).

**WILLIAM O. DOUGLAS (1898-1980):** Widely regarded as one of the most brilliant, eccentric, and independent persons to serve on the Court, William Douglas sat as an associate justice for thirty-six years, seven months — longer than any other justice. Born in poverty in Minnesota, he spent his early years in Yakima, Washington. Although financially hard pressed, he managed to go east to study law at Columbia Law School, where he taught before joining the Yale faculty in 1929. President Roosevelt named him to the newly created Securities and Exchange Commission in 1934, and Douglas became its chairman in 1937. Roosevelt nominated him to be an associate justice in 1939. Douglas's early opinions gave little hint of the controversy that would surround him in later years. Indeed, Roosevelt came close to choosing him as his running mate in 1944 — a decision that would have made him President on Roosevelt's death a year later. In subsequent years, however, Douglas's controversial statements both on and off the bench, his strong support for unpopular political causes, and his unconventional lifestyle (he was married four times) stirred up a whirlwind of political opposition. Congress twice began impeachment proceedings against him, although neither effort came close to success. A prodigiously rapid worker, Douglas often ridiculed his colleagues for complaining about the Court's workload. By his own account, he once assisted a colleague who had fallen behind in his work by ghostwriting a majority opinion that responded to his own dissent. He often finished his work for the term early and retreated to his nearly inaccessible summer home in Yakima, to which lawyers were forced to trek when emergency matters arose. Critics claimed that his opinions showed the signs of haste; admirers emphasized the forceful, blunt manner in which he cut through legal doctrine to reach the core issue in a case. His opinions were marked by a fierce commitment to individual rights and distrust of government power. See V. Countryman, Douglas of the Supreme Court (1959); W. Douglas, The Court Years 1939-1975 (1980); W. Douglas, Go East Young Man (1974).

**ABE FORTAS (1910-1984):** Founder of the Washington law firm Arnold, Fortas, and Porter, Abe Fortas provided behind-the-scenes advice to Democratic politicians for years before his appointment to the Court in 1965. As a young man, Fortas held a series of jobs in the Roosevelt administration, including under-secretary of the interior under Harold Ickes. After entering private practice, Fortas found time to defend victims of McCarthyism and to litigate several important civil rights cases, including Gideon v. Wainwright, 372 U.S. 335 (1963). In 1948, Fortas successfully represented Congressman Lyndon Johnson when his forty-eight-vote victory in the Democratic senatorial primary was challenged. (The election earned Johnson the nickname "Landslide Lyndon.") Fortas became one of Johnson's close friends, and when Justice Goldberg resigned to become United Nations ambassador, Johnson appointed him to the Court. In 1968, when Chief Justice Warren indicated that he intended to retire, Johnson chose Fortas as Warren's successor. The nomination had long-term consequences that neither man could have foreseen. Republicans and conservative Democrats charged Johnson with "cronyism" and ultimately forced him to withdraw the nomination, but not before it was revealed that Fortas had received $15,000 to teach a course at a local university while on the bench. The next year Life magazine revealed that Fortas had accepted and then returned $20,000 from a charitable foundation controlled by the family of an indicted stock manipulator. Although denying any wrongdoing, Fortas resigned from the Court. As a consequence, President Nixon was able to fill two vacancies early in his term, thereby helping to fulfill his campaign promise to "roll back" the Warren Court revolution. See L. Kalman, Abe Fortas: A Biography (1990); B. Murphy, Fortas: The Rise and Ruin of a Supreme Court Justice (1988).

**FELIX FRANKFURTER (1882-1965):** An immigrant from Austria, Felix Frankfurter grew up in poverty on New York's lower east side. Before his appointment to the Court by President Roosevelt in 1939, he taught at the Harvard Law School, helped found The New Republic, served in a variety of public positions, and provided important, informal advice to Roosevelt in formulating the New Deal. Frankfurter's scholarly writings contributed significantly to understanding of administrative law, labor law, and the relationship between federal and state courts. As a justice, Frankfurter's career was marked by a preoccupation with problems of judicial legitimacy and self-restraint.

He frequently clashed with Justices Douglas and Black, also Roosevelt appointees, over the "preferred position" of the first amendment and the incorporation doctrine. His concern over the countermajoritarian aspect of judicial review led him to argue for deference to legislative judgment in such landmark cases as Dennis v. United States, 341 U.S. 494 (1951), and Baker v. Carr, 369 U.S. 186 (1962). See P. Kurland, Felix Frankfurter on the Supreme Court (1970); J. Lash, From the Diaries of Felix Frankfurter (1974).

**RUTH BADER GINSBURG (1933- ):** When Ruth Bader Ginsburg graduated from law school, one of her mentors suggested to Justice Felix Frankfurter that he take her on as a law clerk. Despite Ginsburg's brilliant law school record (earned while caring for an infant daughter), Justice Frankfurter told her sponsor that he just was not ready to hire a woman. Thirty-three years after this rebuff, Ginsburg assumed her seat on the Supreme Court. In the intervening years, Ginsburg gained fame as the first tenured woman professor at the Columbia Law School; as the director of the Women's Rights Project of the American Civil Liberties Union, where she won many pioneering victories in the legal battle against gender discrimination; and as a judge on the U.S. Court of Appeals for the District of Columbia Circuit. She has been called "the Thurgood Marshall of gender equality law" and is said to be "as responsible as any one person for legal advances that women made under the Equal Protection Clause." As a lower court judge, however, she gained a reputation for caution and sometimes disappointed her more activist supporters. A strong defender of abortion rights, she has nonetheless criticized Roe v. Wade for rejecting a narrower approach to the abortion question that might have "served to reduce rather than to fuel controversy."

**JOHN MARSHALL HARLAN (1899-1971):** The grandson of the first Justice Harlan, John Harlan was appointed to the Court by President Eisenhower in 1955. Before his appointment, Harlan spent a quarter of a century in practice with a prominent Wall Street law firm, served as chief counsel to the New York State Crime Commission, and sat briefly on the Court of Appeals for the Second Circuit. On the Court, Justice Harlan became the intellectual leader of the "conservative" wing, often dissenting from "activist" decisions during the stewardship of Chief Justice Warren. He defended the values of federalism and never accepted the incorporation of the bill of rights against the states. Nor was he ever reconciled to the Court's broad reading of the equal protection clause, especially when strict scrutiny was utilized to defend "fundamental" values. There was also a strong libertarian strain in Justice Harlan's opinions, however. His belief in federalism and rejection of "judicial activism" did not prevent him from finding, for example, that the due process clause precluded the states from restricting the use of contraceptives by married couples. He also wrote for the Court in a series of important first amendment decisions, narrowly construing federal statutes prohibiting subversive advocacy and defending the right of a Vietnam War protestor to wear a jacket inscribed with the message "Fuck the Draft." It was in the latter case that Harlan proclaimed that "one man's vulgarity is another's lyric." During his tenure, Harlan was widely respected, even by opponents of his philosophy, for his thoroughness, candor, and civility. Although he often disagreed publicly with Justice Black, they were close friends in private. They were hospitalized together during their final illnesses and died within a short period of each other. See D. Shapiro, The Evolution of a Judicial Philosophy: Selected Opinions and Papers of Justice John M. Harlan. (1969).

**OLIVER WENDELL HOLMES, JR. (1841-1935):** Oliver Wendell Holmes, the son of a famous poet and essayist, survived three wounds in the Civil War. He had already enjoyed a distinguished career as a practitioner, author, professor, and justice on the Supreme Judicial Court of Massachusetts before his appointment to the Supreme Court by President Roosevelt in 1902. Holmes, then sixty-two years old, seemed to be at the close of his career. A life-long Republican, he was expected to be a loyal supporter of the President on the bench. Few could have anticipated that he would serve on the Court for twenty-nine years, that his tenure would be marked by a fierce independence, and that he would exercise virtually unparalleled influence over modern constitutional theory. Holmes is perhaps best remembered for his formulation of the "clear and present danger test" for subversive advocacy and his rejection of substantive due process as a limitation on state social and economic legislation. His judicial philosophy was marked by skepticism, particularism, and pragmatism. He doubted that general propositions decided particular cases or that broad value judgments could be objectively defended. He thought that the law was necessarily unconcerned with the thought processes of those it regulated, and that it had no independent existence apart from what people did in response to what judges said. For twenty-five years, he walked daily the two and one-half miles from his home to the Court, never missing a session. He finally retired at ninety years of age and died two days before his ninety-fourth birthday. See G. White, Justice Oliver Wendell Holmes: Law and the Inner Self (1993); M. Howe, Justice Oliver Wendell Holmes: The Proving Years (1963); M. Howe, Justice Oliver Wendell Holmes: The Shaping Years (1957).

**CHARLES EVANS HUGHES (1862-1948):** After defeating William Randolph Hearst for the governorship of New York, Charles Evans Hughes served as governor for one term and part of another until 1910, when President Taft appointed him to the Court. In 1916, Hughes resigned to run for the presidency on the Republican and Progressive tickets against Woodrow Wilson. On election eve, he went to bed thinking that he was President, but when the final returns were counted, he had lost by a scant twenty-three electoral votes. Hughes returned to New York law practice until President Harding appointed him secretary of state. In 1930, President Hoover returned Hughes to the

Court, this time as chief justice. Hughes served as chief justice during the tumultuous eleven-year period when the Court blocked much of President Roosevelt's New Deal, then survived a direct attack on its independence, and finally reconciled itself to the fundamental changes wrought by Roosevelt's program. Throughout this period, Hughes occupied a centrist position. Although closely identified with the conservative New York bar, he often joined the liberals on the Court who dissented from invalidation of social and economic legislation. But he also defended the institutional independence of the Court when it was attacked by President Roosevelt. At a crucial point in the "Court-packing" controversy, Hughes sent a letter to Senator Wheeler arguing that the Court was current in its work, and that the addition of new justices would create serious inefficiencies. Upon his retirement in 1941, Justice Frankfurter likened his leadership ability to that of "Toscanini lead[ing] an orchestra." See M. Pusey, Charles Evans Hughes (1951).

**ROBERT H. JACKSON (1892-1954):** A skillful advocate and brilliant legal stylist, Robert Jackson rose quickly in the early Roosevelt administration, eventually becoming one of President Roosevelt's closest advisors. After serving as counsel to the Internal Revenue Bureau, where he won a $750,000 judgment against former Treasury Secretary Andrew W. Mellon, Jackson served successively as assistant attorney general, solicitor general, and attorney general. President Roosevelt named him to the Supreme Court in 1941 to fill the seat vacated by Justice Stone when Stone was appointed chief justice. Jackson is perhaps best remembered for his graceful prose and his subtle and original efforts to articulate a coherent theory of separation of powers in his opinions in such cases as Youngstown Sheet & Tube Co. v. Sawyer, 342 U.S. 579 (1952), and Korematsu v. United States, 323 U.S. 214 (1944). In 1945, while still on the Court, Jackson served as the chief U.S. prosecutor at the Nuremburg war crimes trial. This exposure to German fascism may have influenced Jackson's subsequent approach to constitutional interpretation. Many of his later first amendment opinions, for example, were preoccupied with the attempt to draw a bright line between protected freedom of conscience and unprotected speech that threatened the public peace and order. Jackson's willingness to permit government regulation of subversive or abusive advocacy in cases such as Dennis v. United States, 341 U.S. 494 (1951), and Terminiello v. Chicago, 337 U.S. 1 (1949), brought him into sharp conflict with Justices Black and Douglas — conflict that was exacerbated by deteriorating personal relationships. When Chief Justice Stone died, it was reported that several justices threatened to resign if Jackson was elevated to the chief justiceship. Jackson never became chief justice, but remained on the Court until his death in 1954. See E. Gerhart, America's Advocate: Robert A. Jackson (1958); G. White, The American Judicial Tradition ch. 11 (1976).

**ELENA KAGAN (1960- ):** Named to the Supreme Court by Barack Obama in 2010, Elena Kagan is the first person in almost forty years nominated to the

Court without judicial experience. After graduating magna cum laude from Harvard Law School, she clerked for Justice Thurgood Marshall, who nicknamed her "Shorty" because of her 5'3" height. She then embarked on a distinguished academic career, first at the University of Chicago Law School and then at Harvard Law School, where she eventually became the first woman dean. For four years she served President Clinton as Associate White House Counsel, Deputy Assistant to the President for Domestic Policy, and Deputy Director of the Domestic Policy Council. In 2009, President Obama named her Solicitor General of the United States. Kagan is known for her powerful intellect, effective writing style, and puckish sense of humor.

**ANTHONY M. KENNEDY (1936- ):** President Reagan's effort to fill the seat vacated by the retirement of Justice Powell, who was widely viewed as a "swing vote" on a number of important issues, sparked an extraordinary controversy about the future direction of the Supreme Court. His first nominee, Robert Bork, was defeated on the Senate floor after a long and bitter debate that pitted "originalists" against those who would treat the Constitution as incorporating values not directly derived from the text. His second nominee, Douglas Ginsburg, was forced to withdraw from consideration after it was revealed that he had used marijuana. In the wake of these events, the Senate greeted with relief the nomination of Anthony Kennedy, a relatively colorless and nonideological conservative. After graduating from Harvard Law School in 1961, Kennedy worked as a lawyer and lobbyist in California until his appointment to the Ninth Circuit by President Ford in 1975. Since joining the Supreme Court, he has been a reliable conservative. He criticized his colleagues for "trivializing constitutional adjudication" by engaging in a "jurisprudence of minutiae" in its enforcement of the establishment clause and for moving "from 'separate but equal' to 'unequal but benign'" in upholding an affirmative action plan. However, he joined some of his liberal colleagues when he twice cast the deciding vote to uphold the first amendment right of protestors to burn the American flag and disappointed some of his conservative supporters when he coauthored a joint opinion with Justices Souter and O'Connor declining to overrule Roe v. Wade.

**THURGOOD MARSHALL (1908-1993):** The son of a primary school teacher and a club steward, Thurgood Marshall became the first black to serve on the Court when he was appointed by President Johnson in 1967. But Marshall had already made an enduring mark on American legal history decades before his judicial career began. After graduating first in his class from Howard Law School, Marshall began his long involvement with the National Association for the Advancement of Colored People. For two decades, he traveled across the country coordinating the NAACP's attack on segregation in housing, employment, voting, public accommodations, and especially education. His most famous victory during this period came in Brown v. Board of

Education, 347 U.S. 483 (1954), where he successfully argued that segregated public education violated the equal protection clause. In 1961, President Kennedy nominated him to serve on the U.S. Court of Appeals for the Second Circuit. Although southern senators blocked his confirmation for a year, he finally assumed his seat, where he served until 1965 when President Johnson appointed him solicitor general. As a justice, Marshall was known primarily for his unstinting defense of racial and other minorities, his liberal interpretation of free speech and press guarantees, his "multi-tiered" theory of equal protection analysis, and his fervent opposition to capital punishment. See M. Tushnet, Making Civil Rights Law: Thurgood Marshall and the Supreme Court, 1931-1961 (1994).

**JAMES C. McREYNOLDS (1862-1946):** Although remembered today primarily as one of the "four horsemen of reaction" who helped block Franklin Roosevelt's New Deal, James McReynolds first came to public attention as a vigorous "trust buster" in the Theodore Roosevelt and Wilson administrations. In the year that he served as Wilson's attorney general, he angered many members of Congress and of the administration with his arrogance and ill-temper. President Wilson named him to the Court in 1914 largely to quiet the controversy. His judicial career was marked by an unyielding commitment to strict constructionism and conservative principles. His personal manner continued to alienate many of his colleagues. After The Gold Clause Cases were decided in 1935, he proclaimed, "Shame and humiliation are on us now. Moral and financial chaos may confidently be expected." Chief Justice Taft remarked that McReynolds "has a continual grouch" and "seems to delight in making others uncomfortable." Widely accused of antisemitism, McReynolds conspicuously failed to sign the letter of affection and regret drafted by his brethren on Justice Brandeis's retirement from the Court.

**SANDRA DAY O'CONNOR (1930- ):** The first woman ever to serve on the Court, Sandra Day O'Connor was appointed by President Reagan in 1981. O'Connor was a classmate of Justice Rehnquist at the Stanford Law School, where she was an editor of the Stanford Law Review. Despite her outstanding academic achievements, O'Connor found it difficult to locate a job on graduation. When she applied to the firm in which future Attorney General William French Smith was a partner, she was offered the position of secretary. After briefly serving as deputy county attorney for San Mateo County in California, she worked as a civilian attorney for the army while her husband served his tour of duty. She then spent eight years as a mother, homemaker, and volunteer while her three children grew up. When she resumed her legal career, she became an assistant attorney general in Arizona. In 1970, she was elected to the Arizona senate and eventually became majority leader. She then served on the Superior Court for Maricopa County and the Arizona Court of Appeals. Although her nomination to the Supreme Court was opposed by some conservatives, Justice O'Connor frequently aligned herself with the conservative wing of the Court. However, she has shown a preference for a balancing approach to constitutional law and case-by-case particularism — a stance that has created conflict with Justice Scalia, who claims to favor a rule-based approach. She initially urged her colleagues to reconsider its analysis of the abortion question in Roe v. Wade, but later surprised many by coauthoring an important opinion preserving Roe's central holding at a time when many thought it would be overruled. She wrote for a five-to-four majority in Mississippi University for Women v. Hogan, 458 U.S. 718 (1982), to invalidate a state nursing school's single-sex admissions policy. Widely respected for her incisive and informed questioning at oral argument, O'Connor is known for her deference to the political branches of government, for her defense of federalism, and for her original approach to the problem of church-state relations. See Comment, The Emerging Jurisprudence of Justice O'Connor, 52 U. Chi. L. Rev. 389 (1985).

**LEWIS F. POWELL, JR. (1907-1998):** After graduating from Washington & Lee Law School, Lewis Powell took a graduate degree in law from Harvard Law School. He then returned to his native Virginia, where he joined one of Richmond's most prestigious law firms. As president of the Richmond school board during a period of intense controversy concerning school desegregation, Powell gained a reputation as a racial moderate. Despite intense pressure from those advocating "massive resistance," he insisted on keeping the schools open. Powell was elected president of the American Bar Association in 1964. In that capacity, he worked to establish a legal services program within the Office of Economic Opportunity and spoke out against civil disobedience and "parental permissiveness." In 1971, President Nixon fulfilled his promise to name a southerner to the Court by selecting Powell to fill the vacancy created by the resignation of Justice Black. A few years after his appointment, Powell seemed to speak for the South in his concurring opinion in Keyes v. School District, 413 U.S. 189 (1973), in which he argued that there was no significant legal distinction between northern and southern school segregation. Over time, Powell gained the reputation as an ad hoc "balancer," often casting the critical "swing vote" in important decisions. In Regents of the University of California v. Bakke, 438 U.S. 265 (1978), Trimble v. Gordon, 430 U.S. 762 (1977), and Branzburg v. Hayes, 408 U.S. 665 (1972), for example, he controlled the disposition even though he was the only justice adopting his particular view of affirmative action, the rights of nonmarital children, and press rights, respectively. See J. Jeffries, Justice Lewis F. Powell, Jr. (1994).

**WILLIAM H. REHNQUIST (1924-2005):** After graduation from Stanford Law School, William Rehnquist came to Washington in 1952 to clerk for Associate Justice Robert Jackson. During his clerkship, he wrote a controversial memorandum for Justice Jackson supporting the constitutionality of "separate but equal" education for blacks. When the memorandum surfaced years later during Rehnquist's confirmation hearings, he explained that it represented Jackson's views and not his own. Following his clerkship, Rehnquist moved to Phoenix, Arizona, where he became involved in Republican politics. A strong supporter of Barry Goldwater, Rehnquist headed the Justice Department's Office of Legal Counsel in the Nixon administration. President Nixon named him to the Court in 1971, and President Reagan named him chief justice in 1986. Chief Justice Rehnquist is known for his commitment to judicial restraint and majoritarianism. His opinions in the areas of equal protection, due process, and free speech consistently reflect a narrow construction of constitutional rights. For example, he would limit strict scrutiny under the equal protection clause to cases involving racial discrimination. Unlike conservative justices of an earlier era, however, Rehnquist would maintain the same deferential stance when reviewing state legislation arguably interfering with private markets and the free flow of commerce. (See, for example, his opinion for the Court in Posadas de Puerto Rico Associates v. Tourism Co. of Puerto Rico, 478 U.S. 328 (1986), and his dissenting opinion in Kassel v. Consolidated Freightways Corp., 450 U.S. 662 (1981).) Nonetheless, Rehnquist has supported judicial intervention to protect the prerogatives of the states from federal interference and to place constitutional limits on affirmative action programs arguably discriminating in favor of racial minorities. See Shapiro, Mr. Justice Rehnquist: A Preliminary View, 90 Harv. L. Rev. 293 (1976).

**JOHN G. ROBERTS (1955- )** : John Roberts was born in Buffalo, New York, in 1955. He attended Harvard College and Harvard Law School. After graduating from law school in 1979, Roberts served as a law clerk to Judge Henry Friendly on the U.S. Court of Appeals for the Second Circuit and then to Justice William Rehnquist on the U.S. Supreme Court. From 1981 to 1982, he served in the Reagan administration as a Special Assistant to U.S. Attorney General William French Smith, and from 1982 to 1986 he served as Associate Counsel to the President. Roberts then entered law practice at the Washington, D.C.-based law firm of Hogan & Hartson, but left to serve as Principal Deputy Solicitor General from 1989 to 1993 under President George H. W. Bush. In this capacity, he argued thirty-nine cases for the government before the Supreme Court, prevailing in twenty-five of them. In 1992, George H. W. Bush nominated Roberts to the U.S. Court of Appeals for the D.C. Circuit, but no Senate vote was held, and Roberts's nomination expired when Bush left office after losing the 1992 presidential election. Roberts then returned to Hogan & Hartson, where he became head of the firm's appellate practice and argued another thirty-nine cases before the Supreme Court, making him one of the most experienced Supreme Court advocates in the nation. On July 19, 2005, President George W. Bush nominated Roberts to the U.S. Supreme Court to fill a vacancy that would be left by the announced retirement of Sandra Day O'Connor. But following the death of Chief Justice

William Rehnquist on September 3, 2005, President Bush withdrew Roberts's nomination as O'Connor's successor and nominated Roberts to succeed Rehnquist. The Senate approved his appointment on September 29, 2005, by a vote of 78-22.

**ANTONIN SCALIA (1936- ):** The son of an Italian immigrant, Antonin Scalia was the first Italian-American to be appointed to the Supreme Court. A former law professor and assistant attorney general, he earned a reputation as an intelligent, hardworking, and dedicated conservative while serving as a judge on the U.S. Court of Appeals for the District of Columbia Circuit. Since his elevation to the Supreme Court, Justice Scalia has become known for his forceful opposition to constitutional balancing tests and to reliance on nontextual sources of interpretation. This posture has most often led him to "conservative" outcomes. He is a strong defender of executive prerogatives and is perhaps the Court's most vigorous opponent of affirmative action and abortion rights. The same posture has occasionally led him to vote with the Court's "liberals," however, especially on free speech and search and seizure questions. He is widely admired for his independence and intellectual integrity and for the clarity and forcefulness of his opinions, especially when in dissent.

**SONIA SOTOMAYOR (1954- ):** Justice Sotomayor is the daughter of a factory worker with a third-grade education who died when she was nine, and a nurse who raised her as a single mother. She grew up in a public housing project in the South Bronx. After graduating valedictorian of her high school class, she enrolled at Princeton, where she graduated summa cum laude, and then Yale Law School, where she was an editor of the Yale Law Journal. She served as a prosecutor and in private practice until she was appointed to the United States District Court by George H. W. Bush. In 1995, she issued a ruling that effectively ended the Major League Baseball strike, a decision that, according to a reporter for the Philadelphia Inquirer, caused her to join "the ranks of Joe DiMaggio, Willie Mays, Jackie Robinson, and Ted Williams." In 1998, President Clinton appointed her to the United States Court of Appeals for the Second Circuit, where she served as the first Latina on that court. Nominated by Barack Obama, she joined the Supreme Court in 2009. Since her elevation, Justice Sotomayor has generally voted with the Court's liberal wing. She has become known for her probing questions at oral argument and her mastery of the record in complex cases.

**DAVID HACKETT SOUTER (1939- ):** Prior to his nomination to the Supreme Court by President Bush, David Souter was a virtual unknown. In his long career as a justice on the New Hampshire Supreme Court, a judge on the New Hampshire trial court, and New Hampshire's attorney general, he seldom had occasion to express his views on contentious constitutional issues such as abortion and affirmative action. Indeed, some critics suggested that President Bush, mindful of the searing controversy surrounding the nomination of Judge Bork, selected Souter principally because he lacked a "paper trail." But although Souter had little experience in constitutional adjudication, he came to the Court with solid intellectual credentials. A Rhodes scholar and graduate of the Harvard Law School, he was praised by liberals and conservatives alike for his intelligence and fair-mindedness. The counsel for the New Hampshire State Democratic Party and president of the New Hampshire Bar Association characterized him as "an enormous intellectual" and "about 135 pounds — and about 120 pounds of brain." Before his appointment, Justice Souter lived by himself in a ramshackle New Hampshire farmhouse laden with stacks of books. Friends said that he liked to work seven days a week, taking time out to hike and listen to classical music. As a justice, Souter is known for careful, lawyer-like opinions and his moderate, nonideological stance toward controversial constitutional issues.

**JOHN PAUL STEVENS (1920- ):** A graduate of Northwestern Law School, John Paul Stevens clerked for Justice Wiley B. Rutledge before joining a Chicago law firm specializing in antitrust work. He taught part time at the University of Chicago and Northwestern Law Schools until his appointment to the Seventh Circuit Court of Appeals in 1970. Although a registered Republican, Justice Stevens was never active in partisan politics. President Ford elevated him to the Supreme Court in 1975. Stevens is known for his independence and an unwillingness to be bound by rigid formulas. He rejected the position that equal protection analysis can be reduced to various "tiers" of review, for example, arguing that various factors must be weighed under the same standard in every case to ensure that the state has met its obligation to govern impartially. And in free speech cases, Stevens staked out his own theory that fits comfortably within neither the traditional "liberal" nor the "conservative" ideology. See, e.g., Smith v. United States, 431 U.S. 291 (1977); Young v. American Mini Theatres, 427 U.S. 50 (1976).

**POTTER STEWART (1915-1985):** Son of the Republican mayor of Cincinnati, Potter Stewart became active in Ohio Republican politics at an early age. He was twice elected to the city council and served one term as vice mayor before President Eisenhower appointed him to the Sixth Circuit Court of Appeals in 1954. In 1958, Eisenhower elevated him to the Supreme Court, where he served until his retirement in 1981. Although his political background was conservative, Stewart occupied a centrist position on the Court. He frequently voted with the liberal justices on first amendment issues (an orientation perhaps influenced by his experience as editor of a student newspaper while at Yale), but with conservative justices on equal protection issues. On many questions, his position simply could not be predicted in advance, and he had little difficulty in changing his mind about views he had expressed in earlier opinions. Perhaps his most famous opinion was a concurrence in Jacobellis v. Ohio, 378 U.S. 184 (1964), in which he said of "hard core" pornography, "I shall not today attempt further to define the kinds of material I understand to be embraced within that shorthand description; and perhaps I could never succeed in intelligibly doing so. But I know it when I see it, and the motion picture involved in this case is not that." Although sometimes ridiculed, this statement in some ways summarized Stewart's judicial philosophy, which tended to be particularistic, intuitive, and pragmatic.

**HARLAN FISKE STONE (1872-1946):** For twenty-five years, Harlan Fiske Stone practiced law with a Wall Street law firm and served as a professor and the dean of the Columbia Law School. In 1924, President Coolidge appointed Stone, his old friend and classmate, to head a Department of Justice demoralized by the Teapot Dome scandal. A year later Coolidge appointed Stone to the Court. Although a Republican and moderate conservative, Stone sided with the wing of the Court willing to uphold New Deal programs during the great controversy that engulfed the Court in the early 1930s. In 1941, President Roosevelt elevated Stone to chief justice, an appointment that Archibald MacLeish called "the perfect word spoken at the perfect moment." Justice Stone's footnote 4 in United States v. Carolene Products, 304 U.S. 144 (1938), is doubtless the most famous footnote in constitutional law and has formed the basis of much of modern constitutional theory. During his twenty-one years on the bench, Stone occupied every seat from junior associate justice, to senior associate justice, to chief justice — a feat accomplished by no other justice. He died "with his boots on" — stricken while reading a dissenting opinion from the bench in 1946. See A. Mason, Harlan Fiske Stone: A Pillar of the Law (1956); G. White, The American Judicial Tradition ch. 10 (1976); Dunham, Mr. Chief Justice Stone, in A. Dunham and P. Kurland, Mr. Justice 229-251 (1956).

**GEORGE SUTHERLAND (1862-1942):** A friend and close advisor to President Harding, George Sutherland was appointed to the Court in 1922. Before his appointment, he served in the U.S. Senate for twelve years, where he developed a reputation as an authority on constitutional questions and a conservative who nonetheless occasionally supported progressive causes. While on the Court, he was the intellectual leader of the conservative wing. He strongly objected to what he considered the evisceration of the contract clause and vigorously opposed the constitutionality of minimum wage laws. See Home Building & Loan Association v. Blaisdell, 290 U.S. 398 (1934); Adkins v. Children's Hospital, 261 U.S. 525 (1923). But his concern for the rights of the individual and broad reading of the due process clause also led him to write for the majority in Powell v. Alabama, 287 U.S. 45 (1932), which reversed the conviction of the "Scottsboro Boys" and began the process of applying constitutionally based rules of criminal procedure to the states. See J. Paschal, Mr. Justice Sutherland: A Man against the State (1951).

**WILLIAM HOWARD TAFT (1857-1930):** The only person to serve as both President and chief justice, William Howard Taft's career was marked by genial conservatism and a commitment to the institutional independence of each branch of the federal government. Taft served as secretary of war in Theodore Roosevelt's administration and became one of Roosevelt's closest advisors. With support from Roosevelt, he was elected President in 1908. Soon after his inauguration, however, he and Roosevelt split, and he lost his bid for reelection in 1912, when Roosevelt splintered the Republican vote by running as an independent. After leaving the presidency, Taft taught constitutional law at Yale University and served for a year as president of the American Bar Association. Along with several other former ABA presidents, Taft fought to block Louis Brandeis's nomination to the Court in 1916. President Harding named Taft chief justice in 1921. Taft was responsible for passage of the Judiciary Act of 1925, which gave the Supreme Court effective control over its own appellate jurisdiction and for the appropriation of funds for construction of the present Supreme Court building. See A. Mason, William Howard Taft: Chief Justice (1964).

**CLARENCE THOMAS (1948- ):** Born into grinding poverty in segregated coastal Georgia, Clarence Thomas became the second African American and one of the youngest justices to join the Court when he was appointed by President Bush in 1991. He was confirmed by the Senate to fill the seat vacated by the retirement of Thurgood Marshall after extraordinary confirmation hearings that opened with a moving account of his personal saga and closed with charges of sexual harassment leveled against him by Anita Hill, who had worked with him at the Department of Education and the Equal Employment Opportunity Commission. A graduate of the Yale Law School, he served as assistant secretary for civil rights at the Department of Education and chair of the Equal Employment Opportunity Commission in the Reagan administration. During his controversial seven-year stewardship of the EEOC, Thomas's fierce opposition to affirmative action antagonized liberals and members of the civil rights community. In 1989, President Bush appointed Thomas to the U.S. Court of Appeals for the District of Columbia, where he served for fifteen months before his elevation to the Supreme Court. Known as a staunch conservative, Thomas's extrajudicial writings suggest an interest in natural law as a basis for constitutional adjudication. Since joining the Court, he has written a series of distinctive dissents and concurrences, often demonstrating a willingness to reject settled precedent in favor of his understanding of the constitutional text. On racial issues, he strongly opposes what he considers liberal condescension in the form of affirmative action and the assumption that majority black institutions are necessarily inferior.

**WILLIS VAN DEVANTER (1859-1941):** A lawyer's lawyer, William Van Devanter invariably sided with the conservative wing of the Court, but, unlike some of his colleagues, never resorted to divisive ideological rhetoric. Instead, he relied on his mastery of technical doctrine to become a "master of formulas that decided cases without creating precedents." Van Devanter, who was active in Republican politics in Wyoming, came to Washington during the McKinley administration and was named to the Eighth Circuit Court of Appeals by Theodore Roosevelt. When President Taft nominated him to serve as an associate justice, William Jennings Bryan complained that he was "the judge that held that two railroads running parallel to each other for two thousand miles were not competing lines, one of the roads being that of Union Pacific," one of Van Devanter's former clients. It has been said that Van Devanter came to the Court "fully equipped with a lawyer's understanding of federal jurisdiction, a frontiersman's knowledge of Indian affairs, and a native hostility to governmental regulation." His years on the Court were marked by a concern for technical jurisdictional questions and opposition to government intervention in all forms. His retirement in June of 1937 gave Franklin Roosevelt his first appointment and helped defuse the crisis created by the Court's opposition to the New Deal.

**EARL WARREN (1891-1974):** Both vilified and canonized during his tenure, Earl Warren presided as chief justice over one of the most tumultuous and portentous periods in the Court's history. The emotions that he aroused are hard to reconcile with his political stance, which was, essentially, centrist and pragmatic. As Republican governor of California, he denounced "communistic radicals" and supported the wartime order to forcibly evacuate Japanese Americans. (The Court subsequently upheld the constitutionality of the evacuation in Korematsu v. United States, 323 U.S. 214 (1944).) In his later years as governor, however, he developed the reputation as a progressive and proposed state programs for prepaid medical insurance and liberal welfare benefits. In 1948, he ran for Vice President on the ticket headed by Thomas Dewey. In 1952, he mounted his own presidential effort. At the Republican convention, however, he threw his support behind Dwight Eisenhower. President Eisenhower repaid Warren by nominating him as chief justice in 1953 — a nomination Eisenhower later called "the biggest damn-fool mistake I ever made." Perhaps Warren's greatest accomplishment on the Court was his painstaking and successful effort to maintain a united front as the Court overturned the separate but equal doctrine in Brown v. Board of Education, 347 U.S. 873 (1954), and then confronted southern violence and intransigence. Warren himself believed that his opinion in Reynolds v. Sims, 377 U.S. 533 (1964), establishing the one person, one vote formula, was of greater significance. In the end, however, it may have been his opinions in the field of criminal procedure — especially Miranda v. Arizona, 384 U.S. 436 (1966) — that attracted the most controversy. This controversy tended to obscure the fact that there was a strong conservative and moralistic tone to many of Warren's opinions. He opposed constitutional protection for "pornographic" literature, for example, and dissented in Shapiro v. Thompson, 394 U.S. 618 (1969), when the Court invalidated durational residency requirements for welfare recipients. Warren was distrustful of complex doctrinal argument. His opinions were thus marked by a confident, intuitively grounded insistence on fair play and fundamental justice. See B. Schwartz, Superchief (1983); E. Warren, The Memoirs of Earl Warren (1977); G. White, Earl Warren (1982).

**BYRON R. WHITE (1917-2002):** An outstanding scholar-athlete, Byron "Whizzer" White was first in his class at the University of Colorado, a Rhodes scholar, and a professional football player with the Detroit Lions before beginning his legal career. White served in the navy during World War II and graduated from Yale Law School magna cum laude. After serving as law clerk to Chief Justice Fred Vinson, he returned to his native Colorado where he practiced with a prominent Denver law firm for fourteen years. A long-time friend of John Kennedy, White headed Kennedy's preconvention presidential campaign in Colorado in 1960 and subsequently became chairman of National Citizens for Kennedy. After the election, Kennedy named him deputy attorney general and in 1962 elevated him to the Court. As a justice, White was known as a strong advocate of school desegregation and a defender of the rights of minorities. Although more ready than his colleagues to find legislation lacking in a "rational basis" when challenged under "low-level" equal protection review, he also criticized his colleagues for too aggressive use of substantive due process analysis. For example, joined only by Justice Rehnquist, White dissented in Roe v. Wade, 410 U.S. 113 (1973), which held that women have a constitutionally protected liberty interest in securing abortions. White opposed many of the Warren Court decisions extending new protections to criminal defendants and in later years often voted to limit the scope of those holdings. See Dennis J. Hutchinson, The Man Who Once Was Whizzer White (1998).

# First Amendment Timeline

1785    James Madison's Memorial and Remonstrance

1786    Virginia Bill for Religious Liberty

1798    The Sedition Act of 1798

1879    Reynolds v. United States

1917    Masses Publishing Co. v. Patten

1919    Schenck v. United States
        Abrams v. United States

1925    Gitlow v. New York

1927    Whitney v. California

1939    Schneider v. State
        Hague v. CIO

1940    Cantwell v. Connecticut

1941    Bridges v. California
        Cox v. New Hampshire

1942    Chaplinsky v. New Hampshire
        Valentine v. Chrestensen

1943    Martin v. City of Struthers
        West Virginia Board of Education v. Barnette

1947     Everson v. Board of Education
         United Public Workers v. Mitchell

1949     Terminiello v. Chicago
         Kovacs v. Cooper

1951     Feiner v. New York
         Dennis v. United States

1952     Beauharnais v. Illinois
         Adler v. Board of Education

1957     Yates v. United States
         Roth v. United States

1958     NAACP v. Alabama

1959     Barenblatt v. United States

1960     Talley v. California
         Shelton v. Tucker

1961     Konigsberg v. State Bar

1962     Engel v. Vitale

1963     Abington School District v. Schempp
         Sherbert v. Verner
         Edwards v. South Carolina
         NAACP v. Button
         Gibson v. Florida Legislative Investigating Committee

1964     New York Times v. Sullivan

1965     United States v. Seeger
         Cox v. Louisiana
         Freedman v. Maryland

1966     Adderley v. Florida
         Elfbrandt v. Russell

1967     Robel v. United States

1968     Epperson v. Arkansas
         O'Brien v. United States
         Pickering v. Board of Education

1969    Brandenburg v. Ohio
        Watts v. United States
        Gregory v. City of Chicago
        Stanley v. Georgia
        Tinker v. Des Moines Independent Community School District
        Street v. New York
        Red Lion Broadcasting Co. v. FCC

1970    Schacht v. United States

1971    Lemon v. Kurtzman
        Cohen v. California
        New York Times v. United States (Pentagon Papers Case)

1972    Gooding v. Wilson
        Grayned v. City of Rockford
        Police Department of Chicago v. Mosley
        Branzburg v. Hayes

1973    Broadrick v. Oklahoma
        Miller v. California
        Paris Adult Theatre I v. Slaton

1974    Gertz v. Robert Welch, Inc.
        Lehman v. City of Shaker Heights
        Spence v. Washington
        Miami Herald Publishing Co. v. Tornillo

1975    Cox Broadcasting Corp. v. Cohn
        Erznoznik v. City of Jacksonville
        Southeastern Promotions v. Conrad

1976    Nebraska Press Association v. Stuart
        Virginia Board of Pharmacy v. Virginia Consumers Council
        Young v. American Mini-Theaters
        Greer v. Spock
        Buckley v. Valeo
        Elrod v. Burns

1977    Wooley v. Maynard

1978    Landmark Communications v. Virginia
        FCC v. Pacifica Foundation
        First National Bank of Boston v. Bellotti
        Houchins v. KQED

1980    Central Hudson v. Public Service Commission
        Snepp v. United States
        PruneYard Shopping Center v. Robins
        Richmond Newspapers v. Virginia

1981    Widmar v. Vincent

1982    New York v. Ferber
        Board of Education of Island Trees v. Pico
        NAACP v. Clairborne Hardware Co.

1983    Perry Educators' Association v. Perry Local Educators' Association
        Regan v. Taxation with Representation
        Minneapolis Star & Tribune v. Minnesota Commissioner of
        Revenue

1984    Lynch v. Donnelly
        Roberts v. Jaycees
        FCC v. League of Women Voters

1985    Dun & Bradstreet v. Greenmoss Builders

1986    Posadas De Puerto Rico Associates v. Tourism Co.
        City of Renton v. Playtime Theatres

1988    Hustler Magazine v. Falwell

1989    Texas v. Johnson

1990    Employment Division, Department of Human Resources v. Smith
        United States v. Eichman
        Austin v. Michigan Chamber of Commerce

1991    Rust v. Sullivan
        Barnes v. Glen Theatre

1992    R.A.V. v. City of St. Paul
        International Society for Krishna Consciousness v. Lee

1993    Wisconsin v. Mitchell
        Lamb's Chapel v. Center Moriches
        Religious Freedom Restoration Act

1994    City of LaDue v. Gilleo
        Madsen v. Women's Health Center
        Turner Broadcasting v. FCC (Turner I)

1995    Rosenberger v. Rector of the University of Virginia
        Hurley v. Irish-American Gay, Lesbian, Bisexual Group

1996    Denver Area Educational Telecommunications Consortium v. FCC

1997    City of Boerne v. Flores
        Agostini v. Felton
        Reno v. American Civil Liberties Union
        Turner v. FCC (Turner II)

1998    NEA v. Finley

2000    Boy Scouts of America v. Dale

2002    Planned Parenthood v. American Coalition of Life Activists
        Ashcroft v. Free Speech Coalition
        Zelman v. Simmons-Harris

2003    Virginia v. Black
        United States v. American Library Association
        McConnell v. Federal Election Commission

2004    Ashcroft v. American Civil Liberties Union

2007    Federal Election Commission v. Wisconsin Right to Life

2008    Davis v. Federal Election Commission

2009    Pleasant Grove City, Utah v. Summum

2010    United States v. Stevens
        Christian Legal Society Chapter v. Martinez
        Citizens United v. Federal Election Commission
        Holder v. Humanitarian Law Project

2011    Snyder v. Phelps
        Brown v. Entertainment Merchants Association
        Arizona Free Enterprise Club's Freedom PAC v. Bennett

2012    United States v. Alvarez
        Hosanna-Tabor Evangelical Lutherna Church and School v.
        EEOC

2013    Agency for International Development v. Alliance for Open Society
        International

2014    McCutcheon v. Federal Election Commission

2015    Walker v. Texas Div. Sons of Confederate Veterans, Inc.

# The First Amendment

# PART I

## Freedom of Expression

# I

# The History and Philosophy of Free Expression

The first amendment provides that "Congress shall make no law [abridging] the freedom of speech, or of the press; or the right of the people peaceably to assemble, and to petition the Government for a redress of grievances." Consider Justice Black's position: "The phrase 'Congress shall make no law' is composed of plain words, easily understood. [The] language [is] absolute. [Of] course the decision to provide a constitutional safeguard for [free speech] involves a balancing of conflicting interests. [But] the Framers themselves did this balancing when they wrote the [Constitution]. Courts have neither the right nor the power [to] make a different [evaluation]." Black, The Bill of Rights, 35 N.Y.U. L. Rev. 865, 874, 879 (1960).

The Court has never accepted Black's view. Rather, it has consistently held that "abridging" and "the freedom of speech" require interpretation, and that restraints on free expression may be "permitted for appropriate reasons." Elrod v. Burns, 427 U.S. 347, 360 (1976). This section examines two sources that might aid interpretation: the history and philosophy underlying the first amendment.

## Note: The History of Free Expression

1. *The English background.* The notion that government "shall make no law [abridging] the freedom of speech, or of the press" received only gradual acceptance in Anglo-American law. Indeed, throughout much of English history the crown and Parliament attempted vigorously to suppress opinions deemed pernicious. Three forms of restraint were most commonly employed: the licensing of the press; the doctrine of constructive treason; and the law of seditious libel.

a. *Licensing.* The invention of printing greatly magnified the danger posed by "undesirable" opinions, and shortly after the first book was printed in

3

England in 1476, the crown claimed an authority to control printing presses as a right of prerogative. The manuscript of any work intended for publication had to be submitted to crown officials empowered to censor objectionable passages and to approve or deny a license for the printing of the work. Anything published without an imprimatur was criminal. This system of "prior restraint" remained in effect until 1694, when the authorizing legislation expired and was not renewed. The decision not to renew licensing resulted not from any commitment to free expression but rather from considerations of expediency, for licensing had proved ineffective, difficult to enforce, and conducive to bribery. See generally L. Levy, Emergence of a Free Press ch. 1 (1985); F. Siebert, Freedom of the Press in England, 1476–1776 chs. 2–3, 6–12 (1952).

b. *Constructive treason.* The law of treason in England derived from the statute 25 Edward III (1352), which defined the crime as (1) compassing or imagining the king's death, (2) levying war against the king, or (3) adhering to his enemies. During the latter part of the seventeenth century, the English judges ruled that mere written or printed matter, as well as overt acts, could constitute treason. John Twyn was the first printer to suffer under this extension of the law of treason. Government officers searched Twyn's home and seized the proofs of a book suggesting that the king was accountable to the people, and that the people were entitled to self-governance. Twyn was convicted of constructive treason, hanged, drawn, and quartered.

Although constructive treason was invoked in only a few cases, the doctrine posed a serious threat to freedom of expression, for the few instances in which conviction and execution occurred served to remind potential publishers of the fate that awaited those who violated the law. The doctrine was abandoned after 1720 because juries were often reluctant to convict, the death penalty was in many cases considered too drastic, and the procedure was too detailed. See generally Siebert, supra, at 265–269.

c. *Seditious libel.* The doctrine of seditious libel first entered Anglo-American jurisprudence in a 1275 statute outlawing "any false news or tales whereby discord or occasion of discord or slander may grow between the king and his people." Violations were punished by the king's council sitting in the "starred chamber." The point of departure for the modern law of seditious libel was Sir Edward Coke's report of a Star Chamber case of 1606, which stated three central propositions: (1) A libel against a private person may be punished criminally because it may provoke revenge and thus cause a breach of the peace. (2) A libel against a government official is an even greater offense, "for it concerns not only the breach of the peace, but also the scandal of government." (3) Although the essence of the crime as fixed by the statute of 1275 was the falsity of the libel, even a true libel may be criminally punished.

The theory underlying seditious libel was explained by Chief Justice Holt in 1704: "If people should not be called to account for possessing the people with an ill opinion of the government, no government can subsist. For it is very necessary for all governments that the people should have a good opinion of it." Rex v. Tutchin, 14 Howell's State Trials 1095, 1128 (1704). Thus, a true libel is especially dangerous, for unlike a false libel, the dangers of truthful criticism cannot be defused by disproof. It was thus an oft-quoted maxim after 1606 that "the greater the truth the greater the libel."

In practice, then, seventeenth-century judges punished as seditious libel any "written censure upon any public man whatever for any conduct whatever, or upon any law or institution whatever." 2 J. Stephen, A History of the Criminal Law of England 350 (1883). As one commentator has observed, "no single method of restricting the press was as effective as the law of seditious libel as it was developed and applied by the common-law courts in the latter part of the seventeenth century." Siebert, supra, at 269. For general discussion, see Hamburger, The Development of the Law of Seditious Libel and the Control of the Press, 37 Stan. L. Rev. 661 (1985).

In 1769, Blackstone summarized the law as follows:

> The liberty of the press [consists] in laying no *previous* restraints upon publications, and not in freedom from censure for criminal matter when published. [To] subject the press to the restrictive power of a licenser [is] to subject all freedom of sentiment to the prejudices of one man, and make him the arbitrary and infallible judge of all controverted points in learning, religion, and government. But to punish (as the law does at present) any dangerous or offensive writings, which, when published, shall on a fair and impartial trial be adjudged of a pernicious tendency, is necessary for the preservation of peace and good order, of government and religion, the only solid foundations of civil liberty.

4 W. Blackstone, Commentaries on the Laws of England *151–152.

2. *The colonial background.* The image of colonial America as a society in which freedom of expression was cherished seems largely inaccurate. Although colonial America was the scene of extraordinary diversity of opinion on religion, politics, social structure, and other subjects, each community "tended to be a tight little island clutching its own respective orthodoxy and [eager] to banish or extralegally punish unwelcome dissidents." Levy, supra, at 16.

Formal legal restraints on expression, however, were relatively rare. Licensing expired in 1725, and although there were hundreds of trials for seditious libel in England during the seventeenth and eighteenth centuries, there were not more than half a dozen such cases in colonial America. The most famous of these trials involved the prosecution of John Peter Zenger in New York in 1735. Zenger, publisher of the New York Weekly Journal, was charged with seditious libel by the Governor General of New York, whom he had criticized. Zenger argued unsuccessfully to the judge that the truth of the libel should be an absolute defense. The jury, responding to the popularity of Zenger's cause, disregarded the judge's instructions and returned a verdict of not guilty.

Although common law prosecutions for seditious libel were rare, the popularly elected colonial assemblies, imitating Parliament, assumed and vigorously exercised the power to punish "seditious" expression. Any criticism of an assembly or its members was likely to be regarded as a seditious scandal against the government punishable as a "breach of privilege." Levy, supra, at 14. To cite just one example, James Franklin, the older brother of Ben, ran a brief notice in his New England Courant that the government was preparing a ship to pursue coastal pirates "sometime this month, wind and weather permitting." The insinuation that the government was not dealing effectively with the pirates angered Massachusetts's popularly elected assembly. Franklin was arrested, and after a pro forma hearing, the assembly resolved that he had committed "a High affront to this Government." Franklin was imprisoned for the remainder of the session.

3. *The first amendment.* Scholars have long puzzled over the actual intentions of the framers of the first amendment. The primary dispute is over whether the framers intended to adopt the Blackstonian view — that freedom of speech consists entirely in the freedom from prior restraints — or whether they intended some broader meaning. Consider the following views.

a. Z. Chafee, Free Speech in the United States 18–20 (1941):

If we [consider] what mischief in the existing law the [framers] wished to [remedy], we can be sure that it was not [licensing]. This had expired in England in 1695, and in the colonies by 1725. [There] was no need to go to all the trouble of pushing through a constitutional amendment just to settle an issue that had been dead for decades. What the framers did have plenty of reason to fear was an entirely different danger to political writers and speakers. For years the government here and in England had substituted for [licensing] rigorous and repeated prosecutions for seditious libel [and] for years these prosecutions were opposed by liberal opinion and popular agitation.

b. Levy, supra, at xii–xv:

[The proposition has been conventionally accepted] that it was the intent of the American Revolution or the Framers of the First Amendment to abolish the common law of seditious libel. [The] evidence suggests that the proposition is suppositious and unprovable. [We] may even have to confront the possibility that the intentions of the Framers were not the most [libertarian]. But this should be expected because the Framers were nurtured on the crabbed historicism of Coke and the narrow conservatism of Blackstone, as well as Zenger's case. The ways of thought of a lifetime are not easily broken. The Declaration of Independence severed the political connection with England but the American states continued the English common-law system except as explicitly rejected by statute. If the Revolution produced any radical libertarians on the meaning of freedom of speech and press, they were not present at the Constitutional Convention or the First Congress, which drafted the Bill of Rights. Scholars and judges have betrayed a penchant for what John P. Roche called "retrospective symmetry," by giving to present convictions a patriotic lineage and tradition — in this case, the fatherhood of the "Framers."

For critical analyses of this view, see D. Rabban, Free Speech in Its Forgotten Years (1997); Rabban, An Ahistorical Historian: Leonard Levy on Freedom of Expression in Early American History, 37 Stan. L. Rev. 795 (1985); Mayton, From a Legacy of Suppression to the "Metaphor of the Fourth Estate," 39 Stan. L. Rev. 139 (1986).

The framers themselves were unsure what a constitutional guarantee of "freedom of the speech or of the press" would mean. Benjamin Franklin observed, for example, that "Few of us, I believe, have distinct ideas of its nature and extent," and Alexander Hamilton asked, "Who can give it any definition which would not leave the utmost latitude for evasion?" See Meyerson, The Neglected History of the Prior Restraint Doctrine, 34 Ind. L. Rev. 295, 320 (2001).

4. *The relevance of history.* To what extent, if any, is the preceding history relevant to interpretation of the first amendment? Is the English common law important because it was what the framers rejected or because it was what they accepted? Is it plausible that states that themselves punished seditious libel intended to prohibit Congress from punishing it? And given the enormous changes in the media and politics since the adoption of the first amendment, to what extent, if any, should the intent of the framers control the contemporary resolution of first amendment issues?

5. *The Sedition Act of 1798.* The first serious challenge to freedom of expression in the United States came with the Sedition Act of 1798. Act of July 14, 1798, 1 Stat. 596. The United States was on the verge of war with France, and many of the ideas generated by the French Revolution aroused fear and hostility in segments of the U.S. population. A bitter political and philosophical debate raged between the Federalists, then in power, and the Republicans.

Against this backdrop, the Federalists enacted the Sedition Act of 1798. The act prohibited the publication of

false, scandalous, and malicious [writings] against the government of the United States, or either house of the Congress of the United States, or the President of the United States, with intent to defame [them]; or to bring them [into] contempt or disrepute; or to excite against them [the] hatred of the good people of the United States. . . .

The act provided further that truth would be a defense and that malicious intent was an element of the crime. Thus, as the Federalists emphasized, the act eliminated those aspects of the English common law that had been the focus of attack during the eighteenth century. See Levy, supra, at xi.

The Sedition Act was vigorously enforced, but only against members or supporters of the Republican Party. Prosecutions were brought against the four leading Republican newspapers. The cases, often tried before openly hostile Federalist judges, resulted in ten convictions and no acquittals. Moreover, in the hands of these judges, the procedural reforms of the act proved largely illusory.

Consider, for example, the plight of Matthew Lyon, a Republican congressman from Vermont. During his reelection campaign, Lyon published an article in which he attacked the Adams administration, asserting that under President Adams "every consideration of the public welfare [was] swallowed up in a continual grasp for power, in an unbounded thirst for ridiculous pomp, foolish adulation, and selfish avarice." At Lyon's trial, the judge instructed the jury to find malicious intent unless the statement "could have been uttered with any other intent than that of making odious or contemptible the President and the government, and bringing them both into disrepute." Although Lyon was technically free to prove the "truth" of his statement in his defense, this was hardly possible, given the nature of the statement. Lyon was convicted and sentenced to a fine of $1,000 and four months in prison. The Federalist press rejoiced, but Lyon became an instant martyr and was reelected while in jail. See Trial of Matthew Lyon, in F. Wharton, State Trials 333 (1849).

The Supreme Court did not rule on the constitutionality of the Sedition Act, but it was upheld without dissent by the lower federal courts and by three Supreme Court justices sitting on circuit. The act expired of its own force on March 3, 1801. President Jefferson thereafter pardoned all those who had been convicted under the act, and Congress eventually repaid most of the fines. It is generally agreed that the act was a factor in the defeat of the Federalists in the election of 1800. Significant cases under the Sedition Act are printed in Wharton, supra. The story of the enforcement of the act is told in G. Stone, Perilous Times: Free Speech in Wartime 15–78 (2004). What is the significance of the fact that the Sedition Act was approved by many of the same people who had earlier approved the first amendment?

6. *From the Sedition Act of 1798 to the Espionage Act of 1917.* The Supreme Court did not directly consider the first amendment's guarantee of free expression until Congress enacted the Espionage Act of 1917 at the outset of World War I. See Chapter II A infra. This is not to say, however, that controversies over free speech did not arise in the years between the Sedition Act of 1798 and the Espionage Act of 1917. See G. Stone, supra, 79–134 (free speech during the Civil War); M. Curtis, Free Speech: The People's Darling Privilege (2000) (abolitionist speech and free speech during the Civil War); D. Rabban, Free Speech in Its Forgotten Years (1997) (free speech between 1870 and 1920).

### Note: The Philosophy of Free Expression

"Intuition at first may suggest that an individual ought to have more freedom to speak than he has liberty in other areas. There would seem to be some truth in the adage, 'sticks and stones can break my bones, but words will never hurt me.' Yet speech often hurts. It can offend, injure reputation, fan prejudice or passion, and ignite the world. Moreover, a great deal of other conduct that the state regulates has less harmful potential." Wellington, On Freedom of Expression, 88 Yale L.J. 1105, 1106–1107 (1979). Why, then, should expression have greater immunity from government regulation than most other forms of human conduct? Why should society prohibit the making of any law "abridging the freedom of speech"?

1. *Search for truth: the "marketplace of ideas."* The search for truth rationale for the protection of free expression rests on the premise that "when men have realized that time has upset many fighting faiths, they may come to believe even more than they believe the very foundations of their own conduct that the ultimate good desired is better reached by free trade in ideas — that the best test of truth is the power of the thought to get itself accepted in the competition of the market, and that truth is the only ground upon which their wishes safely can be carried out." Abrams v. United States, 250 U.S. 616, 630 (1919) (Holmes, J., dissenting).

The search for truth rationale was first fully enunciated by John Stuart Mill in On Liberty (1859):

> [The] peculiar evil of silencing the expression of an opinion is, that it is robbing the human race; posterity as well as the existing generation; those who dissent from the opinion, still more than those who hold it. . . . First: the opinion which it is attempted to suppress [may] be true. Those who desire to suppress it [are] not infallible. They have no authority to decide the question for all mankind, and exclude every other person from the means of judging. [Of course, it is not the case] that truth always triumphs over persecution. [But the] real advantage which truth has [is] that when an opinion is true, it may be extinguished once, twice, or many times, but in the course of ages there will generally be found persons to rediscover it, until [eventually] it has made such head as to withstand all subsequent attempts to suppress it. . . .
>
> [Second: the received opinion may be true. But however true an opinion] may be, if it is not fully, frequently, and fearlessly discussed, it will be held as a dead dogma, not a living truth. [He] who knows only his own side of the case, knows little of that. [Even if] the received opinion [is] true, a conflict with the opposite error is essential to a clear apprehension and deep feeling of its truth. . . .
>
> [Finally:] the conflicting doctrines, instead of being one true and the other false, [may] share the truth between them; and the nonconforming opinion [may be] needed to supply the remainder of the truth, of which the received doctrine embodies only a part. [Every] opinion which embodies somewhat of the portion of truth which the common opinion omits, ought to be considered precious.

Consider the following observations.

a. Baker, Scope of the First Amendment Freedom of Speech, 25 UCLA L. Rev. 964, 974–978 (1978):

> [The] hope that the marketplace leads to truth, or even to the best or most desirable decision, [is] implausible. [First, experience as well as discussion

contributes to understanding. Thus,] restrictions on experience-generating conduct are as likely as restrictions on [debate] to stunt the progressive development of understanding, [but the marketplace theory gives no] constitutional protection [to] experience-producing conduct. [Second, the marketplace theory assumes] that people [use] their rational capacities to eliminate distortion caused by the form and frequency of message presentation. [This] assumption cannot be accepted. Emotional or "irrational" appeals have great [impact]. [Finally, in practice,] the marketplace of ideas appears improperly biased in favor of presently dominant groups.

b. Greenawalt, Free Speech Justifications, 89 Colum. L. Rev. 119, 135–136 (1989):

The critical question is not how well truth will advance absolutely in conditions of freedom, but how well it will advance in conditions of freedom as compared with some alternative set of conditions. Suppose one were highly pessimistic about the capacity of people to ascertain important kinds of truths, but believed that governments that suppress ideas almost always manage to promote [falsehoods]. One might then support freedom of speech as less damaging to truth than an alternative social practice. One's overall judgment on this subject must depend on a delicate judgment about people's responses to claimed truth, about the effects of inequality of private power over what is communicated, and about the soundness of government determinations about valid ideas.

c. Wellington, supra, at 1130–1132:

In the long run, true ideas do tend to drive out false ones. The problem is that the short run may be very long, that one short run follows hard upon another, and that we may become overwhelmed by the inexhaustible supply of freshly minted, often very seductive, false ideas. [Moreover,] most of us do believe that the book is closed on some issues. Genocide is an example. [Truth] may win, and in the long run it may almost always win, but millions of Jews were deliberately and systematically murdered in a very short period of time. [Before] those murders occurred, many individuals must have come "to have false beliefs."

2. *Self-governance.* The self-governance rationale is most closely identified with the work of Alexander Meiklejohn:

[The] Constitution [ordains] that all authority [to] determine common action, belongs to "We, the People."[Under this system, free men are governed] by themselves. [What,] then, does the First Amendment forbid? [The] town meeting suggests an answer. That meeting is called to discuss [and] to decide matters of public policy. [The] voters, therefore, must be made as wise as possible. [And] this, in turn, requires that so far as time allows, all facts and interests relevant to the problem shall be fully and fairly presented. . . .

The First Amendment, then, is not the guardian of unregulated talkativeness. It does not require that, on every occasion, every citizen shall take part in public debate. [Rather,] the vital point [is] that no suggestion of policy shall be denied a hearing because it is on one side of the issue rather than another. [Citizens] may not be barred [from speaking] because their views are thought to be false or dangerous. [The] reason for this equality of status in the field of ideas lies deep in the very foundation of the self-governing process. When men govern themselves, it is they — and no one else — who must pass judgment upon unwisdom and unfairness and danger. [Just] so far as, at any point, the citizens who are to decide an issue are denied acquaintance with information or opinion [which] is relevant to that issue, just so far the result must be ill-considered. [It] is that mutilation of the thinking process of the community against which the First Amendment [is] directed. The principle of the freedom of speech [is] not a Law of Nature or of Reason in the abstract. It is a deduction from the basic American agreement that public issues shall be decided by universal suffrage.

A. Meiklejohn, Free Speech and Its Relation to Self-Government 15–16, 24–27, 39 (1948).
Consider the following observations.
a. Chafee, Book Review, 62 Harv. L. Rev. 891, 899–900 (1949):

The most serious weakness in Mr. Meiklejohn's argument is that it rests on his supposed boundary between public speech and private speech. That line is extremely blurred. [The] truth is that there are public aspects to practically every subject. [Moreover, if Mr. Meiklejohn's public speech excludes scholarship,] art and literature, it is shocking to deprive these vital matters of the protection of [the] First Amendment. [Valuable] as self-government is, it is in itself only a small part of our lives. That a philosopher should subordinate all other activities to it is indeed surprising.

b. Meiklejohn's response:

The First Amendment [protects] the freedom of those activities of thought and communication by which we "govern." [But] voting is merely the external expression of a wide and diverse number of activities by means of which citizens attempt to meet the responsibilities of making judgments, which that freedom to govern lays upon them. [Self-government] can exist only insofar as the voters acquire the intelligence, integrity, sensitivity, and generous devotion to the general welfare that, in theory, casting a ballot is assumed to express. [Thus,] there are many forms of thought and expression within the range of human communications from which the voter derives the [necessary] knowledge, intelligence, [and] sensitivity to human values. [These], too, must suffer no abridgment of their freedom. [These include:] 1. Education, in all its phases. [2.] The achievements of philosophy and the sciences. [3.] Literature and the arts. [4.] Public discussions of public issues.

Meiklejohn, The First Amendment Is an Absolute, 1961 Sup. Ct. Rev. 245, 255–257.

c. Bork, Neutral Principles and Some First Amendment Problems, 47 Ind. L.J. 1, 26–28 (1971):

> Professor Alexander Meiklejohn seems correct when he says: "The First Amendment [protects] the freedom of those activities of thought and communication by which we 'govern.'" [But Meiklejohn goes] further and would extend the protection of the first amendment beyond speech that is explicitly political. [I disagree.] [There is, of course,] an analogy between criticism of official behavior and the publication of a novel like Ulysses, for the latter may form attitudes that ultimately affect politics. But it is an analogy, not an identity. Other human activities and experiences also form personality, teach and create attitudes just as much as does the novel, but no one would on that account [suggest] that the first amendment strikes down regulations of economic activity, control of entry into trade, laws about sexual behavior, marriage and the like. Yet these activities, in their capacity to create attitudes that ultimately impinge upon the political process, are more like literature and science than literature and science are like political speech. If the dialectical progression is not to become an analogical stampede, the protection of the first amendment must be cut off when it reaches the outer limits of political speech. [The] notion that all valuable types of speech must be protected by the first amendment confuses the constitutionality of laws with their wisdom. Freedom of nonpolitical speech rests, as does freedom for other valuable forms of behavior, upon the enlightenment of society and its elected representatives.

d. Sunstein, Free Speech Now, 59 U. Chi. L. Rev. 255, 301, 304–306 (1992):

> [The] First Amendment is principally about political deliberation. [We should] treat speech as political when it is both intended and received as a contribution to public deliberation about some issue. [An] approach that affords special protection to political speech, thus defined, is justified on numerous grounds. [It] receives firm support from history — not only from the Framers' theory of free expression, but also from the development of that principle through the history of American law. [In] addition, an insistence that government's burden is greatest when political speech is at issue responds well to the fact that here government is most likely to be biased. [Finally], this approach protects speech when regulation is most likely to be harmful. Restrictions on political speech have the distinctive feature of impairing the ordinary channels for political [change]. If there are controls on commercial advertising [or artistic and scientific expression], it always remains possible to argue that such controls should be lifted. [But] if the government forecloses political argument, the democratic corrective is unavailable. [Taken] in concert, these considerations suggest that government should be under a special burden of justification when it seeks to control speech intended and received as a contribution to public deliberation.

e. Post, Participatory Democracy and Free Speech, 97 Va. L. Rev. 477, 482-483, 486 (2011):

> [T]he best possible explanation of the shape of First Amendment doctrine is the value of democratic governance. [Democracy] refers to a certain relationship between persons and their government. Democracy is achieved when those who are subject to law believe that they are also potential authors of law. [The] value of democratic legitimation occurs [through] processes of communication in the public sphere. [The] function of public discourse is to enable persons to experience the value of self-government. [Public] discourse includes all communicative processes deemed necessary for the formation of public opinion.

Consider Volokh, The Trouble with "Public Discourse" as a Limitation on Free Speech Rights, 97 Va. L. Rev. 567 (2011): "If 'the speech by which public opinion is formed' is especially protected and other speech lacks full protection, then we need to define this category's boundaries with some precision. Yet both the phrase and the label 'public discourse' [are] inadequate to the task." Do the following constitute "public discourse": (1) a conversation between two friends over a beer about politics; (2) an exhibition of 19th century French art; (3) a teacher's out-of-class discussion of contraceptive use with junior high school students; (d) publication of a trade secret?

f. R. Collins & D. Skover, On Dissent: Its Meaning in America 103, 115-116 (2013):

> [The First Amendment] safeguards the speech of those who refute our creeds, reject our values, renounce our government, and even repudiate our very way of life. This uniquely American principle of free speech provides a haven for irritating ranters and irksome rogues who feel the need to spoil our parade. In short, it protects the voice of the other. [In] one way or the other, the idea of dissent finds followers in every ideological camp. [As] Benjamin Franklin observed "[i]t is the first responsibility of every citizen to question authority." [The] First Amendment sometimes converts illegal action into lawful action; it transforms what was seen as anarchy into what may be viewed as democratic engagement; and it reconfigures the relationship between society and its critics.

3. *Self-fulfillment.* Consider the following views:

a. Richards, Free Speech and Obscenity Law: Toward a Moral Theory of the First Amendment, 123 U. Pa. L. Rev. 45, 62 (1974):

> [People] are not to be constrained to communicate or not to communicate, to believe or not to believe, to associate or not to associate. The value placed on this cluster of ideas derives from the notion of self-respect that comes from a mature person's full and untrammelled exercise of capacities central to human rationality. Thus, the significance of free expression rests on the central human capacity to create and express symbolic systems, such as speech, writing, pictures, and [music]. Freedom of expression permits and encourages the exercise

of these [capacities]. In so doing, it nurtures and sustains the self-respect of the mature person. [The] value of free expression, in this view, rests on its deep relation to self-respect arising from autonomous self-determination without which the life of the spirit is meager and slavish.

b. Bork, supra, at 25:

[The self-fulfillment/autonomy rationale does] not distinguish speech from any other human activity. An individual may develop his faculties or derive pleasure from trading on the stock market, [working] as a barmaid, engaging in sexual activity, [or] in any of thousands of other endeavors. Speech [can] be preferred to other activities [on the basis of this rationale] only by ranking forms of personal gratification. [One] cannot, on neutral grounds, choose to protect speech [on this basis] more than [one] protects any other claimed freedom.

4. *Other rationales.* Although courts and commentators have focused primarily on the search for truth, self-governance, and self-fulfillment/autonomy rationales for the protection of free expression, some other rationales merit note.

a. *The checking value.* Consider Blasi, The Checking Value in First Amendment Theory, 1977 Am. B. Found. Res. J. 521, 527–542:

[Another rationale for the protection of free expression] is the value that free speech [can] serve in checking the abuse of power by public officials. [The] central premise of the checking value is that the abuse of official power is an especially serious evil [because of government's unique] capacity to employ legitimized violence. [The] government's monopoly of legitimized violence means [that the] check on government must come from the power of public opinion. [Thus,] the checking value grows out of democratic theory, but it is the democratic theory of John Locke [and] not that of Alexander Meiklejohn. Under [this] view of democracy, the role of the ordinary citizen is not so much to contribute on a continuing basis to the formation of public policy as to retain a veto power to be employed when the decisions of officials pass certain bounds.

b. *The tolerant society.* Consider L. Bollinger, The Tolerant Society: Freedom of Speech and Extremist Speech in America 9–10, 107 (1986):

[While] free speech theory has traditionally focused on the value of the protected activity (speech), [the theory offered here] seeks a justification by looking at the disvalue of the [frequently intolerant] response to that activity. [The] rationality and wisdom of choosing the course of tolerance can be derived from a neglected insight — namely, that the problematic feelings evoked [by] speech activity are precisely the same kinds of feelings evoked by a myriad of interactions in the society, not the least of which are the reactions we take toward nonspeech behavior. [The free speech principle] involves a special act of carving out one area of social interaction for extraordinary self-restraint, the purpose of which is to develop and demonstrate a social capacity to control feelings evoked by a host of social encounters. [The free speech principle is thus] concerned with nothing less than helping to shape the intellectual character of the society.

c. *Free speech and the development of character*. Consider Blasi, Free Speech and Good Character: From Milton to Brandeis to the Present, in L. Bollinger and G. Stone, Eternal Vigilance: Free Speech in the Modern Era 61, 62, 84–85 (2002):

[A] culture that prizes and protects expressive liberty nurtures in its members certain character traits such as inquisitiveness, distrust of authority, willingness to take initiative, and the courage to confront evil. Such character traits are valuable [for] their instrumental contribution to the collective well-being, social as well as political. [The] most important [consequence] of protecting free speech is the intellectual and moral pluralism, and thus disorder in a sense, thereby engendered. In matters of belief, conventional structures of authority are weakened, rebellion is facilitated, closure is impaired. Persons who live in a free-speech regime are forced to cope with persistent, and frequently intractable, differences of understanding. For most of us that is a painful challenge. . . . Being made to take account of such differences shapes our character.

d. *Free speech and conservative libertarianism*. For an argument that much of modern free speech doctrine grows out of libertarian conceptions that also support expansion of property and gun rights and opposition to redistributive legislation, see Heyman, The Conservative-Libertarian Turn in First Amendment Jurisprudence, 117 W. Va. L. Rev. 231 (2014). See also Seidman, The Dale Problem: Property and Speech under the Regulatory State, 75 U. Chi. L. Rev. 1541 (2008).

5. *Philosophy and the first amendment*. To what extent, if any, are these rationales for the protection of free expression relevant to interpretation of the first amendment? Consider Bloustein, The Origin, Validity, and Interrelationships of the Political Values Served by Freedom of Expression, 33 Rutgers L. Rev. 372, 381 (1981): "[There] is no evidence [that these rationales were] discussed or debated during the period of the drafting and adoption of the [first] amendment [and we may thus conclude] that whatever validity and authority they may have do *not* derive directly from the intentions of the drafters." From where, then, do the validity and authority of these rationales derive? If the theories are valid, should it matter whether they were entertained by the Framers?

To what extent do these rationales, if relevant to interpretation of the first amendment, provide a coherent and workable basis for the decision of actual cases? Note that in some instances it may be necessary to choose among the competing rationales. For example, the self-fulfillment/autonomy rationale does not support a distinction between political and nonpolitical expression, whereas the self-governance theory seems to compel that distinction. Despite such potential conflicts, most commentators agree that any "adequate conception of freedom of speech must [draw] upon several strands of theory in order to protect a rich variety of expressional modes." L. Tribe, American Constitutional Law 789 (2d ed. 1988). As one commentator has observed, in the "democratic state," which "is founded on a tradition of free inquiry," the "attainment of knowledge," the "consensual participation in government," and the "dignity of self-expression" are "so interdependent that they really represent three aspects [of] a single value; their relationships define a kind of culture, embracing the individual, the state, and the system of knowledge, art and other such values that we call liberal." Bloustein, supra, at 395.

## Note: Organization

The remaining chapters in this part explore the Supreme Court's interpretation of the first amendment's guarantee of free speech, press, assembly, and petition. These chapters are structured in accordance with two distinctions that have played a central role in the Court's analysis. First, there is the distinction between content-based and content-neutral restrictions. Content-based restrictions restrict communication because of the message conveyed. Laws prohibiting the publication of "confidential" information, forbidding the hiring of teachers who advocate the violent overthrow of government, or banning the display of the swastika in certain neighborhoods illustrate this type of restriction. Content-neutral restrictions, on the other hand, restrict communication without regard to the message conveyed. Laws prohibiting noisy speeches near a hospital, banning the erection of billboards in residential communities, or requiring the disclosure of the names of all leafleteers are examples. The Court has generally employed different standards to test the constitutionality of these two types of restrictions.

Second, there is the distinction within the realm of content-based restrictions between "high" and "low" value expression. The Court has long adhered to the view that there are certain categories of expression that do not appreciably further the values underlying the first amendment. Examples are obscenity, commercial advertising, and false statements of fact. The Court has traditionally held that such categories of expression are either unprotected or only marginally protected by the first amendment.

In line with these distinctions, Chapters II and III focus primarily on government efforts to suppress "high" value speech; Chapter IV explores "low" value expression; Chapter V examines content-neutral restrictions and the issue of content-neutrality; and Chapter VI explores the "freedom of the press." The point of this structure is not to insulate these distinctions from challenge. It is rather to illuminate the Court's jurisprudence while at the same time facilitating critical scrutiny of the Court's analysis.

# II

## Content-Based Restrictions:
## Dangerous Ideas and Information

In what circumstances, if any, may government, consonant with the first amendment, restrict speech because the expression of particular ideas or items of information might cause some harm to government, to private individuals, or to society in general? In addressing this question, this chapter examines four separate, but related, problems: speech that may induce hearers or listeners to engage in unlawful conduct; speech that "threatens" harm to others; speech that provokes a hostile audience response; and speech that discloses confidential information. In its effort to deal with these problems, the Court has struggled to identify the relevant considerations. The task is not easy. How serious must the harm be before speech may be suppressed? How likely must the harm be? How imminent must it be? Should it matter whether the speaker intended to cause the harm? Can these and other considerations be integrated into a single, coherent standard?

## A. SPEECH THAT "CAUSES" UNLAWFUL CONDUCT

The question whether government may constitutionally restrict expression because it might persuade, incite, or otherwise "cause" readers or listeners to engage in unlawful conduct has long absorbed the Court's attention. This was the first issue of first amendment interpretation to capture the Court's sustained interest, and the debate within the Court over this question has produced some of the most powerful and most eloquent opinions in the Court's history. That the question has played so central a role in the evolution of first amendment theory is not surprising, for it focuses on government efforts to restrict advocacy in many respects similar to the traditional concept of seditious libel and thus implicates values at the very core of the first amendment.

The Supreme Court first confronted this issue in a series of cases concerning agitation against the war and the draft during World War I. Such agitation was not uncommon:

> [When] the U.S. first entered the war, [many] influential groups of people were apathetic if not actually hostile to fighting. [Organizations] which identified themselves as against the war, [such as the Socialist Party of America], made strong gains during 1917 [and] over three hundred thirty thousand draft evaders or delinquents were reported during the war. [Antiwar] sentiment did not pose a threat of revolution or violence, but it did pose a threat of spreading disaffection which could paralyze the war effort. [Attorney] General Thomas Gregory, referring to war opponents in November, 1917, stated, "May God have mercy on them, for they need expect none from an outraged people and an avenging government."

R. Goldstein, Political Repression in Modern America 105–108 (1978).

Two months after our entry into the First World War, Congress enacted the Espionage Act of 1917. Although the act was directed primarily toward such matters as espionage and the protection of military secrets, the third section of title I of the act made it a crime when the nation is at war for any person (1) willfully to "make or convey false reports or false statements with intent to interfere" with the military success of the United States or "to promote the success of its enemies"; (2) willfully to "cause or attempt to cause insubordination, disloyalty, mutiny, or refusal of duty, in the military or naval forces of the United States"; or (3) willfully to "obstruct the recruiting or enlistment service of the United States." Violations were punishable by fines of up to $10,000, prison sentences of up to twenty years, or both. Act of June 15, 1917, ch. 30, tit. I, §3, 40 Stat. 219.

Eleven months later, Congress enacted the Sedition Act of 1918. The 1918 act, which was repealed in 1921, made it criminal, among other things, for any person to say anything with intent to obstruct the sale of war bonds; to utter, print, write, or publish any disloyal, profane, scurrilous, or abusive language intended to cause contempt or scorn for the form of government of the United States, the Constitution, or the flag; to urge the curtailment of production of war materials with the intent of hindering the war effort; or to utter any words supporting the cause of any country at war with the United States or opposing the cause of the United States. Act of May 16, 1918, ch. 75, §1, 40 Stat. 553.

During the war years, federal authorities initiated approximately two thousand prosecutions under these acts. Most of these prosecutions were brought under the 1917 statute. The opinions that follow represent three distinct analyses of the issue.

**SHAFFER v. UNITED STATES, 255 F. 886 (9th Cir. 1919).** Shaffer was convicted of violating the Espionage Act of 1917. The indictment alleged that Shaffer had mailed a book, The Finished Mystery, which contained several "treasonable, disloyal, and seditious utterances," specifying the following passages in particular:

> Standing opposite to these Satan has placed [a] certain delusion which is best described by the word patriotism, but which in reality is murder, the spirit of the very devil. [If] you say it is a war of defense against wanton and intolerable aggression, I must reply that [it] has yet to be proved that Germany has any intention or desire of attacking us. [The] war itself is wrong. Its prosecution will be a crime. There is not a question raised, an issue involved, a cause at stake, which is worth the life of one blue-jacket on the sea or one khaki-coat in the trenches.

The Court of Appeals for the Ninth Circuit affirmed the conviction: "It is true that disapproval of war and the advocacy of peace are not crimes under the Espionage Act; but the question here [is] whether the natural and probable tendency and effect of [the publication] are such as are calculated to produce the result condemned by the statute. [It cannot] be said, as a matter of law, that the reasonable and natural effect of [the] publication was not to obstruct [the] recruiting or enlistment service, and thus to injure the service of the United States. Printed matter may tend to obstruct [the] service, even if it contains no mention of recruiting or enlistment, and no reference to the military service of the United States. [The] service may be obstructed by attacking the justice of the cause for which the war is waged, and by undermining the spirit of loyalty which inspires men to enlist or to register for conscription in the service of their country. [To] teach that patriotism is murder and the spirit of the devil, and that the war against Germany was wrong and its prosecution a crime, is to weaken patriotism and the purpose to enlist or to render military service in the war. . . .

"It is argued that the evidence fails to show that [Shaffer] committed the act willfully and intentionally. But there is enough in the evidence to show the hostile attitude of his mind against the prosecution of the war by the United States, and that the books were intentionally concealed on his premises. He must be presumed to have intended the natural and probable consequences of what he knowingly did."

## Masses Publishing Co. v. Patten
244 F. 535 (S.D.N.Y. 1917)

[In July 1917, the postmaster of New York, acting on the direction of the Postmaster General, advised the plaintiff, a publishing company engaged in the production of a monthly revolutionary journal called The Masses, that the

August issue of the journal would be denied access to the mails under the Espionage Act of 1917. The Masses regularly featured a remarkable collection of writers, poets, playwrights, and philosophers, including Max Eastman, John Reed, Vachel Lindsay, Emma Goldman, Carl Sandburg, Bertrand Russell, Louis Untermeyer, and Sherwood Anderson. Iconoclastic, impertinent, and confrontational, it was filled with sparkling social satire, intellectual commentary, and political criticism. Plaintiff applied for a preliminary injunction to forbid the postmaster to refuse to accept the August issue for mailing. While objecting generally that the whole purport of the issue was in violation of the law, on the ground that it tended to produce a violation of the law, to encourage the enemies of the United States, and to hamper the government in the conduct of the war, the postmaster specified four cartoons and four pieces of text as especially falling within the act.]

LEARNED HAND, DISTRICT JUDGE. . . .

It must be remembered at the outset, and the distinction is of critical consequence throughout, that no question arises touching the war powers of Congress. It may be that Congress may forbid the mails to any matter which tends to discourage the successful prosecution of the war. It may be that the fundamental personal rights of the individual must stand in abeyance, even including the right of the freedom of the press, though that is not here in question. . . .

[The postmaster's] position is that to arouse discontent and disaffection among the people with the prosecution of the war and with the draft tends to promote a mutinous and insubordinate temper among the troops. This [is] true; men who become satisfied that they are engaged in an enterprise dictated by the unconscionable selfishness of the rich, and effectuated by a tyrannous disregard for the will of those who must suffer and die, will be more prone to insubordination than those who have faith in the cause and acquiesce in the means. Yet to interpret the word "cause" so broadly would [involve] necessarily as a consequence the suppression of all hostile criticism, and of all opinion except what encouraged and supported the existing policies, or which fell within the range of temperate argument. It would contradict the normal assumption of democratic government that the suppression of hostile criticism does not turn upon the justice of its substance or the decency and propriety of its temper. Assuming that the power to repress such opinion may rest in Congress in the throes of a struggle for the very existence of the state, its exercise is so contrary to the use and wont of our people that only the clearest expression of such a power justifies the conclusion that it was intended.

The [postmaster's] position, therefore, in so far as it involves the suppression of the free utterance of abuse and criticism of the existing law, or of the policies of the war, is not, in my judgment, supported by the language of the statute. Yet there has always been a recognized limit to such expressions. [One] may not counsel or advise others to violate the law as it stands. Words are not only the keys of persuasion, but the triggers of action, and those which have no purport but to counsel the violation of law cannot by any latitude of interpretation be a part of that public opinion which is the final source of government in a democratic state. [To] counsel or advise a man to an act is to urge upon him either that it is his interest or his duty to do it. While, of course, this may be accomplished as well by indirection as expressly, since words carry the meaning that they impart, the definition is exhaustive, I think, and I shall use it. Political agitation, by the passions it arouses or the convictions it engenders, may in fact stimulate men to the violation of law. Detestation of existing policies is easily transformed into forcible resistance of the authority which puts them in execution, and it would be folly to disregard the causal relation between the two. Yet to assimilate agitation, legitimate as such, with direct incitement to violent resistance, is to disregard the tolerance of all methods of political agitation which in normal times is a safeguard of free government. The distinction is not a scholastic subterfuge, but a hard-bought acquisition in the fight for freedom, and the purpose to disregard it must be evident when the power exists. If one stops short of urging upon others that it is their duty or their interest to resist the law, it seems to me one should not be held to have attempted to cause its violation. If that be not the test, I can see no escape from the conclusion that under this section every political agitation which can be shown to be apt to create a seditious temper is illegal. I am confident that by such language Congress had no such revolutionary purpose in view.

It seems to me, however, quite plain that none of the language and none of the cartoons in this paper can be thought directly to counsel or advise insubordination or mutiny, without a violation of their meaning quite beyond any tolerable understanding. I come, therefore, to the third phrase of the section, which forbids any one from willfully obstructing the recruiting or enlistment service of the United States. I am not prepared to assent to the plaintiff's position that this only refers to acts other than words, nor that the act thus defined must be shown to have been successful. One may obstruct without preventing, and the mere obstruction is an injury to the service; for it throws impediments in its way. Here again, however, since the question is of the expression of opinion, I construe the sentence, so far as it restrains public utterance, as [limited] to the direct advocacy of resistance to the recruiting and enlistment service. If so, the inquiry is narrowed to the question whether any of the challenged matter may be said to advocate resistance to the draft, taking the meaning of the words with the utmost latitude which they can bear.

As to the cartoons it seems to me quite clear that they do not fall within such a test. Certainly the nearest is that entitled "Conscription," and the most that can be said of that is that it may breed such animosity to the draft as will promote resistance and strengthen the determination of those disposed to be recalcitrant. There is no intimation that, however hateful the draft may be, one is in duty bound to resist it, certainly none that such resistance is to one's interest. I cannot, therefore, [assent] to the assertion that any of the cartoons violate the act.

The text offers more embarrassment. The poem to Emma Goldman and Alexander Berkman, at most, goes no further than to say that they are martyrs in the cause of love among nations. Such a sentiment holds them up to admiration, and hence their conduct to possible emulation. The paragraph in which the editor offers to receive funds for their appeal also expresses admiration for them, but goes no further. The paragraphs upon conscientious objectors are of the same kind. They go no further than to express high admiration for those who have held and are holding out for their convictions even to the extent of resisting the law. [That] such comments have a tendency to arouse emulation in others is clear enough, but that they counsel others to follow these examples is not so plain. Literally at least they do not, and while, as I have said, the words are to be taken, not literally, but according to their full import, the literal meaning is the starting point for interpretation. One may admire and approve the course of a hero without feeling any duty to follow him. There is not the least implied intimation in these words that others are under a duty to follow. The most that can be said is that, if others do follow, they will get the same admiration and the same approval. Now, there is surely an appreciable distance between esteem and emulation; and unless there is here some advocacy of such emulation, I cannot see how the passages can be said to fall within the law. [The] question before me is quite the same as what would arise upon a motion to dismiss an indictment at the close of the proof: Could any reasonable man say, not that the indirect result of the language might be to arouse a seditious disposition, for that would not be enough, but that the language directly advocated resistance to the draft? I cannot think that upon such language any verdict would stand. . . .

It follows that the plaintiff is entitled to the usual preliminary injunction.

## Schenck v. United States

249 U.S. 47 (1919)

Mr. Justice Holmes delivered the opinion of the court. . . .

[The defendants were convicted of conspiracy to violate section 3 of the Espionage Act of 1917 by circulating "to men who had been called and accepted for military service" a document "alleged to be calculated" to obstruct the recruiting and enlistment service.]

The document in question, upon its first printed side, recited the 1st section of the Thirteenth Amendment, said that the idea embodied in it was violated by the Conscription Act, and that a conscript is little better than a convict. In impassioned language it intimated that conscription was despotism in its worst form and a monstrous wrong against humanity, in the interest of Wall Street's chosen few. It said: "Do not submit to intimidation"; but in form at least confined itself to peaceful measures, such as a petition for the repeal of the act. The other and later printed side of the sheet was headed, "Assert Your Rights." It stated reasons for alleging that anyone violated the Constitution when he refused to recognize "your right to assert your opposition to the draft," and went on: "If you do not assert and support your rights, you are helping to deny or disparage rights which it is the solemn duty of all citizens and residents of the United States to retain." It described the arguments on the other side as coming from cunning politicians and a mercenary capitalist press, and even silent consent to the Conscription Law as helping to support an infamous conspiracy. It denied the power to send our citizens away to foreign shores to shoot up the people of other lands, and added that words could not express the condemnation such cold-blooded ruthlessness deserves, etc., etc., winding up, "You must do your share to maintain, support, and uphold the rights of the people of this country." Of course the document would not have been sent unless it had been intended to have some effect, and we do not see what effect it could be expected to have upon persons subject to the draft except to influence them to obstruct the carrying of it out. The defendants do not deny that the jury might find against them on this point.

But it is said, suppose that that was the tendency of this circular, it is protected by the First Amendment to the Constitution. Two of the strongest expressions are said to be quoted respectively from well-known public men. It well may be that the prohibition of laws abridging the freedom of speech is not confined to previous restraints, although to prevent them may have been the main purpose, as intimated in Patterson v. Colorado, 205 U.S. 454, 462. We admit that in many places and in ordinary times the defendants, in saying all that was said in the circular, would have been within their constitutional rights. But the character of every act depends upon the circumstances in which it is done. The most stringent protection of free speech would not protect a man in falsely shouting fire in a theater, and causing a panic. It does not even protect a man from an injunction against uttering words that may have all the effect of force. The question in every case is whether the words used are used in such circumstances and are of such a nature as to create a clear and present danger that they will bring about the substantive evils that Congress has a right to prevent. It is a question of proximity and degree. When a nation is at war many things that might be said in time of peace are such a hindrance to its effort that their utterance will not be endured so long as men fight, and that no Court could regard them as protected by any constitutional right. It seems to be admitted that if an actual obstruction of the recruiting service were proved, liability for words that produced that effect might be enforced. The Statute of 1917, in §4, punishes conspiracies to obstruct as well as actual obstruction. If the act, (speaking, or circulating a paper,) its tendency and the intent with which it is done, are the same, we perceive no ground for saying that success alone warrants making the act a crime. Goldman v. United States, 245 U.S. 474, 477. Indeed, that case might be said to dispose of the present contention if the precedent covers all media concludendi. But as the right to free speech was not referred to specially we have thought fit to add a few words. . . .

Judgments affirmed.

## *Note:* **Shaffer, Masses,** *and* **Schenck**

1. *The facts of* Masses. The following is one of the poems in the August 17 issues of The Masses magazine that led to the postmaster's action (Goldman and Berkman were in prison for obstructing the draft):

"A TRIBUTE"
JOSEPHINE BELL

. . .

Emma Goldman and Alexander Berkman
Are in prison tonight,
But they have made themselves elemental forces,
Like the water that climbs down the rocks:
Like the wind in the leaves:
Like the gentle night that holds us:
They are working on our destinies:
They are forging the love of the nations:

. . . . . . . . .

Tonight they lie in prison.

2. *Bad tendency. Shaffer* reflects the then-prevailing view of the lower federal courts — that speech could constitutionally be punished as an attempt to cause some forbidden or otherwise undesirable conduct if the natural and reasonable tendency of the expression might be to bring about the conduct, and if the speaker intended such a result. Under this view, intent could be inferred from the tendency of the speech itself, on the theory that one intends the natural and foreseeable consequences of one's acts. Through the twin doctrines of bad tendency and constructive intent, decisions like *Shaffer* routinely converted criticism of the war and the draft into criminal attempts to cause insubordination or obstruct recruiting. The relatively modest provisions of the 1917 act were thus converted into essentially open-ended restrictions on seditious expression. For detailed accounts of this era, see G. Stone, Perilous Times: Free Speech in Wartime 135–234 (2004); Z. Chafee, Free Speech in the United States 36–108 (1941); Rabban, The Emergence of Modern First Amendment Theory, 50 U. Chi. L. Rev. 1205 (1983).

3. *Express incitement.* Although Judge Hand technically limited himself in *Masses* to a mere interpretation of the Espionage Act, the opinion has clear constitutional overtones, and, as Hand himself made clear in private correspondence, *Masses* was "a distinctive, carefully considered alternative to the prevalent analyses of free speech issues." Gunther, Learned Hand and the Origins of Modern First Amendment Doctrine: Some Fragments of History, 27 Stan. L. Rev. 719, 720 (1975). In effect, Hand attempted in *Masses* to articulate a categorical, per se rule that would be "hard, conventional, difficult

to evade." Id. at 749. Unlike the *Shaffer* and *Schenck* analyses, Judge Hand focused on the content of the speech rather than on the intent of the speaker or the consequences of the communication. Under Judge Hand's formula, the dispositive factor was whether the speaker employed express words of incitement. As Judge Hand intimated in his opinion and made explicit in correspondence, if the effect of such speech "upon the hearers is only to counsel them to violate the law, it is unconditionally illegal." Id. at 765. But if the speaker refrains from such incitement, the speech may not be restrained. Consider the following propositions.

a. *Hand's analysis of express incitement is underprotective of free speech.* Judge Hand's analysis accords little, if any, constitutional protection to express advocacy of criminal conduct. Is this defensible on the ground, urged by Judge Hand, that "words [which] have no purport but to counsel the violation of law cannot by any latitude of interpretation be a part of that public opinion which is the final source of government in a democratic state"? Consider Bork, Neutral Principles and Some First Amendment Problems, 47 Ind. L. Rev. 1, 31 (1971):

> Advocacy of law violation is a call to set aside the results that political speech has produced. The process of the "discovery and spread of political truth" is damaged or destroyed if the outcome is defeated by a minority that makes law enforcement, and hence the putting of political truth into practice, impossible or less effective. There should, therefore, be no constitutional protection for any speech advocating the violation of the law.

See also Stromberg v. California, 283 U.S. 359 (1931) ("The maintenance of the opportunity for free political discussion to the end that government may be responsible to the will of the people and that changes may be obtained *by lawful means* is a fundamental principle of our constitutional system."). Even if express incitement is constitutionally "valueless," might there nonetheless be practical or institutional reasons to protect it? Consider T. Emerson, The System of Freedom of Expression 51–53 (1970):

> Groups which [would] abolish democratic institutions [do] not operate in a political vacuum. They advance other ideas that may be valid [and] groups [expressing] the prohibited views usually represent real grievances, which should be heard. [Moreover, suppression] of any group in a society destroys the atmosphere of freedom essential to the life and progress of a healthy community.

Should the rhetorical or hyperbolic use of express incitement ("Kill the umpire!") be constitutionally protected?

b. *The Hand formula is overprotective of the "clever" inciter.* Judge Hand's theory distinguishes between the speaker who uses express words of incitement and the speaker who specifically intends to incite but is clever enough to avoid the use of such language. Is this sensible? Consider the following arguments: (1) The express inciter is more dangerous because he is more likely to be effective. (2) Case-by-case inquiries into actual subjective intent are too slippery to provide adequate protection to innocent speakers. As Zechariah Chafee observed, "It is only in times of popular panic and indignation that freedom of speech becomes important as an institution, and it is precisely in those times that the protection of the jury proves [illusory]. 'Men believed during [the period of the Espionage Act prosecutions] that the only verdict in a war case, which could show loyalty, was a verdict of guilty.'" Chafee, supra, at 70. Thus, to avoid the dangers of "erroneous" fact-finding, and protect the rights of innocent dissenters, it is necessary to focus on more objective considerations than intent. (3) What really matters under the first amendment is not the intent of the speaker but the value of the expression. Since the clever inciter has not used "words [which] have no purport but to counsel the violation of law," the value of his speech is indistinguishable from that of the speaker who utters the same words with a more honorable intent.

c. *The Hand formula is overprotective of the dangerous speaker.* Suppose during a famine that a speaker angrily asserts "to an excited mob assembled before the house of a corn-dealer" that "corn-dealers are starvers of the poor," thus inflaming the mob to burn down the corn-dealer's house. J. S. Mill, On Liberty ch. 3 (1859). Is it sensible to accord absolute protection to such a speaker, without regard to the potential dangers of his speech, merely because he does not use express language of incitement? Consider the following arguments: (1) It is the actor, and not the speaker, who ultimately brings about the harm. Government should thus direct its punishment and deterrence toward actors, not speakers. (2) A central premise of the first amendment is that government may not restrict expression because it does not trust citizens to make wise decisions if they are exposed to the expression. Such "paternalism" is fundamentally at odds with the very notion of free expression. (3) As Judge Hand argued, "If that be not the test, I can see no escape from the conclusion that [every] political agitation which can be shown to be apt to create a seditious temper is illegal."

4. *The fate of* Masses. Judge Hand's opinion was reversed on appeal. Masses Publishing Co. v. Patten, 246 F. 24 (2d Cir. 1917). The court of appeals flatly rejected Judge Hand's construction of the act: "If the natural and reasonable effect of what is said is to encourage resistance to a law, and the words are used in an endeavor to persuade to resistance, it is immaterial that the duty to resist is not mentioned, or the interest of the persons addressed in resistance is not suggested." Other reactions to Judge Hand's formulation were equally unsupportive, and after 1921 Judge Hand himself abandoned his advocacy of the *Masses* approach. Parts of the formula, however, have reappeared in contemporary tests of subversive advocacy. See *Yates* and *Brandenburg*, infra, this chapter. The Masses itself was soon driven out of business, and its editors were prosecuted under the Espionage Act of 1917.

5. *Clear and present danger.* Whence does Justice Holmes derive the clear and present danger standard? Is Justice Holmes's famous reference to the false shout of fire helpful? Such speech, Justice Holmes implies, may be restricted because it creates a clear and present danger of panic. But suppose the shout is *true*. Would that change the analysis?

Was there a clear and present danger in *Schenck*? Of what? That the war effort would be jeopardized? That the recruiting and enlistment service would grind to a halt? That a single person might be influenced to refuse induction or not enlist? How should we deal with the possibility that there may be many Schencks?

Was Holmes's clear and present danger standard designed to supplant the prevailing bad tendency/constructive intent test? Note that the jury instructions in *Schenck* could not have embodied the clear and present danger standard, which did not yet exist. Why, then, didn't the Court remand for a new trial?

Consider the Court's decisions in *Frohwerk* and *Debs*, handed down on the same day in the spring of 1919, exactly one week after *Schenck*. Consider also the Court's decision, and Justice Holmes's dissent, in *Abrams*, handed down the following fall.

**FROHWERK v. UNITED STATES, 249 U.S. 204 (1919).** As a result of his participation in the preparation and publication of a series of articles in the Missouri Staats Zeitung, a German language newspaper, Frohwerk was convicted under the Espionage Act of 1917 of conspiring to cause disloyalty, mutiny, and refusal of duty in the military and naval forces of the United States. Frohwerk was sentenced to a fine and to ten years' imprisonment. The Court, speaking through Justice Holmes, unanimously rejected Frohwerk's contention that his conviction violated the first amendment. Illustrative of the articles was one that declared "it a monumental and inexcusable mistake to send our soldiers to France" and described our participation in the war as "outright murder."

Justice Holmes began his analysis by observing that the first amendment "cannot have been, and obviously was not, intended to give immunity for every possible use of language. Neither Hamilton nor Madison, nor any other competent person then or later ever supposed that to make criminal the counseling of murder within the jurisdiction of Congress would be an unconstitutional interference with free speech." Justice Holmes then turned to the crux of the issue: "It may be that all this may be said or written even in time of war in circumstances that would not make it a crime. [But] we must take the case on the record as it is, and on the record it is impossible to say that it might not have been found that the circulation of the paper was in quarters where a little breath would be enough to kindle a flame [and that that] fact was known and relied upon by those who sent the paper out." Justice Holmes therefore concluded that "we find ourselves unable to say that the articles could not furnish a basis for a conviction."

*Rosca*
*Paulstin*
*concurrent*

DEBS v. UNITED STATES, 249 U.S. 211 (1919). As a result of a speech delivered to a public assembly in Canton, Ohio, in July of 1918, Eugene V. Debs, national leader of the Socialist Party, was convicted under the Espionage Act of 1917 of attempting to obstruct the recruiting and enlistment service of the United States. Debs was sentenced to a prison term of ten years. The Supreme Court, speaking once again through Justice Holmes, unanimously rejected Debs's claim that the conviction violated the first amendment. Justice Holmes noted at the outset that "[the] main theme of the speech was socialism, its growth, and a prophecy of its ultimate success. With that we have nothing to do, but [if] one purpose of the speech, whether incidental or not does not matter, was to oppose [the] war, and if, in all the circumstances, that would be its probable effect, it would not be protected."

Turning to the speech itself, Justice Holmes observed that Debs had specifically praised several persons who previously had been convicted of aiding or encouraging others to refuse induction, and that toward the end of his address Debs had told his audience that "you need to know that you are fit for something better than slavery and cannon fodder." In such circumstances, Justice Holmes concluded that Debs's first amendment claim had in practical effect been "disposed of in [*Schenck*]." Justice Holmes emphasized that the jury in *Debs* had been "most carefully instructed that they could not find the defendant guilty for advocacy of any of his opinions unless the words used had as their natural tendency and reasonably probable effect to obstruct the recruiting service [and] unless the defendant had the specific intent to do so in his mind." As in *Frohwerk*, Justice Holmes made no reference in *Debs* to "clear and present danger."

In 1920, while in prison, Debs was the Socialist candidate for President. He again received almost a million votes. President Harding released him from prison in 1921.

Other representative prosecutions under the Espionage Act include the following:

(a) Rose Pastor Stokes was convicted for saying, "I am for the people and the government is for the profiteers," during an antiwar talk to the Women's Dining Club of Kansas City. Although there were no soldiers — and indeed no one eligible for the draft — in her intended audience, the government successfully argued that she had violated the act because "our armies . . . can operate and succeed only so far as they are supported and maintained by the folks at home," and Stokes's statement had the tendency to "chill enthusiasm, extinguish confidence, and retard cooperation" of mothers, sisters, and sweethearts. She was sentenced to ten years in prison.

(b) The Reverend Clarence H. Waldron was convicted for distributing a pamphlet stating that "if Christians [are] forbidden to fight to preserve the Person of their Lord and Master, they may not fight to preserve themselves, or any city they should happen to dwell in." The government charged that in distributing this pamphlet Waldron had obstructed the recruiting service. He was sentenced to fifteen years in prison.

(c) Robert Goldstein was convicted for producing and exhibiting a motion picture about the American Revolution. The Spirit of '76 depicted Paul Revere's ride, the signing of the Declaration of Independence, and Washington at Valley Forge. But it also included a scene accurately portraying the Wyoming Valley Massacre, in which British soldiers bayoneted women and children. The government charged that this could promote insubordination because it negatively portrayed America's ally in the war against Germany. Goldstein was sentenced to ten years in prison. See G. Stone, Perilous Times: Free Speech in Wartime 170–173 (2004).

## Abrams v. United States

250 U.S. 616 (1919)

[Although czarist Russia, like the United States, had declared war on Germany, the Bolsheviks, on seizing power, signed a peace treaty with Germany. In the summer of 1918, the United States sent a contingent of marines to Vladivostok and Murmansk. The defendants in *Abrams*, a group of Russian immigrants who were self-proclaimed socialists and anarchists, perceived the expedition as an attempt to "crush the Russian Revolution." In protest, they distributed several thousand copies of each of two leaflets, one of which was written in English, the other in Yiddish. The leaflets, which were thrown from a window and circulated secretly, called for a general strike. The defendants were arrested by the military police, and after a controversial trial, they were convicted of conspiring to violate various provisions of the 1918 amendments to the Espionage Act of 1917. The overall flavor of the trial is captured in the trial judge's remarks just prior to sentencing:

> These defendants took the stand. They talked about capitalists and producers, and I tried to figure out what a capitalist and what a producer is as contemplated by them. After listening carefully to all they had to say, I came to the conclusion that a capitalist is a man with a decent set of clothes, a minimum of $1.25 in his pocket, and a good character. And when I tried to find out what the prisoners had produced, I was unable to find out anything at all. So far as I can learn, not one of them ever produced so much as a single potato. The only thing they know how to raise is hell, and to direct it against the government of the United States. [But] we are not going to help carry out the plans mapped out by the Imperial German Government, and which are being carried out by Lenin and Trotsky. I have heard of the reported fate of the poor little daughters of the Czar, but I won't talk about that now. I might get mad. I will now sentence the prisoners.

The defendants were sentenced to prison terms ranging from three to twenty years. The Supreme Court affirmed the convictions on two counts: one charging a violation of the provision prohibiting conspiracy "to incite, provoke or encourage resistance to the United States" (count 3); the other charging a violation of the provision prohibiting conspiracy to urge curtailment of the production of war materials "with intent [to] cripple or hinder the United States in the prosecution of the war" (count 4). Speaking for the Court, Justice Clarke summarily rejected the defendants' first amendment argument, noting simply that "[this] contention is sufficiently discussed and is definitely negatived in [*Schenck*] and [*Frohwerk*]."]

MR. JUSTICE HOLMES dissenting. . . .

The first of these leaflets says that the President's cowardly silence about the intervention in Russia reveals the hypocrisy of the plutocratic gang in Washington. It intimates that "German militarism combined with allied capitalism to crush the Russian revolution."[It] says that there is only one enemy of the workers of the world and that is capitalism; that it is a crime for workers of America, &c., to fight the workers' republic of Russia, and ends "Awake! Awake, you Workers of the World! Revolutionists." A note adds "It is absurd to call us pro-German. We hate and despise German militarism more than do you hypocritical tyrants. We have more reasons for denouncing German militarism than has the coward of the White House."

The other leaflet, headed "Workers — Wake Up," with abusive language says that [the] hypocrites shall not fool the Russian emigrants and friends of Russia in America. It tells the Russian emigrants that they now must spit in the face of the false military propaganda by which their sympathy and help to the prosecution of the war have been called forth and says that with the money they have lent or are going to lend "they will make bullets not only for the Germans but also for the Workers Soviets of Russia," and further, "Workers in the ammunition factories, you are producing bullets, bayonets, cannon, to murder not only the Germans, but also your dearest, best, who are in Russia and are fighting for freedom." It then appeals to the same Russian emigrants at some length not to consent to the "inquisitionary expedition to Russia," and says that the destruction of the Russian revolution is "the politics of the march to Russia." The leaflet winds up by saying "Workers, our reply to this barbarous intervention has to be a general strike!," and after a few words on the spirit of revolution, exhortations not to be afraid, and some usual tall talk ends "Woe unto those who will be in the way of progress. Let solidarity live! The Rebels."

[After describing the leaflets, Justice Holmes argued that the conviction under the fourth count was invalid because the defendants did not have the intent, required by the act, "to cripple or hinder the United States in the prosecution of the war." The defendants' specific intent, Justice Holmes maintained, was to help Russia, with whom we were not at war. Although conceding that "the word *intent* as vaguely used in ordinary legal discussion means no more than knowledge at the time of the act that the consequences said to be intended will ensue," Justice Holmes insisted that "this statute must be taken to use its words in a strict and accurate sense." Otherwise, Justice Holmes reasoned, the act would "be absurd," for it would make it criminal for one who thought "we were wasting money on aeroplanes" successfully to advocate curtailment if such curtailment later turned out "to hinder the United States in the prosecution of the war." Justice Holmes then passed to what he referred to as "a more important aspect of the case" — the first amendment.]

I never have seen any reason to doubt that the questions of law that alone were before this Court in the cases of *Schenck*, *Frohwerk* and *Debs* were rightly decided. I do not doubt for a moment that by the same reasoning that would justify punishing persuasion to murder, the United States constitutionally may punish speech that produces or is intended to produce a clear and imminent danger that it will bring about forthwith certain substantive evils that the United States constitutionally may seek to prevent. The power undoubtedly is greater in time of war than in time of peace because war opens dangers that do not exist at other times.

But as against dangers peculiar to war, as against others, the principle of the right to free speech is always the same. It is only the present danger of immediate evil or an intent to bring it about that warrants Congress in setting a limit to the expression of opinion where private rights are not concerned. Congress certainly cannot forbid all effort to change the mind of the country. Now nobody can suppose that the surreptitious publishing of a silly leaflet by an unknown man, without more, would present any immediate danger that its opinions would hinder the success of the government arms or have any appreciable tendency to do so. Publishing those opinions for the very purpose of obstructing, however, might indicate a greater danger and at any rate would have the quality of an attempt. So I assume that the second leaflet if published for the purposes alleged in the fourth count might be punishable. But [I] do not see how anyone can find the intent required by the statute in any of the defendants' words. The second leaflet is the only one that affords even a foundation for the charge, and there, without invoking the hatred of German militarism expressed in the former one, it is evident from the beginning to the end that the only object of the paper is to help Russia and stop American intervention there against the popular government — not to impede the United States in the war that it was carrying on. To say that two phrases taken literally might import a suggestion of conduct that would have interference with the war as an indirect and probably undesired effect seems to me by no means enough to show an attempt to produce that effect.

In this case sentences of twenty years imprisonment have been imposed for the publishing of two leaflets that I believe the defendants had as much right to publish as the Government has to publish the Constitution of the United States now vainly invoked by them. Even if I am technically wrong and enough can be squeezed from these poor and puny anonymities to turn the color of legal litmus paper; I will add, even if what I think the necessary intent were shown; the most nominal punishment seems to me all that possibly could be inflicted, unless the defendants are to be made to suffer not for what the indictment alleges but for the creed that they avow — a creed that I believe to be the creed of ignorance and immaturity when honestly held, as I see no reason to doubt that it was held here, but which, although made the subject of examination at the trial, no one has a right even to consider in dealing with the charges before the Court.

Persecution for the expression of opinions seems to me perfectly logical. If you have no doubt of your premises or your power and want a certain result with all your heart you naturally express your wishes in law and sweep away all opposition. To allow opposition by speech seems to indicate that you think the speech impotent, as when a man says that he has squared the circle, or that you do not care whole-heartedly for the result, or that you doubt either your power or your premises. But when men have realized that time has upset many fighting faiths, they may come to believe even more than they believe the very foundations of their own conduct that the ultimate good desired is better reached by free trade in ideas — that the best test of truth is the power of the thought to get itself accepted in the competition of the market, and that truth is the only ground upon which their wishes safely can be carried out. That at any rate is the theory of our Constitution. It is an experiment, as all life is an experiment. Every year if not every day we have to wager our salvation upon some prophecy based upon imperfect knowledge. While that experiment is part of our system I think that we should be eternally vigilant against attempts to check the expression of opinions that we loathe and believe to be fraught with death, unless they so imminently threaten immediate interference with the lawful and pressing purposes of the law that an immediate check is required to save the country. I wholly disagree with the argument of the Government that the First Amendment left the common law as to seditious libel in force. History seems to me against the notion. I had conceived that the United States through many years had shown its repentance for the Sedition Act of 1798, by repaying fines that it imposed. Only the emergency that makes it immediately dangerous to leave the correction of evil counsels to time warrants making any exception to the sweeping command, "Congress shall make no law . . . abridging the freedom of speech." Of course I am speaking only of expressions of opinion and exhortations, which were all that were uttered here, but I regret that I cannot put into more impressive words my belief that in their conviction upon this indictment the defendants were deprived of their rights under the Constitution of the United States.

Mr. Justice Brandeis concurs with the foregoing opinion.

## Note: Abrams *and the Emergence of the Holmes/Brandeis Tradition*

1. *Historical context.* For a lively telling of the full story of the *Abrams* case, see R. Polenberg, Fighting Faiths (1987). The defendants in *Abrams* were a

fascinating group. One of Abrams's codefendants, Mollie Steimer, arrived at Ellis Island in 1913 with her parents and her five brothers and sisters, part of the flood of immigrants fleeing poverty and anti-Semitism in czarist Russia. Two days after her arrival, the fifteen-year-old Steimer went to work in a grimy garment factory amid the crowded tenements of New York's Lower East Side. Faced with continuing hardship and bleak prospects for the future, she began to explore radical literature and soon became a committed anarchist.

At the time of her trial, she was only twenty years old. At four feet nine inches and less than ninety pounds she was tiny, but she was tough as nails. After her conviction, she was sentenced to fifteen years in prison. In 1922, she was ordered deported to the Soviet Union. When she was informed of this action, she refused to leave the federal penitentiary, because there was a threatened railroad strike and she would not ride on a train run by strikebreakers. After the strike was resolved, she was shipped back to Russia.

Once there, she immediately began protesting the injustices of Soviet society. In 1923, the Soviets deported Steimer to Germany. Few other people have the distinction of having been deported by both the United States and the Soviet Union. In 1933, when Hitler came to power, Steimer fled to Paris. Her Jewish and anarchist identities caught up with her, however, and after the Nazis occupied France she escaped to Mexico. Steimer died in Cuernavaca in 1980 at the age of eighty-two. See G. Stone, Perilous Times: Free Speech in Wartime 138–140, 232–233 (2004).

2. *The Holmes transformation.* Most commentators have concluded that Justice Holmes moved from a narrow construction of the first amendment in *Schenck, Frohwerk,* and *Debs* to a more civil libertarian position in his dissent in *Abrams.* Holmes apparently was influenced during the summer of 1919 by a lively set of exchanges about free speech with Learned Hand, Zechariah Chafee, and Harold Laski.

T. Healy, The Great Dissent: How Oliver Wendell Holmes Changed His Mind — and Changed the History of Free Speech in America 201, 343 (2013), provides a full account of Holmes's transformation. It began with a chance encounter with Learned Hand on a train in the summer of 1919. In the following months, Holmes came "under considerable pressure to rethink" his position. His opinions in *Schenck, Frohwerk,* and *Debs* were "attacked in the pages of the New Republic" by University of Chicago law professor Ernst Freund and in "the Harvard Law Review, challenged in correspondence with Learned Hand, confronted over tea by [Harvard law professor] Zechariah Chafee." The political theorist Harold Laski "fed him one book after another espousing a liberal view of free speech," and a young Felix Frankfurter "tried to arrange for him to write a piece on tolerance in the Atlantic Monthly." Although initially resistant to the criticism, Holmes came around. In 1922, Holmes confessed in a letter to Chafee that before the summer of 1919, when it came to issues of free speech and tolerance, "I was simply ignorant." See also G. Stone, Perilous Times: Free Speech in Wartime 198–211 (2004); Rabban,

The Emergence of Modern First Amendment Doctrine, 50 U. Chi. L. Rev. 1207, 1208–1209, 1311–1317 (1983).

3. *The administrability of clear and present danger.* Is Justice Holmes's formulation of clear and present danger in *Abrams* administratively workable? Judge Hand was largely unimpressed with Justice Holmes's effort. As he wrote to Chafee,

> I am not wholly in love with Holmesey's test, [for once] you admit that the matter is one of degree, [you] give to Tomdickandharry, D.J., so much latitude that the jig is at once up. Besides [the] Nine Elder Statesmen have not shown themselves wholly immune from the "herd instinct" and what seems "immediate and direct" to-day may seem very remote next year even though the circumstances surrounding the utterance be unchanged. I own I should prefer a qualitative formula, hard, conventional, difficult to evade.

In short, Judge Hand preferred "a test based upon the nature of the utterance itself." Gunther, Learned Hand and the Origins of Modern First Amendment Doctrine: Some Fragments of History, 27 Stan. L. Rev. 719, 749 (1975).

4. *Was there a clear and present danger in* Abrams? Consider Wigmore's criticism:

> [The *Abrams* dissent] is dallying with the facts and the law. [If] these [individuals] could, without the law's restraint, urge munition workers to a general strike and armed violence, then others could lawfully do so; and a thousand disaffected undesirables, aliens and natives alike, were ready and waiting to do so. [If] such urgings were lawful, every munitions factory in the country could be stopped by them. The relevant amount of harm that one criminal act can effect is no measure of its criminality, and no measure of the danger of its criminality.

Wigmore, Abrams v. United States: Freedom of Speech and Freedom of Thuggery in War-Time and Peace-Time, 14 Ill. L. Rev. 539, 549–550 (1920).

5. *The rationale of clear and present danger.* Consider the following rationales for the clear and present danger standard: (a) The test balances competing speech and societal interests — speech is important, so government can restrict it only when there is an "emergency"; an "emergency" exists only if the danger is "clear" and "present." (b) The test marks off a broad area of protected expression to avoid Judge Hand's concern in *Masses* that government not be permitted to render unlawful "every political agitation which can be shown to be apt to create a seditious temper." (c) The test is designed to reduce the risk that government, in the guise of preventing "danger," will in fact suppress expression because it disapproves of the substantive message.

6. *"Sentences of twenty years imprisonment."* Holmes is clearly appalled that the defendants in *Abrams* were sentenced to terms "of twenty years imprisonment." He implies that the only plausible explanation for such severe punishment is that the defendants were being "made to suffer" not for any actual

harm they might have caused to the nation (which he regards as trivial), but because of the government's hostility to their ideas (which he regards as impermissible). Suppose, then, that the defendants had been sentenced to a fine of $100 instead of to twenty years in prison. Should that have changed Holmes's analysis or the result? Should the nature or severity of the penalty be relevant to the constitutionality of a restriction of speech? See Coenen, Of Speech and Sanctions: Toward a Penalty-Sensitive Approach to the First Amendment, 112 Colum. L. Rev. 991 (2012).

7. *Other Espionage Act decisions.* In several post-*Abrams* decisions, the Court, over the dissents of Justices Holmes and Brandeis, upheld further convictions under the Espionage Act. See Pierce v. United States, 252 U.S. 239 (1920); Schaefer v. United States, 251 U.S. 466 (1920). See also Gilbert v. Minnesota, 254 U.S. 325 (1920).

8. *The "Red Scare."* After World War I and the Russian Revolution, the United States entered a period of intense antiradicalism. In the years 1919 and 1920, an era known as the "Red Scare," two-thirds of the states enacted laws prohibiting the advocacy of criminal syndicalism and criminal anarchy. In addition, two-thirds of the states adopted "red flag" laws, which made it a crime to display a red flag with a seditious intent. On the Red Scare, see G. Stone, supra, at 220–226; Z. Chafee, Free Speech in the United States 141–168 (1941). It was not long before the Court had to rule on the constitutionality of such legislation.

## Gitlow v. New York

268 U.S. 652 (1925)

Mr. Justice Sanford delivered the opinion of the Court.

Benjamin Gitlow was indicted in the Supreme Court of New York, with three others, for the statutory crime of criminal anarchy. [He] was separately tried, convicted, and sentenced to imprisonment. . . .

The contention here is that the statute, by its terms and as applied in this case, is repugnant to the due process clause of the Fourteenth Amendment. Its material provisions are: . . .

> §161. *Advocacy of criminal anarchy.* Any person [who] advocates, advises, or teaches the duty, necessity or propriety of overthrowing [organized] government by force or violence, or by assassination of [any] of the executive officials of government, or by any unlawful means, [is] guilty of a felony. . . .

[The] defendant is a member of the Left Wing Section of the Socialist Party, a dissenting branch or faction of that party formed in opposition to its dominant policy of "moderate Socialism." [The] Left Wing Section was organized nationally at a conference in New York City in June, 1919, attended by ninety delegates from twenty different States. The conference elected a National Council, of which the defendant was a member, and left to it the adoption of a "manifesto." This was published in The Revolutionary Age, the official organ of the Left Wing. The defendant [arranged] for the printing [and publication of the first issue of the paper, which contained the Left Wing Manifesto].

[The indictment charged that, as a result of his involvement in the publication of the manifesto, he "had advocated, advised and taught the duty, necessity and propriety of overthrowing and overturning organized government by force, violence and unlawful means." The Court conceded that there "was no evidence of any effect resulting from the publication and circulation of the Manifesto."]

The statute does not penalize the utterance or publication of abstract "doctrine" or academic discussion having no quality of incitement to any concrete action. It is not aimed against mere historical or philosophical essays. It does not restrain the advocacy of changes in the form of government by constitutional and lawful means. What it prohibits is language advocating, advising or teaching the overthrow of organized government by unlawful means. These words imply urging to action. . . .

The Manifesto, plainly, is neither the statement of abstract doctrine nor, as suggested by counsel, mere prediction that industrial disturbances and revolutionary mass strikes will result spontaneously in an inevitable process of evolution in the economic system. It advocates and urges in fervent language mass action which shall progressively foment industrial disturbances and through political mass strikes and revolutionary mass action overthrow and destroy organized parliamentary government. It concludes with a call to action in these words: "The proletariat revolution and the Communist reconstruction of society — *the struggle for these* — is now indispensable. . . . The Communist International calls the proletariat of the world to the final struggle!" This [is] the language of direct incitement. [That] the jury were warranted in finding that the Manifesto advocated not merely the abstract doctrine of overthrowing organized government by force, violence and unlawful means, but action to that end, is clear.

For present purposes we may and do assume that freedom of speech and of the press — which are protected by the First Amendment from abridgment by Congress — are among the fundamental personal rights and "liberties" protected by the due process clause of the Fourteenth Amendment from impairment by the States. . . .

It is a fundamental principle, long established, that the freedom of speech and of the press which is secured by the Constitution, does not confer an absolute right to speak or publish, without responsibility, whatever one may choose, or an unrestricted and unbridled license that gives immunity for every possible use of language and prevents the punishment of those who abuse this freedom. [A] State may punish utterances endangering the foundations of organized government and threatening its overthrow by unlawful means. These imperil its own existence as a constitutional State. Freedom of speech and press [does] not deprive a State of the primary and essential right of self preservation. . . .

By enacting the present statute the State has determined, through its legislative body, that utterances advocating the overthrow of organized government by force, violence and unlawful means, are so inimical to the general welfare and involve such danger of substantive evil that they may be penalized in the exercise of its police power. That determination must be given great weight. Every presumption is to be indulged in favor of the validity of the statute. Mugler v. Kansas, 123 U.S. 623, 661. [That] utterances inciting to the overthrow of organized government by unlawful means, present a sufficient danger of substantive evil to bring their punishment within the range of legislative discretion, is clear. Such utterances, by their very nature, involve danger to the public peace and to the security of the State. They threaten breaches of the peace and ultimate revolution. And the immediate danger is none the less real and substantial, because the effect of a given utterance cannot be accurately foreseen. The State cannot reasonably be required to measure the danger from every such utterance in the nice balance of a jeweler's scale. A single revolutionary spark may kindle a fire that, smouldering for a time, may burst into a sweeping and destructive conflagration. It cannot be said that the State is acting arbitrarily or unreasonably when in the exercise of its judgment as to the measures necessary to protect the public peace and safety, it seeks to extinguish the spark without waiting until it has enkindled the flame or blazed into the conflagration. It cannot reasonably be required to defer the adoption of measures for its own peace and safety until the revolutionary utterances lead to actual disturbances of the public peace or imminent and immediate danger of its own destruction; but it may, in the exercise of its judgment, suppress the threatened danger in its incipiency. . . .

We cannot hold that the present statute is an arbitrary or unreasonable exercise of the police power of the State unwarrantably infringing the freedom of speech or press; and we must and do sustain its constitutionality.

This being so it may be applied to every utterance — not too trivial to be beneath the notice of the law — which is of such a character and used with such intent and purpose as to bring it within the prohibition of the statute. [In] other words, when the legislative body has determined generally, in the constitutional exercise of its discretion, that utterances of a certain kind involve such danger of substantive evil that they may be punished, the question whether any specific utterance coming within the prohibited class is likely, in and of itself, to bring about the substantive evil, is not open to consideration. It is sufficient that the statute itself be constitutional and that the use of the language comes within its prohibition. . . .

Affirmed.

Mr. Justice Holmes, dissenting.

Mr. Justice Brandeis and I are of opinion that this judgment should be reversed. The general principle of free speech, it seems to me, must be taken to be included in the Fourteenth Amendment, in view of the scope that has been given to the word "liberty" as there used, although perhaps it may be accepted with a somewhat larger latitude of interpretation than is allowed to Congress by the sweeping language that governs, or ought to govern, the laws of the United States. If I am right, then I think that the criterion sanctioned by the full court in [*Schenck*] applies: "The question in every case is whether the words used are used in such circumstances and are of such a nature as to create a clear and present danger that they will bring about the substantive evils that [the state] has a right to prevent." It is true that in my opinion this criterion was departed from in [*Abrams*], but the convictions that I expressed in that case are too deep for it to be possible for me as yet to believe that it [has] settled the law. If what I think the correct test is applied, it is manifest that there was no present danger of an attempt to overthrow the government by force on the part of the admittedly small minority who shared the defendant's views. It is said that this Manifesto was more than a theory, that it was an incitement. Every idea is an incitement. It offers itself for belief, and, if believed, it is acted on unless some other belief outweighs it, or some failure of energy stifles the movement at its birth. The only difference between the expression of an opinion and an incitement in the narrower sense is the speaker's enthusiasm for the result. Eloquence may set fire to reason. But whatever may be thought of the redundant discourse before us, it had no chance of starting a present conflagration. If, in the long run, the beliefs expressed in proletarian dictatorship are destined to be accepted by the dominant forces of the community, the only meaning of free speech is that they should be given their chance and have their way.

If the publication of this document had been laid as an attempt to induce an uprising against government at once, and not at some indefinite time in the future, it would have presented a different question. The object would have been one with which the law might deal, subject to the doubt whether there was any danger that the publication could produce any result; or, in other words, whether it was not futile and too remote from possible consequences. But the indictment alleges the publication and nothing more.

### Note: "Abstract Doctrine" versus "Urging to Action"

1. *Incitement.* Justice Sanford emphasized repeatedly in *Gitlow* that the New York statute was not directed against "abstract doctrine," "academic discussion," "historical or philosophical essays," or "advocacy of changes in the form of government by constitutional and lawful means." Rather, it restricted only "urging to action," "incitement to [concrete] action," and "the language of direct incitement." Justice Sanford thus seemed to be suggesting an analysis reminiscent of that of Judge Hand in *Masses*, arguing implicitly that whatever

protection might be appropriate for "abstract doctrine" or for general political discussion, express "incitement" of unlawful conduct is an entirely different matter. Is Justice Holmes's reply to this argument that "every idea is an incitement" a satisfactory response?

2. *The marketplace of ideas.* In *Abrams*, Justice Holmes maintained that as an "experiment" our Constitution embraced the "theory" that "the best test of truth is the power of the thought to get itself accepted in the competition of the market." The market, however, is not perfect and in *Gitlow* Justice Holmes conceded that, "if, in the long run, the beliefs expressed in proletarian dictatorship are destined to be accepted by the dominant forces of the community, the only meaning of free speech is that they should be given their chance and have their way." What about ideas that, if accepted, would refuse to permit other ideas to compete in the "market"? Are some evils so grave that we cannot afford to "experiment"?

Consider Stone, Reflections on the First Amendment: The Evolution of the American Jurisprudence of Free Expression, 131 Proc. J. Am. Phil. Soc'y. 251, 253 (1987):

> [The central principle of first amendment jurisprudence is that] the Government may *never* restrict the expression of particular ideas because it fears that citizens may adopt those ideas in the political process. As Alexander Meiklejohn explained, this principle is rooted "in the very foundations of the self-governing process," for when individuals "govern themselves it is they — and no one else — who must pass judgment upon unwisdom, unfairness and danger." Under this view, "no suggestion of policy" may be denied a hearing "because someone in control thinks it unwise."
>
> Now, there is an anomaly in this principle, [for] if the essential goal is to preserve self-governance, why can't citizens, acting in their capacity as self-governors, decide that certain policies are simply out-of-bounds and thus prohibit further debate on such issues? Under this view, it is not the Government, as some independent entity, that is closing off debate, but citizens themselves, and they are doing so through the very self-governing process that the First Amendment is designed to promote.
>
> The answer, I think, is that the First Amendment [places] out of bounds any law that attempts to freeze public debate at a particular moment in time. Under this view, a majority at any moment has the power to decide an issue of policy for itself, but it has no power irrevocably to decide that issue for future citizens by preventing them from continuing to debate the issue. This is [what] Justice Holmes described as the great First Amendment "experiment."

Is there a difference under the marketplace theory between advocacy of change through political processes and advocacy of change through criminal conduct? Must those who seek to implement their ideas by the use of force or violence "be given their chance" to "have their way"?

## Whitney v. California

274 U.S. 357 (1927)

MR. JUSTICE SANFORD delivered the opinion of the Court.

[In 1919, Anita Whitney attended the national convention of the Socialist Party in Chicago as a delegate of the local Oakland branch of the party. At this convention, the party split between the "radicals" and the old-line Socialists. The radicals, supported by the Oakland branch delegates, formed the Communist Labor Party and promulgated a platform similar in style and substance to the Left Wing Manifesto at issue in *Gitlow*. Shortly thereafter, Whitney attended a convention held in Oakland for the purpose of organizing a California branch of the Communist Labor Party. At this convention, she sponsored a moderate resolution calling for the achievement of the party's goals through the political process. This resolution was defeated, however, and the convention adopted the more militant national platform. Whitney remained at the convention until it adjourned and remained a member of the party. As a result of her activities at the Oakland convention, she was charged with violating the California Criminal Syndicalism Act, which prohibited any person to knowingly become a member of any organization that advocates "the commission of crime, sabotage, or unlawful acts of force and violence or unlawful methods of terrorism as a means of accomplishing a change in industrial ownership or control, or effecting any political change." For an excellent account of Ms. Whitney's life and of the trial and appellate proceedings in the case, see Blasi, The First Amendment and the Ideal of Civic Courage: The Brandeis Opinion in Whitney v. California, 29 Wm. & Mary L. Rev. 653 (1988).]

The first count of the information, on which the conviction was had, charged that [at the Oakland convention] the defendant, in violation of the Criminal Syndicalism Act, "did then and there [knowingly] became a member of [a group] organized [to advocate] criminal syndicalism." . . .

[At her trial, Whitney] testified that it was not her intention that the Communist Labor Party of California should be an instrument of terrorism or violence. [But by] enacting the provisions of the Syndicalism Act the State has declared, [for an individual] to knowingly be or become a member of [an organization that advocates criminal syndicalism] involves such danger to the public peace and the security of the State [that] these acts should be penalized in the exercise of its police power. That determination must be given great weight. . . .

The essence of the offense denounced by the Act [partakes] of the nature of a criminal conspiracy. [That] such united and joint action involves even greater danger to the public peace and security than the isolated utterances and acts of individuals, is clear. We cannot hold that, as here applied, the Act is an unreasonable or arbitrary exercise of the police power of the State. . . .

Affirmed.

MR. JUSTICE BRANDEIS, concurring. . . .

[Although] the rights of free speech and assembly are fundamental, they are not in their nature absolute. Their exercise is subject to restriction, if the particular restriction proposed is required in order to protect the state from destruction or from serious injury, political, economic or moral. That the necessity which is essential to a valid restriction does not exist unless speech would produce, or is intended to produce, a clear and imminent danger of some substantive evil which the state constitutionally may seek to prevent has been settled. See [*Schenck*].

It is said to be the function of the legislature to determine whether at a particular time and under the particular circumstances the formation of, or assembly with, a society organized to advocate criminal syndicalism constitutes a clear and present danger of substantive evil; and that by enacting the law here in question the legislature of California determined that question in the affirmative. [The] legislature must obviously decide, in the first instance, whether a danger exists which calls for a particular protective measure. But where a statute is valid only in case certain conditions exist, the enactment of the statute cannot alone establish the facts which are essential to its validity. . . .

This court has not yet fixed the standard by which to determine when a danger shall be deemed clear; how remote the danger may be and yet be deemed present; and what degree of evil shall be deemed sufficiently substantial to justify resort to abridgment of free speech and assembly as the means of protection. To reach sound conclusions on these matters, we must bear in mind why a state is, ordinarily, denied the power to prohibit dissemination of social, economic and political doctrine which a vast majority of its citizens believes to be false and fraught with evil consequence.

Those who won our independence believed that the final end of the state was to make men free to develop their faculties; and that in its government the deliberative forces should prevail over the arbitrary. They valued liberty both as an end and as a means. They believed liberty to be the secret of happiness and courage to be the secret of liberty. They believed that freedom to think as you will and to speak as you think are means indispensable to the discovery and spread of political truth; that without free speech and assembly discussion would be futile; that with them, discussion affords ordinarily adequate protection against the dissemination of noxious doctrine; that the greatest menace to freedom is an inert people; that public discussion is a political duty; and that this should be a fundamental principle of the American government. They recognized the risks to which all human institutions are subject. But they knew that order cannot be secured merely through fear of punishment for its infraction; that it is hazardous to discourage thought, hope and imagination; that fear breeds repression; that repression breeds hate; that hate menaces stable government; that the path of safety lies in the opportunity to discuss freely supposed grievances and proposed remedies; and that the fitting remedy for evil counsels is good ones. Believing in the power of reason as applied through public discussion, they eschewed silence coerced by law — the argument of force in its worst form. Recognizing the occasional tyrannies of governing majorities, they amended the Constitution so that free speech and assembly should be guaranteed.

Fear of serious injury cannot alone justify suppression of free speech and assembly. Men feared witches and burned women. It is the function of speech to free men from the bondage of irrational fears. To justify suppression of free speech there must be reasonable ground to fear that serious evil will result if free speech is practiced. There must be reasonable ground to believe that the danger apprehended is imminent. There must be reasonable ground to believe that the evil to be prevented is a serious one. Every denunciation of existing law tends in some measure to increase the probability that there will be violation of it. Condonation of a breach enhances the probability. Expressions of approval add to the probability. Propagation of the criminal state of mind by teaching syndicalism increases it. Advocacy of lawbreaking heightens it still further. But even advocacy of violation, however reprehensible morally, is not a justification for denying free speech where the advocacy falls short of incitement and there is nothing to indicate that the advocacy would be immediately acted on. The wide difference between advocacy and incitement, between preparation and attempt, between assembling and conspiracy, must be borne in mind. In order to support a finding of clear and present danger it must be shown either that immediate serious violence was to be expected or was advocated, or that the past conduct furnished reason to believe that such advocacy was then contemplated.

Those who won our independence by revolution were not cowards. They did not fear political change. They did not exalt order at the cost of liberty. To courageous, self-reliant men, with confidence in the power of free and fearless reasoning applied through the processes of popular government, no danger flowing from speech can be deemed clear and present, unless the incidence of the evil apprehended is so imminent that it may befall before there is opportunity for full discussion. If there be time to expose through discussion the falsehood and fallacies, to avert the evil by the processes of education, the remedy to be applied is more speech, not enforced silence. Only an emergency can justify repression. Such must be the rule if authority is to be reconciled with freedom. Such, in my opinion, is the command of the Constitution. It is, therefore, always open to Americans to challenge a law abridging free speech and assembly by showing that there was no emergency justifying it.

Moreover, even imminent danger cannot justify resort to prohibition of these functions essential to effective democracy, unless the evil apprehended is relatively serious. Prohibition of free speech and assembly is a measure so stringent that it would be inappropriate as the means for averting a relatively trivial harm to society. A police measure may be unconstitutional merely because the remedy, although effective as means of protection, is unduly harsh or oppressive. Thus, a state might, in the exercise of its police power, make any trespass upon the land of another a crime, regardless of the results or of the intent or purpose of the trespasser. It might, also, punish an attempt, a conspiracy, or an incitement to commit the trespass. But it is hardly conceivable that this court would hold constitutional a statute which punished as a felony the mere voluntary assembly with a society formed to teach that pedestrians had the moral right to cross unenclosed, unposted, waste lands and to advocate their doing so, even if there was imminent danger that advocacy would lead to a trespass. The fact that speech is likely to result in some violence or in destruction of property is not enough to justify its suppression. There must be the probability of serious injury to the state. Among freemen, the deterrents ordinarily to be applied to prevent crime are education and punishment for violations of the law, not abridgment of the rights of free speech and assembly.

The California Syndicalism Act recites, in §4:

> [This] act concerns and is necessary to the immediate preservation of the public peace and safety, for the reason that at the present time large numbers of persons are going from place to place in this state advocating, teaching and practicing criminal syndicalism. . . .

This legislative declaration satisfies the requirement of the Constitution of the state concerning emergency legislation. [But] it does not preclude inquiry into the question whether, at the time and under the circumstances, the conditions existed which are essential to validity under the Federal Constitution. As a statute, even if not void on its face, may be challenged because invalid as applied, [the] result of such an inquiry may depend upon the specific facts of the particular case. Whenever the fundamental rights of free speech and assembly are alleged to have been invaded, it must remain open to a defendant to present the issue whether there actually did exist at the time a clear danger; whether the danger, if any, was imminent; and whether the evil apprehended was one so substantial as to justify the stringent restriction interposed by the legislature. The legislative declaration, like the fact that the statute was passed and was sustained by the highest court of the state, creates merely a rebuttable presumption that these conditions have been satisfied. [For technical reasons, Justice Brandeis ultimately voted to uphold the conviction.]

MR. JUSTICE HOLMES joins in this opinion.

### Note: The Brandeis Concurrence and the Road to Dennis

1. *Clear and present danger.* Justice Brandeis attempted in Whitney to explicate the underlying rationale of the clear and present danger standard. Was his reliance on the intent of the framers historically sound? Note that Justice

Brandeis's conception of the function of free speech differs markedly from that of Justice Holmes. Whereas Justice Holmes speaks of "free trade in ideas," Justice Brandeis emphasizes the "development of the faculties" and the "deliberative" process, and suggests that "public discussion is a political duty" and that "the greatest menace to freedom is an inert people." See Blasi, The First Amendment and the Ideal of Civic Courage: The Brandeis Opinion in Whitney v. California, 29 Wm. & Mary L. Rev. 653 (1988). For a historical analysis of the Brandeis concurrence, see Collins and Skover, Curious Concurrence: Justice Brandeis's Vote in Whitney v. California, 2005 Sup. Ct. Rev. 333.

2. *The persuasion principle.* Justice Brandeis emphasized that, if the danger is not imminent, "the remedy to be applied is more speech, not enforced silence." Is the opportunity for counterspeech an adequate explanation of the imminence requirement? Consider Strauss, Persuasion, Autonomy, and Freedom of Expression, 91 Colum. L. Rev. 334–336, 346–347, 353–356 (1991):

The government may not suppress speech on the ground that it is too persuasive. Except, perhaps, in extraordinary circumstances, the government may not restrict speech because it fears, however justifiably, that the speech will persuade those who hear it to do something of which the government disapproves. [This] principle [unifies] much of first amendment law.

[T]he persuasion principle can[not] be justified on consequentialist grounds. [Justice Brandeis's] opinion in *Whitney* [argues that "good counsels"] are a "remedy" for "evil counsels." [The] suggestion is that "more" speech can accomplish practically everything that suppression could accomplish. [If] this were true, the persuasion principle would be easy to justify. [But] there will be many occasions on which this optimistic view is an illusion. The problem with the "more speech" approach is that it is not unusual for people to be persuaded to do bad things, and it will not always be possible to talk them out of it. . . .

Brandeis's opinion in *Whitney*, in addition to suggesting a consequentialist argument, uses terms that we would today say reflect a conception of human autonomy: "the final end of the State" is to make people "free to develop their faculties," and liberty is valuable "both as an end and as a means." [The] persuasion principle can be defended on autonomy grounds in the following way: Violations of the persuasion principle are similar in kind [to] lies that are told for the purpose of influencing behavior. Violating the persuasion principle is wrong for some of the same reasons that lies of this kind are wrong: both involve a denial of autonomy in the sense that they interfere with a person's control over her own reasoning processes. [When] the government violates the persuasion principle, it has determined that people [will] pursue [the government's] objectives, instead of their own.

3. *Association.* In the pre-*Whitney* cases, the various defendants were prosecuted for engaging personally in prohibited expression. The California Criminal Syndicalism Act, however, declared it unlawful for any person

knowingly to be a *member* of any organization that engages in unlawful advocacy. *Whitney* thus posed, but did not necessarily answer, three new questions: First, is the act of associating with others for expression-related purposes in itself protected by the first amendment? Second, assuming association is a protected first amendment activity, in what circumstances, if any, can the state constitutionally punish membership in an organization that engages in unlawful advocacy? The Court in *Whitney* held "knowing" membership unprotected. Is that the appropriate line? Third, how does the Holmes-Brandeis conception of clear and present danger apply to association? Recall the argument of Wigmore that the legislature should be permitted to consider the cumulative danger posed by many individually harmless speakers in deciding whether there is sufficient danger to warrant the suppression of speech. On the "right to associate" as a distinct first amendment right, see Bhagwat, *Associational Speech*, 120 Yale L.J. 978 (2011).

4. *A new direction?* In the decade following *Whitney*, the Court handed down three decisions concerning subversive advocacy and the right of association. Although the Court did not expressly reconsider its earlier decisions in these cases, in each case the Court found a technical way to invalidate the conviction. Thus, after an era of nine consecutive affirmances of convictions for subversive advocacy, the Court in the next decade offered three consecutive reversals. See Fiske v. Kansas, 274 U.S. 380 (1927); De Jonge v. Oregon, 299 U.S. 353 (1937); Herndon v. Lowry, 301 U.S. 242 (1937).

5. *Clear and present danger from* Whitney *to* Dennis. In the quarter-century between *Whitney* and *Dennis*, the Court embraced clear and present danger as the appropriate test for a wide range of first amendment issues. See, e.g., Chapter 5.A, infra (leafleting); Cantwell v. Connecticut, Section B of this chapter, infra (hostile audience); Bridges v. California, Chapter 4.C, infra (contempt by publication); Terminiello v. Chicago, Section B of this chapter, infra (breach of peace). See also Strong, Fifty Years of "Clear and Present Danger": From *Schenck* to *Brandenburg* — and Beyond, 1969 Sup. Ct. Rev. 41.

Although there were no major Supreme Court decisions concerning subversive advocacy during World War II, there were several prosecutions of individuals under both the Espionage Act of 1917 and the Smith Act of 1940. Most often, these were prosecutions of individuals who were leaders of fascist organizations in the United States. See R. Steele, Free Speech in the Good War (1999); M. St. George and L. Dennis, The Great Sedition Trial of 1944 (1946); G. Stone, Perilous Times: Free Speech in Wartime 252–283 (2004).

6. *The war on communism.* With its 1951 decision in *Dennis*, the Court continued its quest for a satisfactory solution to the problem of subversive advocacy. During the post–World War II "cold war" era, fears over national security once again generated wide-ranging federal and state restrictions on "radical" speech. These restrictions included extensive loyalty programs, emergency detention plans, attempts to "outlaw" the Communist Party,

requirements that all so-called communist-front and communist-action organizations register with the government, and extensive legislative investigations
of suspected "subversives." *Dennis*, which involved the prosecution under the
Smith Act of the national leaders of the Communist Party of the United States,
represents but one facet of this era.

## Dennis v. United States
341 U.S. 494 (1951)

Mr. Chief Justice Vinson announced the judgment of the Court and an
opinion in which Mr. Justice Reed, Mr. Justice Burton and Mr. Justice
Minton join.

Petitioners were indicted for violation of the conspiracy provisions of the Smith
Act during the period of April 1945, to July, 1948. [A] verdict of guilty as to all the
petitioners was returned by the jury. [The] Court of Appeals affirmed. . . .

Sections 2 and 3 of the Smith Act provide as follows:

> Sec. 2. It shall be unlawful for any person to knowingly or willfully advocate,
> abet, advise, or teach the duty, necessity, desirability, or propriety of over-
> throwing or destroying any government in the United States by force or violence,
> or by the assassination of any officer of such government. . . .
> Sec. 3. It shall be unlawful for any person to attempt to commit, or to conspire
> to commit, any of the acts prohibited by the provisions of . . . this title.

The indictment charged the petitioners with willfully and knowingly conspiring (1) to organize as the Communist Party of the United States of America
a society, group and assembly of persons who teach and advocate the overthrow
and destruction of the Government of the United States by force and violence,
and (2) knowingly and willfully conspiring to advocate and teach the duty and
necessity of overthrowing and destroying the Government of the United States
by force and violence. . . .

The trial of the case extended over nine months, six of which were devoted
to the taking of evidence, resulting in a record of 16,000 pages. Our limited
grant of the writ of certiorari has removed from our consideration any question
as to the sufficiency of the [evidence]. Whether on this record petitioners did
in fact advocate the overthrow of the Government by force and violence is not
before us, and we must base any discussion of this point upon the conclusion
[of] the Court of Appeals, which [held] that the record in this case amply
supports the necessary finding of the jury that petitioners, the leaders of the
Communist Party in this country, [intended] to initiate a violent revolution
whenever the propitious occasion appeared. . . .

[The petitioners attack] the statute on the grounds that by its terms it prohibits academic discussion of the merits of Marxism-Leninism, that it stifles

ideas and is contrary to all concepts of a free speech and a free press. [But the] very language of the Smith Act [demonstrates that it] is directed at advocacy, not discussion. Thus, the trial judge properly charged the jury that they could not convict if they found that petitioners did "no more than pursue peaceful studies and discussions or teaching and advocacy in the realm of ideas." . . .

[In *Gitlow* and *Whitney*, the] legislature had found that a certain kind of speech was, itself, harmful and unlawful. [In such circumstances, the Court held that the test was] whether the statute was "reasonable." [Although] no case subsequent to *Whitney* and *Gitlow* has expressly overruled the majority opinions in those cases, there is little doubt that subsequent opinions have inclined toward the Holmes-Brandeis rationale. . . .

In this case we are [thus] squarely presented with the application of the "clear and present danger" test, and must decide what that phrase imports. We first note that [overthrow] of the Government by force and violence is certainly a substantial enough interest for the Government to limit speech. [If], then, this interest may be protected, the literal problem which is presented is what has been meant by the use of the phrase "clear and present danger." . . .

Obviously, the words cannot mean that before the Government may act, it must wait until the putsch is about to be executed, the plans have been laid and the signal is awaited. If Government is aware that a group aiming at its overthrow is attempting to indoctrinate its members and to commit them to a course whereby they will strike when the leaders feel the circumstances permit, action by the Government is required. The argument that there is no need for Government to concern itself, for Government is strong, it possesses ample powers to put down a rebellion, it may defeat the revolution with ease needs no answer. For that is not the question. Certainly an attempt to overthrow the Government by force, even though doomed from the outset because of inadequate numbers or power of the revolutionists, is a sufficient evil for Congress to prevent. The damage which such attempts create both physically and politically to a nation makes it impossible to measure the validity in terms of the probability of success, or the immediacy of a successful attempt. . . .

Chief Judge Learned Hand, writing for the majority below, interpreted the phrase as follows: "In each case [courts] must ask whether the gravity of the 'evil,' discounted by its improbability, justifies such invasion of free speech as is necessary to avoid the danger." [We] adopt this statement of the rule. As articulated by Chief Judge Hand, it is as succinct and inclusive as any other we might devise at this time. It takes into consideration those factors which we deem relevant, and relates their significances. More we cannot expect from words.

Likewise, we are in accord with the court below, which affirmed the trial court's finding that the requisite danger existed. The mere fact that from the period 1945 to 1948 petitioners' activities did not result in an attempt to overthrow the Government by force and violence is of course no answer to the fact that there was a group that was ready to make the attempt. The formation by petitioners of such a highly organized conspiracy, with rigidly disciplined members subject to call when the leaders, these petitioners, felt that the time had come for action, coupled with the inflammable nature of world conditions, similar uprisings in other countries, and the touch-and-go nature of our relations with countries with whom petitioners were in the very least ideologically attuned, convince us that their convictions were justified on this score. And this analysis disposes of the contention that a conspiracy to advocate, as distinguished from the advocacy itself, cannot be constitutionally restrained, because it comprises only the preparation. It is the existence of the conspiracy which creates the danger. . . .

[Affirmed.]

MR. JUSTICE CLARK took no part in the consideration or decision of this case.

MR. JUSTICE FRANKFURTER, concurring. . . .

Primary responsibility for adjusting the interests which compete in the situation before us of necessity belongs to the Congress. [We] are to set aside the judgment of those whose duty it is to legislate only if there is no reasonable basis for it. [After canvassing the entire corpus of the Court's first amendment jurisprudence, Justice Frankfurter set forth the following conclusions.]

First. Free-speech cases are not an exception to the principle that we are not legislators, that direct policy-making is not our province. [Second.] A survey of the relevant decisions indicates that the results which we have reached are on the whole those that would ensue from careful weighing of conflicting interests. [Third.] Not every type of speech occupies the same position on the scale of values. [On] any scale of values, [speech advocating the overthrow of the government by force and violence] ranks low. Throughout our decisions there has recurred a distinction between the statement of an idea which may prompt its hearers to take unlawful action, and advocacy that such action be taken. . . .

These general considerations underlie decision of the case before us. On the one hand is the interest in security. [In] determining whether application of the statute to the defendants is within the constitutional powers of Congress, we [must consider] whatever is relevant to a legislative judgment. [We] may take account of evidence brought forward at this trial and elsewhere, much of which has long been common knowledge, [that] would amply justify a legislature in concluding that recruitment of additional members of the Party would create a substantial danger to national security.

On the other hand is the interest in free speech. The right to exert all governmental powers in aid of maintaining our institutions and resisting their physical overthrow does not include intolerance of opinions and speech that cannot do harm although opposed and perhaps alien to dominant, traditional opinion. [Moreover, a] public interest is not wanting in granting freedom to speak their minds even to those who advocate the overthrow of the Government by force. For, as the evidence in this case abundantly illustrates, coupled with such advocacy is criticism of defects in our society. [We must also recognize that suppressing] advocates of overthrow inevitably will also silence critics who do not advocate overthrow but fear that their criticism may be so construed. [It] is self-delusion to think that we can punish [the defendants] for their advocacy without adding to the risks run by loyal citizens who honestly believe in some of the reforms these defendants advance. It is a sobering fact that in sustaining the convictions before us we can hardly escape restriction on the interchange of ideas. . . .

It is not for us to decide how we would adjust the clash of interests which this case presents were the primary responsibility for reconciling it ours. Congress has determined that the danger created by advocacy of overthrow justifies the ensuing restriction on freedom of speech. [To] make validity of legislation depend on judicial reading of events still in the womb of time [is] to charge the judiciary with duties beyond its equipment. . . .

Mr. Justice Jackson, concurring. . . .

I would save [the clear and present danger standard], unmodified, for application as a "rule of reason" in the kind of case for which it was devised. When the issue is criminality of a hot-headed speech on a street corner, or circulation of a few incendiary pamphlets, or parading by some zealots behind a red flag, [it] is not beyond the capacity of the judicial process to gather, comprehend, and weigh the necessary materials for decision whether it is a clear and present danger of substantive evil or a harmless letting off of steam. [But] unless we are to hold our government captive in a judge-made verbal trap, we must approach the problem of a well-organized, nation-wide conspiracy [as] realistically as our predecessors faced the trivialities that were being prosecuted until they were checked with a rule of reason. . . .

The highest degree of constitutional protection is due to the [individual]. But even an individual cannot claim that the Constitution protects him in advocating or teaching overthrow of government by force or violence. [I] think direct incitement by speech or writing can be made a crime, and I think there can be a conviction without also proving that the odds favored its success by 99 to 1, or some other extremely high ratio. . . .

Mr. Justice Black, dissenting. . . .

[The] other opinions in this case show that the only way to affirm these convictions is to repudiate directly or indirectly the established "clear and present danger" rule. This the Court does in a way which greatly restricts the protections afforded by the First Amendment. The opinions for affirmance indicate that the chief reason for jettisoning the rule is the expressed fear that advocacy of Communist doctrine endangers the safety of the Republic. Undoubtedly, a governmental policy of unfettered communication of ideas does entail dangers. To the Founders of this Nation, however, the benefits derived from free expression were worth the risk. . . .

Public opinion being what it now is, few will protest the conviction of these Communist petitioners. There is hope, however, that in calmer times, when present pressures, passions and fears subside, this or some later Court will restore the First Amendment liberties to the high preferred place where they belong in a free society.

MR. JUSTICE DOUGLAS, dissenting.

If this were a case where those who claimed protection under the First Amendment were teaching the techniques of sabotage, the assassination of the President, the filching of documents from public files, the planting of bombs, the art of street warfare, and the like, I would have no doubts. The freedom to speak is not absolute; the teaching of methods of terror and other seditious conduct should be beyond the pale. [This] case was argued as if those were the facts. [But] the fact is that no such evidence was introduced at the trial. . . .

So far as the present record is concerned, what petitioners did was to organize people to teach and themselves teach the Marxist-Leninist doctrine contained chiefly in four books: Stalin, Foundations of Leninism (1924); Marx and Engels, Manifesto of the Communist Party (1848); Lenin, The State and Revolution (1917); History of the Communist Party of the Soviet Union (B.) (1939). . . .

The opinion of the Court does not outlaw these texts nor condemn them to the fire, as the Communists do literature offensive to their creed. But if the books themselves are not outlawed, if they can lawfully remain on library shelves, by what reasoning does their [use] become a crime? [The] Act, as construed, requires the element of intent — that those who teach the creed believe in it. The crime then depends not on what is taught but on who the teacher is. That is to make freedom of speech turn not on *what is said*, but on the *intent* with which it is said. Once we start down that road we enter territory dangerous to the liberties of every citizen. . . .

There comes a time when even speech loses its constitutional immunity. Speech innocuous one year may at another time fan such destructive flames that it must be halted in the interests of the safety of the Republic. That is the meaning of the clear and present danger test. When conditions are so critical that there will be no time to avoid the evil that the speech threatens, it is time to call a halt. . . .

[If] we are to take judicial notice of the threat of Communists within the nation, it should not be difficult to conclude that *as a political party* they are of little consequence. [Communism] in the world scene is no bogeyman; but Communism as a political faction or party in this country plainly is. Communism has been so thoroughly exposed in this country that it has been crippled as a political force. Free speech has destroyed it as an effective political party. . . .

How it can be said that there is a clear and present danger that this advocacy will succeed is, therefore, a mystery. [In] America, [the Communists] are miserable merchants of unwanted ideas; their wares remain unsold. The fact that their ideas are abhorrent does not make them powerful. [Thus], if we are to proceed on the basis of judicial notice, it is impossible for me to say that the Communists in this country are so potent or so strategically deployed that they must be suppressed for their speech. . . .

## *Note:* Dennis *and the Communist "Conspiracy"*   Clear/present substantive evil

1. *Clear and present danger: the Holmes/Brandeis formulation.* Could the Holmes/Brandeis formulation of clear and present danger sensibly be applied in *Dennis*? What "substantive evil" must be clear and present? Actual overthrow? Attempted overthrow? Conspiracy to overthrow? Conspiracy to advocate overthrow?

2. *Clear and present danger: the* Dennis *formulation.* Note that Judge Learned Hand, the author of *Masses,* also wrote the opinion for the court of appeals in *Dennis.* By the time of *Dennis,* Judge Hand had come to accept that *Masses* had found "little professional support." As he put it, he had "bid a long farewell to my little toy ship which set out quite bravely on the shortest voyage ever made." As a lower court judge "who took seriously his obligation to follow Supreme Court precedents," Judge Hand did his best to make sense of "an array of rulings on 'clear and present danger' — a standard he disliked from the outset." Although upholding the convictions under his reformulated version of the standard, Judge Hand "insisted repeatedly" that the prosecution was "a mistake." As he wrote a friend shortly after the decision, we "should never have prosecuted those birds. . . . So far as all this will do anything, it will encourage the faithful and maybe help the [Party's] Committee on Propaganda." G. Gunther, Learned Hand: The Man and the Judge 600–603 (1994). Was Hand's opinion in *Dennis* a betrayal of the position he had staked out in *Masses*? Note that the Smith Act prohibited only the express advocacy of unlawful conduct. Consider G. Stone, Perilous Times: Free Speech in Wartime 402 (2004):

> In June 1951, [Hand] wrote Frankfurter, "[S]o far as the constitution goes, I cannot see why it should protect any speech which contains 'aid[ing], abetting, counsel[ing]' etc., to *violate* any law." Six months later he wrote [that] "every society which promulgates a law means that it shall be obeyed until it is changed, and any society which lays down means by which its laws can be changed makes those means exclusive. . . . If [this be] so, how in God's name can an incitement to do what will be unlawful if done, be itself lawful?" In this sense, then, not only was Learned Hand faithfully following Supreme Court precedents rather than his own inclinations in *Dennis,* but his own inclinations would have led him to the very same outcome, though for quite different reasons.

Is the *Dennis* version of clear and present danger "simply the remote bad tendency test dressed up in modern style"? M. Shapiro, Freedom of Speech:

The Supreme Court and Judicial Review 65 (1966). In his concurring opinion in *Whitney*, Justice Brandeis first introduced the "seriousness" element as a means of intensifying the clear and present danger standard. The *Dennis* formulation, however, uses "gravity" to dilute the standard. Is this dilution unreasonable? If government may restrict speech that creates an immediate 70 percent chance of a relatively modest evil (such as persuading a few persons to refuse induction), shouldn't it also be permitted to restrict speech that creates a less immediate 30 percent chance of a very serious evil (such as attempted overthrow of government)? See Posner, The Speech Market and the Legacy of *Schenck*, in L. Bollinger and G. Stone, Eternal Vigilance: Free Speech in the Modern Era 121, 125–126 (2002).

3. *Deference.* In *Gitlow* and *Whitney*, the Court held that when a legislature expressly prohibits a certain category of expression, the judiciary must defer to the legislative judgment so long as it is reasonable. Is this the "correct" approach to judicial review? The Court's present position on the deference issue is set out in Landmark Communications, Inc. v. Virginia, 435 U.S. 829 (1978):

> Deference to a legislative finding cannot limit judicial inquiry when First Amendment rights are at stake. "[A legislative declaration] does not preclude enquiry into the question whether, at the time and under the circumstances, the conditions existed which are essential to validity under the Federal Constitution." [A] legislature appropriately inquires into and may declare the reasons impelling legislative action but the judicial function commands analysis of whether the specific conduct charged falls within the reach of the statute and if so whether the legislation is consonant with the Constitution. Were it otherwise, the scope of freedom of speech and of the press would be subject to legislative definition and the function of the First Amendment as a check on legislative power would be nullified.

4. *The Smith Act in context — other anticommunist activity.* As noted earlier, in the post–World War II "cold war" era the federal government launched an intensive campaign against the Communist Party and its adherents that reached far beyond the Smith Act. Consider the following:

a. Because of a fear that communist officers of labor organizations might misuse their influence by calling strikes as a means of disrupting commerce and industry, section 9(h) of the Labor-Management Relations Act of 1947 prohibited the enforcement of employee representation rights of any labor union whose officers failed to execute affidavits that they were not members of the Communist Party. See American Communications Association v. Douds, 339 U.S. 382 (1950) (upholding section 9(h)).

b. The Internal Security Act of 1950 created a complex regulatory scheme requiring all "Communist-action organizations" to register with the Attorney General and to disclose a wide range of information, including membership lists. The act also established the Subversive Activities Control Board to administer the scheme and provided that, once a board order to register became final, various sanctions would automatically be imposed on the organization and its members. See Communist Party v. Subversive Activities Control Board, 367 U.S. 1 (1961) (upholding the registration requirement).

c. Both the state and federal governments created extensive loyalty programs for government employees, and at both the state and federal levels legislative committees were used extensively to investigate communist "infiltration." See Barenblatt v. United States, 360 U.S. 109 (1959) (upholding a contempt citation of a witness before a congressional investigating committee who refused to answer questions about his past and present membership in the Communist Party); Gibson v. Florida Legislative Investigating Committee, 372 U.S. 539 (1963) (invalidating a contempt citation of a witness before a state legislative investigating committee who refused to answer questions about whether certain identified members of the Communist Party were members of the NAACP).

d. There were also efforts during this era to prevent the importation of communist doctrine from abroad. See Lamont v. Postmaster General, 381 U.S. 301 (1965) (invalidating restrictions on the mailing of foreign "communist political propaganda"); Kleindienst v. Mandel, 408 U.S. 753 (1972) (upholding a law declaring foreign communists ineligible to visit the United States).

e. During this period, the FBI launched a wide-ranging campaign of anticommunist activities, including a program designed extralegally to "expose, disrupt, and otherwise neutralize" the domestic communist movement. Consider the 1976 findings of a Senate committee:

> The Government has often undertaken the secret surveillance of citizens of the basis of their political beliefs, even when those beliefs posed no threat of violence or illegal acts. [The] Government, operating primarily through secret informants, [has] swept in vast amounts of information about the personal lives, views, and associations of American citizens. Investigations of groups deemed potentially dangerous — and even of groups suspected of associating with potentially dangerous organizations — have continued for decades, despite the fact that those groups did not engage in unlawful activity. [FBI] headquarters alone has developed over 500,000 domestic intelligence files. [The] targets of intelligence activity have included political adherents of the right and the left, ranging from activists to casual supporters.

Senate Select Committee to Study Governmental Operations with Respect to Intelligence Activities, Final Report, Intelligence Activities and the Rights of Americans, Book II, S. Doc. No. 13133–4, 94th Cong., 2d Sess. 5–9 (1976). See also F. Donner, The Age of Surveillance (1980); A. Theoharis, Spying on Americans (1978).

5. *Understanding* Dennis. Consider Wiecek, The Legal Foundations of Domestic Anticommunism: The Background of Dennis v. United States, 2001 Sup. Ct. Rev. 375, 377–379, 417, 428–429:

> The [anticommunist] crusade after World War II [demonized] Communists, endowing them with extraordinary powers and malignity, making them both covert and ubiquitous. [Communists] became The Other. Popular culture, in movies like *On the Waterfront* [and] *Invasion of the Body Snatchers* effectively delivered this image to a mass audience. [The] manufactured image of the domestic Communist, cultivated and propagated by J. Edgar Hoover, the Catholic Church, the American Legion, and political opportunists, made of Communists something less than full humans, full [citizens]. [To] resist the ideological and emotional pressures of the Cold War era would have required superhuman wisdom and equanimity. Whatever else might be said of the Justices of the *Dennis* Court, the majority of them did not have those qualities.

Consider also Wells, Fear and Loathing in Constitutional Decision-Making, 2005 Wis. L. Rev. 115, 117–119:

> The [argument] that courts ought to protect civil liberties in times of crisis is an attractive one. [But courts] remain subject to the same passions, fears, and prejudices that sweep the rest of the nation. [Nowhere] is this more evident than in [*Dennis*]. [The evidence against the defendants] was weak, as there was no proof that they agreed to overthrow or advocate overthrow of the government. . . . Conventional wisdom roundly condemns *Dennis*, attributing the result to a Cold War hysteria that gripped the country and infected the judges' reasoning. [Conventional] wisdom, however, provides few answers regarding how to guard against *Dennis*'s failings in the future. We cannot simply assume that judges armed with an understanding of past errors will act courageously. [What] we need, then, is a doctrine that can counteract the effects of fear and prejudice that lead to such action. . . .

## Note: *The Road to* Brandenburg

1. *Revising the* Dennis *approach: advocacy of doctrine versus advocacy of action.* Following *Dennis*, federal authorities initiated Smith Act prosecutions against more than 120 individuals constituting the secondary leadership of the Communist Party. By 1957, the government had secured convictions in almost all of these prosecutions. In Yates v. United States, 354 U.S. 298 (1957), however, the Court, in a six-to-one decision, adopted a narrow interpretation of the Smith Act to avoid constitutional doubts and overturned the convictions of several members of the Communist Party for conspiracy to violate the act. Justice Harlan delivered the opinion:

> [We are] faced with the question whether the Smith Act prohibits advocacy [of] forcible overthrow as an abstract principle, divorced from any effort to instigate

action to that end, so long as such advocacy [is] engaged in with evil intent. We hold that it does not.

The distinction between advocacy of abstract doctrine and advocacy directed at promoting unlawful action is one that has been consistently recognized in the opinions of this Court, [and] was heavily underscored in [*Gitlow*]. [We] need not, however, decide the issue before us in terms of constitutional compulsion, for our first duty is to construe this statute. In doing so we should not assume that Congress chose to disregard a constitutional danger zone so clearly marked. . . .

[We reject the proposition] that mere doctrinal justification of forcible overthrow, if engaged in with the intent to accomplish overthrow, is punishable [under] the Smith Act. That sort of advocacy, even though uttered with the hope that it may ultimately lead to violent revolution, is too remote from concrete action to be regarded as the kind of indoctrination preparatory to action which was condemned in *Dennis*. [The] essential distinction is that those to whom the advocacy is addressed must be urged to *do* something, now or in the future, rather than merely to *believe* in something.

Harlan's opinion in *Yates* was greeted with puzzlement. One newspaper at the time characterized it as "a masterpiece of hair-splitting" and scholars characterized it as "complex, scholarly, and painfully dull" and as "a sort of *Finnegan's Wake* of impossibly nice distinctions." Nonetheless, "the Justice Department, faced with Yates's insistence upon proof of advocacy to '*do* something, now or in the future, rather than merely to *believe* in something,' soon admitted that 'we cannot satisfy the evidentiary requirements laid down by the Supreme Court' and dismissed" all remaining Smith Act conspiracy cases then pending. R. Lichtman, The Supreme Court and McCarthy Era Repression: One Hundred Decisions 95–96 (2012).

What is the basis of Justice Harlan's distinction between advocacy of action and advocacy of belief? Is it premised on the relative dangerousness of the expression? On the relative "value" of the speech? Consider Gunther, Learned Hand and the Origins of Modern First Amendment Doctrine: Some Fragments of History, 27 Stan. L. Rev. 719, 753 (1975):

Harlan found a way to curtail prosecutions under the Smith Act even though the constitutionality of the Act had been sustained in *Dennis*. He did it by [reading] the statute in terms of constitutional presuppositions; and he strove to find standards "manageable" by judges and capable of curbing jury discretion. He insisted on strict statutory standards of proof emphasizing the actual speech of the [defendants]. Harlan claimed to be interpreting *Dennis*. In fact, [*Yates*] represented doctrinal evolution in a new direction.

2. *Post-*Yates *Decisions.* For cases following *Yates* that were influenced by the distinction it drew, see Kingsley International Pictures Corp. v. Regents of New York, 360 U.S. 684 (1959) (holding unconstitutional a New York statute prohibiting the issuance of a license to exhibit nonobscene motion pictures

that "portray 'acts of sexual immorality [as] desirable, acceptable, or proper patterns of behavior;'" the Court held that as applied to a movie of Lady Chatterley's Lover, the statute was unconstitutional because the Constitution "protects advocacy of the opinion that adultery may sometimes be proper, no less than advocacy of socialism or the single tax."); Bond v. Floyd, 385 U.S. 116 (1966) (holding unconstitutional the refusal of the Georgia House of Representatives to seat Julian Bond, a duly elected representative, because of his statements, and statements to which he subscribed, criticizing the policy of the federal government in Vietnam and the operation of the selective service system; the Court explained that, although the statement in question expressed sympathy with, and support for, those who refused to respond to a military draft, that statement "alone cannot be interpreted as a call to unlawful refusal to be drafted."); Scales v. United States, 367 U.S. 203 (1961) (holding that a "blanket prohibition" of knowing membership in organizations "having both legal and illegal aims" might pose "a real danger that legitimate political expression or association would be impaired"; to avoid this danger, the Court interpreted the Smith Act as making membership unlawful only if the individual was an "active" member and not merely a "nominal, passive, inactive or purely technical" member, with knowledge of the organization's illegal advocacy, and with the "specific intent" to further the organization's illegal ends).

## Brandenburg v. Ohio
395 U.S. 444 (1969)

Per Curiam.

The appellant, a leader of a Ku Klux Klan group, was convicted under the Ohio Criminal Syndicalism statute of "advocat[ing] . . . the duty, necessity, or propriety of crime, sabotage, violence, or unlawful methods of terrorism as a means of accomplishing industrial or political reform" and of "voluntarily assembl[ing] with any society, group or assemblage of persons formed to teach or advocate the doctrines of criminal syndicalism." He was fined $1,000 and sentenced to one to 10 years' imprisonment. . . .

The record shows that a man, identified at trial as the appellant, telephoned an announcer-reporter on the staff of a Cincinnati television station and invited him to come to a Ku Klux Klan "rally" to be held at a farm in Hamilton County. With the cooperation of the organizers, the reporter and a cameraman attended the meeting and filmed the events. Portions of the films were later broadcast on the local station and on a national network.

The prosecution's case rested on the films and on testimony identifying the appellant as the person who communicated with the reporter and who spoke at the rally. The State also introduced into evidence several articles appearing in the film, including a pistol, a rifle, a shotgun, ammunition, a Bible, and a red hood worn by the speaker in the films.

One film showed 12 hooded figures, some of whom carried firearms. They were gathered around a large wooden cross, which they burned. No one was present other than the participants and the newsman who made the film. Most of the words uttered during the scene were incomprehensible when the film was projected, but scattered phrases could be understood that were derogatory of Negroes and, in one instance, of Jews. Another scene on the same film showed the appellant, in Klan regalia, making a speech. The speech, in full, was as follows:

> This is an organizers' meeting. We have had quite a few members here today which are — we have hundreds, hundreds of members throughout the State of Ohio. I can quote from a newspaper clipping from the Columbus Ohio Dispatch, five weeks ago Sunday morning. The Klan has more members in the State of Ohio than does any other organization. We're not a revengent organization, but if our President, our Congress, our Supreme Court, continues to suppress the white, Caucasian race, it's possible that there might have to be some revengence taken. We are marching on Congress July the Fourth, four hundred thousand strong. From there we are dividing into two groups, one group to march on St. Augustine, Florida, the other group to march into Mississippi. Thank you.

The second film showed six hooded figures one of whom, later identified as the appellant, repeated a speech very similar to that recorded on the first film. The reference to the possibility of "revengence" was omitted, and one sentence was added: "Personally, I believe the nigger should be returned to Africa, the Jew returned to Israel." Though some of the figures in the films carried weapons, the speaker did not.

The Ohio Criminal Syndicalism Statute was enacted in 1919. From 1917 to 1920, identical or quite similar laws were adopted by 20 States and two territories. . . . In 1927, this Court sustained the constitutionality of California's Criminal Syndicalism Act, [the] text of which is quite similar to that of the laws of Ohio. [*Whitney.*] The Court upheld the statute on the ground that, without more, "advocating violent means to effect political and economic change involves such danger to the security of the State that the State may outlaw it." [But]*Whitney* has been thoroughly discredited by later decisions. See [*Dennis*]. These later decisions have fashioned the principle that the constitutional guarantees of free speech and free press do not permit a State to forbid or proscribe advocacy of the use of force or of law violation except where such advocacy is directed to inciting or producing imminent lawless action and is likely to incite or produce such action.[1] As we [have said], "the

---

1. It was on the theory that the Smith Act [embodied] such a principle and that it had been applied only in conformity with it that this Court sustained the Act's constitutionality. [*Dennis.*] That this was the basis for *Dennis* was emphasized in [*Yates*], in which the Court overturned convictions for advocacy of the forcible overthrow of the Government under the Smith Act, because the trial judge's instructions had allowed convictions for mere advocacy, unrelated to its tendency to produce forcible action.

mere abstract teaching [of] the moral propriety or even moral necessity for a resort to force and violence, is not the same as preparing a group for violent action and steeling it to such action." See also [*Bond*]. A statute which fails to draw this distinction impermissibly intrudes upon the freedoms guaranteed by the First and Fourteenth Amendments. It sweeps within its condemnation speech which our Constitution has immunized from governmental control. Cf. [*Yates*]. . . .

Measured by this test, Ohio's Criminal Syndicalism Act cannot be sustained. [Neither] the indictment nor the trial judge's instructions to the jury in any way refined the statute's bald definition of the crime in terms of mere advocacy not distinguished from incitement to imminent lawless action.

Accordingly, we are here confronted with a statute which, by its own words and as applied, purports to punish mere advocacy and to forbid, on pain of criminal punishment, assembly with others merely to advocate the described type of action. Such a statute falls within the condemnation of the First and Fourteenth Amendments. The contrary teaching of [*Whitney*] cannot be supported, and that decision is therefore overruled.

Reversed.

MR. JUSTICE BLACK, concurring.

I agree with the views expressed by Mr. Justice Douglas in his concurring opinion in this case that the "clear and present danger" doctrine should have no place in the interpretation of the First Amendment. I join the Court's opinion, which, as I understand it, simply cites [*Dennis*] but does not indicate any agreement on the Court's part with the "clear and present danger" doctrine on which *Dennis* purported to rely.

MR. JUSTICE DOUGLAS, concurring. . . .

I see no place in the regime of the First Amendment for any "clear and present danger" test, whether strict and tight as some would make it, or free-wheeling as the Court in *Dennis* rephrased it. When one reads the opinions closely and sees when and how the "clear and present danger" test has been applied, great misgivings are aroused. First, the threats were often loud but always puny and made serious only by judges so wedded to the status quo that critical analysis made them nervous. Second, the test was so twisted and perverted in *Dennis* as to make the trial of those teachers of Marxism an all-out political trial which was part and parcel of the cold war that has eroded substantial parts of the First Amendment. . . .

The line between what is permissible and not subject to control and what may be made impermissible and subject to regulation is the line between ideas and overt acts. The example usually given by those who would punish speech is the case of one who falsely shouts fire in a crowded theatre. This is, however, a classic case where speech is brigaded with action. [They] are indeed inseparable and a prosecution can be launched for the overt acts actually caused. Apart from rare instances of that kind, speech is, I think, immune from prosecution. . . .

## Note: The Brandenburg Formulation

1. *The meaning of* Brandenburg. Although the Court maintained that the pre-*Brandenburg* "decisions [fashioned] the principle" adopted in *Brandenburg*, the case seems to have gone far beyond settled law. Indeed, it has been said that the *Brandenburg* formulation would "have demanded the contrary result in [both] the early Espionage Act cases and the later Communist cases," J. Ely, Democracy and Distrust 115 (1980), and that *Brandenburg* combined "the most [speech] protective ingredients of the *Masses* emphasis with the most useful elements of the clear and present danger heritage" to produce "the most speech-protective standard yet evolved by the Supreme Court." Gunther, Learned Hand and the Origins of Modern First Amendment Doctrine: Some Fragments of History, 27 Stan. L. Rev. 719, 754, 755 (1975). More specifically, *Brandenburg* has been interpreted as requiring "three things: (1) express advocacy of law violation; (2) the advocacy must call for *immediate* law violation; and (3) the immediate law violation must be *likely* to occur." Schwartz, Holmes versus Hand: Clear and Present Danger or Advocacy of Unlawful Action?, 1994 Sup. Ct. Rev. 209, 240-241.

Thus interpreted, and particularly when viewed in the light of *Yates* and *Bond*, *Brandenburg* appears by implication to accord absolute protection to the speaker so long as he does not use express words of incitement. If this is so, does *Brandenburg* suggest that, as a general first amendment principle, expression should be absolutely protected against direct criminal prohibition, regardless of dangerousness and intent, so long as it is not of "low" first amendment value?

2. *The lessons of history.* Consider Stone, Free Speech in the Twenty-First Century: Ten Lessons from the Twentieth Century, 36 Pepp. L. Rev. 273 (2008):

> As a result of its experience in the *Schenck-Brandenburg* line of decisions, the Court learned three very practical lessons about the workings of "the system of free expression" — lessons that have come to play a critical role in shaping contemporary First Amendment jurisprudence.
>
> First, the Court learned about the *chilling effect*. That is, the Court learned that people are easily deterred from exercising their freedom of speech. This is so because individual speakers usually gain very little personally from signing a petition, marching in a demonstration, handing out leaflets, or posting on a blog. [Thus,] if they know they might go to jail for speaking, they will often forego their right to speak. This makes perfect sense for each individual. But if many individuals make this same decision, the net effect may be to mutilate the thought process of the community. The Court's gradual recognition of this "chilling effect," and of the consequent power of government to use intimidation to

silence its critics, was a critical insight in shaping twentieth-century free speech doctrine.

Second, the Court learned about the *pretext effect*. That is, the Court learned that government officials will often defend their restrictions of speech on grounds quite different from their real motivations for the suppression, which will often be [to] silence their critics, [insulate] themselves from criticism, and preserve their own authority. . . .

Third, the Court learned about the *crisis effect*. That is, the Court learned that in times of crisis, real or imagined, citizens and public officials tend to panic [and] to rush headlong to suppress speech that they demonize as dangerous, subversive, disloyal, or treasonable. Painful experience with this "crisis effect," especially during World War I and the Cold War, led the Court to embrace what Professor Vincent Blasi has termed a "pathological perspective" in crafting First Amendment doctrine. That is, the Court attempts to structure First Amendment doctrine to anticipate and to guard against the worst of times.

On the pathological perspective, see Blasi, The Pathological Perspective and the First Amendment, 85 Colum. L. Rev. 449, 449–500 (1985). On cost-benefit analysis and the problem of analyzing low-probability, high-magnitude harms (such as violent revolution), see Masur, Probability Thresholds, 92 Iowa L. Rev. 1293, 1296–1298 (2007).

3. *Subsequent decisions.* The Court has adhered to *Brandenburg* in Hess v. Indiana, 414 U.S. 105 (1973) (reversing the conviction for disorderly conduct of an individual who shouted, "We'll take the fucking street later [or again]," during an antiwar demonstration); and NAACP v. Claiborne Hardware Co., 458 U.S. 886 (1982) (holding that a statement by an NAACP official in a public speech in support of a boycott that "[if] we catch any of you going in any of them racist stores, we're gonna break your damn neck" was protected by the first amendment because it did not incite immediate lawless action and because the "mere *advocacy* of the use of force or violence does not remove speech from the protection of the First Amendment").

4. *Additional variations.* In light of *Brandenberg*, if you were a lawyer hired by the plaintiff in the following cases, how would you answer first amendment objections:

a. A fourteen-year-old boy was found hanging in his closet with a copy of Hustler on the floor beneath his feet, opened to an article entitled "Orgasms of Death," which detailed the procedures for autoerotic asphyxiation. The plaintiff brings a lawsuit against the magazine. See Herceg v. Hustler Magazine, Inc., 814 F.2d 1017 (5th Cir. 1987) (invalidating a civil jury verdict against Hustler on these facts because *Brandenburg* was not satisfied).

b. There is compelling evidence that the television movie Born Innocent, which described a rape using a "plumber's helper," caused just such a rape of a nine-year-old girl by a group of teenage boys who had just seen Born Innocent shortly before. See Olivia N. v. National Broadcasting Co., 178 Cal. Rptr. 888 (Ct. App. 1981) (holding that, even though the movie caused the rape, the rule in *Brandenburg* immunized NBC because no intent to injure could be shown).

c. A publisher distributes a book, entitled Hit Man, that extolled the lifestyle of contract murderers and offers detailed instructions on how to commit a contract murder. Following these instructions precisely, X kills Y in a contract murder, and Y's survivors thereafter sued the publisher for damages. See Rice v. The Paladin Enterprises, 128 F.3d 233 (4th Cir. 1997) (holding that *Brandenburg* does not control this situation and that the publisher could be held liable because the publisher "had intended . . . that the publication would be used by criminals to execute the crime of murder for hire").

5. *From* Schenck *to* Brandenburg, *and beyond.* Consider Bollinger, Epilogue, in L. Bollinger and G. Stone, Eternal Vigilance: Free Speech in the Modern Era 1, 312–313 (2002):

> The question for the future [is] whether the scope of First Amendment rights articulated in the *Brandenburg* era reflects the distilled wisdom of historical experience, which makes it more likely to survive in future periods of social upheaval, or whether the *Brandenburg* era will turn out to be just one era among many, in which the freedom of speech varies widely and more or less according to the sense of security and tolerance prevailing in the nation at the time. The fact that the last thirty years since *Brandenburg* have been remarkably peaceful and prosperous means that the understandings we now have about the meaning of free speech have not really been tested. By the standards we now apply (that is, through the eyes of *Brandenburg*), just about every time the country has felt seriously threatened the First Amendment has retreated.

**HOLDER v. HUMANITARIAN LAW PROJECT, 130 S. Ct. 2705 (2010).** A federal statute declares it unlawful for any person knowingly to provide "material support" to a designated foreign terrorist organization. "Material support" includes, among other things, "training, expert advice or assistance." Plaintiffs wanted to train two designated foreign terrorist organizations, which engage in political and humanitarian as well as violent terrorist activities, how to use international law to resolve disputes peacefully, and how to engage in political advocacy to pursue their goals.

Plaintiffs asserted that the statute violates the first amendment because it does not require the government to prove that, in assisting these organizations, plaintiffs specifically intended to further the organizations' unlawful activities. Plaintiffs relied on *Scales*, in which the Court had held that an individual could not constitutionally be punished for being a "knowing" member of the Communist Party, which had "both legal and illegal aims," unless the government proved that the individual specifically intended to promote the Party's illegal aims (i.e., in the context of *Scales*, "to bring about the overthrow of government as speedily as circumstances would permit").

The Court, in a six-to-three decision, upheld the material support provision. Writing for the Court, Chief Justice Roberts distinguished *Scales* on the ground that it dealt with mere membership, rather than with "material support." He observed that "[e]veryone agrees that the Government's interest in combating terrorism is an urgent objective of the highest order." The plaintiffs maintained, however, that their speech was intended to "advance only the legitimate activities of the designated terrorist organizations, not their terrorism." Chief Justice Roberts responded that Congress had made specific findings that "any form of material support furnished 'to' a foreign terrorist organization" will have "harmful effects," regardless of the intent of the speaker. For example, such "support frees up other resources within the organization that may be put to violent ends" and "helps lend legitimacy to foreign terrorist groups — legitimacy that makes it easier for those groups to persist, to recruit members, and to raise funds — all of which facilitate more terrorist attacks."

Chief Justice Roberts insisted that the conclusions of Congress and the Executive about the dangers of such support are "entitled to deference" because the statute "implicates sensitive and weighty interests of national security and foreign affairs." Although "we do not defer to the Government's reading of the First Amendment, even when such interests are at stake," it is also the case that in these circumstances "conclusions must often be based on informed judgment rather than concrete evidence, and that reality affects what we may reasonably insist on from the Government" in terms of proof of danger. "Given the sensitive interests in national security and foreign affairs at stake, the political branches have adequately substantiated their determination that, to serve the Government's interest in preventing terrorism, it was necessary to prohibit providing material support in the form of training [and] expert advice [to] foreign terrorist groups, even if the supporters meant to promote only the groups' nonviolent ends."

Finally, Chief Justice Roberts made clear that "we in no way suggest that a regulation of independent speech would pass constitutional muster, even if the Government were to show that such speech benefits foreign terrorist organizations," and we "do not suggest that Congress could extend the same prohibition on material support [to] domestic organizations."

Justice Breyer, joined by Justices Ginsburg and Sotomayor, dissented: "In my view, the Government has not made the strong showing necessary to justify under the First Amendment the criminal prosecution of those who engage [in] the communication and advocacy of political ideas and lawful means of achieving political ends. ["Coordination"] with a group that engages in unlawful activity [does] not deprive the plaintiffs of the First Amendment's [protection]. [The] First Amendment protects advocacy of even *unlawful* action so long as that advocacy is not 'directed to inciting or producing *imminent lawless action* and . . . *likely to incite or produce* such action.' [Quoting *Brandenburg*.] Here the plaintiffs seek to advocate peaceful, *lawful* action to secure *political* ends; and they seek to teach others how to do the same. . . .

"[W]here, as here, a statute applies criminal penalties [for such speech], I should think we would scrutinize the statute and justifications 'strictly' — to determine whether the prohibition is justified by a 'compelling' need that cannot be 'less restrictively' accommodated. [I] doubt that the statute [can] survive any reasonably applicable First Amendment standard. [The] majority emphasizes that it [must] defer strongly to Congress' 'informed judgment.' [But] 'whenever the fundamental rights of free speech and assembly are alleged to be invaded, it must remain open [for judicial] determination whether there actually did exist at the time a clear danger; whether the danger, if any, was imminent; and whether the evil apprehended was one so substantial as to justify the stringent restriction interposed by the legislature.' [Quoting Justice Brandeis in *Whitney*.] [And] the fact that other nations may like us less for granting [First Amendment] protection cannot in and of itself carry the day. . . .

"I would read the statute as criminalizing First-Amendment protected pure speech [only] when the defendant knows or intends that those activities will assist the organization's unlawful terrorist actions. Under this reading, the Government would have to show, at a minimum, that such defendants provided support that they knew was significantly likely to help the organization pursue its unlawful terrorist aims. [This] reading does not require the Government to undertake the difficult task of proving which, as between peaceful and non-peaceful purposes, a defendant specifically preferred; knowledge is enough."

Under the Court's approach, could a lawyer be convicted for filing a brief on behalf of an alleged terrorist asserting that his constitutional rights had been violated? Consider Cole, The First Amendment's Borders: The Place of Holder v. Humanitarian Law Project in First Amendment Doctrine, 6 Harv. L. & Poly. Rev. 147, 149 (2012):

> If this is the type of scrutiny that content-based laws enacted in the name of national security are to receive in the future, the scope of political freedom has been significantly narrowed. For the first time in history, the Court upheld the criminalization of speech advocating only nonviolent, lawful ends on the ground that such speech might unintentionally assist a third party in criminal wrongdoing.

## Note: Abridgment of Speech Other Than by Direct Criminal Prohibition

1. *Disclosure.* Up to now, we have focused on direct criminal prohibitions of speech or association. But there are other forms of regulation that may "abridge" the freedom of expression. In some circumstances, for example, government may "chill" the exercise of free expression merely by disclosing

it. This is especially likely where the individual's speech or association is unpopular. Should such an "indirect" abridgment of speech trigger the same standards of constitutional review as direct criminal prohibition? Consider the following decisions:

a. In Barenblatt v. United States, 360 U.S. 109 (1959), an instructor at Vassar College was subpoenaed to appear as a witness before a subcommittee of the House Committee on Un-American Activities during an inquiry into alleged Communist infiltration into the field of education. He was held in contempt of Congress for refusing to answer questions about his past and present membership in the Communist Party. The Court, in a five-to-four decision, held that this did not violate the first amendment.

b. In Gibson v. Florida Legislative Investigating Committee, 372 U.S. 539 (1963), the Florida legislature created a committee to investigate the infiltration of Communists into various organizations. Gibson, who was president of the Miami branch of the NAACP, was adjudged in contempt for refusing to disclose whether fourteen individuals previously identified as Communists were members of the NAACP. The Court, in an opinion by Justice Goldberg, distinguished *Barenblatt* and held that Gibson's conviction violated the first amendment:

> In *Barenblatt*, [it] was a refusal to answer [questions] concerning [membership] in the Communist Party which supported [the] conviction. [Here, however,] the entire thrust of the demands on the petitioner was that he disclose whether [certain] persons were members of the NAACP, itself a concededly legitimate and nonsubversive organization. [Such organizations do not] automatically forfeit their rights to privacy of association simply because the general subject matter of the legislative inquiry is Communist subversion or infiltration. [The] record in this case is insufficient to show a substantial connection between the Miami branch of the NAACP and Communist activities which [is] an essential prerequisite to demonstrating the immediate, substantial, and subordinating state interest necessary to sustain [the committee's] right of inquiry into the membership lists of the association.

After *Brandenburg* and *Scales*, what showing must the government make before "infiltrating" an allegedly "terrorist" organization with informers? Can the government investigate an organization because its advocacy raises concerns about possible future violence even if its speech does not meet the requirements of *Brandenburg*? See Rosenthal, First Amendment Investigations and the Inescapable Pragmatism of the Common Law of Free Speech, 86 Ind. L.J. 1 (2011).

2. *Public employees.* Does firing a public employee for her speech pose the same constitutional issue as criminally punishing a citizen for her speech? Suppose the government refuses to hire an applicant for a position with the police department because she was once a member of an organization that

advocates terrorism as a means of political change. Do *Brandenburg* and *Scales* govern these situations? Consider the following views:

a. McAuliffe v. Mayor of New Bedford, 155 Mass. 216, 29 N.E. 517 (1892) (in which Justice Holmes, speaking for the Supreme Judicial Court of Massachusetts, upheld a rule prohibiting police officers to "solicit money [for] any political purpose whatever"):

> The petitioner may have a constitutional right to talk politics, but he has no constitutional right to be a policeman. There are few employments for hire in which the servant does not agree to suspend his constitutional rights of free speech, as well as of idleness, by the implied terms of his contract. The servant cannot complain, as he takes the employment on the terms which are offered him.

b. Frost & Frost Trucking Co. v. Railroad Commission, 271 U.S. 583, 593–594 (1926):

> It would be a palpable incongruity to strike down an act of state legislation which [strips] the citizen of rights guaranteed by the federal Constitution, but to uphold an act by which the same result is accomplished under the guise of a surrender of a right in exchange for a valuable privilege which the State threatens otherwise to withhold. [It] is inconceivable that guarantees embedded in the Constitution [may] thus be manipulated out of existence.

The Court has generally followed *Frost* rather than *McAuliffe*. In Perry v. Sindermann, 408 U.S. 593, 597 (1972), for example, the Court announced that, "even though a person has no 'right' to a valuable government benefit and even though the government may deny him the benefit for any number of reasons, [it may not do so] on a basis that infringes his constitutionally protected interests — especially, his interest in freedom of speech."

Does the rejection of *McAuliffe* suggest that the first amendment rights of government employees are coextensive with those of private individuals? Consider Pickering v. Board of Education, 391 U.S. 563, 568 (1968):

> [The] State has interests as an employer in regulating the speech of its employees that differ significantly from those it possesses in [regulating] the speech of the citizenry in general. The problem in any case is to arrive at a balance between the interests of the [employee], as a citizen, in commenting upon matters of public concern, and the interests of the State, as an employer, in promoting the efficiency of the public services it performs through its employees.

3. *Subversive advocacy and the rights of public employees.* At the height of the post–World War II Communist scare, more than one-sixth of the total civilian labor force was subject to some sort of loyalty qualification, and the federal

government and most of the states excluded from many areas of public employment individuals who had been members of a "subversive" organization. What interests are served by the government's refusal to employ such individuals? Consider Israel, Elfbrandt v. Russell: The Demise of the Oath?, 1966 Sup. Ct. Rev. 193, 219:

> [At] least three different state interests are commonly advanced to justify disqualification of individuals from public employment on the basis of membership in organizations advocating the violent overthrow of government: (1) The elimination of persons who present a potential for sabotage, espionage, or other activities directly injurious to national security. (2) The elimination of persons who are likely to be either incompetent or untrustworthy in the performance of their duties. (3) The elimination of persons who, aside from any question of danger or fitness, simply are not considered deserving of a government position because they oppose the basic principles on which the government is founded.

In what circumstances are these interests sufficient to justify a restriction on the subversive advocacy or associations of public employees?

4. *A first answer*. In Adler v. Board of Education, 342 U.S. 485 (1952), the Court upheld a New York law providing that no person who becomes a member of any organization that advocates the violent overthrow of government, with knowledge of the organization's proscribed advocacy, "shall be appointed to any [position] in a public school":

> A teacher works in a sensitive area in a schoolroom. There he shapes the attitude of young minds towards the society in which they live. [That] the school authorities have the right and the duty to screen [teachers] as to their fitness to maintain the integrity of the schools [cannot] be doubted. One's associates, past and present, as well as one's conduct, may properly be considered in determining [fitness]. If, under [the] New York law, a person is found to be unfit and is disqualified from employment in the public school system because of membership in a [subversive] organization, he is not thereby denied the right of free speech and assembly. His freedom of choice between membership in the organization and employment in the school system might be limited, but [such] limitation is not one the State may not make in the exercise of its police power to protect the schools from pollution and thereby to defend its own existence.

5. *A second answer*. In Elfbrandt v. Russell, 384 U.S. 11 (1966), the Court invalidated an Arizona statute requiring all state employees to take an oath that they are not "knowingly" a member of the Communist Party or of "any other organization" having for "one of its purposes" the overthrow of the government of Arizona:

> We recognized in *Scales* that [a] "blanket prohibition of association with a group having both legal and illegal aims" would pose "a real danger that legitimate

political expression or association would be impaired." [Those] who join an organization but do not share its unlawful purposes and who do not participate in its unlawful activities surely pose no threat, either as citizens or as public employees. [A] law which applies to membership without the "specific intent" to further the illegal aims of the organization infringes unnecessarily on protected freedoms. It rests on the doctrine of "guilt by association" which has no place here. [Such] a law cannot stand.

Is *Elfbrandt's* extension of *Scales* to the public employment context warranted? Does *Elfbrandt* suggest that the government may not refuse to employ an individual because of her advocacy or associations unless such advocacy or associations could constitutionally be declared unlawful?

6. *The reach of* Elfbrandt: Robel. In United States v. Robel, 389 U.S. 258 (1967), appellee, a member of the Communist Party who had worked at a shipyard for ten years "without incident," was charged with violating section 5(a)(1)(D) of the Subversive Activities Control Act of 1950, which prohibited any "knowing" member of a communist-action organization "to engage in any employment in any defense facility." The Court held that section 5(a)(1)(D) was an "unconstitutional abridgment of the right of association protected by the First Amendment":

> The Government [emphasizes] that the purpose of §5(a)(1)(D) is to reduce the threat of sabotage and espionage in the Nation's defense plants. The Government's interest in such a prophylactic measure is not insubstantial. But [the] means chosen to implement that governmental purpose in this instance cut deeply into the right of association. Section 5(a)(1)(D) [casts] its net across a broad range of associational activities, indiscriminately trapping membership which can be constitutionally punished [see *Scales*] and membership which cannot be so proscribed. [See *Elfbrandt*.] It is made irrelevant to the statute's operation that an individual may be a passive or inactive [member], that he may be unaware of the organization's unlawful aims, or that he may disagree with those unlawful aims. It is also made irrelevant that [the individual] may occupy a nonsensitive position in a defense facility. Thus, §5(a)(1)(D) contains the fatal defect of overbreadth because it seeks to bar employment both for association which may be proscribed and for association which may not be proscribed. [This] the Constitution will not tolerate.

After *Robel*, in what circumstances, if any, may the government refuse to employ an individual in a defense facility because of that individual's membership in a "terrorist" organization, where the individual's membership does not meet the requirements of *Scales*?

7. Brandenburg *and public employees.* Suppose a public school teacher publicly advocates the use of cocaine. Can she be fired even though such advocacy would not meet the requirements of *Brandenburg*? Does it matter whether the expression occurs on school premises? During class? Can a public

school require a public school teacher to answer whether she has ever been a member of an organization that supports terrorism? For a comparative perspective, see Attis v. Board of School Trustees, 35 C.R.R.2d 1 (1996) (Canadian court upholding a rule prohibiting a public school teacher from making anti-Semitic statements and distributing anti-Semitic materials even during off-duty hours).

8. *The first amendment rights of students.* May a public university deny official recognition to a student group because it advocates the use of violence to effect change? Consider Healy v. James, 408 U.S. 169 (1972):

> [In] 1969–70, [a] climate of unrest prevailed on many college campuses in this country. There had been widespread civil disobedience on some college campuses, accompanied by the seizure of buildings, vandalism, and arson. Some colleges had been shut down altogether, while at others files were looted and manuscripts destroyed. SDS chapters on some of those campuses had been a catalytic force during this period. . . .
>
> [The College argues that its denial of recognition to SDS was justified because SDS adheres to] a philosophy of violence and disruption. [But as] repugnant as these views may [be], the mere expression of them would not justify the denial of First Amendment rights. Whether petitioners did in fact advocate a philosophy of "destruction" thus becomes immaterial. The College, acting here as the instrumentality of the State, may not restrict speech or association simply because it finds the views expressed by any group to be abhorrent. [The] critical line [is] the line between mere advocacy and advocacy "directed to inciting or producing imminent lawless action and . . . likely to incite or produce such action." [*Brandenburg.*]

See also Papish v. Board of Curators of the University of Missouri, 410 U.S. 667 (1973) (a state university may not expel a student for distributing on campus a newspaper containing a political cartoon depicting policemen raping the Statue of Liberty); Tinker v. Des Moines Independent Community School District, 393 U.S. 503 (1969) (a public school may not discipline students for wearing black armbands to school to publicize their objections to the war in Vietnam in the absence of a showing that the "forbidden conduct would 'materially and substantially interfere with the requirements of appropriate discipline in the operation of the school'").

On the other hand, in Morse v. Frederick, 551 U.S. 393 (2007), the Court upheld the suspension of a high school student for displaying at a school-sponsored event a fourteen-foot-long banner bearing the phrase "BONG Hits 4 JESUS," on the theory that *Tinker* does not apply when a student's speech does not contribute to political debate and "can reasonably be regarded as encouraging illegal drug use."

9. *The first amendment rights of soldiers.* Does a soldier have a constitutional right to attempt to persuade other soldiers not to obey orders? Should *Brandenburg* govern? Consider Parker v. Levy, 417 U.S. 733 (1974), in which a

captain in the army told enlisted personnel that "[the] United States is wrong in being involved in the Viet Nam War. I would refuse to go to Viet Nam if ordered to do so. I don't see why any colored soldier would go to Viet Nam; they should refuse to go [and] if sent should refuse to fight because they are discriminated against [in] the United States, and they are sacrificed and discriminated against in Viet Nam by being given all the hazardous duty." As a consequence of such statements, appellee was court-martialed for "conduct unbecoming an officer and gentleman." The Court, in a five-to-three decision, upheld the conviction:

> [The] military is, by necessity, a specialized society separate from civilian society. [It has] developed laws and traditions of its [own]. "An army is not a deliberative body. [No] question can be left open as to the right to command in the officer, or the duty of obedience in the soldier." [While] members of the military are not excluded from the protection granted by the First Amendment, the different character of the military community and of the military mission requires a different application of those protections. The fundamental necessity for obedience [may] render permissible within the military that which would be constitutionally impermissible outside it. [Appellee's] conduct, that of a commissioned officer publicly urging enlisted personnel to refuse to obey orders which might send them into combat, was unprotected under the most expansive notions of the First Amendment.

## B.  SPEECH THAT PROVOKES A HOSTILE AUDIENCE REACTION

This section examines the circumstances, if any, in which government may restrict speech because the ideas expressed might provoke a hostile audience response. To what extent does the first amendment protect the speaker whose expression provokes a "breach of the peace"? Must society tolerate speech that leads to fistfights, riots, or even mob violence? Is there a danger that, in attempting to maintain order, we may invite a "heckler's veto"?

**TERMINIELLO v. CHICAGO, 337 U.S. 1 (1949).** Terminiello was convicted of disorderly conduct based on a speech he delivered under the following circumstances: "The auditorium was filled to capacity with over eight hundred persons present. [Outside] a crowd of about one thousand persons gathered to protest against the meeting. A cordon of policemen was assigned to maintain order; but they were not able to prevent several disturbances. The crowd outside was angry and turbulent." Members of the crowd threw stink bombs and broke windows. Terminiello goaded his opponents, referring to them as "slimy scum," "snakes," and "bedbugs." In his condemnation of various political and racial groups, Terminiello "followed, with fidelity that [was] more than coincidental, the pattern of European fascist leaders." The Court found it unnecessary to decide the case on its facts. At Terminiello's trial, the jury was instructed that it could convict if it found that his speech included expression that "stirs the public to anger, invites dispute, brings about a condition of unrest, or creates a disturbance." The Court held that this instruction violated the first amendment:

> A function of free speech under our system of government is to invite dispute. It may indeed best serve its high purpose when it induces a condition of unrest, creates dissatisfaction with conditions as they are, or even stirs people to anger. [That] is why freedom of speech, though not absolute, [is] nevertheless protected against censorship or punishment, unless shown likely to produce a clear and present danger of a serious substantive evil that rises far above public inconvenience, annoyance, or unrest.

*Terminiello* stands for the proposition that speech may not be restricted because the ideas expressed offend the audience. What is the reason for this limitation? Because there is no clear and present danger? Because the harm is too insubstantial? Because the justification for suppression is fundamentally at odds with basic first amendment principles? Are no ideas sufficiently offensive to justify suppression on this basis?

## Cantwell v. Connecticut
310 U.S. 296 (1940)

MR. JUSTICE ROBERTS delivered the opinion of the Court.
[In an effort to proselytize and solicit contributions, Jesse Cantwell, a Jehovah's Witness, played a phonograph record that sharply attacked the Roman Catholic religion to persons he encountered on the street. As a result of these activities, Cantwell was charged with inciting a breach of the peace.] . . .
When clear and present danger of riot, disorder, interference with traffic upon the public streets, or other immediate threat to public safety, peace, or order, appears, the power of the State to prevent or punish is obvious. Equally obvious is it that a State may not unduly suppress free communication of views, religious or other, under the guise of conserving desirable conditions. . . .
Having these considerations in mind, we note that Jesse Cantwell, on April 26, 1938, was upon a public street, where he had a right to be, and where he had a right peacefully to impart his views to others. There is no showing that his deportment was noisy, truculent, overbearing or offensive. He requested of two pedestrians permission to play to them a phonograph record. The permission was granted. It is not claimed that he intended to insult or affront the hearers by playing the record. It is plain that he wished only to interest them in his

propaganda. The sound of the phonograph is not shown to have disturbed residents of the street, to have drawn a crowd, or to have impeded traffic. Thus far he had invaded no right or interest of the public or of the men accosted.

The record [embodies] a general attack on all organized religious systems as instruments of Satan and injurious to man; it then singles out the Roman Catholic Church for strictures couched in terms which naturally would offend not only persons of that persuasion, but all others who respect the honestly held religious faith of their fellows. The hearers were in fact highly offended. One of them said he felt like hitting Cantwell and the other that he was tempted to throw Cantwell off the street. The one who testified he felt like hitting Cantwell said, in answer to the question "Did you do anything else or have any other reaction?" "No, sir, because he said he would take the victrola and he went." . . .

Cantwell's conduct, in the view of the court below, considered apart from the effect of his communication upon his hearers, did not amount to a breach of the peace. One may, however, be guilty of the offense if he commit acts or make statements likely to provoke violence and disturbance of good order, even though no such eventuality be intended. Decisions to this effect are many, but examination discloses that, in practically all, the provocative language which was held to amount to a breach of the peace consisted of profane, indecent, or abusive remarks directed to the person of the hearer. We find in the instant case no assault or threatening of bodily harm, no truculent bearing, no intentional discourtesy, no personal abuse. On the contrary, we find only an effort to persuade a willing listener to buy a book or to contribute money in the interest of what Cantwell, however misguided others may think him, conceived to be true religion.

In the realm of religious faith, and in that of political belief, sharp differences arise. In both fields the tenets of one man may seem the rankest error to his neighbor. To persuade others to his own point of view, the pleader, as we know, at times, resorts to exaggeration, to vilification of men who have been, or are, prominent in church or state, and even to false statement. But the people of this nation have ordained in the light of history, that, in spite of the probability of excesses and abuses, these liberties are, in the long view, essential to enlightened opinion and right conduct on the part of the citizens of a democracy. . . .

Although the contents of the record not unnaturally aroused animosity, we think that, in the absence of a statute narrowly drawn to define and punish specific conduct as constituting a clear and present danger to a substantial interest of the State, the petitioner's communication, considered in the light of the constitutional guarantees, raised no such clear and present menace to public peace and order as to render him liable to conviction of the common law offense in question. . . .

Reversed.

## Feiner v. New York

340 U.S. 315 (1951)

Mr. Chief Justice Vinson delivered the opinion of the Court.

Petitioner was convicted of the offense of disorderly conduct. . . .

*Facts*

On the evening of March 8, 1949, petitioner [was] addressing [a street-corner] meeting [in] the City of Syracuse. [The] police received a telephone complaint concerning the meeting, and two officers were detailed to investigate. [They] found a crowd of about seventy-five or eighty people, both Negro and white, filling the sidewalk and spreading out into the street. Petitioner, standing on a large wooden box on the sidewalk, was addressing the crowd through a loud-speaker system attached to an automobile. Although the purpose of his speech was to urge his listeners to attend a meeting to be held that night in the Syracuse Hotel, in its course he was making derogatory remarks concerning President Truman, the American Legion, the Mayor of Syracuse, and other local political officials. [Feiner referred to Truman as a "bum," to the mayor as a "champagne-sipping bum" who "does not speak for the Negro people," and to the American Legion as "a Nazi Gestapo."]

The police officers made no effort to interfere with petitioner's speech, but were first concerned with the effect of the crowd on both pedestrian and vehicular traffic. [The] crowd was restless and there was some pushing, shoving and milling around. . . .

At this time, petitioner was speaking in a "loud, high-pitched voice." He gave the impression that he was endeavoring to arouse the Negro people against the whites, urging that they rise up in arms and fight for equal rights. The statements before such a mixed audience "stirred up a little excitement." Some of the onlookers made remarks to the police about their inability to handle the crowd and at least one threatened violence if the police did not act. There were others who appeared to be favoring petitioner's arguments. Because of the feeling that existed in the crowd both for and against the speaker, the officers finally "stepped in to prevent it from resulting in a fight." One of the officers approached the petitioner, not for the purpose of arresting him, but to get him to break up the crowd. He asked petitioner to get down off the box, but the latter refused to accede to his request and continued talking. The officer waited for a minute and then demanded that he cease talking. Although the officer had thus twice requested petitioner to stop over the course of several minutes, petitioner not only ignored him but continued talking. During all this time, the crowd was pressing closer around petitioner and the officer. Finally, the officer told petitioner he was under arrest and ordered him to get down from the box, reaching up to grab him. Petitioner stepped down, announcing over the microphone that "the law has arrived, and I suppose they will take over now." In all, the officer had asked petitioner to get down off the box three times over a space of four or five minutes. Petitioner had been speaking for over a half hour.

*Asked 3 times*

On these facts, petitioner was specifically charged with violation of §722 of the Penal Law of New York, the pertinent part of which is set out in the margin.[1] . . .

We are not faced here with blind condonation by a state court of arbitrary police action. [The] courts below recognized petitioner's right to hold a street meeting at this locality, to make use of loud-speaking equipment in giving his speech, and to make derogatory remarks concerning public officials and the American Legion. They found that the officers in making the arrest were motivated solely by a proper concern for the preservation of order and protection of the general welfare, and that there was no evidence which could lend color to a claim that the acts of the police were a cover for suppression of petitioner's views and opinions. Petitioner was thus neither arrested nor convicted for the making or the content of his speech. Rather, it was the reaction which it actually engendered.

The language of [*Cantwell*] is appropriate here. ". . . When clear and present danger of riot, disorder, interference with traffic upon the public streets, or other immediate threat to public safety, peace, or order, appears, the power of the State to prevent or punish is obvious." . . .

We are well aware that the ordinary murmurings and objections of a hostile audience cannot be allowed to silence a speaker, and also mindful of the possible danger of giving overzealous police officials complete discretion to break up otherwise lawful public meetings. [But] we are not faced here with such a situation. It is one thing to say that the police cannot be used as an instrument for the suppression of unpopular views, and another to say that, when as here the speaker passes the bounds of argument or persuasion and undertakes incitement to riot, they are powerless to prevent a breach of the peace. . . .

Affirmed.

[A concurring opinion of Justice Frankfurter and a dissenting opinion of Justice Douglas, in which Justice Minton concurred, are omitted.]

MR. JUSTICE BLACK, dissenting.

The record before us convinces me that petitioner, a young college student, has been sentenced to the penitentiary for the unpopular views he expressed on matters of public interest while lawfully making a street-corner speech. . . .

The Court's opinion apparently rests on this reasoning: The policeman, under the circumstances detailed, could reasonably conclude that serious

---

1. "Section 722. Any person who with intent to provoke a breach of the peace, or whereby a breach of the peace may be occasioned, commits any of the following acts shall be deemed to have committed the offense of disorderly conduct:

"1. Uses offensive, disorderly, threatening, abusive or insulting language, conduct or behavior;

"2. Acts in such a manner as to annoy, disturb, interfere with, obstruct, or be offensive to others;

"3. Congregates with others on a public street and refuses to move on when ordered by the police. . . .

fighting or even riot was imminent; therefore he could stop petitioner's speech to prevent a breach of peace; accordingly, it was "disorderly conduct" for petitioner to continue speaking in disobedience of the officer's request. As to the existence of a dangerous situation on the street corner, it seems far-fetched to suggest that the "facts" show any imminent threat of riot or uncontrollable disorder. It is neither unusual nor unexpected that some people at public street meetings mutter, mill about, push, shove, or disagree, even violently, with the speaker. Indeed, it is rare where controversial topics are discussed that an outdoor crowd does not do some or all of these things. Nor does one isolated threat to assault the speaker forebode disorder. Especially should the danger be discounted where, as here, the person threatening was a man whose wife and two small children accompanied him and who, so far as the record shows, was never close enough to petitioner to carry out the threat.

Moreover, assuming that the "facts" did indicate a critical situation, I reject the implication of the Court's opinion that the police had no obligation to protect petitioner's constitutional right to talk. The police of course have power to prevent breaches of the peace. But if, in the name of preserving order, they ever can interfere with a lawful public speaker, they first must make all reasonable efforts to protect him. Here the policeman did not even pretend to try to protect petitioner. According to the officers' testimony, the crowd was restless but there is no showing of any attempt to quiet it; pedestrians were forced to walk into the street, but there was no effort to clear a path on the sidewalk; one person threatened to assault petitioner but the officers did nothing to discourage this when even a word might have sufficed. Their duty was to protect petitioner's right to talk, even to the extent of arresting the man who threatened to interfere. Instead, they shirked that duty and acted only to suppress the right to speak.

Finally, I cannot agree with the Court's statement that petitioner's disregard of the policeman's unexplained request amounted to such "deliberate defiance" as would justify an arrest or conviction for disorderly conduct. On the contrary, I think that the policeman's action was a "deliberate defiance" of ordinary official duty as well as of the constitutional right of free speech. For at least where time allows, courtesy and explanation of commands are basic elements of good official conduct in a democratic society. Here petitioner was "asked" then "told" then "commanded" to stop speaking, but a man making a lawful address is certainly not required to be silent merely because an officer directs it. Petitioner was entitled to know why he should cease doing a lawful act. Not once was he told. I understand that people in authoritarian countries must obey arbitrary orders. I had hoped that there was no such duty in the United States. . . .

## Note: *The Search for Mechanisms of Control*

1. *Incitement to riot.* Is *Feiner* consistent with *Cantwell*? Because Feiner triggered a clear and present danger? Because he passed "the bounds of

argument or persuasion" and undertook "incitement to riot"? In what sense did Feiner "incite to riot"? Does "incitement" mean the same thing here as in the subversive advocacy context?

2. *Police orders.* Note that Feiner, unlike Cantwell, disobeyed a specific police order to stop speaking. What is the appropriate role of the police? Does the first amendment require the police to arrest the hostile members of the audience rather than to stop the speaker? Suppose the officers on the scene need support. Must they call in additional officers rather than stop the speaker? May an individual who is prosecuted for refusing to obey a police order to stop speaking assert the unconstitutionality of the order in his defense?

3. *Licensing.* Kunz v. New York, 340 U.S. 290 (1951), decided on the same day as *Feiner*, concerned the constitutionality of a city ordinance declaring it unlawful to hold public worship meetings on the streets without first obtaining a permit from the police commissioner. Kunz, an ordained Baptist minister, was issued a permit in 1946, but the permit was revoked after a hearing at which it was determined that Kunz had ridiculed and denounced other religious beliefs in such a way as to cause disorder. Thereafter, the city denied Kunz's permit applications, and in 1948 he was convicted for holding a meeting without a permit in violation of the ordinance. The Court did not decide whether a permit could constitutionally be denied on the ground that the speaker had previously caused disorder, holding instead that the permit scheme was invalid on its face because it failed to provide clear standards to guide the discretion of the official charged with administering the scheme. On standardless licensing, see Chapter III.B, infra.

4. *Permit fees and the hostile audience.* In Forsythe County, Georgia v. The Nationalist Movement, 505 U.S. 123 (1992), the Court invalidated a municipal ordinance that authorized permit fees for parades, demonstrations, marches, and similar activities, up to a maximum of $1,000, based in part on the anticipated expense necessary to maintain the public order. The Court, in an opinion by Justice Blackmun, explained:

> The county envisions that the administrator [will] assess a fee to cover "the cost of necessary and reasonable protection of persons participating or observing [said] activity." [To perform this function, the administrator] "must necessarily examine the content of the message that is conveyed," [estimate] the response of others to that content, and judge the number of police necessary to meet that response. The fee assessed will depend on the administrator's measure of the amount of hostility likely to be created by the speech based on its content. Those wishing to express views unpopular with bottle throwers, for example, may have to pay more for their permit [Speech] cannot be financially burdened, any more than it can be punished or banned, simply because it might offend a hostile mob. "[Regulations] which permit the Government to discriminate on the basis of the content of the message cannot be tolerated under the First Amendment." [The county] contends that the $1,000 cap on the fee [saves] its constitutionality. [But neither] the $1,000 cap [nor] even some lower nominal cap [could] save the

ordinance because in this context the level of the fee is irrelevant. A tax based on the content of speech does not become more constitutional because it is a small tax.

5. A *"far cry" from* Feiner. In Edwards v. South Carolina, 372 U.S. 229 (1963), petitioners, 187 black high school and college students, walked to the South Carolina State House grounds, an area open to the general public, to protest discrimination. About thirty law enforcement officers, who had advance knowledge of the demonstration, were present. Petitioners walked in an orderly manner through the grounds carrying placards bearing such messages as "I am proud to be a Negro" and "Down with segregation." A crowd of about two hundred to three hundred onlookers gathered; although some were identified as "possible trouble makers," there were no threatening remarks, hostile gestures, or offensive comments. There was no significant interference with either vehicular or pedestrian traffic. After thirty to forty-five minutes, police authorities informed petitioners that they would be arrested if they did not disperse within fifteen minutes. One of the demonstrators then delivered a "religious harangue," inspiring petitioners to sing several patriotic songs while loudly clapping their hands and stamping their feet. After fifteen minutes, petitioners were arrested. They were convicted of the common law crime of breach of the peace.

The Court, in an opinion by Justice Stewart, held that the convictions "infringed the petitioners' constitutionally protected rights of free speech, free assembly, and freedom to petition for redress of their grievances." *Edwards*, the Court explained, "was a far cry" from *Feiner*. Here, "there was no violence or threat of violence on [the part of the petitioners], or on the part of any member of the crowd watching them." Moreover, "police protection at the scene was at all times sufficient to meet any foreseeable possibility of disorder." In the Court's view, then, petitioners had been convicted because "the opinions which they were peaceably expressing were sufficiently opposed to the views of the majority of the community to attract a crowd and necessitate police protection." The Constitution, however, "does not permit a State to make criminal the peaceful expression of unpopular views." The Court thus concluded that, "as in [*Terminiello*], the Courts of South Carolina have defined a criminal offense so as to permit conviction of the petitioners if their speech 'stirred people to anger, invited public dispute, or brought about a condition of unrest. A conviction resting on any of those grounds may not stand.'"

6. A *"far cry" from* Feiner II. In Cox v. Louisiana, 379 U.S. 536 (1965), Cox, an ordained minister, led a demonstration of approximately two thousand black students to protest the arrest the previous day of twenty-three black students who had picketed stores that maintained segregated lunch counters. The demonstration was to take place at the local courthouse, which contained the parish jail in which the twenty-three students were confined. The

demonstrators walked to the courthouse in an orderly manner, two or three abreast. As they neared the courthouse, the police chief stopped the procession and inquired as to their purpose. Cox stated that they would sing the national anthem and a freedom song and recite the Lord's Prayer and the pledge of allegiance, and that he would deliver a short speech. The police chief instructed Cox to confine the demonstration to the west side of the street, across the street from the courthouse. The demonstrators lined up on the west sidewalk about five deep, spread along almost the entire length of the block. A group of about one hundred to three hundred whites, mostly court-house personnel, gathered across the street on the steps of the courthouse. Seventy-five to eighty policemen, several members of the fire department, and a fire truck were stationed in the street between the two groups.

The demonstration proceeded according to plan until Cox, in the course of his speech, said: "It's lunch time. Let's go eat. There are twelve stores we are protesting. [These stores won't accept your money at one of their counters.] This is an act of racial discrimination. These stores are open to the public. You are members of the public." These remarks caused some "muttering" and "grumbling" among the white onlookers. The sheriff, deeming Cox's appeal to the students to sit in at the lunch counters to be "inflammatory," ordered the demonstrators to disperse. When Cox and the students ignored the sheriff, the police fired tear gas, causing the demonstrators to flee. The following day, Cox was arrested. He was thereafter convicted of breach of the peace.

In a unanimous decision, the Court overturned Cox's conviction. Justice Goldberg, speaking for the Court, found "no conduct which the State had a right to prohibit as a breach of the peace." The Court rejected the state's contention that the conviction could be sustained because "violence was about to erupt." The demonstrators themselves "were not violent and threatened no violence." Indeed, there was "no indication that the mood of the students was ever hostile, aggressive, or unfriendly." The fear of violence was thus "based upon the reaction of the group of white citizens looking on from across the street." Although there were some "mutterings," there was no evidence "that any member of the white group threatened violence." In any event, the police and other personnel present "could have handled the crowd." The Court thus concluded that the facts of *Cox* "are strikingly similar" to *Edwards* and, like *Edwards*, "a far cry" from *Feiner*.

7. A *"far cry"* from Feiner III. In Gregory v. City of Chicago, 394 U.S. 111 (1969), Gregory led a march of about eighty-five protesters to the home of Chicago Mayor Richard Daley to protest segregation in the city's public schools. The protesters, accompanied by about one hundred police, arrived at the mayor's home at 8:00 P.M. and began marching continuously around the block. For the first thirty minutes, they sang civil rights songs and chanted slogans criticizing the mayor and referring to him as a "snake." After 8:30, the protesters marched quietly but continued to carry sharply critical placards. In the next hour, the crowd of white onlookers grew rapidly to more than one

thousand, and, as the evening wore on, they became increasingly unruly. In several instances, spectators attempted physically to block the march. There were threatening shouts such as "Get out of here niggers — go back where you belong or we will get you out of here," and rocks and eggs were thrown at the marchers. At about 9:30, the police officer in charge informed Gregory that "the situation was dangerous and becoming riotous" and asked Gregory to lead the marchers out of the area. When Gregory refused, he and the other protesters were arrested. They were thereafter convicted under Chicago's disorderly conduct ordinance, which declared it unlawful for any person to make "any improper noise, riot, disturbance, breach of the peace, or diversion tending to a breach of the peace."

The Court, in an opinion by Chief Justice Warren, unanimously overturned the convictions. The Court announced that "this is a simple case." Noting that "there is no evidence in this record that petitioners' conduct was disorderly," the Court concluded that "convictions so totally devoid of evidentiary support violate due process."

8. *Evaluation.* Why were these cases "a far cry" from *Feiner?* Consider the following possibilities: (a) The demonstrators in these cases did not pass "the bounds of argument or persuasion and undertake incitement to riot"; (b) there was less likelihood in these cases of an imminent violent response; (c) the police were better able to handle the situations in *Edwards, Cox,* and *Gregory.* Were these cases really "a far cry" from *Feiner,* or do they limit its precedential force? Do the results in *Edwards, Cox,* and *Gregory* suggest that the Court has implicitly embraced a set of principles for dealing with the hostile audience problem analogous to those articulated at approximately the same time for dealing with the problem of subversive advocacy? Should the state *ever* be allowed to stop or punish a speaker because of a hostile audience response? Consider the argument that even allowing for that possibility will only invite threats of violence and discriminatory law enforcement against unpopular speakers. Might it be best simply to say: "Never"?

What is "low" value speech in this context? The difficulties of defining "incitement" in cases like *Cantwell, Feiner, Edwards,* and *Cox* have already been noted. Consider also *Chaplinsky* and the "fighting words" doctrine.

## Chaplinsky v. New Hampshire
315 U.S. 568 (1942)

MR. JUSTICE MURPHY delivered the opinion of the Court.

Appellant, a member of the sect known as Jehovah's Witnesses, was convicted in the municipal court of Rochester, New Hampshire, for violation of Chapter 378, §2, of the Public Laws of New Hampshire:

> No person shall address any offensive, derisive or annoying word to any other person who is lawfully in any street or other public place, nor call him by an

offensive or derisive name, nor make any noise or exclamation in his presence and hearing with intent to deride, offend or annoy him, or to prevent him from pursuing his lawful business or occupation.

The complaint charged that appellant,

with force and arms, in a certain public place in said city of Rochester, to wit, on the public sidewalk on the easterly side of Wakefield Street, near unto the entrance of the City Hall, did unlawfully repeat, the words following, addressed to the complainant, that is to say, "You are a God damned racketeer" and "a damned Fascist and the whole government of Rochester are Fascists or agents of Fascists," the same being offensive, derisive and annoying words and names. . . .

*spoken fighting words*

There is no substantial dispute over the facts. Chaplinsky was distributing the literature of his sect on the streets of Rochester on a busy Saturday afternoon. Members of the local citizenry complained to the City Marshal, Bowering, that Chaplinsky was denouncing all religion as a "racket." Bowering told them that Chaplinsky was lawfully engaged, and then warned Chaplinsky that the crowd was getting restless. Some time later, a disturbance occurred and the traffic officer on duty at the busy intersection started with Chaplinsky for the police station, but did not inform him that he was under arrest or that he was going to be arrested. On the way, they encountered Marshal Bowering, who had been advised that a riot was under way and was therefore hurrying to the scene. Bowering repeated his earlier warning to Chaplinsky, who then addressed to Bowering the words set forth in the complaint.

Chaplinsky's version of the affair was slightly different. He testified that, when he met Bowering, he asked him to arrest the ones responsible for the disturbance. In reply, Bowering cursed him and told him to come along. Appellant admitted that he said the words charged in the complaint, with the exception of the name of the Deity.

Over appellant's objection the trial court excluded, as immaterial, testimony relating to appellant's mission "to preach the true facts of the Bible," his treatment at the hands of the crowd, and the alleged neglect of duty on the part of the police. This action was approved by the court below, which held that neither provocation nor the truth of the utterance would constitute a defense to the charge. . . .

Allowing the broadest scope to the language and purpose of the Fourteenth Amendment, it is well understood that the right of free speech is not absolute at all times and under all circumstances. There are certain well-defined and narrowly limited classes of speech, the prevention and punishment of which have never been thought to raise any Constitutional problem. These include the lewd and obscene, the profane, the libelous, and the insulting or "fighting" words — those which by their very utterance inflict injury or tend to incite an immediate breach of the peace. It has been well observed that such utterances are no essential part of any exposition of ideas, and are of such slight social value as a step to truth that any benefit that may be derived from them is clearly outweighed by the social interest in order and morality. "Resort to epithets or personal abuse is not in any proper sense communication of information or opinion safeguarded by the Constitution, and its punishment as a criminal act would raise no question under that instrument."[*Cantwell.*] . . .

On the authority of its earlier decisions, the state court declared that the statute's purpose was to preserve the public peace, no words being "forbidden except such as have a direct tendency to cause acts of violence by the persons to whom, individually, the remark is addressed." It was further said:

> The word "offensive" is not to be defined in terms of what a particular addressee thinks. . . . The test is what men of common intelligence would understand would be words likely to cause an average addressee to fight. . . . The English language has a number of words and expressions which by general consent are "fighting words" when said without a disarming smile. . . . Such words, as ordinary men know, are likely to cause a fight. So are threatening, profane or obscene revilings. Derisive and annoying words can be taken as coming within the purview of the statute as heretofore interpreted only when they have this characteristic of plainly tending to excite the addressee to a breach of the peace. . . . The statute, as construed, does no more than prohibit the face-to-face words plainly likely to cause a breach of the peace by the addressee, words whose speaking constitutes a breach of the peace by the speaker — including "classical fighting words," words in current use less "classical" but equally likely to cause violence, and other disorderly words, including profanity, obscenity and threats.

We are unable to say that the limited scope of the statute as thus construed contravenes the Constitutional right of free expression. It is a statute narrowly drawn and limited to define and punish specific conduct lying within the domain of state power, the use in a public place of words likely to cause a breach of the peace. . . .

Nor can we say that the application of the statute to the facts disclosed by the record substantially or unreasonably impinges upon the privilege of free speech. Argument is unnecessary to demonstrate that the appellations "damned racketeer" and "damned Fascist" are epithets likely to provoke the average person to retaliation, and thereby cause a breach of the peace.

The refusal of the state court to admit evidence of provocation and evidence bearing on the truth or falsity of the utterances, is open to no Constitutional objection. Whether the facts sought to be proved by such evidence constitute a defense to the charge, or may be shown in mitigation, are questions for the state court to determine. Our function is fulfilled by a determination that the challenged statute, on its face and as applied, does not contravene the Fourteenth Amendment.

Affirmed.

## Note: Fighting Words

1. *The actual facts of* Chaplinsky. According to Blasi and Shiffrin, The Real Story of West Virginia Board of Education v. Barnette, in Dorf, ed., Constitutional Law Stories 433 (2004), here is what really happened in the case:

> In April of 1940, Walter Chaplinsky, a vociferous Jehovah's Witness preaching in Rochester, New Hampshire, was surrounded by a group of men who scornfully invited him to salute the flag. While one veteran attempted to pummel Chaplinsky, the town marshal looked on, warned the Witness that things were turning ugly, but refused to arrest the assailant. After the marshal left, the assailant returned with a flag and attempted to impale Chaplinsky on the flagpole, eventually pinning him onto a car while other members of the crowd began to beat him. A police officer then arrived, not to detain or disperse members of the mob but to escort Chaplinsky to the police station. En route, the officer and others who joined the escort directed epithets at the hapless Witness. When Chaplinsky responded in kind, calling the marshal who had reappeared "a damn fascist and a racketeer," he was arrested for, and later convicted of, using offensive language in public.

Does the divergence between these "real" facts and the facts recited in the Court's opinion have any implication for first amendment doctrine? If you were Chaplinski's lawyer in the Supreme Court and if the facts were not in the record, is there any way you could have informed the Court of the facts? If you somehow succeeded in doing so, would it have made any difference in the outcome?

2. *The two-level theory.* Building on dictum in *Cantwell*, the Court in *Chaplinsky* first fully enunciated what Professor Harry Kalven later termed the "two-level" theory of speech, under which speech is either "protected" or "unprotected" by the first amendment according to the Court's assessment of its relative "value." Kalven, The Metaphysics of the Law of Obscenity, 1960 Sup. Ct. Rev. 1, 10. The analytical underpinnings and historical evolution of this theory, and the other varieties of "unprotected" speech mentioned in *Chaplinsky*, such as the "obscene" and the "libelous," are examined more fully in Chapter 4, infra.

3. *Fighting words as "low" value speech.* Why was Chaplinsky's expression unprotected by the first amendment? Because it consisted of "epithets or personal abuse"? What distinguishes an "epithet" from bona fide criticism? The following arguments might be advanced for the proposition that fighting words are of only "low" first amendment value:

a. Fighting words are unprotected because, as "epithets or personal abuse," they are intended to inflict harm rather than to communicate ideas, and thus are not really "speech" at all. They are "verbal assaults," more akin to a "punch in the mouth" than to constitutionally protected expression of opinion. See

Greenawalt, Insults and Epithets: Are They Protected Speech?, 42 Rutgers L. Rev. 287, 291–298 (1990). If Chaplinsky had actually punched Bowering, could he successfully claim that this was a constitutionally protected expression of his evaluation of Bowering's performance of his duties?

b. Fighting words are unprotected because they are "likely to provoke the average person to retaliation, and thereby cause a breach of the peace." On this view, the doctrine is merely an application of the Holmes/Brandeis version of clear and present danger. But is name-calling really likely to cause the *average* addressee to fight? Is the focus on the *average*, rather than the *actual*, addressee consistent with the Holmes/Brandeis formulation? How should we deal with the possibility that men may be more prone than women to respond with violence?

c. Fighting words are unprotected because they are "no essential part of any exposition of ideas." Does the Court undervalue the use of personal insults to dramatize one's point? Is the emotive impact worth protecting? Even if fighting words are not "essential" to the exposition of ideas, is this in itself a basis for holding them unprotected? Is it, in conjunction with other factors, a relevant consideration?

4. *Fighting words?* Consider whether the following constitute "fighting words": (a) Cantwell's phonograph record, which charged that Roman Catholicism "has by means of fraud and deception brought untold sorrow and suffering upon the people" and "operates the greatest racket ever employed amongst men and robs the people of their money," when played, as it was, to Roman Catholics. (b) Terminiello's speech, in which he called his opponents, who were outside the hall, "slimy scum," "snakes," and "bedbugs." (c) Kunz's public prayer meetings, in which he labeled Catholicism "a religion of the devil," declared that the Pope is "the anti-Christ," and described Jews as "Christ-killers" and "garbage that [should] have been burnt in the incinerators [of Nazi Germany]." (d) Gregory's repeated references to Mayor Daley as a "snake." Consider also the Court's post-*Chaplinsky* decisions:

a. In Street v. New York, 394 U.S. 576 (1969), Street, on learning that James Meredith, a civil rights leader, had been shot, burned an American flag in public. A small crowd gathered, and Street said, "We don't need no damn flag. [If] they let that happen to Meredith we don't need an American flag." The state argued, among other things, that Street could constitutionally be convicted for this speech because of "the possible tendency of [his] words to provoke violent retaliation." The Court disagreed: "Though it is conceivable that some listeners might have been moved to retaliate upon hearing [Street's] disrespectful words, we cannot say that [his] remarks were so inherently inflammatory as to come within that small class of 'fighting words' which are 'likely to provoke the average person to retaliation, and thereby cause a breach of the peace.' [Citing *Chaplinsky*.]"

b. In Cohen v. California, 403 U.S. 15 (1971), Cohen wore a jacket bearing the words "Fuck the Draft" in a corridor of a courthouse. As a consequence, he was convicted under a California statute prohibiting any person "maliciously and willfully [to disturb] the peace or quiet of any neighborhood or person [by] offensive conduct." The state courts interpreted the phrase "offensive conduct" as "behavior which has a tendency to provoke *others* to acts of violence." In overturning the conviction, the Court rejected the state's argument that Cohen's speech constituted fighting words: "While the four-letter word displayed by Cohen in relation to the draft is not uncommonly employed in a personally provocative fashion, in this instance it was clearly not 'directed to the person of the hearer.' [Citing *Cantwell*.] No individual actually or likely to be present could reasonably have regarded the words on appellant's jacket as a direct personal insult."

c. In Gooding v. Wilson, 405 U.S. 518 (1972), Gooding said to a police officer attempting to restore access to an army induction center during an antiwar demonstration, "White son of a bitch, I'll kill you" and "You son of a bitch, I'll choke you to death." He was thereafter convicted under a Georgia statute prohibiting any person to "use to or of another, and in his [presence] opprobrious words or abusive language, tending to cause a breach of the peace." The Court found it unnecessary to decide whether Gooding's speech could constitutionally be punished under a properly drawn statute, holding instead that the Georgia law was overbroad and hence unconstitutional on its face because the state courts had repeatedly interpreted it as reaching clearly protected expression. As examples of this overbreadth, the Court noted that the state courts had failed to construe the statute as "limited in application, as in *Chaplinsky*, to words that 'have a direct tendency to cause acts of violence by the person to whom, individually, the remark is addressed,'" and further that the state courts had previously interpreted the statute as authorizing conviction even if, because of surrounding circumstances, the addressee might "'not be able at the time [of the remark] to assault and beat another,'" so long as "'it might still tend to cause a breach of the peace at some future time.'" The Court emphasized that this went beyond the fighting words doctrine, which reached only utterances tending "to incite an immediate breach of the peace." On the overbreadth doctrine, see Chapter III.A, infra.

d. Rosenfeld v. New Jersey, 408 U.S. 901 (1972); Lewis v. New Orleans, 408 U.S. 913 (1972); and Brown v. Oklahoma, 408 U.S. 914 (1972), were decided as companion cases. In *Rosenfeld*, the appellant, in the course of a public school board meeting attended by approximately 150 people, about forty of whom were children, used the noun "mother-fucker" on four occasions to describe the teachers, the school board, the town, and the country. In *Lewis*, while the police were engaged in arresting appellant's son, she called them "god-damn-mother-fucker police." In *Brown*, appellant, a member of the Black Panthers, spoke by invitation to a large audience at the University of Tulsa's chapel. During the question-and-answer period, he referred to some police officers as "mother-fucking fascist pig cops" and to one officer in particular as a "black mother-fucking pig." Each appellant was convicted under a state law prohibiting, in varying forms, the use of profanity in public. In each case, the Court summarily vacated the judgment and reversed for reconsideration in light of *Gooding*.

e. In Texas v. Johnson, 491 U.S. 397 (1989), the Court invalidated a Texas statute that prohibited any person to "desecrate" the American flag "in a way that the actor knows will seriously offend [others] likely to observe or discover his action," as applied to an individual who publicly burned the flag in symbolic protest of national policy. The Court held that this "expressive conduct" did not fall within the fighting words doctrine because "no reasonable onlooker would have regarded [the defendant's] generalized expression of dissatisfaction with the policies of the Federal Government as a direct personal insult or an invitation to exchange fisticuffs."

5. *Fighting words reconsidered.* It has been suggested that the post-*Chaplinsky* decisions establish that the doctrine applies only to the use of insulting and provocative epithets that describe a particular individual and are addressed specifically to that individual in a face-to-face encounter. See Gard, Fighting Words as Free Speech, 58 Wash. U. L.Q. 531 (1980). Are these limitations defensible? Should the doctrine apply when an insult descriptive of a group is directed to an individual member of that group? Are insults descriptive of a group less likely to provoke a violent response? Are they, because of their generality, more likely to be of "high" first amendment value?

The Court has not upheld a conviction on the basis of the fighting words doctrine since *Chaplinsky*. It has been argued that the Court's post-*Chaplinsky* decisions have so narrowed the doctrine as to render it meaningless, and that the doctrine is "nothing more than a quaint remnant of an earlier morality that has no place in a democratic society dedicated to the principle of free expression." Gard, supra, at 536. Do you agree?

6. *The problem of underinclusion.* Suppose a law restricts only a subset of fighting words, such as (a) fighting words directed against blacks, (b) fighting words concerning religion, or (c) fighting words uttered in bars. Are such restrictions necessarily constitutional because the category of fighting words is itself "unprotected" by the first amendment? Are such restrictions subject to scrutiny, even though the category is "unprotected," because of the inequalities created by the decision to restrict less than the entire category? This issue is addressed in R.A.V. v. City of St. Paul, Chapter IV.H, infra.

### Note: *The* Skokie *Controversy*

In 1977, the Village of Skokie, a northern Chicago suburb, had a population of about 70,000 persons, 40,000 of whom were Jewish. Approximately 5,000 of the Jewish residents were survivors of Nazi concentration camps during World War II. In March 1977, Frank Collin, leader of the National Socialist Party of America, informed village officials that the party intended to hold a peaceable public assembly in Skokie on May 1 to protest the village's requirement that a $350,000 insurance bond be posted before the village's parks could be used for purposes of assembly. Collin explained that the demonstration would last twenty to thirty minutes and would consist of thirty to fifty demonstrators marching in single file in front of the village hall. The marchers would wear uniforms reminiscent of those worn by members of the Nazi Party in Germany under Hitler, and they would wear swastika emblems or armbands. The marchers would carry a party banner containing a swastika emblem and signs bearing such messages as "White Free Speech" and "Free Speech for the White Man."

Village officials filed suit, seeking to enjoin the marchers from wearing their uniforms, displaying the swastika, or distributing or displaying any materials "which incite or promote hatred against persons of Jewish faith or ancestry." The complaint alleged that the march, as planned, was a "deliberate and willful attempt to exacerbate the sensitivities of the Jewish population in Skokie and to incite racial and religious hatred" and that the display of the swastika in Skokie "constitutes a symbolic assault against large numbers of the residents of the plaintiff village and an incitation to violence and retaliation."

At a hearing before the trial court, the village presented evidence that some fifteen to eighteen Jewish organizations, along with various other anti-Nazi organizations, planned to hold a counterdemonstration to protest the march. Between 12,000 and 15,000 persons were expected to participate in the counterdemonstration. The village also presented evidence that there had already been many threats of violence, and that, if the party was permitted to demonstrate, "an uncontrollably violent situation would develop" and "bloodshed would occur." Finally, the village presented the testimony of a survivor of a Nazi concentration camp to the effect that for him and other survivors, "the swastika is a symbol that his closest family was killed by the Nazis, and that the lives of him and his children are not presently safe." The village maintained that the display of the swastika in such circumstances amounted to the intentional infliction of emotional harm. The witness testified further that, although he did not "intend to use violence against" the marchers, he did "not know if he [could] control himself." On April 29, the trial judge granted the injunction. The National Socialist Party appealed.

After the issuance of the injunction, the Illinois appellate courts refused to stay the injunction pending appeal, and the Illinois Supreme Court denied a petition for direct, expedited appeal. The party then sought a stay in the Supreme Court of the United States, which treated the petition as a petition for certiorari, granted the writ, and summarily reversed the state court's denial of the stay. In a five-to-four decision, the Court characterized the denial of the stay as a "final judgment for purposes of our jurisdiction" because it

finally determined the merits of petitioners' claim that the outstanding injunction will deprive them of rights protected by the First Amendment during the period of appellate review which, in the normal course, may take a year or more to complete. If a State seeks to impose a restraint of this kind, it must provide strict procedural safeguards, [including] immediate appellate review. [Absent] such review, the State [must] allow a stay.

On remand, the Illinois appellate court in July modified the injunction, so as to enjoin the party only from displaying the swastika. Skokie v. National Socialist Party of America, 366 N.E.2d 347 (Ill. App. Ct. 1977). The following January the Illinois Supreme Court held the entire injunction invalid. Skokie v. National Socialist Party of America, 373 N.E.2d 21 (Ill. 1978).

During the course of the injunction litigation, Skokie enacted a series of ordinances designed to block the march. These ordinances (1) required applicants for parade permits to procure $300,000 in public liability insurance and $50,000 in property damage insurance; (2) prohibited the "dissemination of any material [including signs and clothing of symbolic significance] which promotes and incites hatred against persons by reason of their race, national origin, or religion, and is intended to do so"; and (3) prohibited anyone to demonstrate "on behalf of any political party while wearing a military-style uniform." All three ordinances were held to violate the first amendment. Collin v. Smith, 578 F.2d 1197 (7th Cir.), aff'g 477 F. Supp. 676 (N.D. Ill. 1978). With the march scheduled for June 25, 1978, the village requested the Supreme Court to stay the ruling of the court of appeals. The Court denied the stay, Justices Blackmun and Rehnquist dissenting. Smith v. Collin, 436 U.S. 953 (1978).

On June 22, Collin cancelled the march. He explained that he had used the threat of a march in Skokie as a means to win the right to demonstrate in Chicago, a right he had won while the Skokie litigation was proceeding. On July 9, 1978, the party held an hour-long rally in Chicago at which four hundred riot-helmeted policemen protected the twenty-five Nazi demonstrators. There were seventy-two arrests and some rock and bottle throwing, but no serious violence.

Consider Douglas-Scott, The Hatefulness of Protected Speech: A Comparison of the American and European Approaches, 7 Wm. & Mary Bill Rts. J. 305, 309, 317, 343–345 (1999):

[Controls] on free speech long have been permitted in many European countries to curb incitement to race hatred. [For] example, in the United Kingdom, Part III of the Public Order Act of 1986 prohibits behavior intended to or likely to have the result of stirring up racial hatred. [The European approach to free speech emphasizes] particular values — dignity, protection of personal identity, and equality. [This] approach recognizes a different sort of harm caused by the abuse of freedom than the danger of imminent lawless action required under American law. The *Brandenburg* requirement that violence be imminent before hateful speech may be proscribed is objectionable. . . .

European case law looks not only to the harm caused by such expression, but also proceeds from a particular conception of individual personality and psychology. [European] case law rejects a conception of individuals as beings who merely should be left to their own devices to make up their own minds about the value of expression in the public domain, to be free to ignore it, or to counter it with more speech. Such an approach isolates human beings by forcing them to take the consequences of painful conduct and ignores the particular susceptibility of certain groups to injury, especially when the offense of the speech seems to be targeted at such groups because of their identity. [Surely] it is not enough for societies that claim to be committed to the ideals of social and political equality and respect for individual dignity to remain neutral and passive when threats to these values exist. Sometimes the state must act to show its solidarity with vulnerable minority groups and its commitment to equality.

Consider also Bollinger, The Skokie Legacy: Reflections on an "Easy Case" and Free Speech Theory, 80 Mich. L. Rev. 617, 629–631 (1982):

[The] free speech principle is grounded as much in a desire to avoid being the slaves of our own intolerant impulses as it is in a desire to preserve an unshackled freedom to speak one's mind as one wishes. [From] this perspective upholding a right of free speech in a case like the Skokie case seems to make the most sense. [One] can understand [the] choice to protect the free speech activities of Nazis, but not because people should value their message in the slightest or believe it should be seriously entertained, not because a commitment to self-government or rationality logically demands that such ideas be presented for consideration, not because a line could not be drawn that would exclude this ideology without inevitably encroaching on ideas that one likes — not for any of these reasons nor others related to them that are a part of the traditional baggage of the free speech argumentation; but rather because the danger of intolerance towards ideas is so pervasive an issue in our social lives, the process of mastering a capacity for tolerance so difficult, that it makes sense somewhere in the system to attempt to confront that problem and exercise more self-restraint than may be otherwise required. [On] this basis, then, tolerance becomes [a] symbolic act indicating an awareness of the risks and dangers of intolerance and a commitment to developing a certain attitude toward the ideas and beliefs of others.

May a police officer be fired for marching in a Nazi Party demonstration? For contributing to an alleged Islamist terrorist organization?

**SNYDER v. PHELPS, 131 S. Ct. 1207 (2011).** Suppose the Nazis had marched in Skokie without prior warning. Could individual residents who were shocked and outraged by their conduct have sued them for damages for the intentional infliction of emotional distress? Consider *Snyder.*

For at least twenty years, the congregation of the Westboro Baptist Church in Topeka, Kansas, picketed hundreds of military funerals to communicate its belief that God hates the United States for its tolerance of homosexuality, particularly in America's military. As part of this campaign, Fred Phelps, who founded the church, and six Westboro Baptist parishioners traveled to

Maryland to picket the funeral of Marine Lance Corporal Matthew Snyder, who was killed in Iraq in the line of duty. The picketing took place on public land approximately one thousand feet from the church where the funeral was held. The picketers peacefully displayed their signs — stating, for example, "Thank God for Dead Soldiers," "Fags Doom Nations," "America is Doomed," and "You're Going to Hell" — for about thirty minutes before the funeral began.

Matthew Snyder's father (Snyder) saw the tops of the picketers' signs when driving to the funeral, but did not learn what was written on them until watching a news broadcast later that night. Snyder filed a civil action against Phelps and Westboro asserting a state tort claim for intentional infliction of emotional distress. A jury held Westboro liable for millions of dollars in compensatory and punitive damages. The trial judge reduced the punitive damages award, but left the verdict otherwise intact. The court of appeals reversed, concluding that Westboro's statements were entitled to first amendment protection. The Supreme Court affirmed.

Chief Justice Roberts delivered the opinion of the Court: "Whether the First Amendment prohibits holding Westboro liable for its speech in this case turns largely on whether that speech is of public or private concern, as determined by all the circumstances of the case. [The] First Amendment reflects 'a profound national commitment to the principle that debate on public issues should be uninhibited, robust, and wide-open.' That is because 'speech concerning public affairs is more than self-expression; it is the essence of self-government.' [Accordingly], 'speech on public issues occupies the highest rung of the hierarchy of First Amendment values, and is entitled to special protection.' . . .

"Speech deals with matters of public concern when it can 'be fairly considered as relating to any matter of political, social, or other concern to the community' or when it 'is a subject of legitimate news interest; that is, a subject of general interest and of value and concern to the public.' [Deciding] whether speech is of public or private concern requires us to examine the 'content, form, and context' of that speech, as revealed by the whole record. [The] 'content' of Westboro's signs plainly relates to broad issues of interest to society at large, rather than matters of 'purely private concern.' [While] these messages may fall short of refined social or political commentary, the issues they highlight — the political and moral conduct of the United States and its citizens, the fate of our Nation, [and] homosexuality in the military [are] matters of public import. The signs certainly convey Westboro's position on those issues, in a manner designed [to] reach as broad a public audience as possible. . . .

"Snyder goes on to argue that Westboro's speech should be afforded less than full First Amendment protection [because] the church members exploited the funeral 'as a platform to bring their message to a broader audience.' There is no doubt that Westboro chose to stage its picketing at the Naval

Academy, the Maryland State House, and Matthew Snyder's funeral to increase publicity for its views and because of the relation between those sites and its views — in the case of the military funeral, because Westboro believes that God is killing American soldiers as punishment for the Nation's sinful policies. [Westboro's] choice of where and when to conduct its picketing is not beyond the Government's regulatory reach — it is 'subject to reasonable time, place, or manner restrictions.' [But the] record confirms that any distress occasioned by Westboro's picketing turned on the content and viewpoint of the message conveyed, rather than any interference with the funeral itself. A group of parishioners standing at the very spot where Westboro stood, holding signs that said 'God Bless America' and 'God Loves You,' would not have been subjected to liability. It was what Westboro said that exposed it to tort damages. [Given] that Westboro's speech was at a public place on a matter of public concern, [it] cannot be restricted simply because it is upsetting or arouses contempt. 'If there is a bedrock principle underlying the First Amendment, it is that the government may not prohibit the expression of an idea simply because society finds the idea itself offensive or disagreeable.'

"The jury here was instructed that it could hold Westboro liable for intentional infliction of emotional distress based on a finding that Westboro's picketing was 'outrageous.' 'Outrageousness,' however, is a highly malleable standard with 'an inherent subjectiveness about it which would allow a jury to impose liability on the basis of the jurors' tastes or views, or perhaps on the basis of their dislike of a particular expression.' In a case such as this, a jury is 'unlikely to be neutral with respect to the content of [the] speech,' posing 'a real danger of becoming an instrument for the suppression of . . . vehement, caustic, and sometimes unpleasan[t]' expression. Such a risk is unacceptable; 'in public debate [we] must tolerate insulting, and even outrageous, speech in order to provide adequate "breathing space" to the freedoms protected by the First Amendment.' [For] all these reasons, the jury verdict imposing tort liability on Westboro for intentional infliction of emotional distress must be set aside."

Justice Alito dissented: "Our profound national commitment to free and open debate is not a license for the vicious verbal assault that occurred in this case. [Phelps and Westboro] have strong opinions on certain moral, religious, and political issues, and the First Amendment ensures that they have almost limitless opportunities to express their views. They may write and distribute books, articles, and other texts; they may create and disseminate video and audio recordings; they may circulate petitions; they may speak to individuals and groups in public forums and in any private venue that wishes to accommodate them; they may picket peacefully in countless locations; they may appear on television and speak on the radio; they may post messages on the Internet and send out e-mails. And they may express their views in terms that are 'uninhibited,' 'vehement,' and 'caustic.' It does not follow, however, that they may intentionally inflict severe emotional injury on private persons at a time of intense emotional sensitivity by launching vicious verbal attacks that make no contribution to public debate. [I] think it is clear that the First Amendment does not entirely preclude liability for the intentional infliction of emotional distress by means of speech."

Suppose you are a state legislature and learn of the following events, which occur in your district: A gay teenager dies in a car accident and the members of the Westboro Baptist Church picket his funeral. Their speech is directed specifically at the parents of the boy, rather than at the general public. Their signs charge that the son died because he was gay, condemn the parents for failing to "correct" their son's homosexuality, and blame them for his death. Is it possible to draft a statute that is consistent with Snyder but that reaches this conduct? In the years since *Snyder*, many states have enacted "buffer-zone" laws that prohibit any picketing within a certain distance of a funeral within a certain time before and after the funeral. Are such laws constitutional? See Heyman, To Drink the Cup of Fury: Funeral Picketing, Public Discourse, and the First Amendment, 45 Conn. L. Rev. 101 (2012).

## C.  CLASSIFIED INFORMATION

### New York Times Co. v. United States; United States v. Washington Post Co.
403 U.S. 713 (1971)

[On June 12–14, 1971, the New York Times and, on June 18, the Washington Post published excerpts from a top-secret Defense Department study of the Vietnam War. The study, which was commissioned by Robert McNamara in 1967, filled forty-seven volumes and reviewed in great detail the formulation of U.S. policy toward Indochina, including military operations and secret diplomatic negotiations. The newspapers obtained the study, known popularly as the Pentagon Papers, from Daniel Ellsberg, a former Pentagon official. The government filed suit in federal district courts in New York and Washington, D.C., seeking to enjoin further publication of the materials, claiming that such publication would interfere with national security and would lead to the death of soldiers, the undermining of our alliances, the inability of our diplomats to negotiate, and the prolongation of the war. Between June 15 and June 23, the cases worked their way through the federal courts, and on June 26, the Supreme Court heard argument. On June 30, the Court issued its decision. Restraining orders remained in effect throughout the Court's deliberations.]

Per Curiam.

We granted certiorari in these cases in which the United States seeks to enjoin the New York Times and the Washington Post from publishing the contents of a classified study entitled "History of U.S. Decision-Making Process on Viet Nam Policy."

"Any system of prior restraints of expression comes to this Court bearing a heavy presumption against its constitutional validity." [The] Government "thus carries a heavy burden of showing justification for the imposition of such a restraint." [The] District Court for the Southern District of New York in the New York Times case and the District Court for the District of Columbia and the Court of Appeals for the District of Columbia Circuit in the Washington Post case held that the Government had not met that burden. We agree.

The judgment of the Court of Appeals for the District of Columbia Circuit is therefore affirmed. The order of the Court of Appeals for the Second Circuit is reversed and the case is remanded with directions to enter a judgment affirming the judgment of the District Court for the Southern District of New York. The stays entered June 25, 1971, by the Court are vacated. The judgments shall issue forthwith.

So ordered.

MR. JUSTICE BLACK, with whom MR. JUSTICE DOUGLAS joins, concurring. . . .

[Every] moment's continuance of the injunctions against these newspapers amounts to a flagrant, indefensible, and continuing violation of the First Amendment. [For] the first time in the 182 years since the founding of the Republic, the federal courts are asked to hold that the First Amendment does not mean what it says, but rather means that the Government can halt the publication of current news of vital importance to the people of this country. . . .

In the First Amendment the Founding Fathers gave the free press the protection it must have to fulfill its essential role in our democracy. The press was to serve the governed, not the governors. The Government's power to censor the press was abolished so that the press would remain forever free to censure the Government. The press was protected so that it could bare the secrets of government and inform the people. Only a free and unrestrained press can effectively expose deception in government. . . .

[We] are asked to hold that despite the First Amendment's emphatic command, the Executive Branch, the Congress, and the Judiciary can make laws enjoining publication of current news and abridging freedom of the press in the name of "national security." . . .

The word "security" is a broad, vague generality whose contours should not be invoked to abrogate the fundamental law embodied in the First Amendment. The guarding of military and diplomatic secrets at the expense of informed representative government provides no real security for our Republic.

MR. JUSTICE DOUGLAS, with whom MR. JUSTICE BLACK joins, concurring. . . .

These disclosures may have a serious impact. But that is no basis for sanctioning a previous restraint on the press. [The] dominant purpose of the First Amendment was to prohibit the widespread practice of governmental suppression of embarrassing information. It is common knowledge that the First Amendment was adopted against the widespread use of the common law of seditious libel to punish the dissemination of material that is embarrassing to the powers-that-be. [A] debate of large proportions goes on in the Nation over our posture in Vietnam. That debate antedated the disclosure of the contents of the present documents. The latter are highly relevant to the debate in progress.

Secrecy in government is fundamentally anti-democratic, perpetuating bureaucratic errors. Open debate and discussion of public issues are vital to our national health. On public questions there should be "uninhibited, robust, and wide-open" debate. . . .

The stays in these cases that have been in effect for more than a week constitute a flouting of the principles of the First Amendment. . . .

MR. JUSTICE BRENNAN, concurring.

The error that has pervaded these cases from the outset was the granting of any injunctive relief whatsoever, interim or otherwise. The entire thrust of the Government's claim throughout these cases has been that publication of the material sought to be enjoined "could," or "might," or "may" prejudice the national interest in various ways. But the First Amendment tolerates absolutely no prior judicial restraints of the press predicated upon surmise or conjecture that untoward consequences may result. Our cases, it is true, have indicated that there is a single, extremely narrow class of cases in which the First Amendment's ban on prior judicial restraint may be overridden. Our cases have thus far indicated that such cases may arise only when the Nation "is at war," [*Schenck*], during which times "[n]o one would question but that a government might prevent actual obstruction to its recruiting service or the publication of the sailing dates of transports or the number and location of troops." Near v. Minnesota, [Chapter III.B, infra]. Even if the present world situation were assumed to be tantamount to a time of war, or if the power of presently available armaments would justify even in peacetime the suppression of information that would set in motion a nuclear holocaust, in neither of these actions has the Government presented or even alleged that publication of items from or based upon the material at issue would cause the happening of an event of that nature. "[T]he chief purpose of [the First Amendment's]

---

* Freedman v. Maryland, 380 U.S. 51 (1965), and similar cases regarding temporary restraints of allegedly obscene materials are not in point. For those cases rest upon the proposition that "obscenity is not protected by the freedoms of speech and press." [Here] there is no question but that the material sought to be suppressed is within the protection of the First Amendment; the only question is whether, notwithstanding that fact, its publication may be enjoined for a time because of the presence of an overwhelming national interest.

guaranty [is] to prevent previous restraints upon publication." [*Near.*] Thus, only governmental allegation and proof that publication must inevitably, directly, and immediately cause the occurrence of an event kindred to imperiling the safety of a transport already at sea can support even the issuance of an interim restraining order. [Every] restraint issued in this case, whatever its form, has violated the First Amendment — and not less so because that restraint was justified as necessary to afford the courts an opportunity to examine the claim more thoroughly. Unless and until the Government has clearly made out its case, the First Amendment commands that no injunction may issue.

MR. JUSTICE STEWART, with whom MR. JUSTICE WHITE joins, concurring.

In the governmental structure created by our Constitution, the Executive is endowed with enormous power in the two related areas of national defense and international relations. This power, largely unchecked by the Legislative and Judicial branches, has been pressed to the very hilt since the advent of the nuclear missile age. . . .

In the absence of the governmental checks and balances present in other areas of our national life, the only effective restraint upon executive policy and power in the areas of national defense and international affairs may lie in an enlightened citizenry — in an informed and critical public opinion which alone can here protect the values of democratic government . . .

Yet it is elementary that the successful conduct of international diplomacy and the maintenance of an effective national defense require both confidentiality and secrecy. Other nations can hardly deal with this Nation in an atmosphere of mutual trust unless they can be assured that their confidences will be kept. And within our own executive departments, the development of considered and intelligent international policies would be impossible if those charged with their formulation could not communicate with each other freely, frankly, and in confidence. In the area of basic national defense the frequent need for absolute secrecy is, of course, self-evident.

I think there can be but one answer to this dilemma, if dilemma it be. The responsibility must be where the power is. If the Constitution gives the Executive a large degree of unshared power in the conduct of foreign affairs and the maintenance of our national defense, then under the Constitution the Executive must have the largely unshared duty to determine and preserve the degree of internal security necessary to exercise that power successfully. [It] is clear to me that it is the constitutional duty of the Executive — as a matter of sovereign prerogative and not as a matter of law as the courts know law — through the promulgation and enforcement of executive regulations, to protect the confidentiality necessary to carry out its responsibilities in the fields of international relations and national defense.

This is not to say that Congress and the courts have no role to play. Undoubtedly Congress has the power to enact specific and appropriate criminal laws to protect government property and preserve government secrets. . . .

*If they want to restrict then put laws in place*

But in the cases before us we are asked neither to construe specific regulations nor to apply specific laws. We are asked, instead, to perform a function that the Constitution gave to the Executive, not the Judiciary. We are asked, quite simply, to prevent the publication by two newspapers of material that the Executive Branch insists should not, in the national interest, be published. I am convinced that the Executive is correct with respect to some of the documents involved. But I cannot say that disclosure of any of them will surely result in direct, immediate, and irreparable damage to our Nation or its people. That being so, there can under the First Amendment be but one judicial resolution of the issues before us. I join the judgments of the Court.

MR. JUSTICE WHITE, with whom MR. JUSTICE STEWART joins, concurring.

I concur in today's judgments, but only because of the concededly extraordinary protection against prior restraints enjoyed by the press under our constitutional system. I do not say that in no circumstances would the First Amendment permit an injunction against publishing information about government plans or operations. Nor, after examining the materials the Government characterizes as the most sensitive and destructive, can I deny that revelation of these documents will do substantial damage to public interests. Indeed, I am confident that their disclosure will have that result. But I nevertheless agree that the United States has not satisfied the very heavy burden that it must meet to warrant an injunction against publication in these cases, at least in the absence of express and appropriately limited congressional authorization for prior restraints in circumstances such as these.

The Government's position is simply stated: The responsibility of the Executive for the conduct of the foreign affairs and for the security of the Nation is so basic that the President is entitled to an injunction against publication of a newspaper story whenever he can convince a court that the information to be revealed threatens "grave and irreparable" injury to the public interest; and the injunction should issue whether or not the material to be published is classified, whether or not publication would be lawful under relevant criminal statutes enacted by Congress, and regardless of the circumstances by which the newspaper came into possession of the information.

*Too Broad →*

At least in the absence of legislation by Congress, based on its own investigations and findings, I am quite unable to agree that the inherent powers of the Executive and the courts reach so far as to authorize remedies having such sweeping potential for inhibiting publications by the press. . . .

[Prior] restraints require an unusually heavy justification under the First Amendment; but failure by the Government to justify prior restraints does not measure its constitutional entitlement to a conviction for criminal publication. That the Government mistakenly chose to proceed by injunction does not mean that it could not successfully proceed in another way. . . .

The Criminal Code contains numerous provisions potentially relevant to these cases. [Section] 793(e)[8] makes it a criminal act for any unauthorized possessor of a document "relating to the national defense" either (1) willfully to communicate or cause to be communicated that document to any person not entitled to receive it or (2) willfully to retain the document and fail to deliver it to an officer of the United States entitled to receive it. . . .

It is thus clear that Congress has addressed itself to the problems of protecting the security of the country and the national defense from unauthorized disclosure of potentially damaging information. [It] has not, however, authorized the injunctive remedy against threatened publication. It has apparently been satisfied to rely on criminal sanctions and their deterrent effect on the responsible as well as the irresponsible press. I am not, of course, saying that either of these newspapers has yet committed a crime or that either would commit a crime if it published all the material now in its possession. That matter must await resolution in the context of a criminal proceeding if one is instituted by the United States. . . .

MR. JUSTICE MARSHALL, concurring.

I believe the ultimate issue in these cases [is] whether this Court or the Congress has the power to make law. . . .

The problem here is whether in these particular cases the Executive Branch has authority to invoke the equity jurisdiction of the courts to protect what it believes to be the national interest. [In] some situations it may be that under whatever inherent powers the Government may have, as well as the implicit authority derived from the President's mandate to conduct foreign affairs and to act as Commander in Chief, there is a basis for the invocation of the equity jurisdiction of this Court as an aid to prevent the publication of material damaging to "national security," however that term may be defined.

It would, however, be utterly inconsistent with the concept of separation of powers for this Court to use its power of contempt to prevent behavior that Congress has specifically declined to prohibit. [The] Constitution provides that Congress shall make laws, the President execute laws, and courts interpret

---

8. Section 793(e) of 18 U.S.C. provides that:

(e) Whoever having unauthorized possession of, access to, or control over any document, writing, code book, signal book, sketch, photograph, photographic negative, blueprint, plan, map, model, instrument, appliance, or note relating to the national defense, or information relating to the national defense which information the possessor has reason to believe could be used to the injury of the United States or to the advantage of any foreign nation, willfully communicates, delivers, transmits or causes to be communicated, delivered, or transmitted, or attempts to communicate, deliver, transmit or cause to be communicated, delivered, or transmitted the same to any person not entitled to receive it, or willfully retains the same and fails to deliver it to the officer or employee of the United States entitled to receive it; is guilty of an offense punishable by 10 years in prison, a $10,000 fine, or both.

laws. [It] did not provide for government by injunction in which the courts and the Executive Branch can "make law" without regard to the action of Congress. [It] is clear that Congress has specifically rejected passing legislation that would have clearly given the President the power he seeks here and made the current activity of the newspapers unlawful. When Congress specifically declines to make conduct unlawful it is not for this Court to redecide those issues — to overrule Congress. . . .

MR. CHIEF JUSTICE BURGER, dissenting.

[In] these cases, the imperative of a free and unfettered press comes into collision with another imperative, the effective functioning of a complex modern government and specifically the effective exercise of certain constitutional powers of the Executive. Only those who view the First Amendment as an absolute in all circumstances — a view I respect, but reject — can find such cases as these to be simple or easy.

These cases are not simple for another and more immediate reason. We do not know the facts of the cases. No District Judge knew all the facts. No Court of Appeals judge knew all the facts. No member of this Court knows all the facts. . . .

I suggest we are in this posture because these cases have been conducted in unseemly haste. [It] seems reasonably clear now that the haste precluded reasonable and deliberate judicial treatment of these cases and was not warranted. The precipitate action of this Court aborting trials not yet completed is not the kind of judicial conduct that ought to attend the disposition of a great issue. . . .

It is not disputed that the Times has had unauthorized possession of the documents for three to four months, during which it has had its expert analysts studying them, presumably digesting them and preparing the material for publication. During all of this time, the Times, presumably in its capacity as trustee of the public's "right to know," has held up publication for purposes it considered proper and thus public knowledge was delayed. No doubt this was for a good reason; the analysis of 7,000 pages of complex material drawn from a vastly greater volume of material would inevitably take time and the writing of good news stories takes time. But why should the United States Government, from whom this information was illegally acquired by someone, along with all the counsel, trial judges, and appellate judges be placed under needless pressure? After these months of deferral, the alleged "right to know" has somehow and suddenly become a right that must be vindicated instanter. . . .

I would affirm the Court of Appeals for the Second Circuit and allow the District Court to complete the trial aborted by our grant of certiorari, meanwhile preserving the status quo in the Post case. I would direct that the District Court on remand give priority to the Times case to the exclusion of all other business of that court but I would not set arbitrary deadlines. . . .

We all crave speedier judicial processes but when judges are pressured as in these cases the result is a parody of the judicial function.

MR. JUSTICE HARLAN, with whom THE CHIEF JUSTICE and MR. JUSTICE BLACK-
MUN join, dissenting. . . .

With all respect, I consider that the Court has been almost irresponsibly
feverish in dealing with these cases.

Both the Court of Appeals for the Second Circuit and the Court of Appeals
for the District of Columbia Circuit rendered judgment on June 23. The New
York Times' petition for certiorari, its motion for accelerated consideration
thereof, and its application for interim relief were filed in this Court on June 24
at about 11 A.M. The application of the United States for interim relief in the
*Post* case was also filed here on June 24 at about 7:15 P.M. This Court's order
setting a hearing before us on June 26 at 11 A.M., a course which I joined only to
avoid the possibility of even more peremptory action by the Court, was issued
less than 24 hours before. The record in the *Post* case was filed with the Clerk
shortly before 1 P.M. on June 25; the record in the *Times* case did not arrive
until 7 or 8 o'clock that same night. The briefs of the parties were received less
than two hours before argument on June 26.

This frenzied train of events took place in the name of the presumption
against prior restraints created by the First Amendment. Due regard for the
extraordinarily important and difficult questions involved in these litigations
should have led the Court to shun such a precipitate timetable. . . .

Forced as I am to reach the merits of these cases, I dissent from the opinion
and judgments of the Court. [It] is plain to me that the scope of the judicial
function in passing upon the activities of the Executive Branch of the Government in the field of foreign affairs is very narrowly restricted. This view is, I
think, dictated by the concept of separation of powers upon which our
constitutional system rests. . . .

The power to evaluate the "pernicious influence" of premature disclosure is
not, however, lodged in the Executive alone. I agree that, in performance of its
duty to protect the values of the First Amendment against political pressures,
the judiciary must review the initial Executive determination to the point of
satisfying itself that the subject matter of the dispute does lie within the proper
compass of the President's foreign relations power. Constitutional considerations forbid "a complete abandonment of judicial control." [Moreover], the
judiciary may properly insist that the determination that disclosure of the
subject matter would irreparably impair the national security be made by
the head of the Executive Department concerned — here the Secretary of
State or the Secretary of Defense — after actual personal consideration by
that officer. . . .

But in my judgment the judiciary may not properly go beyond these two
inquiries and redetermine for itself the probable impact of disclosure on the
national security.

[T]he very nature of executive decisions as to foreign policy is political, not
judicial. Such decisions are wholly confided by our Constitution to the political

departments of the government, Executive and Legislative. They are delicate, complex, and involve large elements of prophecy. They are and should be undertaken only by those directly responsible to the people whose welfare they advance or imperil. They are decisions of a kind for which the Judiciary has neither aptitude, facilities nor responsibility and which has long been held to belong in the domain of political power not subject to judicial intrusion or inquiry.

Chicago & Southern Air Lines v. Waterman Steamship Corp., 333 U.S. 103, 111 (1948) (Jackson, J.).

Even if there is some room for the judiciary to override the executive determination, it is plain that the scope of review must be exceedingly narrow. I can see no indication in the opinions of either the District Court or the Court of Appeals in the Post litigation that the conclusions of the Executive were given even the deference owing to an administrative agency, much less that owing to a co-equal branch of the Government operating within the field of its constitutional prerogative. . . .

Pending further hearings in each case conducted under the appropriate ground rules, I would continue the restraints on publication. I cannot believe that the doctrine prohibiting prior restraints reaches to the point of preventing courts from maintaining the status quo long enough to act responsibly in matters of such national importance as those involved here.

MR. JUSTICE BLACKMUN, dissenting.

The First Amendment, after all, is only one part of an entire Constitution. Article II of the great document vests in the Executive Branch primary power over the conduct of foreign affairs and places in that branch the responsibility for the Nation's safety. Each provision of the Constitution is important, and I cannot subscribe to a doctrine of unlimited absolutism for the First Amendment at the cost of downgrading other provisions. First Amendment absolutism has never commanded a majority of this Court. [What] is needed here is a weighing, upon properly developed standards, of the broad right of the press to print and of the very narrow right of the Government to prevent. Such standards are not yet developed. The parties here are in disagreement as to what those standards should be. But even the newspapers concede that there are situations where restraint is in order and is constitutional. . . .

I therefore would remand these cases to be developed expeditiously, of course, but on a schedule permitting the orderly presentation of evidence from both sides. . . .

The Court, however, decides the cases today the other way. I therefore add one final comment.

I strongly urge, and sincerely hope, that these two newspapers will be fully aware of their ultimate responsibilities to the United States of America. Judge Wilkey, dissenting in the District of Columbia case [concluded] that there were a number of examples of documents that, if in the possession of the Post, and if published, "could clearly result in great harm to the nation," and he defined "harm" to mean "the death of soldiers, the destruction of alliances, the greatly increased difficulty of negotiation with our enemies, the inability of our diplomats to negotiate. . . ." I, for one, have now been able to give at least some cursory study not only to the affidavits, but to the material itself. I regret to say that from this examination I fear that Judge Wilkey's statements have possible foundation. I therefore share his concern. I hope that damage has not already been done. If, however, damage has been done, and if, with the Court's action today, these newspapers proceed to publish the critical documents and there results therefrom "the death of soldiers, the destruction of alliances, the greatly increased difficulty of negotiations with our enemies, the inability of our diplomats to negotiate," to which list I might add the factors of prolongation of the war and of further delay in the freeing of United States prisoners, then the Nation's people will know where the responsibility for these sad consequences rests.

### Note: The Pentagon Papers Controversy

1. *Prior restraint.* The Court emphasized repeatedly that the injunction in the New York Times was a "prior restraint," and that a prior restraint bears a special "presumption against its constitutional validity." Why is an injunction more threatening to the values underlying the first amendment than a criminal prosecution for publication of the same material? For analysis of the doctrine of prior restraint, see Chapter III.B infra.

2. *The Pentagon Papers: too much haste?* Publication of the Pentagon Papers offered the public valuable insights into the processes of government decision-making involving the Vietnam War. Moreover, by disclosing that the Eisenhower administration's attempt to undermine the new communist regime in North Vietnam directly involved the United States in the breakdown of the 1954 Geneva settlement, that the Johnson administration took steps toward waging an overt war against North Vietnam a full year before it disclosed the depth of its involvement to the American public, and that the infiltration of men and arms from North Vietnam into South Vietnam was more important as a means of publicly justifying our involvement than for its military effects, publication of the Papers sharpened the public's understanding of the war and altered public attitudes toward a central issue of American policy.

At the same time, however, one must ask whether, as the dissenters charged, the Court acted with "unseemly haste" in permitting publication of the documents. In light of the extraordinary seriousness of the government's contentions and the almost overwhelming length of the study, should the Court have permitted the injunctions to remain in effect pending a more thorough judicial determination of the risks? Was the Court, in other words, playing fast and loose with the national security? Consider in this regard Justice Brennan's argument that the very notion of an injunction against expression pending final resolution of the controversy is inherently incompatible with the first amendment.

3. *The Pentagon Papers: injunctions and the national security.* Note that the per curiam opinion did not define the precise circumstances in which a court may enjoin the publication of information relating to the national security. Does the standard enunciated by Justice Stewart, that there must be proof that the disclosure will "surely result in direct, immediate, and irreparable damage to our Nation or its people," come closest to representing the view of the Court? Why was that standard not satisfied in the *Pentagon Papers* case?

4. *The Pentagon Papers: criminal prosecution?* Suppose the New York Times and the Washington Post had been criminally prosecuted for their publication of the Pentagon Papers. What standard should govern? Is section 793(e) of the Federal Code, reproduced in footnote 8 of Justice White's opinion, constitutional? Should disclosure of historical information be absolutely protected? For such an argument, see Volokh, Freedom of Speech, Permissible Tailoring and Transcending Strict Scrutiny, 144 U. Pa. L. Rev. 2417, 2425–2431 (1996).

Suppose the government claimed in this hypothetical criminal prosecution that the newspapers' disclosure of some of the historical information weakened our alliances, increased the difficulty of negotiating with other nations, prolonged the war, and delayed the release of American prisoners of war. Could the newspapers constitutionally be convicted? Are these sorts of issues, as Justice Harlan suggested, beyond the competence of courts? Consider the following arguments: (a) The Executive may consciously or unconsciously err on the side of suppression in order to prevent the revelation of potentially embarrassing information. (b) Newspapers, eager to boost sales, may undervalue the interest in national security.

In considering the Pentagon Papers controversy, recall the problem of the *true* cry of "fire." Even though the true cry may create a clear and present danger that some persons will be injured in the dash for the exit, the benefits of the speech may outweigh the harm. Do the decisions examined in this section, taken together, "leave little doubt that, except in cases involving imminent national military catastrophe, the Court will not permit previous restraints upon, or subsequent punishment for, publication in a mass medium of accurate information that the publisher has lawfully acquired"? Cox, Foreword: Freedom of Expression in the Burger Court, 94 Harv. L. Rev. 1, 17 (1980).

5. *Disclosure of the NSA surveillance program.* In January 2006, the New York Times publicly disclosed that President George W. Bush had secretly authorized the National Security Agency to intercept international telephone calls and e-mails between individuals inside the United States and individuals outside the United States whenever the NSA had "a reasonable basis to conclude that one party to the communication is a member of al Qaeda, affiliated with al Qaeda, or a member of an organization affiliated with al Qaeda, or

working in support of al Qaeda." Critics of the program charged that it violated the Foreign Intelligence Surveillance Act of 1978, which prohibits such surveillance in the absence of probable cause and a warrant. Defenders of the program argued that FISA violates the inherent authority of the "President as commander in chief of the Army and Navy."

Attorney General Alberto Gonzales raised the possibility that the United States might prosecute the New York Times for violating the Espionage Act of 1917. Gonzales maintained that the disclosure of the program seriously undermined the national security by alerting terrorists to its existence. Suppose the United States had indicted the New York Times under section 793(e). If you were representing the New York Times, what standard would you argue should apply in deciding whether the publication was protected by the first amendment? Note that the United States has never criminally prosecuted the press for publishing secret government information.

Suppose that in 2005 the NSA secretly broke the al Qaeda code, enabling the United States to thwart several terrorist attacks. Suppose further that in 2008 a newspaper published this information, with the result that the terrorists changed their cipher. If you were an attorney working in the Justice Department, would you recommend prosecution of the newspaper?

Consider Stone, Government Secrecy v. Freedom of the Press, 1 Harv. L. & Pol'y. Rev. 185, 203–204 (2007):

> [The] reason for protecting the publication of the Pentagon Papers was not only that the disclosure would not "surely result in direct, immediate, and irreparable damage" to the nation, but also that the Pentagon Papers made a meaningful contribution to informed public discourse. Suppose a newspaper accurately reports that American troops in Iraq recently murdered twenty insurgents in cold blood. As a result of this publication, insurgents quite predictably kidnap and murder twenty Americans. Could the newspaper constitutionally be punished for disclosing the initial massacre? I would argue that it could not. Even if there were a clear and present danger that the retaliation would follow, the information is simply too important to the American people to punish its publication.
>
> What this suggests is that to justify the criminal punishment of the press for publishing classified information, the government must prove that the publisher knew that (a) it was publishing classified information, (b) the publication of which would result in likely, imminent, and serious harm to the national security, *and* (c) the publication of which would not meaningfully contribute to public debate.

In Posen, The Leaky Leviathan: Why the Government Condemns and Condones Unlawful Disclosures of Information, 127 Harv. L. Rev. 512, 515 (2013), the author argues that

> [most] components of the executive branch have never prioritized criminal, civil, or administrative enforcement against leakers; that a nuanced set of

informal social controls has come to supplement, and nearly supplant, the formal disciplinary scheme; that much of what we call leaking occurs in a gray area between full authorization and no [authorization]; that the executive's toleration of these disclosures is a rational, power-enhancing strategy and not simply a product of prosecutorial limitations, a feature, not a bug, of the system; and that to untangle these dynamics is to illuminate important facets of presidential power, bureaucratic governance, and the national security state in America today.

If this analysis is correct, does the occasional criminal prosecution of selected leakers pose a constitutional problem?

For an historical analysis of government secrecy and an argument that "by seeking to keep secret so much for so long, the secrecy system cheapens and undermines our vital secrets," see F. Schwarz, Jr., Democracy in the Dark: The Seduction of Government Secrecy (2015). See also H. Kitrosser, Reclaiming Accountability: Transparency, Executive Power, and the U.S. Constitution (2015) (tying excessive secrecy to constitutional theories that defend broad executive power).

6. *Restricting speech because it was obtained illegally.* Suppose a reporter gains access to confidential government information through an unlawful wiretap of a senator. Can the reporter be criminally punished for the wiretap? Can her newspaper be prohibited from publishing the information? Suppose the newspaper learns of the information as the result of a third party's unlawful act, such as theft of a document or an unlawful wiretap. Can the newspaper be enjoined, criminally punished, or held civilly liable for invasion of privacy for publishing the information? See Bartnicki v. Vopper, 532 U.S. 514 (2001), in which the Court held that federal and state anti-wiretap statutes cannot constitutionally be applied to a radio station that broadcasts the tape of an unlawfully intercepted telephone call, where the subject of the call was a matter of public concern and the broadcaster did not participate directly in the unlawful wiretap, even though the broadcaster knew that the material had been obtained unlawfully. Does this make any sense?

7. *Public employees.* The Court suggested in *Pentagon Papers* that the state may keep information from the press by prohibiting government employees from disclosing that information. Suppose the government had prosecuted Daniel Ellsberg for releasing the Pentagon Papers. Should the government have greater authority to prohibit its employees from disclosing confidential information to the press than to prohibit the press from publishing such information once it comes into its hands? If an ultimate concern of the first amendment is the "public's right to know," isn't that right undermined just as much by restrictions on the press's ability to obtain information as by restrictions on its ability to publish?

Consider Snepp v. United States, 444 U.S. 507 (1980), in which Snepp, a former CIA agent, published a book about certain CIA activities in South

Vietnam in violation of an express condition of his employment contract with the CIA in which he promised not to publish "any information or material relating to the Agency, its activities or intelligence activities generally, either during or after the term of [his] employment, [without] specific prior approval by the Agency." The Court, in a six-to-three decision, held that Snepp "breached a fiduciary obligation and that the proceeds of his breach are impressed with a constructive trust." The Court explained that the "Government has a compelling interest in protecting both the secrecy of information important to our national security and the appearance of confidentiality so essential to the effective operation of our foreign intelligence service." The Court concluded that the "agreement that Snepp signed is a reasonable means for protecting this vital interest."

Consider the following views:

a. The public employee gains access to confidential government information only by virtue of her employment. Thus, for government to prohibit her disclosure of such information does not limit any first amendment right the employee would have but for such employment.

b. Easterbrook, Insider Trading, Secret Agents, Evidentiary Privileges, and the Production of Information, 1981 Sup. Ct. Rev. 309, 345–347:

> Snepp [struck] a bargain. He learned of the CIA's activities by agreeing to limit his speech about them. [So] long as he enters into the agreement without fraud or coercion, he has made a judgment that he is better off with the agreement (and its restraints) than without; he can hardly complain that his rights have been reduced. [Constitutional] rights are waived every day.

c. Sunstein, Government Control of Information, 74 Cal. L. Rev. 889, 915 (1986):

> [The] first amendment is largely a structural provision. [Its] purpose is not only to protect private autonomy, but also to preserve a certain form of government. Citizens may often find it in their interest to give up rights of free speech in exchange for benefits from government. For many, these rights are not extremely valuable as individual possessions. But if government is permitted to obtain enforceable waivers, the aggregate effect may be considerable, and the deliberative processes of the public will be skewed. [Waivers] of first amendment rights thus affect people other than government employees, and effects on third parties are a classic reason to proscribe waivers. The analogy [is] to government purchases of voting rights, which are impermissible even if voters willingly assent.

d. A. Bickel, The Morality of Consent 79–82 (1975):

> The government is entitled to keep things private and will attain as much privacy as it can get away with politically by guarding its privacy internally; but with few exceptions involving the highest probability of very grave consequences, it may

not do so effectively. It is severely limited as to means, being restricted, by and large, to enforcing security at the source. [Yet] the power to arrange security at the source, looked at in itself, is great, and if it were nowhere countervailed it would be quite frightening. [But] there *is* countervailing power. The press, by which is meant anybody, not only the institutionalized print and electronic press, can be prevented from publishing only in extreme and quite dire circumstances. [It] is a disorderly situation surely. But if we ordered it we would have to sacrifice one of two contending values — privacy or public discourse — which are ultimately irreconcilable. If we should let the government censor as well as withhold, that would be too much dangerous power, and too much privacy. If we should allow the government neither to censor nor to withhold, that would provide for too little privacy of decision-making and too much power in the press.

e. Sunstein, supra, at 901–902, 904:

[Bickel's] equilibrium theory is vulnerable because it does not address three critical matters: the actual incentives of the press and the government; the respective power of the countervailing forces; and what the proper baseline for evaluating outcomes should be. [The] equilibrium theory [is] impressionistic and relies on premises that are both unsupported and unlikely. The sharp distinction between rights of access and rights of publication thus rests on unstable foundations.

In deciding whether government may constitutionally prohibit an employee's disclosure of particular "confidential" information, should courts consider not only the potential danger but also the potential value of the disclosure? For example, may an employee disclose "classified" information if it reveals a substantial abuse of power?

8. *Snowden*. If Edward Snowden returns to the United States, could he be prosecuted and convicted, consistent with the First Amendment, for disclosing to journalists and thus to the world massive amounts of classified information about previously secret NSA surveillance programs? Consider the following positions:

a. Snowden accepted a position of trust in his relation to the government. He did not have to accept his job, but he did. A clear condition of that job was his voluntary agreement not to disclose any classified information. That agreement is binding. Period.

b. An individual government employee should never have the authority, on his own say, to override the judgments of the elected representatives of the American people and to decide for the nation that classified information should be disclosed to friends and foes alike. The question is who gets to decide when classified information should be made public. It should not be any tomdickandharry government employee or private contractor with a security clearance who thinks he knows better than the President, the Congress, and the courts about how best to protect the nation's security.

c. Suppose the disclosure of the previously secret programs renders them ineffective in the future, thus seriously damaging the nation's ability to ferret out possible terrorist plots. Should Snowden nonetheless have a first amendment defense if, upon learning about the previously secret programs, the public opposes them as a matter of policy? If the programs are found to have been illegal? If some of the programs he disclosed were illegal and others were legal?

d. Does your view on any of these positions change if the prosecution is directed against the newspaper publishing Snowden's revelations rather than against Snowden himself?

9. *"Technical" information.* Suppose, in addition to general historical information, the Pentagon Papers had disclosed blueprints of secret military weapons, the identity of covert agents abroad, or secret codes. Is the disclosure of such information more readily subject to restriction? See Symposium, National Security and the First Amendment, 26 Wm. & Mary L. Rev. 715 (1985). Do you agree that "the law need not treat differently the crime of one man who sells a bomb to terrorists and that of another who publishes an instructional manual for terrorists on how to build their own bombs out of old Volkswagen parts"? L. Tribe, American Constitutional Law 837 (2d ed. 1988). For analysis of the constitutional status of technical data, see Sunstein, supra, at 905–912.

10. *Facts and the First Amendment.* Note that in many cases the government is attempting to restrict the dissemination of facts rather than opinions. The seminal conception of the first amendment was about the "marketplace of ideas." How do facts fit into this marketplace? Should government efforts to restrict the dissemination of facts be treated the same way as government efforts to restrict the dissemination of ideas? In addition to the cases in this section, consider also the following: (a) an anti-abortion group publishes on its Web site the names and addresses of abortion providers; (b) a newspaper publishes the name of a rape victim; (c) a reporter discloses the names of covert American agents in Iran. See Bhagwat, Details: Specific Facts and the First Amendment, 86 So. Cal. L. Rev. 1 (2012).

### Note: The Progressive Controversy

In February 1979, Howard Morland, a freelance writer, completed an article for The Progressive magazine, entitled The H-Bomb Secret — How We Got It, Why We're Telling It. The article, which was based on information contained in publicly available literature and Morland's interviews of various scientists and government officials, was designed to demonstrate the ineffectiveness and undesirability of a government system of classification and secrecy. Uncertain of the potential legal consequences of publication, The Progressive delivered a copy of the manuscript to the Department of Energy

(DOE), requesting verification of its "technical accuracy." Officials in the DOE determined that, although Morland had relied on no classified documents, the article nonetheless contained information that the Atomic Energy Act required to be classified as "restricted data." They therefore requested The Progressive not to publish the article without first permitting government officials to work with the magazine to recast the manuscript to eliminate the restricted data. The Progressive informed the DOE that it intended to publish the article without alteration.

The following day, March 8, the United States filed suit in federal district court, seeking to enjoin publication of the restricted data. The United States maintained that the suit was authorized by the Atomic Energy Act, which authorized injunctive relief to prohibit any person from disclosing restricted data, defined in the act as including any data concerning "design, manufacture, or utilization of atomic weapons," "with reason to believe such data will be utilized to injure the United States or to secure an advantage to any foreign nation." On March 9, the court issued a temporary restraining order against publication of the article. On March 26, the court held a hearing on the issuance of a preliminary injunction.

After considering several complex affidavits submitted by experts on both sides, the court found that at least some of the information in the article may not have been in the public domain. More important, "the article provides a more comprehensive, accurate, and detailed analysis of the overall construction and operation of a thermonuclear weapon than any publication to date in the public literature." The court found further that the article does not "provide a 'do-it-yourself' guide for the hydrogen bomb," but "could possibly provide sufficient information to allow a medium size nation to move faster in developing a hydrogen weapon" and "could provide a ticket to by-pass blind alleys."

The court granted the preliminary injunction. United States v. The Progressive, Inc., 467 F. Supp. 990 (W.D. Wis. 1979). The court noted that, although the purpose of the article was to "alert the people of this country to the false illusion of security created by the government's futile efforts at secrecy" and to "provide the people with needed information to make informed decisions on an urgent issue of public concern," it could "find no plausible reason why the public needs to know the technical details about hydrogen bomb construction to carry on an informed debate on this issue." Moreover, the information at issue, the court observed, deals "with the most destructive weapon in the history of mankind," and an erroneous decision against the government could "involve human life itself and on such an awesome scale." In light of this "disparity of risk," the court held that the injunction was warranted. The court distinguished the *Pentagon Papers* decision on the grounds that (1) the information disclosed in that case involved "historical data relating to events that occurred some three to twenty years previously"; (2) "no cogent arguments were advanced by the government" in that case "as to why the article affected national security except that publication might cause some embarrassment to the United States"; and (3) there was no specific statutory authorization of the injunction in that case.

The government's suit against The Progressive was dismissed on October 1, 1979, while pending in the U.S. Court of Appeals for the Seventh Circuit, because similar information concerning the construction of the hydrogen bomb was published independently by others. See generally Powe, The H-Bomb Injunction, 61 U. Colo. L. Rev. 55 (1990).

Suppose a terrorist posts on the Internet instructions on how to make out of common household materials a bomb that is sufficiently powerful to destroy a large building. Can this be prohibited?

Consider also Haig v. Agee, 453 U.S. 280 (1981), in which the Court upheld the revocation of Agee's passport because he engaged in activities abroad that caused "serious damage to the national security." Specifically, Agee, a former employee of the Central Intelligence Agency, engaged in a campaign "to expose CIA officers and agents and to take the measures necessary to drive them out of the countries where they are operating." Although Agee did not expressly incite "anyone to commit murder," there was evidence that his disclosures resulted in "episodes of violence against the persons and organizations identified." The Court rejected Agee's claim that the passport revocation violated his rights under the first amendment: "Long ago, [this] Court recognized that 'No one would question but that a government might prevent actual obstruction to its recruiting service or the publication of the sailing dates of transports or the number and location of troops.'[*Near,* Chapter III.B, infra.] Agee's disclosures [have] the declared purpose of obstructing intelligence operations and the recruiting of personnel. They are clearly not protected by the Constitution."

Is *Agee* consistent with the *Pentagon Papers* decision? Are Agee's disclosures "not protected" because they consisted of "technical," rather than "historical," information? Because they were designed to effect change not through the political process but by directly obstructing the operations of government? Consider the constitutionality of the Intelligence Identities Protection Act, 50 U.S.C. §421 (1982), which prohibits any person "with reason to believe that such activities would impair or impede the foreign intelligence activities of the United States, [to disclose] any information that identifies an individual as a covert agent, [if the disclosure is part of a] pattern of activities intended to identify or expose covert action."

Consider also the Arms Export Control Act, 22 U.S.C. §2778 (1982), which authorizes compilation of a list of items that may not be exported without a license from the State Department. This list includes not only physical objects but also information "that can be used or adapted for use" in the production, operation, or maintenance of the armaments listed and "any technology which advances the state of the art or establishes a new art in any area of significant military applicability." Export of technical data is defined to apply to disclosure to foreign nationals in the United States, including disclosure through participation in symposia.

### Note: The WikiLeaks Controversy

WikiLeaks is an international online organization created by Julian Assange. It publishes submissions of classified data from anonymous sources. In November 2010, WikiLeaks collaborated with major global media organizations to release thousands of classified U.S. State Department diplomatic cables allegedly leaked to WikiLeaks by Army Private Bradley Manning. The cables included revelations of the views of American diplomats relating to such matters as the Middle East peace process, nuclear disarmament, actions in the War on Terror, climate change, and U.S. intelligence and counterintelligence activities.

Floyd Abrams was one of the lawyers who argued the *Pentagon Papers* case for the New York Times. Consider his views, expressed in a 2011 speech, about WikiLeaks:

> In making public 77,000 U.S. confidential military reports from Afghanistan, [WikiLeaks] included over 100 names of confidential Afghan sources of information to our nation, putting them at risk of retaliation by the Taliban. [There] are simply too many examples of WikiLeaks' having released materials of significant harm with only the slightest potential public benefit. There was the release, for example, of a classified cable that listed facilities around the world whose disruption, not to say destruction, would threaten American security. There was, as well, the release of a classified report describing the radio frequency that [American jammers in Iraq] used to cut off signals to remotely detonated explosives. The report gives information, quite specific in nature, of how the jammers function and which frequencies they stop. When criticized for releasing the classified document which related to some jammers then still in use, Mr. Assange responded by saying "WikiLeaks represents whistleblowers in the same way that lawyers represent their clients — fairly and impartially. Our 'job' is to safely and impartially conduct the whistleblower's message to the public, not to inject our own nationality or beliefs." [If WikiLeaks] is nothing more or less than a conduit for the transmission of secrets from sources to the public [then] it is not engaged in journalism. . . . Consider [that] Mr. Assange has acknowledged that [before releasing 77,000 classified documents,] he and his colleagues had *read* only 2,000 of them. [My] point is not that WikiLeaks has not played some useful role. It has. But it has too often behaved recklessly. . . .

In such circumstances, can Manning, Assange, and WikiLeaks be criminally punished for their actions?

## Note: Dangerous Ideas and Information — Final Thoughts

In what circumstances, if any, may government, consonant with the first amendment, restrict speech of "high" first amendment value because, if left unchecked, it might cause some harm to government, private individuals, or society in general? As the foregoing materials illustrate, the Court's efforts to define the perimeters of government power in this regard have focused primarily on the clear and present danger standard. Has that standard served well? In a different context, Justice Holmes, the author of the clear and present danger standard, warned of "the need of scrutinizing the reasons for the rules which we follow, and of not being contented with hollow forms of words merely because they have been used very [often]. We must think things not words, or at least we must constantly translate our words into the facts for which they stand, if we are to keep to the real and the true." O. Holmes, Collected Legal Papers 238 (1920). Has the Court been sensitive to this admonition, or has it "tended to seek [solutions] for problems of freedom of speech by invocation of magic phrases rather than hard rationalizations, if not by way of resolving the issues then by way of covering them up"? Kurland, The Irrelevance of the Constitution: The First Amendment's Freedom of Speech and Freedom of Press Clauses, 29 Drake L. Rev. 1, 5 (1979–1980).

Has the Court, in its results, been underprotective of free speech? Has it been overprotective? A canvass of what the Court has done may be more illuminating than an emphasis on what it has said. The Court has not upheld a direct prohibition of speech because it might induce readers or listeners to engage in criminal activity since *Dennis* (1951), and it has not upheld a direct prohibition of speech for this reason in the absence of express advocacy of crime since the Espionage Act cases following World War I. The Court has not upheld a restriction on speech because it might provoke a hostile audience response since *Feiner* (1951). With the exception of *Agee*, it has never upheld a restriction on the publication of truthful information because the government would prefer to keep it confidential. Has clear and present danger come to mean essentially absolute protection?

On the other hand, does it really matter what the Court says or does? Consider Nagel, How Useful Is Judicial Review in Free Speech Cases?, 69 Cornell L. Rev. 302, 304–305 (1984):

> [It] is not self-evident [that] the legal rules adopted by the Court [have] had any useful systemic consequences. [A] wide range of factors coalesce to determine the amount of tolerance [in a society], including: educational levels, [economic] conditions, international politics, institutional rivalries [and] insecurities caused by flux in social [status]. Adjudication is an unlikely mechanism for controlling such large and complex factors. [The] causes of intolerance and censorship — as well as the cures — lie far beyond the sound and fury of particular cases.

# III

## Overbreadth, Vagueness,
## and Prior Restraint

This section represents a brief interlude in our analysis of content-based restrictions. It focuses not on what speech government may restrict but rather on how government may restrict speech. The doctrines examined in this section may be explored either as a distinct unit or as they arise in the course of the preceding and succeeding material.

In interpreting the first amendment, courts have often focused not only on what speech is "protected" but also on what means of restriction are constitutionally permissible. Indeed, "courts have [come] to realize that procedural guarantees play [a] large role in protecting freedom of speech; [for like] the substantive rules themselves, insensitive procedures can 'chill' the right of free expression. Accordingly, wherever first amendment claims are involved, sensitive procedural devices are necessary." Monaghan, First Amendment "Due Process," 83 Harv. L. Rev. 518, 518–519 (1970).

The overbreadth, vagueness, and prior restraint doctrines have played an especially important role in this aspect of first amendment jurisprudence. Under each of these doctrines, courts may invalidate restrictions on expression because the means of suppression are impermissible, even though the particular speech at issue might constitutionally be restricted by some other means.

## A. OVERBREADTH AND VAGUENESS

### Gooding v. Wilson
405 U.S. 518 (1972)

[During an antiwar demonstration at an army induction center, police attempted to move appellee and his companions away from the door of the center. A scuffle ensued, and appellee said to several of the officers, "You son of a bitch, I'll choke you to death"; "White son of a bitch, I'll kill you"; and "You son of a bitch, if you ever put your hands on me again, I'll cut you all to pieces." Appellee was thereafter convicted of using opprobrious words and abusive language in violation of Georgia Code Ann. §26-6303, which provided: "Any person who shall, without provocation, use to or of another, and in his presence [opprobrious] words or abusive language, tending to cause a breach of the peace [shall] be guilty of a misdemeanor." The Supreme Court affirmed a decision of the U.S. Court of Appeals granting appellee's petition for federal habeas corpus relief.]

MR. JUSTICE BRENNAN delivered the opinion of the Court. . . .

Section 26-6303 punishes only spoken words. It can therefore withstand appellee's attack upon its facial constitutionality only if, as authoritatively construed by the Georgia courts, it is not susceptible of application to speech, although vulgar or offensive, that is protected by the First and Fourteenth Amendments. [Only] the Georgia courts can supply the requisite construction, since of course "we lack jurisdiction authoritatively to construe state legislation." [It] matters not that the words appellee used might have been constitutionally prohibited under a narrowly and precisely drawn statute. At least when statutes regulate or proscribe speech and when "no readily apparent construction suggests itself as a vehicle for rehabilitating the statutes in a single prosecution,"[the] transcendent value to all society of constitutionally protected expression is deemed to justify allowing "attacks on overly broad statutes with no requirement that the person making the attack demonstrate that his own conduct could not be regulated by a statute drawn with the requisite narrow specificity." [This] is deemed necessary because persons whose expression is constitutionally protected may well refrain from exercising their rights for fear of criminal sanctions provided by a statute susceptible of application to protected expression. . . .

The constitutional guarantees of freedom of speech forbid the States to punish the use of words or language not within "narrowly limited classes of speech." [Chaplinsky.] [Statutes] must be carefully drawn or be authoritatively construed to punish only unprotected speech and not be susceptible of application to protected expression. "Because First Amendment freedoms need breathing space to survive, government may regulate in the area only with narrow specificity." . . .

Appellant does not challenge these principles but contends that the Georgia statute is narrowly drawn to apply only to a constitutionally unprotected class of words — "fighting" words — "those which by their very utterance inflict injury or tend to incite an immediate breach of the peace." [Chaplinsky.] In Chaplinsky, we sustained a conviction under [a statute] which provided: "No person shall address any offensive, derisive or annoying word to any other person who is lawfully in any street or other public place, nor call him by any offensive or derisive name. . . ." Chaplinsky was convicted for addressing to another on a public sidewalk the words, "You are a God damned racketeer," and "a damned Fascist and the whole government of Rochester are Fascists or agents of Fascists." Chaplinsky challenged the constitutionality of the statute as inhibiting freedom of expression because it was vague and indefinite. The Supreme Court of New Hampshire, however, "long before the words for which Chaplinsky was convicted," sharply limited the statutory language "offensive, derisive or annoying word" to "fighting" words. . . .

In view of that authoritative construction, this Court held: "We are unable to say that the limited scope of the statute as thus construed contravenes the Constitutional right of free expression. It is a statute narrowly drawn and limited to define and punish specific conduct lying within the domain of state power, the use in a public place of words likely to cause a breach of the peace." . . .

Appellant argues that the Georgia appellate courts have by construction limited the prescription of §26-6303 to "fighting" words, as the New Hampshire Supreme Court limited the New Hampshire statute. [We] have, however, made our own examination of the Georgia cases, both those cited and others discovered in research. That examination brings us to the conclusion, in agreement with the courts below, that the Georgia appellate decisions have not construed §26-6303 to be limited in application, as in *Chaplinsky*, to words that "have a direct tendency to cause acts of violence by the person to whom, individually, the remark is addressed."

[The dictionary definitions of "opprobrious" and "abusive" give them greater reach than "fighting" words.] Webster's Third New International Dictionary (1961) defined "opprobrious" as "conveying or intended to convey disgrace," and "abusive" as including "harsh insulting language." Georgia appellate decisions have construed §26-6303 to apply to utterances that, although within these definitions, are not "fighting" words as *Chaplinsky* defines them. In Lyons v. State, 94 Ga. App. 570, 95 S.E.2d 478 (1956), a conviction under the statute was sustained for [appellee's] awakening 10 women scout leaders on a camp-out by shouting, "Boys, this is where we are going to spend the night." "Get the G — d — bed rolls out . . . let's see how close we can come to the G — d — tents." Again, in Fish v. State, 124 Ga. 416, 52 S.E. 737 (1905), the Georgia Supreme Court held that a jury question was presented by the remark, "You swore a lie." Again, Jackson v. State, 14 Ga. App. 19, 80 S.E. 20 (1913), held that a jury question was presented by the words addressed to another, "God damn you, why don't you get out of the road?" Plainly, although "conveying . . . disgrace" or "harsh insulting language," these were not words "which by their very utterance . . . tend to incite an immediate breach of the peace." [*Chaplinsky*.] Indeed, the Georgia Court of Appeals in Elmore v. State, 15 Ga. App. 461, 83 S.E. 799 (1914), construed "tending to cause a breach of the peace" as [including the possibility that the addressee might retaliate at some time in the future].

Moreover, in Samuels v. State, 103 Ga. App. 66, 67, 118 S.E.2d 231, 232 (1961), the Court of Appeals, in applying another statute, adopted from a textbook the common-law definition of "breach of the peace" [that] makes it a "breach of peace" merely to speak words offensive to some who hear them. [Because] earlier appellate decisions applied §26-6303 to utterances where there was no likelihood that the person addressed would make an immediate violent response, it is clear that the standard allowing juries to determine guilt "measured by common understanding and practice" does not limit the application of §26-6303 to "fighting" words defined by *Chaplinsky*. [Unlike] the construction of the New Hampshire statute by the New Hampshire Supreme Court, the Georgia appellate courts have not construed §26-6303 "so as to avoid all constitutional difficulties." . . .

Affirmed. *for Appellee*

MR. JUSTICE POWELL and MR. JUSTICE REHNQUIST took no part in the consideration or decision of this case.

MR. CHIEF JUSTICE BURGER, dissenting.

I fully join in Mr. Justice Blackmun's dissent against the bizarre result reached by the Court. It is not merely odd, it is nothing less than remarkable that a court can find a state statute void on its face, not because of its language — which is the traditional test — but because of the way courts of that State have applied the statute in a few isolated cases, decided as long ago as 1905 and generally long before this Court's decision in [*Chaplinsky*]. Even if all of those cases had been decided yesterday, they do nothing to demonstrate that the narrow language of the Georgia statute has any significant potential for sweeping application to suppress or deter important protected speech. . . .

The Court apparently acknowledges that the conduct of the defendant in this case is not protected by the First Amendment, and does not contend that the Georgia statute is so ambiguous that he did not have fair notice that his conduct was prohibited. Nor does the Court deny that under normal principles of constitutional adjudication, appellee would not be permitted to attack his own conviction on the ground that the statute in question might in some hypothetical situation be unconstitutionally applied to the conduct of some party not before the Court. . . .

As the Court itself recognizes, if the First Amendment overbreadth doctrine serves any legitimate purpose, it is to allow the Court to invalidate statutes because their language demonstrates their potential for sweeping improper applications posing a significant likelihood of deterring important First Amendment speech — not because of some insubstantial or imagined potential for occasional and isolated applications that go beyond constitutional bounds. [The] actual and apparent danger to free expression [in] the case at hand is at best strained and remote. . . .

MR. JUSTICE BLACKMUN, with whom THE CHIEF JUSTICE joins, dissenting. . . .

The Court would justify its conclusion by unearthing a 66-year-old decision [of] the Supreme Court of Georgia, and two intermediate appellate court cases over 55 years old, [broadly] applying the statute in those less permissive days, and by additional reference to (a) a 1956 Georgia intermediate appellate court decision, [which], were it the first and only Georgia case, would surely not support today's decision, and (b) another intermediate appellate court decision [relating], not to §26-6303, but to another statute. . . .

I wonder, now that §26-6303 is voided, just what Georgia can do if it seeks to proscribe what the Court says it still may constitutionally proscribe. The natural thing would be to enact a new statute reading just as §26-6303 reads. But it, too, presumably would be overbroad unless the legislature would add words to the effect that it means only what this Court says it may mean and no more. . . .

*Doesn't like use of old cases, inapplicable*

*GA legislatures hands are tied now*

### Note: Overbreadth

1. *The nature of overbreadth.* The traditional "as applied" mode of judicial review tests the constitutionality of legislation as it is applied to particular facts on a case-by-case basis. Suppose, for example, a state law prohibits any person from "advocating criminal conduct." Under "as applied" review, this law could constitutionally be applied to any expression that satisfies the requirements of *Brandenburg.* That the law fails "on its face" to comport with the strictures of *Brandenburg* is, under this approach, irrelevant.

The first amendment overbreadth doctrine, on the other hand, tests the constitutionality of legislation in terms of its *potential* applications. Under this approach, a state law prohibiting any person from "advocating unlawful conduct" is unconstitutional "on its face" because the law purports to forbid expression that the state may not constitutionally prohibit. That an individual defendant's own speech could constitutionally be restricted under a more narrowly drawn statute is irrelevant.

In effect, then, the overbreadth doctrine is an exception both to the traditional "as applied" mode of judicial review and to the general rule that an individual has no standing to litigate the rights of third persons. See United States v. Raines, 362 U.S. 17 (1960); Barrows v. Jackson, 346 U.S. 249 (1953); see also Note, Standing to Assert Constitutional Jus Tertii, 88 Harv. L. Rev. 423 (1974).

2. *Justifications and criticisms of overbreadth.* The overbreadth doctrine is "highly protective of first amendment interests, not only because it sometimes

prescribes invalidation of an entire provision but also because of the alacrity with which it can accomplish that result." Note, The First Amendment Overbreadth Doctrine, 83 Harv. L. Rev. 844, 846 (1970). Are you persuaded by Justice Brennan's explanation in *Gooding* that this exception to ordinary standing rules is "necessary because persons whose expression is constitutionally protected may well refrain from exercising their rights for fear of criminal sanctions provided by a statute susceptible of application to protected expression"? Are you persuaded that "one of the evils of an overly broad statute is its potential for selective enforcement" and that the doctrine is thus justified because "it can minimize [this] danger by restricting the occasions for enforcement"? Karst, Equality as a Central Principle in the First Amendment, 43 U. Chi. L. Rev. 20, 38 (1975).

*Chilling effect?*

What are the costs of the overbreadth doctrine? Consider the following objections: (a) Because the doctrine permits an individual whose own rights have *not* been violated to "go free" or to otherwise benefit because the statute might conceivably interfere with the rights of others, it unjustifiably frustrates legitimate state interests. (b) The doctrine enables the Court to act "as if it had a roving commission" to find and to cure unconstitutionality and is thus inconsistent with a fundamental premise of judicial review — that judicial resolution of constitutional controversies is warranted only when unavoidable. A. Cox, The Warren Court 18 (1968). (c) The doctrine necessarily requires the decision of questions not actually presented by the record and thus results in the resolution of important constitutional issues in a "sterile," abstract context, without the depth and texture ordinarily provided by a concrete factual setting. A. Bickel, The Least Dangerous Branch 115–116 (1962). (d) The doctrine may promote judicial disingenuousness, for it invites the Court to escape possibly difficult decisions concerning the constitutionality of the statute "as applied" so long as it can hypothesize potentially unconstitutional applications not actually before the Court. (e) Because the Court may invalidate a statute for overbreadth without explaining precisely how the statute should have been drafted to pass constitutional muster, invocation of the doctrine "lacks intellectual coherence" and may leave legislatures with little or no guidance on how to avoid the Court's objections in the future. Id. at 53.

3. *The problem of narrowing construction.* As noted in *Gooding,* the statute at issue in *Chaplinsky* was clearly overbroad on its face but was saved by the state court's narrowing construction. When may a court narrowly construe a facially overbroad statute to save it from invalidation? In affirming the conviction of Gooding, could the Georgia Supreme Court have limited the statute to "fighting words" and thus avoided overbreadth invalidation? Was the legislative intent too clear in *Gooding* to permit a narrowing interpretation? Would a narrowing construction by the Georgia Supreme Court have come too late to affect Gooding?

Consider Osborne v. Ohio, 495 U.S. 103 (1990), in which the Court upheld a child pornography statute as construed by the state supreme court on appeal in the same case. Although the statute, as written, was unconstitutionally overbroad, the Court held that it was saved from invalidation by the state supreme court's narrowing construction, and that the statute, as construed, could "'be applied to conduct occurring prior to the construction, provided such application affords fair warning to the defendant.'" In *Osborne*, the Court concluded that the statute afforded "fair warning" because the defendant "would not [have been] surprised to learn that his possession of [the] photographs at issue [constituted] a crime."

Note that the Supreme Court of the United States had no authority to adopt a narrowing construction in *Gooding*. Is that sensible? Wouldn't a narrowing construction have involved a less drastic exercise of federal power than invalidation? Consider Virginia v. American Booksellers Association, Inc., 484 U.S. 383 (1988), in which the Court, rather than speculate on the reach of an ambiguous state statute, certified to the Virginia Supreme Court the question whether the challenged statute actually covered those acts of expression that gave rise to the overbreadth challenge. Is this a sensible approach?

Suppose that, while a criminal prosecution is on appeal, the state legislature amends the challenged statute to eliminate the unconstitutional overbreadth. May the defendant still take advantage of the fact that the statute was overbroad at the time he violated it? See Massachusetts v. Oakes, 491 U.S. 576 (1989) (defendant may still assert overbreadth).

4. *Broadrick: requiring "substantial" overbreadth*. Chief Justice Burger maintained in *Gooding* that the overbreadth doctrine should be invoked only when there is "a significant likelihood of deterring important First Amendment speech." In Broadrick v. Oklahoma, 413 U.S. 601 (1973), the Court, in a five-to-four decision, expressly adopted such a limitation. *Broadrick* involved a state law restricting the political activities of civil servants. The plaintiffs conceded that the state could constitutionally prohibit civil servants from doing what they had done — solicit funds for political candidates. They argued, however, that the law was unconstitutionally overbroad because it attempted also to prohibit civil servants from engaging in such relatively innocuous and thus constitutionally protected activities as displaying political bumper stickers and buttons.

The Court, in an opinion by Justice White, observed that under the overbreadth doctrine, litigants "are permitted to challenge a statute not because their own rights of free expression are violated, but because of a judicial prediction or assumption that the statute's very existence may cause others not before the court to refrain from constitutionally protected speech or expression." Terming the doctrine "strong medicine," the Court argued that, although laws, "if too broadly worded, may deter protected speech to some unknown extent, there comes a point where that effect — at best a prediction — cannot, with confidence, justify invalidating a statute on its face and so prohibiting a State from enforcing the statute against conduct that is admittedly within its power to proscribe." Thus, the Court concluded, "we believe that the overbreadth of a statute must not only be real, but substantial as well, judged in relation to the statute's plainly legitimate sweep." Applying that standard to the statute in *Broadrick*, the Court concluded that, because the statute "regulates a substantial spectrum of conduct that [is] manifestly subject to state regulation," it "is not substantially overbroad [and] whatever overbreadth may exist should [thus] be cured through case-by-case analysis of the fact situations to which its sanctions, assertedly, may not be applied."

In dissent, Justice Brennan described *Broadrick* "as a wholly unjustified retreat from fundamental and previously well-established [principles]." Although conceding that the Court had "never held that a statute should be held invalid on its face merely because it is possible to conceive of a single impermissible application," and that "in that sense a requirement of substantial overbreadth is already implicit in the doctrine," Justice Brennan faulted the Court for leaving "obscure" the contours of its arguably new conception of overbreadth. The Court, Justice Brennan noted, "makes no effort to define what it means by 'substantial overbreadth'" and "no effort to explain why the overbreadth of the Oklahoma Act, while real, is somehow not quite substantial." Indeed, "no more guidance is provided" on that question "than the Court's conclusory assertion that appellants' showing here falls below the line."

5. *The impact of* Broadrick. In Los Angeles City Council v. Taxpayers for Vincent, 466 U.S. 789 (1984), the Court offered the following elaboration:

> The concept of "substantial overbreadth" is not readily reduced to an exact definition. It is clear, however, that the mere fact that one can conceive of some impermissible applications of a statute is not sufficient to render it susceptible to an overbreadth challenge. On the contrary, [there] must be a realistic danger that the statute itself will significantly compromise recognized First Amendment protections of parties not before the Court for it to be facially challenged on overbreadth grounds.

How should "substantiality" be measured: By the total number of unconstitutional applications? By the ratio of possible constitutional to possible unconstitutional applications? Should the state have to justify even an "insubstantial" overbreadth? See Redish, The Warren Court, the Burger Court and the First Amendment Overbreadth Doctrine, 78 Nw. U. L. Rev. 1031, 1067 (1983) (the "logical question [is] whether [a] more narrowly drawn [law] would inadequately achieve the state's goal"); Fallon, Making Sense of Overbreadth, 100 Yale L.J. 853, 894 (1991) (in deciding when overbreadth is "intolerably substantial," courts should weigh the state's substantive interest in being able to "employ a standard that is broader than less restrictive substitutes" against "the First Amendment interest in avoiding [the] chilling effect on constitutionally protected conduct" — the "farther [the] chilled conduct lies from the central concerns of the First Amendment [the] more [a] court should hesitate about declaring a [statute] void for overbreadth").

The ultimate impact of *Broadrick* remains obscure. See New York v. Ferber, 458 U.S. 747 (1982), Chapter IV.F, infra (upholding as not substantially overbroad a child pornography statute prohibiting any person to produce, exhibit, or sell any material depicting any "performance" by a child under the age of sixteen that includes "actual or simulated sexual intercourse, deviate sexual intercourse, sexual bestiality, masturbation, sado-masochistic abuse, or lewd exhibition of the genitals"); Houston v. Hill, 482 U.S. 451 (1987) (invalidating as substantially overbroad an ordinance prohibiting any person to "assault, strike or in any manner oppose, molest, abuse or interrupt any policeman in the execution of his duty"); Board of Airport Commissioners of Los Angeles v. Jews for Jesus, Inc., 482 U.S. 569 (1987) (invalidating as substantially overbroad a regulation prohibiting any person "to engage in First Amendment activities within the Central Terminal Area at Los Angeles International Airport"); National Endowment for the Arts v. Finley, 524 U.S. 569 (1998), Chapter V.B, infra (upholding as not substantially overbroad a federal statute directing the NEA, in establishing procedures to judge the artistic merit of grant applications, to "tak[e] into consideration general standards of decency and respect for the diverse beliefs and values of the American public").

### Note: Vagueness

1. *The danger of vagueness.* Although not all overbroad laws are vague (e.g., "No person may expressly advocate criminal conduct"), and not all vague laws are overbroad (e.g., "No person may engage in any speech that the state may constitutionally restrict"), there is in most circumstances a close relation between the two doctrines. As a matter of due process, a law is void on its face if it is so vague that persons "of common intelligence must necessarily guess at its meaning and differ as to its application." Connally v. General Construction Co., 269 U.S. 385, 391 (1926). A law that fails to define clearly the conduct it proscribes "may trap the innocent by not providing fair warning" and may in practical effect impermissibly delegate "basic policy matters to policemen, judges and juries for resolution on an ad hoc and subjective basis, with the attendant dangers of arbitrary and discriminatory application." Grayned v. Rockford, 408 U.S. 104, 108–109 (1972).

These concerns are present whenever a law is vague, whether or not it touches on expression. The vagueness doctrine has special bite in the first amendment context, however, for "where First Amendment interests are affected, a precise statute 'evincing a legislative judgment that certain specific conduct [be] proscribed,' assures us that the legislature has focused on the First Amendment interests and determined that other governmental policies compel regulation." Moreover, "where a vague statute '[abuts] upon sensitive areas of basic First Amendment freedoms,' it 'operates to inhibit the exercise of [those] freedoms.'" Uncertain meanings inevitably lead citizens to "'steer far wider of the unlawful zone' [than] if the boundaries of the forbidden areas were clearly marked." Id. at 109 & n.5; see also Smith v. Goguen, 415 U.S. 566, 572–573 (1974). In at least some instances, in other words, it may be difficult to determine whether a vague law proscribes — or purports to proscribe — constitutionally protected expression. In such circumstances, vague laws, like overbroad laws, may have a significant chilling effect and may invite selective enforcement. See Amsterdam, The Void-for-Vagueness Doctrine in the Supreme Court, 109 U. Pa. L. Rev. 67 (1960).

2. *How "vague" is "too vague"?* The degree of constitutionally tolerable vagueness "is not calculable with precision; in any particular area, the legislature confronts a dilemma: to draft with narrow particularity is to risk nullification by easy evasion of the legislative purpose; to draft with great generality is to risk ensnarement of the innocent in a net designed for others." L. Tribe, American Constitutional Law 1033 (2d ed. 1988). How vague must a law be for it to be held void on its face? Should it matter whether the vagueness is "avoidable"? Whether it is "substantial"? Consider the following:

a. A city ordinance provides that "no person, while on public or private grounds adjacent to any building in which a school [is] in session, shall willfully make [any] noise or diversion which disturbs or tends to disturb the peace or good order of such school." In Grayned v. City of Rockford, 408 U.S. 104 (1972), the Court rejected a vagueness challenge because "we think it is clear what the ordinance as a whole prohibits."

b. A Massachusetts statute provides that any person who "publicly mutilates, tramples upon, defaces or treats contemptuously the flag of the United States" shall be guilty of a misdemeanor. In Smith v. Goguen, 415 U.S. 566 (1974), the Court invalidated the statute because the statutory prohibition on treating the flag "contemptuously" failed "to draw reasonably clear lines between the kinds [of] treatment that are criminal and those that are not."

3. *Vagueness and standing.* When a law is overbroad, or at least substantially overbroad, an individual may assert its unconstitutionality, even if his own expression is unprotected. Is a similar waiver of traditional standing rules warranted in the vagueness context? If the law is vague as to its coverage of the individual's own expression, the problem does not arise, for the vagueness in such circumstances violates the individual's own right to due process. Suppose, however, the individual's own expression is so clearly within the statutory prohibition that he could not reasonably have been misled. See Smith v. Goguen, supra (invalidating as unconstitutionally vague on its face a statute prohibiting any person to treat the flag of the United States "contemptuously" because the statute is so vague that "no standard of conduct is specified at all"); Young v. American Mini Theatres, 427 U.S. 50 (1976) (declining to invalidate as unconstitutionally vague on its face an ordinance restricting the exhibition of sexually explicit movies where the ordinance is "unquestionably applicable" to the claimants' speech and the Court was "not persuaded" that the

"ordinance [would] have a significant [chilling] effect on the exhibition of films protected by the First Amendment").

1 5

## B.  PRIOR RESTRAINT

The doctrine of prior restraint has its roots in the sixteenth- and seventeenth-century English licensing systems under which all printing presses and printers were licensed by the state and no book or pamphlet could lawfully be published without the prior approval of a government censor. With the expiration of this system in England in 1695, the right of the press to be free from licensing gradually assumed the status of a common law right. Blackstone's definition of freedom of the press illustrates the importance of the doctrine of prior restraint in eighteenth-century thought: "The liberty of the press is indeed essential to the nature of a free state; but this consists in laying no *previous* restraints upon publications, and not in freedom from censure for criminal matter when published." 4 W. Blackstone, Commentaries *151–152.

Even after adoption of the first amendment, Justice Story and other early American commentators accepted the view that liberty of the press was limited to "the right to publish without any previous restraint or license." J. Story, Commentaries on the Constitution of the United States §1879 (1833); see also 2 J. Kent, Commentaries on American Law 23 (2d ed. 1832). Moreover, in its 1907 decision in Patterson v. Colorado, 205 U.S. 454, 462 (1907), the Court, speaking through Justice Holmes, announced that the Constitution prohibited "all such *previous restraints* upon publications as had been practiced by other governments," but not "the subsequent punishment of such as may be deemed contrary to the public welfare." And, although the Court, speaking again through Justice Holmes, recognized a dozen years later in *Schenck* that "the prohibition of laws abridging the freedom of speech is not confined to previous restraints," the doctrine of prior restraint has continued to play a central role in the jurisprudence of the first amendment. As indicated in the *Pentagon Papers* decision, Chapter II.C, the Court has steadfastly held that there is a special presumption under the first amendment against the use of prior restraints.

Like the vagueness and overbreadth concepts, the doctrine of prior restraint is concerned with the permissible means of restricting speech. A prior restraint may thus be invalid even if the particular expression at issue could constitutionally be restricted by some other means, such as subsequent criminal prosecution. Although the historical origins of the doctrine are clear, its analytical and functional underpinnings are often puzzling. Apart from historical considerations, why are prior restraints special? After all, "whether the sanction be fine or imprisonment for criminal violation or fine or imprisonment for violation of [a prior restraint], the judicial sanction takes its bite after the [expression.]" Freund, The Supreme Court and Civil Liberties, 4 Vand. L. Rev. 533, 537–538 (1951).

# Lovell v. Griffin

303 U.S. 444 (1938)

MR. CHIEF JUSTICE HUGHES delivered the opinion of the Court.

Appellant, Alma Lovell, was convicted in the Recorder's Court of the City of Griffin, Georgia, of the violation of a city ordinance and was sentenced to imprisonment for fifty days in default of the payment of a fine of fifty dollars. . . .

The ordinance in question is as follows:

*Can't circulate literature w/o approval from city Mngr*

> Section 1. That the practice of distributing, either by hand or otherwise, circulars, handbooks, advertising, or literature of any kind, whether said articles are being delivered free, or whether same are being sold, within the limits of the City of Griffin, without first obtaining written permission from the City Manager of the City of Griffin, such practice shall be deemed a nuisance, and punishable as an offense against the City of Griffin. . . .

The violation, which is not denied, consisted of the distribution without the required permission of a pamphlet and magazine in the nature of religious tracts, setting forth the gospel of the "Kingdom of Jehovah." Appellant did not apply for a permit. . . .

The ordinance in its broad sweep prohibits the distribution of "circulars, handbooks, advertising, or literature of any kind." [The] ordinance is not limited to "literature" that is obscene or offensive to public morals or that advocates unlawful conduct. [The] ordinance embraces "literature" in the widest sense. [Moreover, the] ordinance prohibits the distribution of literature of any kind at any time, at any place, and in any manner without a permit from the City Manager.

We think that the ordinance is invalid on its face. Whatever the motive which induced its adoption, its character is such that it strikes at the very foundation of the freedom of the press by subjecting it to license and censorship. The struggle for the freedom of the press was primarily directed against the power of the licensor. It was against that power that John Milton directed his assault by his "Appeal for the Liberty of Unlicensed Printing." And the liberty of the press became initially a right to publish "*without* a license what formerly could be published only *with* one." While this freedom from previous restraint upon publication cannot be regarded as exhausting the guaranty of liberty, the prevention of that restraint was a leading purpose in the adoption of the constitutional provision. . . .

Legislation of the type of the ordinance in question would restore the system of license and censorship in its baldest form. . . .

As the ordinance is void on its face, it was not necessary for appellant to seek a permit under it. She was entitled to contest its validity in answer to the charge against her. . . .

Reversed.


MR. JUSTICE CARDOZO took no part in the consideration and decision of this case.


### Note: Licensing as Prior Restraint

1. *Standardless licensing*. What is the special vice of the licensing scheme in *Lovell*? Why not simply uphold the scheme on its face but permit any person whose application for a license is unconstitutionally denied to challenge that denial in court? Is the Court's primary concern in *Lovell* the absence of standards to guide the city manager's discretion? See Kagan, Private Speech, Public Purpose: The Role of Governmental Motive in First Amendment Doctrine, 63 U. Chi. L. Rev. 415, 459–463 (1996) ("the rule against standardless licensing [serves the] function of flushing out bad motives by establishing a safeguard against administrative action based on the content of expression").

In City of Lakewood v. Plain Dealer Publishing Co., 486 U.S. 750 (1988), the Court applied the *Lovell* principle to invalidate an ordinance that gave a mayor standardless discretion to grant or deny permits to place newsracks on public property. The Court explained that the evils of standardless licensing "can be effectively alleviated only through a facial challenge":

> First, the mere existence of the licensor's unfettered discretion [intimidates] parties into censoring their own speech, even if the discretion and power are never actually abused. [Self-censorship] is immune to an "as applied" challenge, for it derives from the individual's own actions, not an abuse of government power. [Only] standards limiting the licensor's discretion will eliminate this danger by adding an element of certainty to fatal self-censorship. And only a facial challenge can effectively test the statute for these standards.
>
> Second, the absence of express standards makes it difficult to distinguish, "as applied," between a licensor's legitimate denial of a permit and its illegitimate abuse of censorial power. Standards provide the guideposts that check the licensor and allow courts quickly and easily to determine whether the licensor is discriminating against disfavored speech. Without these guideposts, post hoc rationalizations by the licensing official and the use of shifting or illegitimate criteria are far too easy, making it difficult for courts to determine in any particular case whether the licensor is permitting favorable, and suppressing unfavorable, expression.

Following *Lovell*, the Court has repeatedly held that a state "cannot vest restraining control over the right to speak [in] an administrative official where there are no appropriate standards to guide his action." Kunz v. New York, 340 U.S. 290, 295 (1951) (permit required for religious meetings); see also Shuttlesworth v. City of Birmingham, 394 U.S. 147 (1969) (permit required for parades); Staub v. City of Baxley, 355 U.S. 313 (1958) (permit required to solicit members for dues-paying organization); Saia v. New York, 334 U.S. 558 (1948) (permit required to operate sound amplifiers in public); Forsyth County, Georgia v. The Nationalist Movement, 505 U.S. 123 (1992) (even nominal permit fees for marches, demonstrations, and parades cannot be imposed in the absence of clear standards governing the setting of fees).

2. *Licensing with standards.* Suppose the authority of licensing officials to deny a permit is explicitly limited to only those circumstances in which the proposed expression could constitutionally be punished in a subsequent criminal prosecution. Would such a scheme, like that in *Lovell*, be unconstitutional on its face? Assume, for example, a state may constitutionally prohibit any person to participate in a parade that would physically interfere with another, ongoing parade. To prevent such conflicts from occurring, could the state constitutionally prohibit any person to participate in a parade without first obtaining a permit, where the licensing officials are authorized to deny a permit only on a finding that the proposed parade would physically interfere with another, previously authorized parade? Cf. Cox v. New Hampshire, 312 U.S. 569 (1941), Chapter V.B, infra. Or assume a state may constitutionally make criminal the exhibition of "obscene" motion pictures. May the state constitutionally create a licensing board to which all movies must be submitted prior to public exhibition, where the board is authorized to deny a license only on a finding that a movie is "obscene"? So long as the standards are clear, precise, and in conformity with the standards employed in subsequent criminal prosecutions, is there any reason to erect a special presumption against "prior" restraints?

3. *The objections to licensing.* Consider Emerson, The Doctrine of Prior Restraint, 20 Law & Contemp. Probs. 648, 656–660 (1955):

> [(1)] A system of prior restraint normally brings within the complex of government machinery a far greater amount of communication than a system of subsequent punishment. [The] pall of government control is, thus, likely to hang more pervasively over the area of communication.
>
> [(2)] Under a system of subsequent punishment, the communication has already been made before the government takes action. [Under] a system of prior restraint, the communication, if banned, never reaches the market place at all. Or the communication may be withheld until the issue of its release is finally settled, at which time it may have become obsolete.
>
> [(3)] A system of prior restraint is so constructed as to make it easier, and hence more likely, that in any particular case the government will rule adversely to free

expression. [A] government official thinks longer and harder before deciding to undertake the serious task of subsequent punishment. [Under] a system of prior restraint, he can reach the result by a simple stroke of the pen.

[(4)] Under a system of prior restraint, the issue of whether a communication is to be suppressed or not is determined by an administrative rather than a criminal procedure. This means that the procedural protections built around the criminal prosecution [are] not applicable to a prior restraint.

[(5)] A system of prior restraint usually operates behind a screen of informality and partial concealment that seriously curtails opportunity for public appraisal and increases the chances of discrimination and other abuse.

[(6)][As] common experience [shows, the] attitudes, drives, emotions, and impulses [of licensers] all tend to carry them to excesses. [The] function of the censor is to censor. He has a professional interest in finding things to suppress. [These factors combine to produce] unintelligent, overzealous, and usually absurd administration.

[(7)] A system of prior restraint is, in general, more readily and effectively enforced than a system of subsequent punishment. [A] penal proceeding to enforce a prior restraint normally involves only a limited and relatively simple issue — whether or not the communication was made without prior approval. The objection to the content or manner of the communication need not be demonstrated. And furthermore, the violation of a censorship order strikes sharply at the status of the licenser, whose prestige thus becomes involved and whose power must be vindicated.

How weighty are these concerns? In light of these concerns, should licensing ever be permitted?

4. *The* Freedman *case: procedural safeguards.* In Freedman v. Maryland, 380 U.S. 51 (1965), appellant, in violation of a state motion picture censorship statute, exhibited a film, conceded by the state not to be obscene or otherwise violative of the statutory standards, without first submitting it to the State Board of Censors for review. In a unanimous decision, the Court, speaking through Justice Brennan, held the statute invalid. At the outset, the Court emphasized that the statute was unconstitutional not because it might "prevent even the first showing of a film whose exhibition may legitimately be the subject of an obscenity prosecution," but rather because the administration of the censorship system "presents peculiar dangers to constitutionally protected speech." The Court explained that

unlike a prosecution for obscenity, a censorship proceeding puts the initial burden on the exhibitor or distributor. Because the censor's business is to censor, there inheres the danger that he may well be less responsive than a court — part of an independent branch of government — to the constitutionally protected interests in free expression. And if it is made unduly onerous, by reason of delay or otherwise, to seek judicial review, the censor's determination may in practice be final.

The Court thus concluded that "a noncriminal process which requires the prior submission of a film to a censor avoids constitutional infirmity only if it takes place under procedural safeguards designed to obviate the dangers of a censorship system."

The Court then identified and explained several constitutionally required safeguards:

> First, the burden of proving that the film is unprotected expression must rest on the [censor]. Second, while the State may require advance submission of all films, in order to proceed effectively to bar all showings of unprotected films, the requirement cannot be administered in a manner which would lend an effect of finality to the censor's determination whether a film constitutes protected expression. [Because] only a judicial determination in an adversary proceeding ensures the necessary sensitivity to freedom of expression, only a procedure requiring a judicial determination suffices to impose a valid final restraint.
>
> [To] this end, the exhibitor must be assured, by statute or authoritative judicial construction, that the censor will, within a specified brief period, either issue a license or go to court to restrain showing the film. Any restraint imposed in advance of a final judicial determination on the merits must similarly be limited to preservation of the status quo for the shortest fixed period compatible with sound judicial resolution. Moreover, [the] procedure must also assure a prompt final judicial decision, to minimize the deterrent effect of an interim and possibly erroneous denial of a license. Without these safeguards, it may prove too burdensome to seek review of the censor's determination.

Because the Maryland scheme did not contain these procedural safeguards, the Court held it unconstitutional on its face. Justices Douglas and Black concurred on the ground that no "form of censorship — no matter how speedy or prolonged it may be — is permissible."

5. *The* Freedman *safeguards.* Should the *Freedman* safeguards be deemed a minimum requirement before *any* licensing scheme may pass constitutional muster? What about the parade permit scheme, noted earlier? See Blasi, Prior Restraints on Demonstrations, 68 Mich. L. Rev. 1481, 1536–1552 (1970); Monaghan, First Amendment "Due Process," 83 Harv. L. Rev. 518, 541–543 (1970). See Thomas v. Chicago Park District, 534 U.S. 316 (2002) (a content-neutral licensing scheme regulating the time, place, and manner of use of a public forum need not employ the procedural safeguards required by *Freedman* because such a scheme "does not authorize a licensor to pass judgment on the content of speech").

To what extent do the *Freedman* safeguards mitigate the dangers of licensing? Does it follow from *Freedman* that a licensing scheme is always constitutional so long as (a) the licenser's authority to deny a permit is limited to only those circumstances in which the expression could constitutionally be subjected to subsequent criminal prosecution and (b) the *Freedman* safeguards are employed? *Freedman* involved the licensing of motion pictures. Can government constitutionally require that all *books* be submitted to a board of censors prior to publication in order to screen out those that are obscene or include libelous statements?

# Near v. Minnesota
283 U.S. 697 (1931)

[A Minnesota statute provided for the abatement, as a public nuisance, of a "malicious, scandalous and defamatory newspaper, magazine or other periodical." The statute provided further that there "shall be available the defense that the truth was published with good motives and for justifiable ends." In November 1927, a county attorney sought to invoke this statute against The Saturday Press, which had run a series of articles charging "in substance that a Jewish gangster was in control of gambling, bootlegging and racketeering in Minneapolis, and that law enforcing officers and agencies were not energetically performing their duties." The Saturday Press was especially critical of the Chief of Police, who was charged "with gross neglect of duty, illicit relations with gangsters, and with participation in graft." Pursuant to the statute, a state trial court perpetually enjoined The Saturday Press and its owners from publishing or circulating "any publication whatsoever which is a malicious, scandalous or defamatory newspaper." The Supreme Court reversed.]

MR. CHIEF JUSTICE HUGHES delivered the opinion of the Court. . . .
[The] object of the statute is not punishment, in the ordinary sense, but suppression of the offending newspaper or periodical. The reason for the enactment, as the state court has said, is that prosecutions to enforce penal statutes for libel do not result in "efficient repression or suppression of the evils of scandal." . . .
[The statute provides] that public authorities may bring [the] publisher of a newspaper or periodical before a judge upon a charge of conducting a business of publishing scandalous and defamatory matter [and] unless [the] publisher is able [to prove] that the charges are true and are published with good motives and for justifiable ends, his newspaper or periodical is suppressed and further publication is made punishable as a contempt. This is of the essence of censorship.
The question is whether a statute authorizing such proceedings [is] consistent with the conception of the liberty of the press as historically conceived and guaranteed. In determining the extent of the constitutional protection, it has been generally, if not universally, considered that it is the chief purpose of the guaranty to prevent previous restraints upon publication. [The] protection even as to previous restraint is not absolutely unlimited. But the limitation has been recognized only in exceptional cases. [No] one would question but

that a government might prevent actual obstruction to its recruiting service or the publication of the sailing dates of transports or the number and location of troops. On similar grounds, the primary requirements of decency may be enforced against obscene publications. The security of the community life may be protected against incitements to acts of violence and the overthrow by force of orderly government. [These] limitations are not applicable here. . . .

The fact that for approximately one hundred and fifty years there has been almost an entire absence of attempts to impose previous restraints upon publications relating to the malfeasance of public officers is significant of the deep-seated conviction that such restraints would violate constitutional right. Public officers, whose character and conduct remain open to debate and free discussion in the press, find their remedies for false accusations in actions under libel laws providing for redress and punishment, and not in proceedings to restrain the publication of newspapers and periodicals. [The] fact that the liberty of the press may be abused by miscreant purveyors of scandal does not make any the less necessary the immunity of the press from previous restraint in dealing with official misconduct. Subsequent punishment for such abuses as may exist is the appropriate remedy, consistent with constitutional privilege. . . .

The statute in question cannot be justified by reason of the fact that the publisher is permitted to show, before injunction issues, that the matter published is true and is published with good motives and for justifiable ends. If such a statute, authorizing suppression and injunction on such a basis, is constitutionally valid, it would be equally permissible for the legislature to provide that at any time the publisher of any newspaper could be brought before a court, or even an administrative officer (as the constitutional protection may not be regarded as resting on mere procedural details) and required to produce proof of the truth of his publication, or of what he intended to publish, and of his motives, or stand enjoined. If this can be done, the legislature may provide machinery for determining in the complete exercise of its discretion what are justifiable ends and restrain publication accordingly. And it would be but a step to a complete system of censorship. The recognition of authority to impose previous restraint upon publication in order to protect the community against the circulation of charges of misconduct, and especially of official misconduct, necessarily would carry with it the admission of the authority of the censor against which the constitutional barrier was erected. . . .

For these reasons we hold the statute, so far as it authorized the proceedings in this action [to] be an infringement of the liberty of the press guaranteed by the Fourteenth Amendment. . . .

Judgment reversed.

MR. JUSTICE BUTLER, dissenting. . . .

The Minnesota statute does not operate as a *previous* restraint on publication within the proper meaning of that phrase. It does not authorize administrative control in advance such as was formerly exercised by the licensers and censors but prescribes a remedy to be enforced by a suit in equity. In this case there was previous publication made in the course of the business of regularly producing malicious, scandalous and defamatory periodicals. [There] is no question of the power of the State to denounce such transgressions. The restraint authorized is only in respect of continuing to do what has been duly adjudged to constitute a nuisance. [It] is fanciful to suggest similarity between the granting or enforcement of the decree authorized by this statute to prevent *further* publication of malicious, scandalous and defamatory articles and the *previous restraint* upon the press by licensers as referred to by Blackstone and described in the history of the times to which he alludes. . . .

It is well known, as found by the state supreme court, that existing libel laws are inadequate effectively to suppress evils resulting from the kind of business and publications that are shown in this case. The doctrine that measures such as the one before us are invalid because they operate as previous restraints [exposes][every individual] to [the] false and malicious assaults of any insolvent publisher who [may] put into effect [programs] for oppression, blackmail or extortion.

The judgment should be affirmed.

MR. JUSTICE VAN DEVANTER, MR. JUSTICE MCREYNOLDS, and MR. JUSTICE SUTHERLAND concur in this opinion.

### Note: Injunction as Prior Restraint

1. *Injunctions, criminal prosecutions, and licensing.* Assuming arguendo, as the Court apparently did in *Near*, that the speech prohibited by the injunction could constitutionally be punished in a subsequent criminal prosecution, why is the injunction invalid? Why isn't the injunction a *preferable* means of restraint? After all, unlike a criminal statute, an injunction is directed to a specific individual and is thus less likely to have a broad chilling effect. Moreover, unlike the licensing schemes in *Lovell* and *Freedman*, the injunctions in *Near* and the *Pentagon Papers* case did not require prepublication submission to a censor for review. And, unlike licensing schemes, injunctions are issued and administered by judges rather than by censors whose "business is to censor." In what sense, then, is the injunction a prior restraint?

2. *Injunctions: Are they too effective?* It has been suggested that injunctions are especially threatening to free speech because they are more likely than criminal statutes to be obeyed. Does this make sense? If an injunction prohibits only speech that could constitutionally be punished in a subsequent criminal prosecution, is the greater effectiveness of the injunction a bad thing?

Suppose an injunction prohibits speech that could not constitutionally be punished in a subsequent criminal prosecution. Is the greater effectiveness of the injunction now a bad thing?

Are injunctions in fact more likely than criminal statutes to be obeyed? It has been argued that injunctions have a special "mystique," causing individuals to accord them an unusually high degree of respect, and that injunctions are more likely to be obeyed because they are more likely to be enforced. Injunctions, after all, are directed at specific individuals, thus increasing the probability that violations will be detected, and violations may be viewed as a direct affront to the issuing judge's authority, thus increasing the likelihood that violations will be punished. On the other hand, punishments imposed for violations of injunctions are typically less severe than those for violations of criminal statutes, thus reducing the potential costs of violation. For analyses of these issues, see O. Fiss, The Civil Rights Injunction 71–73 (1978); Barnett, The Puzzle of Prior Restraint, 29 Stan. L. Rev. 539, 551–552 (1977); Blasi, Toward a Theory of Prior Restraint: The Central Linkage, 66 Minn. L. Rev. 11, 24–49 (1981).

3. *The collateral bar rule.* It has been suggested that the critical feature of injunctions, making them far more likely to be obeyed than criminal statutes, and thus appropriately rendering them prior restraints, is the rule, applicable to injunctions generally, that an injunction "must be obeyed until it is set aside, and that persons subject to the [injunction] who disobey it may not defend against the ensuing charge of criminal contempt on the ground that the order was erroneous or even unconstitutional." Barnett, supra, at 552. In the ordinary criminal prosecution, the defendant may assert the unconstitutionality of the statute as a defense. Thus, an individual whose planned expression is prohibited by a statute he believes to be invalid may elect to gamble and speak in defiance of the statute on the assumption that, if prosecuted, he will be able to persuade a court of the statute's unconstitutionality. An individual confronted with an injunction, however, has no such option, for under the "collateral bar" rule, "persons subject to an injunctive order issued by a court with jurisdiction are expected to obey that decree until it is modified or reversed, even if they have proper grounds to object to the order." GTE Sylvania v. Consumers Union, 445 U.S. 375, 386 (1980). This rule, which derives from the notion that "respect for judicial process is a small price to pay for the civilizing hand of law," has been held applicable even to injunctions directed against expression. In Walker v. City of Birmingham, 388 U.S. 307, 321 (1967), for example, a state trial court convicted eight black ministers of criminal contempt for leading mass street parades in violation of a temporary restraining order enjoining them from participating in such parades without first obtaining a permit as required by a city ordinance. The Court, invoking the collateral bar rule, upheld the contempt convictions without passing on the constitutionality of the injunction.

The collateral bar rule may have a significant impact on an individual's willingness to disobey even a patently unconstitutional order, for if the individual violates the injunction, he is subject to punishment even if the injunction is invalid. Consider Barnett, supra, at 553:

> [The rule places the individual] in a trilemma of chilling effects unique to a prior restraint situation. [He] can comply with the order and take no legal steps, thereby accepting the suppression. [He] can appeal the order directly, [but] must obey the interim restraint while [he] does so. [Or he] can [speak] in the face of [the] order, but only at the price of forfeiting [his] legal and constitutional objections to the order and thus, in all probability, embracing a contempt conviction.

With the collateral bar rule in force, the state in effect orders the enjoined individual to delay his speech unless and until a court lifts the injunction, whether or not the injunction itself is constitutionally permissible. The rule is thus strong medicine. In *Near*, for example, The Saturday Press was silenced for four years while courts debated the constitutionality of the injunction. In the *Progressive* controversy, Chapter II.B, supra, the injunction remained in force for seven months, and in the *Skokie* controversy, Chapter II.B, supra, the injunction prohibited the Nazis from marching for more than eight months before it was set aside.

Does the existence of the collateral bar rule justify the observation that, whereas a "criminal statute chills," an injunction "freezes"? A. Bickel, The Morality of Consent 61 (1975). Does it justify the characterization of injunctions as prior restraints? See Jeffries, Rethinking Prior Restraint, 92 Yale L.J. 409 (1983). For a general analysis of the collateral bar rule, see Palmer, Collateral Bar and Contempt: Challenging a Court Order after Disobeying It, 88 Cornell L. Rev. 215 (2002).

4. *When is an injunction not a prior restraint?* Consider the following:

a. Suppose state law provides that the collateral bar rule is inapplicable to injunctions against expression. See cases cited in Rendleman, Free Press — Fair Trial: Review of Silence Orders, 52 N.C. L. Rev. 127, 153 n.181, 154 nn.182–185 (1973). Should injunctions in such a jurisdiction be treated as prior restraints?

b. In Pittsburgh Press Co. v. Pittsburgh Commission on Human Relations, 413 U.S. 376 (1973), the commission, after a hearing, found that the Pittsburgh Press had violated a city ordinance by displaying "help wanted" advertisements in its daily newspaper under headings designating job preference by sex. The commission therefore issued an order prohibiting the newspaper from carrying sex-designated ads in the future. In upholding the order, the Court explained that a criminal statute cast in such terms would be constitutionally permissible and then observed:

> [We have] never held that all injunctions are impermissible. [The] special vice of a prior restraint is that communication will be suppressed, either directly or by

inducing excessive caution in the speaker, before an adequate determination that it is unprotected by the First Amendment. The present order does not endanger arguably protected speech. Because the order is based on a continuing course of repetitive conduct, this is not a case in which the Court is asked to speculate as to the effect of publication. Cf. [*Pentagon Papers* case]. Moreover, [because] no interim relief was granted, the order will not have gone into effect before our final determination that the actions of Pittsburgh Press were unprotected.

Consider Redish, The Proper Role of the Prior Restraint Doctrine in First Amendment Theory, 70 Va. L. Rev. 53, 55, 58 (1984):

[Injunctions, like licensing schemes,] are appropriately disfavored [because] of the coincidental harm to fully protected expression that results [when] a *preliminary* restraint [is] imposed prior to a decision on the merits of a *final* restraint. [Such] interim restraints present a threat to first amendment rights not found in subsequent punishment schemes — the threat that expression will be abridged, if only for a short time, prior to a full and fair hearing before an independent judicial forum to determine the scope of the speaker's constitutional right. [Thus,] the doctrine should strike down [injunctions only if they are] imposed *prior* to a full and fair judicial hearing.

c. Should it matter whether an injunction is directed at the content of the restricted speech? Consider Madsen v. Women's Health Center, Inc., 512 U.S. 753 (1994), in which the Court held that an injunction prohibiting particular named individuals from demonstrating within thirty-six feet of an abortion clinic was not a "prior restraint" because the injunction was issued "not because of the content of petitioners' expression," but "because of their prior unlawful conduct" in earlier demonstrations. Consider also an injunction prohibiting the use of loudspeakers in demonstrations within one hundred feet of a hospital, school, or abortion clinic. In *Madsen*, the Court suggested that content-neutral injunctions are not "prior restraints," but that they nonetheless should be tested by more "rigorous" standards than other forms of content-neutral restrictions because injunctions "carry greater risks of censorship and discriminatory application than do general ordinances."

5. *Prior restraint revisited.* Consider Freund, The Supreme Court and Civil Liberties, 4 Vand. L. Rev. 533, 539 (1951): "In sum, it will hardly do to place 'prior restraint' in a special category for condemnation. What is needed is a pragmatic assessment of its operation in the particular circumstances. The generalization that prior restraint is particularly obnoxious in civil liberties cases must yield to more particularistic analysis."

# IV

## Content-Based Restrictions:
## "Low" Value Speech

As suggested in Chapter II, the Court has articulated a two-level theory of free expression. Some speech, in other words, is said to possess only "low" first amendment value and is therefore accorded less than full constitutional protection. The two-level theory has its roots in the famous dictum of Chaplinsky v. New Hampshire, Chapter II.B, supra:

> There are certain well-defined and narrowly limited classes of speech, the prevention and punishment of which have never been thought to raise any Constitutional problem. These include the lewd and obscene, the profane, the libelous, and the insulting or "fighting" words — those which by their very utterance inflict injury or tend to incite an immediate breach of the peace. It has been well observed that such utterances are no essential part of any exposition of ideas, and are of such slight social value as a step to truth that any benefit that may be derived from them is clearly outweighed by the social interest in order and morality.

This section examines the "low" value theory in depth. In so doing, it poses a number of central first amendment questions: Is the very concept of low value speech inherently incompatible with the guarantee of free expression? That is, does the determination that certain types of speech are of "slight social value as a step to truth" compel the Court to make "value judgments concerned with the content of expression, a role foreclosed to it by the basic theory of the First Amendment"? T. Emerson, The System of Freedom of Expression 326 (1970). Is the Court's exercise of this power tolerable so long as it confines itself to defining low value speech in terms of discrete categories of expression rather than in terms of particular "good" or "bad" ideas? How is the Court to determine what speech is of low first amendment value? What follows from a determination that a certain category of expression is of low first amendment value? Is such expression wholly outside the protection of the first amendment, as suggested by *Chaplinsky*, or does such a determination trigger a form of "categorical balancing," according such speech some, but less than "full," first amendment protection?

It has been argued that the two-level theory is essential to "any well-functioning system of free expression" because without it one of two "unacceptable" results would follow — either (1) "the burden of justification imposed on government" when it regulates high value speech, such as pure political expression, "would have to be lowered," or (2) "the properly stringent standards applied to efforts to regulate" high value speech would have to be applied to low value speech, with the result that government would not be able to regulate speech "that in all probability should be regulated." C. Sunstein, The Partial Constitution 233–234 (1993). Is there any answer to this argument?

Consider Lakier, The Invention of Low-Value Speech, 128 Harv. L. Rev. 2166 (2015):

> By emphasizing the historical basis of the low-value categories, the Court has attempted to depict the distinction between high and law-value speech as the product of something other than the perhaps idiosyncratic value judgments and preferences of its individual members. . . .
>
>     There is little historical evidence, however, to back up the Court's claim that the categories of low-value speech we recognize [today] constituted, in the eighteenth and nineteenth centuries, well-defined and narrowly limited exceptions to the ordinary constitutional rule. . . .
>
>     [Eighteenth] and nineteenth century courts appled the same constitutional principles to the regulation of high-value speech as they applied to the regulation of low-value speech. The general rule [was] that speech — no matter how valuable it might be — could be sanctioned criminally whenever it threatened [to] "disturb the public peace or . . . subvert the government." But almost no speech or writing could be enjoined in advance without violating the constitutional prohibition against prior [restraints]. . . .
>
>     By forcing courts to determine the constitutional value of speech by means of a historical test that does not illuminate original understandings of what speech is worth protecting, the [low-value speech doctrine] threatens to create a set of doctrinal distinctions that rest either on hidden value-judgments [or] are the product of factors that are constitutionally irrelevant.

This section examines several categories of arguably "low" value expression — false statements of fact; nonnewsworthy disclosures of "private" facts; threats; commercial advertising; obscenity; child pornography; depictions of animal cruelty; violent expression; lewd, profane, and indecent speech; and hate speech and pornography.

# A.  FALSE STATEMENTS OF FACT

The Supreme Court has long maintained that "[under] the First Amendment there is no such thing as a false idea. However pernicious an opinion may seem, we depend for its correction not on the conscience of judges and juries but on the competition of other ideas." Gertz v. Robert Welch, Inc., infra this chapter. Government, in other words, may not restrict the expression of an idea or opinion because of *its* determination that the idea or opinion is "false." What, though, of false statements of *fact*? Recall Justice Holmes's example of the "false cry of fire."

The problem of false statements of fact arises most often in the context of defamation. At the time of adoption of the first amendment, civil and criminal actions for defamation were commonplace, and in *Chaplinsky* the Court expressly included libel within the class of utterances that "are no essential part of any exposition of ideas, and are of such slight social value as a step to truth that any benefit that may be derived from them is clearly outweighed by the social interest in order and morality." A decade later, in Beauharnais v. Illinois, infra, this chapter, the Court announced that libelous utterances are not "within the area of constitutionally protected speech," and, accordingly, that "no one would contend that [they] may be punished only upon a showing" of clear and present danger.

## New York Times v. Sullivan
376 U.S. 254 (1964)

MR. JUSTICE BRENNAN delivered the opinion of the Court.

We are required in this case to determine for the first time the extent to which the constitutional protections for speech and press limit a State's power to award damages in a libel action brought by a public official against critics of his official conduct.

Respondent L. B. Sullivan is one of the three elected Commissioners of the City of Montgomery, Alabama. [He] brought this civil libel action against the four individual petitioners, who are Negroes and Alabama clergymen, and against petitioner the New York Times. . . .

Respondent's complaint alleged that he had been libeled by statements in a full-page advertisement that was carried in the New York Times on March 29, 1960. Entitled "Heed Their Rising Voices," the advertisement [described the civil rights movement in the South and concluded with an appeal for funds].

Of the 10 paragraphs of text in the advertisement, the third and a portion of the sixth were the basis of respondent's claim of libel. They read as follows:

Third paragraph:

In Montgomery, Alabama, after students sang "My Country, 'Tis of Thee" on the State Capital steps, their leaders were expelled from school, and truckloads of police armed with shotguns and tear-gas ringed the Alabama State College campus. When the entire student body protested to state authorities by refusing to re-register, their dining hall was padlocked in an attempt to starve them into submission.

Sixth paragraph:

Again and again the Southern violators have answered Dr. King's peaceful protests with intimidation and violence. They have bombed his home almost killing his wife and child. They have assaulted his person. They have arrested him seven times — for "speeding," "loitering" and similar "offenses." And now they have charged him with "perjury" — a *felony* under which they could imprison him for *ten years*. . . .

Although neither of these statements mentions respondent by name, he contended that the word "police" in the third paragraph referred to him as the Montgomery Commissioner who supervised the Police Department, so that he was being accused of "ringing" the campus with police. He further claimed that the paragraph would be read as imputing to the police, and hence to him, the padlocking of the dining hall in order to starve the students into submission. As to the sixth paragraph, he contended that since arrests are ordinarily made by the police, the statement "They have arrested [Dr. King] seven times" would be read as referring to him. . . .

It is uncontroverted that some of the statements contained in the two paragraphs were not accurate descriptions of events which occurred in Montgomery. Although Negro students staged a demonstration on the State Capitol steps, they sang the National Anthem and not "My Country, 'Tis of Thee." Although nine students were expelled by the State Board of Education, this was not for leading the demonstration at the Capitol, but for demanding service at a lunch counter in the Montgomery County Courthouse on another day. Not the entire student body, but most of it, had protested the expulsion. [The] campus dining hall was not padlocked on any occasion. [Although] the police were deployed near the campus in large numbers on three occasions, they did not at any time "ring" the campus. [Dr.] King had not been arrested seven times, but only four. . . .

Respondent made no effort to prove that he suffered actual pecuniary loss as a result of the alleged libel.[3]

The trial judge submitted the case to the jury under instructions that the statements in the advertisement were "libelous per se" and were not privileged, so that petitioners might be held liable if the jury found that they had published the advertisement and that the statements were made "of and

3. Approximately 394 copies of the edition of the Times containing the advertisement were circulated in Alabama. Of these, about 35 copies were distributed in Montgomery County. The total circulation of the Times for that day was approximately 650,000 copies. . . .

concerning" respondent. The jury was instructed that, because the statements were libelous per se, "the law . . . implies legal injury from the bare fact of publication itself," "falsity and malice are presumed," "general damages need not be alleged or proved but are presumed," and "punitive damages may be awarded by the jury even though the amount of actual damages is neither found nor shown." [The jury returned a judgment for respondent in the amount of $500,000.]

We reverse the judgment. We hold that the rule of law applied by the Alabama courts is constitutionally deficient for failure to provide the safeguards for freedom of speech and of the press that are required by the First and Fourteenth Amendments in a libel action brought by a public official against critics of his official conduct. We further hold that under the proper safeguards the evidence presented in this case is constitutionally insufficient to support the judgment for respondent.

## I

We may dispose at the outset of [respondent's argument that the judgment of the state court is insulated from constitutional scrutiny because] "The Fourteenth Amendment is directed against State action and not private action." That proposition has no application to this case. Although this is a civil lawsuit between private parties, the Alabama courts have applied a state rule of law which petitioners claim to impose invalid restrictions on their constitutional freedoms of speech and press. It matters not that that law has been applied in a civil action and that it is common law only. [The] test is not the form in which state power has been applied but, whatever the form, whether such power has in fact been exercised. . . .

## II . . .

Respondent relies heavily, as did the Alabama courts, on statements of this Court to the effect that the Constitution does not protect libelous publications. Those statements do not foreclose our inquiry here. None of the cases sustained the use of libel laws to impose sanctions upon expression critical of the official conduct of public officials. [In] deciding the question now, we are compelled by neither precedent nor policy to give any more weight to the epithet "libel" than we have to other "mere labels" of state law. [Like] insurrection, contempt, advocacy of unlawful acts, breach of the peace, obscenity, solicitation of legal business, and the various other formulae for the repression of expression that have been challenged in this Court, libel can claim no talismanic immunity from constitutional limitations. It must be measured by standards that satisfy the First Amendment.

[We] consider this case against the background of a profound national commitment to the principle that debate on public issues should be uninhibited, robust, and wide-open, and that it may well include vehement, caustic, and sometimes unpleasantly sharp attacks on government and public officials. See [*Terminiello,* Chapter II.B, supra]. The present advertisement, as an expression of grievance and protest on one of the major public issues of our time, would seem clearly to qualify for the constitutional protection. The question is whether it forfeits that protection by the falsity of some of its factual statements and by its alleged defamation of respondent.

Authoritative interpretations of the First Amendment guarantees have consistently refused to recognize an exception for any test of truth — whether administered by judges, juries, or administrative officials — and especially one that puts the burden of proving truth on the speaker. [Erroneous] statement is inevitable in free debate, [and] it must be protected if the freedoms of expression are to have the "breathing space" that they "need ... to survive." ...

Injury to official reputation affords no more warrant for repressing speech that would otherwise be free than does factual error. Where judicial officers are involved, this Court has held that concern for the dignity and reputation of the courts does not justify the punishment as criminal contempt of criticism of the judge or his decision. [*Bridges.*] If judges are to be treated as "men of fortitude, able to thrive in a hardy climate,"[surely] the same must be true of other government officials, such as elected city commissioners. Criticism of their official conduct does not lose its constitutional protection merely because it is effective criticism and hence diminishes their official reputations.

If neither factual error nor defamatory content suffices to remove the constitutional shield from criticism of official conduct, the combination of the two elements is no less inadequate. This is the lesson to be drawn from the great controversy over the Sedition Act of 1798, which first crystallized a national awareness of the central meaning of the First Amendment. ...

Although the Sedition Act was never tested in this Court, the attack upon its validity has carried the day in the court of history. Fines levied in its prosecution were repaid by Act of Congress on the ground that it was unconstitutional. [Jefferson], as President, pardoned those who had been convicted and sentenced under the Act and remitted their fines. [These] views reflect a broad consensus that the Act, because of the restraint it imposed upon criticism of government and public officials, was inconsistent with the First Amendment. ...

What a State may not constitutionally bring about by means of a criminal statute is likewise beyond the reach of its civil law of libel. The fear of damage awards under a rule such as that invoked by the Alabama courts here may be markedly more inhibiting than the fear of prosecution under a criminal statute. [Alabama], for example, has a criminal libel law [which] allows as punishment upon conviction a fine not exceeding $500 and a prison sentence of six months. [The] judgment awarded in this case — without the need for any proof of actual pecuniary loss — was one thousand times greater than the maximum fine provided by the Alabama criminal statute, and one hundred times greater than that provided by the Sedition Act. [Whether] or not a newspaper can survive a succession of such judgments, the pall of fear and timidity imposed upon those who would give voice to public criticism is an atmosphere in which the First Amendment freedoms cannot survive. . . .

The state rule of law is not saved by its allowance of the defense of truth. [A] rule compelling the critic of official conduct to guarantee the truth of all his factual assertions — and to do so on pain of libel judgments virtually unlimited in amount — leads to a comparable "self-censorship." Allowance of the defense of truth, with the burden of proving it on the defendant, does not mean that only false speech will be deterred.[10] [Under] such a rule, would-be critics of official conduct may be deterred from voicing their criticism, even though it is believed to be true and even though it is in fact true, because of doubt whether it can be proved in court or fear of the expense of having to do so. They tend to make only statements which "steer far wider of the unlawful zone." [The] rule thus dampens the vigor and limits the variety of public debate. It is inconsistent with the First and Fourteenth Amendments.

The constitutional guarantees require, we think, a federal rule that prohibits a public official from recovering damages for a defamatory falsehood relating to his official conduct unless he proves that the statement was made with "actual malice" — that is, with knowledge that it was false or with reckless disregard of whether it was false or not. . . .

Such a privilege for criticism of official conduct is appropriately analogous to the protection accorded a public official when *he* is sued for libel by a private citizen. In Barr v. Matteo, 360 U.S. 564, 575, this Court held the utterance of a federal official to be absolutely privileged if made "within the outer perimeter" of his duties. The States accord the same immunity to statements of their highest officers. [The] reason for the official privilege is said to be that the threat of damage suits would otherwise "inhibit the fearless, vigorous, and effective administration of policies of government" and "dampen the ardor of all but the most resolute, or the most irresponsible, in the unflinching discharge of their duties."[Analogous] considerations support the privilege for the citizen-critic of government. It is as much his duty to criticize as it is the official's duty to administer. [As] Madison [said,] "the censorial power is in the people over the Government, and not in the Government over the people." . . .

---

10. Even a false statement may be deemed to make a valuable contribution to public debate, since it brings about "the clearer perception and livelier impression of truth, produced by its collision with error." Mill, On Liberty (Oxford: Blackwell, 1947), at 15; see also Milton, Areopagitica in Prose Works (Yale, 1959), Vol. II, at 561.

## III

We hold today that the Constitution delimits a State's power to award damages for libel in actions brought by public officials against critics of their official conduct. Since this is such an action,[23] the rule requiring proof of actual malice is applicable. . . .

Since respondent may seek a new trial, we deem that considerations of effective judicial administration require us to review the evidence in the present record to determine whether it could constitutionally support a judgment for respondent. [The] proof presented to show actual malice lacks the convincing clarity which the constitutional standard demands. [Although] there is evidence that the Times published the advertisement without checking its accuracy against the news stories in the Times' own files, [we] think the evidence against the Times supports at most a finding of negligence in failing to discover the misstatements, and is constitutionally insufficient to show the recklessness that is required for a finding of actual malice. . . .

We also think the evidence was constitutionally defective in another respect: it was incapable of supporting the jury's finding that the allegedly libelous statements were made "of and concerning" respondent. [The state courts embraced the proposition that criticism of government action could be treated as criticism of the officials responsible for that action for purposes of a libel suit.]

This proposition has disquieting implications for criticism of government conduct. [It would transmute] criticism of government, however impersonal it may seem on its face, into personal criticism, and hence potential libel, of the officials of whom the government is composed. [We] hold that such a proposition may not constitutionally be utilized to establish that an otherwise impersonal attack on governmental operations was a libel of an official responsible for those operations. . . .

Reversed and remanded.

MR. JUSTICE BLACK, with whom MR. JUSTICE DOUGLAS joins, concurring. . . .

"Malice," even as defined by the Court, is an elusive, abstract concept, hard to prove and hard to disprove. The requirement that malice be proved provides at best an evanescent protection for the right critically to discuss public affairs and certainly does not measure up to the sturdy safeguard embodied in the First Amendment. . . .

---

23. We have no occasion here to determine how far down into the lower ranks of government employees the "public official" designation would extend for purposes of this rule, or otherwise to specify categories of persons who would or would not be included. Nor need we here determine the boundaries of the "official conduct" concept. It is enough for the present case that respondent's position as an elected city commissioner clearly made him a public official, and that the allegations in the advertisement concerned what was allegedly his official conduct as Commissioner in charge of the Police Department. . . .

The half-million-dollar verdict [gives] dramatic proof [that] state libel laws threaten the very existence of an American press virile enough to publish unpopular views on public affairs and bold enough to criticize the conduct of public officials. [There] is no reason to believe that there are not more such huge verdicts lurking just around the corner for the Times or any other newspaper or broadcaster which might dare to criticize public officials. In fact, briefs before us show that in Alabama there are now pending eleven libel suits by local and state officials against the Times seeking $5,600,000, and five such suits against the Columbia Broadcasting System seeking $1,700,000.

In my opinion the Federal Constitution has dealt with this deadly danger to the press in the only way possible without leaving the free press open to destruction — by granting the press an absolute immunity for criticism of the way public officials do their public duty. Compare Barr v. Matteo, 360 U.S. 564. Stopgap measures like those the Court adopts are in my judgment not enough. . . .

[In a separate concurring opinion, Justice Goldberg, joined by Justice Douglas, maintained that the first amendment affords "an absolute, unconditional privilege to criticize official conduct," but noted that "defamatory statements directed against the private conduct of a public official or private citizen" may be different, for "purely private defamation has little to do with the political ends of a self-governing society."]

## Note: "The Central Meaning" of New York Times v. Sullivan

1. *The central meaning of the first amendment.* Professors Meiklejohn and Kalven maintained that the *New York Times* decision "is [an] occasion for dancing in the streets." Kalven, The *New York Times* Case: A Note on "The Central Meaning of the First Amendment," 1964 Sup. Ct. Rev. 191, 221 n.125. Consider id. at 208–209:

> The Court did not simply, in the face of an awkward history, definitively put to rest the status of the Sedition Act. More important, it found in the controversy over seditious libel the clue to "the central meaning of the First Amendment." The choice of language was unusually apt. The Amendment has a "central meaning" — a core of protection of speech without which democracy cannot function, without which, in Madison's phrase, "the censorial power" would be in the Government over the people and not "in the people over the Government." This is not the whole meaning of the Amendment. There are other freedoms protected by it. But at the center there is no doubt what speech is being protected and no doubt why it is being protected. The theory of the freedom of speech clause was put right side up for the first time. [The] central meaning of the Amendment is that seditious libel cannot be made the subject of government sanction.

IV.   Content-Based Restrictions

2. *Low value?* Does *New York Times* reject the view of *Chaplinsky* and *Beauharnais* that false statements of fact are of "slight social value" and hence not "within the area of constitutionally protected speech"? Consider footnote 10. Is the Court's primary concern with the protection of false statements of fact or with the risk that libel laws might generate a self-censorship that invades the zone of "high" value speech?

3. *Categorical balancing.* Consider Nimmer, The Right to Speak from *Times* to *Time:* First Amendment Theory Applied to Libel and Misapplied to Privacy, 56 Cal. L. Rev. 935, 942–943 (1968):

> [*New York Times*] points the way to the employment of the balancing process on the [categorical level]. That is, the Court employs balancing [for] the purpose of [determining when certain categories of speech can be restricted] within the meaning of the first amendment. [By] in effect holding that [false statements of fact can be restricted when they are] knowingly and recklessly false [the] Court implicitly [balanced] certain competing policy considerations.

Is such "categorical balancing" an appropriate way to formulate first amendment doctrine? Contrast the "definitional balancing" in *New York Times* with that in *Brandenburg.* How does each treat the issue of intent? For a critique of categorical balancing, see Aleinikoff, Constitutional Law in the Age of Balancing, 96 Yale L.J. 943, 979.

4. *Is* New York Times *overprotective of false speech?* Consider the following views:

a. Even if the first amendment protects false statements of fact in the sense that government may not criminally punish them, does it necessarily follow that newspapers should not have to pay for the costs of their speech? Why should the first amendment require the victims of false statements to bear the loss and in effect to *subsidize* newspapers?

b. *New York Times* rests on the assumption that the marketplace of ideas will function better with the Court's rule than without it. But the opposite assumption seems at least equally plausible. First, self-censorship is not intrinsically a bad thing. It all depends on what speech is discouraged. Although traditional libel law may "chill" more valuable speech than the *New York Times* rule, it also "chills" more false speech. It is by no means clear that the effect of *New York Times* will be to improve the overall quality of public debate. Second, *New York Times* may actually reduce "the quality of information [available to the public by eliminating jury judgments] as to the truth or falsity of some accusations." Nagel, How Useful Is Judicial Review in Free Speech Cases?, 69 Cornell L. Rev. 302, 323 (1984). Finally, *New York Times* may so expose public officials to journalistic abuse that it will drive capable persons away from government service, thus frustrating, rather than furthering, the political process.

Consider. Kendrick, Speech, Intent, and the Chilling Effect, 54 Wm. & Mary L. Rev. 1633 (2013):

> The chilling-effect account holds some appeal. [But] there are reasons to doubt [it]. An argument based on the chilling effect necessarily rests on suppositions about the deterrent effects of law. These suppositions in turn rest upon predictions about the behavior of speakers under counterfactual conditions. Meanwhile, the selection of a remedy, such as an intent requirement, rests on similar predictions about the remedy's speech-protective effects. In short, both the detection of a problem and the imposition of a remedy rest upon intractable empirical suppositions. [In fact], the chilling effect provides at best a weak justification for existing intent requirements in First Amendment law. [Although] at first blush these requirements might seem acceptable as a matter of rough empirical surmise, in reality they often fail to persuade.

c. Dun & Bradstreet v. Greenmoss Builders, 472 U.S. 749 (1985) (White, J., concurring):

> Instead of escalating the plaintiff's burden of proof to an almost impossible level, [the Court] could have achieved [its] goal by limiting the recoverable damages to a level that would not unduly threaten the press. Punitive [and presumed damages] might have been prohibited, or limited. Had that course been taken and the common-law standard of liability been retained, the defamed public official, upon proving falsity, could at least have had a judgment to that effect. His reputation would then be vindicated; and to the extent possible, the misinformation circulated would have been countered. He might also have recovered a modest amount, enough perhaps to pay his litigation expenses. [In] this way, both First Amendment and reputational interests would have been far better served.

d. Epstein, Was New York Times v. Sullivan Wrong?, 53 U. Chi. L. Rev. 782, 797, 804 (1986):

> The general tendency in defamation cases has always been for a powerful rule of strict liability. [In] strict liability the probability of recovery is relatively large and the damages can be kept relatively small. With actual malice the probability of recovery is relatively small and damages are relatively large. It takes little mathematical sophistication to realize that if success is more likely with strict liability, and damages are more generous with actual malice, it becomes uncertain whether the total liabilities [are] greater under the strict liability rule or the actual malice rule.

Epstein concludes that, once one takes into account "litigation costs" and "reputational effects," the common law rule of strict liability is preferable to the actual malice rule of New York Times v. Sullivan.

5. *Is* New York Times *underprotective of false speech?* Consider the following views:

a. Anderson, Libel and Press Self-Censorship, 53 Tex. L. Rev. 422, 424–425, 436 (1975):

> [*New York Times* will not prevent self-censorship because] it does little to reduce the cost of defending against libel claims. Instead, it perpetuates a system of censorship [in] which the relevant question is not whether a story is libelous, but whether the subject is likely to sue, and if so, how much it will cost to defend. [The decision] has failed to alleviate this problem primarily because it usually has no effect until a case reaches the trial stage.

b. Smolla, Let the Author Beware: The Rejuvenation of the American Law of Libel, 132 U. Pa. L. Rev. 1, 4–7, 12, 91–93 (1984):

> The data show a trend toward more generous jury awards, and a corresponding trend toward the media settling suits at a substantial cost. [One] study showed that thirty out of forty-seven damage awards included punitive damages, and seven of those punitive damage awards were for $1 million or more. [The] prospect of such lucrative awards is likely to entice more potential defamation plaintiffs to bring [suit]. A failure to adjust defamation doctrine [can] be expected to have a severe impact on the media. [Many] media outlets [defend] libel actions under the peril of shutdown if they lose. [One] alternative to current law is to allow punitive damages only when the plaintiff, in addition to proving actual malice, proves common law ill-will malice. [Preferably,] punitive damages should be [abolished altogether].

6. *The limits of* New York Times. What does the Court mean by "reckless disregard"? Does *New York Times* implicitly prohibit criminal prosecutions for libel of public officials? Are all public employees "public officials" within the meaning of *New York Times*?

Consider the following decisions, which shed light on these and related issues: Milkovich v. Lorain Journal Co., 497 U.S. 1 (1990) (a statement "must be provable as false before there can be liability"); Harte-Hanks Communications v. Connaughton, 491 U.S. 657 (1989) (neither failure to comply with "professional standards" nor publication of falsehood in order to increase profits is in itself sufficient to establish "actual malice," but "purposeful avoidance of the truth" may be sufficient); Philadelphia Newspapers, Inc. v. Hepps, 475 U.S. 767 (1986) (the "plaintiff must bear the burden of proving that the statements at issue are false"); Monitor Patriot Co. v. Roy, 401 U.S. 265 (1971) ("a charge of criminal conduct, no matter how remote in time or place, can never be irrelevant to an official's or a candidate's fitness for office for purposes of application of" *New York Times*); St. Amant v. Thompson, 390 U.S. 727 (1968) (failure to investigate or otherwise seek corroboration prior to publication is not reckless disregard for the truth unless the publisher acts with a "high degree of awareness of [probable] falsity"); Garrison v. Louisiana, 379 U.S. 64 (1964) (first amendment does not absolutely prohibit criminal prosecution for libel even of public officials, but *New York Times* standard applies).

Perhaps the most important question remaining after *New York Times* was whether the privilege it recognized governed only libel of public officials or whether it extended to libel of other persons as well.

**CURTIS PUBLISHING CO. v. BUTTS; ASSOCIATED PRESS v. WALKER**, 388 U.S. 130 (1967). In these companion cases, the Court examined the question whether a libel action brought by an individual who is a "public figure," but not a "public official," must also be governed by the *New York Times* standard. Butts brought an action for libel, alleging that the defendant had published an article falsely accusing him of conspiring to "fix" a football game between the University of Georgia and the University of Alabama. At the time of the article, Butts was the athletic director of the University of Georgia, a state university, but was employed by the Georgia Athletic Association, a private corporation. Butts had served previously as head football coach at the university and had an established national reputation. In the companion case, Walker sued the Associated Press for libel, claiming that it had distributed a news dispatch falsely reporting that, when a riot erupted on the campus of the University of Mississippi because of federal efforts to enforce court-ordered desegregation, Walker had taken command of the crowd, encouraged it to use violence, and personally led a charge against the federal marshals. Walker, a private citizen at the time of the riot and publication, had pursued a distinguished military career and was a figure of national prominence. In each case, the jury found the defendant liable under state law, the trial judge approved a damage award of about $500,000, and the defendant maintained that *New York Times* should govern and that it thus could not be held liable without proof that it had published the story either knowing it to be false or with reckless disregard for the truth.

In a sharply divided set of opinions, the Court held the *New York Times* standard applicable to "public figures" as well as to "public officials," and, further, that both Butts and Walker constituted "public figures" for purposes of the rule. Chief Justice Warren, joined by Justices Brennan and White, observed that "increasingly in this country, the distinctions between governmental and private sectors are blurred," and that many individuals "who do not hold public office at the moment are nevertheless intimately involved in the resolution of important public questions or, by reason of their fame, shape events in areas of concern to society at large." Moreover, Chief Justice Warren argued, "as a class these 'public figures' have as ready access as 'public officials' to mass media of communication, both to influence policy and to counter criticism of their views and activities." Thus, Chief Justice Warren concluded, "differentiation between 'public figures' and 'public officials' and adoption of separate standards of proof for each have no basis in law, logic, or First

Amendment policy." Justice Black, joined by Justice Douglas, maintained that "the First Amendment was intended to leave the press [absolutely] free from the harassment of libel judgments," but accepted the narrower rationale of Chief Justice Warren "'in order for the Court to be able at this time to agree on [a disposition of] this important case.'" Justice Harlan, joined by Justices Clark, Stewart, and Fortas, concurred in the result.

Is the extension of *New York Times* to "public figures" mandated by "the central meaning of the first amendment"?

**GERTZ v. ROBERT WELCH, INC., 418 U.S. 323 (1974).** In 1968, a Chicago policeman named Nuccio shot and killed a youth named Nelson. The state prosecuted Nuccio and obtained a conviction for murder. The Nelson family retained Gertz, a Chicago attorney, to represent them in civil litigation against Nuccio. In 1969, respondent, publisher of American Opinion, a monthly outlet for the views of the John Birch Society, ran an article in which it accused Gertz of being the architect of a "frame-up" of Nuccio and stated that Gertz had a criminal record and long-standing communist affiliations. Gertz filed this action for libel. After the jury returned a $50,000 verdict for Gertz, the trial court entered judgment for respondent, concluding that the *New York Times* standard applied to any discussion of a "public issue."

The Supreme Court, in an opinion by Justice Powell, reversed: "The principal issue in this case is whether a newspaper or broadcaster that publishes defamatory falsehoods about an individual who is neither a public official nor a public figure may claim a constitutional privilege against liability for the injury inflicted by those statements. [We] begin with the common ground. Under the First Amendment there is no such thing as a false idea. However pernicious an opinion may seem, we depend for its correction not on the conscience of judges and juries but on the competition of other ideas. But there is no constitutional value in false statements of fact. Neither the intentional lie nor the careless error materially advances society's interest in 'uninhibited, robust, and wide-open' debate on public issues. [New York Times Co. v. Sullivan.] They belong to that category of utterances which 'are no essential part of any exposition of ideas, and are of such slight social value as a step to truth that any benefit that may be derived from them is clearly outweighed by the social interest in order and morality.'[*Chaplinsky*.]

"Although the erroneous statement of fact is not worthy of constitutional protection, it is nevertheless inevitable in free debate. [And] punishment of error runs the risk of inducing a cautious and restrictive exercise of the constitutionally guaranteed freedoms of speech and press. Our decisions recognize that a rule of strict liability that compels a publisher or broadcaster to guarantee the accuracy of his factual assertions may lead to intolerable self-censorship. [The] First Amendment requires that we protect some falsehood in order to protect speech that matters.

"The need to avoid self-censorship by the news media is, however, not the only societal value at issue. If it were, this Court would have embraced long ago the view that publishers and broadcasters enjoy an unconditional and indefeasible immunity from liability for defamation. [The] legitimate state interest underlying the law of libel is the compensation of individuals for the harm inflicted on them by defamatory falsehood. We would not lightly require the State to abandon this purpose, for [the] individual's right to the protection of his own good name 'reflects [our] basic concept of the essential dignity and worth of every human being — a concept at the root of any decent system of ordered [liberty].' . . .

"The *New York Times* standard defines the level of constitutional protection appropriate to the context of defamation of a public person. [We] have no difficulty in distinguishing among defamation plaintiffs. The first remedy of any victim of defamation is self-help — using available opportunities to contradict the lie or correct the error and thereby to minimize its adverse impact on reputation. Public officials and public figures usually enjoy significantly greater access to the channels of effective communication and hence have a more realistic opportunity to counteract false statements than private individuals normally enjoy. Private individuals are therefore more vulnerable to injury, and the state interest in protecting them is correspondingly greater.

"[Moreover, an] individual who decides to seek governmental office must accept certain necessary consequences of that involvement in public affairs. He runs the risk of closer public scrutiny than might otherwise be the case. [Those] classed as public figures stand in a similar position. [For] the most part those who attain this status have assumed roles of especial prominence in the affairs of society. Some occupy positions of such persuasive power and influence that they are deemed public figures for all purposes. More commonly, those classed as public figures have thrust themselves to the forefront of particular public controversies in order to influence the resolution of the issues involved. In either event, they invite attention and comment.

"Even if the foregoing generalities do not obtain in every instance, the communications media are entitled to act on the assumption that public officials and public figures have voluntarily exposed themselves to increased risk of injury from defamatory falsehood concerning them. No such assumption is justified with respect to a private individual. He has not accepted public office or assumed an 'influential role in ordering society.' [He] has relinquished no part of his interest in the protection of his own good name, and consequently he has a more compelling call on the courts for redress of injury inflicted by defamatory falsehood. Thus, private individuals are not only more vulnerable to injury than public officials and public figures; they are also more deserving of recovery.

"For these reasons we conclude that the States should retain substantial latitude in their efforts to enforce a legal remedy for defamatory falsehood injurious to the reputation of a private individual. The extension of the *New York Times* test [to defamatory falsehoods relating to private persons if the statements concerned matters of general or public interest] would abridge this legitimate state interest to a degree that we find unacceptable. [We] hold that, so long as they do not impose liability without fault, the States may define for themselves the appropriate standard of liability for a publisher or broadcaster of defamatory falsehood injurious to a private individual. . . .

"[We] endorse this approach in recognition of the strong and legitimate state interest in compensating private individuals for injury to reputation. But this countervailing state interest extends no further than compensation for actual injury. [We] hold that the States may not permit recovery of presumed or punitive damages, at least when liability is not based on a showing of knowledge of falsity or reckless disregard for the truth."

*reckless disregard for truth*

Justice Douglas dissented: "The Court describes this case as a return to the struggle of 'defin[ing] the proper accommodation between the law of defamation and the freedoms of speech and press protected by the First Amendment.' [I] would suggest that the struggle is a quite hopeless one, for, in light of the command of the First Amendment, no 'accommodation' of its freedoms can be 'proper' except those made by the Framers themselves."

Justice Brennan dissented: "[We] strike the proper accommodation between avoidance of media self-censorship and protection of individual reputations only when we require States to apply the [*New York Times*] knowing-or-reckless-falsity standard in civil libel actions concerning media reports of the involvement of private individuals in events of public or general interest."

Justice White dissented: "To me, it is quite incredible to suggest that threats of libel suits from private citizens are causing the press to refrain from publishing the truth. I know of no hard facts to support that proposition, and the Court furnishes none. [In] any event, if the Court's principal concern is to protect the communications industry from large libel judgments, it would appear that its new requirements with respect to general and punitive damages would be ample protection. Why it also feels compelled to escalate the threshold standard of liability I cannot fathom, particularly when this will eliminate in many instances the plaintiff's possibility of securing a judicial determination that the damaging publication was indeed false, whether or not he is entitled to recover money damages. Under the Court's new rules, the plaintiff must prove not only the defamatory statement but also some degree of fault accompanying it. The publication may be wholly false and the wrong to him unjustified, but his case will nevertheless be dismissed for failure to prove negligence or other fault on the part of the publisher. I find it unacceptable to distribute the risk in this manner and force the wholly innocent victim to bear the injury; for, as between the two, the defamer is the only culpable party. It is he who circulated a falsehood that he was not required to publish."

Chief Justice Burger also filed a dissenting opinion.

## Note: Public and Private Figures, Public and Private Speech

1. *Was Gertz a "public figure"?* Consider Justice Powell's analysis of this question:

> [The public figure] designation may rest on either of two alternative bases. In some instances an individual may achieve such pervasive fame or notoriety that he becomes a public figure for all purposes and in all contexts. More commonly, an individual voluntarily injects himself or is drawn into a particular public controversy and thereby becomes a public figure for a limited range of issues. In either case such persons assume special prominence in the resolution of public questions.
>
> Petitioner has long been active in community and professional affairs. He has served as an officer of local civic groups and of various professional organizations, and he has published several books and articles on legal subjects. Although petitioner was consequently well known in some circles, he had achieved no general fame or notoriety in the community. [Absent] clear evidence of general fame or notoriety in the community, and pervasive involvement in the affairs of society, an individual should not be deemed a public personality for all aspects of his life. It is preferable to reduce the public-figure question to a more meaningful context by looking to the nature and extent of an individual's participation in the particular controversy giving rise to the defamation.
>
> In this context it is plain that petitioner was not a public figure. He played a minimal role at the coroner's inquest, and his participation related solely to his representation of a private client. He took no part in the criminal prosecution of Officer Nuccio. Moreover, he never discussed either the criminal or civil litigation with the press and was never quoted as having done so. He plainly did not thrust himself into the vortex of this public issue, nor did he engage the public's attention in an attempt to influence its outcome. We are persuaded that the trial court did not err in refusing to characterize petitioner as a public figure for the purpose of this litigation.

2. *Public figures.* What arguments would you make on behalf of the plaintiffs and defendants in the following situations:

a. Plaintiff was divorced by Russell Firestone, the scion of one of America's wealthiest families. Time magazine erroneously reported that the divorce was granted on the ground of adultery. Plaintiff sued Time for libel. In Time, Inc. v. Firestone, 424 U.S. 448 (1976), the Court rejected Time's claim that Mrs. Firestone was a public figure: "[She] did not assume any role of especial prominence in the affairs of society, other than perhaps Palm Beach society, and she did not thrust herself to the forefront of any particular public controversy in order to influence the resolution of the issues involved in it."

b. In the late 1950s, in a widely publicized case, plaintiff was convicted of contempt for his refusal to appear before a grand jury investigating Soviet espionage. Sixteen years later, defendant published a book erroneously identifying plaintiff as a Soviet agent. Plaintiff sued for libel. In Wolston v. Reader's

Digest Association, 443 U.S. 157 (1979), the Court rejected the publisher's claim that plaintiff was a "limited-purpose public figure." The Court emphasized that plaintiff had not "engaged the attention of the public in an attempt to influence the resolution of the issues involved" and explained that one who commits a crime does not become a public figure, even for the purpose "of comment on a limited range of issues relating to his conviction," for "[to] hold otherwise would create an 'open season' for all who sought to defame persons convicted of a crime."

c. Over the course of several years, various federal agencies spent almost half a million dollars funding plaintiff's research into aggressive monkey behavior. Senator Proxmire awarded the federal agencies his Golden Fleece of the Month Award, an award designed to publicize what Proxmire believed to be the most egregious examples of wasteful government spending. Claiming Proxmire's description of his research to be inaccurate, plaintiff sued for libel. In Hutchinson v. Proxmire, 443 U.S. 111 (1979), the Court rejected Proxmire's argument that plaintiff was a "limited-purpose public figure" for the "purpose of comment on his receipt of federal funds for research projects." The Court concluded that plaintiff "at no time assumed any role of public prominence in the broad question of concern about expenditures," and that "neither his applications for federal grants nor his publications in professional journals can be said to have invited that degree of public attention and comment on his receipt of federal grants essential to meet the public figure level."

3. *The need for vindication.* Justice White expressed concern in *Gertz* that the Court's decision would eliminate the private plaintiff's opportunity to vindicate himself by obtaining a judicial declaration of falsity. Is there any way to deal with this concern after *Gertz*? Consider Freund, Political Libel and Obscenity, 42 F.R.D. 491, 497 (1966): "Plaintiffs [should] be permitted to request a special verdict, so that if there is a verdict for the defendant based solely and simply on [the *New York Times* or *Gertz* privileges, the jury could nevertheless find] that the utterances were untrue." Consider also Justice Brennan's suggestion in *Gertz* that states could enact statutes "not requiring proof of fault, which provide for an action for retraction or for publication of a court's determination of falsity if the plaintiff is able to demonstrate that false statements have been published concerning his activities." Would such a statute violate the first amendment "right" of newspapers not to publish information against their will? See Miami Herald Publishing Co. v. Tornillo, 418 U.S. 241 (1974), Chapter VI.D, infra.

4. *The limits of Gertz.* Does *Gertz*'s "fault" standard govern all libelous statements not involving public officials or public figures, whether or not such statements concern matters of "general or public interest"? Is the *Gertz* privilege available only to media defendants? Note Justice Powell's consistent references to the media. Can denial of the privilege to nonmedia defendants be justified on the ground that the "press" is entitled to special constitutional protection?

**DUN & BRADSTREET v. GREENMOSS BUILDERS, 472 U.S. 749** (1985). Petitioner, a credit reporting agency, provides subscribers with financial information about businesses. Petitioner sent a report to five subscribers indicating that respondent, a construction contractor, had filed a voluntary petition for bankruptcy. This report was inaccurate. In respondent's defamation action against petitioner, the trial judge instructed the jury that it could award presumed and punitive damages without a showing of "actual malice." The jury returned a verdict in favor of respondent and awarded $50,000 in compensatory or presumed damages and $300,000 in punitive damages. The Supreme Court, in a five-to-four decision, affirmed the judgment.

Justice Powell's plurality opinion was joined by Justices Rehnquist and O'Connor: "We have never considered whether the *Gertz* balance obtains when the defamatory statements involve no issue of public concern. [The] state interest [here] is identical to the one weighed in *Gertz*. [The] First Amendment interest, on the other hand, is less important than the one weighed in *Gertz*. We have long recognized that not all speech is of equal First Amendment importance. It is speech on 'matters of public concern' that is 'at the heart of the First Amendment's protection.' In contrast, speech on matters of purely private concern is of less First Amendment concern. [When the state regulates such expression], 'There is no threat to the free and robust debate of public issues, [and] there is no potential interference with a meaningful dialogue of ideas concerning self-government.' [While] such speech is not totally unprotected by the First Amendment, its protections are less stringent. [In] light of the reduced constitutional value of speech involving no matters of public concern, we hold that the state interest adequately supports awards of presumed and punitive damages — even absent a showing of 'actual malice.'"

Chief Justice Burger and Justice White concurred in the judgment. Justice Brennan, joined by Justices Marshall, Blackmun, and Stevens, dissented on the ground that, under *Gertz*, respondent "should be required to show actual malice to receive presumed or punitive damages."

### Note: Other False Statements of Fact

In *Gertz*, the Court again made explicit its conclusion that "there is no constitutional value in false statements of fact." Nonetheless, in its *New York Times/Gertz* line of authority, the Court granted substantial first amendment protection to false statements of fact in the libel context to avoid "self-censorship" and "to protect speech that matters." How should false statements of fact be dealt with in other contexts? Consider the following:

a. Suppose an individual falsely asserts that a particular law was enacted because a majority of the legislators had been "paid off." In what circumstances, if any, may government criminally punish an individual for factually false utterances that defame government itself?

b. Recall section 3 of the Espionage Act of 1917, Chapter II, supra: "Whoever, when the United States is at war, shall willfully make or convey false reports [with] intent to interfere with [the] success of the military [forces] of the United States [shall be guilty of a felony]." Is the act constitutional in light of the *New York Times*/*Gertz* line of authority? If you were a member of Congress, how might you redraft it to satisfy the first amendment? For discussion of the prosecution of an American Nazi under this provision during World War II, see G. Stone, Perilous Times: Free Speech in Wartime 258–275 (2004).

c. The problem of false statements of fact arises often in the context of political campaigns. Suppose, for example, a supporter of a candidate's opponent falsely accuses the candidate of some impropriety. So long as the candidate can meet the demands of *New York Times*, he can, of course, sue for libel. That may be small consolation, however, if he loses the election. To avoid that result, can the candidate obtain an injunction against further dissemination of the falsehood? Can a state electoral commission prohibit distribution of any campaign literature containing the falsehood? Suppose, instead of defaming an opponent, a candidate or his supporters falsely inflate the candidate's own qualifications. In what circumstances, and by what means, may such speech be restricted? See Pestrak v. Ohio Elections Commission, 926 F.2d 573 (6th Cir. 1991) (upholding state election commission's restriction on the dissemination of false statements in the context of political campaigns); Tomei v. Finley, 512 F. Supp. 695 (N.D. Ill. 1981) (granting a preliminary injunction against a candidate's use of a misleading campaign slogan); Stone, The Rules of Evidence and the Rules of Public Debate, 1993 U. Chi. Legal F. 127, 137–141 (arguing that such restrictions are invalid because of the "great danger" inherent in permitting "government to involve itself in the political process in this manner"); Marshall, False Campaign Speech and the First Amendment, 53 U. Pa. L. Rev. 285, 299 (2004) ("authorizing the government to decide what is true or false in campaign speech opens the door to partisan abuse"); Ashdown, Distorting Democracy: Campaign Lies in the 21st Century, 20 Wm. & Mary B. Rts. J. 1085 (2012).

d. In a state law defamation action filed by attorney Johnnie Cochran, a California trial court found that defendant Tory had falsely claimed that Cochran owed him money, picketed Cochran's office with signs containing insults, and pursued him in public, chanting similar insults, in order to coerce Cochran into paying Tory money to get him to desist from such defamatory activity. Because Tory was judgment-proof, the California court enjoined him from continuing in this conduct. Is such a prior restraint permissible in these circumstances? See Tory v. Cochran, 544 U.S. 734 (2004) (invalidating the injunction in light of Cochran's death).

**UNITED STATES v. ALVAREZ, 132 S. Ct. 2537 (2012).** The federal Stolen Valor Act makes it a crime for any person to falsely state that he was "awarded any decoration or medal authorized by Congress for the Armed

Forces of the United States." At a public meeting, Alvarez falsely stated that he had received the Congressional Medal of Honor. This statement was made not to secure any particular benefit, but as "a pathetic attempt to gain respect that eluded him." He was prosecuted and convicted for violating the act. The Supreme Court held the act unconstitutional.

Justice Kennedy delivered a plurality opinion joined by Chief Justice Roberts and Justices Ginsburg and Sotomayor: "The Government [argues] that false statements 'have no First Amendment value in themselves,' and [are thus] beyond constitutional protection. [But the] Court has never endorsed the categorical rule [that] false statements receive no First Amendment protection." Although conceding that some false statements could be restricted, including defamatory statements, perjury, and fraudulent statements intended to extract something from another, Justice Kennedy noted that the Stolen Valor Act applies broadly, without regard to whether anyone else is harmed by the falsehood. "Permitting the government to decree this speech to be a criminal offense [without regard to the circumstances] would endorse government authority to compile a list of subjects about which false statements are punishable. That governmental power has no clear limiting principle. Our constitutional tradition stands against the idea that we need Oceania's Ministry of Truth [citing George Orwell's Nineteen Eighty-Four]. Were the Court to hold that the interest in truthful discourse alone is sufficient to sustain a ban on speech, [it] would give government a broad censorial power unprecedented in [our] constitutional tradition."

Although agreeing that the "Government's interest in protecting the integrity of the Medal of Honor is beyond question," Justice Kennedy concluded that in order to satisfy "exacting scrutiny" the restriction must "be 'actually necessary' to achieve" the government's interests. Here, the "Government points to no evidence [that] the public's general perception of military awards is diluted by false claims such as those made by Alvarez." Moreover, the "Government has not shown, and cannot show, why counterspeech would not suffice to achieve its interest." Indeed, if the government really wants to address this interest it can simply create an online database that "could list Congressional Medal of Honor winners." It would then "be easy to verify and expose false claims." In such circumstances, Justice Kennedy held that the act was unconstitutional.

Justice Breyer, joined by Justice Kagan, concurred. Justice Breyer argued that "intermediate scrutiny" was appropriate in this situation, because "false factual statements are less likely than are true factual statements to make a valuable contribution to the marketplace of ideas [and] the government often has good reasons to prohibit such false speech." Although noting that the Court "has frequently [said] that false factual statements enjoy little First Amendment protection," Justice Breyer observed that this does not mean "no protection at all." After all, he argued, false "factual statements can serve useful human objectives." In social contexts, for example, they can "prevent embarrassment, protect privacy, shield a person from prejudice, provide the sick with comfort, or preserve a child's innocence; in public contexts [they can] stop a panic or otherwise preserve calm in the face of danger."

Moreover, Justice Breyer noted, there are dangers to free speech in allowing the government to punish even lies. As the Court recognized in New York Times v. Sullivan, "the threat of criminal prosecution for making a false statement can inhibit the speaker from making true statements, thereby 'chilling' a kind of speech that lies at the First Amendment's heart." In addition, he recognized, the inevitability of inaccurate statements in public discourse "provides a weapon to a government broadly empowered to prosecute falsity without more. And those who are unpopular may fear that the government will use that weapon selectively, say by prosecuting a pacifist who supports his cause by (falsely) claiming to have been a war hero, while ignoring members of other political groups who might make similar claims."

Like Justice Kennedy, though, Justice Breyer conceded that the government can constitutionally restrict some types of factually false statements, such as fraud, defamation, perjury, false statements about terrorist threats, and impersonation of a government official. But in such instances, he reasoned, "limitations of context, requirements of proof of injury, and the like, narrow the statute to a subset of lies where specific harm is more likely to occur," whereas the "statute before us lacks any such limiting features." Because the "government has provided no convincing explanation as to why a more finely tailored statute would not work," he concluded that "the statute as presently drafted works disproportionate constitutional harm. It consequently fails intermediate scrutiny, and so violates the First Amendment."

Justice Alito, joined by Justices Scalia and Thomas, dissented: "The [act] was enacted to stem an epidemic of false claims about military decorations. [It] is a narrow statute that presents no threat to the freedom of speech. The statute reaches only knowingly false statements about hard facts directly within a speaker's personal knowledge. These lies have no value in and of themselves, and proscribing them does not chill any valuable speech. [Moreover,] the Act is strictly viewpoint neutral. [It] applies equally to all false statements, whether they tend to disparage or commend the Government, the military, or the system of military honors.

"[At the same time, these lies] inflict substantial harm. In many instances, the harm is tangible in nature: Individuals often falsely represent themselves as award recipients in order to obtain financial or other material rewards. [In] other cases the harm is less tangible, but nonetheless significant. The lies proscribed by the [act] tend to debase the distinctive honor of military awards. [It] is well recognized in trademark law that the proliferation of cheap imitations of luxury goods blurs the "'signal" given out by the purchasers of the originals.'[Surely] it was reasonable for Congress to conclude that the goal of preserving the integrity of our country's top military honors is at least as worthy as that of protecting the prestige associated with fancy watches and designer handbags. . . .

"Time and again, this Court has recognized that as a general matter false factual statements possess no intrinsic First Amendment value. [There] are more than 100 federal criminal statutes that punish false statements made in connection with areas of federal agency concern. [Of course,] there are broad areas in which any attempt by the state to penalize purportedly false speech would present a grave and unacceptable danger of suppressing truthful speech. [But] the Stolen Valor Act presents no risk at all that valuable speech will be suppressed. The speech punished by the Act is not only verifiably false and entirely lacking in intrinsic value, but it also fails to serve any instrumental purpose that the First Amendment might protect. . . .

"The plurality [worries] that a decision sustaining the Stolen Valor Act might prompt Congress and the state legislatures to enact laws criminalizing lies about 'an endless list of subjects.' The plurality apparently fears that we will see laws making it a crime to lie about civilian awards such as college degrees. [This] concern is likely unfounded. With very good reason, military honors have traditionally been regarded as quite different from civilian awards. [In] any event, if the plurality's concern is not entirely fanciful, it falls outside the purview of the First Amendment. [If] there is a problem with, let us say, a law making it a criminal offense to falsely claim to have been a high school valedictorian, the problem is not the suppression of speech but the misuse of the criminal law, which should be reserved for conduct that inflicts or threatens truly serious societal harm. The objection to this hypothetical law would be the same as the objection to a law making it a crime to eat potato chips during the graduation ceremony. [The] safeguard against such laws is democracy, not the First Amendment. Not every foolish law is unconstitutional."

Is there any good reason not to allow the government to punish "knowingly false statements about hard facts directly within a speaker's personal knowledge"? Because an individual knows to a virtual certainty whether or not he's won the Congressional Medal of Honor, does enforcement of the Stolen Valor Act pose *any* realistic risk of chilling valuable speech? Consider Han, Autobiographical Lies and the First Amendment's Protection of Self-Defining Speech, 87 N.Y.U. L. Rev. 70, 97–102 (2012):

The interest in individual self-definition [recognizes] people's fundamental interest in controlling the contours of their public personas. [Statements] about ourselves are typically the most direct way by which we craft our personas for others. [Of] course, we do not paint the same picture of ourselves for every person. The persona we construct for our friends is different from the one we construct for our employers, parents, or spouses. [The] interest in self-definition is rooted in an autonomy-based conception of the First Amendment. [We] often lie about ourselves as a means of controlling how we portray ourselves to the world. [Truthful] autobiographical statements [are] often as deceptive as false ones. For example, people often select the true facts they disclose about themselves in order to create a false impression for a particular audience. [It] thus seems incorrect to say that only true speech legitimately advances the self-definition interest.

Assuming Justice Alito is correct that the government can constitutionally punish "knowingly false statements about hard facts directly within a speaker's personal knowledge," because such speech has no first amendment value and such a restriction chills no valuable speech, should it matter that the Stolen Valor Act punishes only some speech falling within the category, but not other speech falling within it? For example, is it constitutional for the government to punish "knowingly false statements about hard facts directly within a speaker's personal knowledge" if the statements relate to military medals but not if they relate to college degrees? Is there any first amendment problem in the government's picking and choosing which of those statements to punish and which to leave alone? Is Justice Alito right that such choices pose no first amendment issue? See R.A.V. v. City of St. Paul, this chapter, infra.

**HUSTLER MAGAZINE v. FALWELL, 485 U.S. 46 (1988).** Hustler magazine published a "parody" of an advertisement concerning the nationally known minister Jerry Falwell. The relevant item contained the name and picture of Reverend Falwell and an "interview" in which Falwell says that his "first time" was during a drunken incestuous rendezvous with his mother in an outhouse. Small print at the bottom of the page noted "ad parody — not to be taken seriously." Falwell brought suit for libel and intentional infliction of emotional distress. The jury found against Falwell on the libel claim because the ad parody could not "reasonably be understood as describing actual facts" about Falwell. The jury found in favor of Falwell on the intentional infliction of emotional distress claim, however, and awarded $100,000 in compensatory damages and $50,000 in punitive damages. The court of appeals affirmed. The Supreme Court, in a unanimous decision, reversed.

Chief Justice Rehnquist wrote the opinion: "The sort of robust political debate encouraged by the First Amendment is bound to produce speech that is critical of [public officials and public figures]. Such criticism, inevitably, will not always be reasoned or moderate; public figures as well as public officials will be subject to 'vehement, caustic, and sometimes unpleasantly sharp attacks.' [New York Times.]

"Of course, this does not mean that *any* speech about a public figure is immune from sanction in the form of damages. [To the contrary, because] false statements of fact are particularly valueless, [we have consistently held since New York Times] that a public figure may hold a speaker liable for the damage to reputation caused by publication of a defamatory falsehood, but only if the statement was made 'with knowledge that it was false or with reckless disregard of whether it was false or not.' . . .

"Respondent argues [that] a different standard should apply in this case because here the State seeks to prevent not reputational damage, but the severe emotional distress suffered by the person who is the subject of an offensive publication. In respondent's view, [so] long as the utterance was intended to inflict emotional distress, was outrageous, and did in fact inflict serious emotional distress, it is of no constitutional import whether the statement was a fact or an opinion, or whether it was true or false. It is the intent to cause injury that is the gravamen of the tort, and the State's interest in preventing emotional harm simply outweighs whatever interest a speaker may have in speech of this type.

"Generally speaking the law does not regard the intent to inflict emotional distress as one which should receive much [solicitude]. But [while a] bad motive may be deemed controlling for purposes of tort liability in other areas of the law, we think the First Amendment prohibits such a result in the area of public debate about public figures. Were we to hold otherwise, there can be little doubt that political cartoonists and satirists would be subjected to damage awards without any showing that their work falsely defamed its subject. [The] appeal of the political cartoon or caricature is often based on exploration of unfortunate physical traits or politically embarrassing events — an exploration often calculated to injure the feelings of the subject of the portrayal. The art of the cartoonist is often not reasoned or evenhanded, but slashing and one-sided. . . .

"Respondent contends, however, that the caricature in question was so 'outrageous' as to distinguish it from more traditional political cartoons. [If] it were possible by laying down a principled standard to separate the one from the other, public discourse would probably suffer little or no harm. But we doubt that there is any such standard, and we are quite sure that the pejorative description 'outrageous' does not supply one. 'Outrageousness' in the area of political and social discourse has an inherent subjectiveness about it which would allow a jury to impose liability on the basis of the jurors' tastes or views, or perhaps on the basis of the dislike of a particular expression. An 'outrageousness' standard thus runs afoul of our longstanding refusal to allow damages to be awarded because the speech in question may have an adverse emotional impact on the audience. . . .

"Admittedly, these oft-repeated First Amendment principles [are] subject to limitations. We recognized in *Pacifica Foundation* [section G, infra] that [profanity] is 'not entitled to absolute constitutional protection under all circumstances.' In [*Chaplinsky*] we held that a state could lawfully punish an individual for the use of insulting or 'fighting [words].' These limitations are but recognition of the observation in [*Dun & Bradstreet*] that this Court has 'long recognized that not all speech is of equal First Amendment importance.' But the sort of expression involved in this case does not seem to us to be governed by any exception to the general First Amendment principles stated above.

*Actual malice needed*

"We conclude that public figures and public officials may not recover for the tort of intentional infliction of emotional distress by reason of publications such as the one here at issue without showing in addition that the publication contains a false statement of fact which was made with 'actual malice,' i.e., with knowledge that the statement was false or with reckless disregard as to whether or not it was true . . ."

Suppose X posts online a parody analogous to the one in *Hustler* about Y, a nonpublic figure whom he particularly dislikes. Can Y sue X for intentional infliction of emotional distress? Recall *Snyder v. Phelps*. Can Y sue X for invasion of privacy? Suppose X calls Y and pretending to be a doctor falsely tells Y that Y's son has been killed in a car accident. Can Y sue X for intentional infliction of emotional distress in that situation after *Snyder* and *Hustler*?

Did the Court in *Hustler* give sufficient weight to Falwell's dignitary interests? Consider *Strauss Caricature*, 75 BVerfGE 369 (1987), in which the German Constitutional Court reviewed a civil action for damages brought by Bavarian Prime Minister Franz Josef Strauss against the magazine *Konkret*, which had published a series of disparaging cartoons portraying Strauss as a rutting pig. One cartoon, for example, depicted a pig, clearly drawn to be a caricature of Strauss, copulating with other pigs dressed in judicial robes. Noting that individual dignity is a "preferred constitutional value," the court held that the cartoons were not protected by Germany's constitutional guarantee of freedom of speech. The court explained that by depicting the Prime Minister as a pig engaged in bestial sexual conduct, the cartoons were clearly "intended to devalue the person concerned as a person, to deprive him of his dignity as a human being," and therefore went "too far" to merit constitutional protection. See Ronald Krotoszynski, The First Amendment in Cross-Cultural Perspective 112 (2006); Carmi, Dignity — The Enemy from Within: A Theoretical and Comparative Analysis of Human Dignity as a Free Speech Justification, 9 U. Pa. J. Const. L. 957 (2007).

## B.   "NONNEWSWORTHY" DISCLOSURES OF "PRIVATE" INFORMATION

In the *Pentagon Papers* case, the Supreme Court took a strong position against government efforts to prohibit the publication of truthful information. In the years since, the Court has extended this position beyond the context of classified national security information. In Landmark Communications, Inc. v. Virginia, 435 U.S. 829 (1978), for example, the Court invalidated a state statute making it a crime for any person to divulge information regarding confidential matters pending before the state's Judicial Inquiry and Review Commission. Although the state argued that the disclosure of confidential information about pending investigations would create a clear and present danger to the effective operation of the commission by chilling the willingness of individuals to file complaints, the Court held that if the state wanted to protect this interest it had to do so by means other than restricting the press's publication of truthful information, for example, by adopting "careful internal procedures" to preserve confidentiality and by prohibiting participants in the commission's proceedings from divulging confidential information.

Similarly, in Nebraska Press Association v. Stuart, 427 U.S. 539 (1976), the Court unanimously held unconstitutional a judge's order, issued in anticipation of a trial for a multiple murder that had attracted widespread news coverage, that restrained newspapers and broadcasters from disseminating accounts of confessions made by the accused or any other facts "strongly implicative" of the accused. The Court explained that even though the Constitution guarantees trial "by an impartial jury," and that a trial judge therefore "has a major responsibility" to protect the rights of a defendant against unduly prejudicial pretrial publicity, the judge must use alternative means to mitigate the danger, such as changing the trial venue, postponing the trial, questioning prospective jurors about their knowledge, sequestering jurors, and restricting what the lawyers, police, and witnesses may "say to anyone."

Are some types of information so private and so nonnewsworthy, however, that government can constitutionally restrict their publication on the theory that, unlike the information in *Pentagon Papers*, *Landmark Communications*, and *Nebraska Press*, they are of only "low" first amendment value?

## Cox Broadcasting Corp. v. Cohn
420 U.S. 469 (1975)

MR. JUSTICE WHITE delivered the opinion of the Court.

The issue before us in this case is whether, consistently with the First and Fourteenth Amendments, a State may extend a cause of action for damages for invasion of privacy caused by the publication of the name of a deceased rape victim which was publicly revealed in connection with the prosecution of the crime.

In August 1971, appellee's 17-year-old daughter was the victim of a rape and did not survive the incident. Six youths were soon indicted for murder and rape. Although there was substantial press coverage of the crime and of subsequent developments, the identity of the victim was not disclosed pending trial, perhaps because of Ga. Code Ann. §26-9901 (1972), which makes it a misdemeanor to publish or broadcast the name or identity of a rape victim. In April 1972, some eight months later, the six defendants appeared in court. . . .

In the course of the proceedings that day, appellant Wassell, a reporter covering the incident for his employer, learned the name of the victim from an examination of the indictments which were made available for his inspection in the courtroom. That the name of the victim appears in the indictments and that the indictments were public records available for inspection are not disputed. Later that day, Wassell broadcast over the facilities of station WSB-TV, a television station owned by appellant Cox Broadcasting Corp., a news report concerning the court proceedings. The report named the victim of the crime and was repeated the following day.

In May 1972, appellee brought an action for money damages against appellants, relying on §26-9901 and claiming that his right to privacy had been invaded by the television broadcasts giving the name of his deceased daughter. Appellants admitted the broadcasts but claimed that they were privileged under [the] First and Fourteenth Amendments. . . .

Georgia stoutly defends both §26-9901 and the State's common-law privacy action challenged here. Its claims are not without force, for powerful arguments can be made, and have been made, that however it may be ultimately defined, there *is* a zone of privacy surrounding every individual, a zone within which the State may protect him from intrusion by the press, with all its attendant publicity. Indeed, the central thesis of the root article by Warren and Brandeis, The Right to Privacy, 4 Harv. L. Rev. 193, 196 (1890), was that the press was overstepping its prerogatives by publishing essentially private information and that there should be a remedy for the alleged abuses.[16]

More compellingly, the century has experienced a strong tide running in favor of the so-called right of privacy. "[I]n one form or another, the right of privacy is by this time recognized and accepted in all but a very few jurisdictions." W. Prosser, Law of Torts 804 (4th ed.). . . .

These are impressive credentials for a right of privacy. [The] version of the privacy tort now before us — termed in Georgia "the tort of public disclosure," [is] that in which the plaintiff claims the right to be free from unwanted publicity about his private affairs, which, although wholly true, would be offensive to a person of ordinary sensibilities. [In] this sphere of collision between claims of privacy and those of the free press, the interests on both sides are plainly rooted in the traditions and significant concerns of our society. Rather than address the broader question whether truthful publications may ever be subjected to civil or criminal liability, [it] is appropriate to focus on the narrower interface between press and privacy that this case presents, namely,

16. "Of the desirability — indeed of the necessity — of some such protection [of the right of privacy], there can, it is believed, be no doubt. The press is overstepping in every direction the obvious bounds of propriety and of decency. Gossip is no longer the resource of the idle and of the vicious, but has become a trade, which is pursued with industry as well as effrontery. To satisfy a prurient taste the details of sexual relations are spread broadcast in the columns of the daily papers. To occupy the indolent, column upon column is filled with idle gossip, which can only be procured by intrusion upon the domestic circle. The intensity and complexity of life, attendant upon advancing civilization, have rendered necessary some retreat from the world, and man, under the refining influence of culture, has become more sensitive to publicity, so that solitude and privacy have become more essential to the individual; but modern enterprise and invention have, through invasions upon his privacy, subjected him to mental pain and distress, far greater than could be inflicted by mere bodily injury. . . ."

whether the State may impose sanctions on the accurate publication of the name of a rape victim obtained from public records — more specifically, from judicial records which are maintained in connection with a public prosecution and which themselves are open to public inspection. We are convinced that the State may not do so.

[In] a society in which each individual has but limited time and resources with which to observe at first hand the operations of his government, he relies necessarily upon the press to bring to him in convenient form the facts of those operations. [With] respect to judicial proceedings in particular, the function of the press serves to guarantee the fairness of trials and to bring to bear the beneficial effects of public scrutiny upon the administration of justice. [The] commission of crime, prosecutions resulting from it, and judicial proceedings arising from the prosecutions [are] without question events of legitimate concern to the public and consequently fall within the responsibility of the press to report the operations of government. . . .

[Moreover, the] interests in privacy fade when the information involved already appears on the public record. [The] publication of truthful information available on the public record contains none of the indicia of those limited categories of expression, such as "fighting" words, which "are no essential part of any exposition of ideas, and are of such slight social value as a step to truth that any benefit that may be derived from them is clearly outweighed by the social interest in order and morality."[*Chaplinsky.*]

By placing the information in the public domain on official court records, the State must be presumed to have concluded that the public interest was thereby being served. Public records by their very nature are of interest to those concerned with the administration of government, and a public benefit is performed by the reporting of the true contents of the records by the media. . . .

We are reluctant to embark on a course that would make public records generally available to the media but forbid their publication if offensive to the sensibilities of the supposed reasonable man. Such a rule would make it very difficult for the media to inform citizens about the public business and yet stay within the law. The rule would invite timidity and self-censorship and very likely lead to the suppression of many items that would otherwise be published and that should be made available to the public. At the very least, the First and Fourteenth Amendments will not allow exposing the press to liability for truthfully publishing information released to the public in official court records. If there are privacy interests to be protected in judicial proceedings, the States must respond by means which avoid public documentation or other exposure of private information. Their political institutions must weigh the interests in privacy with the interests of the public to know and of the press to publish. Once true information is disclosed in public court documents open to public inspection, the press cannot be sanctioned for publishing it. In this instance as in others reliance must rest upon the judgment of those who decide what to publish or broadcast. . . .

Reversed.

[Concurring opinions of Chief Justice Burger and Justices Powell and Douglas are omitted, as is Justice Rehnquist's dissenting opinion, which argues that there is a "want of jurisdiction."]

### Note: Invasion of Privacy and the First Amendment

1. *The reach of* Cox Broadcasting. For similar decisions, see The Florida Star v. B.J.F., 491 U.S. 524 (1989) (newspaper cannot be held liable in damages for publishing a rape victim's name where the name was obtained from a publicly released police report); Oklahoma Publishing Co. v. District Court, 430 U.S. 308 (1977) (reporter cannot be prohibited from disclosing the name of a juvenile offender where the name was obtained at court proceedings that were open to the public); Smith v. Daily Mail Publishing Co., 443 U.S. 97 (1979) (newspaper cannot be punished for publishing the name and photograph of a juvenile offender where the newspaper had learned the suspect's name from several witnesses to the shooting and from police and prosecutors at the scene).

2. *Other sources of information.* Suppose a reporter learns the name of a rape victim from a witness rather than from a public document or proceeding. In light of *Cox*, what arguments would you make for both sides in the following situations:

a. William Sidis was a famous child prodigy in 1910. His name and prowess were well known to newspaper readers of the period. At the age of eleven, he lectured to distinguished mathematicians on the subject of four-dimensional bodies, and at the age of sixteen, he graduated from Harvard College amid considerable public attention. Thereafter, Sidis sought to live as unobtrusively as possible, and his name disappeared from public view. In 1937, however, The New Yorker ran a biographical sketch of Sidis in its Where Are They Now? section. The article described Sidis's early achievements, his general breakdown, and his attempts to conceal his identity through his chosen career as an insignificant clerk. The article further described in intimate detail Sidis's enthusiasm for collecting streetcar transfers, his interest in the lore of the Okamakammessett Indians, and his personal lifestyle and habits. Sidis sued for invasion of privacy. Sidis v. F-R Publishing Corp., 113 F.2d 806 (2d Cir. 1940).

b. Dorothy Barber suffered from a rare condition that caused her to lose weight, even though she ate often. In its Medicine section, Time magazine reported on Barber's condition, disclosing her name and publishing a photograph that showed "her face, head and arms, with bedclothes over her chest." The article was titled Starving Glutton. Barber sued for invasion of privacy. Barber v. Time, Inc., 348 Mo. 1199, 159 S.W.2d 291 (1942).

c. In 1956, Marvin Briscoe and another man hijacked a truck. After paying his debt to society, Briscoe abandoned his life of crime, led an exemplary life, and made many friends who were unaware of the incident in his earlier life. In 1967, Reader's Digest published an article on The Big Business of Hijacking, which reported: "Typical of many beginners, Marvin Briscoe and [another man] stole a 'valuable-looking' truck in Danville, Ky., and then fought a gun battle with the local police only to learn that they had hijacked four bowling-pin spotters." Briscoe sued for invasion of privacy. Briscoe v. Reader's Digest Association, 4 Cal. 3d 529, 483 P.2d 34, 93 Cal. Rptr. 866 (1971).

3. *Nonnewsworthiness and "low" value.* As Justice White suggested in *Cox Broadcasting,* in most states the truthful disclosure of "private" facts concerning an individual constitutes a tort if the disclosure would be "highly offensive" to a reasonable person and is not in itself newsworthy. Is the tort of public disclosure compatible with the first amendment? Should it matter that the harm caused by such speech cannot be corrected by counterspeech? That there is no significant "risk that government will [use the tort to] insulate itself from the critical views of its enemies"? L. Tribe, American Constitutional Law 889 (2d ed. 1988).

Is "nonnewsworthy" information of "low" first amendment value? Consider Bloustein, The First Amendment and Privacy: The Supreme Court Justice and the Philosopher, 28 Rutgers L. Rev. 41, 56–57 (1974): "[The] weight to be given 'the public interest in obtaining information' should depend on whether or not the information is relevant to the public's governing purposes. 'Public interest,' taken to mean curiosity, must be distinguished from 'public interest,' taken to mean value to the public of receiving information of governing importance. There is [no first amendment] right to satisfy public curiosity and publish lurid gossip about private lives."

On the other hand, consider Zimmerman, Requiem for a Heavyweight: A Farewell to Warren and Brandeis's Privacy Tort, 68 Cornell L. Rev. 291, 332–334 (1983):

> [Contemporary] society [uses] knowledge about the private lives of individual members [to] preserve and enforce social norms. [By] providing people with a way to learn about social groups to which they do not belong, gossip increases intimacy and a sense of community among disparate groups and individuals. [It] is a basic form of information exchange that teaches about other lifestyles and attitudes, and through which community values are changed or reinforced. [Perceived] in this way, gossip contributes directly to the first amendment "marketplace of ideas."

Even if "nonnewsworthy" information has only "low" first amendment value, might there nonetheless be sound reasons to reject such a standard?

In *Gertz*, the Court expressed "doubt" as to "the wisdom of committing [the task of deciding what information is relevant to self-government] to the conscience of judges." Is the "nonnewsworthiness" concept simply too vague to protect first amendment rights? Consider Kalven, Privacy in Tort Law — Were Warren and Brandeis Wrong?, 31 Law & Contemp. Probs. 326, 336 (1966): "What is at issue [is] whether the claim of privilege is not so overpowering as virtually to swallow the tort. [Surely] there is force to the simple contention that whatever is in the news media is by definition newsworthy, that the press must in the nature of things be the final arbiter of newsworthiness."

4. *The interest in "privacy."* Are the interests protected by the public disclosure tort of sufficient importance to justify a restriction of even "low" value expression? How would you compare the gravity of the harm caused by speech that "invades privacy" with the gravity of the harm in the incitement, fighting words, and libel contexts? Consider Bloustein, supra, at 54: "In [public disclosure] cases the individual has been profaned by laying a private life open to public view. The intimacy and private space necessary to sustain individuality and human dignity has been impaired by turning a private life into a public spectacle. The innermost region of being [has] been bruised by exposure to the world." On the other hand, consider Posner, The Right of Privacy, 12 Ga. L. Rev. 393, 419 (1978): "If what is revealed is something the individual has concealed for purposes of misrepresenting himself to others, the fact that disclosure is offensive to him and of limited interest to the public at large is no better reason for protecting his privacy than if a seller advanced such arguments for being allowed to continue to engage in false advertising of his goods."

Consider also Gewirtz, Privacy and Speech, 2001 Sup. Ct. Rev. 139, 179, 185–189:

[Why] is the name of a rape victim a matter of legitimate public concern? The fact of the rape or even the name of the alleged perpetrator is one thing, but the victim's name is ordinarily not something the public profits from knowing. [The] flavor of the Court's [opinions] is that [it] will find any conceivable escape hatch for media liability. [Supreme] courts and constitutional courts in most other democracies give greater weight to values of privacy [when] they conflict with free speech claims [citing cases from Great Britain, Germany, India and Canada]. [To] other countries, our current free speech doctrines seem to have become quite extreme.

5. *"Revenge porn."* Would a prohibition on "revenge porn" be constitutional? "Revenge porn" refers to the practice of posting nude or sexually suggestive photographs on line without the consent of the person who is photographed. Consider the following proposed statute:

An actor commits criminal invasion of privacy if the actor harms another person by knowingly disclosing an image of another person whose intimate parts are exposed or who is engaged in a sexual act, when the actor knows that the other person did not consent to the disclosure and when the actor knows that the other person expected that the image would be kept private, under circumstances where the other person had a reasonable expectation that the image would be kept private. The fact that a person has consented to the possession of an image by another person does not imply consent to disclose that image more broadly.

D. Citron, Hate Crimes in Cyberspace (2014). The proposed statute contains exceptions for "lawful and common practices of law enforcement, criminal reporting, legal proceedings; or medical treatment," for the reporting of unlawful conduct, for voluntary exposures in public or commercial settings, and for disclosures that relate to the public interest.

Is the statute constitutional? If so, how (if at all) is this disclosure different from unconsented disclosure of verbal descriptions of sexual acts or from disclosure of embarrassing information gained through an intimate relationship?

6. *Unlawfully obtained information.* In *Cox Broadcasting*, the Court emphasized that the information had been obtained lawfully by the press from government documents. Suppose, however, the information is obtained unlawfully. In Bartnicki v. Vopper, 532 U.S. 514 (2001), a radio station aired a tape of a telephone conversation that the station received from an anonymous source. In the circumstances, the station knew that the tape had been made in violation of federal and state anti-wiretap statutes. The Court held that these statutes could not constitutionally be applied to the radio station because the topic of the call was a matter of public concern (collective-bargaining negotiations between a union representing teachers at a public high school and the local school board) and the broadcaster had not participated directly in the unlawful interception (even though the broadcaster knew that the material had been obtained unlawfully). Without deciding whether there might be some circumstances in which the privacy interest is "strong enough to justify the application" of the statute, such as when there is disclosure of "domestic gossip [of] purely private concern," the Court held that the enforcement of the statute in this case "implicates core purposes of the First Amendment because it imposes sanctions on the publication of truthful information of public concern." In this situation, "privacy concerns give way when balanced against the interest in publishing matters of public importance." Recall the *Pentagon Papers* case. Suppose in *Bartnicki* that the radio station itself had unlawfully intercepted the phone call. Should that lead to a different result?

## C.   THREATS

A "threat" is generally defined as "a statement of an intention to inflict pain, injury, damage, or other hostile action on someone if she does not do something the person making the statement wants her to do." In what circumstances, and for what reasons, can the state constitutionally punish individuals who make threats? Are threats of only "low" first amendment value?

**BRIDGES v. CALIFORNIA, 314 U.S. 252 (1941).** *Bridges* arose out of litigation between two rival unions. While a motion for new trial was pending, Bridges, president of the union against whom the trial judge had ruled, published a copy of a telegram he had sent to the Secretary of Labor describing the judge's decision as "outrageous" and suggesting that, if the decision were enforced, his union would call a strike that would tie up the port of Los Angeles. As a result of this publication, Bridges was found guilty of contempt of court.

In an opinion by Justice Black, the Court held the contempt conviction unconstitutional: "The 'clear and present danger' language of the *Schenck* case has afforded practical guidance in a great variety of cases in which the scope of constitutional protections of freedom of expression was in issue. [What] finally emerges from the 'clear and present danger' cases is a working principle that the substantive evil must be extremely serious and the degree of imminence extremely high before utterances can be punished. . . .

"Let us assume that the telegram could be construed as an announcement of Bridges' intention to call a strike, something which [neither] the general law of California nor the court's decree prohibited. With an eye on the realities of the situation, we cannot assume that Judge Schmidt was unaware of the possibility of a strike as a consequence of his decision. If he was not intimidated by the facts themselves, we do not believe that the most explicit statement of them could have sidetracked the course of justice."

Justice Frankfurter, joined by Chief Justice Stone and Justices Roberts and Byrnes, dissented: "Of course freedom of speech and of the press [should] be employed in comment upon the work of [courts]. But [freedom] of expression can hardly carry implications that nullify the guarantees of impartial trials. [Comment,] however forthright[,] is one thing. Intimidation with respect to specific matters still in judicial suspense, quite another. [To be punishable, a publication] must refer to a matter under consideration and constitute in effect a threat to its impartial disposition. It must be calculated to create an atmospheric pressure incompatible with rational, impartial adjudication. But to interfere with justice it need not succeed. As with other offenses, the state should be able to proscribe attempts that fail because of the danger that attempts may succeed. . . .

"The publication of the telegram was regarded by the state supreme court as 'a threat that if an attempt was made to enforce the decision, the ports of the entire Pacific Coast would be tied up.' [This] occurred immediately after counsel had moved to set aside the judgment which was criticized, so unquestionably there was a threat to litigation obviously alive. It would be inadmissible dogmatism for us to say that in the context of the immediate case [this] could not have dominated the mind of the judge before whom the matter was pending."

––––––––––––––

Is clear and present danger the correct standard in a case like *Bridges*? Is Justice Frankfurter correct in asserting that Bridges "threatened" the judge? Should a threat be thought of as only "low" value speech "because it operates more like a physical action than [a] communication of ideas or emotions"? Gey, The Nuremberg Files and the First Amendment Value of Threats, 78 Tex. L. Rev. 541, 591–593 (2000). See K. Greenawalt, Speech, Crime and the Uses of Language 94 (1989) (the first amendment does not protect speech that "involves the creation of prospective harmful consequences in order to achieve one's objective").

Consider the following situations: (1) X threatens to kill Judge Y unless she acquits Z. (2) X threatens to disclose that Judge Y is having a lesbian relationship unless she acquits Z. (3) X threatens to oppose Judge Y's reelection unless she acquits Z. (4) X threatens to call a general strike unless Judge Y convicts Z. If a "threat" is subject to regulation because it affects behavior by coercion rather than by persuasion, does that rationale support any distinction among situations (1), (2), (3), and (4)?

**WATTS v. UNITED STATES, 394 U.S. 705 (1969).** Petitioner, during a public rally at the Washington Monument, stated to a small group of persons: "I have already received my draft classification as 1-A and I have got to go for my physical this Monday coming. I am not going. If they ever make me carry a rifle the first man I want to get in my sights is L.B.J." For this remark, petitioner was convicted of violating a federal statute prohibiting any person "knowingly and willfully [to make] any threat to take the life of or to inflict bodily harm upon the President of the United States." Although conceding that the statute was constitutional "on its face," the Court reversed the conviction on the ground that "the kind of political hyperbole indulged in by petitioner" did not constitute a "threat" within the meaning of the statute. Petitioner's "only offense," the Court concluded, "was 'a kind of very crude offensive method of stating a political opposition to the President.'" Do you agree that the statute is constitutional "on its face"? Is a threat to kill the President of "low" first amendment value?

**PLANNED PARENTHOOD v. AMERICAN COALITION OF LIFE ACTIVISTS, 290 F.3d 1058 (9th Cir. 2002).** Suppose defendant establishes a Web site (called the "Nuremberg Files") that states that its purpose is to "collect dossiers on abortionists in anticipation that one day we may be able to hold them on trial for crimes against humanity," lists the names and addresses of abortion providers, includes photographs of abortion providers in Wild-

West-style "Wanted" posters, and crosses out the names of abortion providers who have been murdered. Can this expression be restricted on the ground that the Web site constitutes "incitement"? On the ground that it constitutes a "threat"? Should it matter that the Web site was established after an unrelated individual had murdered three abortion providers after distributing similar posters naming them as "Wanted" persons?

The Court of Appeals for the Ninth Circuit, in a six-to-five en banc decision, held that the operators of the Nuremberg Files Web site could be held liable in damages and enjoined because the site constituted an unprotected threat: "If ACLA had merely endorsed or encouraged the violent actions of others, its speech would be protected. [Citing *Brandenburg*.] However, while advocating violence is protected, threatening a person with violence is not. [Although the] posters contain no language that is [literally] a threat, whether a particular statement may properly be considered to be a threat is governed by an objective standard — whether a reasonable person would foresee that the statement would be interpreted by those to whom the maker communicates the statement as a serious expression of intent to harm or assault. [It] is not necessary that the defendant intend to, or be able to carry out his threat; the only intent requirement for a true threat is that the defendant intentionally or knowingly communicate the [threat] *with the intent to intimidate*. [It] is making a threat to intimidate that makes ACLA's conduct unlawful. . . .

"The true threats analysis [in this case] turns on the poster pattern. [The Web site does not contain] any language that is overtly threatening. [It] is use of the 'Wanted'-type format in the context of the poster pattern — poster followed by murder — that constitutes the threat. Because of the pattern, a 'Wanted'-type poster naming a specific doctor who provides abortions was perceived by physicians, who are providers of reproductive health services, as a serious threat of death or bodily harm. [The] posters are a true threat because, [like] burning crosses, they connote something they do not literally say, yet both the actor and the recipient get the message. To the doctor who performs abortions, these posters meant 'You'll be shot or killed.' [As] a direct result of having [a] poster out on them, physicians wore bulletproof vests and took other extraordinary security measures to protect themselves and their families. ACLA had every reason to foresee that its expression [would] elicit this reaction. Physicians' fear did not simply happen; ACLA intended to intimidate them from doing what they do. This [is] conduct that [lacks] any protection under the First Amendment. Violence is not a protected value. Nor is a true threat of violence with intent to intimidate."

The dissenting judges argued as follows: "[I]t is not illegal — and cannot be made so — merely to say things that would frighten or intimidate the listener. For example, when a doctor says, 'You have cancer and will die within six months,' it is not a threat, even though you almost certainly will be frightened. [By] contrast, 'If you don't stop performing abortions, I'll kill you' is a true threat and surely illegal. The difference between a true threat and protected expression is this: A true threat warns of violence or other harm that the speaker controls. . . .

"[As the majority argues,] because context matters, the statements [in this case] could reasonably be interpreted as an effort to intimidate plaintiffs into ceasing their abortion-related activities. If that were enough to strip the speech of First Amendment protection, there would be nothing left to decide. But the Supreme Court has told us that '[s]peech does not lose its protected character . . . simply because it may embarrass others *or coerce them into action.*' [*Claiborne Hardware.*] In other words, some forms of intimidation enjoy constitutional protection. The majority does not point to any statement by defendants that they intended to inflict bodily harm on plaintiffs, nor is there any evidence that defendants took any steps whatsoever to plan or carry out physical violence against anyone. Rather, the majority relies on the fact that 'the poster format itself had acquired currency as a death threat for abortion providers.' [But none of the doctors who were killed were killed by anyone connected with this Web page.]

"The majority tries to fill this gaping hole in the record by noting that defendants 'kn[ew] the fear generated among those in the reproductive health services community who were singled out for identification on a "wanted"-type poster.' But a statement does not become a true threat because it instills fear in the listener; as noted above, many statements generate fear in the listener, yet are not true threats and therefore may not be punished or enjoined consistent with the First Amendment. In order for the statement to be a threat, it must send the message that the speakers themselves — or individuals acting in concert with them — will engage in physical violence. [Yet] the opinion points to no evidence that defendants [would] have been understood by a reasonable listener as saying that *they* will cause the harm.

"From the point of view of the victims, it makes little difference whether the violence against them will come from the makers of the posters or from unrelated third parties; bullets kill their victims regardless of who pulls the trigger. But it makes a difference for the purpose of the First Amendment. Speech — especially political speech, as this clearly was — may not be punished or enjoined unless it falls into one of the narrow categories of unprotected speech recognized by the Supreme Court: true threat, incitement, fighting words, etc. [The] posters can be viewed, at most, as a call to arms for *other* abortion protesters to harm plaintiffs. However, the Supreme Court made it clear that under *Brandenburg,* encouragement or even advocacy of violence is protected by the First Amendment [unless the harm is both likely and imminent]. . . .

"The Nuremberg Files website is clearly an expression of a political point of view. The posters and the website are designed both to rally political support for the views espoused by defendants, and to intimidate plaintiffs and others like them into desisting abortion related activities. This political agenda may not be to the liking of many people — political dissidents are often unpopular — but the speech, including the intimidating message, does not constitute a direct threat because there is no evidence [that] the speakers intend to resort to physical violence if their threat is not heeded. We have recognized that statements communicated directly to the target are much more likely to be true threats than those, as here, communicated as part of a public protest. [In] deciding whether the coercive speech is protected, it makes a big difference whether it is contained in a private communication — a face-to-face confrontation, a telephone call, a dead fish wrapped in newspaper — or is made during the course of public discourse. The reason for this distinction is obvious: Private speech is aimed only at its target. Public speech, by contrast, seeks to move public opinion and to encourage those of like mind. Coercive speech that is part of public discourse enjoys far greater protection than identical speech made in a purely private context. In this case, defendants said nothing remotely threatening, yet they find themselves cruci-fied financially. Who knows what other neutral statements a jury might imbue with a menacing meaning based on the activities of unrelated parties. . . ."

---

See Rothman, Freedom of Speech and True Threats, 25 Harv. J.L. & Pub. Poly. 283 (2001) (to prove a "true" threat, the prosecution should have to prove (1) that the speaker knowingly or recklessly made a statement that would frighten or intimidate the victim with the threat of harm; (2) that the speaker knowingly or recklessly suggested that the threat would be carried out by the speaker or his coconspirators; and (3) that a reasonable person who heard the statement would conclude that it was meant to threaten the victim with harm).

In what circumstances, if any, might the display of a swastika or a burning cross constitute a "true threat"? Suppose a black family moves into an all-white community and the next day wakes up to discover a burning cross on the street in front of their home. Can the persons who erected the cross be punished for making a threat? In the incitement situation, the Court, following the leading of Judge Learned Hand in *Masses*, seems to require that for incitement of unlawful conduct to come within the low value category of express incitement, the incitement must be *express*. Is a burning cross an *express* threat? Does it make any sense to require express incitement but not express threats? On cross-burning as a threat, see Virginia v. Black, this chapter, infra.

Can an individual be punished for threatening words if she does not intend for them to be perceived as a threat? In Elonis v. United States, 135 S. Ct. 2001 (2015), the petitioner posted on Facebook a series of threatening statements directed toward his wife and others. He was convicted under a federal statute making it a crime to transmit in interstate commerce "any threat . . . to injure the person of another." The trial court instructed the jury that it could convict if a reasonable person would regard the statements as threats and declined to instruct the jury that the petitioner had to intend to communicate a threat. The Supreme Court, per Chief Justice Roberts, reversed the conviction, but declined to reach the constitutional question. As a matter of statutory construction, the Court held that the government was required to prove more than mere negligence. However, the majority did not specify what mental state was required.

Two separate opinions, written by Justice Alito, concurring in part and dissenting in part, and by Justice Thomas, dissenting, rejected a constitutional requirement of intent to threaten. Justice Alito thought that the statute required no more than recklessness — disregard of a risk of which the perpetrator was aware — and that this requirement was sufficient to satisfy the first amendment.

> True threats inflict great harm and have little if any social value. . . .
> [Whether] or not the person making a threat intends to cause harm, the damage is the same. . . .
> We have sometimes cautioned that it is necessary to "exten[d] a measure of stratetic protection" to otherwise unprotected false statements of fact in order to ensure enough "'breathing space'" for protected speech. But we have also held that the laws provides adequate breathing space when it requires proof that false statements were made with reckless disregard of their falsity. Requiring proof of recklessness is similarly sufficient here.

Justice Thomas read the statute as requiring neither intent nor recklessness and would have held that neither requirement was constitutionally mandatory. His view was based largely on state statutes and English precedent at the time of the framing that, in his judgment, did not require intent or recklessness with regard to whether words would be perceived as threats.

## D. COMMERCIAL ADVERTISING

Although the *Chaplinsky* dictum made no reference to commercial advertising, only a month after *Chaplinsky* the Court added commercial advertising to its list of "unprotected" expression in Valentine v. Chrestensen, 316 U.S. 52 (1942). In *Chrestensen*, the Court upheld a prohibition on the distribution of any "handbill [or] other advertising matter [in] or upon any street." Although conceding that a similar prohibition on noncommercial expression would violate the first amendment, the Court announced, without explanation or analysis, that the amendment imposed "no such restraint on government as respects purely commercial advertising." See also Breard v. Alexandria, 341 U.S. 622 (1951) (upholding a prohibition on door-to-door solicitation of magazine subscriptions).

Despite *Chrestensen*, the precise contours and rationale of the commercial advertising doctrine remained obscure. The mere presence of a commercial motive, for example, was not deemed dispositive, as evidenced by the Court's continued protection of books, movies, newspapers, and other forms of expression produced and sold for profit. Moreover, in New York Times v. Sullivan, this chapter, supra, the Court rejected an argument that the paid "political" advertisement there at issue was unprotected commercial expression:

> The publication here was not a "commercial" advertisement in the sense in which the word was used in *Chrestensen*. It communicated information, expressed opinion, recited grievances, [and] protested claimed abuses. [That] the Times was paid for publishing the advertisement is as immaterial in this connection as is the fact that newspapers and books are sold. [Any] other conclusion would discourage newspapers from carrying "editorial advertisements" of this type, and so might shut off an important outlet for the promulgation of information and ideas by persons who do not themselves have access to publishing facilities.

In the 1970s, the Court began to narrow the scope of the commercial speech doctrine. In Bigelow v. Virginia, 421 U.S. 809 (1975), for example, the Court reversed the conviction of an individual who, prior to the Court's decision in Roe v. Wade, 410 U.S. 113 (1973), and in violation of Virginia law, published in his newspaper an advertisement announcing the availability of legal abortions in New York. The Court distinguished *Chrestensen* on the ground that the advertisement in *Bigelow* "did more than simply propose a commercial transaction. It contained factual material of clear 'public interest.'" The Court emphasized that *Chrestensen*'s holding was "distinctly a limited one."

## Virginia State Board of Pharmacy v. Virginia Citizens Consumer Council
425 U.S. 748 (1976)

[An organization of prescription drug consumers challenged as violative of the first and fourteenth amendments a Virginia statute providing that a pharmacist licensed in Virginia is guilty of unprofessional conduct if he "publishes, advertises, or promotes, directly or indirectly, in any manner whatsoever, any amount, price, fee, premium, discount, rebate or credit terms [for] any drugs which may be dispensed only by prescription." Although drug prices varied strikingly throughout the state and even within the same locality, the challenged law effectively prevented the dissemination of any prescription drug price information, since only licensed pharmacists were authorized to dispense such drugs. A three-judge district court held the law invalid. The Supreme Court affirmed.]

MR. JUSTICE BLACKMUN delivered the opinion of the Court. . . . [*]

## IV

The appellants contend that the advertisement of prescription drug prices is outside the protection of the First Amendment because it is "commercial speech." There can be no question that in past decisions the Court has given some indication that commercial speech is unprotected. [Discussing *Chrestensen*, *Breard*, and *Bigelow*.] . . .

[The] question whether there is a First Amendment exception for "commercial speech" is squarely before us. Our pharmacist does not wish to editorialize on any subject, cultural, philosophical, or political. He does not wish to report any particularly newsworthy fact, or to make generalized observations even about commercial matters. The "idea" he wishes to communicate is simply this: "I will sell you the X prescription drug at the Y price." Our question, then, is whether this communication is wholly outside the protection of the First Amendment.

## V

We begin with several propositions that already are settled or beyond serious dispute. It is clear, for example, that speech does not lose its First Amendment protection because money is spent to project it, as in a paid advertisement of one form or another. [Citing New York Times v. Sullivan.] Speech likewise is protected even though it is carried in a form that is "sold" for profit, [and] even though it may involve a solicitation to purchase or otherwise pay or contribute money . . . .

If there is a kind of commercial speech that lacks all First Amendment protection, therefore, it must be distinguished by its content. Yet the speech whose content deprives it of protection cannot simply be speech on a commercial subject. No one would contend that our pharmacist may be prevented from being heard on the subject of whether, in general, pharmaceutical prices should be regulated, or their advertisement forbidden. Nor can it be dispositive that a commercial advertisement is noneditorial, and merely

---

[*] [At the outset, Justice Blackmun rejected a claim that, even if first amendment protection attached to the flow of drug price information, it is a protection enjoyed only by advertisers and not by the appellees, who were mere recipients of such information. Justice Blackmun reasoned that, "where a speaker exists, [the] protection afforded is to the communication, to its source and to its recipients both." Thus, "if there is a right to advertise, there is a reciprocal [first amendment] right to receive the advertising." — EDS.]

reports a fact. Purely factual matter of public interest may claim protection. . . .

Our question is whether speech which does "no more than propose a commercial transaction" is so removed from any "exposition of ideas,"[*Chaplinsky*], and from "'truth, science, morality, and arts in general, in its diffusion of liberal sentiments on the administration of Government,'" that it lacks all protection. Our answer is that it is not.

Focusing first on the individual parties to the transaction that is proposed in the commercial advertisement, we may assume that the advertiser's interest is a purely economic one. That hardly disqualifies him from protection under the First Amendment. The interests of the contestants in a labor dispute are primarily economic, but it has long been settled that both the employee and the employer are protected by the First Amendment when they express themselves on the merits of the dispute in order to influence its outcome. [We] know of no requirement that, in order to avail themselves of First Amendment protection, the parties to a labor dispute need address themselves to the merits of unionism in general or to any subject beyond their immediate dispute. . . .

As to the particular consumer's interest in the free flow of commercial information, that interest may be as keen, if not keener by far, than his interest in the day's most urgent political debate. Appellees' case in this respect is a convincing one. Those whom the suppression of prescription drug price information hits the hardest are the poor, the sick, and particularly the aged. A disproportionate amount of their income tends to be spent on prescription drugs; yet they are the least able to learn, by shopping from pharmacist to pharmacist, where their scarce dollars are best spent. When drug prices vary as strikingly as they do, information as to who is charging what becomes more than a convenience. It could mean the alleviation of physical pain or the enjoyment of basic necessities.

Generalizing, society also may have a strong interest in the free flow of commercial information. Even an individual advertisement, though entirely "commercial," may be of general public interest. The facts of decided cases furnish illustrations: advertisements stating that referral services for legal abortions are available, [*Bigelow*]; that a manufacturer of artificial furs promotes his product as an alternative to the extinction by his competitors of fur-bearing mammals, and that a domestic producer advertises his product as an alternative to imports that tend to deprive American residents of their jobs. [Obviously,] not all commercial messages contain the same or even a very great public interest element. There are few to which such an element, however, could not be added. Our pharmacist, for example, could cast himself as a commentator on store-to-store disparities in drug prices, giving his own and those of a competitor as proof. We see little point in requiring him to do so, and little difference if he does not.

Moreover, there is another consideration that suggests that no line between publicly "interesting" or "important" commercial advertising and the opposite kind could ever be drawn. Advertising, however tasteless and excessive it sometimes may seem, is nonetheless dissemination of information as to who is producing and selling what product, for what reason, and at what price. So long as we preserve a predominantly free enterprise economy, the allocation of our resources in large measure will be made through numerous private economic decisions. It is a matter of public interest that those decisions, in the aggregate, be intelligent and well informed. To this end, the free flow of commercial information is indispensable. [And] if it is indispensable to the proper allocation of resources in a free enterprise system, it is also indispensable to the formation of intelligent opinions as to how that system ought to be regulated or altered. Therefore, even if the First Amendment were thought to be primarily an instrument to enlighten public decisionmaking in a democracy, we could not say that the free flow of information does not serve that goal.

Arrayed against these substantial individual and societal interests are a number of justifications for the advertising ban. These have to do principally with maintaining a high degree of professionalism on the part of licensed pharmacists. Indisputably, the State has a strong interest in maintaining that professionalism. . . .

Price advertising, it is argued, will place in jeopardy the pharmacist's expertise and, with it, the customer's health. It is claimed that the aggressive price competition that will result from unlimited advertising will make it impossible for the pharmacist to supply professional services in the compounding, handling, and dispensing of prescription drugs. Such services are time consuming and expensive; if competitors who economize by eliminating them are permitted to advertise their resulting lower prices, the more painstaking and conscientious pharmacist will be forced either to follow suit or to go out of business. It is also claimed that prices might not necessarily fall as a result of advertising. If one pharmacist advertises, others must, and the resulting expense will inflate the cost of drugs. [Finally] it is argued that damage will be done to the professional image of the pharmacist. This image, that of a skilled and specialized craftsman, attracts talent to the profession and reinforces the better habits of those who are in it. Price advertising, it is said, will reduce the pharmacist's status to that of a mere retailer.

The strength of these proffered justifications is greatly undermined by the fact that high professional standards, to a substantial extent, are guaranteed by the close regulation to which pharmacists in Virginia are subject. [At] the same time, we cannot discount the Board's justifications entirely. The Court regarded justifications of this type sufficient to sustain the advertising bans challenged on due process and equal protection grounds. [Citing, e.g., Williamson v. Lee Optical of Oklahoma, 348 U.S. 483 (1955).]

The challenge now made, however, is based on the First Amendment. This casts the Board's justifications in a different light, for on close inspection it is seen that the State's protectiveness of its citizens rests in large measure on the advantages of their being kept in ignorance. The advertising ban does not directly affect professional standards one way or the other. It affects them only through the reactions it is assumed people will have to the free flow of drug price information. . . .

It appears to be feared that if the pharmacist who wishes to provide low cost, and assertedly low quality, services is permitted to advertise, he will be taken up on his offer by too many unwitting customers. They will choose the low-cost, low-quality service and drive the "professional" pharmacist out of business. They will respond only to costly and excessive advertising, and end up paying the price. They will go from one pharmacist to another, following the discount, and destroy the pharmacist-customer relationship. They will lose respect for the profession because it advertises. All this is not in their best interests, and all this can be avoided if they are not permitted to know who is charging what.

There is, of course, an alternative to this highly paternalistic approach. That alternative is to assume that this information is not in itself harmful, that people will perceive their own best interests if only they are well enough informed, and that the best means to that end is to open the channels of communication rather than to close them. If they are truly open, nothing prevents the "professional" pharmacist from marketing his own assertedly superior product, and contrasting it with that of the low-cost, high-volume prescription drug retailer. But the choice among these alternative approaches is not ours to make or the Virginia General Assembly's. It is precisely this kind of choice, between the dangers of suppressing information, and the dangers of its misuse if it is freely available, that the First Amendment makes for us. . . .

## VI

In concluding that commercial speech, like other varieties, is protected, we of course do not hold that it can never be regulated in any way. Some forms of commercial speech regulation are surely permissible. We mention a few only to make clear that they are not before us and therefore are not foreclosed by this case.

There is no claim, for example, that the prohibition on prescription drug price advertising is a mere time, place, and manner restriction. We have often approved restrictions of that kind provided that they are justified without reference to the content of the regulated speech, that they serve a significant governmental interest, and that in so doing they leave open ample alternative channels for communication of the information. [Whatever] may be the proper bounds of time, place, and manner restrictions on commercial speech, they are plainly exceeded by this Virginia statute, which singles out speech of a particular content and seeks to prevent its dissemination completely.

Nor is there any claim that prescription drug price advertisements are forbidden because they are false or misleading in any way. Untruthful speech, commercial or otherwise, has never been protected for its own sake. [*Gertz.*]

Obviously, much commercial speech is not provably false, or even wholly false, but only deceptive or misleading. We foresee no obstacle to a State's dealing effectively with this problem.[24] The First Amendment, as we construe it today, does not prohibit the State from insuring that the stream of commercial information flows cleanly as well as freely. . . .

Also, there is no claim that the transactions proposed in the forbidden advertisements are themselves illegal in any way. [Finally,] the special problems of the electronic broadcast media are likewise not in this case. . . .

What is at issue is whether a State may completely suppress the dissemination of concededly truthful information about entirely lawful activity, fearful of that information's effect upon its disseminators and its recipients. Reserving other questions,[25] we conclude that the answer to this one is in the negative.

The judgment of the District Court is affirmed.

[Justice Stevens did not participate. Chief Justice Burger concurred in an opinion emphasizing the reservations set out in footnote 25. Justice Stewart concurred in an opinion emphasizing that government still should be free to regulate false or misleading commercial advertising.]

Mr. Justice Rehnquist, dissenting.

The logical consequences of the Court's decision in this case, a decision which elevates commercial intercourse between a seller hawking his wares and

24. In concluding that commercial speech enjoys First Amendment protection, we have not held that it is wholly undifferentiable from other forms. There are commonsense differences between speech that does "no more than propose a commercial transaction," and other varieties. Even if the differences do not justify the conclusion that commercial speech is valueless, and thus subject to complete suppression by the State, they nonetheless suggest that a different degree of protection is necessary to insure that the flow of truthful and legitimate commercial information is unimpaired. The truth of commercial speech, for example, may be more easily verifiable by its disseminator than, let us say, news reporting or political commentary, in that ordinarily the advertiser seeks to disseminate information about a specific product or service that he himself provides and presumably knows more about than anyone else. Also, commercial speech may be more durable than other kinds. Since advertising is the sine qua non of commercial profits, there is little likelihood of its being chilled by proper regulation and forgone entirely.

Attributes such as these, the greater objectivity and hardiness of commercial speech, may make it less necessary to tolerate inaccurate statements for fear of silencing the speaker. [They] may also make it appropriate to require that a commercial message appear in such a form, or include such additional information, warnings, and disclaimers, as are necessary to prevent its being deceptive. [They] may also make inapplicable the prohibition against prior restraints. . . .

25. We stress that we have considered in this case the regulation of commercial advertising by pharmacists. Although we express no opinion as to other professions, the distinctions, historical and functional, between professions may require consideration of quite different factors. Physicians and lawyers, for example, do not dispense standardized products; they render professional *services* of almost infinite variety and nature, with the consequent enhanced possibility for confusion and deception if they were to undertake certain kinds of advertising.

a buyer seeking to strike a bargain to the same plane as has been previously reserved for the free marketplace of ideas, are far reaching indeed. Under the Court's opinion the way will be open not only for dissemination of price information but for active promotion of prescription drugs, liquor, cigarettes, and other products the use of which it has previously been thought desirable to discourage. Now, however, such promotion is protected by the First Amendment so long as it is not misleading or does not promote an illegal product or enterprise. . . .

The Court speaks of the consumer's interest in the free flow of commercial information, particularly in the case of the poor, the sick, and the aged. It goes on to observe that "society also may have a strong interest in the free flow of commercial information." [One] need not disagree with either of these statements in order to feel that they should presumptively be the concern of the Virginia Legislature, which sits to balance these and other claims in the process of making laws such as the one here under attack. The Court speaks of the importance in a "predominantly free enterprise economy" of intelligent and well-informed decisions as to allocation of resources. While there is again much to be said for the Court's observation as a matter of desirable public policy, there is certainly nothing in the United States Constitution which requires the Virginia Legislature to hew to the teachings of Adam Smith in its legislative decisions regulating the pharmacy profession. E.g., Nebbia v. New York, 291 U.S. 502 (1934); Olsen v. Nebraska, 313 U.S. 236 (1941). . . .

The Court insists that the rule it lays down is consistent even with the view that the First Amendment is "primarily an instrument to enlighten public decisionmaking in a democracy." I had understood this view to relate to public decisionmaking as to political, social, and other public issues, rather than the decision of a particular individual as to whether to purchase one or another kind of shampoo. It is undoubtedly arguable that many people in the country regard the choice of shampoo as just as important as who may be elected to local, state, or national political office, but that does not automatically bring information about competing shampoos within the protection of the First Amendment. . . .

In the case of "our" hypothetical pharmacist, he may now presumably advertise not only the prices of prescription drugs, but may attempt to energetically promote their sale so long as he does so truthfully. Quite consistently with Virginia law requiring prescription drugs to be available only through a physician, "our" pharmacist might run any of the following representative advertisements in a local newspaper:

Pain getting you down? Insist that your physician prescribe Demerol. You pay a little more than for aspirin, but you get a lot more relief.

Can't shake the flu? Get a prescription for Tetracycline from your doctor today.

Don't spend another sleepless night. Ask your doctor to prescribe Seconal without delay.

Unless the State can show that these advertisements are either actually untruthful or misleading, it presumably is not free to restrict in any way commercial efforts on the part of those who profit from the sale of prescription drugs to put them in the widest possible circulation. But such a line simply makes no allowance whatever for what appears to have been a considered legislative judgment in most States that while prescription drugs are a necessary and vital part of medical care and treatment, there are sufficient dangers attending their widespread use that they simply may not be promoted in the same manner as hair creams, deodorants, and toothpaste. The very real dangers that general advertising for such drugs might create in terms of encouraging, even though not sanctioning, illicit use of them by individuals for whom they have not been prescribed, or by generating patient pressure upon physicians to prescribe them, are simply not dealt with in the Court's opinion. . . .

## Note: Virginia Pharmacy *and "the Free Flow of Commercial Information"*

1. *Is commercial speech of "low" first amendment value?* Consider the following:

a. Jackson and Jeffries, Commercial Speech: Economic Due Process and the First Amendment, 65 Va. L. Rev. 1, 17–18, 30–31 (1979):

> [The Court's conclusion in *Virginia Pharmacy* that commercial speech is relevant to self-government is] a non sequitur. It apparently rests on the assertion that because regulation of the free enterprise system is a matter of political choice, commercial advertising that plays a part in the functioning of the free enterprise system is *for that reason* politically significant speech. But in terms of relevance to political decisionmaking, advertising is neither more nor less significant than a host of other market activities that legislatures concededly may regulate. [The] decisive point is the absence of any principled distinction between commercial soliciting and other aspects of economic activity. [In *Virginia Pharmacy*,] economic due process is resurrected, clothed in the ill-fitting garb of the first amendment.

For a critique of this argument, see Shiffrin, The First Amendment and Economic Regulation: Away from a General Theory of the First Amendment, 78 Nw. U. L. Rev. 1212, 1225–1239 (1983).

b. Redish, The First Amendment in the Marketplace: Commercial Speech and the Values of Free Expression, 39 Geo. Wash. L. Rev. 429, 433, 441–444 (1971):

> If the individual is to achieve the maximum degree of material satisfaction permitted by his resources, he must be presented with as much information as possible concerning the relative merits of competing products. After receiving

the competing information, the individual will then be in a position [to] rationally decide which combination of features best satisfies his personal needs. [Viewed in this light,] informational commercial speech furthers legitimate first amendment purposes. When the individual is presented with rational grounds for preferring one product or brand over another, he is encouraged to consider the competing information [and to] exercise his abilities to reason and think; this aids him towards the intangible goal of rational self-fulfillment.

Compare R. Collins and D. Skover, The Death of Discourse 77, 80, 105, 114 (1996):

On the eve of the twenty-first century, America's marketplace of ideas has largely become a junkyard of commodity ideology. [Today's] mass advertising often has less to do with products than lifestyles, less to do with facts than image, and less to do with reason than romance. [In modern mass advertising, entire] categories of commercial communication are essentially bereft of any real informational content. [If] commercial communication is safe [in the free speech marketplace], it is not because it *actually* furthers the First Amendment's traditional values of rational decisionmaking and self-realization. [The] real reason for constitutional protection of modern mass advertising is less ennobling: It is speech in the service of selling.

c. Coase, Advertising and Free Speech, 6 J. Legal Stud. 1, 2, 14 (1977):

It seems to be believed that [if the government intervened in the market for ideas, it] would be inefficient and wrongly motivated. [How] different is the government assumed to be when we come to economic regulation. In this area government is considered to be competent in action and pure in motivation. [Since] we are concerned with [the] same government, why is it that it is regarded as incompetent and untrustworthy in the one market and efficient and reliable in the other? [It] seems to me that the arguments [used] to support freedom in the market for ideas are equally applicable in the market for goods.

Compare Scanlon, Freedom of Expression and Categories of Expression, 40 U. Pitt. L. Rev. 519, 541 (1979): "[Commercial speech deserves less than full first amendment protection because] we regard the government as much less partisan in the competition between commercial firms than in the struggle between religious or political views."

Consider also Stone, Ronald Coase's First Amendment, 54 J. Law & Econ. 367, 374 (2011):

As both logic and history teach, the temptation of public officials to use government power to stifle criticism and distort public debate poses a direct threat to the very existence of a self-governing society. Such behavior not only gives those in power a continuing political advantage over their challengers but also enables them to prevent any criticism or even discussion of their actions. It therefore freezes policies in place. In the sphere of economic regulation, however, that is not the case. As long as free speech is guaranteed, even an inefficient and rent-seeking economic regulation can be publicly criticized and ultimately changed. From a constitutional standpoint, economic freedom simply does not stand on the same footing as freedom of speech.

d. Blasi, The Pathological Perspective and the First Amendment, 85 Colum. L. Rev. 449, 486, 488 (1985):

Commercial advertising was never a concern in any of the historical political struggles over freedom of expression. The first amendment claimants in disputes over commercial advertising often are sophisticated and driven by the profit motive. The speech in question is brief and intended to evoke a reflexive, even if somewhat delayed, response from listeners. There is a strong tradition of government regulation of [advertising]. [Perhaps] most important, [the] spectacle of voluminous litigation over [product] advertising, conducted in the name of the first amendment, [would] undercut [society's] belief that first amendment freedoms represent a noble commitment well worth preserving even in the face of serious anxieties, risks, and costs. [Thus, we should] exclude commercial advertising from the protection of the first amendment.

e. Justice Powell's opinion for the Court in Ohralik v. Ohio State Bar, 436 U.S. 447 (1978):

In rejecting the notion [that expression concerning purely commercial transactions] "is wholly outside the protection of the First Amendment," [we] were careful [in *Virginia Pharmacy* not to discard] the "commonsense distinction between speech proposing a commercial transaction [and] other varieties of speech." [Indeed,] to require a parity of constitutional protection for commercial and noncommercial speech alike could invite dilution, simply by a leveling process, of the force of the Amendment's guarantee with respect to the latter kind of speech. Rather than subject the First Amendment to such a devitalization, we have instead afforded commercial speech a limited measure of protection, commensurate with its subordinate position in the scale of First Amendment values. . . .

f. Brudney, The First Amendment and Commercial Advertising, 53 B.C. L. Rev. 1153, 1179, 1168 (2013):

It has been suggested that because it is speech and serves a communicative function, commercial speech is entitled to the same protection against government regulation as other protected [speech]. As a predicate for First Amendment protection, however, commercial speech's communicative function may not be sufficient to justify such protection. . . .

[This is so because,] in much commercial speech, the speaker's concern is primarily, or only, with the choices to be made by individual consumers for their personal benefit, rather than for the benefit of society as a whole. The question that each consumer is presumed to ask in making his choice is: "What is good, or best, for me?" [But in the case of traditionally protected speech] the question the addressee or member of the audience is presumed to ask is: "What is good, or best, for the community or society?" Such an inquiry is not of central concern to the speaker-seller or indeed to the listener-buyer [in the context of commercial speech]. . . .

2. *What is "commercial" speech?* In *Virginia Pharmacy*, the Court reaffirmed that the content of the speech, rather than the speaker's commercial or profit motivation, is determinative. What matters, in other words, is not whether the speaker is out to make money, but whether the expression does "no more than propose a commercial transaction." Is this definition satisfactory? Does a billboard displaying a cigarette package in a pastoral setting constitute "commercial" speech under this definition? What about corporate issue advertising that describes the corporation, its activities, or its policies without explicitly identifying any of the corporation's products or services? Consider Comment, First Amendment Protection for Commercial Advertising: The New Constitutional Doctrine, 44 U. Chi. L. Rev. 205, 236 (1976): "[Commercial speech should be defined as] (1) speech that refers to a specific brand name product or service, (2) made by a speaker with a financial interest in the sale of the advertised product or service, in the sale of a competing product or service, or in the distribution of the speech, (3) that does not advertise an activity itself protected by the first amendment."

In Bolger v. Youngs Drug Products Corp., 463 U.S. 60 (1983), the Court held that various "informational pamphlets" dealing with contraceptives constituted "commercial" speech. "One of [the] pamphlets, 'Condoms and Human Sexuality,' specifically [referred] to a number of Trojan-brand condoms manufactured by [Youngs] and [described] the advantages of each type. [Another], 'Plain Talk about Venereal Disease,' [discussed] condoms without any specific reference to those manufactured by [Youngs]." The Court explained:

> The mere fact that these pamphlets are conceded to be advertisements clearly does not compel the conclusion that they are commercial speech. [Citing New York Times v. Sullivan.] Similarly, the reference to a specific product does not by itself render the pamphlets commercial speech. Finally, the fact that Youngs has an economic motivation for mailing the pamphlets would clearly be insufficient by itself to turn the materials into commercial speech. [The] combination of *all* these characteristics, however, provides strong support for [the] conclusion that the informational pamphlets [are] commercial speech. [Moreover, the pamphlets] constitute commercial speech notwithstanding the fact that they contain discussions of important public issues such as venereal disease and family planning. [Advertising] which "links a product to a current public debate" is not thereby entitled to the constitutional protection afforded noncommercial

speech. [Finally, that] a product is referred to generically [and not by brand name] does not [remove] it from the realm of commercial speech. [For] a company with sufficient control of the market for a product may be able to promote the product without reference to specific brand names. [Indeed, in] this case, Youngs describes itself as "the leader in the manufacture and sale" of contraceptives.

3. *Raffirmations of* Virginia Pharmacy. In the years immediately after *Virginia Pharmacy*, the Court reaffirmed and expanded its protection of truthful, nondeceptive commercial speech. See Bates v. State Bar of Arizona, 433 U.S. 350 (1977) (invalidating a state court rule prohibiting attorney advertising, as applied to a newspaper advertisement stating "DO YOU NEED A LAWYER? Legal Services at Very Reasonable Fees" and listing fees for a variety of services, such as uncontested divorce, uncontested adoption, uncontested non-business bankruptcy, and name change); Linmark Associates v. Township of Willingboro, 431 U.S. 85 (1977) (invalidating an ordinance prohibiting the display of "For Sale" or "Sold" signs on all but model homes so as to discourage "white flight" as neighborhood became racially integrated; Carey v. Population Services International, 431 U.S. 678 (1977) (invalidating a prohibition on the advertising of contraceptives because the state's concerns "that advertisements of contraceptive products would be offensive and embarrassing to those exposed to them, and that permitting them would legitimate sexual activity of young people" are "classically not justifications validating the suppression of expression protected by the First Amendment.") See also Bolger v. Youngs Drug Products Corp., 463 U.S. 60 (1983) (invalidating a federal statute prohibiting the mailing of unsolicited advertisements for contraceptives because the interest in shielding "recipients of mail from materials that they are likely to find offensive" is not sufficiently substantial to justify the suppression of "protected speech").

**CENTRAL HUDSON GAS v. PUBLIC SERVICE COMMISSION OF NEW YORK, 447 U.S. 557 (1980).** The commission permitted electric utilities to engage in institutional and informational advertising, but, to further the conservation of energy, prohibited such utilities to engage in promotional advertising designed to stimulate the use of electricity. The Court, in an opinion by Justice Powell, held the order invalid. After observing that the "Constitution [accords] a lesser protection to commercial speech than to other constitutionally guaranteed expression," the Court maintained that in its prior decisions, it had implicitly "developed" a "four-part analysis" for commercial speech cases:

"[First], we must determine whether the expression is protected by the First Amendment. For commercial speech to come within that provision, it at least must concern lawful activity and not be misleading. [Second], we ask whether the asserted governmental interest is substantial. [Third, if] both inquiries yield positive answers, we must determine whether the regulation directly advances the governmental interest. [And fourth], if the governmental interest could be served as well by a more limited restriction on commercial speech, the excessive restrictions cannot survive."

Applying this analysis to the ban on promotional advertising, the Court noted that the "Commission does not claim that the expression at issue is either inaccurate or relates to unlawful activity." Moreover, "in view of our country's dependence on energy resources beyond our control, no one can doubt the importance of energy conservation. Plainly, therefore, the state interest asserted is substantial." Further, "the State's interest in energy conservation is directly advanced by the Commission order." Thus, "the critical inquiry" is whether the commission's complete suppression of speech ordinarily protected by the first amendment is "no more extensive than necessary to further the State's interest." The Court found the complete ban on promotional advertising to be too "extensive" because the commission "has not demonstrated that its interest in conservation cannot be protected adequately by more limited regulation of [the] format and content of Central Hudson's advertising. It might, for example, require that the advertisements include information about the relative efficiency and expense of the offered service." The Court thus concluded that, "in the absence of a showing that more limited speech regulation would be ineffective, we cannot approve the complete suppression of Central Hudson's advertising."

Justice Blackmun, joined by Justice Brennan, concurred, but argued that the Court's standard weakened the protection accorded commercial advertising in *Virginia Pharmacy*. Justice Rehnquist dissented. He argued that New York's order is essentially "an economic regulation to which virtually complete deference should be accorded by this Court," for "in terms of constitutional values," the ban on promotional advertising is "virtually indistinguishable" from a decision of the commission to raise the price of electricity in order to conserve energy.

## Note: *Truthful, Nondeceptive Commercial Advertising*

1. *Retreat?* Confirming Justice Blackmun's concern that *Central Hudson* seemed to retreat from the Court's prior understanding of the first amendment's protection of truthful, nondeceptive commercial advertising, in a few post–*Central Hudson* decisions the Court did seem to take a relatively deferential approach to laws regulating commercial advertising.

In Posadas de Puerto Rico Associates v. Tourism Co. of Puerto Rico, 478 U.S. 328 (1986), for example, the Court, in a five-to-four decision, upheld a Puerto Rican statute that prohibited any advertising of legal casino gambling aimed at the residents of Puerto Rico. In an opinion by Justice Rehnquist, the Court explained that Puerto Rico apparently believed that "[excessive] casino gambling among local residents [would] produce serious harmful effects" similar to those that had "motivated the vast majority of the 50 States to prohibit casino gambling." The Court held this was a "substantial" government interest and declared that the law directly advanced that interest, within the meaning of *Central Hudson*.

In response to the argument that, having chosen to legalize casino gambling for residents of Puerto Rico, the first amendment prohibited the legislature from using restrictions on advertising to accomplish its goal of reducing demand for such gambling, the Court reasoned that because "the government could have enacted a wholesale prohibition of the underlying conduct" it was permissible for the government to take the "less intrusive step of allowing the conduct, but reducing the demand through restrictions on advertising." The Court observed that "the greater power to completely ban casino gambling necessarily includes the lesser power to ban advertising of casino gambling," and that it would "be a strange constitutional doctrine which would concede to the legislature the authority to totally ban a product or activity, but deny to the legislature the authority to forbid the stimulation of demand for the product or activity through advertising." After *Posadas*, could a state constitutionally ban all cigarette advertising?

See also Florida Bar v. Went for It, 515 U.S. 618 (1995) (upholding a rule of the Florida bar prohibiting any lawyer to send "a written communication to a prospective client for the purpose of obtaining professional employment if [the] communication concerns an action for personal injury [arising out of] an accident [involving] the person to whom the communication is addressed," because the challenged rule protects "in a direct and material way" the "privacy and tranquility of personal injury victims [against] intrusive, unsolicited contact by lawyers").

2. *Retreat from retreat.* The retreat from *Virginia Pharmacy* was short-lived, however. Consider the following decisions:

a. In Rubin v. Coors Brewing Co., 514 U.S. 476 (1995), the Court invalidated section 205(e)(2) of the Federal Alcohol Administration Act, which prohibited beer labels from displaying alcohol content. The government had argued that the labeling ban was necessary to prevent "strength wars" among brewers who, without regulation, would seek to compete in the marketplace based on the potency of their beer.

b. In Greater New Orleans Broadcasting Association, Inc. v. United States, 527 U.S. 173 (1999), the Court unanimously invalidated 18 U.S.C. §1304, which prohibited radio and television broadcasters from carrying advertisements about privately operated commercial casino gambling, as applied to broadcast stations located in states where such gambling is legal.

c. In 44 Liquormart, Inc. v. Rhode Island, 517 U.S. 484 (1996), the Court invalidated a Rhode Island statute prohibiting "advertising in any manner whatsoever" of the price of any alcoholic beverage, except for price tags or signs displayed within licensed premises and not visible from the street:

"[When] a State [prohibits] the dissemination of truthful, nonmisleading commercial [messages], there is [little] reason to depart from the rigorous review that the First Amendment generally demands. [Bans] against truthful, nonmisleading commercial speech [usually] rest solely on the offensive assumption that the public will respond 'irrationally' to the truth. The First Amendment directs us to be especially skeptical of regulations that seek to keep people in the dark for what the government perceives to be their own good. . . .

"The State [cannot] satisfy the requirement that its restriction on speech be no more extensive than necessary. It is perfectly obvious that alternative forms of regulation that would not involve any restriction on speech would be more likely to achieve the State's goal of promoting temperance. [Higher] prices can be maintained [by] increased taxation. Per capita purchases could be limited as is the case with prescription drugs. Even educational campaigns focused on the problems [of] drinking might prove to be more effective. [Thus,] the price advertising ban cannot survive the more stringent constitutional review that *Central Hudson* [concluded] was appropriate for the complete suppression of truthful, nonmisleading commercial speech."

Justice Thomas filed a concurring opinion: "In cases such as this, in which the government's asserted interest is to keep legal users of a product or service ignorant in order to manipulate their choices in the marketplace, [the state's interest] is per se illegitimate and can no more justify regulation of 'commercial' speech than it can justify regulation of 'noncommercial' speech. [I] would [hold that] all attempts to dissuade legal choices by citizens by keeping them ignorant are impermissible."

d. In Lorillard Tobacco Co. v. Reilly, 533 U.S. 525 (2001), the Court invalidated Massachusetts regulations governing the advertising of cigarettes, smokeless tobacco products, and cigars. The regulations prohibited outdoor advertising of such products within one thousand feet of a public playground or elementary or secondary school: "The State's interest in preventing under-age tobacco use is substantial, and even compelling, but it is no less true that the sale and use of tobacco products by adults is a legal activity. [Tobacco] retailers and manufacturers have an interest in conveying truthful information about their products to adults, and adults have a corresponding interest in receiving truthful information about tobacco products. [The State] has failed to show that [these regulations] are not more extensive than necessary to advance the State's substantial interest in preventing underage tobacco use."

In a concurring opinion, Justice Thomas argued that "there is no 'philosophical or historical basis for asserting that "commercial" speech is of "lower value" than "noncommercial" speech.'" Thus, the "asserted government interest in keeping people ignorant by suppressing expression 'is per se illegitimate and can no more justify regulation of "commercial" speech than it can justify regulation of "noncommercial" speech.'"

e. Thompson v. Western States Medical Center, 535 U.S. 357 (2002), concerned the regulation of drug compounding, a process by which a pharmacist combines ingredients to create a medication tailored to the needs of an individual patient. Compounding is typically used to prepare medications that are not commercially available. It is a traditional component of the practice of pharmacy. The federal Food, Drug and Cosmetic Act of 1938 prohibits any person to manufacture or sell any "new drug" without prior FDA approval. Until the early 1990s, the FDA left the regulation of drug compounding to the States. In the early 1990s, however, the FDA became increasingly concerned about the practice. In 1997, Congress enacted the Food and Drug Administration Modernization Act, which, among other things, expressly exempted compounded drugs from the FDA's standard drug approval requirements if, but only if, the providers of those drugs did not advertise them.

The Court, in a five-to-four decision, held this restriction unconstitutional: "[The] Government [notes] that the FDCA's [general] drug approval requirements are critical to the public health [because the safety] of a new drug needs to be established by rigorous, scientifically valid clinical studies, [rather than by the] impressions of individual doctors, who cannot themselves compile sufficient [data]. [But] 'because obtaining FDA approval for a new drug is a costly process, requiring [such] approval of all drug products compounded by pharmacies for the particular needs of an individual patient would, as a practical matter, eliminate the practice of compounding, and thereby [eliminate] compounded drugs for those patients who have no alternative treatment.' [Thus], the Government needs to be able to draw a line between small-scale compounding and large-scale drug manufacturing. That line must distinguish compounded drugs produced on such a small scale that they could not [realistically] undergo [costly] safety and efficacy testing from drugs produced and sold on a large enough scale that they could undergo such testing and therefore must do so.

"The Government argues that the FDAMA's speech-related provisions provide just such a line [because they] use advertising as the trigger for requiring FDA approval — essentially, as long as pharmacists do not advertise particular compounded drugs, they may sell [them] without first [obtaining] FDA approval. If they advertise their compounded drugs, however, FDA approval is required. [The] Government argues [that] Congress' decision to limit the FDAMA's compounding exemption to pharmacies that do not engage in promotional activity was 'rationally calculated' to avoid creating 'a loophole that would allow unregulated drug manufacturing to occur under the guise of pharmacy compounding.'

"[The] Government has failed to demonstrate that the speech restrictions are 'not more extensive than is necessary to serve [its] interest[s].' [Several] non-speech related means of drawing a line between compounding and large-scale manufacturing might be possible here. [For] example, the Government could ban the use of 'commercial scale manufacturing [for] compounding drug products.' [It could cap] the amount of any particular compounded drug

[that] a pharmacist may make or sell in a given period of time. [The] Government has not offered any reason why these possibilities, alone or in combination, would be insufficient to prevent compounding from occurring on such a scale as to undermine the new drug approval process. . . .

"The dissent describes another governmental interest — an interest in prohibiting the sale of compounded drugs to 'patients who may not clearly need them.' [Aside] from the fact that this concern rests on the questionable assumption that doctors would prescribe unnecessary medications, [this] concern amounts to a fear that people would make bad decisions if given truthful information about compounded drugs. We have previously rejected the notion that the Government has an interest in preventing the dissemination of truthful commercial information in order to prevent members of the public from making bad decisions with the information. [Citing *Virginia Pharmacy* and *44 Liquormart.*]"

Justice Breyer, joined by Chief Justice Rehnquist and Justices Stevens and Ginsburg, dissented: "There is considerable evidence that consumer oriented advertising will create strong consumer-driven demand for a particular drug, [and] there is strong evidence that doctors will often respond affirmatively to a patient's request for a specific drug that the patient has seen advertised. [I] do not deny that the statute restricts the circulation of some truthful information. [Nonetheless], this Court has not previously held that commercial advertising restrictions automatically violate the First Amendment. Rather, the Court has applied a more flexible test. [It] has done so because it has concluded that, from a constitutional perspective, commercial speech does not warrant application of the Court's strictest speech-protective tests. [The] Court, in my view, gives insufficient weight [in this case] to the Government's regulatory rationale, and too readily assumes the existence of practical alternatives. It thereby applies the commercial speech doctrine too strictly."

f. Sorrell v. IMS Health, Inc., 131 S. Ct. 2653 (2011), involved the process of "detailing," by which pharmaceutical manufacturers market their drugs to doctors. This typically involves a salesperson's (or "detailer's") visit to a doctor's office to persuade the doctor to prescribe a particular brand-name drug. Knowledge of the doctor's prescription practices — called "prescriber-identifying information" — enables the detailer to determine which doctors are likely to be interested in particular drugs and how best to present the sales pitch. Pharmacies receive prescriber-identifying information whenever they fill prescriptions. Many pharmacies sell this information to data miners, who then analyze the information and sell it to pharmaceutical manufacturers, who then give it to their detailers to enable them to refine their marketing approach and increase sales. In 2007, Vermont enacted legislation prohibiting pharmacies from selling prescriber-identifying information for the purpose of marketing prescription drugs.

The Court, in a six-to-three decision, held in an opinion by Justice Kennedy that this law violated the first amendment: "[The State] contends that [its law] advances important public policy goals by lowering the costs of medical services and promoting public health. If prescriber-identifying information were available for use by detailers, the State contends, then detailing would be effective in promoting brand-name drugs that are more expensive and less safe than generic alternatives. [While these] goals may be proper, [the law] does not advance them in a permissible way. [Those] who seek to censor [expression] often assert that disfavored speech has adverse effects. But the 'fear that people would make bad decisions if given truthful information' cannot justify content-based burdens on speech. [Citing *Thompson, Virginia Board of Pharmacy,* and *44 Liquormart*]."

Justice Breyer, joined by Justices Ginsburg and Kagan, dissented: "[O]ur cases make clear that the First Amendment offers considerably less protection to the maintenance of a free marketplace for goods and services [than for] a marketplace that provides access to social, political, esthetic, moral, and other ideas and experiences. [To] apply a 'heightened' standard of review [in a case like this] would risk what then-Justice Rehnquist [once described] as a 'retur[n] to the bygone era of *Lochner*.'[By] inviting courts to scrutinize whether a State's legitimate regulatory interests can be achieved in less restrictive ways whenever they touch (even indirectly) upon commercial speech, today's majority risks repeating the mistakes of the past."

3. *The implications of* Rubin, Greater New Orleans, 44 Liquormart, Lorillard, Thompson, *and* Sorrell. After these six decisions, can you envision any circumstances in which the Court would uphold the regulation of truthful, nondeceptive commercial advertising of a lawful product or service because the advertising might cause consumers to make undesirable decisions? What about advertising directed at children? Can the state constitutionally ban cigarette advertisements in school newspapers? In comic books?

## Note: Other Regulations of Commercial Advertising

1. *Regulating the means of commercial advertising.* The cases considered above involved restrictions on the advertising of particular services or products. Suppose the government restricts *all* commercial advertising, as a class. How might that affect the analysis? Consider City of Cincinnati v. Discovery Network, 507 U.S. 410 (1993). In 1989, Cincinnati authorized respondent companies to place sixty-two freestanding newsracks on public property for the purpose of distributing free magazines that consisted primarily of advertisements for respondents' services. In 1990, motivated by its interest in the safety and attractive appearance of its streets and sidewalks, Cincinnati revoked respondents' permits on the ground that the magazines were "commercial handbills" whose distribution on public property could be prohibited. The Court, in an opinion by Justice Stevens, invalidated the restriction:

[Respondents] do [not] question the substantiality of the city's interest in safety and esthetics. [The critical issue is whether the city has met its burden under

*Central Hudson* and *Board of Trustees of SUNY v. Fox*] to establish a "reasonable fit" between its legitimate interests [and] its [ban] on newsracks dispensing "commercial handbills." . . .

The city argues that there is a close fit [because] every decrease in the number of such dispensing devices necessarily effects an increase in safety and an improvement in the attractiveness of the cityscape. [This is] an insufficient justification for the discrimination against respondents' use of newsracks that are no more harmful than the [1,500 to 2,000 noncommercial newsracks that the city permits]. The major premise supporting the city's argument is the proposition that commercial speech has only a low value. Based on that premise, the city contends that the fact that assertedly more valuable publications are allowed to use newsracks does not undermine its judgment that its esthetic and safety interests are stronger than the interest in allowing commercial speakers to have similar access to the reading public.

We cannot agree. [In] this case, the distinction [between commercial and noncommercial speech] bears no relationship whatsoever to the particular interests that the city has asserted. It is therefore an impermissible means of responding to the city's admittedly legitimate interests. [Respondents'] newsracks are no greater an eyesore than the newsracks permitted to remain on Cincinnati's sidewalks. [In] the absence of some basis for distinguishing between "newspapers" and "commercial handbills" that is relevant to an interest asserted by the city, we are unwilling to recognize Cincinnati's bare assertion that the "low value" of commercial speech is a sufficient justification for its selective and categorical ban on newsracks dispensing "commercial handbills."

Chief Justice Rehnquist, joined by Justices White and Thomas, dissented, arguing that one "would have thought that the city [could] have decided to place the burden of its regulatory scheme on less protected speech [without] running afoul of the First Amendment."

2. *Regulating commercial billboards.* In light of *Discovery Network*, how would you expect the Court to rule on the constitutionality of a city ordinance banning all commercial (but not political or public service) billboards? Consider Metromedia, Inc. v. San Diego, 453 U.S. 490 (1981), which involved the constitutionality of a San Diego ordinance prohibiting virtually all outdoor advertising display signs. The ordinance was designed to eliminate hazards to pedestrians and motorists and to improve the appearance of the city. Although the Court invalidated the ordinance as applied to *noncommercial* advertising, it sustained the ordinance as applied to *commercial* messages. The Court explained that the "critical" question concerned "the third of the *Central Hudson* criteria: Does the ordinance 'directly advance' governmental interests in traffic safety and in the appearance of the city?" Although noting that there was no direct evidence in the record "to show any connection between billboards and traffic safety," the Court was reluctant "to disagree with the accumulated, common-sense judgments of local lawmakers [that] billboards are real and substantial hazards to traffic safety. There is nothing here to suggest that these judgments are unreasonable." Similarly, although noting that

"esthetic judgments are necessarily subjective," the Court concluded that the city's esthetic judgment was reasonable. Can *Metromedia* be squared with *Discovery Network*?

3. *Regulating commercial spam.* Commercial advertisers often send unsolicited, bulk e-mails to thousands of recipients. This has the potential to overwhelm individuals' electronic mailboxes and thus to discourage the use of e-mail generally. Could Congress constitutionally prohibit any person to send unsolicited commercial advertisements via e-mail? Could it constitutionally prohibit any person to send unsolicited commercial advertisements via regular mail?

4. *Regulating commercial advertisements of unlawful products or services.* The Court has repeatedly stated that commercial advertisements offering to enter into unlawful transactions are not protected by the first amendment. See, e.g., Hoffman Estates v. Flipside, 455 U.S. 489 (1982) ("government may regulate or ban entirely" commercial "speech proposing an illegal transaction"). Is this reconcilable with *Brandenburg*?

5. *Regulating factually false commercial advertising.* In footnote 24 of *Virginia Pharmacy*, the Court offered several arguments as to why factually false commercial speech may constitutionally be regulated more extensively than other forms of factually false expression. Consider the following criticisms: (a) "Commercial speech is not necessarily more verifiable than other speech. There may well be uncertainty about some quality of a product, such as the health effect of eggs. [On] the other hand, political speech is often quite verifiable by the speakers. A political candidate knows the truth about his own past and present intentions, yet misrepresentations on these subjects are immune from state regulation." Farber, Commercial Speech and First Amendment Theory, 74 Nw. U. L. Rev. 372, 385–386 (1979). (b) "[It] is also incorrect to distinguish commercial from political expression on the ground that the former is somehow hardier because of the inherent profit motive. It could just as easily be said that we need not fear that commercial magazines and newspapers will cease publication for fear of government regulation, because they are in business for profit." Redish, The Value of Free Speech, 130 U. Pa. L. Rev. 591, 633 (1982).

6. *Regulating deceptive or misleading commercial advertising. Virginia Pharmacy* suggests that commercial advertising may be regulated or prohibited, even if it is not factually false, if it is deceptive or misleading. Is this defensible? The Court observed in *Gertz* that "there is no constitutional value in false statements of fact." Can the same be said of misleading or deceptive expression? Do you agree with the Court in *Central Hudson* that, since "the First Amendment's concern for commercial speech is based on the informational function of advertising, [there] can be no constitutional objection to the suppression of commercial messages that [are] more likely to deceive the public than to inform it"? When is an advertisement "misleading"? See Friedman v. Rogers, 440 U.S. 1 (1979) (upholding a state statute prohibiting the practice of

optometry under "any trade name" as a permissible restriction of misleading advertising); Peel v. Attorney Registration & Disciplinary Commission of Illinois, 496 U.S. 91 (1990) (rejecting a state's claim that it is "inherently misleading" for lawyers to hold themselves out as "specialists" in particular fields); Ibanez v. Florida Department of Business and Professional Regulation, 512 U.S. 136 (1994) (rejecting a state's claim that it is "inherently misleading" for an attorney truthfully to advertise that she is also a certified public accountant).

7. *Compelled disclosure.* In Zauderer v. Office of Disciplinary Counsel, 471 U.S. 626 (1985), an attorney advertised in a certain type of case, "if there is no recovery, no legal fees are owed by our clients." The Court upheld a disciplinary rule requiring the attorney to disclose in the advertisement that clients would have to pay "costs" even if the lawsuits were unsuccessful. The Court explained that "because the extension of First Amendment protection to commercial speech is justified principally by the value to consumers of the information such speech provides," the state may constitutionally require advertisers to disclose specific information in their advertisements if that requirement is "reasonably related to the State's interest in preventing deception of consumers."

8. *Compelled commercial speech.* The Agricultural Marketing Agreement Act of 1937, which is designed to maintain orderly agricultural markets, authorizes collective action by groups of agricultural producers on such matters as uniform prices, product standards, and generic advertising. The cost of such collective action, which must be approved by two-thirds of the affected producers, is covered by compulsory assessments on the producers. In Glickman v. Wileman Brothers & Elliott, Inc., 512 U.S. 1145 (1997), the Court held that marketing orders promulgated by the Secretary of Agriculture, which assessed respondent producers for the cost of generic advertising of California tree fruits, did not violate respondents' first amendment rights, even though respondents objected to the requirement that they pay for such advertising. The Court explained:

> [The] regulatory scheme at issue [is distinguishable] from laws that we have found to abridge [the] First Amendment [see Chapter VI.C, infra] [because] they do not compel the producers to endorse or to finance any political or ideological views. [None] of the advertising in this record promotes any particular message other than encouraging consumers to buy California tree fruit. Neither the fact that respondents may prefer to foster that message independently in order to promote and distinguish their own products, nor the fact that they think more or less money should be spent fostering it, makes this case comparable to those in which an objection rested on political or ideological disagreement with the content of the message. The mere fact that the objectors believe their money is not being well spent "does not mean [that] they have a First Amendment complaint."

In such circumstances, the Court concluded that the wisdom of the overall program "is simply a question of economic policy for Congress and the

Executive to resolve." Justice Souter, joined by Chief Justice Rehnquist and Justices Scalia and Thomas, dissented.

See also United States v. United Foods, 533 U.S. 405 (2001) (invalidating a federal statute requiring producers of fresh mushrooms to fund a common advertising program promoting mushroom sales on the ground that, unlike the situation in *Glickman*, where the compelled assessments were ancillary to a comprehensive regulatory scheme, the requirements in *United Foods* were not part of such a comprehensive scheme); Johanns v. Livestock Marketing Association, 544 U.S. 550 (2005) (upholding a federal statute imposing an assessment on all sales of cattle to fund, among other things, beef promotional campaigns on the ground that, unlike the situation in *United Foods*, the promotional materials in this case are "government speech" rather than government-compelled private speech because the Secretary of Agriculture directly controls "every word" in the promotional materials). See Post, Compelled Subsidization of Speech: Johanns v. Livestock Marketing Association, 2005 Sup. Ct. Rev. 195. For more on the problem of government speech, see Chapter V.B.

## E.  OBSCENITY

In the first reported obscenity case in the United States, a Pennsylvania court declared it an offense at common law to exhibit for profit a picture of a nude couple. Commonwealth v. Sharpless, 2 Serg. & Rawle 91 (1815). Despite *Sharpless*, there were few serious efforts to restrict "obscene" expression prior to the Civil War. In the late 1860s, however, Anthony Comstock, a grocer, initiated a campaign to suppress obscenity. Comstock's efforts resulted in the enactment of antiobscenity legislation in virtually every state. In applying this legislation, most courts adopted the *Hicklin* definition of obscenity: The "test of obscenity" is "whether the tendency of the matter [is] to deprave and corrupt those whose minds are open to such immoral influences." Regina v. Hicklin, 3 L.R-Q.B. 360, 371 (1868). Under this test, which resulted in the suppression of such works as Theodore Dreiser's An American Tragedy and D. H. Lawrence's Lady Chatterley's Lover, a work could be deemed obscene because of the potential effect of even isolated passages on the most susceptible readers or viewers. See Commonwealth v. Friede, 271 Mass. 318, 171 N.E. 472 (1930) (An American Tragedy); Commonwealth v. DeLacey, 271 Mass. 327, 171 N.E. 455 (1930) (Lady Chatterley's Lover).

In an influential decision reviewing the suppression of James Joyce's Ulysses in the early 1930s, a federal court rejected the *Hicklin* test and adopted instead a standard focusing on the effect on the average person of the dominant theme of the work as a whole. United States v. One Book Called "Ulysses," 5 F. Supp. 182 (S.D.N.Y. 1933), aff'd, 72 F.2d 705 (2d Cir. 1934). On the evolution of obscenity doctrine in this era, see Gillers, A Tendency to Deprave and

Corrupt: The Transformation of American Obscenity Law from *Hicklin* to *Ulysses II*, 85 Wash. U. L. Rev. 215 (2007).

Throughout this era, it was generally assumed that the first amendment posed no barrier to the suppression of obscenity. Indeed, the *Chaplinsky* dictum prominently featured the "obscene" in its catalogue of "unprotected" utterances. The Supreme Court first considered the obscenity issue in a 1948 case arising out of New York's attempt to suppress Memoirs of Hecate County, a highly regarded book written by Edmund Wilson, one of America's foremost literary critics. The Court divided equally on the issue, however, and thus affirmed the conviction without opinion. Doubleday & Co. v. New York, 335 U.S. 848 (1948).

Nine years later, in Roth v. United States, infra, the Court finally addressed the obscenity question. There have been two distinct periods in the Court's efforts to come to grips with obscenity. The first period, which lasted from the 1957 decision in *Roth* until 1973, was dominated by the Warren Court's frustrating and largely unsuccessful efforts to define "obscenity." The second period, which began with the Court's 1973 decisions in Miller v. California and Paris Adult Theatre I v. Slaton, infra, has been dominated by the Court's subsequent efforts to reformulate the doctrine. This section focuses on three questions: Is obscenity "low" value speech? What is "obscenity"? What interests justify the suppression of obscenity?

**ROTH v. UNITED STATES; ALBERTS v. CALIFORNIA, 354 U.S. 476 (1957).** Roth was convicted of violating a federal statute prohibiting any person to mail any "obscene" publication. Alberts was convicted of violating a California statute prohibiting any person to write, print, or sell any "obscene" writing. The Supreme Court affirmed the convictions. Justice Brennan delivered the opinion of the Court:

"The dispositive question is whether obscenity is utterance within the area of protected speech and press. [All] ideas having even the slightest redeeming social importance — unorthodox ideas, controversial ideas, even ideas hateful to the prevailing climate of opinion — have the full protection of the guarantees, unless excludable because they encroach upon the limited area of more important interests. But implicit in the history of the First Amendment is the rejection of obscenity as utterly without redeeming social importance. [Thirteen] of the 14 States which by 1792 had ratified the Constitution [provided] for the prosecution of libel, and all of those States made either blasphemy or profanity, or both, statutory crimes. [In] light of this history, it is apparent [that] obscenity, [like] libel, [was] outside the protection intended for speech and press. [We therefore] hold that obscenity is not within the area of constitutionally protected speech or press. [Accordingly,] obscene material [may be suppressed] without proof [that it will] create a clear and present danger of antisocial conduct.

"However, sex and obscenity are not synonymous. Obscene material is material which deals with sex in a manner appealing to prurient interest.

The portrayal of sex, e.g., in art, literature, and scientific works, is not itself sufficient reason to deny material the constitutional protection of freedom of speech and press. Sex, a great and mysterious motive in human life, has indisputably been a subject of absorbing interest to mankind through the ages; it is one of the vital problems of human interest and public concern. [It] is therefore vital that the standards for judging obscenity safeguard the protection of freedom of speech and press for material which does not treat sex in a manner appealing to prurient interest. [The proper test is] whether to the average person, applying contemporary community standards, the dominant theme of the material taken as a whole appeals to the prurient interest."

*prurient interest test*

Chief Justice Warren concurred in the result: "It is not the book that is on trial; it is a person. [The] defendants [in] these cases [were] plainly engaged in the commercial exploitation of the morbid and shameful craving for materials with prurient effect. [State] and Federal Governments can constitutionally punish such conduct. That is all that [we] need to decide."

*const to punish*

Justice Harlan concurred in the result in *Alberts*, but dissented in *Roth* on the ground that the states have broader authority to regulate obscene expression than the federal government, which may restrict only "hard-core pornography."

Justice Douglas, joined by Justice Black, dissented: "I do not think that the problem can be resolved by the Court's statement that 'obscenity is not expression protected by the First Amendment.' [There] is no special historical evidence that literature dealing with sex was intended to be treated in a special manner by those who drafted the First Amendment. [Moreover,] I reject [the] implication that problems of freedom of speech [are] to be resolved by weighing against the values of free expression, the judgment of the Court that a particular form of expression has 'no redeeming social importance.' The First Amendment [was] designed to preclude courts as well as legislatures from weighing the values of speech against silence. [I] have the same confidence in the ability of our people to reject noxious literature as I have in their capacity to sort out the true from the false in theology, economics, politics, or any other field."

*Show me historical intent*

*Does nt like court passing judgment on speeches value,*

## Note: Obscenity and Free Expression

1. *Entertainment, art, literature, and the first amendment.* Does the first amendment protect not only speech that expressly addresses "public" issues but also "speech" in the form of entertainment, art, and literature? Does the latter form of "speech" have a "subordinate position" in the scale of first amendment values? Consider Kalven, The Metaphysics of the Law of Obscenity, 1960 Sup. Ct. Rev. 1, 15–16:

The classic defense of John Stuart Mill and the modern defense of Alexander Meiklejohn do not help much when the question is why the novel, the poem, the painting, the drama, or the piece of sculpture falls within the protection of the First Amendment. Nor do the famous opinions of Hand, Holmes, and Brandeis. The emphasis is all on truth winning out in a fair fight between competing ideas [and on the] argument that free speech is indispensable to the informed citizenry required to make self-government work. The people need free speech because they vote. [But not] all communications are relevant to the political process. The people do not need novels or dramas or paintings or poems because they will be called upon to vote. Art and belles-lettres do not deal in such ideas — at least not good art or belles-lettres. [Thus] there seems to be a hiatus in our basic free-speech theory.

Consider Meiklejohn's response:

> [There] are many forms of thought and expression within the range of human communications from which the voter derives the knowledge, intelligence, sensitivity to human values: the capacity for sane and objective judgment which, so far as possible, a ballot should express. [The] people do need novels and dramas and paintings and poems, "because they will be called upon to vote." The primary social fact which blocks and hinders the success of our experiment in self-government is that our citizens are not educated for self-government.

Meiklejohn, The First Amendment Is an Absolute, 1961 Sup. Ct. Rev. 245, 256, 263. Does the "self-fulfillment" defense of free expression fill Kalven's "hiatus" and offer a more persuasive rationale for the protection of art, literature, and entertainment?

The Court has generally assumed that nonobscene literature and entertainment are entitled to "full" first amendment protection. In Winters v. New York, 333 U.S. 507, 510 (1948), for example, the Court explained that "[the] line between the informing and the entertaining is too elusive for the protection of the basic right. Everyone is familiar with instances of propaganda through fiction. What is one man's amusement, teaches another's doctrine." See also Schad v. Borough of Mount Ephraim, 452 U.S. 61 (1981) (holding unconstitutional a prohibition on all live entertainment in the borough). For a more thorough explication of the values of aesthetic expression, see Bezanson, Art and the Constitution, 93 Iowa L. Rev. 1593 (2008); Nahmod, Artistic Expression and Aesthetic Theory: The Beautiful, The Sublime and The First Amendment, 1987 Wis. L. Rev. 221; Hamilton, Art Speech, 49 Vand. L. Rev. 73 (1996).

2. *Is obscenity of only "low" first amendment value?* Does obscenity further any of the values underlying the protection of free expression? Consider the following arguments:

a. In *Roth*, the Court argues that the historical evidence shows that obscenity "was outside the protection intended for speech and press." But consider Kalven, supra, at 9: "[The] Court's use of history was so casual as to be [alarming]. Is it clear, for example, that blasphemy can constitutionally be made a crime today? And what would the Court say to an argument along the same lines appealing to the Sedition Act of 1798 as justification for the truly liberty-defeating crime of seditious libel?"

b. Stone, Sex, Violence, and the First Amendment, 74 U. Chi. L. Rev. 1857, 1861–1863 (2007):

> In *Roth*, the Court maintained that "implicit in the history of the First Amendment is the rejection of obscenity as utterly without redeeming social importance." [But] unlike libel, blasphemy, and profanity, obscenity was not unlawful under either English or American law in 1792. . . .
>
> [In] the 1790s, when the United States was contemplating the First Amendment, England was awash with all sorts of sexually explicit material, [and the] first prosecution for obscenity in the United States did not occur until [almost] a quarter-century *after* the adoption of the First Amendment. . . .

c. Schauer, Speech and "Speech" — Obscenity and "Obscenity": An Exercise in the Interpretation of Constitutional Language, 67 Geo. L.J. 899, 906, 922, 923, 926 (1979):

> Certain uses of words, although speech in the ordinary sense, clearly are not speech in the constitutional sense. ["Speech" for first amendment purposes is defined by] the idea of cognitive content, of mental effect, of a communication designed to appeal to the intellectual process. This [includes] the artistic and the emotive as well as the propositional. [But] hardcore pornography is [by definition] designed to produce a purely physical effect. [It is] essentially a physical rather than a mental stimulus. [A] pornographic item is in a real sense a sexual surrogate. [Consider] rubber, plastic, or leather sex aids. It is hard to find any free speech aspects in their sale or use. [The] mere fact that in pornography the stimulating experience is initiated by visual rather than tactile means is irrelevant. [Neither] means constitutes communication in the cognitive sense. [Thus,] hardcore pornography *is* sex, [not "speech"].

For a critique of Schauer's view, see Gey, The Apologetics of Suppression: The Regulation of Pornography as Act and Idea, 86 Mich. L. Rev. 1564 (1988).

d. As the Court observed in *Chaplinsky*, obscenity is "of such slight social value as a step to truth that any benefit that may be derived from [it] is clearly outweighed by the social interest in order and morality." Or as the Court observed in *Roth*, such expression is "utterly without redeeming social importance." But consider Richards, Free Speech and Obscenity Law: Toward a Moral Theory of the First Amendment, 123 U. Pa. L. Rev. 45, 82 (1974):

> [The] First Amendment rests [fundamentally] on the moral liberties of expression, conscience and thought; these liberties are fundamental conditions of the integrity and competence of a person in mastering his life and expressing this mastery to others. [There] is no reason whatsoever to believe that the freedom to determine the sexual contents of one's communications or to be an audience to

section. (b) No television station may broadcast any material that is obscene for children, except between the hours of 11:00 P.M. and 6:00 A.M. (c) No person may post on the Internet any material that is obscene for children. (d) No person may display on any billboard any image that is obscene for children.

4. *The definition of obscenity: Redrup.* The inability of the Court to articulate a definition of obscenity that could command the allegiance of a majority, compounded by the potential relevance of factors extrinsic to the material itself, led to an era of chaos. In Redrup v. New York, 386 U.S. 767 (1967), the Court began the practice of per curiam reversals of convictions for the sale or exhibition of materials that at least five members of the Court, applying their separate tests, deemed not to be obscene. From 1967 to 1973, some thirty-one cases were disposed of in this fashion. The full opinion of the Court in Walker v. Ohio, 398 U.S. 434 (1970), is typical: "The judgment of the Supreme Court of Ohio is reversed. [*Redrup.*]" As Justice Brennan later commented: "[The *Redrup* approach] resolves cases as between the parties, but offers only the most obscure guidance to legislation, adjudication by other courts, and primary conduct. [It] comes as no surprise that judicial attempts to follow our lead conscientiously have often ended in hopeless confusion." Paris Adult Theatre I v. Slaton, 413 U.S. 49, 83 (1973) (Brennan, J., dissenting).

5. *The interests furthered by the suppression of obscenity.* Although debating the definitional issue endlessly, the justices in this era said almost nothing about the nature of the interests that assertedly justified the suppression of obscene expression. As noted earlier, this was due largely to *Roth's* acceptance of the underlying premise of the *Chaplinsky* dictum — obscene utterances are wholly "unprotected" by the first amendment and their restriction thus does not necessitate an inquiry into the nature or substantiality of the state interests.

There was, however, one notable exception to the Court's silence on this issue. In Stanley v. Georgia, 394 U.S. 557 (1969), the Court, speaking through Justice Marshall, held that "the mere private possession of obscene matter cannot constitutionally be made a crime." In reaching this result, the Court announced that the "right to receive information and ideas, regardless of their social worth, [is] fundamental to our free society," and that "in the context of this case — a prosecution for mere possession of printed or filmed matter in the privacy of a person's own home — that right takes on an added dimension," for "also fundamental is the right to be free, except in very limited circumstances, from unwanted governmental intrusions into one's privacy." In light of these interests, "mere categorization of these films as 'obscene' is insufficient justification for such a drastic invasion of personal liberties," for "if the First Amendment means anything, it means that a State has no business telling a man, sitting alone in his own house, what books he may read or what films he may watch."

6. *The implications of* Stanley: *Reidel.* In United States v. Reidel, 402 U.S. 351 (1971), a federal district court, relying on *Stanley,* held a federal statute prohibiting the knowing use of the mails for the delivery of obscene matter

unconstitutional as applied to the distribution of such matter to willing recipients who state that they are adults. The district court reasoned that, "if a
person has the right to receive and possess this material, then someone must
have the right to deliver it to him." The Supreme Court reversed. The Court
explained that the "focus of [*Stanley*] [was] on freedom of mind and thought
and on the privacy of one's home." "Reidel," however, "is in a wholly different
position," for "he has no complaints about governmental violations of his
private thoughts or fantasies, but stands squarely on a claimed First Amendment right to do business in obscenity and use the mails in the process. [*Stanley*] did not overrule *Roth* and we decline to do so now." To the same effect, see
United States v. Thirty-Seven Photographs, 402 U.S. 363 (1971); United States
v. 12 200-Ft. Reels, 413 U.S. 123 (1973); United States v. Orito, 413 U.S. 139
(1973). See also Osborne v. Ohio, 495 U.S. 103 (1990) (holding *Stanley*
inapplicable to the possession of child pornography).

7. *Reformulation.* By 1973, then, the law of obscenity was in a state of
considerable confusion. Two questions were especially troublesome: How
should obscenity be defined? When may it be restricted? In its 1973 decisions
in *Miller* and *Paris Adult Theatre,* the Court attempted to reformulate and
clarify the law.

## Miller v. California

413 U.S. 15 (1973)

Mr. Chief Justice Burger delivered the opinion of the Court.

This is one of a group of "obscenity-pornography" cases being reviewed by
the Court in a re-examination of [the standards] which must be used to identify
obscene material that a State may regulate. . . .

[In this case, appellant] conducted a mass mailing campaign to advertise the
sale of illustrated books, euphemistically called "adult" material. [Appellant's]
conviction was specifically based on his conduct in causing five unsolicited
advertising brochures to be sent through the mail. [The] brochures [consist
primarily] of pictures and drawings very explicitly depicting men and women
in groups of two or more engaging in a variety of sexual activities, with genitals
often prominently displayed. [This] case [thus] involves the application of a
State's criminal obscenity statute to a situation in which sexually explicit
materials have been thrust by aggressive sales action upon unwilling
recipients. . . .

## II

[Obscene] material is unprotected by the First Amendment. [*Roth.*]
[However,] State statutes designed to regulate obscene materials must be

of the First Amendment. [The] First Amendment protects works which, taken as a whole, have serious literary, artistic, political, or scientific value, regardless of whether the government or a majority of the people approve of the ideas these works represent. [But] the public portrayal of hard-core sexual conduct for its own sake, and for the ensuing commercial gain, is a different matter. [There] is no evidence, empirical or historical, that the stern 19th century American censorship of public distribution and display of material relating to sex [in] any way limited or affected expression of serious literary, artistic, political, or scientific ideas. . . .

In sum, we (a) reaffirm the *Roth* holding that obscene material is not protected by the First Amendment; (b) hold that such material can be regulated by the States, subject to the specific safeguards enunciated above, without a showing that the material is *"utterly* without redeeming social value"; and (c) hold that obscenity is to be determined by applying "contemporary community standards." . . .

Vacated and remanded.

MR. JUSTICE DOUGLAS, dissenting. . . .

[The] idea that the First Amendment permits punishment for ideas that are "offensive" to the particular judge or jury sitting in judgment is astounding. No greater leveler of speech or literature has ever been designed. . . .

I do not think we, the judges, were ever given the constitutional power to make definitions of obscenity. If it is to be defined, let the people [decide] by a constitutional amendment what they want to ban as [obscene]. Whatever the choice, the courts will have some guidelines. Now we have none except our own predilections.

MR. JUSTICE BRENNAN, with whom MR. JUSTICE STEWART and MR. JUSTICE MARSHALL join, dissenting.

In my dissent in [*Paris Adult Theatre*, infra], I noted that I had no occasion to consider the extent of state power to regulate the distribution of sexually oriented material [to] unconsenting adults. [I] need not now decide [that question, for] it is clear that under my dissent in *Paris Adult Theatre* the statute under which the prosecution was brought is unconstitutionally overbroad, and therefore invalid on its face. . . .

## Paris Adult Theatre I v. Slaton

413 U.S. 49 (1973)

MR. CHIEF JUSTICE BURGER delivered the opinion of the Court.

[Petitioners are two Atlanta, Georgia, movie theaters and their owners and managers, operating in the style of "adult" theaters. The theaters have a conventional, inoffensive entrance, without any pictures, but with signs indicating that the theaters exhibit "Atlanta's Finest Mature Feature Films." On the door is a sign saying "Adult Theater — You must be 21 and able to prove it. If viewing the nude body offends you, Please Do Not Enter." The local state district attorney filed civil complaints alleging that petitioners were exhibiting to the public for paid admission two allegedly obscene films, Magic Mirror and It All Comes Out in the End, which depict scenes of simulated fellatio, cunnilingus, and group sex intercourse. Respondent's complaints demanded that the two films be declared obscene, and that petitioners be enjoined from exhibiting the films. The trial judge found the films obscene, but dismissed the complaints on the ground that "the display of these films in a commercial theatre, when surrounded by requisite notice to the public of their nature and by reasonable protection against the exposure of these films to minors, is constitutionally permissible." The Georgia Supreme Court reversed and held that exhibition of the films should be enjoined. The U.S. Supreme Court vacated and remanded for reconsideration in light of *Miller.*]

We categorically disapprove the theory [that] obscene, pornographic films acquire constitutional immunity from state regulation simply because they are exhibited for consenting adults only. [Although] we have often pointedly recognized the high importance of the state interest in regulating the exposure of obscene materials to juveniles and unconsenting adults, [this] Court has never declared these to be the only legitimate state interests permitting regulation of obscene material. . . .

In particular, we hold that there are legitimate state interests at stake in stemming the tide of commercialized obscenity, even assuming it is feasible to enforce effective safeguards against exposure to juveniles and to passersby.[7] Rights and interests "other than those of the advocates are involved." [These] include the interest of the public in the quality of life and the total community environment, the tone of commerce in the great city centers, and, possibly, the public safety itself. The Hill-Link Minority Report of the Commission on Obscenity and Pornography indicates that there is at least an arguable correlation between obscene material and crime. Quite apart from sex crimes, however, there remains one problem of large proportions aptly described by Professor Bickel:

> It concerns the tone of the society, the mode, or to use terms that have perhaps greater currency, the style and quality of life, now and in the future. A man may be entitled to read an obscene book in his room, or expose himself indecently there. . . . We should protect his privacy. But if he demands a right to obtain the

7. It is conceivable that an "adult" theater can — if it really insists — prevent the exposure of its obscene wares to juveniles. An "adult" bookstore, dealing in obscene books, magazines, and pictures, cannot realistically make this claim. The legitimate interest in preventing exposure of juveniles to obscene material cannot be fully served by simply barring juveniles from the immediate physical premises of "adult" bookstores, when there is a flourishing "outside business" in these materials.

[The] state interests in protecting children and in protecting unconsenting adults [stand] on a different footing from the other asserted state interests. [But] whatever the strength of [those] interests, [they] cannot be asserted [where, as] in this case, [the] films [were] exhibited only to persons over the age of 21 who viewed them willingly and with prior knowledge of the nature of their contents. [The] justification for the suppression must be found, therefore, in some independent interest in regulating the reading and viewing habits of consenting adults. . . .

In *Stanley* we pointed out that "[t]here appears to be little empirical basis for" the assertion that "exposure to obscene materials may lead to deviant sexual behavior or crimes of sexual violence."[26] [In] any event, we added that "if the State [is] concerned about [sexual] materials inducing antisocial conduct, [we] should adhere to the view that '[a]mong free men, the deterrents ordinarily to be applied to prevent crime are education and punishment for violations of the law. . . . '"

Moreover, in *Stanley* we rejected as "wholly inconsistent with the philosophy of the First Amendment" [the] notion that there is a legitimate state concern in the "control [of] the moral content of a person's thoughts." [That] is not to say, of course, that a State must remain utterly indifferent to — and take no action bearing on — the morality of the community. The traditional description of state police power does embrace the regulation of morals as well as the health, safety, and general welfare of the citizenry. [But] the State's interest in regulating morality by suppressing obscenity, while often asserted, remains essentially unfocused and ill defined. And, since the attempt to curtail unprotected speech necessarily spills over into the area of protected speech, the effort to serve this speculative interest through the suppression of obscene material must tread heavily on rights protected by the First Amendment. [I] would hold, therefore, that at least in the absence of distribution to juveniles or obtrusive exposure to unconsenting adults, the First and Fourteenth Amendments prohibit the State and Federal Governments from attempting [to] suppress sexually oriented materials on the basis of their allegedly "obscene" contents. . . .

[A dissenting opinion by Justice Douglas is omitted.]

### Note: The 1973 Reformulation and Its Aftermath

1. Miller *and* Roth. Does the *Miller* reformulation constitute a "rejection of the fundamental first amendment premises" of *Roth*? Does its elimination of the "utterly without redeeming social value" criterion fatally undermine the notion that obscenity is of only "low" first amendment value?

---

26. Indeed, since *Stanley* was decided, [the] President's Commission on Obscenity and Pornography has concluded: "In sum, empirical research designed to clarify the question has found no evidence to date that exposure to explicit sexual materials plays a significant role in the causation of delinquent or criminal behavior among youth or adults. The Commission cannot conclude that exposure to erotic materials is a factor in the causation of sex crime or sex delinquency. . . ."

2. Miller *and vagueness.* Is the *Miller* reformulation likely significantly to reduce the problems generated by the prior vagueness of the definition of obscenity? Are there any limits on the sorts of "sexual conduct" that might constitutionally be deemed "patently offensive"? In Jenkins v. Georgia, 418 U.S. 153 (1974), the Court, in an opinion by Justice Rehnquist, overturned a state court determination that the highly acclaimed movie Carnal Knowledge was obscene. The Court explained that *Miller* "intended to fix substantive constitutional limitations, deriving from the First Amendment, on the type of material subject to [a determination of patent offensiveness]." As an example, the Court observed that "it would be wholly at odds with this aspect of *Miller* to uphold an obscenity conviction based upon a defendant's depiction of a woman with a bare midriff." As for Carnal Knowledge, the Court noted that "our own viewing of the film satisfies us that [it] could not be found under the *Miller* standards to depict sexual conduct in a patently offensive way." The Court explained that, "while the subject of the picture is, in a broader sense, sex, and there are scenes in which sexual conduct including 'ultimate sexual acts' is to be understood to be taking place, the camera does not focus on the bodies of the actors at such times. There is no exhibition of the actor's genitals, lewd or otherwise, during these scenes. There are occasional scenes of nudity, but nudity alone is not enough to make material legally obscene under the *Miller* standards." Thus, "the film could not, as a matter of constitutional law, be found to depict sexual conduct in a patently offensive way, [and] is therefore not outside the protection of the First and Fourteenth Amendments because it is obscene."

3. *Local versus national standards.* What interests are furthered by the Court's conclusion in *Miller* that "appeal to prurient interest" and "patent offensiveness" may be determined according to local rather than national standards? Consider the following objections to local standards:

a. Smith v. United States, 431 U.S. 291, 313–315 (1977) (Stevens, J., dissenting):

> The geographic boundaries of [a local] community are not easily defined. They are [thus] subject to elastic adjustment to suit the needs of the prosecutor. Moreover, although a substantial body of evidence and decisional law concerning the content of a national standard could have evolved through its consistent use, the derivation of the relevant community standard for each of our countless communities is necessarily dependent on the perceptions of the individuals who happen to compose the jury in a given case.

b. Hamling v. United States, 418 U.S. 87, 144–145 (1974) (Brennan, J., dissenting):

> Under [a local standards approach national] distributors [will] be forced to cope with the community standards of every hamlet into which their goods may wander. [Because] these variegated standards are impossible to discern, national

distributors, fearful of risking the expense and difficulty of defending against prosecution in any of several remote communities, must inevitably [retreat] to debilitating self-censorship. [As a result], the people of many communities will be "protected" far beyond government's constitutional power to deny them access to sexually oriented materials.

4. *Local standards: post-*Miller *decisions.* The Court has handed down several post-*Miller* rulings concerning local standards. See *Jenkins*, supra (in a state obscenity prosecution, jurors need not "apply the standards of a hypothetical statewide community," but may "rely on their understanding of community from which they come"); Hamling v. United States, 418 U.S. 87 (1974) (in a federal obscenity prosecution, jurors need not rely on national standards, but may rely on their "knowledge of the community or vicinage" from which they come); *Paris Adult Theatre*, supra (the first amendment does not "require 'expert' affirmative evidence that the materials [are] obscene when the materials themselves [are] actually placed in evidence"); Pope v. Illinois, 481 U.S. 497 (1987) (a trial court may not use community standards to decide whether a work lacks serious literary, artistic, political, or scientific value, for "the value of a work does not vary from community to community").

5. *Community standards on the Internet.* In Ashcroft v. American Civil Liberties Union, 535 U.S. 564 (2002), the Court held that a federal statute (the Child Online Protection Act) regulating obscene material on the Internet was not invalid on its face because it applies local community standards in determining whether particular material is obscene, even though an individual posting sexually explicit material on the Internet has no control over the geographic areas in which the material is accessible. The majority left open the question, however, whether the statute might be unconstitutional as applied in particular circumstances. As Justice O'Connor observed, "given Internet speakers' inability to control the geographic location of their audience, expecting them to bear the burden of controlling the recipients of their speech [may] be entirely too much to ask, and would potentially suppress an inordinate amount of expression." Justice Stevens would have held the law invalid on its face.

6. *Intent.* What state of mind must the seller or distributor have in an obscenity prosecution? As the incitement and libel cases make clear, intent can play a central role in "definitional" balancing and can do much to reduce problems caused by the vagueness of the underlying concepts.

In Smith v. California, 361 U.S. 147 (1959), appellant was convicted of violating a city ordinance construed by the state courts as imposing strict liability on the proprietor of any bookstore who possessed in his store any book later judicially determined to be obscene — even if the proprietor had no personal knowledge of the contents of the book. The Court held the imposition of strict liability invalid. This feature of the ordinance, the Court noted, "tends to impose a severe limitation on the public's access to constitutionally protected matter. For if the bookseller is criminally liable without knowledge of the contents [he] will tend to restrict the books he sells to those he has inspected." Such a state of affairs would generate a "self-censorship [affecting] the whole public."

In Hamling v. United States, supra, however, the Court approved a jury instruction to the effect that, in order to satisfy its burden on intent, the prosecution need only prove that the defendants "had knowledge of the character of the materials." The Court explained that the prosecution did not need to prove that the defendants knew that the materials were obscene because to "require proof of a defendant's knowledge of the legal status of the materials would permit the defendant to avoid prosecution by simply claiming that he had not brushed up on the law." Is this reconcilable with the Court's analysis of intent in the libel context? Consider Lockhart, Escape from the Chill of Uncertainty: Explicit Sex and the First Amendment, 9 Ga. L. Rev. 533, 563 (1975): "My suggestion is that [the first amendment establishes] as a defense to a criminal obscenity prosecution that the defendant *reasonably believed* that the material involved was not obscene."

7. *The regulation of obscenity.* The procedural issues involved in the regulation of obscenity have proved especially difficult. See, e.g., Times Film Corp. v. Chicago, 365 U.S. 43 (1961) (licensing); Bantam Books v. Sullivan, 372 U.S. 58 (1963) (blacklisting); *Paris Adult Theatre*, supra (injunction); Heller v. New York, 413 U.S. 483 (1973) (search and seizure); Alexander v. United States, 509 U.S. 544 (1993) (forfeiture).

8. *Internet filters for public libraries.* Can a public library use filters on its Internet terminals designed to preclude patrons from accessing obscene Web sites? Suppose the filter is imprecise and inevitably will block access to non-obscene as well as obscene Web sites? See United States v. American Library Association, 539 U.S. 194 (2003).

9. *The end of obscenity?* Consider the following proposition: In the forty years since the Court's 1973 decisions, a combination of technological innovation and changing social mores has rendered the obscenity doctrine irrelevant. The advent of video rentals, DVDs, cable television, and the Internet has completely overwhelmed the capacity of law enforcement to keep up with the flood of sexually oriented material. As more and more individuals have been exposed to more and more of that material, "contemporary community standards" about what is "patently offensive" have evolved (some might say deteriorated) to the point where today virtually nothing is obscene. Rather than focus their limited resources on ferreting out the few extreme images that a jury today might still find obscene, most prosecutors have moved on to more important matters and left obscenity in the dust. Thus, although there are still calls from moral crusaders for government to initiate obscenity prosecutions, such prosecutions now seem more symbolic than real — except, of course, for those few defendants who are unlucky enough to be targeted. Does this seem an accurate statement of reality? If so, is it a good or a bad thing?

10. *Obscenity and substantive due process.* Even if obscenity is not protected by the first amendment, is it protected from prohibition by the doctrine of substantive due process, as articulated in such decisions like Lawrence v. Texas, 539 U.S. 558 (2003) (invalidating state criminal prohibition against sodomy on substantive due process grounds). See Kinsley, Sexual Privacy in the Internet Age: How Substantive Due Process Protects Online Obscenity, 16 Vand. J. Ent. & Tech. L. 103 (2013); Reliable Consultants, Inc. v. Earle, 517 F.3d 738 (5th Cir. 2008) (invalidating on substantive due process grounds a Texas law prohibiting any person to sell, advertise, give away or lend any device "designed or marketed for sexual stimulation").

## F.  CHILD PORNOGRAPHY, ANIMAL CRUELTY, AND VIOLENT EXPRESSION

The Court's conclusion that obscenity can constitutionally be regulated inevitably invited analogies. To what extent does the obscenity doctrine open the door to other forms of speech restriction?

**NEW YORK v. FERBER, 458 U.S. 747 (1982).** Ferber, the proprietor of a Manhattan bookstore specializing in sexually oriented products, was prosecuted for selling two films to an undercover police officer. The films were devoted almost entirely to depicting young boys masturbating. A jury held that the films were not obscene, but convicted Ferber of violating a New York statute prohibiting any person knowingly to produce, promote, direct, exhibit, or sell any material depicting a "sexual performance" by a child under the age of sixteen. The statute defined "sexual performance" as any performance that includes "actual or simulated sexual intercourse, deviate sexual intercourse, sexual bestiality, masturbation, sado-masochistic abuse, or lewd exhibition of the genitals." The Court unanimously upheld the conviction. Justice White delivered the opinion:

"In [the *Chaplinsky* dictum], the Court laid the foundation for the excision of obscenity from the realm of constitutionally protected expression. [For the following reasons, we are persuaded that pornographic depiction of children, like obscenity, is unprotected by the first amendment.]

"First. It is evident beyond the need for elaboration that a state's interest in 'safeguarding the physical and psychological well being of a minor' is 'compelling.' [The] use of children as subjects of pornographic materials is harmful to the physiological, emotional, and mental health of the child.

"Second. The distribution of photographs and films depicting sexual activity by juveniles is intrinsically related to the sexual abuse of children in at least two ways. First, the materials produced are a permanent record of the children's participation and the harm to the child is exacerbated by their circulation.

Second, the distribution network for child pornography must be closed if the production of material which requires the sexual exploitation of children is to be effectively controlled. . . .

"Third. The advertising and selling of child pornography provides an economic motive for and is thus an integral part of the production of such materials, an activity illegal throughout the nation. [Were] the statutes outlawing the employment of children in these films and photographs fully effective, and the constitutionality of these laws have not been questioned, the First Amendment implications would be no greater than that presented by laws against distribution: enforceable production laws would leave no child pornography to be marketed.

"Fourth. The value of permitting live performances and photographic reproductions of children engaged in lewd sexual conduct is exceedingly modest, if not de minimis. We consider it unlikely that visual depictions of children performing sexual acts or lewdly exhibiting their genitals would often constitute an important and necessary part of a literary performance or scientific or educational work. [If] it were necessary for literary or artistic value, a person over the statutory age who perhaps looked younger could be utilized. Simulation outside of the prohibition of the statute could provide another alternative. Nor is there any question here of censoring a particular literary theme or portrayal of sexual activity. The First Amendment interest is limited to that of rendering the portrayal somewhat more 'realistic' by utilizing or photographing children.

"Fifth. Recognizing and classifying child pornography as a category of material outside the protection of the First Amendment is not incompatible with our earlier decisions. [It] is not rare that a content-based classification of speech has been accepted because it may be appropriately generalized that within the confines of the given classification, the evil to be restricted so overwhelmingly outweighs the expressive interests, if any, at stake, that no process of case-by-case adjudication is required. . . .

"There are, of course, limits on the category of child pornography which, like obscenity, is unprotected by the First Amendment. As with all legislation in this sensitive area, the conduct to be prohibited must be adequately defined by the applicable state law, as written or authoritatively construed. [The] test for child pornography is separate from the obscenity standard enunciated in *Miller*, but may be compared to it for purpose of clarity. The *Miller* formulation is adjusted in the following respects: A trier of fact need not find that the material appeals to the prurient interest of the average person; it is not required that sexual conduct portrayed be done so in a patently offensive manner; and the material at issue need not be considered as a whole. . . .

"It remains to address the claim that the New York statute is unconstitutionally overbroad because it would forbid the distribution of material with serious literary, scientific, or educational value or material which does not threaten the harms sought to be combated by the State. [The New York

Court of Appeals, which invalidated the statute,] was understandably concerned that some protected expression, ranging from medical textbooks to pictorials in National Geographic would fall prey to the statute. [Yet] we seriously doubt, and it has not been suggested, that these arguably impermissible applications of the statute amount to more than a tiny fraction of the materials within the statute's reach. [Under] these circumstances, [the statute] is 'not substantially overbroad and whatever overbreadth exists should be cured through case-by-case analysis of the fact situations to which its sanctions, assertedly, may not be applied.' [Broadrick v. Oklahoma, Chapter III.A, supra]. As applied to [Ferber] and to others who distribute similar material, the statute does not violate the First Amendment."

Should the Court have analyzed the New York statute not as a content-based restriction of "unprotected" speech but as a content-neutral restriction on the "means" of expression? Child abuse is unlawful. Consider the following propositions: (1) There is no first amendment right to violate an otherwise valid criminal law that is unrelated to the suppression of free expression merely because the violation would render one's speech more effective. Can one, for example, steal a camera in order to make a movie? Could the government have punished Daniel Ellsberg for "stealing" the Pentagon Papers? (2) There is no first amendment right to depict the commission of a criminal act where the criminal act was committed solely in order to produce the depiction. In other words, if X stabs Y in order to film a real stabbing, X can be punished for the assault. But can the film be banned? If so, is that true of the Pentagon Papers as well?

Consider Bartnicki v. Vopper, 532 U.S. 514 (2001), in which the Court held that federal and state antiwiretap statutes cannot constitutionally be applied to a radio station that broadcasts the tape of an unlawfully intercepted telephone call, where the subject of the call was a matter of public concern and the broadcaster did not participate directly in the unlawful wiretap, even though the broadcaster knew that the material had been obtained unlawfully. The Court expressly distinguished *Ferber* on the ground that *Ferber* involved speech "considered of minimal value." Suppose a documentary filmmaker secretly films the actual sexual abuse of a child in a foster home. Can the government make it unlawful for the filmmaker to show the documentary? Can it require the filmmaker to block out the face and identity of the child?

Suppose a film depicts *simulated* sex between an adult and a child but was made entirely with adult actors or by computer imaging. Can the exhibition of the film be prohibited after *Ferber* on the ground that it will encourage pederasty? What about an animated film?

**ASHCROFT v. THE FREE SPEECH COALITION, 535 U.S. 234 (2002).** The Court invalidated the Child Pornography Prevention Act of 1996 (CPPA), which extended the prohibition against child pornography to sexually explicit images that *appear* to depict minors, but were in fact produced without using real children — either by computer imaging or by using adults who look like children. Justice Kennedy delivered the opinion of the Court:

"By prohibiting child pornography that does not depict an actual child, the statute goes beyond *Ferber*, which distinguished child pornography from other sexually explicit speech because of the State's interest in protecting the children exploited by the production process. [Although the statute] captures a range of depictions [that] do not [harm] any children in the production process, [Congress] decided the materials threaten children in other, less direct, ways. Pedophiles might use the materials to encourage children to participate in sexual activity [or they] might 'whet their own sexual appetites' with the pornographic images, 'thereby increasing the creation and distribution of child pornography and the sexual abuse and exploitation of actual children.' Under these rationales, harm flows from the content of the images, not from the means of their production. In addition, Congress [was concerned that the existence of] computer-generated images [can] can make it harder to prosecute pornographers who [use] real minors. As imaging technology improves, Congress found, it becomes more difficult to prove that a particular picture was produced using actual children. To ensure that defendants possessing child pornography using real minors cannot evade prosecution, Congress extended the ban to virtual child pornography. . . .

"The sexual abuse of a child is a most serious crime and an act repugnant to the moral instincts of a decent people. [Congress] may pass valid laws to protect children from abuse, and it has. The prospect of crime, however, by itself does not justify laws suppressing protected speech. See *Kingsley Pictures*. ('Among free men, the deterrents ordinarily to be applied to prevent crime are education and punishment for violations of the law, not abridgment of the rights of free speech'). . . .

"As a general principle, the First Amendment bars the government from dictating what we see or read or speak or hear. The freedom of speech has its limits; it does not embrace certain categories of speech, including defamation, incitement, obscenity, and pornography produced with real children. While these categories may be prohibited without violating the First Amendment, none of them includes the speech prohibited by the CPPA. . . .

"[T]he CPPA [does not deal with] obscenity. Under *Miller*, the Government must prove that the work, taken as a whole, appeals to the prurient interest, is patently offensive in light of community standards, and lacks serious literary, artistic, political, or scientific value. The CPPA, however, [applies] without regard to the *Miller* requirements. . . .

"The Government seeks to address this deficiency by arguing that speech prohibited by the CPPA is virtually indistinguishable from child pornography, which may be banned without regard to whether it depicts works of value. See *Ferber*. Where the images are themselves the product of child sexual abuse, *Ferber* recognized that the State had an interest in stamping it out without regard to any judgment about its content. The production of the work, not its content, was the target of the statute. The fact that a work contained serious literary, artistic, or other value did not excuse the harm it caused to its child participants. [*Ferber*] upheld a prohibition on the distribution and sale of child pornography, as well as its production, because these acts were 'intrinsically related' to the sexual abuse of children in two ways. First, as a permanent record of a child's abuse, the continued circulation itself would harm the child who had participated. Like a defamatory statement, each new publication of the speech would cause new injury to the child's reputation and emotional well-being. Second, because the traffic in child pornography was an economic motive for its production, the State had an interest in closing the distribution network. [Under] either rationale, the speech had what the Court in effect held was a proximate link to the crime from which it came. . . .

"In contrast to the speech in *Ferber*, [the] CPPA prohibits speech that records no crime and creates no victims by its production. Virtual child pornography is not 'intrinsically related' to the sexual abuse of children, as were the materials in *Ferber*. While the Government asserts that the images can lead to actual instances of child abuse, the causal link is contingent and indirect. The harm does not necessarily follow from the speech, but depends upon some unquantified potential for subsequent criminal acts.

"The Government says these indirect harms are sufficient because, as *Ferber* acknowledged, child pornography rarely can be valuable speech. This argument, however, suffers from two flaws. First, *Ferber*'s judgment about child pornography was based upon how it was made, not on what it communicated. [Second,] *Ferber* did not hold that child pornography is by definition without value. On the contrary, the Court recognized some works in this category might have significant value, but relied on virtual images — the very images prohibited by the CPPA — as an alternative and permissible means of expression. *Ferber*, then, not only referred to the distinction between actual and virtual child pornography, it relied on it as a reason supporting its holding. *Ferber* provides no support for a statute that eliminates the distinction and makes the alternative mode criminal as well.

"The CPPA [is thus] inconsistent with *Miller* and finds no support in *Ferber*. The Government seeks to justify its prohibitions in other ways. It argues that the CPPA is necessary because pedophiles may use virtual child pornography to seduce children. There are many things innocent in themselves, however, such as cartoons, video games, and candy, that might be used for immoral purposes, yet we would not expect those to be prohibited because they can be misused. The Government, of course, may punish adults who provide unsuitable materials to children, see *Ginsberg*, and it may enforce criminal penalties for unlawful solicitation. The precedents establish, however, that speech within the rights of adults to hear may not be silenced completely in an attempt to shield children from it. [Here, the] evil in question depends upon the actor's unlawful conduct, conduct defined as criminal quite apart from any link to the speech in question. This establishes that the speech ban is not narrowly drawn.

The objective is to prohibit illegal conduct, but this restriction goes well beyond that interest by restricting the speech available to law-abiding adults.

"The Government submits further that virtual child pornography whets the appetites of pedophiles and encourages them to engage in illegal conduct. This rationale cannot sustain the provision in question. The mere tendency of speech to encourage unlawful acts is not a sufficient reason for banning it. [The] Court's First Amendment cases draw vital distinctions between words and deeds, between ideas and conduct. The government may not prohibit speech because it increases the chance an unlawful act will be committed 'at some indefinite future time.' [The] Government has shown no more than a remote connection between speech that might encourage thoughts or impulses and any resulting child abuse. Without a significantly stronger, more direct connection, the Government may not prohibit speech on the ground that it may encourage pedophiles to engage in illegal conduct. . . .

"Finally, the Government says that the possibility of producing images by using computer imaging makes it very difficult for it to prosecute those who produce pornography by using real children. Experts, we are told, may have difficulty in saying whether the pictures were made by using real children or by using computer imaging. The necessary solution, the argument runs, is to prohibit both kinds of images. The argument, in essence, is that protected speech may be banned as a means to ban unprotected speech. This analysis turns the First Amendment upside down. The Government may not suppress lawful speech as the means to suppress unlawful speech. Protected speech does not become unprotected merely because it resembles the latter."

Justice Thomas filed a concurring opinion in which he observed that "if technological advances" eventually reach a point where they actually (as opposed to speculatively) "thwart prosecution of 'unlawful speech,' the Government may well have a compelling interest [in] regulating some narrow category of 'lawful speech' in order to enforce effectively laws against pornography made through the abuse of real children."

Justice O'Connor, joined in part by Chief Justice Rehnquist and Justice Scalia, dissented in part. Justice O'Connor concluded that the CPPA was unconstitutional insofar as it restricts material created by using youthful-looking adults, but that it was constitutional insofar as it restricts virtual-child pornography. With respect to the latter, Justice O'Connor argued that if the CPPA is narrowly construed to limit only computer-generated images that are "virtually indistinguishable" from real child pornography, it would satisfy "strict scrutiny" because it would then be narrowly tailored to serve the compelling governmental interest in eliminating real child pornography. She also noted that if any work falling within this category in fact has serious social, political, literary or scientific value, the possible "overbreadth" of the law in that regard could be considered in an "as applied" challenge. On the other hand, Justice O'Connor concurred with the Court in invalidating the law insofar as it restricts material created with youthful-looking adults because such material would not pose the same problem to the enforcement of the prohibition on actual child pornography as material created using computer images.

### Note: Child Pornography

1. *Morphing.* Another provision of the CPPA, not at issue in this case, prohibits the use of computer morphing to alter the images of real children so they appear to be engaged in sexual activity. Is this different from the issues addressed in *Ashcroft*? The Court noted in passing that because such morphed images "implicate the interests of real children" they are closer to the issue considered in *Ferber*. Might this better be analyzed as a form of libel?

2. *Permissible limits on movies that appear to involve child porngraphy.* Suppose that you were a member of Congress concerned about the effects of *Ashcroft*. Is it possible to write a statute satisfying at least some of your concerns without running afoul of the decision? See United States v. Williams, 553 U.S. 285 (2008) (upholding the Prosecutorial Remedies and Other Tools to End the Exploitation of Children Today Act (the PROTECT Act), which made it a crime for any person "knowingly" to "advertise, promote, present, distribute, or solicit through the mails, or in interstate or foreign commerce [any] material or purported material in a manner that reflects the belief, or that is intended to cause another to believe, that the material or purported material is, or contains, [a] visual depiction of an actual minor engaging in sexually explicit conduct.") Would a statute that prohibited images that appeared to depict minors but that allowed to the defendant an affirmative defense if the defendant could prove that the image had been created without the abuse of a real child satisfy the first amendment?

3. *Child pornography in the home.* In Osborne v. Ohio, 495 U.S. 103 (1990), the Court held that Stanley v. Georgia does not extend to the private possession of child pornography. The Court, in an opinion by Justice White, explained: "[The] interests underlying child pornography prohibitions far exceed the interests justifying [the] law at issue in *Stanley*. [In] *Stanley*, Georgia primarily sought to proscribe the private possession of obscenity because it was concerned that obscenity will poison the mind of its viewers. [The] difference here is obvious: the State does not rely on a paternalistic interest in regulating [the defendant's] mind. Rather, [the law is designed] to protect the victims of child pornography; it hopes to destroy a national market for the exploitative use of children." Justices Brennan, Marshall, and Stevens dissented.

**UNITED STATES v. STEVENS, 559 U.S. 460 (2010).** 18 U.S.C. §48 establishes a criminal penalty of up to five years in prison for anyone who knowingly "creates, sells, or possesses a depiction of animal cruelty" for "commercial gain" in interstate or foreign commerce. A depiction of "animal cruelty" is defined as one "in which a living animal is intentionally maimed, mutilated, tortured, wounded, or killed," if that conduct violates federal or state law where "the creation, sale, or possession takes place." The law exempts from the prohibition any depiction "that has serious religious, political, scientific, educational, journalistic, historical, or artistic value."

The legislative background of section 48 focused primarily on the interstate market for "crush videos," which depict women crushing small animals like mice and hamsters to death with their bare feet or while wearing high-heeled shoes, sometimes while talking to the animals in a kind of dominatrix patter. Apparently these depictions appeal to persons with a very specific sexual fetish. The acts depicted in crush videos are typically prohibited by the animal cruelty laws enacted by all fifty states and the District of Columbia, but because crush videos rarely disclose the participants' identities, prosecution of the underlying conduct is often impossible.

This case involved an application of section 48 not to crush videos, but to depictions of dogfighting. Dogfighting is unlawful in all fifty states and the District of Columbia, and has been restricted by federal law since 1976. Robert Stevens ran a business, "Dogs of Velvet and Steel," and an associated Web site, through which he sold videos of pit bulls engaging in dogfights and attacking other animals. His videos included contemporary footage of dogfights in Japan (where such conduct is legal) as well as footage of American dogfights from the 1960s and 1970s. On the basis of these videos, Stevens was convicted of violating section 48. The court of appeals declared section 48 facially unconstitutional and vacated Stevens's conviction.

In an eight-to-one decision, the Supreme Court affirmed. Chief Justice Roberts delivered the opinion of the Court:

"The Government's primary submission is that §48 necessarily complies with the Constitution because the banned depictions of animal cruelty, as a class, are categorically unprotected by the First Amendment. We disagree. . . .

"From 1791 to the present, [the] First Amendment has 'permitted restrictions upon the content of speech in a few limited areas,' [including, for example, obscenity, defamation, threats, and incitement]. [Citing *Chaplinsky*.] The Government argues that 'depictions of animal cruelty' should be added to the list. It contends that depictions of 'illegal acts of animal cruelty' that are 'made, sold, or possessed for commercial gain' necessarily 'lack expressive value,' and may accordingly 'be regulated as *unprotected* speech.' [The] prohibition of animal cruelty [has] a long history in American law, [but] we are unaware of any similar tradition excluding *depictions* of animal cruelty from 'the freedom of speech' codified in the First Amendment. . . .

"The Government contends that 'historical evidence' about the reach of the First Amendment is not 'a necessary prerequisite for regulation today,' and that categories of speech may be exempted from the First Amendment's protection without any long-settled tradition of subjecting that speech to regulation. Instead, the Government points to Congress's 'legislative judgment that ... depictions of animals being intentionally tortured and killed [are] of such minimal redeeming value as to render [them] unworthy of First Amendment protection,' and asks the Court to uphold the ban on the same basis. The Government thus proposes that a claim of categorical exclusion should be considered under a simple balancing test: 'Whether a given category of speech enjoys First Amendment protection depends upon a categorical balancing of the value of the speech against its societal costs.' [Quoting Brief for United States].

"As a free-floating test for First Amendment coverage, that sentence is startling and dangerous. The First Amendment's guarantee of free speech does not extend only to categories of speech that survive an ad hoc balancing of relative social costs and benefits. The First Amendment itself reflects a judgment by the American people that the benefits of its restrictions on the Government outweigh the costs. Our Constitution forecloses any attempt to revise that judgment simply on the basis that some speech is not worth it. ...

"When we have identified categories of speech as fully outside the protection of the First Amendment, it has not been on the basis of a simple cost-benefit analysis. [Our decisions] cannot be taken as establishing a freewheeling authority to declare new categories of speech outside the scope of the First Amendment. Maybe there are some categories of speech that have been historically unprotected, but have not yet been specifically identified or discussed as such in our case law. But if so, there is no evidence that 'depictions of animal cruelty' is among them. We need not foreclose the future recognition of such additional categories to reject the Government's highly manipulable balancing test as a means of identifying them. ...

"We read §48 to create a criminal prohibition of alarming breadth. [The] only thing standing between defendants who sell such depictions and five years in federal prison — other than the mercy of a prosecutor — is the statute's exceptions clause. Subsection (b) exempts from prohibition 'any depiction that has serious religious, political, scientific, educational, journalistic, historical, or artistic value.' The Government argues that this clause substantially narrows the statute's reach: News reports about animal cruelty have 'journalistic' value; pictures of bullfights in Spain have 'historical' value; and instructional hunting videos have 'educational' value. [But much valuable speech under the First Amendment does not] fall within one of the enumerated categories. [Most] hunting videos, for example, are not obviously instructional in nature, [but] 'have primarily entertainment value.' [The] Government offers no principled explanation why these depictions of hunting or depictions of Spanish bullfights would be *inherently* valuable while those of Japanese dogfights are not. ...

"The Government explains that the language of §48(b) was largely drawn from our opinion in Miller v. California, which excepted from its definition of obscenity any material with 'serious literary, artistic, political, or scientific value.' According to the Government, this incorporation of the *Miller* standard into §48 is therefore surely enough to answer any First Amendment objection. In *Miller* we held that 'serious' value shields depictions of sex from regulation as obscenity. We did not, however, determine that serious value could be used as a general precondition to protecting *other* types of speech in the first place. *Most* of what we say to one another lacks 'religious, political, scientific, educational, journalistic, historical, or artistic value' (let alone serious value), but it is still sheltered from government regulation. [Thus,] the protection of the First Amendment presumptively extends to many forms of speech that do not qualify for the serious-value exception of §48(b), but nonetheless fall within the broad reach of §48(c)."

Why are depictions of animal cruelty different from depictions of child sexual abuse? Consider Chief Justice Roberts's explanation: "In *Ferber*, [we] classified child pornography as [unprotected speech]. We noted that the State [had] a compelling interest in protecting children from abuse, and that the value of using children in these works (as opposed to simulated conduct or adult actors) was *de minimis*. But our decision did not rest on this 'balance of the competing interests' alone. We made clear that *Ferber* presented a special case: The market for child pornography was 'intrinsically related' to the underlying abuse, and was 'an integral part of the production of such materials, an activity illegal throughout the Nation.' As we noted, '[i]t rarely has been suggested that the constitutional freedom for speech and press extends its immunity to speech or writing used as an integral part of conduct in violation of a valid criminal statute.' *Ferber* thus grounded its analysis in a previously recognized, long-established category of unprotected speech." Is this persuasive?

The Court held in *Ferber* and *Ashcroft* that the government can constitutionally prohibit the sale or exhibition of child pornography only because the government has a "compelling" interest in "safeguarding the physical and psychological well-being of a minor." The Court explained that the prohibition of child pornography serves this "compelling" interest in two ways: (1) by drying up the market for such materials and thereby eliminating the incentive to create them; and (2) by protecting the victims from the emotional and psychological harm caused by the continued circulation of the images. Does the government have a similarly "compelling" argument in the animal cruelty context?

Consider the following arguments: (1) As evidenced by the many circumstances (including hunting and slaughtering food animals) in which we permit cruelty to animals, we clearly do not take the interest in preventing animal cruelty as seriously as we take the interest in preventing child sexual abuse, which is never permitted. (2) Unlike people, animals have no consciousness of the continuing exhibition of the depiction of their abuse and therefore suffer no comparable emotional or psychological injury.

Justice Alito was the lone dissenter: "The Court strikes down in its entirety a valuable statute [that] was enacted not to suppress speech, but to prevent horrific acts of animal cruelty — in particular, the creation and commercial exploitation of 'crush videos,' a form of depraved entertainment that has no social value. The Court's approach [is] unwarranted. [The] most relevant of our prior decisions is *Ferber*. [In] *Ferber*, an important factor — I would say the most important factor — was that child pornography involves the commission of a crime that inflicts severe personal injury to the 'children who are made to engage in sexual conduct for commercial purposes.' [As] later noted in Ashcroft v. Free Speech Coalition, in *Ferber* '[t]he production of the work, not its content, was the target of the statute.' [*Ferber* also] emphasized [that] these underlying crimes could not be effectively combated without targeting the distribution of child pornography. [And, finally,] the *Ferber* Court noted that the value of child pornography 'is exceedingly modest, if not *de minimis*,' and that any such value was 'overwhelmingly outweigh[ed]' by 'the evil to be restricted.'

"All three of these characteristics are shared by §48, as applied to crush videos. [It] must be acknowledged that §48 differs from a child pornography law in an important respect: preventing the abuse of children is certainly much more important than preventing the torture of the animals used in crush videos. But while protecting children is unquestionably *more* important than protecting animals, the Government also has a compelling interest in preventing the torture depicted in crush videos. [The] animals used in crush videos are living creatures that experience excruciating pain. [Applying] the principles set forth in *Ferber*, I would hold that crush videos are not protected by the First Amendment."

Suppose that you were a member of Congress concerned about the impact of *Stevens*. Is it possible to draft a statute that meets at least some of your concerns without running afoul of the decision? Within months of the decision in *Stevens*, Congress amended section 48. The new provision, titled "Animal Crush Videos," defines an "animal crush video" as "any photograph, motion-picture film, video or digital recording, or electronic image" that (1) "depicts actual conduct in which one or more living non-human mammals, birds, reptiles, or amphibians is intentionally crushed, burned, drowned, suffocated, impaled or otherwise subjected to serious bodily injury" and (2) "is obscene." The statute exempts any visual depiction of "customary and normal veterinary or agricultural husbandry practices," "the slaughter of animals for food," or "hunting, trapping or fishing." Is this statute constitutional? See United States v. Richards, 755 F. 3d 269 (2014) (holding that statute was facially constitutional).

**BROWN v. ENTERTAINMENT MERCHANTS ASSOCIATION, 131 S. Ct. 2729 (2011).** In *Brown*, the Court invalidated a California law imposing restrictions on violent video games. Justice Scalia delivered the opinion of the Court: "California Assembly Bill 1179 prohibits the sale or rental of 'violent video games' to [minors]. The Act covers games 'in which the range of options available to a player includes killing, maiming, dismembering, or sexually assaulting an image of a human being, if those acts are depicted' in a manner that 'a reasonable person, considering the game as a whole, would find appeals to a deviant or morbid interest of minors,' that is 'patently offensive to prevailing standards in the community as to what is suitable for minors,' and that 'causes the game, as a whole, to lack serious literary, artistic, political, or scientific value for minors.' . . .

"[V]ideo games qualify for First Amendment protection. The Free Speech Clause exists principally to protect discourse on public matters, but we have long recognized that it is difficult to distinguish politics from entertainment, and dangerous to try. [Like] the protected books, plays, and movies that preceded them, video games communicate ideas — and even social messages — through many familiar literary devices (such as characters, dialogue, plot, and music) and through features distinctive to the medium (such as the player's interaction with the virtual world). That suffices to confer First Amendment protection. [W]hatever the challenges of applying the Constitution to ever-advancing technology, 'the basic principles of freedom of speech and the press, like the First Amendment's command, do not vary' when a new and different medium for communication appears.

"The most basic of those principles is this: '[A]s a general matter, . . . government has no power to restrict expression because of its message, its ideas, its subject matter, or its content.' There are of course exceptions. "'From 1791 to the present,' . . . the First Amendment has "permitted restrictions upon the content of speech in a few limited areas]."' These limited areas — such as obscenity [*Roth*], incitement [*Brandenburg*], and fighting words [*Chaplinsky*] — represent 'well-defined and narrowly limited classes of speech, the prevention and punishment of which have never been thought to raise any Constitutional problem.' Last Term, in *Stevens*, we held that new categories of unprotected speech may not be added to the list by a legislature that concludes certain speech is too harmful to be tolerated. [There] was no American tradition of forbidding the *depiction of* animal cruelty — though States have long had laws against *committing* it. [As] in *Stevens*, California has tried to make violent-speech regulation look like obscenity regulation, [but] the obscenity exception to the First Amendment does not cover whatever a legislature finds shocking, but only depictions of 'sexual conduct.'

"[B]ecause speech about violence is not obscene, it is of no consequence that California's statute mimics the New York statute regulating obscenity for minors that we upheld in *Ginsberg*. [The] California Act [does] not adjust the boundaries of an existing category of unprotected speech to ensure that a definition designed for adults is not uncritically applied to children. California does not argue that it is empowered to prohibit selling offensively violent works *to adults*. . . . Instead, it wishes to create a wholly new category of content-based regulation that is permissible only for speech directed at children. That is unprecedented and mistaken. [No] doubt a State possesses legitimate power to protect children from harm, but that does not include a free-floating power to restrict the ideas to which children may be exposed. [California's] argument would fare better if there were a long standing tradition in this country of specially restricting children's access to depictions of violence, but there is none. Certainly the *books* we give children to read — or read to them when they are younger — contain no shortage of gore. [As] her just deserts for trying to poison Snow White, the wicked queen is made to dance in red hot slippers 'till she fell dead on the [floor].' Hansel and Gretel (children!) kill their captor by baking her in an oven. High-school reading lists are full of similar fare. Homer's Odysseus blinds Polyphemus the Cyclops by grinding out his eye with a heated stake. [And] Golding's Lord of the Flies recounts how a schoolboy called Piggy is savagely murdered *by other children* while marooned on an island. . . .

"California claims that video games present special problems because they are 'interactive,' [but as] Judge Posner has observed, all literature is interactive. '[T]he better it is, the more interactive. . . . ' American Amusement Machine Assn. v. Kendrick, 244 F.3d 572, 577 (CA7 2001). [Justice] Alito has done considerable independent research to identify video games in which 'the violence is astounding.' 'Victims are dismembered, decapitated, disemboweled, set on fire, and chopped into little pieces. . . . Blood gushes, splatters, and pools.' Justice Alito recounts all these disgusting video games in order to disgust us — but disgust is not a valid basis for restricting expression. . . .

"Because the Act imposes a restriction on the content of protected speech, it is invalid unless California can demonstrate that it passes strict scrutiny — that is, unless it is justified by a compelling government interest and is narrowly drawn to serve that interest. [California] cannot meet that standard. At the outset, it acknowledges that it cannot show a direct causal link between violent video games and harm to minors. [Indeed,] the State's evidence is not compelling. California relies primarily [on a few] research psychologists whose studies purport to show a connection between exposure to violent video games and harmful effects on children. These studies have been rejected by every court to consider them, and with good reason: They do not prove that violent video games *cause* minors to *act* aggressively (which would at least be a beginning). Instead, '[n]early all of the research is based on correlation, not evidence of causation, and most of the studies suffer from [significant] flaws in methodology.' [Even] taking for granted [the conclusion] that violent video games produce some effect on children's feelings of aggression, those effects are both small and indistinguishable from effects produced by other media. [It appears that] the 'effect sizes' of children's exposure to violent video games are 'about the same' as that produced by their exposure to [cartoons] starring Bugs Bunny or the Road Runner, [or] video games like Sonic the Hedgehog that are rated 'E' (appropriate for all ages), or even when they 'vie[w] a picture of a gun.'

"Of course, California has (wisely) declined to restrict Saturday morning cartoons, the sale of games rated 'E' for young children, or the distribution of pictures of guns. The consequence is that its regulation is wildly underinclusive when judged against its asserted justification, which in our view is alone enough to defeat it. Underinclusiveness raises serious doubts about whether the government is in fact pursuing the interest it invokes, rather than disfavoring a particular speaker or viewpoint. Here, California has singled out the purveyors of video games for disfavored treatment — at least when compared to booksellers, cartoonists, and movie producers — and has given no persuasive reason why.

"The Act is also seriously underinclusive in another respect. The California Legislature is perfectly willing to leave this dangerous, mind-altering material in the hands of children so long as one parent (or even an aunt or uncle) says it's OK. [That] is not how one addresses a serious social problem.

"California claims that the Act is justified in aid of parental authority: By requiring that the purchase of violent video games can be made only by adults, the Act ensures that parents can decide what games are appropriate. [But] California cannot show that the Act's restrictions meet a substantial need of parents who wish to restrict their children's access to violent video games but cannot do so. The video-game industry has in place a voluntary rating system designed to inform consumers about the content of games. [Moreover,] the Act's purported aid to parental authority is vastly overinclusive. Not all of the children who are forbidden to purchase violent video games on their own have parents who *care* whether they purchase violent video games. While some of the legislation's effect may indeed be in support of what some parents of the restricted children actually want, its entire effect is only in support of what the State thinks parents *ought* to want. This is not the narrow tailoring to 'assisting parents' that restriction of First Amendment rights requires."

Justice Alito, joined by Chief Justice Roberts, concurred in the result because "the law's definition of 'violent video game' is impermissibly vague." Justice Alito argued that it was unnecessary to go beyond that conclusion to resolve the case, but he nonetheless suggested that he disagreed "with the approach taken in the Court's opinion." He reasoned that in "considering the application of unchanging constitutional principles to new and rapidly evolving technology, [we] should not jump to the conclusion that new technology is fundamentally the same as some older thing with which we are familiar. And we should not hastily dismiss the judgment of legislators, who may be in a better position than we are to assess the implications of new technology."

Justice Thomas dissented: "The Court's decision [does] not comport with the original public understanding of the First Amendment. [The] practices and beliefs of the founding generation establish that 'the freedom of speech,' as originally understood, does not include a right to speak to minors (or a right of minors to access speech) without going through the minors' parents or guardians. [Because] the Constitution is a written instrument, 'its meaning does not alter.' 'That which it meant when adopted, it means now.' [The] founding generation would not have considered it an abridgment of 'the freedom of speech' to support parental authority by restricting speech that bypasses minors' parents."

Justice Breyer also dissented: "In my view, California's statute provides 'fair notice' of what is prohibited,' and consequently is not impermissibly vague. [I] can find no vagueness-related differences between California's law and the New York law upheld in *Ginsberg*. . . .

"Like the majority, I believe that the California law must be 'narrowly tailored' to further a 'compelling interest,' without there being a 'less restrictive' alternative that would be 'at least as effective.' [But] I would not apply this strict standard 'mechanically.' Rather, in applying it, I would evaluate the degree to which the statute injures speech-related interests, the nature of the potentially-justifying 'compelling interests,' the degree to which the statute furthers that interest, the nature and effectiveness of possible alternatives, and, in light of this evaluation, whether, overall, 'the statute works speech-related harms . . . out of proportion to the benefits that the statute seeks to provide.' First Amendment standards applied in this way are difficult but not impossible to satisfy. [Citing his dissenting opinion in Holder v. Humanitarian Law Project.] . . .

"California's law imposes no more than a modest restriction on expression. [All] it prevents is a child or adolescent from buying, without a parent's assistance, a gruesomely violent video [game]. The interest that California advances in support of the statute is compelling. As the Court has previously described that interest, it consists of both (1) the 'basic' parental claim 'to authority in their own household to direct the rearing of their children,' which makes it proper to enact 'laws designed to aid discharge of [parental] responsibility, and (2) the State's 'independent interest in the well-being of its youth.' [Quoting *Ginsberg*.] Both interests are present here. . . .

"[Moreover,] there is considerable evidence that California's statute significantly furthers this compelling interest. [There] are many scientific studies that support California's views. [Some] of these studies [explain] that the closer a child's behavior comes, not to watching, but to *acting* out horrific violence, the greater the potential psychological harm. [Of course, experts] debate the conclusions of all these studies [and] critics have produced studies [that] reach different conclusions. [I], like most judges, lack the social science expertise to say definitively who is right. [But unlike] the majority, I would find sufficient grounds in these studies [for] this Court to defer to an elected legislature's conclusion that the video games in question are particularly likely to harm children. . . .

"I add that the majority's [conclusion] creates a serious anomaly in First Amendment law. [What] sense does it make to forbid selling to a 13-year-old boy a magazine with an image of a nude woman, while protecting a sale to that 13-year-old of an interactive video game in which he actively, but virtually, binds and gags the woman, then tortures and kills her?"

Are video games "speech" within the meaning of the first amendment? Are games such as bingo, blackjack, chess, and baseball "speech"? After *Brown*, how would you analyze the constitutionality of a state law prohibiting anyone to engage in mixed martial arts?

## G.  THE LEWD, THE PROFANE, AND THE INDECENT

In what circumstances, if any, may government restrict the public use of profane or sexually oriented, but nonobscene, expression because of its offensive character? Recall that in *Chaplinsky* the Court's list of utterances ("the prevention and punishment of which have never been thought to raise any Constitutional problem") expressly included not only "fighting words," the "libelous," and the "obscene," but also the "lewd" and the "profane." Moreover, in explaining why such utterances are "unprotected," the Court in *Chaplinsky* noted not only that they might "tend to incite an immediate breach of the peace," but also that they might "by their very utterance inflict injury."

### Cohen v. California
403 U.S. 15 (1971)

MR. JUSTICE HARLAN delivered the opinion of the Court.

This case may seem at first blush too inconsequential to find its way into our books, but the issue it presents is of no small constitutional significance.

Appellant Paul Robert Cohen was convicted in the Los Angeles Municipal Court of violating that part of California Penal Code §415 which prohibits "maliciously and willfully disturb[ing] the peace or quiet of any neighborhood or person . . . by . . . offensive conduct. . . ." He was given 30 days' imprisonment. The facts upon which his conviction rests are detailed in the opinion of the [state court]:

> On April 26, 1968, the defendant was observed in the Los Angeles County Courthouse in the corridor outside [of] the municipal court wearing a jacket bearing the words "Fuck the Draft." There were women and children present in the corridor. The defendant was arrested. The defendant testified that he wore the jacket [as] a means of informing the public of the depth of his feelings against the Vietnam War and the draft.
>
> The defendant did not engage in, nor threaten to engage in, nor did anyone as the result of his conduct in fact commit or threaten to commit any act of violence. The defendant did not make any loud or unusual noise, nor was there any evidence that he uttered any sound prior to his arrest. . . .

[We reverse.]

## I

In order to lay hands on the precise issue which this case involves, it is useful first to canvass various matters which this record does *not* present.

The conviction quite clearly rests upon the asserted offensiveness of the *words* Cohen used, [for] the State certainly lacks power to punish Cohen for [the] message the inscription conveyed. [Moreover], this is not [an] obscenity case. Whatever else may be necessary to give rise to the States' broader power to prohibit obscene expression, such expression must be, in some significant way, erotic. [*Roth.*] It cannot plausibly be maintained that this vulgar allusion to the Selective Service System would conjure up such psychic stimulation in anyone likely to be confronted with Cohen's crudely defaced jacket.

This Court has [held] that the States are free to [ban] so-called "fighting words," those personally abusive epithets which, when addressed to the ordinary citizen, [are] inherently likely to provoke violent reaction. [*Chaplinsky.*] While the four-letter word displayed by Cohen in relation to the draft is not uncommonly employed in a personally provocative fashion, in this instance it was clearly not "directed to the person of the hearer." No] individual actually or likely to be present could reasonably have regarded the words on appellant's jacket as a direct personal insult. Nor do we have here an instance of the exercise of the State's police power to prevent a speaker from intentionally provoking a given group to hostile reaction. Cf. [*Feiner*]. There [is] no showing that anyone who saw Cohen was in fact violently aroused or that appellant intended such a result.

Finally, in arguments before this Court much has been made of the claim that Cohen's distasteful mode of expression was thrust upon unwilling or unsuspecting viewers, and that the State might therefore legitimately act as it did in order to protect the sensitive from otherwise unavoidable exposure to appellant's crude form of protest. Of course, the mere presumed presence of unwitting listeners or viewers does not serve automatically to justify curtailing all speech capable of giving offense. [While] this Court has recognized that government may properly act in many situations to prohibit intrusion into the privacy of the home of unwelcome views and ideas which cannot be totally banned from the public dialogue, e.g., Rowan v. Post Office Dept., 397 U.S. 728 (1970), we have at the same time consistently stressed that "we are often 'captives' outside the sanctuary of the home and subject to objectionable speech." [The] ability of government, consonant with the Constitution, to shut off discourse solely to protect others from hearing it is, in other words, dependent upon a showing that substantial privacy interests are being invaded in an essentially intolerable manner. Any broader view of this authority would effectively empower a majority to silence dissidents simply as a matter of personal predilections.

In this regard, persons confronted with Cohen's jacket were in a quite different posture than, say, those subjected to the raucous emissions of sound trucks blaring outside their residences. Those in the Los Angeles courthouse could effectively avoid further bombardment of their sensibilities simply by averting their eyes. And, while it may be that one has a more substantial claim to a recognizable privacy interest when walking through a courthouse corridor than, for example, strolling through Central Park, surely it is nothing like the interest in being free from unwanted expression in the confines of one's own home. . . .

## II

Against this background, the issue flushed by this case stands out in bold relief. It is whether California can excise, as "offensive conduct," one particular scurrilous epithet from the public discourse, either upon the theory [that] its use is inherently likely to cause violent reaction or upon a more general assertion that the States, acting as guardians of public morality, may properly remove this offensive word from the public vocabulary.

The [first rationale] is plainly untenable. At most it reflects an "undifferentiated fear or apprehension of disturbance [which] is not enough to overcome the right to freedom of expression." [We] have been shown no evidence that substantial numbers of citizens are standing ready to strike out physically at whoever may assault their sensibilities with execrations like that uttered by Cohen. There may be some persons about with such lawless and violent proclivities, but that is an insufficient base upon which to erect, consistently with constitutional values, a governmental power to force persons who wish to ventilate their dissident views into avoiding particular forms of expression. The argument amounts to little more than the self-defeating proposition that to avoid physical censorship of one who has not sought to provoke such a response by a hypothetical coterie of the violent and lawless, the States may more appropriately effectuate that censorship themselves. . . .

Admittedly, it is not so obvious that the First and Fourteenth Amendments must be taken to disable the States from punishing public utterance of this unseemly expletive in order to maintain what they regard as a suitable level of discourse within the body politic. We think, however, that examination and reflection will reveal the shortcomings of a contrary viewpoint.

At the outset, we cannot overemphasize that, in our judgment, most situations where the State has a justifiable interest in regulating speech will fall within one or more of the various established exceptions, discussed above but not applicable here, to the usual rule that governmental bodies may not prescribe the form or content of individual expression. Equally important to our conclusion is the constitutional backdrop against which our decision must be made. The constitutional right of free expression is powerful medicine in a society as diverse and populous as ours. It is designed and intended to remove governmental restraints from the arena of public discussion, putting the decision as to what views shall be voiced largely into the hands of each of us, in the hope that use of such freedom will ultimately produce a more capable citizenry and more perfect polity and in the belief that no other approach would comport with the premise of individual dignity and choice upon which our political system rests. See [*Whitney* (Brandeis, J., concurring)].

To many, the immediate consequence of this freedom may often appear to be only verbal tumult, discord, and even offensive utterance. These are, however, within established limits, in truth necessary side effects of the broader enduring values which the process of open debate permits us to achieve. That the air may at times seem filled with verbal cacophony is, in this sense not a sign of weakness but of strength. We cannot lose sight of the fact that, in what otherwise might seem a trifling and annoying instance of individual distasteful abuse of a privilege, these fundamental societal values are truly implicated. . . .

Against this perception of the constitutional policies involved, we discern certain more particularized considerations that peculiarly call for reversal of this conviction. First, the principle contended for by the State seems inherently boundless. How is one to distinguish this from any other offensive word? Surely the State has no right to cleanse public debate to the point where it is grammatically palatable to the most squeamish among us. Yet no readily ascertainable general principle exists for stopping short of that result were we to affirm the judgment below. For, while the particular four-letter word being litigated here is perhaps more distasteful than most others of its genre, it is nevertheless often true that one man's vulgarity is another's lyric. Indeed, we think it is largely because governmental officials cannot make principled distinctions in this area that the Constitution leaves matters of taste and style so largely to the individual.

Additionally, we cannot overlook the fact, because it is well illustrated by the episode involved here, that much linguistic expression serves a dual communicative function: it conveys not only ideas capable of relatively precise, detached explication, but otherwise inexpressible emotions as well. In fact, words are often chosen as much for their emotive as their cognitive force. We cannot sanction the view that the Constitution, while solicitous of the cognitive content of individual speech, has little or no regard for that emotive function which, practically speaking, may often be the more important element of the overall message sought to be communicated. . . .

Finally, and in the same vein, we cannot indulge the facile assumption that one can forbid particular words without also running a substantial risk of suppressing ideas in the process. Indeed, governments might soon seize upon the censorship of particular words as a convenient guise for banning the expression of unpopular views. We have been able, as noted above, to discern little social benefit that might result from running the risk of opening the door to such grave results.

It is, in sum, our judgment that, absent a more particularized and compelling reason for its actions, the State may not, consistently with the First and Fourteenth Amendments, make the simple public display here involved of this single four-letter expletive a criminal offense. . . .

Reversed.

MR. JUSTICE BLACKMUN, with whom THE CHIEF JUSTICE and MR. JUSTICE BLACK join.

I dissent. . . .

Cohen's absurd and immature antic, in my view, was mainly conduct and little speech. [Further,] the case appears to me to be well within the sphere of [*Chaplinsky*], where Mr. Justice Murphy, a known champion of First Amendment freedoms, wrote for a unanimous bench. As a consequence, this Court's agonizing over First Amendment values seems misplaced and unnecessary.

[Justice White dissented on other grounds.]

### Note: Profanity, *Cohen, and the Captive Audience*

1. *Profanity as "low" value speech.* Does *Cohen* repudiate *Chaplinsky*'s assumption that profanity is of only "low" first amendment value? If obscenity has "no redeeming social value," why isn't the same true of profanity? Consider the following proposition: Profanity has "high" first amendment value because (a) its use may be necessary to convey "otherwise inexpressible emotions," (b) its suppression creates "a substantial risk of suppressing ideas in the process," and (c) there exists "no readily ascertainable general principle" for distinguishing between prohibitable and nonprohibitable offensive language.

Consider W. Berns, The First Amendment and the Future of American Democracy 200 (1976):

> This country managed to live most of its years under rules, conventional and legal, that forbade the public use of profanity [and] it would be an abuse of language to say that its freedom was thereby restricted in any important respect. Now, suddenly, and for reasons that ought to persuade no one, we are told that it is a violation of the First Amendment for the law to enforce these rules; that however desirable it might be to see them preserved, there is no way for the law to do this except by threatening the freedom of all speech. [Do] we really live in a world so incapable of communication that it can be said that "one man's vulgarity is another's lyric"?

2. *Profanity and fighting words.* As evident in *Chaplinsky*, the problems of fighting words and profanity are closely related. In *Cohen*, however, the Court "made clear that [the phrase 'fighting words'] was no longer to be understood as

a euphemism for controversial or dirty talk but was to require instead a quite unambiguous invitation to a brawl." J. Ely, Democracy and Distrust 114 (1980). The Court thus recognized in *Cohen* that the fighting words and profanity problems are analytically distinct — although fighting words typically involve the use of profanity, this is not essential; although fighting words usually involve insults directed personally to the addressee, the problem of profanity is not so limited; and although the fighting words doctrine is designed primarily to forestall an addressee's violent response, government efforts to suppress offensive language are designed primarily to raise the level of public discourse and to protect the sensibilities of an unconsenting audience. The fighting words doctrine is examined in Chapter II.B, supra.

3. *Profanity: manner or content?* Is a law restricting the use of profanity in public more akin to a law restricting the public expression of an "offensive" idea or to a law restricting the use of an "offensive" means of expression? Compare, for example, a law prohibiting the expression of "offensive ideas" in a public park, a law prohibiting the use of profanity in a public park, and a law prohibiting the use of loudspeakers in a public park. Is the prohibition on profanity more akin to the prohibition on loudspeakers because both are directed against "consequences unrelated" to the particular ideas expressed? Cox, Foreword: Freedom of Expression in the Burger Court, 94 Harv. L. Rev. 1, 40 (1980). Is it more akin to the prohibition on "offensive ideas" because the "harms of shock and offense [flow] entirely from the communicative content of [the] message"? Ely, supra, at 114.

Consider the following views:

a. Haiman, Speech v. Privacy: Is There a Right Not to Be Spoken To?, 67 Nw. U. L. Rev. 153, 189 (1972):

> The problem with the position [that prohibitions on the use of profanity are merely restrictions on the manner of expression] is that the form and content of communications are so inextricably tied that to control the former is, in fact, to modify the latter. [For] example, it can hardly be maintained that phrases like, "Repeal the Draft," "Resist the Draft," or "The Draft Must Go" convey essentially the same message as "Fuck the Draft." Clearly something is lost in the translation.

b. Stone, Content Regulation and the First Amendment, 25 Wm. & Mary L. Rev. 189, 243–244 (1983):

> Governmental efforts to limit speech because it is offensively *noisy* [do] not implicate the same kind of censorial or heckler's veto concerns as governmental efforts to limit speech because the *ideas* are offensive. Analytically, offense at language is more like offense at noise than offense at ideas. [Moreover, although] restrictions on the use of profanity may affect some speakers more than others, [this] is also true of most content-neutral restrictions.

4. *Why does "fuck" offend?* Consider C. Fairman, *FUCK: Word Taboo and Protecting Our First Amendment Liberties* 27–29, 44–45, 55, 60 (2009):

In every culture, there are both taboo acts [and] taboo words. [There] are typical categories of taboo. [Body] effluvia — feces, urine, menstrual fluid, snot, and semen — are often subject to taboo. Sex organs and sex acts are also frequently taboo targets. [Collectively], they all deal with situations in which one is at risk of serious harm. [Our] bodily fluids not only harbor disease but can contaminate others. . . .

I can wrap my mind around cleanliness taboos such as [don't] play with your feces, etc. But how does this transform into a taboo against saying *shit*? It's as if Prohibition in the 1920s forbade not just the sale of alcohol but saying the word *whiskey* as well. [The] transmutation has a scientific explanation. Let me use effluvia taboos as an illustration. Researchers in public health and hygiene [contend] that our hygiene instincts are the product of disgust. [Seeing] a disgust trigger (like vomit or pus) automatically produces a subconscious hygienic reaction. Disgust helps us avoid those things that were associated with the risk of disease in our evolutionary past. [Even] thinking about our excretions (and the body parts associated with them) generates disgust. Because the disgust reaction is involuntary, hearing the words triggers the response. . . .

[There are two forms of the word *fuck*. They] can be labeled as $Fuck^1$ and $Fuck^2$. $Fuck^1$ means literally "to copulate." . . . $Fuck^2$ doesn't have any intrinsic meaning at all. Rather, it's merely a word that has offensive force. It can be substituted for other swear words. It [can] express all kinds of emotions. [As in "Fuck the draft."] The critical relationship between $Fuck^1$ and $Fuck^2$ is the migration of usage. *Fuck* starts out [as a] sexual reference [with] taboo attached. Over time, the referential meaning of $Fuck^1$ gave way to the emotional meanings of $Fuck^2$. The taboo that first attached to $Fuck^1$ migrates to emotional $Fuck^2$ despite its nonsexual meaning. The sexual reference is gone, but the taboo remains. . . .

When you hear fuck, your brain automatically produces an emotional reaction to the word's taboo — all those unhealthy feelings and fears about sex. You can't stop this reflexive processing of the taboo, but you do have choices on how to react. [Some people] don't merely refrain from using the word; they're crusaders designed to stomp out its use, [including] nonsexual *Fuck*.

5. *The captive audience.* Does Justice Harlan undervalue the interests of the "audience" in *Cohen*? Consider A. Bickel, The Morality of Consent 72 (1975): "There is such a thing as verbal violence, a kind of cursing, assaultive speech that amounts to almost physical aggression. [The sort of speech at issue in *Cohen*] constitutes an assault." As noted in *Chaplinsky*, such profanities "by their very utterance inflict injury." Why, then, can't such expression be suppressed? Is the interest in protecting the sensibilities of unconsenting individuals against such "assaults" simply too insubstantial to justify restrictions on "offensive" expression? Note Justice Harlan's conclusion in *Cohen* that "[the] ability of government [to] shut off discourse solely to protect others from

hearing it is [dependent] upon a showing that substantial privacy interests are being invaded in an essentially intolerable manner."

Consider the following:

a. Suppose Congress enacts a law authorizing any homeowner who no longer wishes to receive mail from a particular person or organization to instruct the Postmaster General to direct that person or organization to refrain from further mailings to the homeowner. Consider Rowan v. Post Office Department, 397 U.S. 728 (1970):

> In today's complex society we are inescapably captive audiences for many purposes, but a sufficient measure of individual autonomy must survive to permit every householder to exercise control over unwanted mail. To make the householder the exclusive and final judge of what will cross his threshold undoubtedly has the effect of impeding the flow of ideas, information, and arguments that, ideally, he should receive and consider. [But] nothing in the Constitution compels us to listen to or view any unwanted communication, whatever its merit. [The] ancient concept that "a man's home is his castle" into which "not even the king may enter" has lost none of its vitality, [and we] therefore categorically reject the argument that [an individual] has a right under the Constitution [to] send unwanted material into the home of another.

b. Suppose Congress enacts a law prohibiting any person to mail to another any materials containing profanity or photographs revealing bare human pubic areas without the recipient's prior written consent. In Bolger v. Youngs Drug Products Corp., 463 U.S. 60 (1983), the Court invalidated a federal statute prohibiting the mailing of unsolicited advertisements for contraceptives. The Court explained:

> We [have] recognized the important interest in allowing addressees to give notice to a mailer that they wish no further mailings [citing *Rowan*]. But we have never held that the government itself can shut off the flow of mailings to protect those recipients who might potentially be offended. The First Amendment "does not permit the government to prohibit speech as intrusive unless the 'captive' audience cannot avoid objectionable speech." [The] "short, regular, journey from mail box to trash can [is] an acceptable burden, at least so far as the Constitution is concerned."

In light of *Rowan* and *Bolger*, could Congress constitutionally require all televisions to have a chip that enables the owner to block out unwanted channels or shows? Could it constitutionally require all televisions to have a chip that enables the owner to block out only unwanted channels or shows that are rated as especially violent or sexual? See Balkin, Media Filters, the V-Chip, and the Foundations of Broadcast Regulation, 45 Duke L.J. 1131 (1996).

c. Suppose a city operates a public bus system and each bus contains twenty interior advertising spaces available for lease by private persons. May the city, to protect the sensibilities of "captive" commuters, exclude such "highly offensive" messages as "Welfare Is Black Theft," "God Is Dead," and "Abortion Is Murder"? Is this a situation in which, as in *Cohen*, the audience "could effectively avoid further bombardment of their sensibilities simply by averting their eyes"? Suppose the city excludes ads that contain profanity? Nudity? Cf. Lehman v. City of Shaker Heights, 418 U.S. 298 (1974) (plurality opinion upholding city policy permitting the display of commercial but not generally more "controversial" political or public issue advertisements in the interior of city buses), Chapter V.B, infra. Note that in the bus situation, unlike the situation in *Cohen*, the city could protect the "captive" audience by adopting a content-neutral restriction excluding *all* speech. Is a content-neutral restriction preferable to a "narrower" restriction based on content? Consider Stone, supra, at 280: "If a 'true' captive audience exists, the state may protect the sensibilities of unwilling listeners by banning all speech, regardless of content. It should never, however, be permitted to use the captive audience as a lever for censorship." Should that conclusion, however justified as applied to offensive ideas, apply also to the use of profanity and to the display of "lewd" pictures?

**ERZNOZNIK v. JACKSONVILLE, 422 U.S. 205 (1975).** In *Erznoznik*, the Court invalidated a Jacksonville, Florida, ordinance that declared it a public nuisance for any drive-in movie theater to exhibit any motion picture "in which the human male or female bare buttocks, human female bare breasts, or human bare pubic areas are shown, if such motion picture [is] visible from any public street or place." Justice Powell delivered the opinion of the Court:

"[The city] concedes that its ordinance sweeps far beyond the permissible restraints on obscenity [and] thus applies to films that are protected by the First Amendment. [Nevertheless], it maintains that any movie containing nudity which is visible from a public place may be suppressed as a nuisance. . . .

"[The city's] primary argument is that it may protect its citizens against unwilling exposure to materials that may be offensive. Jacksonville's ordinance, however, does not protect citizens from all movies that might offend; rather it singles out films containing nudity, presumably because the lawmakers considered them especially offensive to passersby. [A] State or municipality may protect individual privacy by enacting reasonable time, place, and manner regulations applicable to all speech irrespective of content. [But] when government [undertakes] selectively to shield the public from some kinds of speech on the ground that they are more offensive than others, the First Amendment strictly limits its power. [Absent extraordinary circumstances], the burden normally falls upon the viewer to 'avoid further bombardment of [his] sensibilities simply by averting [his] eyes.' [*Cohen.*] [The] limited privacy interest of persons on the public streets cannot justify this censorship of otherwise protected speech on the basis of its content. . . .

"[The city] also attempts to support the ordinance as an exercise of the city's undoubted police power to protect children. [But] the ordinance is not directed [only] against sexually explicit [nudity]. Rather, it sweepingly forbids display of all films containing *any* uncovered buttocks or breasts, irrespective of context or pervasiveness. [Clearly] all nudity cannot be deemed obscene even as to minors. [Thus], if Jacksonville's ordinance is intended to regulate expression accessible to minors it is overbroad in its proscription. . . .

"[Finally, the city attempts] to justify the ordinance [on the ground] that nudity on a drive-in movie screen distracts passing motorists, thus slowing the flow of traffic and increasing the likelihood of accidents. [But] the legislative classification is strikingly underinclusive. There is no reason to think that a wide variety of other scenes in the customary screen diet, ranging from soap opera to violence, would be any less distracting to the passing motorist."

Justice Douglas filed a concurring opinion.

Chief Justice Burger, joined by Justice Rehnquist, dissented: "Whatever validity the notion that passersby may protect their sensibilities by averting their eyes may have when applied to words printed on an individual's jacket, see [*Cohen*], it distorts reality to apply that notion to the outsize screen of a drive-in movie theater. [It] is not unreasonable for lawmakers to believe that public nudity on a giant screen, visible at night to hundreds of [drivers], may have a tendency to divert attention from their task and cause accidents. [Moreover], those persons who legitimately desire to [view such films] are not foreclosed from doing so. [Such films may be] exhibited [in] indoor theaters [and in any] drive-in movie theater [whose] screen [is shielded] from public view. Thus, [the challenged] ordinance [is] not a restriction of any 'message.' [The] First Amendment interests involved in this case are trivial at best." Justice White also dissented.

**FCC v. PACIFICA FOUNDATION, 438 U.S. 726 (1978).** At about 2 o'clock in the afternoon on October 30, 1973, a New York radio station, owned by Pacifica Foundation, broadcast George Carlin's monologue entitled "Filthy Words." In this twelve-minute monologue, Carlin discussed "the words you couldn't say on the public, ah, airwaves, um, the ones you definitely wouldn't say, ever." He proceeded to list those words ("shit, piss, fuck, cunt, cocksucker, motherfucker, and tits"), which he described as the "ones that will curve your spine [and] grow hair on your hands," and then repeated them in a variety of colloquialisms. The recording includes frequent laughter from the live audience. A few weeks later, a man who had heard the broadcast while driving with his young son wrote a letter complaining to the Commission.

Pacifica responded to the complaint by explaining that the monologue had been played during a program about contemporary society's attitude toward language and that, immediately before its broadcast, listeners had been advised that it included "sensitive language which might be regarded as offensive to some." Pacifica characterized Carlin as "a significant social satirist" who uses "words to satirize as harmless and essentially silly our attitudes towards those words." There were no other complaints about the broadcast.

The Commission issued a declaratory order granting the complaint. Characterizing Carlin's language as "patently offensive," though not obscene, the Commission explained that such "indecent" speech should be regulated by principles analogous to those found in the law of nuisance. Specifically, the Commission announced that broadcasters may not air language that describes sexual or excretory activities or organs in terms that are patently offensive as measured by contemporary community standards at times of the day when children are likely to be in the audience. Although the Commission did not impose formal sanctions, it stated that the complaint would be "associated with the station's license [file]." . . .

The Court upheld the Commission, although there was no majority opinion. In a plurality opinion, joined by Chief Justice Burger and Justice Rehnquist, Justice Stevens noted that a "requirement that indecent language be avoided will have its primary effect on the form, rather than the content, of serious communication. There are few, if any, thoughts that cannot be expressed by the use of less offensive language." Although affirming that "the government must remain neutral in the marketplace of ideas," Stevens maintained that the FCC's action had nothing to do with the substance of Carlin's political ideas or opinions. Rather, the Commission objected only to the "way" in which Carlin expressed those ideas. In such circumstances, "we must consider its context in order to determine whether the Commission's action was constitutionally permissible."

Applying that approach, Justice Stevens upheld the FCC's order: "The broadcast media have established a uniquely pervasive presence in the lives of all Americans. Patently offensive, indecent material presented over the airwaves confronts the citizen, not only in public, but also in the privacy of the home, where the individual's right to be left alone plainly outweighs the First Amendment rights of an intruder. [*Rowan.*] Because the broadcast audience is constantly tuning in and out, prior warnings cannot completely protect the listener or viewer from unexpected program content. [Moreover], broadcasting is uniquely accessible to children, even those too young to read. Although Cohen's written message might have been incomprehensible to a first grader, Pacifica's broadcast could have enlarged a child's vocabulary in an instant. Other forms of offensive expression may be withheld from the young without restricting the expression at its source. Bookstores and motion picture theaters, for example, may be prohibited from making indecent material available to children. [Citing *Ginsberg*, section E, supra.] The ease with which children may obtain access to broadcast material, coupled with the concerns recognized in *Ginsberg*, amply justify special treatment of indecent broadcasting.

"It is appropriate [to] emphasize the narrowness of our holding. [As] Mr. Justice Sutherland wrote, a 'nuisance may be merely a right thing in the wrong place, — like a pig in the parlor instead of the barnyard.' [We] simply hold that when the Commission finds that a pig has entered the parlor, the exercise of its regulatory power does not depend on proof that the pig is obscene."

Justice Powell, joined by Justice Blackmun, filed a concurring opinion: "The Commission sought to 'channel' the monologue to hours when the fewest unsupervised children would be exposed to it. [This] consideration provides strong support for the Commission's holding. [The] Commission properly held that [the] language involved in this case is as potentially degrading and harmful to children as representations of many erotic acts. In most instances, the dissemination of this kind of speech to children may be limited without also limiting willing adults' access to it. [The] difficulty is that such a physical separation of the audience cannot be accomplished in the broadcast media. [In] my view, the Commission was entitled to give substantial weight to this difference [between the broadcast and other media] in reaching its decision in this case. . . .

The Commission's holding does not prevent willing adults from purchasing Carlin's record, from attending his performances, or, indeed, from reading the transcript reprinted as an appendix to the Court's opinion. [It] does not prevent Pacifica Foundation from broadcasting the monologue during late evening hours when fewer children are likely to be in the audience, nor from broadcasting discussions of the contemporary use of language at any time during the day."

Justice Brennan, joined by Justice Marshall, dissented: "[An] individual's actions in switching on and listening to communications transmitted over the public airways and directed to the public at large do not implicate fundamental privacy interests, even when engaged in within the home. Instead, [these] actions are more properly viewed as a decision to take part, if only as a listener, in an ongoing public discourse. [Moreover], unlike other intrusive modes of communication, such as sound trucks, '[t]he radio can be turned off.' [The Court] fails to accord proper weight to the interests of listeners who wish to hear broadcasts the FCC deems offensive. It permits majoritarian tastes completely to preclude a protected message from entering the homes of a receptive, unoffended minority. No decision of this Court supports such a result. . . .

"[The] government unquestionably has a special interest in the well-being of children and consequently 'can adopt more stringent controls on communicative materials available to youths than on those available to adults.' [But] '[s]peech that is neither obscene as to youths nor subject to some other legitimate proscription cannot be suppressed solely to protect the young from ideas or images that a legislative body thinks unsuitable for them.' [*Erznoznik.*] [Thus, the Court's] result violates in spades the principle of Butler v. Michigan [that government may not] 'reduce the adult population [to] reading only what is fit for children.'"

Justice Stewart, joined by Justices Brennan, White, and Marshall, dissented on the ground that the FCC had statutory authority to regulate only "obscene" material.

### Note: Fleeting Expletives

In 2004, the Federal Communications Commission amended the indecency rule that the Court had upheld twenty-five years earlier in *Pacifica* to provide for the first time that *any* use of indecent words could be actionable, even if the words were not used in a sexual manner and even if they were used spontaneously and only in passing. The 2004 order arose out of several incidents involving so-called fleeting expletives. In one incident, Cher exclaimed during an unscripted acceptance speech at the 2002 Billboard Music Awards, "I've had my critics for the last 40 years saying that I was on my way out every year. Right. So fuck 'em." In another incident, at the 2003 Golden Globe Awards, Bono, upon winning the award for Best Original Song, exclaimed, "This is really, really, fucking brilliant." For these and similar incidents involving fleeting expletives, the FCC levied fines on broadcasters totaling some $8 million. The Commission defended its new rule on the ground that the word "fuck" "is one of the most vulgar, graphic and explicit descriptions of sexual activity in the English language." It therefore argued that its action was necessary to "safeguard the well-being of the nation's children from the most objectionable, most offensive language."

In 2008, the United States Court of Appeals ruled that the FCC lacked statutory authority to punish broadcasters for mere fleeting expletives. In 2009, in FCC v. Fox Television Stations, 556 U.S. 502 (2009), the Supreme Court, in a five-to-four decision, reversed, holding that the FCC did, indeed, have statutory authority for its rule. But the Court remanded the case to the court of appeals to decide whether the FCC's new rule violated the first amendment.

On remand, the court of appeals held that the FCC's indecency policy did, indeed, violate the first amendment because the Commission, in applying its rule, had made ad hoc and inconsistent judgments about the circumstances in which the use of the word "fuck" was forbidden. In FCC v. Fox Television Stations, 132 S. Ct. 2307 (2012) (*Fox II*), the Supreme Court vacated the court of appeals' first amendment holding, but unanimously ruled that the FCC's standard violated the due process clause because the FCC had failed to give the broadcasters fair notice that fleeting expletives could be found indecent.

**SABLE COMMUNICATIONS, INC. v. FCC, 492 U.S. 115 (1989).** The Court unanimously held unconstitutional a federal statute prohibiting the interstate transmission of "indecent" commercial telephone messages ("dial-a-porn" services). In an opinion by Justice White, the Court distinguished the "emphatically narrow holding" of *Pacifica*. The Court explained that telephone communications are different, for they require the caller to take "affirmative steps" to receive the message: "Placing a telephone call is not the same as turning on a radio and being taken by surprise by an indecent message." Moreover, the government's interest in protecting children could be served by various technical means other than a total ban of the transmission of such messages; although some limited numbers of children might be able to defeat these devices, the prohibition "has the invalid effect of limiting the content of adult telephone conversations to that which is suitable for children to hear."

**RENO v. AMERICAN CIVIL LIBERTIES UNION, 521 U.S. 844 (1997).** In an opinion by Justice Stevens, the Court invalidated two sections of the Communications Decency Act of 1996 (CDA) that were designed to protect minors from "indecent" and "patently offensive" communications on the Internet. Section 223(a) prohibited any person from making any communication over the Internet "which is . . . indecent, knowing that the recipient of the communication is under eighteen years of age." Section 223(d) prohibited any person from knowingly sending over the Internet any communication that will be available to a person under eighteen years of age and "that, in context, depicts or describes, in terms patently offensive as measured by contemporary community standards, sexual or excretory activities or organs."

At the outset, the Court distinguished *Pacifica*: "[There] are significant differences between the order upheld in *Pacifica* and the CDA. First, the order in *Pacifica* [focused on] when — rather than whether — it would be permissible to air such a program in that particular medium. The CDA's broad categorical prohibitions are not limited to particular [times]. Second, unlike the CDA, the Commission's declaratory order was not punitive; we expressly refused to decide whether the indecent broadcast 'would justify a criminal prosecution.' Finally, the Commission's order applied to a medium which as a matter of history had 'received the most limited First Amendment protection,' in large part because warnings could not adequately protect the listener from unexpected program content. The Internet, however, has no comparable history. Moreover, [the] risk of encountering indecent material [on the Internet] by accident is remote because a series of affirmative steps is required to access specific material."

The Court next noted "the many ambiguities" concerning the act's coverage, which "render it problematic" for purposes of the first amendment: "For instance, each of the two parts of the CDA uses a different linguistic form. The first uses the word 'indecent,' while the second speaks of material that 'in context, depicts or describes, in terms patently offensive as measured by contemporary community standards, sexual or excretory activities or organs.' Given the absence of a definition of either term, this difference in language will provoke uncertainty among speakers about how the two standards relate to each other and just what they mean. Could a speaker confidently assume that a serious discussion about birth control practices, homosexuality, the First Amendment issues raised by the [text of the broadcast at issue in *Pacifica*], or the consequences of prison rape would not violate the CDA? This uncertainty undermines the likelihood that the CDA has been carefully tailored to the congressional goal of protecting minors from potentially harmful materials."

The Court found this "lack of precision" fatal: "In order to deny minors access to potentially harmful speech, the CDA effectively suppresses a large amount of speech that adults have a constitutional right to receive and to address to one another. That burden on adult speech is unacceptable if less restrictive alternatives would be at least as effective in achieving the legitimate purpose that the statute was enacted to serve. In evaluating the free speech rights of adults, we have made it perfectly clear that '[s]exual expression which is indecent but not obscene is protected by the First Amendment.' [It] is true that we have repeatedly recognized the governmental interest in protecting children from harmful materials. [Citing *Ginsberg; Pacifica.*] But that interest does not justify an unnecessarily broad suppression of speech addressed to adults. As we have explained, the Government may not 'reduc[e] the adult population [to] only what is fit for children.'"

Finally, the Court noted that in enacting these provisions the government had not used the "least restrictive means" for achieving its goal: "The arguments in this Court have referred to possible alternatives such as requiring that indecent material be 'tagged' in a way that facilitates parental control of material coming into their homes, making exceptions for messages with artistic or educational value [and] regulating some portions of the Internet — such as commercial web sites — differently than others, such as chat rooms. Particularly in the light of the absence of any detailed findings by the Congress, or even hearings addressing the special problems of the CDA, we are persuaded that the CDA is not narrowly tailored if that requirement has any meaning at all."

**ASHCROFT v. AMERICAN CIVIL LIBERTIES UNION, 535 U.S. 564 (2004).** In response to *Reno*, Congress enacted the Child Online Protection Act (COPA), which was designed to address the constitutional defects the Court had identified in the Communications Decency Act. COPA imposes criminal penalties of a $50,000 fine and six months in prison for the knowing posting, for "commercial purposes," of World Wide Web content that is "harmful to minors." The act defines material that is "harmful to minors" as: "any communication, picture, image, graphic image file, article, recording, writing, or other matter of any kind that is obscene or that (A) the average person, applying contemporary community standards, would find, taking the material as a whole and *with respect to minors*, is designed to appeal to, or is designed to pander to, the prurient interest; (B) depicts, describes, or represents, in a manner patently offensive *with respect to minors*, an actual or simulated sexual act or sexual contact, an actual or simulated normal or perverted sexual act, or a lewd exhibition of the genitals or post-pubescent female breast; and (C) taken as a whole, lacks serious literary, artistic, political, or scientific value for minors."

COPA defines "minor" as "any person under 17 years of age" and specifies that a person acts for "commercial purposes" only if he "makes a communication, or offers to make a communication, by means of the World Wide Web, that includes any material that is harmful to minors, . . . as a regular course of such person's trade or business, with the objective of earning a profit as a result of such activities." COPA recognizes an affirmative defense for those who attempt to prevent minors from gaining access to the prohibited materials "(A) by requiring use of a credit card, debit account, adult access code, or adult personal identification number; (B) by accepting a digital certificate that verifies age; or (C) by any other reasonable measures that are feasible under available technology."

In a five-to-four decision, the Court held that the federal district court did not "abuse its discretion" in entering a preliminary injunction against enforcement of COPA. In its opinion, written by Justice Kennedy, the Court explained that the district court had issued the preliminary injunction because it found that there "are plausible, less restrictive alternatives to COPA."

The Court continued: "The primary alternative considered by the District Court was blocking and filtering software. [Filters] are less restrictive than COPA. They impose selective restrictions on speech at the receiving end, not universal restrictions at the source. Under a filtering regime, adults without children may gain access to speech they have a right to see without having to identify themselves or provide their credit card information. Even adults with children may obtain access to the same speech on the same terms simply by turning off the filter on their home computers. . . .

"Filters also may well be more effective than COPA. First, a filter can prevent minors from seeing all pornography, not just pornography posted to the Web from America. The District Court noted [that] 40% of harmful-to-minors content comes from overseas. COPA does not prevent minors from having access to those foreign harmful materials. That alone makes it possible that filtering software might be more effective in serving Congress' goals. [It] is not an answer to say that COPA reaches some amount of materials that are harmful to minors; the question is whether it would reach more of them than less restrictive alternatives. In addition, the District Court found that verification systems may be subject to evasion and circumvention, for example by minors who have their own credit cards. [The] Commission on Child Online Protection, a blue-ribbon commission created by Congress, unambiguously found that filters are more effective than age-verification requirements. . . .

"Filtering software, of course, is not a perfect solution to the problem of children gaining access to harmful-to-minors materials. It may block some materials that are not harmful to minors and fail to catch some that are. Whatever the deficiencies of filters, however, the Government failed to introduce specific evidence proving that existing technologies are less effective than the restrictions in COPA. In the absence of a showing as to the relative effectiveness of COPA and the alternatives proposed by respondents, it was not an abuse of discretion for the District Court to grant the preliminary injunction. . . .

"One argument to the contrary is worth mentioning — the argument that filtering software is not an available alternative because Congress may not require it to be used. That argument carries little weight, because Congress undoubtedly may act to encourage the use of filters. [The] need for parental cooperation does not automatically disqualify a proposed less restrictive alternative. [By] enacting programs to promote use of filtering software, Congress could give parents that ability without subjecting protected speech to severe penalties."

Justice Breyer, joined by Chief Justice Rehnquist and Justice O'Connor, dissented: "Like the Court, I would subject the Act to 'the most exacting scrutiny.' [But] my examination of (1) the burdens the Act imposes on protected expression, (2) the Act's ability to further a compelling interest, and (3) the proposed 'less restrictive alternatives' convinces me that the Court is wrong. . . .

"[The] Act, properly interpreted, imposes a burden on protected speech that is no more than modest. [The] Act does not censor the material it covers. Rather, it requires providers of the 'harmful to minors' material to restrict minors' access to it by verifying age. [I] recognize that the screening requirement imposes some burden on adults who seek access to the regulated material, as well as on its providers. The [burden] is, in part, monetary [and, in part, the fear of embarrassment caused by the identification requirement]. Both monetary costs and potential embarrassment can deter potential viewers and, in that sense, the statute's requirements may restrict access to a site. . . .

"I turn next to the question of 'compelling interest,' that of protecting minors from exposure to commercial pornography. No one denies that such an interest is 'compelling.' Rather, the question here is whether the Act, given its restrictions on adult access, significantly advances that interest. [Filtering] software, as presently available, does not solve the 'child protection' problem. It suffers from four serious inadequacies that prompted Congress to pass legislation instead of relying on its voluntary use. First, its filtering is faulty, allowing some pornographic material to pass through without hindrance. [Second], filtering software costs money. Not every family has the $40 or so necessary to install it. Third, filtering software depends upon parents willing to decide where their children will surf the Web and able to enforce that decision. [Fourth], software blocking lacks precision, with the result that those who wish to use it to screen out pornography find that it blocks a great deal of material that is valuable. [Thus], Congress could reasonably conclude that a system that relies entirely upon the use of such software is not an effective system. And a law that adds to that system an age-verification screen requirement significantly increases the system's efficacy. That is to say, at a modest additional cost to those adults who wish to obtain access to a screened program,

In an opinion by Chief Justice Burger, the Court emphasized the "sexual content" of the student's speech:

> [The] penalties imposed in this case were unrelated to any political viewpoint. The First Amendment does not prevent the school officials from determining that to permit a vulgar and lewd speech such as respondent's would undermine the school's basic educational mission. A high school assembly or classroom is no place for a sexually explicit monologue [and] it was perfectly appropriate for the school to disassociate itself to make the point to the pupils that vulgar speech [is] wholly inconsistent with the "fundamental values" of public school education.

## Note: Zoning Theaters with Adult Movies and Bars with Nude Dancing

1. *Zoning adult movie theaters.* In the mid-1970s, Detroit adopted zoning ordinances providing that no adult theater may be located within one thousand feet of any two other "regulated uses" or within five hundred feet of a residential area. Other "regulated uses" included cabarets, bars, hotels, motels, pawnshops, pool halls, shoeshine parlors, and secondhand stores. The ordinance classified a theater as "adult" if it was used to present "material distinguished or characterized by an emphasis on matter depicting, describing or relating to 'Specified Sexual Activities' or 'Specified Anatomical Areas.'"

In Young v. American Mini-Theatres, 427 U.S. 50 (1976), the Court, in an opinion by Justice Stevens, upheld the constitutionality of the ordinances: "In the opinion of urban planners and real estate experts who supported the ordinances, the location of several regulated uses in the same neighborhood tends to attract an undesirable quantity and quality of transients, adversely affects property values, causes an increase in crime, [and] encourages residents and businesses to move elsewhere. [The] ordinances are not challenged on the ground that they impose a limit on the total number of adult theaters which may operate in the city of Detroit. There is no claim that distributors or exhibitors of adult films are denied access to the market or, conversely, that the viewing public is unable to satisfy its appetite for sexually explicit fare. Viewed as an entity, the market for this commodity is essentially unrestrained. [Thus,] apart from the fact that the ordinances treat adult theaters differently from other theaters and the fact that the classification is predicated on the content of material shown in the respective theaters, the regulation of the place where such films may be exhibited does not offend the First Amendment.

"[The Detroit ordinances draw a line] on the basis of content without violating the government's paramount obligation of neutrality in its regulation of protected communication. For the regulation of the places where sexually explicit films may be exhibited is unaffected by whatever social, political, or philosophical message a film may be intended to communicate; whether a motion picture ridicules or characterizes one point of view or another, the effect of the ordinances is exactly the same. [Moreover,] even though we recognize that the First Amendment will not tolerate the total suppression of erotic materials that have some arguably artistic value, it is manifest that society's interest in protecting this type of expression is of a wholly different, and lesser, magnitude than the interest in untrammeled political debate. . . . [Even] though the First Amendment protects communication in this area from total suppression, we hold that the State may legitimately use the content of these materials as the basis for placing them in a different classification from other motion pictures.

"The remaining question is whether the line drawn by these ordinances is justified by the city's interest in preserving the character of its neighborhoods. [The] record discloses a factual basis for the Common Council's conclusion that this kind of restriction will have the desired effect. It is not our function to appraise the wisdom of its decision to require adult theaters to be separated. . . . The city's interest in attempting to preserve the quality of urban life is one that must be accorded high respect [and it] must be allowed a reasonable opportunity to experiment with solutions to admittedly serious problems."

Justice Stewart, joined by Justices Brennan, Marshall, and Blackmun, dissented: "This case does not involve a simple zoning ordinance, or a content-neutral time, place, and manner restriction, or a regulation of obscene expression or other speech that is entitled to less than the full protection of the First Amendment. The kind of expression at issue here is no doubt objectionable to some, but that fact does not diminish its protected status any more than did the particular content of the 'offensive' expression in [Erznoznik or Cohen]. What this case does involve is the constitutional permissibility of selective interference with protected speech whose content is thought to produce distasteful effects. It is elementary that a prime function of the First Amendment is to guard against just such interference. By refusing to invalidate Detroit's ordinance the Court rides roughshod over cardinal principles of First Amendment law, which require that time, place, and manner regulations that affect protected expression be content neutral. . . ."

Presumably, the Court would not uphold a law requiring cable operators to confine antiwar or Nazi programming to certain hours or restricting the location of movie theaters that show racist films or films that portray adultery or homosexuality in a positive light. What, then, explains *Young*? Is it that "indecent" (but nonobscene) speech is of only "low" first amendment value? Is it that regulations of such expression are "viewpoint-neutral"? Does *Young* make any sense? Recall *Denver Area*, supra.

2. *Making sense of* Young? Ten years later, in City of Renton v. Playtime Theatres, 475 U.S. 41 (1986), the Court considered the constitutionality of an ordinance prohibiting adult movie theaters from locating within one thousand feet of any residential zone, single- or multiple-family dwelling, church, park,

or school. In an opinion by Justice Rehnquist, the Court upheld the ordinance. At the outset, the Court observed that "the resolution of this case is largely dictated by [*Young*]." After noting the distinction between "regulations enacted for the purpose of restraining speech on the basis of its content," which "presumptively violate the First Amendment," and "'content-neutral' time, place, and manner regulations," which "are acceptable so long as they are designed to serve a substantial governmental interest and do not unreasonably limit alternative avenues of communication," the Court concluded that, because "the Renton ordinance is aimed not at the *content* of the films, [but] at the *secondary effects* of such theaters on the surrounding community," it is "completely consistent with our definition of 'content-neutral' speech regulations as those that 'are *justified* without regard to the content of the regulated speech.'" This being so, the Court held that the Renton ordinance must be tested as a content-neutral restriction. Applying that standard, the Court echoed its finding in *Young* that "a city's 'interest in attempting to preserve the quality of urban life is one that must be accorded high respect.'"

Justice Brennan, joined by Justice Marshall, dissented. Brennan lamented the Court's "misguided" conclusion that the Renton ordinance was "content-neutral." In Justice Brennan's view, the "fact that adult movie theaters may cause harmful 'secondary' land use effects" does not mean that the regulation is content-neutral. To the contrary, because the ordinance explicitly "discriminates on its face against certain forms of speech based on content," it must be tested as a content-based restriction.

Was the Renton ordinance "content-neutral"? Does it make sense to treat a law that expressly "discriminates on its face against certain forms of speech based on content" more leniently than other content-based laws because it is "justified" in terms of the "secondary effects" of the speech? The issue of content-neutrality is taken up in Chapter V, infra.

3. *Making sense of* Renton? In 1977, the city of Los Angeles conducted a study that concluded that concentrations of adult entertainment establishments are associated with higher crime rates. Accordingly, it enacted an ordinance prohibiting such establishments within one thousand feet of each other or within five hundred feet of a religious institution, school, or public park. In 1983, to close a "loophole" in the original ordinance, the city amended the ordinance to prohibit "more than one adult entertainment business in the same building." Alameda Books, which operated a combined adult book store and adult video arcade in a single location, challenged the amendment on the ground that there was no evidence that combining these two activities in a single location caused higher crime rates. The lower court granted summary judgment to Alameda Books. The Supreme Court reversed. City of Los Angeles v. Alameda Books, 535 U.S. 425 (2002).

Justice O'Connor, joined by Chief Justice Rehnquist and Justices Scalia and Thomas, delivered the plurality opinion: "[In *Renton*,] we stated that the ordinance would be upheld so long as the city [showed] that [it] was designed to serve a substantial government interest and that reasonable alternative avenues of communication remained available. [It was] rational for the city to infer that reducing the concentration of adult operations in a neighborhood, whether within separate establishments or in one large establishment, will reduce crime rates. [We] conclude that the city [has sufficiently] complied with the evidentiary requirement in *Renton* [to withstand a motion for summary judgment]."

Justice Kennedy concurred in the judgment: "If a city can decrease the crime and blight associated with certain speech by the traditional exercise of its zoning power, and at the same time leave the quantity and accessibility of the speech substantially undiminished, there is no First Amendment objection. [But] the purpose and effect of [such] a zoning ordinance must be to reduce secondary effects and not to reduce speech. [In *Renton*,] the Court designated the restriction 'content neutral.' [This] was something of a fiction. [Whether] a statute is content-based or content neutral is something that can be determined on the face of it; if the statute describes speech by content then it is content based. [This ordinance is] content based and we should call [it] so. [Nevertheless], the central holding of *Renton* is sound: [Zoning] regulations do not automatically raise the specter of impermissible content discrimination, even if they are content based, [because the] zoning context provides a built-in legitimate rationale, which rebuts the usual presumption that content-based restrictions are unconstitutional. [But] the necessary rationale for applying intermediate [rather than strict] scrutiny is the promise that zoning ordinances like this one [will] reduce [the] secondary effects without substantially reducing speech."

Justice Souter, joined by Justices Stevens, Ginsburg, and Breyer, dissented: "Because content-based regulation applies to expression by very reason of what is said, it carries a high risk that expressive limits are imposed for the sake of suppressing a message that is disagreeable to listeners or readers, or the government. [The] risk lies in the fact that when a law applies selectively only to speech of particular content, the more precisely the content is identified, the greater is the opportunity for government censorship. [The] capacity of zoning regulations to address the [secondary effects] without eliminating the speech [is] the only possible excuse for [treating them] as akin to time, place and manner regulations. [In] this case, [the] government has not shown that bookstores containing viewing booths [increase] negative secondary effects, [and] we are thus left without substantial justification for viewing the [restriction as content neutral]."

Is it credible to call these regulations "content-neutral"? If not, is there any way to uphold them? Suppose Congress enacts legislation prohibiting any person to post sexually explicit (nonobscene) speech on the Internet, except in a special "domain" (e.g., .sex). Would such a law be constitutional after *Young*, *Renton*, and *Alameda*?

Does it matter whether the zoning law leaves open ample opportunities for adult movie theaters to operate? In *Young* and *Alameda*, the justices seemed to emphasize this point, but in *Renton*, Justice Rehnquist dismissed the concern that the effect of the challenged ordinance was to leave only 5 percent of the city's area available for adult theaters, "some of which was already occupied by existing businesses" and none of which was "commercially viable" for adult theaters, arguing that the first amendment does not compel "the Government to ensure that adult theaters" will be able to obtain sites at "bargain prices."

4. *Nude dancing.* In Schad v. Borough of Mt. Ephraim, 452 U.S. 61 (1981), appellants, who operated an adult bookstore, installed a coin-operated mechanism permitting a customer to watch a live dancer, usually nude, performing behind a glass panel. Appellants were convicted of violating a Mount Ephraim zoning ordinance prohibiting all live entertainment within the borough. The Court, in an opinion by Justice White, held the ordinance invalid. The Court noted that, as a form of entertainment, "nude dancing is not without its First Amendment protections." The Court explained that "this case is not controlled by *Young*," for unlike the situation in *Young*, there was "no evidence" in *Schad* "that the kind of entertainment appellants wish to provide is available in reasonably nearby areas." Chief Justice Burger, joined by Justice Rehnquist, dissented, observing that "to invoke the First Amendment to protect the activity involved in this case trivializes and demeans that great Amendment."

See also California v. LaRue, 409 U.S. 109 (1972) (upholding as "reasonable" under the twenty-first amendment an administrative regulation prohibiting nude dancing in bars and nightclubs that are licensed to sell liquor because of administrative findings that such explicitly sexual performances in establishments licensed to sell liquor tend to promote rape and prostitution and often result in the commission by customers of unlawful public acts of sexuality); New York State Liquor Authority v. Bellanca, 452 U.S. 714 (1981) (upholding a statute prohibiting nude dancing in establishments licensed by the state to sell liquor for on-premises consumption); Newport v. Iacobucci, 479 U.S. 92 (1986) (same); 44 Liquormart, Inc. v. Rhode Island, 517 U.S. 484 (1996) (disavowing *LaRue*'s reliance on the twenty-first amendment and concluding that the twenty-first amendment does not qualify the first amendment's prohibition against laws abridging the freedom of speech).

In Barnes v. Glen Theatre, Inc., 501 U.S. 560 (1991), the Court upheld an Indiana statute prohibiting any person to appear "in a state of nudity" in any "public place," as applied to establishments that present nude dancing as entertainment. Although there was no opinion of the Court, a majority of the justices concluded that nude performance dancing "is expressive conduct within the outer perimeters of the First Amendment." A majority also concluded, however, that the requirement that such dancers wear pasties and a G-string does not violate the first amendment because the nudity statute was not directed at nude dancing as such and had only an "incidental effect" on constitutionally protected activity. See also City of Erie v. Pap's A.M., 529 U.S. 277 (2000) (upholding a city ordinance banning public nudity, as applied to nude performance dancing). For a fuller account of *Barnes* and *Pap's A.M.*, see Chapter V.C, infra.

# H.   HATE SPEECH AND PORNOGRAPHY

## Beauharnais v. Illinois
343 U.S. 250 (1952)

[Beauharnais, president of the White Circle League, organized the distribution of a leaflet setting forth a petition calling on the mayor and city council of Chicago "to halt the further encroachment, harassment and invasion of white people, their property, neighborhoods and persons, by the Negro." The leaflet called for "[one] million self respecting white people in Chicago to unite" and added that, "[if] persuasion and the need to prevent the white race from becoming mongrelized by the negro will not unite us, then the aggressions, [rapes], robberies, knives, guns and marijuana of the negro surely will." Attached to the leaflet was an application for membership in the White Circle League. As a result of his participation in the distribution of this leaflet, Beauharnais was convicted under an Illinois statute declaring it unlawful for any person to [distribute] any publication that "portrays depravity, criminality, unchastity, or lack of virtue of a class of citizens, of any race, color, creed or religion, which [publication] exposes the citizens of any race, color, creed or religion to contempt, derision, or obloquy or which is productive of breach of the peace or riots." At Beauharnais's trial, the judge refused to instruct the jury that, in order to convict, they must find "that the article complained of was likely to produce a clear and present danger of a serious substantive evil that rises far above public inconvenience, annoyance or unrest." The trial judge also refused to consider Beauharnais's offer of proof on the issue of truth, for under Illinois law, the defense of truth is unavailable in a prosecution for criminal libel unless "the truth of all facts in the utterance [be] shown together with good motive for publication." The Supreme Court, in a five-to-four decision, affirmed the conviction.]

MR. JUSTICE FRANKFURTER delivered the opinion of the Court. . . .

Libel of an individual was a common-law crime, and thus criminal in the colonies. Indeed, at common law, truth or good motives was no defense. In the first decades after the adoption of the Constitution, this was changed by judicial decision, statute or constitution in most States, but nowhere was there any suggestion that the crime of libel be abolished. [As we have observed, "libelous] utterances are no essential part of any exposition of ideas, and are of such slight social value as a step to truth that any benefit that may be derived from them is clearly outweighed by the social interest in order and morality. . . ." [*Chaplinsky.*]

No one will gainsay that it is libelous falsely to charge another with being a rapist, robber, carrier of knives and guns, and user of marijuana. The precise question before us, then, is whether the [Constitution] prevents a State from punishing such libels — as criminal libel has been defined, limited and

constitutionally recognized time out of mind — directed at designated collec-
tivities and flagrantly disseminated. [If] an utterance directed at an individual
may be the object of criminal sanctions, we cannot deny to a State power to
punish the same utterance directed at a defined group, unless we can say that
this is a willful and purposeless restriction unrelated to the peace and well-
being of the State.

Illinois did not have to look beyond her own borders or await the tragic
experience of the last three decades to conclude that wilful purveyors of falsehood concerning racial and religious groups promote strife and tend powerfully to obstruct the manifold adjustments required for free, ordered life in a
metropolitan, polyglot community. From the murder of the abolitionist Love-
joy in 1837 to the Cicero riots of 1951, Illinois has been the scene of exacerbated tension between races, often flaring into violence and destruction. In
many of these outbreaks, utterances of the character here in question, so the
Illinois legislature could conclude, played a significant part. . . .

In the face of this history and its frequent obligato of extreme racial and
religious propaganda, we would deny experience to say that the Illinois legislature was without reason in seeking ways to curb false or malicious defamation
of racial and religious groups, made in public places and by means calculated
to have a powerful emotional impact on those to whom it was presented.
[Moreover, it would be] quite outside the scope of our authority [for] us to
deny that the Illinois legislature may warrantably believe that a man's job and
his educational opportunities and the dignity accorded him may depend as
much on the reputation of the racial and religious group to which he willy-
nilly belongs, as on his own merits. This being so, we are precluded from
saying that speech concededly punishable when immediately directed at individuals cannot be outlawed if directed at groups with whose position and
esteem in society the affiliated individual may be inextricably involved.

As to the defense of truth, Illinois in common with many States requires a
showing not only that the utterance state the facts, but also that the publication
be made "with good motives and for justifiable ends." Both elements are
necessary if the defense is to prevail. . . .
– Libelous utterances not being within the area of constitutionally protected
speech, it is unnecessary, either for us or for the State courts, to consider the
issues behind the phrase "clear and present danger." Certainly no one would
contend that obscene speech, for example, may be punished only upon a
showing of such circumstances. Libel, as we have seen, is in the same class.

We find no warrant in the Constitution for denying to Illinois the power to
pass the law here under attack. . . .
Affirmed.

MR. JUSTICE BLACK, with whom MR. JUSTICE DOUGLAS concurs, dissenting. . . .
The Court condones this expansive state censorship by painstakingly analogizing it to the law of criminal libel. As a result of this refined analysis, the

Illinois statute emerges labeled a "group libel law." This label may make the Court's holding more palatable for those who sustain it, but the sugar-coating does not make the censorship less deadly. However tagged, the Illinois law is not that criminal libel which has been "defined, limited and constitutionally recognized time out of mind." For as "constitutionally recognized" that crime has provided for punishment of false, malicious, scurrilous charges against individuals, not against huge groups. This limited scope of the law of criminal libel is of no small importance. It has confined state punishment of speech and expression to the narrowest of areas involving nothing more than purely private feuds. Every expansion of the law of criminal libel so as to punish discussions of matters of public concern means a corresponding invasion of the area dedicated to free expression by the First Amendment. . . .

*slippery slope argument*

Moreover, the leaflet used here was [the] means adopted by an assembled group to enlist interest in their efforts to have legislation enacted. [Freedom] of petition, assembly, speech and press could be greatly abridged by a practice of meticulously scrutinizing every editorial, speech, sermon or other printed matter to extract two or three naughty words on which to hang charges of "group libel." The *Chaplinsky* case makes no such broad inroads on First Amendment freedoms. . . .

If there be minority groups who hail this holding as their victory, they might consider the possible relevancy of this ancient remark: "Another such victory and I am undone."

Mr. Justice Douglas, dissenting. . . .

My view is that if in any case other public interests are to override the plain command of the First Amendment, the peril of speech must be clear and present, leaving no room for argument, raising no doubts as to the necessity of curbing speech in order to prevent disaster. . . .

[Dissenting opinions of Justices Reed and Jackson are omitted.]

## Note: Group Defamation and "Hate Speech"

1. *The* Skokie *controversy.* Reconsider the *Skokie* controversy, Chapter II, supra, in light of *Beauharnais.* Does the display of a swastika constitute "group libel"?

2. *Group defamation as "libel."* Central to Justice Frankfurter's analysis was the conclusion that "group libel," as defined in the Illinois statute, is not "within the area of constitutionally protected speech" and thus need not be tested by the clear and present danger standard. In justifying this conclusion, Justice Frankfurter relied primarily on *Chaplinsky*'s characterization of "libelous" utterances as "unprotected" speech. In New York Times v. Sullivan, however, the Court held that "libel can claim no talismanic immunity from

constitutional limitations." Moreover, the concept of "group libel," held in *Beauharnais* to be "unprotected" expression, was not limited to false statements of fact. Subsequent opinions, however, such as *New York Times* and *Hustler*, have unequivocally held that "libel" is of "low" first amendment value only insofar as it consists of false statements of fact. Do these decisions erode the precedential force of *Beauharnais*? See, e.g., Collin v. Smith, 578 F.2d 1197 (7th Cir. 1978) (the "approach sanctioned [in] *Beauharnais* would [not] pass constitutional muster today").

*Must be false*

3. *False statements of fact.* Suppose the Illinois statute prohibited only false statements of fact that portray "depravity, criminality, unchastity, or lack of virtue of a class of citizens, of any race, color, creed or religion." Are the interests threatened by such expression too diffuse to warrant restriction? Given the statements in the *Beauharnais* leaflet, what sort of showing would be necessary to establish "truth" or "falsity"? Consider Arkes, Civility and the Restriction of Speech: Rediscovering the Defamation of Groups, 1974 Sup. Ct. Rev. 281, 301: "One can think of few things worse than having a jury pronounce on the 'truth' of Beauharnais's charges, with all the solemnity and authority of the legal process. [These] are not the kinds of questions that we typically trust to the judgment of juries."

4. *Other bases for "low" value status.* If the conclusion that group libel constitutes "low" value speech can no longer be sustained solely by invocation of the term "libel," is there any other basis for attributing to such expression only "low" first amendment value? Consider the following arguments:

a. The group libel doctrine is a logical extension of the fighting words doctrine. The fighting words doctrine declares the malicious use of personal epithets to be of "low" first amendment value, see Chapter II, supra; the group libel doctrine accords equivalent treatment to the similarly malicious use of what amount to epithets directed against groups.

b. Group libel is of "low" first amendment value because it operates not by persuasion but by insidiously undermining social attitudes and beliefs, as evidenced by the experience of Nazi Germany. See Riesman, Democracy and Defamation: Control of Group Libel, 42 Colum. L. Rev. 727 (1942). For a description of contemporary anti-Nazi legislation in Germany, see Stein, History against Free Speech: The New German Law against the "Auschwitz" — and Other — Lies, 85 Mich. L. Rev. 277 (1986).

c. It cannot seriously be maintained that the first amendment was intended to protect speech that maliciously "portrays depravity, criminality, unchastity, or lack of virtue of a class of citizens, of any race, color, creed or religion." Just as express language of incitement to crime is incompatible with the fundamental assumptions of our democratic system, and is thus of "low" first amendment value, group libel is likewise of "low" value because it is incompatible with our fundamental commitment to human dignity and equality. Indeed, this issue poses a clash of constitutional rights and calls for the first amendment to be interpreted and applied in light of the fourteenth amendment's equally important guarantee of "equal protection of the laws."

d. Waldron, Dignity and Defamation: The Visibility of Hate, 123 Harv. L. Rev. 1597, 1599-1600, 1627 (2010):

[H]ate speech regulation can be understood as the protection of a certain sort of precious public good: a visible assurance offered by society to all of its members that they will not be subject to abuse, defamation, humiliation, discrimination, and violence on grounds of race, ethnicity, religion, gender, and in some cases sexual orientation. [The] most important aim of these laws [is] simply to diminish the presence of visible hatred in society by protecting the public commitment to their equal standing in society against public denigration. [In] a well-ordered society, [people] know that when they leave home in the morning they can reasonably count on not being discriminated against, humiliated, or terrorized. [When] a society is defaced with anti-Semitic signage, burning crosses, or defamatory racial leaflets, that sort of assurance evaporates. [In a society that tolerates hate speech], people no longer have the benefit of a general public assurance [of] human dignity. [The] security that people look for is security against the soul-shriveling humiliation that accompanies the manifestation of injustice in society.

e. Matsuda, Public Response to Racist Speech: Considering the Victim's Story, 87 Mich. L. Rev. 2320, 2332, 2336-2337, 2357, 2359 (1989):

The claim that a legal response to racist speech is required stems from a recognition of the structural reality of racism in America. Racism, as used here, comprises the ideology of racial supremacy and the mechanisms for keeping selected victim groups in subordinated positions. [Victims of] hate propaganda have experienced [fear, nightmares], post-traumatic stress disorder, hypertension, psychosis, and suicide. [In] order to avoid receiving hate messages, victims [of such speech] have had to quit jobs, forego education, leave their homes, avoid certain public places, curtail their own exercise of free speech rights, and otherwise modify their behavior. . . .

Racist speech is best treated as a *sui generis* category, presenting an idea so historically untenable, so dangerous, and so tied to perpetuation of violence and degradation [that] it is properly treated as outside the realm of protected discourse. [The] identifying characteristics [of] racist hate [speech are]: 1. The message is of racial inferiority; 2. The message is directed against a historically oppressed group; and 3. The message is persecutorial, hateful, and degrading. . . .

How can one argue for censorship of racist hate messages without encouraging a revival of McCarthyism? There is an important difference that comes from human experience, our only source of collective knowledge. [The] doctrines of racial supremacy and racial hatred [are] uniformly rejected. [We] have fought wars and spilled blood to establish [this principle]. The universality of this principle, in a world bereft of agreement on many things, is a mark of collective human progress.

In light of Matsuda's argument that hate speech causes its victims to "curtail their own exercise of free speech rights," can it be said that the regulation of hate speech is justified because it maximizes free expression in the aggregate?

Consider also Powell, As Justice Requires/Permits: The Delimitation of Harmful Speech in a Democratic Society, 16 Law & Ineq. 97, 103, 147–149 (1998):

> [The] insights proffered by critical race and post-modern theorists [suggest] that the classic remedy for harmful speech — that is, more speech — will, in some instances, perpetuate disparities of power and destabilize our sense of self. The marketplace of ideas cannot self-regulate so long as objections to lack of participatory access are subsumed by claims that the liberty interest in expression is primary to the equality interest in participatory access. A self-regulating marketplace presupposes an equal starting line — an assumption that has never been a reality in American political life.
>
> [A decision of the Canadian Supreme Court, Regina v. Keegstra, 2 W.W.R. 1 (1991), illustrates] an alternative way of using democratic principles to valorize liberty and equality. [In *Keegstra*, a Canadian high school teacher was convicted of "communicating statements [that] willfully promote hatred against any identifiable group" for communicating anti-Semitic statements to his students. The Canadian Supreme Court rejected Keegstra's claim that his conviction violated the Canadian Charter of Rights and Freedoms because his speech] was not expression that "serves individual and societal values in a free and democratic society." [This decision reflects] a commitment to both liberty and equality, and mediates between these values by recourse to a collective concern for the underlying values and principles of the society, including social justice. [Commenting] that it is destructive of free expression values themselves, as well as other democratic values, "to treat all expression as equally crucial to those principles at the core" of free expression, the Court suggested that democratic principles recommend viewing free expression as a function of three underlying goals. These goals are truth attainment, ensuring [the] development of self-identity, and most importantly, [the] guarantee that the opportunity for participation in the democratic process is open to all. The Court simultaneously supports these rationales with the observations that hate speech can impede the search for truth, impinge on the autonomy necessary to individual development and subvert the democratic process. Cognizant that the regulation "muzzles the participation of a [few]," the Court remains certain that the loss of that voice is not substantial. [What] is most instructive about the decision is that the Court was willing to employ a democratic calculus.

See also A. Tsesis, Destructive Messages 180, 192 (2002) ("A general consensus among nations holds that hate propaganda [threatens] both outgroup participation in democracy and minority rights. Countries that have enacted laws penalizing the dissemination of hate speech include Austria, Belgium, Brazil, Canada, Cyprus, England, France, Germany, India, Israel, Italy,

Netherlands, and Switzerland. [These] international examples demonstrate that the United States's pure speech jurisprudence is anomalous.").

f. Graber, Old Wine in New Bottles: The Constitutional Status of Unconstitutional Speech, 48 Vand. L. Rev. 349, 352, 364, 367–368, 371–372 (1995):

> Scholars who would ban [hate speech] insist that government can regulate certain expressions of prejudice without violating First Amendment values [because] the First Amendment does not fully protect unconstitutional speech — speech that denies or threatens the realization of fundamental constitutional values. [But what proponents of hate speech regulation] fail to realize is that the leading opponents of free speech in every generation [have] insisted that the First Amendment does not fully protect the right to deny or criticize what their generation regards to be fundamental constitutional values.
>
> [The leading] proponents of restrictions on speech during World War I, [for example, maintained] that persons had no constitutional right to attack what they believed to be the essential principles of republican government. [Similarly,] proponents of the freedom of contract [argued] that the First Amendment did not protect [attacks] on private property because such advocacy [was] unconstitutional speech, [and proponents of restricting the speech of communists asserted] that "[n]o democratic or constitutional principle is violated [when] a democracy acts to exclude those groups from entering the struggle for political power which, if victorious, will not permit that struggle to continue in accordance with the democratic way."

g. Krotoszynski, A Comparative Perspective on the First Amendment: Free Speech, Militant Democracy, and the Primacy of Dignity as a Preferred Constitutional Value in Germany, 79 Tul. L. Rev. 1549, 1550–1551, 1563, 1595, 1608–1609 (2004):

> Critics of the United States Supreme Court's protection of racist speech point to the experience of other constitutional democracies in support of their position. [But at] least in the case of Germany, it is very difficult to claim plausibly that "limited regulation of hate speech does not . . . cause deterioration of the respect accorded free speech." [For] example, the German Constitutional Court has found that preserving the dignity of a dead man outweighed the free expression rights of a living novelist; it has prohibited the publication of a fictional interview involving the wife of the Shah of Iran; it has also enjoined distribution of a docudrama about a gay robber and refused to protect political satire that presented a politician as a rutting pig. [Similarly, it is a crime in Germany for anyone to advocate the violent overthrow of government or to display a swastika in any way that appears] to sympathize with the Third Reich. . . . As a matter of causation, Germany's adoption and enforcement of hate speech laws probably reflect the subordinated position that free speech enjoys vis-à-vis other interests. . . .

h. Post, Racist Speech, Democracy, and the First Amendment, 32 Wm. & Mary L. Rev. 267, 312–317 (1991):

[If] representations in the current literature are accepted as true, [the members of victim groups] confront in public discourse an undifferentiated complex of circumstances in which they are systematically demeaned, stigmatized, ignored; in which the very language of debate resists the articulation of their claims; in which they are harassed, abused, intimidated, and systematically [injured] both individually and collectively. The question [posed is] whether this unacceptable situation would be cured by restraints on speech. . . .

Bluntly expressed, the argument requires us to balance the integrity of public discourse [against] the importance of enhancing the experience [of] members of victim groups. [This] invitation to balance ought to be declined [because] the temptation to balance rests on what might be termed the fallacy of immaculate isolation. The effect on public discourse is acceptable only if it is de minimis, and it is arguably de minimis only when a specific claim is evaluated in isolation from other, similar claims. But no claim is in practice immaculately isolated in this manner. As the flag burning [issue] suggests, there is no shortage of powerful groups contending that uncivil speech [ought] to be "minimally" regulated for highly pressing symbolic reasons. [This] is already plain in the regulations that have proliferated on college campuses, which commonly proscribe not merely speech that degrades persons on the basis of their race, but also [on] the basis of their "color, national origin, religion, sex, sexual orientation, age, handicap, or veteran's status." The claim of de minimis impact loses credibility as the list of claimants to special protection grows longer.

i. R. Kennedy, Nigger 151, 154, 158–159 (2002):

[Proponents] of enhanced hate-speech regulation have typically failed to establish persuasively the asserted predicate for their campaign — that is, that verbal abuse [is] a "rising" [development] demanding countermeasures. Regulationists do cite racist incidents [but] too often the dramatic retelling of an anecdote is permitted to substitute for a more systematic, quantitative analysis. [An] examination of the substance of the regulationists' proposals turns up suggested reforms that are puzzlingly narrow, frighteningly broad, or disturbingly susceptible to discriminatory manipulation. . . .

The cumulative effect of [the Supreme Court's] speech-protective doctrines is a conspicuous toleration of speech [that] many people — in some instances the vast majority of people — find deeply, perhaps even viscerally, obnoxious, including flag burning, pornography, Nazis' taunting of Holocaust survivors, a jacket emblazoned with the phrase "Fuck the Draft," *The Satanic Verses, The Birth of a Nation, The Last Temptation of Christ.* And just as acute wariness [of] censorship has long furthered struggles for freedom of expression in all its many guises, so has resistance against censorship always been an important and positive feature of the great struggles against racist tyranny in the United States, from the fight against slavery to the fight against Jim Crow. For this reason, we may count ourselves fortunate that the anti-hate-speech campaign [has] fizzled and largely subsided. This [effort] was simply not worth the various costs that success would have exacted.

# R.A.V. v. City of St. Paul

505 U.S. 377 (1992)

JUSTICE SCALIA delivered the opinion of the Court.

[After allegedly burning a cross on a black family's lawn, petitioner, a teen-ager, was charged under the St. Paul, Minnesota, Bias-Motivated Crime Ordi-nance, which prohibits the display of a burning cross, a swastika, or other symbol that one knows or has reason to know "arouses anger, alarm or resent-ment in others" on the basis of race, color, creed, religion, or gender. The state supreme court rejected a claim that the ordinance was unconstitutionally overbroad, because the phrase "arouses anger, alarm or resentment in others" had been construed in earlier state cases to limit the ordinance's reach to fighting words within the meaning of *Chaplinsky*. It also rejected the claim that the ordinance was impermissibly content-based, because it was narrowly tailored to serve a compelling governmental interest. The U.S. Supreme Court reversed.]

## I

[We] accept the Minnesota Supreme Court's authoritative statement that the ordinance reaches only those expressions that constitute "fighting words" within the meaning of *Chaplinsky*. [Assuming,] arguendo, that all of the expression reached by the ordinance is proscribable under the "fighting words" doctrine, we nonetheless conclude that the ordinance is facially uncon-stitutional in that it [prohibits] speech solely on the basis of the subjects the speech addresses.

The First Amendment generally prevents government from proscribing speech [because] of disapproval of the ideas expressed. Content-based regula-tions are presumptively invalid. From 1791 to the present, however, our society [has] permitted restrictions upon the content of speech in a few limited areas, which are "of such slight social value as a step to truth that any benefit that may be derived from them is clearly outweighed by the social interest in order and morality." [*Chaplinsky*.] [We] have sometimes said that these categories of expression are "not within the area of constitutionally protected speech." [Such] statements must be taken in context, however. [What] they mean is that these areas of speech can, consistently with the First Amendment, be regulated because of their constitutionally proscribable content (obscenity, defamation, etc.) — not that they are categories of speech entirely invisible to the Constitution, so that they may be made the vehicles for content dis-crimination unrelated to their distinctively proscribable content. Thus, the government may proscribe libel; but it may not make the further content discrimination of proscribing only libel critical of the government, [and although a city may proscribe obscenity, it may not prohibit] only those legally obscene works that contain criticism of the city government. . . .

Even the prohibition against content discrimination [is] not absolute. It applies differently in the context of proscribable speech than in the area of fully protected speech. [When] the basis for the content discrimination consists entirely of the very reason the entire class of speech at issue is proscribable, no significant danger of idea or viewpoint discrimination exists. Such a reason, having been adjudged neutral enough to support exclusion of the entire class of speech from First Amendment protection, is also neutral enough to form the basis of distinction within the class. To illustrate: A State might choose to prohibit only that obscenity which is the most patently offensive in its prurience — i.e., that which involves the most lascivious displays of sexual activity. But it may not prohibit, for example, only that obscenity which includes offensive political messages. And the Federal Government can criminalize only those threats of violence that are directed against the President — since the reasons why threats of violence are outside the First Amendment (protecting individuals from the fear of violence, from the disruption that fear engenders, and from the possibility that the threatened violence will occur) have special force when applied to the person of the President. But the Federal Government may not criminalize only those threats against the President that mention his policy on aid to inner cities. And to take a final example, [a] State may choose to regulate price advertising in one industry but not in others, because the risk of fraud (one of the characteristics of commercial speech that justifies depriving it of full First Amendment protection), is in its view greater there. But a State may not prohibit only that commercial advertising that depicts men in a demeaning fashion. . . .

## II

Applying these principles to the St. Paul ordinance, we conclude that, even as narrowly construed by the Minnesota Supreme Court, the ordinance is facially unconstitutional. Although the phrase in the ordinance, "arouses anger, alarm or resentment in others," has been limited by the Minnesota Supreme Court's construction to reach only those symbols or displays that amount to "fighting words," the remaining, unmodified terms make clear that the ordinance applies only to "fighting words" that insult, or provoke violence, "on the basis of race, color, creed, religion or gender." Displays containing abusive invective, no matter how vicious or severe, are permissible unless they are addressed to one of the specified disfavored topics. Those who wish to use "fighting words" in connection with other ideas — to express hostility, for example, on the basis of political affiliation, union membership, or homosexuality — are not covered. The First Amendment does not permit St. Paul to impose special prohibitions on those speakers who express views on disfavored subjects.

In its practical operation, moreover, the ordinance goes even beyond mere content discrimination, to actual viewpoint discrimination. Displays containing some words — odious racial epithets, for example — would be prohibited to proponents of all views. But "fighting words" that do not themselves invoke race, color, creed, religion, or gender — aspersions upon a person's mother, for example — would seemingly be usable ad libitum in the placards of those arguing in favor of racial, color, etc. tolerance and equality, but could not be used by that speaker's opponents. One could hold up a sign saying, for example, that all "anti-Catholic bigots" are misbegotten; but not that all "papists" are, for that would insult and provoke violence "on the basis of religion." St. Paul has no such authority to license one side of a debate to fight freestyle, while requiring the other to follow Marquis of Queensbury Rules.

What we have here [is] a prohibition of fighting words that contain (as the Minnesota Supreme Court repeatedly emphasized) messages of "bias-motivated" hatred and in particular, as applied to this case, messages "based on virulent notions of racial supremacy." One must wholeheartedly agree with the Minnesota Supreme Court that "it is the responsibility, even the obligation, of diverse communities to confront such notions in whatever form they appear," but the manner of that confrontation cannot consist of selective limitations upon speech. St. Paul's brief asserts that a general "fighting words" law would not meet the city's needs because only a content-specific measure can communicate to minority groups that the "group hatred" aspect of such speech "is not condoned by the majority." The point of the First Amendment is that majority preferences must be expressed in some fashion other than silencing speech on the basis of its content. . . .

The content-based discrimination reflected in the St. Paul ordinance [does] not fall within the exception for content discrimination based on the very reasons why the particular class of speech at issue (here, fighting words) is proscribable. [The] reason why fighting words are categorically excluded from the protection of the First Amendment is not that their content communicates any particular idea, but that their content embodies a particularly intolerable (and socially unnecessary) mode of expressing whatever idea the speaker wishes to convey. St. Paul has not singled out an especially offensive mode of expression — it has not, for example, selected for prohibition only those fighting words that communicate ideas in a threatening (as opposed to a merely obnoxious) manner. Rather, it has proscribed fighting words of whatever manner that communicate messages of racial, gender, or religious intolerance. Selectivity of this sort creates the possibility that the city is seeking to handicap the expression of particular ideas. . . .

Finally, St. Paul [argues] that, even if the ordinance regulates expression based on hostility towards its protected ideological content, this discrimination is nonetheless justified because it is narrowly tailored to serve compelling state interests. Specifically, [it asserts] that the ordinance helps to ensure the basic human rights of members of groups that have historically been subjected to discrimination, including the right of such group members to live in peace where they wish. We do not doubt that these interests are compelling, and that the ordinance can be said to promote them. But the "danger of censorship" presented by a facially content-based statute requires that that weapon be employed only where it is "necessary to serve the asserted [compelling] interest." The existence of adequate content-neutral alternatives thus "undercuts significantly" any defense of such a statute, casting considerable doubt on the government's protestations that "the asserted justification is in fact an accurate description of the purpose and effect of the law." The dispositive question in this case, therefore, is whether content discrimination is reasonably necessary to achieve St. Paul's compelling interests; it plainly is not. An ordinance not limited to the favored topics, for example, would have precisely the same beneficial effect. In fact the only interest distinctively served by the content limitation is that of displaying the city council's special hostility towards the particular biases thus singled out. That is precisely what the First Amendment forbids. . . .

Let there be no mistake about our belief that burning a cross in someone's front yard is reprehensible. But St. Paul has sufficient means at its disposal to prevent such behavior[1] without adding the First Amendment to the fire.

The judgment of the Minnesota Supreme Court is reversed. . . .

JUSTICE WHITE, with whom JUSTICE BLACKMUN and JUSTICE O'CONNOR join, and with whom JUSTICE STEVENS joins except as to Part I(A), concurring in the judgment. . . .

I

A

This Court's decisions have plainly stated that expression falling within certain limited categories so lacks the values the First Amendment was designed to protect that the Constitution affords no protection to that expression. [Nevertheless], the majority holds that the First Amendment protects those narrow categories of expression long held to be undeserving of First Amendment protection — at least to the extent that lawmakers may not regulate some fighting words more strictly than others because of their content. [It] is inconsistent to hold that the government may proscribe an entire category of speech because the content of that speech is evil; but that the government may not treat a subset of that category differently without violating the First

---

1. The conduct might have violated Minnesota statutes [prohibiting "terrorist threats," arson, or criminal damage to property]. [Relocated footnote — EDS.]

Amendment; the content of the subset is by definition worthless and undeserving of constitutional protection. . . .

## II

*overbreadth*

Although I disagree with the Court's analysis, I do agree with its conclusion: The St. Paul ordinance is unconstitutional. However, I would decide the case on overbreadth grounds. [In] construing the St. Paul ordinance, the Minnesota Supreme Court drew upon the definition of fighting words that appears in *Chaplinsky* — words "which by their very utterance inflict injury or tend to incite an immediate breach of the peace." [The court also stated, however,] "the ordinance censors only those displays that one knows or should know will create anger, alarm or resentment based on racial, ethnic, gender or religious bias." [Our] fighting words cases have made clear, however, that such generalized reactions are not sufficient to strip expression of its constitutional protection. The mere fact that expressive activity causes hurt feelings, offense, or resentment does not render the expression unprotected. [Citing, e.g., Cohen v. California; Terminiello v. Chicago.] [Thus, although] the ordinance reaches conduct that is unprotected, it also makes criminal expressive conduct that causes only hurt feelings, offense, or resentment, and is protected by the First Amendment. The ordinance is therefore fatally overbroad and invalid on its face. . . .

JUSTICE BLACKMUN, concurring in the judgment.

I regret what the Court has done in this case. [I] fear that the Court has been distracted from its proper mission by the temptation to decide the issue over "politically correct speech" and "cultural diversity," neither of which is presented here. [I] see no First Amendment values that are compromised by a law that prohibits hoodlums from driving minorities out of their homes by burning crosses on their lawns, but I see great harm in preventing the people of Saint Paul from specifically punishing the race-based fighting words that so prejudice their community.

I concur in the judgment, however, because I agree with Justice White that this particular ordinance reaches beyond fighting words to speech protected by the First Amendment.

JUSTICE STEVENS, concurring in the judgment. . . .

[The] St. Paul ordinance regulates [fighting words] not on the basis of [content], but rather on the basis of the harm the speech causes. [Contrary] to the Court's suggestion, the ordinance regulates [a] subcategory of expression that causes injuries based on "race, color, creed, religion or gender," not a subcategory that involves discussions [of] those characteristics. [Moreover], even if the St. Paul ordinance did regulate fighting words based on its subject matter, such a regulation would, in my opinion, be constitutional. [Subject matter restrictions] generally do not raise the same concerns of government censorship and the distortion of public discourse presented by viewpoint regulations. [Contrary] to the suggestion of the majority, the St. Paul ordinance does not regulate expression based on viewpoint. [The] St. Paul ordinance is evenhanded. In a battle between advocates of tolerance and advocates of intolerance, the ordinance does not prevent either side from hurling fighting words at the other on the basis of their conflicting ideas, but it does bar both sides from hurling such words on the basis of the target's "race, color, creed, religion or gender." To extend the Court's pugilistic metaphor, the St. Paul ordinance simply bans punches "below the belt" — by either party. It does not, therefore, favor one side of any debate. . . .

WISCONSIN v. MITCHELL, 508 U.S. 476 (1993). After viewing the motion picture Mississippi Burning, in which a white man beat a young black who was praying, Mitchell, who is black, urged a group of blacks to assault a young white boy who happened to be walking by. The group, including Mitchell, beat the white boy severely. Mitchell was convicted of aggravated battery, which ordinarily carries a maximum sentence of two years' imprisonment. But because the jury found that Mitchell had intentionally selected his victim because of the boy's race, the maximum sentence for his offense was increased to seven years under the state's hate-crime penalty enhancement statute, which enhances the maximum penalty for an offense whenever the defendant "intentionally selects the person against whom the crime . . . is committed . . . because of the race, religion, color, disability, sexual orientation, national origin or ancestry of that person." The Court overturned the holding of the Wisconsin Supreme Court that the statute violated the first amendment. Chief Justice Rehnquist delivered the opinion for a unanimous Court:

"[A] physical assault is not by any stretch of the imagination expressive conduct protected by the First Amendment. [But this does not end the matter, for] although the statute punishes criminal conduct, it enhances the maximum penalty for conduct motivated by a discriminatory point of view more severely than the same conduct engaged in for some other reason or for no reason at all. Because the only reason for the enhancement is the defendant's discriminatory motive for selecting his victim, Mitchell argues (and the Wisconsin Supreme Court held) that the statute violates the First Amendment by punishing offenders' bigoted beliefs. [But] motive plays the same role under the Wisconsin statute as it does under federal and state antidiscrimination [laws]. Title VII, for example, makes it unlawful for an employer to discriminate against an employee 'because of such individual's race, color, religion, sex, or national origin.' [In Hishon v. King & Spalding, 467 U.S. 69 (1984), we] rejected the argument that Title VII infringed employers' First Amendment rights. . . .

"Nothing in our decision last Term in R.A.V. compels a different result here, [for] whereas the ordinance struck down in R.A.V. was explicitly directed at expression (i.e., 'speech' or 'messages'), the statute in this case is aimed at conduct unprotected by the First Amendment. Moreover, the Wisconsin statute singles out for enhancement bias-inspired conduct because this conduct is thought to inflict greater individual and societal harm. For example, according to the [State], bias-motivated crimes are more likely to provoke retaliatory crimes, inflict distinct emotional harms on their victims, and incite community unrest. The State's desire to redress these perceived harms provides an adequate explanation for its penalty-enhancement provision over and above mere disagreement with offenders' beliefs or biases."

## Note: R.A.V. and Mitchell

1. *The nature of the content-based restriction in* R.A.V. The Court in R.A.V. held that a content-based distinction within a category of expression that can constitutionally be restricted violates the first amendment. Is that sensible? Why does the content-based distinction trouble the Court? Should it matter whether the distinction is based on "subject matter" or "viewpoint"? Consider C. Sunstein, Democracy and the Problem of Free Speech 188–193 (1993):

[The ordinance in *R.A.V.* did] not draw a line between prohibited and permitted points of view. It has not said that one view on an issue [is] permitted, and another proscribed. [To the contrary,] antiwhite and antiblack statements are [treated alike]. In this respect, the law is content-based but viewpoint-neutral. [It] has regulated on the basis of subjects for discussion, not on the basis of viewpoint.

[Of course, the Court in *R.A.V.*] offers a tempting and clever response. [But] the short answer [to the Court's "Marquis of Queensbury" argument] is that the ordinance [does] not embody viewpoint discrimination as that term is ordinarily understood. Viewpoint discrimination occurs if the government takes one side in a debate; it is not established by the fact that in some hypotheticals one side has greater means of expression than another. . . .

We can make the point by reference to statutes that make it a federal crime to threaten the life of the President. The [Court] said in *R.A.V.* that such statutes are permissible. [But] the presidential threat statute involves the same kind of de facto viewpoint discrimination as in *R.A.V.* Imagine the following conversation: John: "I will kill the President." Jill: "I will kill anyone who threatens to kill the President." John has committed a federal crime; Jill has not. . . .

[What *R.A.V.* does involve is a subject matter restriction.] As a class, subject matter restrictions [occupy] a point somewhere between viewpoint-based restrictions and content-neutral ones. [A] subject matter restriction on unprotected speech should probably be upheld if the legislature can plausibly argue that it is counteracting harms rather than ideas. [This standard is easily satisfied in *R.A.V.* because the kinds of fighting words covered by the ordinance have] especially severe social consequences, [and there] is nothing partisan or illegitimate in recognizing that distinctive harms are produced by this unusual class of fighting words.

Assuming a city can constitutionally prohibit all solicitation of contributions within its subway cars, may it permit solicitation of contributions only by groups that address issues relating to abortion? After *R.A.V.*, how would you assess the constitutionality of this policy? This issue, and the issue of subject matter restrictions, are addressed more fully in Chapter V, infra.

2. *Variations on* R.A.V.

a. Consider the following law: "No public official may sue for libel for any statement concerning the performance of her official duties." Is this distinguishable from *R.A.V.*? If so, is it because the "content discrimination is based on the very reason why the particular class of speech at issue is proscribable"? Is it because the state can adequately justify the exemption of defamatory statements concerning the performance of a public official's duties from the "content-neutral" alternative of restricting all defamatory statements governed by New York Times v. Sullivan?

b. After *R.A.V.*, how would you assess the constitutionality of 18 U.S.C. §241, which prohibits any person to "injure, oppress, threaten, or intimidate" others in the enjoyment of their civil rights, as applied to a white person who burns a cross in front of a black person's home?

c. The civil rights laws prohibit an employer from firing an employee because of her race, even though the employer may fire her for many other reasons. Are the civil rights laws invalid after *R.A.V.* because they penalize the employer for his political convictions? That is, if the employer fires an employee because he does not like blacks he is penalized, but if he fires an employee because he does not like Democrats, he is not. Why is *R.A.V.* different? Because the employer is not engaged in "speech"?

d. In United States v. Alvarez, supra, Justices Alito, Scalia, and Thomas voted to uphold the Stolen Valor Act. Can their position be squared with *R.A.V.*?

3. Mitchell *and* R.A.V. On what principle is *Mitchell* consistent with *R.A.V.*? Is the difference that, unlike the defendant in *Mitchell*, the cross-burner was engaged in "speech"? But if cross-burning is "speech," why isn't the act of beating an individual "because of his race" speech as well? After all, the assault "communicates" the defendant's views both to the victim and to observers. Is the assault not "speech" within the meaning of the first amendment because the message is communicated by conduct rather than by words? But then what of cross-burning? Is the difference that in *R.A.V.* the harm was caused by the communicative element of the conduct, whereas in *Mitchell* the harm was caused directly by the conduct itself? But would any of the harms identified by the Court in *Mitchell* to justify the enhanced punishment arise if the act did *not* communicate a message of racial hatred? On the problem of symbolic expression, see Chapter V, infra.

4. *Harassment in the workplace.* Title VII of the 1964 Civil Rights Act prohibits discrimination in conditions of employment by race, religion, national origin, and sex. Courts have held that various kinds of harassment

at work can be so severe that an employee effectively suffers from "discrimination" within the meaning of title VII. Such harassment generally takes two forms. First, there is quid pro quo harassment. This typically arises when an employer conditions an individual's hiring, promotion, or continued employment on sexual involvement, as when a supervisor tells an employee that he will fire her unless she has sex with him. This sort of harassment is generally regarded as an explicit threat that, at least in this context, is not protected by the first amendment.

The second form of harassment is more complex. It may arise when an employer or coworker creates a situation in which the work environment becomes hostile or abusive. Consider the following situations: (a) A white supervisor repeatedly says that black workers are lazy. (b) A male employee repeatedly compliments a female employee on her appearance. (c) Christian employees post pictures of Jesus at their workstations, over the objections of Jewish employees. (d) Male employees post pictures of naked women at their workstations, over the objections of female employees. To what extent, and on what theories, can the government constitutionally prohibit such speech?

Consider the following arguments: (a) Workplace harassment is not speech. It is discrimination. (b) The workplace is for work, not speech. (c) Workplace harassment is private conversation, not public discourse. (d) Workers are a captive audience. (e) Workplace harassment is of "low" first amendment value. For further discussion of workplace harassment, see Estlund, Freedom of Expression in the Workplace and the Problem of Discriminatory Harassment, 75 Tex. L. Rev. 687 (1997); Fallon, Sexual Harassment, Content-Neutrality, and the First Amendment Dog That Didn't Bark, 1994 Sup. Ct. Rev. 1; Volokh, Freedom of Speech and Workplace Harassment, 39 UCLA L. Rev. 1791 (1992); Strauss, Sexist Speech in the Workplace, 25 Harv. C.R.-C.L. L. Rev. 1 (1990).

## Virginia v. Black

538 U.S. 343 (2003)

JUSTICE O'CONNOR announced the judgment of the Court and delivered the opinion of the Court with respect to Parts I, II, and III, and an opinion with respect to Parts IV and V, in which THE CHIEF JUSTICE, JUSTICE STEVENS, and JUSTICE BREYER join.

In this case we consider whether the Commonwealth of Virginia's statute banning cross burning with "an intent to intimidate a person or group of persons" violates the First Amendment. Va. Code Ann. §18.2-423 (1996). We conclude that while a State, consistent with the First Amendment, may ban cross burning carried out with the intent to intimidate, the provision in the Virginia statute treating any cross burning as prima facie evidence of intent to intimidate renders the statute unconstitutional. . . .

I

Respondents Barry Black, Richard Elliott, and Jonathan O'Mara were convicted separately of violating Virginia's cross-burning statute, §18.2-423. That statute provides:

*Statute*

> It shall be unlawful for any person or persons, with the intent of intimidating any person or group of persons, to burn, or cause to be burned, a cross on the property of another, a highway or other public place. . . . Any such burning of a cross shall be prima facie evidence of an intent to intimidate a person or group of persons.

On August 22, 1998, Barry Black led a Ku Klux Klan rally in Carroll County, Virginia. Twenty-five to thirty people attended this gathering, which occurred on private property with the permission of the owner, who was in attendance. The property was located on an open field. . . .

When the sheriff of Carroll County learned that a Klan rally was occurring in his county, he went to observe it from the side of the road. During the approximately one hour that the sheriff was present, about 40 to 50 cars passed the site, a "few" of which stopped to ask the sheriff what was happening on the property. [Rebecca] Sechrist, who was related to the owner of the property where the rally took place, "sat and watched to see wha[t] [was] going on" from the lawn of her in-laws' house. She looked on as the Klan prepared for the gathering and subsequently conducted the rally itself.

During the rally, Sechrist heard Klan members speak about "what they were" and "what they believed in." The speakers "talked real bad about the blacks and the Mexicans." One speaker told the assembled gathering that "he would love to take a .30/.30 and just random[ly] shoot the blacks." The speakers also talked about "President Clinton and Hillary Clinton," and about how their tax money "goes to . . . the black people." Sechrist testified that this language made her "very . . . scared."

At the conclusion of the rally, the crowd circled around a 25- to 30-foot cross. The cross was between 300 and 350 yards away from the road. According to the sheriff, the cross "then all of a sudden . . . went up in a flame." As the cross burned, the Klan played Amazing Grace over the loudspeakers. Sechrist stated that the cross burning made her feel "awful" and "terrible."

When the sheriff observed the cross burning, he informed his deputy that they needed to "find out who's responsible and explain to them that they cannot do this in the State of Virginia." The sheriff then went down the driveway, entered the rally, and asked "who was responsible for burning the cross." Black responded, "I guess I am because I'm the head of the rally." The sheriff then told Black, "[T]here's a law in the State of Virginia that you cannot burn a cross and I'll have to place you under arrest for this."

Black was charged with burning a cross with the intent of intimidating a person or group of persons, in violation of §18.2-423. At his trial, the jury was instructed that "intent to intimidate means the motivation to intentionally put a person or a group of persons in fear of bodily harm. Such fear must arise from the willful conduct of the accused rather than from some mere temperamental timidity of the victim." The trial court also instructed the jury that "the burning of a cross by itself is sufficient evidence from which you may infer the required intent." [The] jury found Black guilty, and fined him $2,500. The Court of Appeals of Virginia affirmed Black's conviction.

On May 2, 1998, respondents Richard Elliott and Jonathan O'Mara, as well as a third individual, attempted to burn a cross on the yard of James Jubilee. Jubilee, an African-American, was Elliott's next-door neighbor in Virginia Beach, Virginia. Four months prior to the incident, Jubilee and his family had moved from California to Virginia Beach. Before the cross burning, Jubilee spoke to Elliott's mother to inquire about shots being fired from behind the Elliott home. Elliott's mother explained to Jubilee that her son shot firearms as a hobby, and that he used the backyard as a firing range.

On the night of May 2, respondents drove a truck onto Jubilee's property, planted a cross, and set it on fire. Their apparent motive was to "get back" at Jubilee for complaining about the shooting in the backyard. Respondents were not affiliated with the Klan. The next morning, as Jubilee was pulling his car out of the driveway, he noticed the partially burned cross approximately 20 feet from his house. After seeing the cross, Jubilee was "very nervous" because he "didn't know what would be the next phase," and because "a cross burned in your yard . . . tells you that it's just the first round."

Elliott and O'Mara were charged with attempted cross burning and conspiracy to commit cross burning. O'Mara pleaded guilty to both counts, reserving the right to challenge the constitutionality of the cross-burning statute. The judge sentenced O'Mara to 90 days in jail and fined him $2,500. The judge also suspended 45 days of the sentence and $1,000 of the fine. At Elliott's trial, the judge [instructed] the jury that the Commonwealth must prove that "the defendant intended to commit cross burning," that "the defendant did a direct act toward the commission of the cross burning," and that "the defendant had the intent of intimidating any person or group of persons." The court did not instruct the jury on the meaning of the word "intimidate," nor on the prima facie evidence provision of §18.2-423. The jury found Elliott guilty of attempted cross burning and acquitted him of conspiracy to commit cross burning. It sentenced Elliott to 90 days in jail and a $2,500 fine. The Court of Appeals of Virginia affirmed the convictions of both Elliott and O'Mara. O'Mara v. Commonwealth, 33 Va. App. 525, 535 S.E.2d 175 (2000).

Each respondent appealed to the Supreme Court of Virginia, arguing that §18.2-423 is facially unconstitutional. The Supreme Court of Virginia consolidated all three cases, and held that the statute is unconstitutional on its face. 262 Va. 764, 553 S.E.2d 738 (2001). It held that the Virginia cross-burning statute "is analytically indistinguishable from the ordinance found unconstitutional in [R.A.V. v. St. Paul]. The Virginia statute, the court held, discriminates on the basis of content since it "selectively chooses only cross burning because of its distinctive message." The court also held that the prima facie evidence provision renders the statute overbroad because "[t]he enhanced probability of prosecution under the statute chills the expression of protected speech." . . .

## II

. . . Burning a cross in the United States is inextricably intertwined with the history of the Ku Klux Klan. [Since at least 1905], cross burnings have been used to communicate both threats of violence and messages of shared ideology. [Often] the Klan used cross burnings as a tool of intimidation and a threat of impending violence. For example, [in] 1941, the Klan burned four crosses in front of a proposed housing project, declaring, "We are here to keep niggers out of your town. . . . When the law fails you, call on us." [These] threats had special force given the long history of Klan violence. [The] Klan continued to use cross burnings to intimidate after World War II. [These] incidents of cross burning, among others, helped prompt Virginia to enact its first version of the cross-burning statute in 1950.

The decision of this Court in Brown v. Board of Education, along with the civil rights movement of the 1950's and 1960's, sparked another outbreak of Klan violence. These acts of violence included bombings, beatings, shootings, stabbings, and mutilations. Members of the Klan burned crosses on the lawns of those associated with the civil rights movement, assaulted the Freedom Riders, bombed churches, and murdered blacks as well as whites whom the Klan viewed as sympathetic toward the civil rights movement.

Throughout the history of the Klan, cross burnings have also remained potent symbols of shared group identity and ideology. The burning cross became a symbol of the Klan itself and a central feature of Klan gatherings. [The] Klan has often published its newsletters and magazines under the name The Fiery Cross. [At] Klan gatherings across the country, cross burning became the climax of the rally or the initiation. [Throughout] the Klan's history, the Klan continued to use the burning cross in their ritual ceremonies. [For] its own members, the cross was a sign of celebration and ceremony. . .

To this day, regardless of whether the message is a political one or whether the message is also meant to intimidate, the burning of a cross is a "symbol of hate." And while cross burning sometimes carries no intimidating message, at other times the intimidating message is the *only* message conveyed. For example, when a cross burning is directed at a particular person not affiliated with the Klan, the burning cross often serves as a message of intimidation, designed to inspire in the victim a fear of bodily harm. Moreover, the history of violence associated with the Klan shows that the possibility of injury or death is not just hypothetical. The person who burns a cross directed at a particular person often is making a serious threat, meant to coerce the victim to comply with the Klan's wishes unless the victim is willing to risk the wrath of the Klan. Indeed, as the cases of respondents Elliott and O'Mara indicate, individuals without Klan affiliation who wish to threaten or menace another person sometimes use cross burning because of this association between a burning cross and violence.

In sum, while a burning cross does not inevitably convey a message of intimidation, often the cross burner intends that the recipients of the message fear for their lives. And when a cross burning is used to intimidate, few if any messages are more powerful.

## III

A . . .

The protections afforded by the First Amendment [are] not absolute, and we have long recognized that the government may regulate certain categories of expression consistent with the Constitution. The First Amendment permits "restrictions upon the content of speech in a few limited areas, which are 'of such slight social value as a step to truth that any benefit that may be derived from them is clearly outweighed by the social interest in order and morality.'" [R.A.V., quoting *Chaplinsky*]. . . .

Thus, for example, a State may punish [a] "true threat." [*Watts*.] "True threats" encompass those statements where the speaker means to communicate a serious expression of an intent to commit an act of unlawful violence to a particular individual or group of individuals. The speaker need not actually intend to carry out the threat. Rather, a prohibition on true threats "protect[s] individuals from the fear of violence" and "from the disruption that fear engenders," in addition to protecting people "from the possibility that the threatened violence will occur." Intimidation in the constitutionally proscribable sense of the word is a type of true threat, where a speaker directs a threat to a person or group of persons with the intent of placing the victim in fear of bodily harm or death. Respondents do not contest that some cross burnings fit within this meaning of intimidating speech, and rightly so. As noted in Part II, *supra*, the history of cross burning in this country shows that cross burning is often intimidating, intended to create a pervasive fear in victims that they are a target of violence.

B

The Supreme Court of Virginia ruled that in light of *R.A.V.*, even if it is constitutional to ban cross burning in a content-neutral manner, the Virginia cross-burning statute is unconstitutional because it discriminates on the basis of content and viewpoint. It is true [that] the burning of a cross is symbolic expression. The reason why the Klan burns a cross at its rallies, or individuals place a burning cross on someone else's lawn, is that the burning cross represents the message that the speaker wishes to communicate. Individuals burn crosses as opposed to other means of communication because cross burning carries a message in an effective and dramatic manner.

The fact that cross burning is symbolic expression, however, does not resolve the constitutional question. [In] R.A.V., we held that a local ordinance that banned certain symbolic conduct, including cross burning, when done with the knowledge that such conduct would "'arouse anger, alarm or resentment in others on the basis of race, color, creed, religion or gender'" was unconstitutional. We held that the ordinance did not pass constitutional muster because it discriminated on the basis of content by targeting only those individuals who "provoke violence" on a basis specified in the law. The ordinance did not cover "[t]hose who wish to use 'fighting words' in connection with other ideas — to express hostility, for example, on the basis of political affiliation, union membership, or homosexuality." This content-based discrimination was unconstitutional because it allowed the city "to impose special prohibitions on those speakers who express views on disfavored subjects."

We did not hold in R.A.V. that the First Amendment prohibits *all* forms of content-based discrimination within a proscribable area of speech. Rather, we specifically stated that some types of content discrimination did not violate the First Amendment: "When the basis for the content discrimination consists entirely of the very reason the entire class of speech at issue is proscribable, no significant danger of idea or viewpoint discrimination exists. Such a reason, having been adjudged neutral enough to support exclusion of the entire class of speech from First Amendment protection, is also neutral enough to form the basis of distinction within the class."

Indeed, we noted that it would be constitutional to ban only a particular type of threat: "[T]he Federal Government can criminalize only those threats of violence that are directed against the President . . . since the reasons why threats of violence are outside the First Amendment . . . have special force when applied to the person of the President." And a State may "choose to prohibit only that obscenity which is the most patently offensive *in its prurience — i.e.*, that which involves the most lascivious displays of sexual activity." Consequently, while the holding of R.A.V. does not permit a State to ban only obscenity based on "offensive *political* messages," or "only those threats against the President that mention his policy on aid to inner cities," the First Amendment permits content discrimination "based on the very reasons why the particular class of speech at issue . . . is proscribable."

Similarly, Virginia's statute does not run afoul of the First Amendment insofar as it bans cross burning with intent to intimidate. Unlike the statute at issue in R.A.V., the Virginia statute does not single out for opprobrium only that speech directed toward "one of the specified disfavored topics." It does not matter whether an individual burns a cross with intent to intimidate because of the victim's race, gender, or religion, or because of the victim's "political affiliation, union membership, or homosexuality." . . .

The First Amendment permits Virginia to outlaw cross burnings done with the intent to intimidate because burning a cross is a particularly virulent form of intimidation. Instead of prohibiting all intimidating messages, Virginia may choose to regulate this subset of intimidating messages in light of cross burning's long and pernicious history as a signal of impending violence. Thus, just as a State may regulate only that obscenity which is the most obscene due to its prurient content, so too may a State choose to prohibit only those forms of intimidation that are most likely to inspire fear of bodily harm. A ban on cross burning carried out with the intent to intimidate is fully consistent with our holding in *R.A.V.* and is proscribable under the First Amendment.

## IV

The Supreme Court of Virginia ruled in the alternative that Virginia's cross-burning statute was unconstitutionally overbroad due to its provision stating that "[a]ny such burning of a cross shall be prima facie evidence of an intent to intimidate a person or group of persons." [The] Supreme Court of Virginia has . . . stated that "the act of burning a cross alone, with no evidence of intent to intimidate, [will] suffice for arrest and prosecution and will insulate the Commonwealth from a motion to strike the evidence at the end of its case-in-chief." . . .

The prima facie evidence provision . . . renders the statute unconstitutional. [The] prima facie provision strips away the very reason why a State may ban cross burning with the intent to intimidate. The prima facie evidence provision permits a jury to convict in every cross-burning case in which defendants exercise their constitutional right not to put on a defense. And even where a defendant [presents] a defense, the prima facie evidence provision makes it more likely that the jury will find an intent to intimidate regardless of the particular facts of the case. The provision permits the Commonwealth to arrest, prosecute, and convict a person based solely on the fact of cross burning itself.

It is apparent that the provision as so interpreted "'would create an unacceptable risk of the suppression of ideas.'" The act of burning a cross may mean that a person is engaging in constitutionally proscribable intimidation. But that same act may mean only that the person is engaged in core political speech. The prima facie evidence provision in this statute blurs the line between these two meanings of a burning cross. As interpreted by the jury instruction, the provision chills constitutionally protected political speech because of the possibility that a State will prosecute — and potentially convict — somebody engaging only in lawful political speech at the core of what the First Amendment is designed to protect.

*Protected in this sense ★*

As the history of cross burning indicates, a burning cross is not always intended to intimidate. Rather, sometimes the cross burning is a statement of ideology, a symbol of group solidarity. It is a ritual used at Klan gatherings, and it is used to represent the Klan itself. Thus, "[b]urning a cross at a political rally would almost certainly be protected expression." . . .

The prima facie provision makes no effort to distinguish among these different types of cross burnings. It [may] be true that a cross burning, even at a political rally, arouses a sense of anger or hatred among the vast majority of citizens who see a burning cross. But this sense of anger or hatred is not sufficient to ban all cross burnings. [The] prima facie evidence provision in this case ignores all of the contextual factors that are necessary to decide whether a particular cross burning is intended to intimidate. The First Amendment does not permit such a shortcut. . . .

JUSTICE STEVENS, concurring.

Cross burning with "an intent to intimidate" unquestionably qualifies as the kind of threat that is unprotected by the First Amendment. For the reasons stated in the separate opinions that Justice White and I wrote in *R.A.V.*, that simple proposition provides a sufficient basis for upholding the basic prohibition in the Virginia statute even though it does not cover other types of threatening expressive conduct. With this observation, I join Justice O'Connor's opinion.

JUSTICE THOMAS, dissenting.

In every culture, certain things acquire meaning well beyond what outsiders can comprehend. That goes for both the sacred, see Texas v. Johnson [Chapter 5.C, infra] (describing the unique position of the American flag in our Nation's 200 years of history), and the profane. I believe that cross burning is the paradigmatic example of the latter.

Although I agree with the majority's conclusion that it is constitutionally permissible to "ban . . . cross burning carried out with intent to intimidate," I believe that the majority errs in imputing an expressive component to the activity in question. [In] our culture, cross burning has almost invariably meant lawlessness and understandably instills in its victims well-grounded fear of physical violence. [This] statute prohibits only conduct, not expression. And, just as one cannot burn down someone's house to make a political point and then seek refuge in the First Amendment, those who hate cannot terrorize and intimidate to make their point. In light of my conclusion that the statute here addresses only conduct, there is no need to analyze it under any of our First Amendment tests. [Because] I would uphold the validity of this statute, I respectfully dissent.

---

* Justice Scalia, joined by Justice Thomas, also filed a separate opinion, concurring in part and dissenting in part.

JUSTICE SOUTER, with whom JUSTICE KENNEDY and JUSTICE GINSBURG join, concurring in the judgment in part and dissenting in part.

I agree with the majority that the Virginia statute makes a content-based distinction within the category of punishable intimidating or threatening expression, [but] I disagree that [the Virginia statute can be saved even in part] from unconstitutionality under the holding in R.A.V. . . .

The [prohibition] of cross burning with intent to intimidate selects a symbol with particular content from the field of all proscribable expression meant to intimidate. [The] issue is whether the statutory prohibition restricted to this symbol falls within one of the exceptions to R.A.V.'s general condemnation of limited content-based proscription within a broader category of expression proscribable generally. [R.A.V.] defines the special virulence exception [this] way: prohibition by subcategory [is] constitutional if it is made "entirely" on the "basis" of "the very reason" that "the entire class of speech at issue is proscribable" at all. The Court explained that when the subcategory is confined to the most obviously proscribable instances, "no significant danger of idea or viewpoint discrimination exists." . . .

The first example of permissible distinction is for a prohibition of obscenity unusually offensive "in its prurience." [Distinguishing] obscene publications on this basis does not suggest discrimination on the basis of the message conveyed. The opposite is true, however, when a general prohibition of intimidation is rejected in favor of a distinct proscription of intimidation by cross burning. The cross may have been selected because of its special power to threaten, but it may also have been singled out because of disapproval of its message of white supremacy, either because a legislature thought white supremacy was a pernicious doctrine or because it found that dramatic, public espousal of it was a civic embarrassment. Thus, there is no kinship between the cross-burning statute and the core prurience example.

Nor does this case present any analogy to the statute prohibiting threats against the President. [The] content discrimination in that statute [reflects] the special risks and costs associated with threatening the President. Again, however, threats against the President are not generally identified by reference to the content of any message that may accompany the threat, let alone any viewpoint, and there is no obvious correlation in fact between victim and message. [Differential] treatment of threats against the President, then, selects nothing but special risks, not special messages. A content-based proscription of cross burning, on the other hand, may be a subtle effort to ban not only the intensity of the intimidation cross burning causes when done to threaten, but also the particular message of white supremacy that is broadcast even by non-threatening cross burning. [I] thus read R.A.V.'s examples of the particular virulence exception as covering prohibitions that are not clearly associated with a particular viewpoint, and that are consequently different from the Virginia statute. . . .

## Note: R.A.V. and Black

Consider the following views:

a. Schauer, Intentions, Conventions, and the First Amendment: The Case of Cross-Burning, 2003 Sup. Ct. Rev. 197, 206–208:

> [Because] Justice O'Connor saw the Virginia statute as singling [out] intimidation with special intimidating power, she concluded [that] the statute was [a] constitutionally permissible prohibition on unprotected intimidation. [But] a closer look at the dynamics of what causes cross-burning to be especially intimidating [makes] the Court's distinction between *Black* and *R.A.V.* difficult to accept. What makes cross-burning more intimidating than, say, flag-burning or leaf-burning, [is] a function of the racist [point] of view it embodies. [Virginia's] belief that burning a cross is especially intimidating is based solely on the viewpoint-based judgment that symbols with one point of view have effects that symbols with another point of view do not have.

b. Gey, A Few Questions About Cross Burning, Intimidation, and Free Speech, 80 Notre Dame L. Rev. 1287, 1373–1374 (2005):

> *Black* is just one example of a disturbing [proliferation] of alternative First Amendment constructs to regulate antisocial speech. These constructs appear uncoordinated by any central principle and seem limited only by the ingenuity of plaintiffs and prosecutors in fitting familiar examples of antisocial speech into the new regulatory patterns. [Some] overriding constitutional framework is needed to limit the expansion of the new categories and constrain the use of flexible terms such as "intimidation" and "terrorism." The *Brandenburg* [explicitness and immediate harm] paradigm was devised to serve precisely that function, if the courts would only use it.

c. In the incitement situation, the Court, following the lead of Judge Learned Hand in *Masses*, seems to require that for incitement of unlawful conduct to come within the "low" value category of express incitement the incitement must be express. Is *Black*'s treatment of threats consistent with that requirement? Is a burning cross an *express* threat? Does it make any sense to require express incitement but not express threats? See Taylor, Free Expression and Expressiveness, 33 N.Y.U. Rev. L. & Soc. Change 375 (2009). Is a noose on someone's front lawn equivalent to a burning cross?

## Note: Pornography and the Victimization of Women

1. *A model statute.* Consider the constitutionality of the following law:

> Pornography is the sexually explicit subordination of women, graphically depicted, whether in words or pictures, that also includes one or more of the

following: (i) women are presented dehumanized as sexual objects, things or commodities; (ii) women are presented as sexual objects who enjoy pain, humiliation or rape; (iii) women are presented as sexual objects tied up or cut up or mutilated or physically hurt; (iv) women are presented in postures of sexual submission or sexual servility, including by inviting penetration; or (v) women are presented as whores by nature. No person may sell, exhibit, or distribute pornography.

2. *Evaluation.* Consider the following views:
a. MacKinnon, Not a Moral Issue, 2 Yale L. & Soc. Poly. Rev. 321, 322–324 (1984):

Obscenity law is concerned with morality, specifically morals from the male point of view, meaning the standpoint of male dominance. The feminist critique of pornography is politics, specifically politics from the women's point of view, meaning the standpoint of the subordination of women to men. Morality here means good and evil; politics means power and powerlessness. Obscenity is a moral idea; pornography is a political practice. The two concepts represent entirely different things. Nudity, explicitness, excess of candor, [these] qualities bother obscenity law when sex is depicted or portrayed. [Sex] forced on real women so that it can be sold at a profit to be forced on other real women; women's bodies trussed and maimed and raped and made into things to be hurt and obtained and accessed and this presented as the nature of women; the coercion that is visible and the coercion that has become invisible — this and more bothers feminists about pornography. Obscenity as such probably does little harm; pornography causes attitudes and behaviors of violence and discrimination which define the treatment and status of half of the population.

b. Clark, Liberalism and Pornography, in Pornography and Censorship 52–57 (D. Copp and S. Wendells eds., 1983):

[Pornography] has very little to do with sex, [but] it has everything to do with [the] use of sexuality as an instrument of active oppression. [Pornography is] a species of hate literature. [It depicts] women [as inviting] humiliating, degrading, and violently abusive [treatment]. [It feeds] traditional male phantasies [and glorifies] the traditional advantages men have enjoyed in relation to exploitation of female sexuality. [Pornography] is a method of socialization; [it] "teaches society to view women as less than human." [It is thus an] affront to [the dignity of women] as equal persons. [Moreover,] role modeling has a powerful effect on human behavior. [People] tend to act out and operationalize the behavior that they see typically acted out around them. [While] the liberal principle behind opposition to censorship is based on a recognition that desirable social change requires public access to information which challenges the beliefs and practices of the status quo, what it does not acknowledge is that information which supports the status quo through providing role models which advocate the use or threat of coercion as a technique of social control directed at a clearly identifiable group depicted as inferior, subordinate, and subhuman, works against the

Does either of these four-factor analyses adequately explain (or at least describe) the Court's decisions?

Consider the following evaluations: (1) The "low" value doctrine demonstrates the sharply limited efficacy of judicial controls on censorship by the majority, for it defines speech as unworthy of protection in precisely those cases where it most seriously threatens majority values and where protection is thus most needed. (2) The "low" value doctrine has served a salutary function, for it has operated as a critical "safety valve," enabling the Court to deal sensibly with somewhat harmful, but relatively insignificant, speech without running the risk of diluting the protection accorded expression at the very heart of the guarantee. (3) The Court's use of the "low" value theory "has been marked by vacillation and uncertainty." It is a highly "result-oriented" approach that is susceptible to an endless expansion of the list of "low" value categories "whenever another kind of expression [gains] a renewed disfavor." To the extent that fighting words, commercial speech, obscenity, and libel are "subject to regulation, it should be because they cause harm and not because they are presumed to be low in communicative value." Shaman, The Theory of Low-Value Speech, 48 S.M.U. L. Rev. 297, 339, 348 (1995).

Low
value
theory

# V

# Content-Neutral Restrictions: Limitations on the Means of Communication and the Problem of Content-Neutrality

Content-neutral restrictions limit expression without regard to its content. They turn neither on their face nor as applied on the content or communicative impact of speech. Such restrictions encompass a broad spectrum of limitations on expressive activity. As we will see, there is dispute about precisely which restrictions are content neutral, but the category arguably includes restrictions ranging from a prohibition on the use of loudspeakers, to a ban on billboards, to a limitation on campaign contributions, to a prohibition on the mutilation of draft cards. To what extent, and in what manner, do content-neutral restrictions implicate the concerns and values underlying the first amendment? How do they differ in this regard from content-based restrictions? Should the doctrines devised to govern content-based restrictions also govern content-neutral restrictions? In exploring these and related questions, this section begins with a search for general principles and then examines four specific areas: the right to a public forum; symbolic speech; regulation of the electoral process; and litigation, association, and the right not to speak. Throughout, this section questions the meaning of "content-neutrality" and tests the occasionally elusive line between content-based and content-neutral restrictions.

## A. GENERAL PRINCIPLES

**SCHNEIDER v. STATE, 308 U.S. 147 (1939).** Appellants, who distributed leaflets on a public street announcing a protest meeting, were convicted or censorship in the city's actions. Nor is there any reason to believe that the overall communications market in San Diego is inadequate. [Thus,] nothing in this record suggests that the ordinance poses a threat to the interests protected by the First Amendment." Chief Justice Burger and Justice Rehnquist agreed with Justice Stevens because "there has been no suggestion that billboards [advance] any particular viewpoint or issue disproportionately." The remaining justices found it unnecessary to address this issue.

**CITY OF LADUE v. GILLEO, 512 U.S. 43 (1994).** In a unanimous opinion, the Court held that a city could not constitutionally prohibit homeowners from displaying signs on their property. The purpose of the ordinance was to minimize "visual clutter." At issue was respondent's desire to place on her front lawn a 24-by-36-inch sign printed with the words "Say No to War in the Persian Gulf, Call Congress Now." Justice Stevens delivered the opinion of the Court:

"Ladue has almost completely foreclosed a venerable means of communication that is both unique and important. [Although] prohibitions foreclosing entire media may be completely free of content or viewpoint discrimination, the danger they pose to freedom of speech is readily apparent — by eliminating a common means of speaking, such measures can suppress too much speech. . . .

"Ladue contends, however, that its ordinance is a mere regulation of the 'time, place, or manner' of speech because residents remain free to convey their desired messages by other means, such as hand-held signs, 'letters, handbills, flyers, telephone calls, newspaper advertisements, bumper stickers, speeches, and neighborhood or community meetings.' However, even regulations [of] time, place, or manner [must] 'leave open ample alternative channels for communication.' In this case, we are not persuaded that adequate substitutes exist for the important medium of speech that Ladue has closed off.

"Displaying a sign from one's own residence often carries a message quite distinct from placing the same sign someplace else, or conveying the same text or picture by other means. Precisely because of their location, such signs provide information about the identity of the 'speaker.' [Moreover, residential] signs are an unusually cheap and convenient form of communication. Especially for persons of modest means or limited mobility, a yard or window sign may have no practical substitute. . . .

"A special respect for individual liberty in the home has long been part of our culture and our law; that principle has special resonance when the government seeks to constrain a person's ability to speak there. Most Americans would be understandably dismayed, given that tradition, to learn that it was illegal to display from their window [a] sign expressing their political views. . . .

"Our decision [by] no means leaves the City powerless to address the ills that may be associated with residential signs. [We] are not confronted here with mere regulations short of a ban. [We] are confident that more temperate measures could in large part satisfy Ladue's stated regulatory needs without harm to the First Amendment rights of its citizens. As currently framed, however, the ordinance abridges those rights."

**BARTNICKI v. VOPPER, 532 U.S. 514 (2001).** During contentious collective-bargaining negotiations between a union representing teachers at a public high school and the local school board, an unidentified person intercepted and recorded a cell phone conversation between the union negotiator and the union president. Vopper, a radio commentator, played a tape of the intercepted conversation on his public affairs talk show in connection with news reports about the settlement. The Court held that Vopper could not be held liable for damages under federal or state wiretap laws for broadcasting the unlawfully recorded phone call.

Justice Stevens delivered the opinion of the Court. The Court accepted that the information on the tapes had been obtained unlawfully by an unknown party, that Vopper had played no part in the illegal interception, that he knew or should have known that the phone call had been intercepted unlawfully, and that "the subject matter of the conversation was a matter of public concern."

The Court explained that the relevant statutes, which prohibited the unauthorized disclosure of unlawfully intercepted communications, were "content-neutral" laws of general applicability. The Court then defined the issue as follows: "Where the punished publisher of information has obtained the information [in] a manner lawful in itself but from a source who has obtained it unlawfully, may the government punish the ensuing publication of that information?" The Court explained that, as a general proposition, "'if a newspaper unlawfully obtains truthful information about a matter of public significance then [government] officials may not constitutionally punish publication of the information, absent a need of the highest order'" [quoting Smith v. Daily Mail Publishing Co.].

The Court identified "two interests served by the statutes — first, the interest in removing an incentive for parties to intercept private conversations, and second, the interest in minimizing the harm to persons whose conversations have been illegally intercepted." With respect to the first of these interests, the Court reasoned that "the normal method of deterring unlawful conduct is to impose an appropriate punishment on the person who engages in it. If the sanctions that presently attach to [these unlawful acts] do not provide sufficient deterrence, perhaps those sanctions should be made more severe. But it would be quite remarkable to hold that speech by a law-abiding possessor of information can be suppressed in order to deter conduct by a non-law abiding third party."

The Court conceded that the second interest "is considerably stronger" because "privacy of communications is an important interest" and "the fear literature broadcast in the streets [since] such activity bears no necessary rela-tionship to the freedom to speak, write, print or distribute information or opinion."

b. "[One] is not to have the exercise of his liberty of expression in appropriate places abridged on the plea that it may be exercised in some other place." Suppose a city permits soapbox orators to make public speeches in only four of its six municipal parks.

c. "That more people may be more easily and cheaply reached by sound trucks [is] not enough to call forth constitutional protection for what those charged with public welfare reasonably think is a nuisance when [alternative] means of publicity are open." Is this consistent with b? Should the existence of alternative means of communication affect the balance?

d. "The dangers of [door-to-door distribution of leaflets] can so easily be controlled by traditional legal methods [that] stringent prohibition can serve no purpose but [the] naked restriction of the dissemination of ideas." Should it matter that the state may be able to achieve part or all of its goals through alternative means that may have a less restrictive effect on expression?

e. "It would be fantastic to suggest that a city has power [to] forbid house-to-house canvassing generally, but that the Constitution prohibits the inclusion in such prohibition of door-to-door [distribution of] printed matter." Should it matter whether a law specifically restricts expression or restricts a broader range of activities in a manner that has only an incidental effect on expression?

f. "There has been no suggestion that billboards heretofore have advanced any particular viewpoint or issue disproportionately. . . . Thus, the ideas billboard advertisers have been presenting are not *relatively* disadvantaged vis-à-vis the messages of those who heretofore have chosen other methods of spreading their views." Should it matter whether a content-neutral restriction has "content-differential" effects?

### Note: The Meaning of "Content-Neutrality"

In most cases, a law's content-neutrality is self-evident. There are several situations, however, in which the matter is more complex:

1. *Communicative impact.* A law may be content-neutral on its face but may turn in application on communicative impact — that is, "on how people will react to what the speaker is saying." J. Ely, Democracy and Distrust 111 (1980). Consider, for example, a law declaring it unlawful for any person to "disturb the peace" by making any public speech that "may cause a hostile audience response." Although such laws are "neutral" on their face, the Court has analyzed them as content-based because it is the content of the message that triggers the restriction. Recall, for example, *Terminiello, Cantwell,* and *Edwards,* Chapter II.B, supra. For analysis of this issue, see Stone, Content Regulation and the First Amendment, 25 Wm. & Mary L. Rev. 189, 207–217

(1983); Rubenfeld, The First Amendment's Purpose, 53 Stan. L. Rev. 767
(2001).

2. *Secondary effects.* A law may be content-based on its face but may be
defended in terms that are unrelated to communicative impact. In *Renton*,
Chapter IV.F, supra, for example, the Court characterized a zoning ordinance
that restricted the location of movie theaters that exhibit movies emphasizing
"specified sexual activities" as "content-neutral" because it was defended not in
terms of the communicative impact of the restricted expression but in terms of
"the secondary effects of such theaters on the surrounding community."

In a separate concurring opinion in Boos v. Barry, 485 U.S. 312 (1988),
Justice Brennan elaborated on his *Renton* dissent:

> I [register] my continuing disagreement with the proposition that an otherwise
> content-based restriction on speech can be recast as "content-neutral" if the
> restriction "aims" at "secondary effects" of the speech. [Such] secondary effects
> offer countless excuses for content-based suppression of political speech. No
> doubt a plausible argument could be made that the political gatherings of
> some parties are more likely than others to attract large crowds causing conges-
> tion, that picketing for certain causes is more likely than other picketing to cause
> visual clutter, or that speakers delivering a particular message are more likely
> than others to attract an unruly audience. [The] *Renton* analysis [plunges] courts
> into [a morass of] notoriously hazardous and indeterminate inquiry. [This] inde-
> terminacy is hardly *Renton*'s worst [flaw, however], for the root problem [is that
> *Renton*] relies on the dubious proposition that a statute which on its face dis-
> criminates based on the content of speech aims not at content but at some
> secondary effect that does not itself affect the operation of the statute.

In decisions since *Renton*, the Court seems to have backed away from the
*Renton* analysis or at least interpreted *Renton* narrowly. In *Boos*, for example,
the Court, in invalidating an ordinance prohibiting the display of any sign
within five hundred feet of a foreign embassy if the sign tends to bring the
foreign government into disrepute, rejected the government's argument that
the ordinance was "content-neutral" under *Renton* because "the real concern
is a secondary effect, namely, our international law obligation to shield diplomats from speech that offends their dignity."

The Court visited the issue again in City of Cincinnati v. Discovery
Network, 507 U.S. 410 (1993), in which the Court invalidated a prohibition
on the use of newsracks on public property for the distribution of commercial
handbills. Although the ordinance on its face distinguished between
commercial and noncommercial publications, the city argued that the challenged prohibition was content-neutral "because the [city's] interests in safety
and esthetics [are] entirely unrelated to the content of [the] publications." The
Court, in an opinion by Justice Stevens, rejected this argument:

> The argument is unpersuasive because the very basis for the regulation is the
> difference in content between ordinary newspapers and commercial speech.

[Under] the city's newsrack policy, whether any particular newsrack falls within the ban is determined by the content of the publication resting inside the news-rack. Thus, by any commonsense understanding of the term, the ban [is] "content-based." [The city's] reliance on *Renton* is misplaced. [We] upheld the regulation [in *Renton*] largely because it was justified, not by an interest in suppressing adult films, but by the city's concern for the "secondary effects" of such theaters on the surrounding neighborhoods. In contrast to the speech at issue in *Renton*, there are no secondary effects attributable to newsracks [containing commercial handbills] that distinguish them from the newsracks Cincinnati permits to remain on its sidewalks.

In City of Los Angeles v. Alameda Books, 535 U.S. 425 (2002), the Court revisited the issue of content-neutrality and secondary effects. Like *Renton*, *Alameda Books* concerned the constitutionality of a zoning ordinance that regulated the location of adult establishments. Although there was no majority opinion, four justices expressly rejected the notion that such regulations should be characterized as "content-neutral." Justice Kennedy described as a "fiction" *Renton*'s designation of such ordinances as "content-neutral" and explained that "whether a statute is content neutral or content based is something that can be determined on the face of it; if the statute describes speech by content, then it is content based." Justice Souter added that "when a law applies selectively only to speech of particular content, the more precisely the content is identified, the greater is the opportunity for government censorship."

3. *Impermissible motive.* A law may be content-neutral on its face but may have been enacted with the purpose of suppressing a particular message. Consider, for example, a law prohibiting any person to destroy a draft card, enacted for the purpose of punishing those individuals who publicly burn their draft cards to protest national policy. Consider McDonald, Speech and Distrust: Rethinking the Content Approach to Protecting the Freedom of Expression, 81 Notre Dame L. Rev. 1347, 1387 (2006):

> Consider [laws] currently being enacted by states that prohibit picketing and demonstrating within a certain distance of funerals shortly before and after a service. These laws are being passed in response to an alleged pastor and members of a church who are using funerals of American soldiers killed in Iraq as opportunities to get out their message that the war and soldiers' deaths constitute divine retribution for the country's tolerant attitude towards homosexuals. Apparently, the church group assembles across the street from such funerals, engaging in expletive-laden chants and displaying signs containing messages such as "Thank God for Dead Soldiers," "Thank God for IEDs" (improvised explosive devices that frequently kill soldiers), and "God Hates Fags."

Should such laws be analyzed as content-based or content-neutral?

4. *Content-differential effects.* Some laws are content-neutral on their face but have content-differential effects. Recall, for example, Justice Black's

observation in *Struthers* that "door to door distribution of circulars is essential to the poorly financed causes of little people." To what extent should this factor convert a content-neutral regulation into one that is treated as content-based? See Williams, Content Discrimination and the First Amendment, 139 U. Pa. L. Rev. 615 (1991) (disparate impact should trigger content-based analysis); Stone, Content-Neutral Restrictions, 54 U. Chi. L. Rev. 46, 81–86 (1987) (disparate impact should merely be a relevant factor in content-neutral analysis).

5. *Speaker-based restrictions.* Is an injunction prohibiting specifically named antiabortion protestors from demonstrating near an abortion clinic content-based or content-neutral? In Madsen v. Women's Health Center, Inc., 512 U.S. 753 (1994), the Court held that such an injunction, issued after the specifically named petitioners had previously violated a narrower order enjoining them from blocking access to the clinic, was content-neutral:

> We [reject] petitioners' contention that the [order is content-based because it] restricts only the speech of antiabortion protestors. [The] injunction, by its very nature, applies only to a particular group. [It] does so, however, because of the group's past actions in the context of a specific dispute. [The] fact that the injunction in the present case did not prohibit activities of those demonstrating in favor of abortion is justly attributable to the lack of any similar demonstrations by those in favor of abortion, and of any consequent request that their demonstrations be regulated by injunction.

Suppose the injunction had prohibited "any antiabortion protestor from demonstrating within thirty-six feet of an abortion clinic"? Would that be content-neutral? Speaker-based restrictions, which treat some speakers differently than others but define the distinction in terms other than content, do not fit neatly within the Court's content-based/content-neutral distinction. For example, suppose a city bans all door-to-door canvassing after 8:00 P.M., except for canvassing by veterans groups. How should such a law be analyzed? For commentary on speaker-based restrictions, see Stone, Content Regulation, supra, at 244–251. See also Regan v. Taxation with Representation, Perry Educators' Association v. Perry Local Educators' Association, and Cornelius v. NAACP Legal Defense and Educational Fund, discussed later in this chapter.

6. *Content or Not?* In McCullen v. Coakley, 135 S. Ct. 2018 (2014), the Supreme Court considered the constitutionality of a Massachusetts statute that made it a crime for any person knowingly to stand on a "public way or sidewalk" within thirty-five feet of an entrance or driveway to any place, other than a hospital, where abortions are performed. The law was designed to eliminate clashes between abortion opponents and advocates of abortion rights that had occurred outside clinics where abortions were performed. The law was challenged by individuals "who approach and talk to women outside such facilities,

attempting to dissuade them from having abortions." According to testimony presented at the trial, such individuals have, over time, "persuaded hundreds of women to forego abortions." The Act exempted persons entering or leaving the facility, employees or agents of the facility, law enforcement and similar personnel, and persons using the sidewalk area solely for the purpose of reaching another destination. The Court, in an opinion by Chief Justice Roberts, invalidated the law as an unconstitutional content-neutral restriction of speech in a traditional public forum.

The challengers also argued, however, that the law was an unconstitutional content-based restriction of speech, because it applied only at facilities that performed abortions and therefore had a disparate impact on those who oppose abortion. Chief Justice Roberts rejected this argument:

"To begin, the Act does not draw content based distinctions on its face. The Act would be content based if it required 'enforcement authorities' to 'examine the content of the message that is conveyed to determine whether' a violation has occurred. But it does not. Whether petitioners violate the Act 'depends' not 'on what they say,' but simply on where they say it. Indeed, petitioners can violate the Act merely by standing in a buffer zone, without displaying a sign or uttering a word.

"It is true, of course, that by limiting the buffer zones to abortion clinics, the Act has the 'inevitable effect' of restricting abortion-related speech more than speech on other subjects. But a facially-neutral law does not become content based simply because it may disproportionately affect speech on certain topics. [The] question in such a case is whether the law is 'justified without reference to the content of the regulated speech.' [The] Massachusetts Act is. Its stated purpose is to 'increase public safety at reproductive health care facilities.' [Obstructed] access and congested sidewalks are problems no matter what caused them. A group of individuals can obstruct clinic access and clog sidewalks just as much when they loiter as when they protest abortion or counsel patients. . . .

"[The challengers argue, however, that] by choosing to pursue these interests only at abortion clinics, [the] Massachusetts Legislature evinced a purpose to 'single out for regulation speech about one particular topic: abortion.' We cannot infer such a purpose from the Act's limited scope. [The] Massachusetts Legislature [enacted the statute] in response to a problem that was, in its experience, limited to abortion clinics. There was a record of crowding, obstruction, and even violence outside such clinics. There were apparently no similar recurring problems associated with other kinds of healthcare facilities [or other kinds of buildings or activities]. In light of the limited nature of the problem, it was reasonable for the Massachusetts Legislature to enact a limited solution. [W]e thus conclude that the Act is neither content nor viewpoint based and therefore need not be analyzed under strict scrutiny."

Justice Scalia, joined by Justices Kennedy and Thomas, filed a concurring opinion in which he maintained that the challenged statute "is content based and fails strict scrutiny": "[It] blinks reality to say [that] a blanket prohibition on

the use of streets and sidewalks where speech on only one politically controversial topic is likely to occur — and where that speech can most effectively be
communicated — is not content based. Would the Court exempt from strict
scrutiny a law banning access to the streets and sidewalks surrounding the site
of the Republican National Convention? Or those used annually to commem-
orate the 1965 Selma-to-Montgomery civil rights marches? Or those outside
the Internal Revenue Service? Surely not. . . .

"The structure of the Act also indicates that it rests on content-based concerns. The goals of 'public safety, patient access to healthcare, and the unob-
structed use of public sidewalks and roadways,' are already achieved by an
earlier-enacted subsection of the statute. [As] the majority recognizes, that
provision is easy to enforce. Thus, the speech-free zones carved out [by the
challenged statute] add nothing to safety and access; what they achieve, and
what they were obviously designed to achieve, is the suppression of speech
opposing abortion. . . .

Justice Alito also filed a concurring opinion: "As the Court recognizes, if the
Massachusetts law discriminates on the basis of viewpoint, it is unconstitutional, and I believe the law clearly discriminates on this ground. [The] Massachusetts statute generally prohibits any person from entering a buffer zone
around an abortion clinic during the clinic's business hours, but the law contains an exemption for 'employees or agents of such facility acting within the
scope of their employment.'

"Thus, during business hours, individuals who wish to counsel against abortion or to criticize the particular clinic may not do so within the buffer zone. If
they engage in such conduct, they commit a crime. By contrast, employees and
agents of the clinic may enter the zone and engage in any conduct that falls
within the scope of their employment. A clinic may direct or authorize an
employee or agent, while within the zone, to express favorable views about
abortion or the clinic, and if the employee exercises that authority, the employee's conduct is perfectly lawful. In short, petitioners and other critics of a clinic
are silenced, while the clinic may authorize its employees to express speech in
support of the clinic and its work. [It is thus] clear on the face of the Massachusetts law that it discriminates based on viewpoint. Speech in favor of the
clinic and its work by employees and agents is permitted; speech criticizing the
clinic and its work is a crime. This is blatant viewpoint discrimination."

# B.   SPEECH ON PUBLIC PROPERTY: THE PUBLIC FORUM

In what circumstances, if any, does the first amendment guarantee the
individual the right to commandeer publicly owned property for the purpose
of exercising the freedom of speech? The Court has been highly solicitous of

the right of owners of *private* property to prevent others from using their property for speech purposes. In *Struthers*, for example, the Court left no doubt that the city could constitutionally "punish those who call at a home in defiance of the previously expressed will of the occupant." More generally, the Court has accepted the view that in most circumstances "an uninvited guest may [not] exercise general rights of free speech on property privately owned," for it "would be an unwarranted infringement of property rights to require them to yield to the exercise of First Amendment rights." Lloyd Corp. v. Tanner, 407 U.S. 551, 568, 567 (1972).

To what extent does the first amendment supersede the "property rights" of the state? Must the state "subsidize" speech by allowing individuals to use publicly owned property for speech purposes? For early commentary on the "public forum," see Kalven, The Concept of the Public Forum: Cox v. Louisiana, 1965 Sup. Ct. Rev. 1; Stone, Fora Americana: Speech in Public Places, 1974 Sup. Ct. Rev. 233.

Public forum theory has evolved along two separate, but related, lines — one governing streets and parks, the other governing all other publicly owned property. The first two parts of this section track this distinction. The remaining two parts of this section examine the problem of inequality of access to public property for speech purposes.

## 1.   The Public Forum: Streets and Parks

**COMMONWEALTH v. DAVIS, 162 Mass. 510, 39 N.E. 113 (1895), aff'd sub nom. DAVIS v. MASSACHUSETTS, 167 U.S. 43 (1897).** Davis, a preacher whose congregation apparently consisted of the crowds on the Boston Common, was convicted under a city ordinance that forbade, among other things, "any public address" on any publicly owned property "except in accordance with a permit from the mayor." The Supreme Judicial Court of Massachusetts, speaking through Justice Holmes, affirmed the conviction. Justice Holmes explained that the ordinance "is directed against free speech generally, [whereas] in fact it is directed toward the modes in which Boston Common may be used," and that, "as representative of the public," the legislature "may and does exercise control over the use which the public may make of such places," and for "the Legislature absolutely or conditionally to forbid public speaking in a highway or public park is no more an infringement of the rights of a member of the public than for the owner of a private house to forbid it in his house." Since the legislature "may end the right of the public to enter upon the public place by putting an end to the dedication to public uses," it necessarily "may take the lesser step of limiting the public use to certain purposes."

On appeal, the Supreme Court unanimously embraced Justice Holmes's position. Chief Justice White, speaking for the Court, maintained that the federal Constitution "does not have the effect of creating a particular and

personal right in the citizen to use public property in defiance of the constitution and laws of the State." Indeed, the "right to absolutely exclude all right
to use, necessarily includes the authority to determine under what circumstances such use may be availed of, as the greater power contains the lesser."[*]

---

Is this a satisfactory resolution of the public forum issue? Consider Stone,
Fora Americana: Speech in Public Places, 1974 Sup. Ct. Rev. 233, 237:
"[Under] the Holmes-White approach, the state possessed the power absolutely to prohibit the exercise of First Amendment rights [on] public property
simply by asserting the prerogatives traditionally associated with the private
ownership of land. [The] problem of the public forum had been 'solved' by
resort to common law concepts of private property."

**HAGUE v. CIO, 307 U.S. 496 (1939).** Forty-two years later, the Court
reopened the question. In *Hague,* the Court considered the constitutionality of
a municipal ordinance forbidding all public meetings in the streets and other
public places without a permit. The city maintained that the ordinance was clearly
constitutional under *Davis.* Although the Court did not directly decide the
question, Justice Roberts, in a plurality opinion, flatly rejected the city's contention
in a dictum that has played a central role in the evolution of public forum theory:

> Wherever the title of streets and parks may rest, they have immemorially been
> held in trust for the use of the public and, time out of mind, have been used for
> purposes of assembly, communicating thought between citizens, and discussing
> public questions. Such use of the streets and public places has, from ancient
> times, been a part of the privileges, immunities, rights, and liberties of citizens.
> The privilege of a citizen of the United States to use the streets and parks for
> communication of views on national questions may be regulated in the interest
> of all; it is not absolute, but relative, and must be exercised in subordination to
> the general comfort and convenience, and in consonance with peace and good
> order; but it must not, in the guise of regulation, be abridged or denied.

Consider Stone, supra, at 238:

> Perhaps the most interesting aspect of the Roberts dictum is its implicit accep-
> tance of the underlying premise of the Holmes-White position — that the public

---

[*] [At the time of *Davis,* the Court had not as yet held the first amendment applicable to the
states, thus undermining the precedential force of *Davis* as a "free speech" decision. It appears
that the primary constitutional issue before the Court concerned dictum in Yick Wo v. Hopkins, 118 U.S. 356 (1886), suggesting that the equal protection clause prohibited all forms of
standardless licensing. This dictum was rejected more clearly in a series of subsequent decisions. See Lieberman v. Van de Carr, 199 U.S. 552 (1905); Gundling v. Chicago, 177 U.S. 183
(1900); Wilson v. Eureka, 173 U.S. 32 (1899). — EDS.]

forum issue must be defined in terms of the common law property rights of the
state. Rather than challenging that premise head-on, Roberts conveniently
adapted it to his own advantage, predicating the public forum right upon established common law notions of adverse possession and public trust. [In effect,
Roberts concluded that] the streets, parks, and similar public places are subject
to what Professor Kalven has termed "a kind of First-Amendment easement."
[Citing Kalven, The Concept of the Public Forum: Cox v. Louisiana, 1965 Sup.
Ct. Rev. 1, 13.] Since such places have been used, "time out of mind," for
purposes of speech and assembly, the Constitution now requires that their
continued use for these purposes not "be abridged or denied."

Is this a sound rationale for the right to a public forum? Note that the
Roberts rationale creates by implication two distinct classes of public property.
Although streets, parks, and similar public places may constitute public fora,
publicly owned property that cannot satisfy the "time out of mind" requirement remains subject to the *Davis* dictum, and access to such places for
purposes of speech and assembly may thus be denied absolutely upon the
state's naked assertion of title. Would it be preferable to base public forum
theory on the notion that access to public property for speech purposes is
essential to effective exercise of first amendment rights?
   Consider C. Sunstein, republic.com 30–32 (2001):

> [The] public forum doctrine promotes three important goals. First, it ensures that
> speakers can have access to a wide array of people. [It allows speakers] to press
> their concerns that might otherwise be ignored by their fellow citizens. [Second,
> the doctrine] allows speakers [to have access] to specific people and specific
> institutions with whom they have a complaint. [The] public forum doctrine
> ensures that you can make your views heard by legislators, for example, by pro-
> testing in front of the state legislature. [Third, the doctrine] increases the likeli-
> hood that people generally will be exposed to a wide variety of people and views.
> [It] tends to ensure a range of experiences that are widely shared [and] a set of
> exposures to diverse views. [These] exposures can help promote understanding.

**SCHNEIDER v. STATE, 308 U.S. 147 (1939).** In *Schneider*, decided only
eight months after *Hague*, the Court held that a city's interest in keeping "the
streets clean and of good appearance" was "insufficient" to justify a municipal
ordinance prohibiting the distribution of leaflets on public property. Although
the Court did not explicitly address the status of *Davis*, the impact of *Hague*
and *Schneider* was made clear several years later in Jamison v. Texas, 318 U.S.
413 (1943), in which the Court, following *Schneider*, invalidated a city ordinance prohibiting the dissemination of leaflets. Relying on *Davis*, the city
maintained that "it has the power absolutely to prohibit the use of the streets
for the communication of ideas." The Court responded: "This same argument,
made in reliance upon the same decision, has been directly rejected by this
Court. [Citing Justice Roberts's concurring opinion in *Hague*.]"

Consider Kalven, supra, at 18–21:

> The result [in *Schneider*] had an impressive bite. Leaflet distribution in public places in a city is a method of communication that carries as an inextricable and expected consequence substantial littering of the streets, which the city has an obligation to keep clean. It is also a method of communication of some annoyance to a majority of people so addressed; that its impact on its audience is very high is doubtful. Yet the constitutional balance in *Schneider* was struck emphatically in favor of keeping the public forum open for this mode of communication. [At stake in *Schneider* was] the immemorial claim of the free man to use the streets as a forum. [The state], the Court was telling us, must recognize the special nature and value of that claim to be on the street. [The] operative theory of the Court, at least for the leaflet situation, is that [the] right to use the streets as a public forum [cannot] be prohibited and can be regulated only for weighty reasons.

How does the *Hague/Schneider* theory of the public forum relate to the analysis of content-neutral restrictions generally? Consider the following propositions:

1. Although the *Hague/Schneider* theory holds that the property rights of the state do not in themselves permit the state absolutely to exclude expression from public property that has been used "time out of mind" for speech purposes, it does not hold that government property rights are irrelevant. Thus, content-neutral restrictions governing streets and parks should be tested by more lenient standards of justification than content-neutral restrictions that do not implicate the property rights of the state.

2. The *Hague/Schneider* theory holds that government property rights are irrelevant when the property has been used "time out of mind" for speech purposes. Thus, content-neutral restrictions governing streets and parks should be tested by the same standards of justification that are used to test content-neutral restrictions that do not implicate the property rights of the state.

3. The *Hague/Schneider* theory holds that the streets and parks are "public fora" in which the state must be especially solicitous of free expression. Thus, content-neutral restrictions governing streets and parks should be tested by more stringent standards of justification than content-neutral restrictions that do not implicate "public forum" rights.

### Note: Regulating the Public Forum

1. *Signs near a courthouse.* In United States v. Grace, 461 U.S. 171 (1983), the Court invalidated a federal statute prohibiting any person to display on the public sidewalks surrounding the Supreme Court building "any flag, banner, or device designed [to] bring into public notice any party, organization or movement." The Court explained that the "public sidewalks forming the

perimeter of the Supreme Court grounds [are] public forums," and that "the government's ability" to restrict expression in such places "is very limited." Indeed, "the government may enforce reasonable time, place, and manner restrictions" in public forums only if "the restrictions 'are content-neutral, are narrowly tailored to serve a significant government interest, and leave open ample alternative channels of communication,'" and it may absolutely prohibit "a particular type of expression" only if the prohibition is "narrowly drawn to accomplish a compelling governmental interest."

The Court held that this statute could not be justified as a means "to maintain proper order and decorum" near the Supreme Court, for a "total ban" was not necessary to achieve these ends. And the restriction could not be justified as a means to prevent the appearance "that the Supreme Court is subject to outside influence," for the restriction did not "sufficiently serve" that purpose "to sustain its validity."

2. *Noise near a school.* In Grayned v. Rockford, 408 U.S. 104 (1972), approximately two hundred demonstrators marched on a public sidewalk about one hundred feet from a public high school to protest the school's racial policies. Appellant, a participant in the demonstration, was convicted of violating a Rockford ordinance prohibiting any "person, while on public or private grounds adjacent to any building in which a school or any class thereof is in session, [to make] any noise or diversion which disturbs or tends to disturb the peace or good order of such school." The Court, in an eight-to-one decision, affirmed the conviction.

The Court explained that, although "the public sidewalk adjacent to school grounds may not be declared off limits for expressive activity, [such] activity may be prohibited if it 'materially disrupts classwork or involves substantial disorder or invasion of the rights of others.'" In this case, the Court held that the "antinoise" ordinance "is narrowly tailored to further Rockford's compelling interest in having an undisrupted school session conducive to the students' learning"; "punishes only conduct which disrupts or is about to disrupt normal school activities"; requires that the "decision [be] made [on] an individualized basis"; and "gives no license to punish anyone because of what he is saying." The Court concluded that "such a reasonable regulation is not inconsistent with the First and Fourteenth Amendments."

3. *Picketing near a home.* In Frisby v. Shultz, 487 U.S. 474 (1988), a group varying in size from eleven to forty people picketed in protest on six occasions within one month on the public street outside the residence of a doctor who performed abortions. The picketing was orderly and peaceful. Thereafter, the town enacted an ordinance that prohibited residential picketing that focuses on and takes place in front of a particular residence. The Court, in a six-to-three decision, upheld the ordinance.

Although emphasizing that "a public street does not lose its status as a traditional public forum because it runs through a residential neighborhood," the Court nonetheless concluded that the ordinance was constitutional because it left "open ample alternative channels of communication" and was "narrowly tailored to serve a significant government interest." The Court found the first requirement "readily" satisfied because the ordinance left pro- testors free to march, proselytize door-to-door, leaflet, and even picket in a manner that did not focus exclusively on a particular residence.

As to the second requirement, the Court observed that "privacy of the home is [of] the highest order in a free and civilized society." Moreover, the "type of picketers banned by [this ordinance] generally do not seek to disseminate a message to the general public, but to intrude upon the targeted resident, and to do so in an especially offensive way. [And] even if some such picketers have a broader communicative purpose, their activity nonetheless inherently and offensively intrudes on residential privacy." Indeed, "even a solitary picket can invade residential privacy, [for the] target of the focused picketing banned by [this] ordinance is [a] 'captive,' [figuratively], and perhaps literally, trapped within the home." The Court thus concluded that the ordinance was "nar- rowly tailored" because "the 'evil' of targeted residential picketing, 'the very presence of an unwelcome visitor at the home,' is 'created by the medium of expression itself.'" Justices Brennan, Marshall, and Stevens dissented.

4. *Sleeping in a park.* In Clark v. Community for Creative Non-Violence, 468 U.S. 288 (1983), the National Park Service permitted CCNV to erect symbolic tent cities, consisting of between twenty and forty tents, in Lafayette Park and on the Mall in Washington, D.C., for the purpose of conducting a round-the-clock demonstration designed to dramatize the plight of the home- less. Pursuant to a National Park Service regulation prohibiting "camping" in these parks, however, the Park Service prohibited CCNV demonstrators from sleeping overnight in the tents. The Court assumed *arguendo* "that overnight sleeping in connection with the demonstration is expressive conduct protected [by] the First Amendment," but upheld the regulation as a "reasonable time, place, and manner restriction."

The Court emphasized that the regulation is "content neutral," that it does not prevent CCNV from demonstrating the "plight of the homeless [in] other ways," and that it "narrowly focuses on the Government's substantial interest in maintaining the parks [in] an attractive and intact condition." The Court rejected CCNV's argument that, once the Park Service decided to permit "the symbolic city of tents," the "incremental benefit to the parks was insuf- ficient to justify the ban on sleeping." Justice Marshall, joined by Justice Brennan, dissented.

Does this mean that members of the Occupy movement could lawfully be ejected from public parks? Is there a first amendment right to "occupy" public parks when the purpose of the occupation is expressive?

5. *Noise in a park.* In Ward v. Rock against Racism, 491 U.S. 781 (1989), the Court upheld a New York City regulation requiring the use of city-provided sound systems and technicians for concerts in the Bandshell in Central Park. The principal justification for the regulation was the city's desire to control

noise levels to avoid undue intrusion into other areas of the park and adjacent residential areas. The Court held that government clearly "'ha[s] a substantial interest in protecting its citizens from unwelcome noise,'" and that the regulation clearly leaves "open ample alternative channels of communication." Justice Marshall, joined by Justices Brennan and Stevens, dissented.

6. *Demonstrating near an abortion clinic.* In Madsen v. Women's Health Center, Inc., 512 U.S. 753 (1994), after petitioners repeatedly violated an injunction prohibiting them from blocking access to an abortion clinic and engaging in other activities that harassed patients and doctors both at the clinic and at their homes, a state court issued a new injunction prohibiting the petitioners from, inter alia, demonstrating within thirty-six feet of the clinic; making excessive noise near the clinic by "singing, chanting, whistling, shouting, yelling, use of bullhorns, auto horns [or] sound amplification equipment"; exhibiting "images observable" by patients within the clinic; approaching patients within three hundred feet of the clinic who did not voluntarily indicate a desire to speak with them; and demonstrating within three hundred feet of the residence of any of the clinic's employees.

The Court upheld the thirty-six-foot buffer zone as a reasonable way to protect "access to the clinic" and the restriction on excessive noise because noise "control is particularly important around hospitals and medical facilities." On the other hand, the Court invalidated the restriction on exhibiting "images observable" to patients within the clinic because the proper remedy is for the clinic to "pull its curtains." It also invalidated that portion of the injunction that prohibited petitioners from "approaching any person seeking services of the clinic 'unless such person indicates a desire to communicate' in an area within 300 feet of the clinic." The Court held that, "[absent] evidence that the protesters' speech is independently proscribable (i.e., 'fighting words' or threats), [this] provision cannot stand." Finally, the Court invalidated the provision enjoining petitioners from demonstrating within 300 feet of the residences of clinic staff. The Court explained that "the 300-foot zone [is] much larger than the zone [upheld] in *Frisby*. [A] limitation of the time, duration of picketing, and number of pickets outside a smaller zone could have accomplished the desired result."

7. *Demonstrating near an abortion clinic II.* In Schenck v. Pro-Choice Network of Western New York, 519 U.S. 357 (1997), several abortion clinics in upstate New York were subjected to a series of large-scale blockades in which antiabortion protesters marched, stood, knelt, or lay in clinic parking lots and doorways, blocking cars from entering the lots and interfering with patients and clinic employees who attempted to enter the clinics. Smaller groups of protesters, called "sidewalk counselors," crowded, jostled, pushed, and yelled and spit at women entering the clinics. Police officers who attempted to control the protests often were harassed by the protesters both verbally and by mail. A federal district court issued an injunction against fifty individuals and three organizations (including Operation Rescue), which,

among other things, (a) prohibited them from demonstrating within fifteen feet of clinic doorways, parking lots, and driveways ("fixed buffer zones"); and (b) prohibited them from demonstrating within fifteen feet of any person or vehicle seeking access to or leaving a clinic ("floating buffer zones").

In upholding the "fixed buffer zones," the Court explained that, in light of the prior conduct of the protesters, the district court "was entitled to conclude" that fixed buffer zones were necessary to prevent the protesters from doing "what they had done before: aggressively follow and crowd individuals right up to the clinic door and then refuse to move, or purposefully mill around parking lot entrances in an effort to impede or block the progress of cars." On the other hand, the Court invalidated the "floating buffer zones" because they would effectively prevent protesters "from communicating a message from a normal conversational distance or handing leaflets to people entering or leaving the clinics [on] the public sidewalks."

8. *Demonstrating near an abortion clinic III.* In Hill v. Colorado, 530 U.S. 703 (2000), the Court, in a six-to-three decision, upheld a Colorado statute that makes it unlawful for any person within one hundred feet of a health care facility to "knowingly approach" within eight feet of another person, without that person's consent, in order to pass "a leaflet or handbill to, [display] a sign to, or [engage] in oral protest, education, or counseling with, such other person." Citing *Frisby*, the Court explained that although the right to free speech "includes the right to attempt to persuade others to change their views, and may not be curtailed simply because the speaker's message may be offensive to his audience," the "protection afforded to offensive messages does not always embrace offensive speech that is so intrusive that the unwilling audience cannot avoid it." Indeed, "no one has a right to press even 'good' ideas on an unwilling recipient," and "none of our decisions has minimized the enduring importance of 'the right to be free' from persistent 'importunity, following and dogging' after an offer to communicate has been declined." The Court thus concluded that the statute "is a valid time, place, and manner regulation [because it] serves governmental interests that are significant and legitimate and [is] 'narrowly tailored' to serve those interests and . . . leaves open ample alternative channels for communication."

9. *Demonstrating near an abortion clinic IV.* In McCullen v. Coakley, 134 S. Ct. 2518 (2014), the Supreme Court invalidated a Massachusetts statute that made it a crime for any person knowingly to stand on a "public way or sidewalk" within thirty-five feet of an entrance or driveway to any place, other than a hospital, where abortions are performed. The law was designed to eliminate clashes between abortion opponents and advocates of abortion rights that had occurred outside clinics where abortions were performed. The law was challenged by individuals "who approach and talk to women outside such facilities, attempting to dissuade them from having abortions." According to testimony presented at the trial, such individuals have, over time, "persuaded hundreds of women to forego abortions."

Chief Justice Roberts authored the opinion of the Court: "[Public ways and sidewalks] occupy a 'special position in terms of First Amendment protection' because of their historic role as sites for discussion and debate. [We] have held that the government's ability to restrict speech in such locations is 'very limited.' [Even if such laws are content-neutral, they must be] "narrowly tailored to serve a significant governmental interest. [For] a content-neutral time, place, or manner regulation to be narrowly tailored, it must not 'burden substantially more speech than is necessary to further the government's legitimate interests.' . . .

"The buffer zones burden substantially more speech than necessary to achieve the Commonwealth's asserted interests. [The] Commonwealth's interests include ensuring public safety outside abortion clinics, preventing harassment and intimidation of patients and clinic staff, and combating deliberate obstruction of clinic entrances. [The Act] itself contains a separate provision [that] prohibits much of this conduct. That provision subjects to criminal punishment '[a]ny person who knowingly obstructs, detains, hinders, impedes or blocks another person's entry to or exit from a reproductive health care facility.' [If] Massachusetts determines that broader prohibitions along the same lines are necessary, it could enact legislation similar to the federal Freedom of Access to Clinic Entrances Act of 1994, which subjects to both criminal and civil penalties anyone who 'by force or threat of force or by physical obstruction, intentionally injures, intimidates or interferes with or attempts to injure, intimidate or interfere with any person because that person is or has been, or in order to intimidate such person or any other person or any class of persons from, obtaining or providing reproductive health services.' [If] the Commonwealth is particularly concerned about harassment, it could also consider an ordinance such as the one adopted in New York City that not only prohibits obstructing access to a clinic, but also makes it a crime 'to follow and harass another person within 15 feet of the premises of a reproductive health care facility.'" . . .

10. *Picketing near military funerals.* In recent years, members of the Westboro Baptist Church have protested at the funerals of American soldiers, carrying placards and shouting such phrases as "Thank God for Dead Soldiers," "God Is Your Enemy," and "Thank God for 9/11." The church's predominant message is one of virulent antihomosexuality, and these protests are designed to convey the message that the United States is being punished for its toleration of such conduct. In Snyder v. Phelps, 131 S. Ct. 1267 (2011), the Supreme Court held that it was unconstitutional to hold church members liable for the tort of intentional infliction of emotional distress. (*Snyder* is discussed in more detail in Chapter II.B, supra.) Suppose that you were a member of Congress concerned about the Church's activities. Would it be possible to draft content-neutral regulations of a public forum that reached the activities? Consider the Respect for America's Fallen Heroes Act, which was enacted in 2006. The act, which governs funerals at national cemeteries,

prohibits any "demonstration" "during the period beginning 60 minutes before and ending 60 minutes" after a funeral at a national cemetery if the demonstration is "within 150 feet of a road pathway, or other route of ingress to or egress from such cemetery property" and the demonstrators willfully make "any noise or diversion that disturbs or tends to disturb the peace or good order" of the funeral or is "within 300 feet of such cemetery" if the demonstration "impedes the access to or egress from such cemetery." The act defines "demonstration" to include "any picketing or similar conduct," "any oration, speech, use of sound amplification equipment" that is not part of the funeral, "the display of any placard, banner, flag, or similar device" that is not part of the funeral, and the "distribution of any handbill, pamphlet, or other written or printed matter" that is not part of the funeral. Is this law a reasonable regulation of public property? Is it content-neutral? See Wells, Privacy and Funeral Protests, 87 N.C. L. Rev. 151 (2008); McAllister, Funeral Picketing Laws and Free Speech, 55 U. Kan. L. Rev. 575 (2007).

11. *Free speech zones.* Consider Zick, Speech and Spatial Tactics, 84 Tex. L. Rev. 581, 584–589 (2006):

> Governments have learned to manipulate geography in a manner that now seriously threatens basic First Amendment principles. [The] state has moved from *regulating* place to actually . . . *creating* places [such as "buffer zones," "free speech zones," and "speech-free zones"] for the express purpose of controlling and disciplining protest and dissent. [By] design, these places mute and even suppress messages, depress participation in social and political protests, and send negative signals to those on the outside regarding those confined within. [Protests in such] places are docile; they are tightly scripted and ineffectual imitations of past social and political movements. [Passively] filing into cages, zones, and other tactical places is an utter capitulation to the status quo. [Such places are] being used to marginalize dissent, to capture and confine it. [Courts] should view [such manipulation of protests] with far greater skepticism than they currently do [and should] take far more seriously the notion that "one is not to have the exercise of his liberty of expression in appropriate places abridged on the please that it may be exercised elsewhere."[Quoting Schneider v. State.]

12. *Unattended structures.* Does an individual have a constitutional right to erect an unattended display in a public park? Suppose, for example, an individual wants to construct a statue, or a cross, or a billboard in such a park. Can the state prohibit this completely? If prohibition is impermissible, what sorts of regulations would be appropriate? In Capitol Square Review & Advisory Board v. Pinette, 515 U.S. 753 (1995), the Court strongly suggested, but did not decide, that "a ban on all unattended displays" might be constitutional. As Justice Stevens explained in a separate opinion, such a display "creates a far greater intrusion on government property and interferes with the Government's ability to differentiate its own message from those of private individuals."

13. *Content neutrality as a formal rule.* Should the Court insist on strict scrutiny for content-based regulation in circumstances where, on the facts of the particular case, the regulation is unlikely to endanger first amendment values? Conversely, should it insist on only intermediate scrutiny where there is a significant risk that a facially content neutral statute it has been gerrymandered because of content? *See* Kendrick, Nonsense on Sidewalks: Content Discrimination in McCullen v. Coakley, 2014 Sup. Ct. Rev. 215, 237:

> Adopting a freewheeling approach, in which intuitions are not channeled into a framework but are imposed directly as law, could have serious ramifications for both the predictability and legitimacy of the Court's jurisprudence. There is something to be said for an approach that, rather than indulging subjective impulses, tries to contain them. When disagreements about a law run so deep, perhaps there are good reasons for approaching the law obliquely, and through predetermined avenues.

Consider in this regard Reed v. Town of Gilbert, 135 S. Ct. 2118 (2015). The Town of Gilbert comprehensively regulated signs in ways that made many distinctions between types of signs. For example, "temporary directional signs relating to a qualifying event" could be no larger than six square feet and could be in place for no longer than twelve hours before the event and one hour afterward. In contrast, "political signs" could be up to thirty-two square feet and could be displayed up to sixty days before a primary election and up to fifteen days following a general election. The Good News Community Church was cited for exceeding the time limits for a sign displaying the time and location of an upcoming service and challenged the regulations as violative of the first amendment. The Court of Appeals treated the signs as content-neutral on the ground that the town's "interests in regulat[ing] temporary signs are unrelated to the content of the sign." The court held that lower-level scrutiny therefore applied and upheld the ordinance.

The Supreme Court, in an opinion written by Justice Thomas, reversed. As the Court explained, the court of appeals had "[skipped] the crucial first step in the content-neutrality analysis: determining whether the law is content neutral on its face. A law that is content based on its face is subject to strict scrutiny regardless of the government's benign motive, content-neutral justification, or lack of 'animus toward the ideas contained' in the regulated speech." The Court went on to note that even if a law is facially content-neutral, it will still be treated as content based if it cannot be justified without reference to the content of the regulated speech or if it was adopted because of disagreement with the message of the speech. But because the town's code was "content based on its face," it was subject to heightened scrutiny whether or not it was motivated by opposition to the message conveyed. According to the Court:

> This type of ordinance may seem like a perfectly rational way to regulate signs, but a clear and firm rule governing content neutrality is an essential means of

protecting the freedom of speech, even if laws that might seem "entirely reasonable" will sometimes be "struck down because of their content-based nature."

Compare Justice Kagan's opinion, joined by Justices Ginsburg and Breyer, concurring in the judgment:

> Given the Court's analysis, many sign ordinances [are] now in jeopardy. . . .
> [Courts will] have to determine that a town has a compelling interest in informing passersby where George Washington slept. And likewise, courts [will] have to find that a town has no way to prevent hidden-driveway mishaps than by specially treating hidden-driveway signs. [The] consequence — unless courts water down strict scrutiny to something unrecognizable — is that our communities will find themselves in an unenviable bind: They will have to either repeal the exemptions that allow for helpful signs on streets and sidewalks, or else lift their sign restrictions altogether and resign themselves to the resulting clutter.
> Although the majority insists that applying strict scrutiny to all such ordinances is "essential" to protecting First Amendment freedoms, I find it challenging to understand why that is so. [Allowing] residents, say, to install a light bulb over "name and address" signs but no others does not distort the marketplace of ideas. Nor does that different treatment give rise to an inference of impermissible government motive.

Justice Kagan would nonetheless have invalidated the ordinance before the Court because "[the] Town of Gilbert's defense of [the ordinance] — most notably, the law's distinctions between directional signs and others — does not pass strict scrutiny, or intermediate scrutiny, or even the laugh test."

Justice Alito, joined by Justices Kennedy and Sotomayor, joined the majority opinion but filed a separate concurring opinion. Justice Breyer filed a separate opinion concurring only in the judgment.

### Note: Devices for Regulating the Public Forum

1. *Licensing.* In Cox v. New Hampshire, 312 U.S. 569 (1941), a group of Jehovah's Witnesses were convicted of violating a state statute prohibiting any "parade or procession" upon a public street without first obtaining a permit. The Court, in a unanimous decision, affirmed the convictions. Chief Justice Hughes, speaking for the Court, explained that, "as regulation of the use of the streets for parades and processions is a traditional exercise of control by local government, the question in a particular case is whether that control is exerted so as not to deny or unwarrantedly abridge the right of assembly and the opportunities for the communication of [thought] immemorially associated with resort to public places."

The Court emphasized that the state court had "construed the statute" as authorizing "the licensing authority" to take into account only "considerations of time, place and manner so as to conserve the public convenience." Such a limited permit requirement had the "obvious advantage" of "giving the public authorities notice in advance so as to afford opportunity for proper policing" and, "in fixing time and place, '[to] prevent confusion by overlapping parades or processions, to secure convenient use of the streets by other travelers, and to minimize the risk of disorder.'" Moreover, the Court emphasized that the state court had stressed that "the licensing board was not vested with arbitrary power [and] that its discretion must be [exercised] 'free [from] unfair discrimination.'" The Court concluded that under this construction of the statute, it is "impossible to say that the limited authority conferred by the licensing provisions [contravened] any constitutional right."

For a critical view, see Baker, Unreasoned Reasonableness: Mandatory Parade Permits and Time, Place, and Manner Regulations, 78 Nw. U. L. Rev. 937 (1983). For analysis of licensing generally, see Chapter III.B, supra. See also Thomas v. Chicago Park District, 534 U.S. 316 (2002) (a content-neutral licensing scheme regulating the time, place and manner of use of a public forum need not employ the *Freedman* safeguards because such a scheme "does not authorize a licensor to pass judgment on the content of speech").

If a city can use a "time, place, and manner"–based licensing scheme for individuals who want to parade on public streets, can it also use such a licensing scheme for speakers who want to go door-to-door to speak with homeowners and distribute literature? In Watchtower Bible & Tract Society v. Village of Stratton, 536 U.S. 150 (2002), the Court, in an eight-to-one decision, held such a scheme unconstitutional. Although acknowledging that the Village's interests in preventing fraud, preventing crime and protecting privacy are "important," the Court nonetheless held that the effect of the licensing scheme on the interests of speakers who want to maintain their anonymity, the administrative burden the scheme imposes on speakers, and the potential impact of the licensing requirement on "spontaneous speech" rendered the ordinance unconstitutional. The Court indicated that such a scheme limited to commercial activities and the solicitation of funds might not be invalid.

2. *Fees.* To what extent may the state charge for use of the public forum? In Murdock v. Pennsylvania, 319 U.S. 105 (1943), the Court held that the state may not impose a "flat license tax [as] a condition to the pursuit of activities whose enjoyment is guaranteed by the First Amendment" where the tax "is not a nominal fee imposed as a regulatory measure to defray the expenses of policing the activities in question." In Cox v. New Hampshire, supra, the licensing statute provided that "every licensee shall pay in advance" a fee ranging from a nominal amount to $300 per day. The state court construed the statute as requiring "a reasonable fixing of the amount of the fee." That is, the amount of the fee must in each instance turn on the size of the "parade or procession," the size of the crowd, and the "public expense of policing" the event. The state court explained that the fee was "not a revenue tax, but one to

meet the expense incident to the administration of the Act and to the maintenance of public order in the matter licensed." The Court held that in such circumstances "there is nothing contrary to the Constitution in the charge of a fee limited to the purpose stated." Moreover, the Court rejected "the suggestion that a flat fee should have been charged," explaining that it is difficult to frame "a fair schedule to meet all circumstances," and that there is "no constitutional ground for denying to local governments that flexibility of adjustment of fees which in the light of varying conditions would tend to conserve rather than impair the liberty sought."

Consider Goldberger, A Reconsideration of Cox v. New Hampshire: Can Demonstrators Be Required to Pay the Costs of Using America's Public Forums?, 62 Tex. L. Rev. 403, 412-413 (1983):

> The Court's approval of [license fees] in *Cox* results from the Court's erroneous assumption that the relationship between a speaker and the government can be treated like a two-party business relationship. [The Court assumes] that the speaker is the primary beneficiary of his use of a public forum. [This] assumption ignores the benefit of the speaker's activities for the entire society. His activities are part of the process by which a democratic society makes informed decisions. [A] proper distribution of costs [would] allocate the costs generated by speech activities to the society as a whole.

Is there a danger that, if the state "is forced to defray administrative costs, it is likely to be more resistant to permit requests"? Blasi, Prior Restraints on Demonstrations, 68 Mich. L. Rev. 1481, 1527 (1970).

During the Skokie controversy, Chapter II.B, supra, the village enacted an ordinance requiring applicants for parade or public demonstration permits to procure public liability insurance in the amount of $350,000 and property damage insurance in the amount of $50,000. Is this ordinance constitutional under the doctrine of *Cox*? Consider Forsyth County, Georgia v. The Nationalist Movement, 505 U.S. 123 (1992), in which the Court invalidated a municipal ordinance that authorized permit fees for parades, demonstrations, marches, and similar activities, up to a maximum of $1,000, based in part on the anticipated expense necessary to maintain the public order. The Court, in an opinion by Justice Blackmun, explained that under this scheme the fee "will depend on the administrator's measure of the amount of hostility likely to be created by the speech." As a result, those "wishing to express views unpopular with bottle throwers [may] have to pay more for their permit." The Court announced that speech "cannot be financially burdened, any more than it can be punished or banned, simply because it might offend a hostile mob," and that "regulations which permit the Government to discriminate on the basis of the content of the message cannot be tolerated under the First Amendment."

3. *Disclosure.* To what extent may the state, in order to prevent abuse, require speakers to disclose their identities? In Talley v. California, 362

U.S. 60 (1960), a distributor of handbills protesting employment discrimination was prosecuted for violating a Los Angeles ordinance prohibiting any person to distribute "any hand-bill [which] does not have printed on [the] face thereof, the name and address of [the] person who printed, wrote, compiled, or manufactured [it]." The Court held the ordinance invalid:

> [It is] urged that this ordinance is aimed at providing a way to identify those responsible for fraud, false advertising and libel. [But] such an identification requirement would tend to restrict freedom to distribute information and thereby freedom of expression. [Anonymous] pamphlets, leaflets, brochures and even books have played an important role in the progress of mankind. Persecuted groups [throughout] history have been able to criticize oppressive practices [either] anonymously or not at all. [Identification] and fear of reprisal might deter perfectly peaceful discussions of public matters of importance. This broad Los Angeles ordinance is subject to the same infirmity.

Justice Clark, joined by Justices Frankfurter and Whittaker, dissented: "[There] is neither allegation nor proof that Talley [would] suffer 'economic reprisal, loss of employment, threat of physical coercion [or] other manifestations of public hostility.' Talley makes no showing whatever to support his contention that a restraint upon his freedom of speech will result from the enforcement of the ordinance. The existence of such a restraint is necessary before we can strike the ordinance down."

See also McIntyre v. Ohio Elections Commission, 514 U.S. 334 (1995), in which the Court invalidated a state statute prohibiting the distribution of campaign literature that does not contain the name and address of the person issuing the literature: "Under our Constitution, anonymous pamphleteering is not a pernicious, fraudulent practice, but an honorable tradition of advocacy and of dissent. Anonymity is a shield from the tyranny of the majority. It thus exemplifies the purpose behind the Bill of Rights, and of the First Amendment in particular: to protect unpopular individuals from retaliation — and their ideas from suppression — at the hand of an intolerant society." See also Buckley v. American Constitutional Law Foundation, 525 U.S. 182 (1999) (invalidating a state law requiring petition circulators to wear a badge identifying them by name).

Are there any circumstances in which compelled disclosure is constitutional? See Buckley v. Valeo, infra (upholding compelled disclosure of campaign contributions). Are there any circumstances in which compelled disclosure is generally constitutional, but is unconstitutional as applied to particular speakers who can demonstrate a meaningful risk of "economic reprisal, loss of employment, threat of physical coercion [or] other manifestations of public hostility"? See NAACP v. Alabama, infra (invalidating an Alabama statute requiring disclosure of the names of members of registered organizations, as applied to the NAACP); Brown v. Socialists Workers '74

Campaign Committee, 459 U.S. 87 (1982) (invalidating the statute compelling disclosure of campaign contributions that had been upheld in *Buckley*, as applied to the Socialist Workers Party).

## 2. *The Public Forum: Other Publicly Owned Property*

If there is a first amendment right to use streets and parks for purposes of expression, to what extent, if any, is there an analogous right to use other publicly owned property, ranging from the grounds surrounding a jail, to a military base, to a state fair? Does the *Hague* dictum's definition of the right to a "public forum" in terms of the common law property rights of the state suggest that the right does not extend to property that has not been used "time out of mind" for speech purposes?

# Adderley v. Florida

385 U.S. 39 (1966)

[About two hundred Florida A. & M. students marched to the county jail to protest the arrest the previous day of several of their schoolmates who had engaged in a civil rights demonstration/ The protestors went directly to the jail entrance, where they were met by a deputy sheriff who explained that they were blocking the entrance to the jail and asked them to move back. The protestors moved back part of the way, where they stood or sat, singing, clapping, and dancing, on the jail driveway and on an adjacent grassy area on the jail premises. This jail entrance and driveway were normally used not by the public, but by the sheriff's department for transporting prisoners and by commercial concerns for servicing the jail. The county sheriff, who was legal custodian of the jail and jail grounds, ordered the students to leave and informed them that, if they did not leave within ten minutes, he would arrest them for trespassing. Some protestors left, but 107 others, including petitioners, remained and were arrested. They were convicted of violating a Florida statute declaring unlawful "every trespass upon the property of another, committed with a malicious and mischievous intent." The Court, in a five-to-four decision, affirmed the convictions.]

MR. JUSTICE BLACK delivered the opinion of the Court. . . .
    [Petitioners maintain that conviction under the trespass statute] unconstitutionally deprives [them] of their rights to freedom of speech, press, assembly, or petition. We hold that it does not. The sheriff, as jail custodian, had power [to] direct that this large crowd of people get off the grounds. There is not a shred of evidence in this record that this power was exercised [because] the sheriff objected to what was being sung or said by the demonstrators or because

he disagreed with the objectives of their protest. The record reveals that he objected only to their presence on that part of the jail grounds reserved for jail uses. There is no evidence at all that on any other occasion had similarly large groups of the public been permitted to gather on this portion of the jail grounds for any purpose. Nothing in the Constitution of the United States prevents Florida from even-handed enforcement of its general trespass statute against those refusing to obey the sheriff's order to remove themselves from what amounted to the curtilage of the jailhouse. The State, no less than a private owner of property, has power to preserve the property under its control for the use to which it is lawfully dedicated. For this reason there is no merit to the petitioners' argument that they had a constitutional right to stay on the property, over the jail custodian's objections, because this "area chosen for the peaceful civil rights demonstration was not only 'reasonable' but also particularly appropriate. . . ." Such an argument has as its major unarticulated premise the assumption that people who want to propagandize protests or views have a constitutional right to do so whenever and however and wherever they please. [We] reject [that concept]. The United States Constitution does not forbid a State to control the use of its own property for its own lawful nondiscriminatory purpose.

These judgments are affirmed.

MR. JUSTICE DOUGLAS, with whom THE CHIEF JUSTICE, MR. JUSTICE BRENNAN, and MR. JUSTICE FORTAS concur, dissenting. . . .

The jailhouse, like an executive mansion, a legislative chamber, a courthouse, or the statehouse itself [is] one of the seats of government, whether it be the Tower of London, the Bastille, or a small county jail. And when it houses political prisoners or those who many think are unjustly held, it is an obvious center for protest. The right to petition for the redress of grievances has an ancient history and is not limited to writing a letter or sending a telegram to a congressman; it is not confined to appearing before the local city council, or writing letters to the President or Governor or Mayor. [Conventional] methods of petitioning may be, and often have been, shut off to large groups of our citizens. [Those] who do not control television and radio, those who cannot afford to advertise in newspapers or circulate elaborate pamphlets may have only a more limited type of access to public officials. Their methods should not be condemned as tactics of obstruction and harassment as long as the assembly and petition are peaceable, as these were.

There is no question that petitioners had as their purpose a protest against the arrest of Florida A. & M. students for trying to integrate public theatres. [There] was no violence; no threat of violence; no attempted jail break; no storming of a prison; no plan or plot to do anything but protest. . . .

We do violence to the First Amendment when we permit this "petition for redress of grievances" to be turned into a trespass action. [To] say that a private owner could have done the same if the rally had taken place on private property is to speak of a different case, as an assembly and a petition for redress of grievances run to government, not to private proprietors.

The Court forgets that prior to this day our decisions have drastically limited the application of state statutes inhibiting the right to go peacefully on public property to exercise First Amendment rights. [Citing Justice Roberts's plurality opinion in *Hague*. There] may be some public places which are so clearly committed to other purposes that their use for the airing of grievances is anomalous. There may be some instances in which assemblies and petitions for redress of grievances are not consistent with other necessary purposes of public property. A noisy meeting may be out of keeping with the serenity of the statehouse or the quiet of the courthouse. No one, for example, would suggest that the Senate gallery is the proper place for a vociferous protest rally. And in other cases it may be necessary to adjust the right to petition for redress of grievances to the other interests inhering in the uses to which the public property is normally put. [See Cox v. New Hampshire.] But this is quite different from saying that all public places are off limits to people with grievances. . . .

### Note: *"No Less Than a Private Owner of Property"?*

1. Davis *revisited?* Does *Adderley* turn on Justice Black's assertion that "the State, no less than a private owner of property, has power to preserve the property under its control for the use to which it is lawfully dedicated"? Does *Adderley* undervalue the interest of the speaker in selecting a "particularly appropriate" location for his speech?

2. *The* Grayned *dictum.* In Grayned v. Rockford, supra, decided in 1972, the Court, although upholding the antinoise ordinance as a reasonable time, place, and manner regulation, offered the following analysis of the public forum issue:

> The nature of a place, "the pattern of its normal activities, dictate the kinds of regulations of time, place, and manner that are reasonable." [The] crucial question is whether the manner of expression is basically incompatible with the normal activity of a particular place at a particular time. Our cases make clear that in assessing the reasonableness of a regulation, we must weigh heavily the fact that communication is involved; the regulation must be narrowly tailored to further the State's legitimate interest.

What are the implications of *Grayned?* Does it reject the central premise of *Adderley?* Consider Stone, Fora Americana: Speech in Public Places, 1974 Sup. Ct. Rev. 233, 251–252:

> In [the *Grayned* dictum], the right to a public forum came of age. No longer does the right to effective freedom of expression turn on the common law property

rights of the state, and no longer does it turn on whether the particular place at issue has historically been dedicated to the exercise of First Amendment rights. The streets, parks, public libraries, and other publicly owned places are all brought under the same roof. In each case, the "crucial question is whether the manner of expression is basically incompatible with the normal activity of a particular place at a particular time."

As events turned out, this celebration proved premature. Consider the following post-*Grayned* decisions.

3. *A military base.* The Fort Dix Military Reservation is a U.S. Army post. Although the federal government exercises exclusive jurisdiction over the base, civilian vehicular traffic is permitted on paved roads within the reservation, and civilians are freely permitted to visit unrestricted areas of the base. In 1972, Benjamin Spock, the People's Party's candidate for President of the United States, requested permission to enter the base to hold a meeting to discuss election issues with service personnel and their dependents. The commanding officer of the base rejected the request, citing a Fort Dix regulation providing that "demonstrations, picketing, sit-ins, protest marches, political speeches and similar activities are prohibited and will not be conducted on the Fort Dix Military Reservation."

In Greer v. Spock, 424 U.S. 828 (1976), the Court, in a six-to-two decision, upheld the regulation. In an opinion by Justice Stewart, the Court rejected "the principle that whenever members of the public are permitted freely to visit a place owned or operated by the Government, then that place becomes a 'public forum' for purposes of the First Amendment." Quoting *Adderley*, the Court explained that "'[t]he State, no less than a private owner of property, has power to preserve the property under its control for the use to which it is lawfully dedicated.'" The Court added that it is "the business of a military installation like Fort Dix to train soldiers, not to provide a public forum," and that the challenged regulation reflects "a considered [policy], objectively and evenhandedly applied, of keeping official military activities [free] of entanglement with partisan political campaigns of any kind [in order to insulate] the military [from] both the reality and the appearance of acting as a handmaiden for partisan political causes or candidates."

Justice Brennan, joined by Justice Marshall, dissented. Justice Brennan maintained that the Court's emphasis on whether the base was a "public forum" was misplaced, for "the determination that a locale is a 'public forum' has never been erected as an absolute prerequisite to all forms of demonstrative First Amendment activity." What is needed, Justice Brennan explained, is a "flexible approach [for] determining when public expression should be protected." Justice Brennan reasoned that the speech in this case was "basically compatible with the activities otherwise occurring" at the base, and he rejected the contention that the interest in "military neutrality" could justify the restriction, for "it borders on casuistry to contend that by evenhandedly permitting public expression to occur in unrestricted portions of a military installation, the military will be viewed as sanctioning the causes there espoused."

4. *A state fair.* The Minnesota State Fair is conducted each year on a 125-acre site. The average daily attendance exceeds 100,000. Minnesota State Fair Rule 6.05 prohibits the sale or distribution of any merchandise, including printed or written material, except from a booth rented from the state. Booths are rented to all comers in a nondiscriminatory manner on a first-come, first-served basis. The rental charge is based on the size and location of the booth. The International Society for Krishna Consciousness (ISKCON), an international religious society espousing the views of the Krishna religion, challenged Rule 6.05 on the ground that it would impair ISKCON's ability effectively to distribute its literature.

In Heffron v. International Society for Krishna Consciousness, 452 U.S. 640 (1981), the Court upheld the rule. In an opinion by Justice White, the Court rejected ISKCON's effort to analogize "the fairgrounds [to] city streets which have 'immemorially been [used] for purposes [of] assembly [and] discussing public questions'":

> A street is continually open, often uncongested, [and] a place where people may enjoy the open air or the company of friends [in] a relaxed environment. The Minnesota Fair [is] a temporary event attracting great numbers of visitors who come to the event for a short period to see [the] host of exhibits [at] the Fair. The flow of the crowd and the demands of safety are more pressing in the context of the Fair. As such, any comparisons to public streets are necessarily inexact.

The Court thus concluded that,

> [given the] threat to the State's interest in crowd control if [all] organizations [could] move freely about the fairgrounds distributing and selling literature and soliciting funds at will, [the] State's interest in confining distribution, selling, and fund solicitation activities to fixed locations is sufficient to satisfy the requirement that a place or manner restriction must serve a substantial state interest.

Justice Brennan, joined by Justices Marshall and Stevens, concurred in part and dissented in part. Although conceding that "the State has a significant interest in maintaining crowd control on its fairgrounds," Justice Brennan concluded that the "booth rule is an overly intrusive means of achieving [that interest]." "A state fair," Justice Brennan maintained, "is truly a marketplace of ideas and a public forum for the communication of ideas and information." Thus, Rule 6.05 constitutes a "significant restriction on First Amendment rights," for "by prohibiting distribution of literature outside the booths, the fair officials sharply limit the number of fairgoers to whom the proselytizers [can] communicate their messages."

5. *A mailbox.* In U.S. Postal Service v. Council of Greenburgh Civic Associations, 453 U.S. 114 (1981), the Court upheld a federal statute prohibiting

the deposit of unstamped "mailable matter" in a letter box approved by the U.S. Postal Service, as applied to appellee civic association, which routinely delivered its messages by placing unstamped notices in the letter boxes of private homes. In an opinion by Justice Rehnquist, the Court explained:

> There is neither historical nor constitutional support for the characterization of a letter box as a public forum. [At least since 1934, when the statute was promulgated,] access to [letter boxes] has been unlawful except under the terms and conditions specified by Congress and the Postal Service. As such, it is difficult to accept appellees' assertion that because it may be somewhat more efficient to place their messages in letter boxes there is a First Amendment right to do so. [Indeed,] it is difficult to conceive of any reason why this Court should treat a letter box differently for First Amendment [purposes] than it has in the past treated the military base in [*Greer* or] the jail [in *Adderley*]. . . . What we hold is the principle reiterated by cases such as [*Adderley*] and [*Greer*], that property owned or controlled by the government which is *not* a public forum may be subject to a prohibition of speech, leafleting, picketing, or other forms of communication without running afoul of the First Amendment. Admittedly, the government must act reasonably in imposing such restrictions [and] the prohibition must be content-neutral. [But] this statute is both a reasonable and content-neutral regulation.

Justices Marshall and Stevens dissented.

6. *A public utility pole.* In Members of the City Council of Los Angeles v. Taxpayers for Vincent, 466 U.S. 789 (1984), the Court upheld a Los Angeles ordinance prohibiting the posting of signs on public property as applied to individuals who tied political campaign signs to public utility poles. Justice Stevens delivered the opinion:

> The ordinance [diminishes] the total quantity of [appellees'] communication in the City. [But] the state [may] curtail speech [in a content-neutral manner if the restriction] "furthers an important or substantial governmental interest [and if the] restriction on [free speech] is no greater than is essential to the furtherance of that interest." [It is undisputed that the] problem addressed by this ordinance — the visual assault [on] citizens [presented] by an accumulation of signs posted on public property — constitutes a significant substantive evil. [Moreover, the] restriction on appellees' expressive activity is [no] broader than necessary to protect the City's interest. [By] banning these signs, the City did no more than eliminate the exact source of the evil it sought to remedy. [Appellees] suggest that the public property covered by the ordinance is [a] "public forum," [but they] fail to demonstrate the existence of a traditional right of access respecting such items as utility poles for purposes [of] communication comparable to that recognized for public streets and parks. [The] mere fact that government property can be used as a vehicle for communication does not mean that the Constitution requires such uses to be permitted.

Justice Brennan, joined by Justices Marshall and Blackmun, dissented.

Is *Vincent* consistent with *Schneider*? Consider Justice Stevens's answer in *Vincent:* "It is true that the esthetic interest in preventing [litter] cannot support a prophylactic prohibition against [leafleting. But the] rationale of *Schneider* is inapposite in the context of this case. [In *Schneider,*] an anti-littering statute could have addressed the substantive evil without prohibiting expressive activity. [Here], the substantive evil — visual blight — is not merely a possible by-product of the activity, but is created by the medium of expression itself. [Thus, the] ordinance curtails no more speech than is necessary to accomplish its purpose."

7. *A post office sidewalk.* In United States v. Kokinda, 497 U.S. 720 (1990), respondents, members of a political advocacy group, set up a table on a side-walk near the entrance to a United States Post Office to distribute literature and solicit contributions. The sidewalk, which is located entirely on Postal Service property, is the sole means by which customers may travel from the parking lot to the post office building. Respondents were convicted of violating a federal regulation prohibiting any person from soliciting contributions "on postal premises." The Court upheld the regulation as applied.

Justice O'Connor, in a plurality opinion joined by Chief Justice Rehnquist and Justices White and Scalia, explained that the "postal sidewalk [does] not have the characteristics of public sidewalks traditionally open to expressive activity." Rather, "the postal sidewalk was constructed solely to provide for the passage of individuals engaged in postal business." Although conceding that individuals had generally "been permitted to leaflet, speak, and picket on postal premises," Justice O'Connor argued this did "not add up to the dedi-cation of postal property to speech activities." Justice O'Connor therefore concluded that "the regulation [must] be analyzed under the standards set forth for nonpublic fora: it must be reasonable and 'not an effort to suppress expression merely because public officials oppose the speaker's view.'" Apply-ing that standard, Justice O'Connor noted that, "based on its long experience with solicitation," the Postal Service had concluded that "solicitation is inher-ently disruptive of the postal service's business" because it "impedes the normal flow of traffic" and "is more intrusive and intimidating than an encounter with a person giving out information." Justice O'Connor concluded that the challenged regulation therefore "passes constitutional muster under [the] usual test for reasonableness." Justice Kennedy concurred in the result. Justice Brennan, joined by Justices Marshall, Blackmun, and Stevens, dissented.

What about an airport terminal?

**INTERNATIONAL SOCIETY FOR KRISHNA CONSCIOUSNESS v. LEE, 505 U.S. 672 (1992).** The Port Authority of New York and New Jersey, which owns and operates three major airports in the New York City area, forbids within the airport terminals the repetitive solicitation of money and

no penhandling

the repetitive sale or distribution of any merchandise, "including but not limited to jewelry, food stuffs, candles, flowers, . . . flyers, brochures, pamphlets, books or any other printed or written material." The regulation governs only the terminal buildings. It does not restrict such activities on the public sidewalks outside the buildings. In a bewildering array of opinions, the Court upheld the ban on solicitation but invalidated the ban on the sale or distribution of literature.

*Solicitation.* Chief Justice Rehnquist delivered the opinion of the Court upholding the ban on solicitation. The Court explained that airport terminals are not traditional public fora because, "given the lateness with which the modern air terminal has made its appearance, it hardly qualifies for the description of having 'immemorially . . . time out of mind' been held in the public trust and used for purposes of expressive activity." Moreover, such terminals have not "been intentionally opened by their operators to such activity." To the contrary, "the frequent and continuing litigation evidencing the operators' objections belies any such claim." Moreover, "airports are commercial establishments funded by use fees and designed to make a regulated profit." The Court thus concluded that, "because it cannot fairly be said that an airport terminal has as a principal purpose 'promoting the free exchange of ideas,'" it is not a public forum.

This being so, the prohibition of solicitation "need only satisfy a requirement of reasonableness," a standard the Court held was easily satisfied because of "the disruptive effect that solicitation may have on business." Specifically, the Court observed that solicitation impedes "the normal flow of traffic," and that such "delays may be particularly costly in this setting, as a flight missed by only a few minutes can result in hours worth of subsequent inconvenience." Moreover, "face to face solicitation presents risk of duress" and "fraud," and it may be especially difficult for airport authorities to enforce rules against such abuses because passengers "frequently are on tight schedules" and are "unlikely to stop and formally complain." Finally, the prohibition is reasonable because solicitation is permitted on the "sidewalk areas outside the terminals," where the "overwhelming" majority of airport users can be reached.

Justice Kennedy, joined by Justices Blackmun, Stevens, and Souter, offered a very different approach to the public forum issue and, contrary to the majority, concluded that airport terminals are public fora. Justice Kennedy complained that "our public forum doctrine ought [not] convert what was once an analysis protective of expression into one which grants the government authority to restrict speech by fiat." Justice Kennedy observed that the Court's analysis, which "holds that traditional public forums are limited to public property which have as their 'principal purpose . . . the free exchanges of ideas,'" as "evidenced by a longstanding historical practice of permitting speech," leaves "the government with almost unlimited authority to restrict speech on its property," for "the critical step in the Court's analysis" is "the government's own definition or decision, unconstrained by an independent duty to respect the speech its citizens can voice" on public property. Justice Kennedy argued that this view "is contrary to the underlying purposes of the public forum doctrine," for "at the heart of our jurisprudence lies the principle that in a free nation citizens must have the right to gather and speak with other persons in public places."

Justice Kennedy therefore argued that the purposes of the public forum doctrine "cannot be given effect unless we recognize that open, public spaces and thoroughfares which are suitable for discourse may be public forums, whatever their historical pedigree and without concern for a precise classification of the property." Indeed, "without this recognition our forum doctrine retains no relevance in times of fast-changing technology and increasing insularity," and the Court's failure to "recognize the possibility that new types of government property may be appropriate forums for speech will lead to a serious curtailment of our expressive activity." Justice Kennedy thus maintained that, "if the objective, physical characteristics of the property at issue and the actual public access and uses which have been permitted by the government indicate that expressive activity would be appropriate and compatible with those uses, the property is a public forum."

Turning to the issue of airport terminals, Justice Kennedy observed that "in these days an airport is one of the few government-owned spaces where people have extended contact with other members of the public." Although an "airport corridor [is] not a street," it bears important "physical similarities" to a street, the relevant areas "are open to the public without restriction," and the "recent history of airports [demonstrates] that when adequate time, place, and manner regulations are in place, expressive activity is quite compatible with the uses of major airports." Justice Kennedy thus found that the public areas of an airport terminal constitute a public forum.

Despite this disagreement with the Court, Justice Kennedy, writing only for himself, concurred that the ban on solicitation was constitutional as "a reasonable time, place, and manner restriction" because of the risks of fraud and duress. Justice Souter, joined by Justices Blackmun and Stevens, adopted Justice Kennedy's analysis of the general public forum issue but dissented on the constitutionality of the ban on solicitation. In Justice Souter's view, "the claim to be preventing coercion is weak" because, "while a solicitor can be insistent," a pedestrian on the street or airport concourse can simply "walk away." Moreover, Justice Souter found the claim to be preventing fraud unpersuasive because, once it is accepted that the terminal is a public forum, the absolute ban on solicitation does not meet "the requirement of narrow tailoring."

*Sale or distribution of literature.* In a plurality opinion, Justice Kennedy, joined by Justices Blackmun, Stevens, and Souter, concluded that the ban on the sale or distribution of literature violated the first amendment. After finding, for the reasons set forth above, that airport terminals are public fora, Justice Kennedy explained that the ban was invalid because "the right to distribute flyers and literature lies at the heart of the liberties guaranteed" by the first

punishment on a person who undertakes to distribute religious literature on the premises of a company-owned town contrary to the wishes of the town's management." The town, a suburb of Mobile, Alabama, known as Chickasaw, was owned by the Gulf Shipbuilding Corporation. The town was freely used by the public, and there was "nothing to distinguish [it] from any other town [except] the fact that the title to the property [belonged] to a private corporation." Appellant, a Jehovah's Witness, attempted to distribute literature on one of the town's sidewalks. She was informed that, pursuant to a formal corporation policy, she could not distribute literature without a permit, and that no permit would be issued her. When asked to leave, she declined. She was eventually convicted of violating a state statute prohibiting any person to enter or remain on the premises of another after having been warned not to do so.

The Court overturned the conviction. Justice Black, speaking for the Court, observed:

> Had the title to Chickasaw belonged not to a private, but to a municipal corporation [it] would have been clear that appellant's conviction must be reversed. [The] State urges [that] the corporation's right to control the inhabitants of Chickasaw is coextensive with the right of a homeowner to regulate the conduct of his guests. We cannot accept that contention. Ownership does not always mean absolute dominion. The more an owner, for his advantage, opens up his property for use by the public in general, the more do his rights become circumscribed by the statutory and constitutional rights of those who use it. [In] our view the circumstance that the property rights to the premises where the deprivation of liberty, here involved, took place, were held by others than the public, is not sufficient to justify the State's permitting a corporation to govern a community of citizens so as to restrict their fundamental liberties and the enforcement of such restraint by the application of a state statute.

2. *Privately owned shopping centers.* Suppose a privately owned shopping center bans all leafleting in the shopping center. Does that violate the first amendment? Consider the following argument:

> [The] similarities between the business block in *Marsh* and the [modern day] shopping center [are] striking. [The] shopping center premises are open to the public to the same extent as the commercial center of a normal town. [Because the] shopping center [is] clearly the functional equivalent of the business district of Chickasaw involved in *Marsh*, [the] State may not delegate the power, through the use of its trespass laws, wholly to exclude those members of the public wishing to exercise their First Amendment rights on the premises in a manner and for a purpose generally consonant with the use to which the property is actually put.

Food Employees Local 590 v. Logan Valley Plaza, 391 U.S. 308 (1968) (holding that the "peaceful [labor] picketing of a business enterprise located within a shopping center" cannot constitutionally be prohibited by the owner of the shopping center). In Hudgens v. NLRB, 424 U.S. 507 (1976), the Court overruled *Logan Valley*. For a critical evaluation, consider C. Sunstein, The Partial Constitution 208 (1993):

> The [Court] has said that the First Amendment is not implicated [in cases like *Hudgens* because] no government regulation of speech is involved. All that has happened is that private property owners have barred people from their land. [But] this is a poor way to understand the situation. [The] owners of the shopping center are able to exclude the protestors only because government has conferred on them a legal right to do so. The conferral of that right is an exercise of state power. It is this action that restricts the speech of the protestors. Surely it is a real question whether the grant of exclusionary power violates the First Amendment.

3. *Does the appropriation of private property for speech purposes violate the constitutional rights of owners?* Suppose the state, in an effort to promote free expression, grants the individual a right under state law to enter on private property for speech purposes. Might that in itself violate the property or speech rights of the property owner? In PruneYard Shopping Center v. Robins, 447 U.S. 74 (1980), a group of high school students who sought to solicit support for their opposition to a United Nations resolution against Zionism set up a card table in the PruneYard Shopping Center and asked passersby to sign petitions. Pursuant to a policy prohibiting any visitor to engage in any publicly expressive activity not directly related to the shopping center's commercial purposes, a security guard ordered the students to leave. The California Supreme Court held that the California Constitution protects "speech and petitioning, reasonably exercised, in shopping centers even when the centers are privately owned." The U.S. Supreme Court rejected PruneYard's contention that the California Supreme Court's decision violated the federal constitutional rights of the shopping center owner. The Court explained:

> [PruneYard contends] that a right to exclude others underlies the Fifth Amendment guarantee against the taking of property without just compensation. [But] "not every destruction or injury to property by governmental action has been held to be a 'taking' in the constitutional sense." [Here, there] is nothing to suggest that preventing [PruneYard] from prohibiting this sort of activity will unreasonably impair the value or use of [the] property as a shopping center. [PruneYard contends further] that a private property owner has a First Amendment right not to be forced by the State to use his property as a forum for the speech of others. [Although there are circumstances in which] a State may not constitutionally require an individual to participate in the dissemination of an ideological message by displaying it on his private property, [this is not such a case. First, PruneYard is] a business establishment that is open to the public to come and go as they please. The views expressed by members of the public in passing out pamphlets or seeking signatures for a petition thus will not likely be

identified with those of the owner. Second, no specific message is dictated by the State to be displayed. [There] consequently is no danger of governmental discrimination for or against a particular message. Finally, [PruneYard] can expressly disavow any connection with the message by simply posting signs in the area where the speakers or handbillers stand.

### 3.   *The Public Forum: Unequal Access and the Problem of Content-Neutrality*

As we have seen, there are many situations in which government can constitutionally restrict expression on public property in a content-neutral manner. Suppose, however, government decides voluntarily to permit some, but not all, speech? For example, the Court held in *Lee* that government can constitutionally prohibit all solicitation in airport terminals. Suppose government decides to permit solicitation by antiabortion groups, or local political candidates, or groups interested in issues relating to air travel?

The issue is one of "underinclusion." That is, such a regulation restricts *less* speech than a broader and concededly constitutional content-neutral restriction. But in so doing, it adopts a potentially problematic inequality. To avoid this inequality, the regulation could be broadened to restrict *more* speech. Does it make sense to say that a law that restricts *more* speech is constitutional but a law that restricts *less* speech is unconstitutional? Recall *R.A.V.*, Chapter IV.H, supra.

Consider Kagan, The Changing Faces of First Amendment Neutrality, 1992 Sup. Ct. Rev. 38–40:

> Such underinclusion [is] a particular kind of content-based restriction. . . . In [most] cases of content-based restrictions, the question [is] the permissibility of the burden placed on the speech affected. Consider, for example, [a] statute that [criminalizes] seditious advocacy. In deciding [on the constitutionality of such a statute], the Court usually will not ask whether the government has a sufficient reason to treat speech of one kind (seditious advocacy) differently from speech of another; rather, the Court will ask merely whether the government has a sufficient reason to restrict the speech actually affected. [In] such a case, the issue is not underinclusion, for the government could not cure the constitutional flaw by extending the restriction to [other speech]. By contrast, in a content-based underinclusion case, equality is all that is at issue.

## Police Department of Chicago v. Mosley
408 U.S. 92 (1972)

MR. JUSTICE MARSHALL delivered the opinion of the Court.

At issue in this case is the constitutionality of [a] Chicago ordinance [providing that a] "person commits disorderly conduct when he knowingly [pickets] or demonstrates on a public way within 150 feet of [any] school building while the school is in [session], provided that this subsection does not prohibit the peaceful picketing of any school involved in a labor dispute. . . ."

[For] seven months prior to the enactment of [this ordinance], Earl Mosley, a federal postal employee, [frequently] picketed Jones Commercial High School in Chicago. During school hours and usually by himself, Mosley would walk the public sidewalk adjoining the school, carrying a sign that read: "Jones High School practices black discrimination. Jones High School has a black quota." His lonely crusade was always peaceful, orderly, and quiet, and was conceded to be so by the city of Chicago. [Mosley brought this action] seeking declaratory and injunctive relief. [We] hold that the ordinance is unconstitutional because it makes an impermissible distinction between labor picketing and other peaceful picketing.

Because Chicago treats some picketing differently from others, we analyze this ordinance in terms of the Equal Protection Clause of the Fourteenth Amendment. Of course, the equal protection claim in this case is closely intertwined with First Amendment interests; the Chicago ordinance affects picketing, which is expressive conduct; moreover, it does so by classifications formulated in terms of the subject of the picketing. As in all equal protection cases, however, the crucial question is whether there is an appropriate governmental interest suitably furthered by the differential treatment.

The central problem with Chicago's ordinance is that it describes permissible picketing in terms of its subject matter. Peaceful picketing on the subject of a school's labor-management dispute is permitted, but all other peaceful picketing is prohibited. The operative distinction is the message on a picket sign. But, above all else, the First Amendment means that government has no power to restrict expression because of its message, its ideas, its subject matter, or its content. [Citing Cohen v. California; New York Times v. Sullivan; Terminiello v. Chicago.] . . .

Necessarily, [then], government may not grant the use of a forum to people whose views it finds acceptable, but deny use to those wishing to express less favored or more controversial views. And it may not select which issues are worth discussing or debating in public facilities. There is an "equality of status in the field of ideas," and government must afford all points of view an equal opportunity to be heard. Once a forum is opened up to assembly or speaking by some groups, government may not prohibit others from assembling or speaking on the basis of what they intend to say. Selective exclusions from a public forum may not be based on content alone, and may not be justified by reference to content alone. . . .

This is not to say that all picketing must always be allowed. We have continually recognized that reasonable "time, place and manner" regulations of picketing may be necessary to further significant governmental interests. [Cox v. New Hampshire; Adderley v. Florida.] Conflicting demands on the same place may compel the State to make choices among potential users and uses. And the State may have a legitimate interest in prohibiting some picketing to protect public order. But these justifications for selective exclusions from a public forum must be carefully scrutinized [and such discriminations] among pickets must be tailored to serve a substantial governmental interest.

In this case, the ordinance itself describes impermissible picketing not in terms of time, place, and manner, but in terms of subject matter. The regulation "thus slip[s] from the neutrality of time, place, and circumstance into a concern about content." This is never permitted. In spite of this, Chicago urges that the ordinance is not improper content censorship, but rather a device for preventing disruption of the school. [Although] preventing school disruption is a city's legitimate concern, Chicago itself has determined that peaceful labor picketing during school hours is not an undue interference with school. Therefore, [Chicago] may not maintain that other picketing disrupts the school unless that picketing is clearly more disruptive than the picketing Chicago already permits. "Peaceful" nonlabor picketing, [however], is obviously no more disruptive than "peaceful" labor picketing. . . .

Similarly, we reject the city's argument that, although it permits peaceful labor picketing, it may prohibit all nonlabor picketing because, as a class, nonlabor picketing is more prone to produce violence than labor picketing. Predictions about imminent disruption from picketing involve judgments appropriately made on an individualized basis, not by means of broad classifications, especially those based on subject matter. [Some] labor picketing is peaceful, some disorderly; the same is true of picketing on other themes. [Given] what Chicago tolerates from labor picketing, the excesses of some nonlabor picketing may not be controlled by a broad ordinance prohibiting both peaceful and violent picketing. Such excesses "can be controlled by narrowly drawn statutes," [focusing] on the abuses and dealing even handedly with picketing regardless of subject matter. [Far] from being tailored to a substantial governmental interest, the discrimination among pickets is based on the content of their expression. Therefore, under the Equal Protection Clause, it may not stand.

Affirmed.

MR. JUSTICE BLACKMUN and MR. JUSTICE REHNQUIST concur in the result.

### Note: Mosley *and the "Equality" of Ideas*

1. *Equality and underinclusion.* Is the Chicago ordinance, absent the labor picketing exemption, a permissible content-neutral restriction? Recall Grayned v. Rockford, supra. If the ordinance is constitutional absent the labor-picketing exemption, should the exemption render it invalid? Is it anomalous that under the Court's reasoning the ordinance would be more likely to

be constitutional if it restricted *more* speech? Consider the following arguments:

(a) The city's willingness to enact the labor exemption undermines the credibility of its asserted justifications for the restriction of nonlabor speech. Thus, even under the ordinary standards of content-neutral review, the restriction of nonlabor picketing may be invalid, even though a restriction of all picketing might be valid.

(b) The standard of review should be higher when the city distinguishes between labor and nonlabor speech than when it acts in a content-neutral manner. That is, from a constitutional perspective, the inequality between labor and nonlabor picketing is more problematic than the broader, but more "equal," restriction of all picketing near a school. (On the other hand, consider the following argument: The standard of review should be especially *lenient* in a case like *Mosley* because the ordinance was designed not to restrict but to expand the opportunities for free expression.)

2. *Subject matter restrictions.* Note that in *Mosley* the content-based restriction was directed not against a particular viewpoint but against an entire subject of discussion — all nonlabor expression. Should the first amendment's hostility to content-based regulation extend not only to restrictions on particular viewpoints but also to restrictions on entire topics? Recall the debate on this issue in R.A.V. v. City of St. Paul, Chapter IV.H, supra. Consider Stone, Restrictions of Speech because of Its Content: The Peculiar Case of Subject-Matter Restrictions, 46 U. Chi. L. Rev. 81, 83, 108 (1978):

> [Although]"subject-matter" distinctions unquestionably regulate content, they [do] not fit neatly within the Court's general framework. [The] Court's rigorous approach to content-based restrictions stems in part from the realization that such restrictions generally have an especially potent viewpoint-differential impact upon the "marketplace of ideas." [Because] they are at least facially viewpoint-neutral, [however, subject-matter restrictions] do not have the same sort of skewing effect on "the thinking process of the community" as restrictions directed against speech taking a particular side in an ongoing debate. Moreover, because of their apparent viewpoint-neutrality, subject-matter restrictions seem much less likely than other forms of content-based restrictions to be the product of government hostility to the ideas suppressed. In general, one is more likely to be hostile to speech espousing a specific point of view than to speech about an entire subject. As a result, one [might] argue that subject-matter restrictions are in general less threatening than other sorts of content-based restrictions and, like content-neutral restrictions, need not be subjected to the most stringent standards of review.

3. *The reach of* Mosley: *residential picketing.* In Carey v. Brown, 447 U.S. 455 (1980), appellees participated in a peaceful demonstration in front of the home of the mayor of Chicago, protesting his alleged failure to support the busing of schoolchildren to achieve racial integration. As a result of this

demonstration, appellees were convicted of violating an Illinois statute declaring it "unlawful to picket before or about the residence [of] any person, except when the residence" is "a place of employment involved in a labor dispute."

The Court held that the residential picketing statute was "constitutionally indistinguishable from the ordinance invalidated in *Mosley*":

> [The] Act accords preferential treatment to the expression of views on one particular subject; information about labor disputes may be freely disseminated, but discussion of all other issues is restricted. [When] government regulation discriminates among speech-related activities in a public forum, the Equal Protection Clause mandates that the legislation be finely tailored to serve substantial state interests, and the justifications offered for and distinctions it draws must be carefully scrutinized. [*Mosley*.] . . .

Justice Rehnquist, joined by Chief Justice Burger and Justice Blackmun, dissented.

4. *The reach of* Mosley: *universities and the problem of religious expression.* The University of Missouri at Kansas City, which officially recognizes more than one hundred student groups and routinely permits such groups to meet in university facilities, adopted a regulation prohibiting the use of university buildings for "purposes of religious worship or religious teaching." Several university students who were members of an organization of evangelical Christian students challenged the regulation.

In Widmar v. Vincent, 454 U.S. 263 (1981), the Court invalidated the regulation:

> [The] campus of a public university, at least for its students, possesses many of the characteristics of a public forum. [At] the same time, however, [a] university differs in significant respects from public forums such as streets or parks. [A] university's mission is education, and [it may] impose reasonable regulations compatible with that mission upon the use of its campus and facilities. [Here, through] its policy of accommodating their meetings, the University has created a forum generally open for use by student groups. [The] Constitution forbids a State to enforce certain exclusions from a forum generally open to the public, even if it was not required to create the forum in the first place. [In] order to justify discriminatory exclusion from a public forum based on the religious content of a group's intended speech, the University [must] show that its regulation is necessary to serve a compelling state interest and that it is narrowly drawn to achieve that end. See [Carey v. Brown]. In this case the University claims a compelling interest in maintaining a strict separation of church and state. [We] agree that the interest of the University in complying with its constitutional obligations may be characterized as compelling. It does not follow, however, that an "equal access" policy would be incompatible with [the establishment clause]. It is possible — perhaps even foreseeable — that religious groups will benefit from access to University facilities. But [a] religious

organization's enjoyment of merely "incidental" benefits does not violate the prohibition against the "primary advancement" of religion.

Justice Stevens concurred in the judgment. Justice White dissented.

See also Lamb's Chapel v. Center Moriches Union Free School District, 508 U.S. 384 (1993) (relying on *Widmar* to invalidate a school district rule permitting school property to be used after school for social, civic, and recreational uses, but prohibiting the use of such property for religious purposes); Rosenberger v. Rector & Visitors of the University of Virginia, 515 U.S. 819 (1995) (relying on *Lamb's Chapel* to invalidate a University of Virginia policy authorizing payment from the Student Activities Fund for the printing costs of a variety of student publications, but prohibiting payment for any student publication that "primarily promotes or manifests a particular belief in or about a deity or an ultimate reality").

5. *The reach of* Mosley: *the "careful scrutiny" standard*. Are there circumstances in which a content-based law, like the ones invalidated in *Mosley*, *Carey*, and *Widmar*, can withstand "careful scrutiny"? See Burson v. Freeman, 504 U.S. 191 (1992) (upholding a law prohibiting the solicitation of votes and the display or distribution of campaign materials within one hundred feet of the entrance to a polling place).

# Lehman v. City of Shaker Heights
418 U.S. 298 (1974)

MR. JUSTICE BLACKMUN announced the judgment of the Court and an opinion, in which THE CHIEF JUSTICE, MR. JUSTICE WHITE, and MR. JUSTICE REHNQUIST join.

This case presents the question whether a city which operates a public rapid transit system and sells [commercial and public service] advertising space for car cards on its vehicles is required by the First and Fourteenth Amendments to accept paid political advertising on behalf of a candidate for public office.

[Petitioner, a candidate for the office of state representative,] sought to promote his candidacy by purchasing car card space on the Shaker Heights Rapid Transit System for the months of August, September, and October. [He] was informed [that], although space was then available, [the] city did not permit political advertising. The system, however, accepted ads from cigarette companies, banks, savings and loan associations, liquor companies, retail and service establishments, churches, and civic and public-service oriented groups. . . .

When petitioner did not succeed in his effort to have his copy accepted, he sought declaratory and injunctive relief in the state courts of Ohio without success. . . . It is urged that the car cards here constitute a public forum protected by the First Amendment, and that there is a guarantee of

Governmental-Proprietary Distinction in Constitutional Law, 66 Va. L. Rev. 1073, 1116 (1980):

> As a regulator of the general public, the government must base its proscription of an activity on the premise that the proscription will act to enhance the general welfare. [As] a procurer or provider of goods and services, however, it may assert a different, more specific kind of interest — the interest of an employer who needs an efficient workforce, a landlord who would prefer not to deal with tenants who do not pay rent, or a purchaser who wishes to contract with a trustworthy seller. This quasi-business interest may adequately support regulation that a court might strike down if applied to the public at large and the state supported it with arguments that it promotes the general welfare. [That government acts in a proprietary capacity, however,] legitimately serves only to identify a state interest not present when the state regulates the general public. It should be but one element in the analysis and should not by itself determine the outcome.

See also International Society for Krishna Consciousness, Inc. v. Lee, supra (invoking the proprietary/governmental distinction in upholding a ban on solicitation in airport terminals); United States v. Kokinda, supra (invoking the distinction in upholding a Postal Service regulation prohibiting any person from soliciting contributions on post office property).

b. *Streetcar passengers are a "captive audience."* Recall Cohen v. California, Chapter IV.G supra: "The ability of government, consonant with the Constitution, to shut off discourse solely to protect others from hearing it is [dependent] upon a showing that substantial privacy interests are being invaded in an essentially intolerable manner." Is that test satisfied in *Lehman*? If so, is the exclusion of all political speech an appropriate device for protecting the sensibilities of captive commuters? Suppose that, after polling its commuters, the city finds that, although the vast majority do not object to the ideas of Democratic and Republican candidates, they "deeply resent" the views expressed by Socialist candidates. Based on this finding, may the city permit Democratic and Republican candidates to purchase car card space to espouse their "inoffensive" ideas, while excluding the "offensive" Socialist messages? For analysis of the "captive" audience, see Chapter IV.G, supra.

c. *"No First Amendment forum is here to be found."* Do you agree with Justice Brennan that, even if the car card space did not inherently constitute a public forum, the city's acceptance of commercial and public service advertisements "created" such a forum? Recall *Widmar*. Consider Emerson, The Affirmative Side of the First Amendment, 15 Ga. L. Rev. 795, 813 (1981): "The dissenters fail to recognize the complications arising when the government is affirmatively promoting expression by providing facilities for a selected area of expression. They argue that, once the 'forum' has been opened, the government may not regulate on the basis of content. The issue before the Court, however, was what the scope of the forum was."

Would any of these "explanations" of *Lehman* justify a content-based restriction defined in terms of viewpoint rather than subject matter?

2. *The reach of* Lehman: *military bases.* In Greer v. Spock, supra, the base commander of the Fort Dix Military Reservation, acting under the authority of a regulation prohibiting "demonstrations, picketing, sit-ins, protest marches, political speeches and similar activities" on the base, denied the request of a political candidate to make a speech on the base to discuss election issues with service personnel and their dependents. The candidate maintained that the regulation was invalid because the ban on civilian access to the base for expressive purposes was not content-neutral: "Civilian speakers have occasionally been invited to the base to address military personnel. The subjects of their talks have ranged from business management to drug abuse. Visiting clergymen have, by invitation, participated in religious services at the base chapel. Theatrical exhibitions and musical productions have also been presented on the base."

The Court upheld the regulation. Although the base was generally open to the public, the Court explained that "the business of a military installation [is] to train soldiers, not to provide a public forum." Moreover, the Court emphasized that there was "no claim that the military authorities discriminated in any way among candidates for public office based upon the candidates' supposed political views." In such circumstances, the ban on partisan political expression was not unconstitutional. Justices Brennan and Marshall dissented. Is *Greer* reconcilable with *Mosley* and *Widmar*?

**PERRY EDUCATORS' ASSOCIATION v. PERRY LOCAL EDUCATORS' ASSOCIATION, 460 U.S. 37 (1983).** The school district of Perry Township, Indiana, operates an interschool mail system to transmit messages among the teachers and between the teachers and the school administration. In addition, some private organizations, such as the YMCA and the Cub Scouts, have been permitted to use the system. After the Perry Educators' Association (PEA) was certified as the exclusive bargaining representative of the district's teachers, the school district and PEA entered into a collective bargaining agreement granting PEA, but no other union, access to the mail system. The Perry Local Educators' Association (PLEA), a rival union, brought this suit claiming that the district's access policy violated the Constitution.

The Court, in a five-to-four decision, upheld the challenged policy. Justice White delivered the opinion: "The existence of a right of access to public property [depends] on the character of the property at issue. [First, there are the] streets and [parks]. In these quintessential public forums, the government may not [enforce] a content-based exclusion [unless the exclusion] is necessary to serve a compelling state interest and [is] narrowly drawn to achieve that end. [*Mosley; Carey.*] [A] second category consists of public property which the state has [voluntarily] opened for use by the public as a place for expressive activity. [Although] a state is not required to indefinitely retain the open upheld the refusal of the Texas Department of Motor Vehicles to approve a license plate featuring the Confederate battle flag on the ground that the plate constituted government, rather than private, speech. In the Court's view, the license plates were not a nonpublic forum because the state was "not simply managing government property, but instead is engaging in expressive conduct." It based this conclusion on the historical context, observers' reasonable interpretation of the messages conveyed by Texas specialty plates, and the effective control that Texas exerted over the design selection process. Justice Alito, joined by Chief Justice Roberts and Justices Scalia and Kennedy, dissented.

5. *Distinctions among means of expression.* In United States v. Kokinda, supra, respondents, members of a political advocacy group, set up a table on a sidewalk near the entrance to a United States Post Office to distribute literature and solicit contributions. The sidewalk is located entirely on post office property and is the sole means by which customers travel from the parking lot to the post office building. Respondents were convicted of violating a regulation prohibiting any person from soliciting contributions on postal premises. The Court upheld the regulation as applied.

In a plurality opinion, Justice O'Connor, joined by Chief Justice Rehnquist and Justices White and Scalia, concluded that the sidewalk is not a "traditional" public forum because the "postal sidewalk at issue does not have the characteristics of public sidewalks traditionally open to expressive activity." Justice O'Connor then rejected the claim that the sidewalk, which was available for all conventional forms of expressive activity other than solicitation, was a "limited-purpose" public forum:

> The Postal Service has not expressly dedicated its sidewalks to any expressive activity. [Although] individuals or groups have been permitted to leaflet, speak, and picket on postal premises, [the] practice of allowing some speech activities on postal property [does] not add up to the dedication of postal property to speech activities. ["The] government does not create a public forum by . . . *permitting* limited discourse, but only by intentionally opening a nontraditional forum for public discourse."[*Cornelius*]. [It] is anomalous [to suggest] that the Service's allowance of some avenues of speech would be relied upon as evidence that it is impermissibly suppressing other speech. If anything, the Service's generous accommodation of some types of speech testifies to its willingness to provide as broad a forum as possible, consistent with its postal mission. [Any other view] would create, in the name of the First Amendment, a disincentive for the Government to dedicate its property to any speech activities at all.

Justice Kennedy concurred in the result. Justice Brennan, joined by Justices Marshall, Blackmun, and Stevens, dissented. Would it be constitutional for the post office to permit only charities eligible to participate in the CFC to distribute literature on this sidewalk?

6. *Speaker-based restrictions.* Note that *Perry, Cornelius,* and *Forbes* involved "speaker-based" restrictions. Such restrictions, which treat some speakers

differently than others, but define the distinction in terms other than content, do not fit neatly within the Court's content-based/content-neutral distinction. In these cases, the Court sharply distinguished speaker-based from viewpoint-based restrictions and, at least in the nonpublic forum context, tested speaker-based restrictions by a standard of reasonableness. But speaker-based restrictions often have clear viewpoint-differential effects. In *Perry*, for example, the challenged policy unquestionably favored some viewpoints over others, for recognized bargaining agents are likely to take consistent and predictable positions on particular issues. Indeed, in some instances, speaker-based restrictions may correlate almost perfectly with viewpoint. Consider, for example, laws granting special subsidies to veterans' organizations or denying tax deductions to individuals who contribute to the Communist Party. How should we deal with such restrictions? See Stone, Content Regulation and the First Amendment, 25 Wm. & Mary L. Rev. 189, 244–251 (1983).

7. *Evaluation.* Consider the Court's categorization of "quintessential," "limited," and "non" public forums. Do these categories make sense? Do you agree that the Court in *Perry* "indulged in a shell game, [throwing] out a circular definition of the public forum"? L. Tribe, Constitutional Choices 207 (1985). Consider the following views:

a. Subject matter classifications should be subjected to closer scrutiny in "quintessential" public forums than in "non" public forums for the same reasons that content-neutral restrictions are subjected to closer scrutiny in quintessential public forums.

b. Whether a particular public facility constitutes a "limited" public forum, rather than a "non" public forum, turns on the amount of speech government has allowed. If the government allows almost all speech, and excludes only a narrow category, as in *Widmar*, it has created a public forum. If it excludes almost all speech, and allows only a narrow category, as in *Lehman, Greer,* and *Perry*, it has not created a public forum.

c. "Classification of public places as various types of forums has only confused judicial opinions by diverting attention from the real first amendment [issues]. Like the fourth amendment, the first amendment 'protects people, not places.' Constitutional protection should depend not on labeling the speaker's physical location but on the first amendment values and governmental interests involved in the case." Farber & Nowak, The Misleading Nature of Public Forum Analysis: Content and Context in First Amendment Adjudication, 70 Va. L. Rev. 1219, 1234 (1984).

### Note: Religious Expression and the Meaning of "Viewpoint Neutrality"

1. *Viewpoint versus subject matter.* In Lamb's Chapel v. Moriches Union Free School District, supra, the Court considered the constitutionality of a

school district rule that permitted after-school social, civic, and recreational uses of school property but prohibited the use of such property for religious purposes. Applying this rule, the school district rejected Lamb's Chapel's request to show on school property religious-oriented films concerning family values and child-rearing. The lower courts upheld the rule on the theory that the school property was "a limited public forum open only for designated purposes," and that access to such a forum "can be based on subject matter [so] long as the distinctions drawn are reasonable [and] viewpoint neutral." The Supreme Court accepted this analysis but nonetheless invalidated the rule because it was not "viewpoint neutral."

In reaching this result, the Court rejected the lower courts' conclusion that the challenged rule was based on subject matter, rather than viewpoint, "because it [would] be applied in the same way to all uses of school property for religious purposes." Although conceding that "all religions and all uses for religious purposes are treated alike under the rule," the Court observed that this "does not answer the critical question" whether it constitutes discrimination "on the basis of viewpoint to permit the school property to be used for the presentation of all views about family issues [except] those dealing with the subject matter from a religious standpoint." The Court reasoned that the "film involved here [dealt] with a subject otherwise permissible under [the rule], and its exhibition was denied solely because the film dealt with the subject from a religious standpoint." The Court therefore concluded that the rule "violates the First Amendment" because it denied "access to a speaker solely to suppress the point of view he espouses on an otherwise included subject."

Consider Stone, The Equal Access Controversy: The Religion Clauses and the Meaning of "Neutrality," 81 Nw. U. L. Rev. 168, 169–170 (1986):

> The protection of political speech, like religious speech, lies at the very core of the first amendment. The Court often has recognized, however, that government may grant special benefits to nonpolitical speech without extending those benefits to political speech, so long as it does not expressly favor any particular political viewpoint. [Citing *Lehman*, *Greer*, and *Cornelius*.] This is so because policies that disadvantage political speech as a class are less threatening to first amendment values than laws that expressly disadvantage specific points of view.
>
> A similar principle [should govern] religious expression. As the Supreme Court has long recognized, the "clearest command" of the religion clauses is that "one religious denomination cannot be officially preferred over another." [Denominational] discrimination in the religious context is the analog of viewpoint discrimination in the political context. [The] corollary is also true, however. Governmental policies that grant special benefits to nonreligious expression as a class should be tested by the same — less demanding — standards that the Court uses to test the constitutionality of governmental policies that grant special benefits to nonpolitical expression as a class. In the religious, as in the political, realm the broader subject-matter classification is less threatening to core first amendment values.

2. Lamb's Chapel *revisited: further debate on the meaning of viewpoint neutrality.* In Rosenberger v. Rector & Visitors of University of Virginia, 515 U.S. 819 (1995), the Court, in a five-to-four decision, invalidated a University of Virginia policy authorizing payment from the Student Activities Fund for the printing costs of a variety of student publications, but prohibiting payment for any student publication that "primarily promotes or manifests a particular belief in or about a deity or an ultimate reality." The suit was brought by a student organization that was denied funding because it publishes a journal that "offers a Christian perspective on both personal and community issues," such as "racism, crisis pregnancy, [and] homosexuality."

The Court, in an opinion by Justice Kennedy, explained that, although the "necessities of confining a forum to the limited and legitimate purposes for which it was created may justify the State in reserving it for certain groups or for the discussion of certain topics," it may not "discriminate against speech on the basis of its viewpoint." The Court then observed that these "same principles apply" to the Student Activities Fund, which the Court described as a "forum," albeit "more in a metaphysical than in a spatial or geographic sense."

Acknowledging that the definition of viewpoint discrimination "is not a precise one," the Court nonetheless concluded that "here, as in *Lamb's Chapel,* viewpoint discrimination is the proper way to interpret the University's" policy. The Court explained that this was so because it was the religious "perspective" of the journal, rather than the "subjects discussed," such as racism, pregnancy, or homosexuality, that resulted in the university's refusal to pay the journal's printing costs.

In dissent, Justice Souter, joined by Justices Stevens, Ginsburg, and Breyer, maintained that the "issue whether a distinction is based on viewpoint does not turn simply on whether a government regulation happens to be applied to a speaker who seeks to advance a particular viewpoint," but "on whether the burden on speech is explained by reference to viewpoint." Thus, citing *Lehman,* Justice Souter observed that "a municipality's decision to prohibit political advertising on bus placards" does not "amount to viewpoint discrimination when in the course of applying this policy it denies space to a person who wishes to speak in favor of a particular political candidate."

Justice Souter argued that it is the "element of taking sides in a public debate that identifies viewpoint discrimination and makes it the most pernicious of all distinctions based on content." Justice Souter reasoned that, given this understanding, there was "no viewpoint discrimination" in this case:

If the [policy] were written [so] as to limit [only] Christian advocacy, [the] discrimination would be based on viewpoint. But that is not what the regulation authorizes; it applies to Muslim and Jewish and Buddhist advocacy as well as Christian. And since it limits funding to activities promoting or manifesting a particular belief not only "in" but "about" a deity or ultimate reality, it applies to agnostics and atheists as well as [to] deists and theists. [Thus, the policy does] not skew debate by funding one position but not its competitors. [It simply denies] funding for hortatory speech that "primarily promotes or manifests" any view on the merits of religion; [it denies] funding for the entire subject matter of religious apologetics.

Justice Souter therefore concluded that this case was distinguishable from *Lamb's Chapel*, where the "regulation did not purport to deny access to any speaker wishing to express a non-religious or expressly antireligious point of view." He concluded that, if the policy at issue in this case "amounts to viewpoint discrimination, the Court has all but eviscerated the line between viewpoint and content."

Recall the debate over a similar issue in R.A.V. v. City of St. Paul, Chapter IV.H, supra. In light of the Court's reasoning in *Lamb's Chapel* and *Rosenberger*, does it follow that the regulation of "obscenity" is also impermissibly viewpoint-based "because it is justified by moral objections to the ideas or messages that sexual speech is said to convey"? Heins, Viewpoint Discrimination, 24 Hastings Const. L.Q. 99, 103 (1996).

3. *Religious speech as viewpoint discrimination: another look.* In Good News Club v. Milford Central School, 533 U.S. 98 (2001), the school district authorized district residents to use school buildings after school hours for "instruction in education, learning, or the arts" and for "social, civic, recreational, and entertainment uses pertaining to the community welfare," but not for "religious purposes." The school district denied a request by the Good News Club, a private Christian organization for children ages six to twelve, to use school property to "sing songs, hear Bible lessons, memorize scripture and pray" on the ground that this constituted "religious purposes."

The Court, in a six-to-three decision, held that this was unconstitutional viewpoint discrimination in a limited public forum. In his opinion for the Court, Justice Thomas explained that "the Club seeks to address a subject otherwise permitted under the rule, the teaching of morals and character, from a religious standpoint." He therefore concluded that this case was indistinguishable from *Lamb's Chapel* and *Rosenberger*.

In dissent, Justice Stevens argued that "speech for 'religious purposes' may reasonably be understood to encompass three different categories. First, there is religious speech that is simply speech about a particular topic from a religious point of view. [Second], there is religious speech that amounts to worship. [Third], there is [speech] that is aimed principally at proselytizing or inculcating a belief in a particular religious faith." In Justice Stevens's view, "the question is whether a school can [create] a limited public forum that admits the first type of religious speech without allowing the other two." He concluded that "just as a school may allow meetings to discuss current events from a political perspective without also allowing organized political recruitment, so too can a school allow discussion of topics such as moral development from a religious (or nonreligious) perspective without thereby opening its forum to religious proselytizing or worship."

In a separate dissenting opinion, Justice Souter, joined by Justice Ginsburg, argued that this case was distinguishable from *Lamb's Chapel* and *Rosenberger* because "Good News intends to use the public school premise not for the mere discussion of a subject from a particular, Christian point of view, but for an evangelical service of worship calling children to commit themselves in an act of Christian conversion." He maintained that the majority's position stands "for the remarkable proposition that any public school opened for civic meetings must be opened for use as a church, synagogue, or mosque."

In a concurring opinion, Justice Scalia responded to the dissenters: "The dissenters emphasize that the religious speech [of the Club is] 'aimed principally at proselytizing or inculcating belief in a particular religious faith.' [But this] does not distinguish the Club's activities from those of [political, social and cultural organizations that also] may seek to inculcate children with their beliefs [and try to]'recruit others to join their respective groups.'"

**CHRISTIAN LEGAL SOCIETY CHAPTER v. MARTINEZ, 130 S. Ct. 2971 (2010).** Hastings College of the Law, a public law school within the University of California system, extends official recognition to student groups through its "Registered Student Organization" (RSO) program. RSOs receive certain benefits, including the use of school funds, facilities, and channels of communication, as well as the use of Hastings' name and logo. In exchange for such recognition, RSOs must abide by certain conditions. All RSOs, for example, must comply with the school's Nondiscrimination Policy, which forbids discrimination on the basis of race, religion, gender, national origin, age, disability, ancestry, and sexual orientation. Hastings interprets this policy to mandate acceptance of *all* students.

In 2004, students at Hastings created the Christian Legal Society by affiliating with a national Christian association that charters student chapters at law schools throughout the country. These chapters must adopt bylaws that, inter alia, require members and officers to sign a "Statement of Faith" and to conduct their lives in accord with prescribed principles. CLS excludes from affiliation anyone who engages in "unrepentant homosexual conduct" or holds religious convictions different from those in the Statement of Faith. Hastings rejected CLS's application for RSO status on the ground that the group excluded students based on religion and sexual orientation. CLS filed this action asserting that Hastings' "accept all-comers" policy violates its first amendment rights of expression and association.

The Court, in a five-to-four decision, rejected CLS's claim. Justice Ginsburg delivered the opinion of the Court: "[Hastings], through its RSO program, established a limited public forum. [See *Rosenberger*]. [The] Court has permitted restrictions on access to a limited public forum, like the RSO program here, [if they are] reasonable and viewpoint neutral. [We first] consider whether Hastings' policy is reasonable. [With] appropriate regard for school administrators' judgment, we review the justifications

Hastings offers in defense of its all-comers requirement. First, the open-access policy 'ensures that the leadership, educational, and social opportunities afforded by [RSOs] are available to all students.' [Second], the all-comers requirement helps Hastings police the written terms of its Nondiscrimination Policy without inquiring into an RSO's motivation for membership restrictions. [Third], the Law School reasonably adheres to the view that an all-comers [policy] 'encourages tolerance, cooperation, and learning among students.' [Fourth], Hastings' policy [conveys] the Law School's decision 'to decline to subsidize with public monies and benefits [discriminatory conduct].' . . .

"The Law School's policy is all the more creditworthy in view of the 'substantial alternative channels' that remain open for [CLS-student] communication to take place. [Student groups] commonly maintain a presence at universities without official school affiliation. Based on the record before us, CLS [hosted] a variety of activities the year after Hastings denied it recognition. [It bears emphasizing] that nonrecognition of a student organization is [not] equivalent to prohibiting its members from speaking. . . .

"CLS [assails] the reasonableness of the all-comers policy [by forecasting] that the policy will facilitate hostile takeovers; if organizations must open their arms to all, CLS contends, saboteurs will infiltrate groups to subvert their mission and message. This supposition strikes us as more hypothetical than real, [but if] students begin to exploit an all-comers policy by hijacking organizations to distort or destroy their missions, Hastings presumably would revisit and revise its policy. . . .

"We next consider whether Hastings' all-comers policy is viewpoint neutral. [It is] hard to imagine a more viewpoint-neutral policy than one requiring *all* student groups to accept *all* comers. [CLS] attacks the regulation by pointing to its effect: The policy is vulnerable to constitutional assault, CLS contends, because 'it systematically and predictably burdens most heavily those groups whose viewpoints are out of favor with the campus mainstream.' [This] argument stumbles from its first step because '[a] regulation that serves purposes unrelated to the content of expression is deemed neutral, even if it has an incidental effect on some speakers or messages but not others.' [Moreover,] Hastings' requirement that student groups accept all [comers] 'is justified without reference to the content [or viewpoint] of the regulated speech.' The Law School's policy aims at the *act* of rejecting would-be group members without reference to the reasons motivating that [behavior]. CLS' conduct — not its Christian perspective — is [what] stands between the group and RSO status. [Finding] Hastings' open-access condition on RSO status reasonable and viewpoint neutral, we reject CLS' free-speech and expressive-association claims."

Note that the Court decided the case on the basis of a stipulation by the parties that Hastings had interpreted and applied the Nondiscrimination Policy as an "accept-all-comers" policy. Would it change the analysis if the

Court had considered the constitutionality of the Nondiscrimination Policy itself — that is, as a policy denying RSO status to organizations discriminating on the basis of certain *particular* characteristics (e.g., race, religion, gender, sexual orientation)?

Does it matter that this case involves a subsidy rather than a prohibition? Suppose, for example, the state made it unlawful for any group or organization to deny membership to any person. Would such a law be constitutional as applied to the Democratic Party, if it wants to exclude Republicans from voting in its upcoming primary? Would it be constitutional as applied to a synagogue that restricts membership only to Jews? Suppose that, instead of prohibiting such selective membership, the state merely denied tax-exempt status to any group or organization that isn't open to all comers.

Consider the Court's response to this question: "CLS, in seeking what is effectively a state subsidy, faces only indirect pressure to modify its membership policies; CLS may exclude any person for any reason if it forgoes the benefits of official recognition. [Our] decisions have distinguished between policies that require action and those that withhold benefits. [The] First Amendment shields CLS against state prohibition of the organization's expressive activity, [but] CLS enjoys no constitutional right to state subvention of its selectivity."

Justice Alito, joined by Chief Justice Roberts and Justices Scalia and Thomas, dissented: "The proudest boast of our free speech jurisprudence is that we protect the freedom to express 'the thought that we hate.' Today's decision rests on a very different principle: no freedom for expression that offends prevailing standards of political correctness in our country's institutions of higher learning. [Hastings] currently has more than 60 registered groups and, in all its history, has denied registration to exactly one: the Christian Legal Society."

Justice Alito maintained that, for procedural reasons, the Nondiscrimination Policy rather than the accept-all-comers policy was properly at issue in the case, and he therefore proceeded to consider the constitutionality of that policy: "[Many RSOs at Hastings] are dedicated to expressing a message. For example, Silenced Right, a pro-life group, [teaches] that 'all human life [is] sacred and has inherent dignity,' while [the] American Constitution Society [seeks] 'to counter [a] narrow conservative vision' of American law. [Under the Nondiscrimination Policy, such groups may exclude members who do not share the organization's views, without losing their RSO status, because discrimination on the basis of political, philosophical, cultural or social viewpoints is not prohibited. The Nondiscrimination Policy] singled out one category of expressive associations for disfavored treatment: groups formed to express a religious message. Only religious groups were required to admit students who did not share their views. An environmentalist group was not required to admit students who rejected global warming. [But] CLS was required to admit avowed atheists. This was patent viewpoint discrimination."

It is no wonder that the Court makes no attempt to defend the constitutionality of the Nondiscrimination Policy."

Although the Court found it unnecessary to consider the constitutionality of the Nondiscrimination Policy because of the parties' stipulation, Justice Stevens filed a separate concurring opinion responding to Justice Alito: "In the dissent's view, by refusing to grant CLS an exemption from the Nondiscrimination Policy, Hastings violated CLS's rights, for by proscribing unlawful discrimination on the basis of religion, the policy discriminated unlawfully on the basis of religion. [But] the Nondiscrimination Policy is content and viewpoint neutral. It does not reflect a judgment by school officials about any student group's speech. [Indeed], it does not regulate expression or belief at all. [What] the policy does reflect is a judgment that discrimination [on] the basis of certain factors, such as race and religion, is less tolerable than discrimination on the basis of other factors."

Justice Alito responded to this argument: "Justice Stevens [argues] that the Nondiscrimination Policy is viewpoint neutral because it 'does not regulate expression or belief at all' but instead regulates conduct. This Court has held, however, that the particular conduct at issue here constitutes a form of expression that is protected by the First Amendment. It is [well] established that the First Amendment shields the right of a group to engage in expressive association by limiting membership to persons whose admission does not significantly interfere with the group's ability to convey its views. [Citing Boy Scouts of America v. Dale, infra.] [Moreover, the Nondiscrimination Policy] also discriminates on the basis of viewpoint regarding sexual morality. CLS has a particular viewpoint on this subject, namely, that sexual conduct outside marriage [is] wrongful. Hastings would not allow CLS to express this viewpoint by limiting membership to persons willing to express a sincere agreement with CLS's views. By contrast, [a] Free Love Club could require members to affirm that they reject the traditional view of sexual morality to which CLS adheres. It is hard to see how this can be viewed as anything other than viewpoint discrimination."

Justice Alito then turned to the "accept-all-comers" version of the Hastings policy: "There can be no dispute that [the first amendment] would not permit a generally applicable law mandating that private religious groups admit members who do not share the group's beliefs. Religious groups like CLS obviously engage in expressive association, and no legitimate state interest could override the powerful effect that an accept-all-comers law would have on the ability of religious groups to express their views. The State of California surely could not demand that all Christian groups admit members who believe that Jesus was merely human. [Muslim] groups could not be forced to admit persons who are viewed as slandering Islam. [But] the Court now holds that Hastings [may] impose these very same requirements on students who wish to [gain the benefits of RSO status]. The Court lists four justifications offered by Hastings in defense of the accept-all-comers policy, [but these justifications] are insufficient. [Moreover], statements in the majority opinion make it seem as if the denial of registration did not hurt CLS at all. [The] majority's emphasis on CLS's ability to endure [by] using private facilities and means of communication [is] quite amazing. This Court does not customarily brush aside a claim of unlawful discrimination with the observation that the effects of the discrimination were really not so bad. . . .

"The Court is also wrong in holding that the accept-all-comers policy is viewpoint neutral. The Court proclaims that it would be 'hard to imagine a more viewpoint-neutral policy,' but I would not be so quick to jump to this conclusion. Even if it is assumed that the policy is viewpoint neutral on its face, there is strong evidence in the record that the policy was announced as a pretext. The adoption of a facially neutral policy for the purpose of suppressing the expression of a particular viewpoint is viewpoint discrimination. Here, CLS has made a strong showing that Hastings's sudden adoption [of] its accept-all-comers policy was a pretext for the law school's unlawful denial of CLS's registration application under the Nondiscrimination Policy. . . .

"I do not think it is an exaggeration to say that today's decision is a serious setback for freedom of expression in this country. [I] can only hope this decision will turn out to be an aberration."

### 4. Unequal Access and the Problem of Government Speech

To what extent, if any, should the principles and doctrines that govern access to public parks, airport terminals, and military bases also govern public auditoriums, school libraries, and government-funded programs to support the arts? To what extent may the government itself engage in speech? When the government speaks, must it do so in an even-handed manner?

SOUTHEASTERN PROMOTIONS v. CONRAD, 420 U.S. 546 (1975). Petitioner, a promoter of theatrical productions, applied to a municipal board charged with managing a city auditorium and a city-leased theater to present the musical "Hair" at the theater. Although no conflicting engagement was scheduled, the board, based on reports that the musical was sexually explicit, involved nudity, and might be "obscene," rejected the application because the production would not be "in the best interest of the community." The Court held that this action constituted an unconstitutional prior restraint. Justice Blackmun, speaking for the Court, explained:

"The elements of prior restraint [were] clearly present in the system by which [the] board regulated the use of its theaters. One seeking to use a theater was required to apply to the board. The board was empowered to determine whether the applicant should be granted permission — in effect, a license or permit — on the basis of its review of the content of the proposed production.

[The board's] action was no less a prior restraint because the public facilities under [its] control happened to be municipal theaters. The Memorial Auditorium and the [city-leased theater] were public forums designed for and dedicated to expressive activities. [Thus, in] order to be held lawful, [the board's] action [must] have been accomplished with procedural safeguards that reduce the danger of suppressing constitutionally protected speech. [We] held in [Freedman v. Maryland, Chapter III.B, supra], that a system of prior restraint runs afoul of the First Amendment if it lacks certain safeguards. [Such] safeguards were lacking here."

Justice Douglas dissented in part and concurred in the result in part: "The critical flaw in this case lies, not in the absence of procedural safeguards, but rather in the very nature of the content screening in which respondents have engaged. [A] municipal theater is no less a forum for the expression of ideas than is a public park, or a sidewalk. [As] soon as municipal officials are permitted to pick and choose [between] those productions which are 'clean and healthful and culturally uplifting' in content and those which are not, the path is cleared for a regime of censorship under which full voice can be given only to those views which meet with the approval of the powers that be."

Justice White, joined by Chief Justice Burger, dissented: "[The District Court described] the play as involving not only nudity but repeated 'simulated acts of anal intercourse, frontal intercourse, heterosexual intercourse, homosexual intercourse, and group intercourse.' Given this description of 'Hair,' the First Amendment in my view does not compel municipal authorities to permit production of the play in municipal facilities. Whether or not a production as described by the District Court is obscene and may be forbidden to adult audiences, it is apparent to me that the [State] could constitutionally forbid exhibition of the musical to children, [Ginsberg v. New York, Chapter IV.E, supra], and that [the city] may reserve its auditorium for productions suitable for exhibition to all citizens of the city, adults and children alike."

Justice Rehnquist also dissented: "[Until] this case the Court has not equated a public auditorium, which must of necessity schedule performances by a process of inclusion and exclusion, with public streets and parks. [Moreover, here] we deal with municipal [action], not prohibiting or penalizing the expression of views in dramatic form [in privately owned theaters], but rather managing its municipal auditorium. [If] it is the desire of the citizens of [the city], who presumably have paid for and own the facilities, that the attractions to be shown there should not be of the kind which would offend any substantial number of potential theatergoers, I do not think the policy can be described as arbitrary or unreasonable. [May] an opera house limit its production to operas, or must it also show rock musicals? May a municipal theater devote an entire season to Shakespeare, or is it required to book any potential producer on a first come, first served basis? These questions are real ones in light of the Court's opinion. [A] municipal theater may not be run by municipal authorities as if it were a private theater, free to judge on a content basis alone which plays it

Thinks municipal theaters should not be subject to this rule wishes to have performed and which it does not. [But] I do not believe fidelity to the First Amendment requires the exaggerated and rigid procedural safeguards which the Court insists upon in this case."

---

What substantive standards should govern the use of municipal auditoriums? Consider Shiffrin, Government Speech, 27 UCLA L. Rev. 565, 584 (1980): "*Conrad* does not appreciate the complicated relationships between public forum doctrine and government interests in speech. *Conrad* supposes that the government could not choose between competing applicants on a content basis. Yet such a supposition denies any legitimate government speech interest." What is the city's "speech interest" in *Conrad?* May the city limit use of the auditorium to the presentation of Shakespeare? To "family" productions? To "competently performed" productions?

Suppose a city allocates $50,000 per year to "promote the arts." What factors may it consider in awarding its grants? Consider the following statute, which was proposed by Senator Jesse Helms in 1990:

> None of the funds authorized to be appropriated pursuant to this Act may be used by [the National Endowment for the Arts] to promote, disseminate, or produce —
>> (1) obscene or indecent material, including but not limited to depictions of sadomasochism, homo-eroticism, the exploitation of children, or individuals engaged in sex acts; or
>> (2) material which denigrates the objects or beliefs of the adherents of a particular religion or non-religion; or
>> (3) material which denigrates, debases, or reviles a person, group, or class of citizens on the basis of race, creed, sex, handicap, age, or national origin.

Are government subsidies of expression less problematic than government restrictions? Is the ordinance in *Mosley* a subsidy or a restriction?

## BOARD OF EDUCATION, ISLAND TREES UNION FREE SCHOOL DISTRICT v. PICO, 457 U.S. 853 (1982).

In 1975, several members of the petitioner Board of Education attended a conference sponsored by a politically conservative organization at which they obtained lists of books described as "objectionable" and as "improper fare for school students." Thereafter, the board removed eleven of the listed books from the district's school libraries "so that Board members could read them." In a press release justifying this action, the board characterized the books as "anti-American, anti-Christian, anti-Semitic, and just plain filthy." Among the books removed were Slaughterhouse Five, by Kurt Vonnegut, Jr.; The Naked Ape, by Desmond Morris; Best Short Stories of Negro Writers, edited by Langston Hughes; Soul on Ice, by Eldridge Cleaver; and Go Ask Alice, of anonymous authorship.

The board appointed a Book Review Committee, consisting of parents and teachers, to recommend whether the books should be retained. Although the committee recommended that most of the books should be retained, the board decided to remove nine of the books and to make one other available subject to parental approval. Respondents, students in the Island Trees school system, brought this action claiming that the board's decision violated the first amendment. The district court, finding that the board acted not on religious or political principles, but "on its belief that the [books] were irrelevant, vulgar, immoral, and in bad taste," granted summary judgment to the board. The court of appeals reversed and remanded for a trial on the merits. The Supreme Court affirmed. Justice Brennan delivered an opinion joined by Justices Marshall and Stevens and joined in part by Justice Blackmun:

"[Although petitioners] rightly possess significant discretion to determine the content of their school [libraries, that] discretion may not be exercised in a narrowly partisan or political manner. If a Democratic school board, motivated by party affiliation, ordered the removal of all books written by or in favor of Republicans, few would doubt that the order violated the [first amendment]. The same conclusion would surely apply if an all-white school board, motivated by racial animus, decided to remove all books authored by blacks or advocating racial equality and integration. Our Constitution does not permit the official suppression of *ideas*. Thus, whether petitioners' removal of the books from their school libraries [violated the first amendment] depends upon the motivation behind petitioners' actions. If petitioners *intended* by their removal decision to deny respondents access to ideas with which petitioners disagreed, and if this intent was the decisive factor in petitioners' decision, then petitioners have exercised their discretion in violation of the Constitution. On the other hand, [an] unconstitutional motivation would *not* be demonstrated if it were shown that petitioners had decided to remove the books at issue because those books were pervasively vulgar [or educationally unsuitable. Such motivations] would not carry the danger of an official suppression of ideas, and thus would not violate respondents' First Amendment rights."

Justice Blackmun filed a concurring opinion: "[Our decisions] yield a general [first amendment] principle: the State may not suppress exposure to ideas — for the sole *purpose* of suppressing exposure to those ideas — absent sufficiently compelling reasons. [I] do not suggest that the State has any affirmative obligation to provide students with information and ideas. [Instead], I suggest that certain forms of state discrimination *between* ideas are improper. [The] State may not act to deny access to any idea simply because state officials disapprove of that idea for partisan or political reasons." Justice White concurred in the judgment.

Justice Rehnquist, joined by Chief Justice Burger and Justice Powell, filed a dissenting opinion: "[When the government] acts as an educator, at least at the elementary and secondary school level, [it] is engaged in inculcating social values and knowledge in relatively impressionable young people. Obviously there are innumerable decisions to be made as to what courses should be taught, what books should be purchased, or what teachers should be employed. [In my view,] it is 'permissible and appropriate for local boards to make educational decisions based upon their personal, social, political and moral views.' [When the managers of a school district decide to remove a book from a school library,] they are not proscribing it as to the citizenry in general, but are simply determining that it will not be included in [the] library. [Actions] by the government as educator do not raise the same First Amendment concerns as actions by the government as sovereign." Chief Justice Burger and Justices Powell and O'Connor also filed dissenting opinions.

---

Do you agree with the plurality that a school board cannot constitutionally remove books "simply because they dislike the ideas" espoused? Consider Justice Powell's evaluation, set forth in his *Pico* dissent: "[Under the plurality's approach, books] may not be removed because they are indecent; extoll violence, intolerance and racism; or degrade the dignity of the individual. [I] would not require a school board to promote ideas and values repugnant to a democratic society."

Suppose that you were corporation counsel working for a city, and school or public library officials wanted advice about whether they could use filters on computer terminals connected to the Internet to prevent students or library patrons from accessing "inappropriate" material. What would you tell them?

**REGAN v. TAXATION WITH REPRESENTATION OF WASHINGTON, 461 U.S. 540 (1983).** In a unanimous decision, the Court upheld a federal statute providing that contributions to an otherwise tax-exempt organization, other than a tax-exempt veterans' organization, are not tax deductible if a substantial part of the organization's activities consists of attempts to influence legislation. Justice Rehnquist delivered the opinion of the Court:

"Congress is not required by the First Amendment to subsidize lobbying. [Respondent contends, however, that the challenged provision is unconstitutional because of its distinction between veterans' and other tax-exempt organizations. We do not agree.] The case would be different if Congress were to discriminate invidiously in its subsidies in such a way as to "'aim[] at the suppression of dangerous ideas.'" [But] veterans' organizations [receive] tax-deductible contributions regardless of the content of [their speech]. We find no indication that the statute was intended to suppress any ideas or any demonstration that it has had that effect. . . .

"It [is] not irrational for Congress to decide that, even though it will not subsidize substantial lobbying by charities generally, it will subsidize lobbying by veterans' organizations. Veterans have [made a unique contribution to the nation]. Our country has a long standing policy of compensating veterans for [this contribution] by providing them with numerous advantages. This policy has 'always been deemed to be legitimate.'"

Justice Blackmun, joined by Justices Brennan and Marshall, filed a concurring opinion: "Because [the] discrimination between veterans' organizations and charitable organizations is not based on the content of their speech, [it] does not deny charitable organizations equal protection of the law. [As] the Court says, a statute designed to discourage the expression of particular views would present a very different question."

---

Consider the following: (1) "No organization, other than a veterans' organization, may demonstrate on a military base." (2) "Contributions to an otherwise tax-exempt organization are not deductible if the organization engages in substantial lobbying activities, unless those activities concern the subject of abortion." (3) "Contributions to an otherwise tax-exempt organization are not deductible if the organization advocates the violent overthrow of government."

In FCC v. League of Women Voters, 468 U.S. 364 (1984), the Court invalidated section 399 of the Public Broadcasting Act of 1967, which prohibited any noncommercial educational station that receives a grant from the Corporation for Public Broadcasting to "engage in editorializing." The Court distinguished *Taxation with Representation* on the ground that, under the statute at issue in *Taxation with Representation*, "a charitable organization could create [an] affiliate to conduct its non-lobbying activities using tax-deductible contributions, and, at the same time, establish [a] separate affiliate to pursue its lobbying efforts without such contributions," whereas in *League of Women Voters*" a noncommercial educational station that receives [even] 1% of its overall income from [the CPB] is barred absolutely from all editorializing." Thus, in *Taxation with Representation* the law prevented only the use of *government funds* for lobbying, whereas in *League of Women Voters* the law prohibited any station that accepted government funds from editorializing, whether or not the editorializing was paid for with government funds.

**RUST v. SULLIVAN, 500 U.S. 173 (1991).** Title X of the Public Health Service Act, enacted in 1970, provides that none of the federal funds appropriated under the act for family planning services "shall be used in programs where abortion is a method of family planning." In 1988, respondent, the Secretary of Health and Human Services, issued new regulations attaching three conditions on the grant of federal funds for title X projects. First, a "[title] X project may not provide counseling concerning the use of abortion or provide referral for abortion as a method of family planning," even upon request.

Second, a title X project may not engage in activities that "encourage, promote or advocate abortion as a method of family planning." Forbidden activities include lobbying for legislation and disseminating materials, providing speakers, and using legal action to increase the availability of abortion. Third, title X projects must be organized so that they are "physically and financially separate" from prohibited abortion activities.

Petitioners, title X grantees and doctors suing on behalf of themselves and their patients, challenged these regulations. The Court, in a five-to-four decision, upheld the regulations. Chief Justice Rehnquist delivered the opinion of the Court:

"Petitioners contend that the regulations violate the first amendment by impermissibly discriminating based on viewpoint because they prohibit 'all discussion about abortion as a lawful option — including counseling, referral, and the provision of neutral and accurate information about ending a pregnancy — while compelling the clinic or counselor to provide information that promotes continuing a pregnancy to term.' [In] Maher v. Roe, [432 U.S. 464 (1977)], we upheld a state welfare regulation under which Medicaid recipients received payments for services related to childbirth, but not for nontherapeutic abortions. The Court rejected the claim that this unequal subsidization worked a violation of the Constitution. We held that the government may 'make a value judgment favoring childbirth over abortion, and . . . implement that judgment by the allocation of public funds.' Here the Government is exercising the authority it possesses under Maher [to] subsidize family planning services [while] declining to 'promote or encourage abortion.' The Government can, without violating the Constitution, selectively fund a program to encourage certain activities it believes to be in the public interest, without at the same time funding an alternate program which seeks to deal with the problem in another way. In so doing, the Government has not discriminated on the basis of viewpoint; it has merely chosen to fund one activity to the exclusion of the other. '[A governmental] decision not to subsidize the exercise of a fundamental right does not infringe that right.' [Quoting Taxation with Representation.] The challenged regulations [are] designed to ensure that the limits of the federal program are observed. [This] is not a case of the Government 'suppressing a dangerous idea,' but of a prohibition on a project grantee or its employees from engaging in activities outside of its scope.

"To hold that the Government unconstitutionally discriminates on the basis of viewpoint when it chooses to fund a program dedicated to advance certain permissible goals, because the program in advancing those goals necessarily discourages alternate goals, would render numerous government programs constitutionally suspect. When Congress established a National Endowment for Democracy to encourage other countries to adopt democratic principles, it was not constitutionally required to fund a program to encourage competing lines of political philosophy such as Communism and Fascism. Petitioners' assertions ultimately boil down to the position that if the government chooses to subsidize one protected right, it must subsidize analogous counterpart rights. But the Court has soundly rejected that proposition. [Citing *Taxation with Representation; Maher.*] Within far broader limits than petitioners are willing to concede, when the government appropriates public funds to establish a program it is entitled to define the limits of that program. [We] have here not the case of a general law singling out a disfavored group on the basis of speech content, but a case of the Government refusing to fund activities, including speech, which are specifically excluded from the scope of the project funded.

"[Relying on *League of Women Voters*, petitioners] contend that the restrictions on the subsidization of abortion-related speech [are] impermissible because they condition the receipt of a benefit [on] the relinquishment of [the constitutional] right to engage in abortion advocacy and counseling. [Petitioners'] reliance on [this case] is unavailing, however, because here the Government is not denying a benefit to anyone, but is instead simply insisting that public funds be spent for the purposes for which they were authorized. The [regulations] do not force the Title X grantee to give up abortion-related speech; they merely require that the grantee keep such activities separate and distinct from Title X activities. [By] requiring that the Title X grantee engage in abortion-related activity separately from activity receiving federal funding, Congress has, consistent with our teaching in *League of Women Voters* and *Taxation with Representation*, not denied it the right to engage in abortion-related activities. Congress has merely refused to fund such activities out of the public fisc. . . .

"This is not to suggest that funding by the Government, even when coupled with the freedom of the fund recipients to speak outside the scope of the Government-funded project, is invariably sufficient to justify government control over the content of expression. For example, this Court has recognized that the existence of a Government 'subsidy,' in the form of Government-owned property, does not justify the restriction of speech in areas that have 'been traditionally open to the public for expressive activity' [or] have been 'expressly dedicated to speech activity.'[ Citing *Kokinda; Hague; Perry.*] In [the] circumstances [of this case, however], the general rule that the Government may choose not to subsidize speech applies with full force."

Justice Blackmun, joined by Justices Marshall and Stevens, dissented: "Until today, the Court has never upheld viewpoint-based suppression of speech simply because that suppression was a condition upon the acceptance of public funds. [Nothing in *Taxation with Representation*] can be said to challenge this long-settled understanding. In [*Taxation with Representation*], the Court upheld a content-neutral provision [and emphasized that the] 'case would be different if Congress were to discriminate invidiously in its subsidies in such a way as to "[aim] at the suppression of dangerous ideas."' [The regulations at issue here are] clearly viewpoint-based. [Indeed, if] a client asks directly about abortion, a Title X physician or counselor is required to say, in essence, that the project does not consider abortion to be an appropriate method of family planning. [The] regulations pertaining to 'advocacy' are even more explicitly viewpoint-based. [The] majority's reliance on the fact that the regulations pertain solely to funding decisions simply begs the question. Clearly, there are some bases upon which government may not rest its decisions to fund or not to fund. For example, [the] majority surely would agree that government may not base its decision to support an activity upon considerations of race. [Our] cases make clear that ideological viewpoint is a similarly repugnant ground upon which to base funding decisions. . . .

"In the cases at bar, the speaker's interest in the communication is both clear and vital. In addressing the family planning needs of their clients, the physicians and counselors who staff Title X projects seek to provide them with the full range of information and options regarding their health and reproductive freedom. Indeed, the legitimate expectations of the patient and the ethical responsibilities of the medical profession demand no less. [When] a client becomes pregnant, the full range of therapeutic alternatives includes the abortion option, and Title X counselors' interest in providing this information is compelling. The Government's articulated interest in distorting the doctor/patient dialogue — ensuring that federal funds are not spent for a purpose outside the scope of the program — falls far short of that necessary to justify suppression of truthful information and professional medical opinion regarding constitutionally protected conduct. [Indeed], it is of no small significance that the speech the Secretary would suppress is truthful information regarding constitutionally protected conduct of vital importance to the listener. One can imagine no legitimate governmental interest that might be served by suppressing such information." Justice O'Connor dissented on statutory grounds.

### Note: The Implications of Rust

1. *Abortions versus smoking.* Suppose government establishes a program to give grants to organizations that help people quit smoking. Does the first amendment require government also to give grants to organizations that encourage people to smoke? Consider the following argument: The cigarette regulation is constitutional, even though *Rust* was wrong. This is so because in the cigarette case the information relates only to the individual's decision whether to smoke, whereas in *Rust* the information relates to the individual's decision whether to exercise a constitutional right (abortion). Along these lines, suppose the government instructs all public defenders not to advise their clients of their rights under the fourth amendment exclusionary rule. Is *Rust* distinguishable? After *Rust*, could the government constitutionally fund the Democratic, but not the Republican, Convention?

2. *Government speech.* At least part of the Court's argument in *Rust* turned on the notion that government does not unconstitutionally discriminate "on

the basis of viewpoint when it chooses to fund a program dedicated to advance certain permissible goals." Consider Rosenberger v. Rector & Visitors of University of Virginia, 515 U.S. 819 (1995), in which the Court invalidated a University of Virginia policy authorizing payment from the Student Activities Fund for the printing costs of a variety of student publications but prohibiting payment for any student publication that "primarily promotes or manifests a particular belief in or about a deity or an ultimate reality." Citing *Rust*, the University argued that it "must have substantial discretion in determining how to allocate scarce resources to accomplish its educational mission," and that the challenged policy was reasonably designed to serve the permissible goal of preserving the separation of church and state. The Court rejected this argument:

> [We] have permitted the government to regulate the content of what is or is not expressed when it is the speaker or when it enlists private entities to convey its own message. [In *Rust*, for example,] the government did not create a program to encourage private speech but instead used private speakers to transmit specific information pertaining to its own program. We recognized that when the government appropriates public funds to promote a particular policy of its own it is entitled to say what it wishes [and] it may take [appropriate] steps to ensure that its message is neither garbled nor distorted by the grantee. It does not follow, however, [that] viewpoint-based restrictions are proper when the [government] does not itself speak or subsidize transmittal of a message it favors but instead expends funds to encourage a diversity of views from private speakers. [The] distinction between the University's own favored message and the private speech of students is evident in the case before us. [The] University declares that the student groups eligible for Student Activities Fund support are not the University's agents, are not subject to its control, and are not its responsibility. Having offered to pay [the printing costs] of private speakers who convey their own messages, the University may not silence the expression of selected viewpoints.

3. *What's wrong with* Rust? Consider Redish and Kessler, Government Subsidies and Free Expression, 80 Minn. L. Rev. 543, 576–577 (1996):

> The problem with the [Court's analysis in *Rust*] is that it allows the government to define its subsidization programs in a wholly unchecked, self-referential manner. [The] fallacy of [this approach] becomes clear if one visualizes the subsidization of private expression exclusively in favor of such ideas as a free-market economic philosophy, or the political theories of Mao Zedong or Rush Limbaugh. [Government] may appropriately choose neutrally to fund works on family planning, on the viability of free-market economic philosophy, or on the wisdom of Mao Zedong's or Rush Limbaugh's political thought. Each of these subsidies would foster First Amendment values by adding to the public's knowledge. [But] government may not foster public acceptance of its own viewpoints on these issues by manipulating private expression [in a viewpoint-based manner].

Consider also Norton, The Measure of Government Speech: Identifying Expression's Source, 88 B.U. L. Rev. 587, 589, 595–597, 629–630 (2008):

> [T]he Supreme Court has shielded the government's expression from Free Speech Clause scrutiny. [Government] speech merits this insulation because it is both inevitable and valuable. In particular, government speech facilitates significant First Amendment interests in sharing knowledge and discovering truth by informing the public on a wide range of topics. [A] message's source can have positive or negative effects on its persuasiveness, depending on observers' assessments of the source's credibility [, and] because public attitudes towards government vary widely [assessments] of government credibility differ too. [One danger of government speech is] that the government may manipulate the public's attitudes towards its views by deliberately obscuring its identity as a message's source. Government speech is thus most valuable and least dangerous when its government source is apparent, enabling the public to more accurately assess the message's credibility. . . .
>
> In *Rust*, [doctors and nurses] delivered the contested counseling [without] any requirement that its governmental origins be disclosed. Under these circumstances, patients might well misunderstand clinic employees to be offering their own independent counsel, rather than speaking as agents required to espouse the government's view. [Because] health professionals may be seen as more credible than the government in this setting based on public perception of their expertise and objectivity, patients may have been misled into evaluating the counseling differently than they would have if the speakers had made clear its governmental source. [*Rust*] thus illustrates the danger of treating expression that fails to satisfy the demands of functional transparency as government speech free from First Amendment scrutiny.

Compare Massaro, Tread on Me!, 17 U. Pa. J. Con L. 365, 402-03 (2014):

> [Freedom] of speech doctrine [should] include an exception to the "government speech" doctrine for the rare circumstances in which the government exerts *so much* expressive power that its actions are tantamount to direct speech regulation. [One] factor, though not the only one, that should be relevant to determining the contours of this caveat is the extent to which government has monopoly power over the information in question. The lack of options matters. We might think we have a choice of horses, but when Thomas Hobson runs the only stable in town, our horse is always the horse that Hobson selects.

In C. Brettschneider, When the State Speaks, What Should it Say? How Democracies Can Protect Expression and Promote Equality (2012), the author argues that states have an obligation to speak so as to promote "democratic persuasion" but only when it speaks in favor of free and equal citizenship.

4. Rust *and* R.A.V. For another twist on the problem of underinclusive, content-based restrictions, see R.A.V. v. City of St. Paul, Chapter IV.H,

supra. Although it may seem that *R.A.V.* and *Rust* pose quite different questions, consider Kagan, The Changing Faces of First Amendment Neutrality, 1992 Sup. Ct. Rev. 29, 31–32:

> *Rust* and *R.A.V.* both raise the same question: If, in a certain setting, the government need not protect or promote any speech at all, may the government choose to protect or promote only speech with a certain content? *Rust* is easily seen in this light. The government [is] not constitutionally required to promote speech through the use of federal funds. May the government then fund whatever speech it wants? [The] question is similar in *R.A.V.* The government is not constitutionally required to tolerate any "fighting words" at all. May the government then permit some but not all fighting words? The question posed in each case is in an important sense the question of First Amendment neutrality in its starkest form: when speech [has] no claim to government promotion or protection, what limitations does the government face in voluntarily advancing some messages, but not all? [Although] the cases have a similar structure, implicate an identical question, and fall within a single [category] of First Amendment [cases, the justices deciding them saw no connection at all].

**NATIONAL ENDOWMENT FOR THE ARTS v. FINLEY, 524 U.S. 569 (1998).** Since its creation by Congress in 1965, the NEA has made more than 100,000 grants, totaling some $3 billion, to promote "public knowledge, education, understanding and appreciation of the arts." In 1989, two provocative works that were supported by NEA grants — a series of homoerotic photographs by Robert Mapplethorpe and a photograph by Andres Serrano that depicted a crucifix immersed in urine ("Piss Christ") — prompted a public controversy that led to a congressional reevaluation of the NEA's funding priorities and procedures. Thus, in 1990 Congress enacted section 954(d)(1), which directs the NEA, in establishing procedures to judge the artistic merit of grant applications, to "[take] into consideration general standards of decency and respect for the diverse beliefs and values of the American public." In implementing this provision, the NEA concluded that it was not required to do anything more than ensure that its peer review panels were constituted in such a way as to represent geographic, ethnic, and aesthetic diversity.

The Court, in an opinion by Justice O'Connor, held that section 954(d)(1) is not unconstitutional "on its face": "Respondents argue that the provision is a paradigmatic example of viewpoint discrimination. [But the challenged provision merely] adds 'considerations' to the grant-making process; it does not preclude awards to projects that might be deemed 'indecent' or 'disrespectful,' [or] even specify that those factors be given any particular weight in reviewing an application. . . .

"[Moreover], the considerations that the provision introduces [do] not engender the kind of directed viewpoint discrimination that would prompt this Court to invalidate a statute on its face. [The considerations enumerated in section 954(d)(1) are] susceptible to multiple interpretations, [and particularly because the NEA considers grant applications through the decisions of many diverse review panels], the provision does not introduce considerations that, in practice, would effectively preclude or punish the expression of particular views."

Although acknowledging that the provision could conceivably be applied in ways that could violate the first amendment, the Court was "reluctant . . . to invalidate legislation 'on the basis of its hypothetical application to situations not before the Court,'" particularly where, as here, there are numerous "constitutional applications" for both the "decency" and the "respect" criteria. For example, "educational programs are central to the NEA's mission," and "it is well-established that 'decency' is a permissible factor where 'educational suitability' motivates its consideration. [Citing *Pico*.]" And "permissible applications of the mandate to consider 'respect for the diverse beliefs and values of the American public' are also apparent, [for the] agency expressly takes diversity into account, giving special consideration to 'projects and productions . . . that reach, or reflect the culture of, a minority, inner city, rural, or tribal community.'"

The Court was unpersuaded that "the language of §954(d)(1) itself will give rise to the suppression of protected expression": "Any content-based considerations that may be taken into account in the grant-making process are a consequence of the nature of arts funding. The NEA has limited resources and it must deny the majority of the grant applications that it receives, including many that propose 'artistically excellent' projects. The agency may decide to fund particular projects for a wide variety of reasons, 'such as the technical proficiency of the artist, the creativity of the work, the anticipated public interest in or appreciation of the work, the work's contemporary relevance, its educational value, its suitability for or appeal to special audiences (such as children or the disabled), its service to a rural or isolated community, or even simply that the work could increase public knowledge of an art form.' [The] very 'assumption' of the NEA is [that] absolute neutrality is simply 'inconceivable.'"

The Court therefore distinguished its decision in *Rosenberger* on the ground that, in "the context of arts funding, in contrast to many other subsidies, the Government does not indiscriminately 'encourage a diversity of views from private speakers.' The NEA's mandate is to make aesthetic judgments, and the inherently content-based 'excellence' threshold for NEA support sets it apart from the subsidy issue in *Rosenberger* — which was available to all student organizations that were 'related to the educational purpose of the University' — and from comparably objective decisions on allocating public benefits, such as access to a school auditorium or a municipal theater [citing *Lamb's Chapel* and *Southeastern Promotions*]."

The Court emphasized that "we have no occasion here to address an as-applied challenge in a situation where the denial of a grant may be shown to be the product of invidious viewpoint discrimination. If the NEA were to leverage its power to award subsidies on the basis of subjective criteria into a penalty on disfavored viewpoints, then we would confront a different case. [Even] in the provision of subsidies, the Government may not 'ai[m] at the suppression of dangerous ideas,' and if a subsidy were 'manipulated' to have a 'coercive effect,' then relief could be appropriate. In addition, as the NEA itself concedes, a more pressing constitutional question would arise if government funding resulted in the imposition of a disproportionate burden calculated to drive 'certain ideas or viewpoints from the marketplace.'"

Justice Scalia, joined by Justice Thomas, concurred in the result: "[Under the challenged provision, to] the extent a particular applicant exhibits disrespect for the diverse beliefs and values of the American public or fails to comport with general standards of decency, the likelihood that he will receive a grant diminishes. [This] unquestionably constitutes viewpoint discrimination. That conclusion is not altered by the fact that the statute does not 'compel' the denial of funding, any more than a provision imposing a five-point handicap on all black applicants for civil service jobs is saved from being race discrimination by the fact that it does not compel the rejection of black applicants. . . .

"[The challenged provision does] not *abridge* the speech of those who disdain the beliefs and values of the American public, nor [does] it *abridge* indecent speech. Those who wish to create indecent and disrespectful art are as unconstrained now as they were before the enactment of this statute. [They] are merely deprived of the [satisfaction] of having the [public] taxed to pay for it. It is preposterous to equate the denial of taxpayer subsidy with measures 'aimed at the *suppression* of dangerous ideas.' The reason that denial of participation in a tax exemption or other subsidy scheme does not necessarily 'infringe' a fundamental right is that — unlike direct restriction or prohibition — such a denial does not, as a general rule, have any 'significant coercive effect.' . . ."

Justice Souter dissented: "The decency and respect proviso mandates viewpoint-based decisions in the disbursement of government subsidies, and the Government has wholly failed to explain why the statute should be afforded an exemption from the fundamental rule of the First Amendment that viewpoint discrimination in the exercise of public authority over expressive activity is unconstitutional. ['If] there is a bedrock principle underlying the First Amendment, it is that the government may not prohibit the expression of an idea simply because society finds the idea itself offensive or disagreeable.' [Because] this principle applies not only to affirmative suppression of speech, but also to disqualification for government favors, Congress is generally not permitted to pivot discrimination against otherwise protected speech on the offensiveness or unacceptability of the views it expresses. [Citing *Rosenberger* and *Lamb's Chapel*.] One need do nothing more than read the text of [this] statute to conclude that Congress's purpose in imposing the decency and respect criteria was to prevent the funding of art that conveys an offensive message; the [provision] on its face is quintessentially viewpoint-based, [for] it penalizes [art] that disrespects the ideology, opinions, or convictions of a significant segment of the American [public, but not] art that reinforces those values. . . .

"[Another] basic strand in the Court's [analysis], and the heart of Justice Scalia's, in effect assumes that whether or not the statute mandates viewpoint discrimination, [government] art subsidies fall within a zone of activity free from First Amendment restraints. [This argument] calls attention to the roles of government-as-speaker and government-as-buyer, in which the government is of course entitled to engage in viewpoint discrimination: if the Food and Drug Administration launches an advertising campaign on the subject of smoking, it may condemn the habit without also having to show a cowboy taking a puff on the opposite page; and if the Secretary of Defense wishes to buy a portrait to decorate the Pentagon, he is free to prefer George Washington over George the Third.

"[But the government] neither speaks through the expression subsidized by the NEA, nor buys anything itself with NEA grants. On the contrary, [in this context] the government acts as a patron, financially underwriting the production of art by private artists [for] independent consumption. [And] outside of the contexts of government-as-buyer and government-as-speaker, we have held time and again that Congress may not 'discriminate invidiously in its subsidies in such a way as to aim at the suppression of ideas.' [As we held in *Rosenberger*, when] the government acts as patron, subsidizing the expression of others, it may not prefer one lawfully stated view over another. [The Court attempts] to distinguish *Rosenberger* on the ground that the student activities funds in that case were generally available to most applicants, whereas NEA funds are disbursed selectively and competitively to a choice few. But the Court in *Rosenberger* [specifically] rejected just this distinction when it held [that] '[t]he government cannot justify viewpoint discrimination among private speakers on the economic fact of scarcity.' Scarce money demands choices, of course, but choices 'on some acceptable [viewpoint] neutral principle,' like artistic excellence; 'nothing in our decision[s] indicates that scarcity would give the State the right to exercise viewpoint discrimination that is otherwise impermissible.'"

**LEGAL SERVICES CORP. v. VELAZQUEZ, 531 U.S. 533 (2001).** In 1974, Congress established the Legal Services Corporation (LSC), whose mission is to distribute funds appropriated by Congress to eligible local grantee organizations "for the purpose of providing financial support for legal assistance in noncriminal proceedings . . . to persons financially unable to afford legal assistance." LSC grantees consist of hundreds of local organizations governed by local boards of directors. In many instances, the grantees are funded by a combination of LSC funds and other public or private sources. The grantee organizations hire and supervise lawyers to provide free legal assistance to indigent clients.

In a five-to-four decision, the Court distinguished *Rust* and held unconstitutional a congressionally imposed restriction prohibiting LSC-funded attorneys from challenging the legality or constitutionality of existing welfare laws. Justice Kennedy delivered the opinion of the Court: "The Court in *Rust* did not place explicit reliance on the rationale that the counseling activities of the doctors under Title X amounted to governmental speech; when interpreting the holding in later cases, however, we have explained *Rust* on this understanding. We have said that viewpoint-based funding decisions can be sustained in instances in which the government is itself the speaker, or instances, like *Rust*, in which the government 'used private speakers to transmit information pertaining to its own program.' As we said in *Rosenberger*, '[w]hen the government disburses public funds to private entities to convey a governmental message, it may take legitimate and appropriate steps to ensure that its message is neither garbled nor distorted by the grantee.' . . .

"[But] '[i]t does not follow . . . that viewpoint-based restrictions are proper when the [government] does not itself speak or subsidize transmittal of a message it favors but instead expends funds to encourage a diversity of views from private speakers. *Rosenberger*. Although the LSC program differs from the program at issue in *Rosenberger* in that its purpose is not to 'encourage a diversity of views,' the salient point is that, like the program in *Rosenberger*, the LSC program was designed to facilitate private speech, not to promote a governmental message. Congress funded LSC grantees to provide attorneys to represent the interests of indigent clients. [In] this vital respect this suit is distinguishable from *Rust*.

"The private nature of the speech involved here, and the extent of LSC's regulation of private expression, are indicated further by the circumstance that the Government seeks to use an existing medium of expression and to control it, in a class of cases, in ways which distort its usual functioning. Where the government uses or attempts to regulate a particular medium, we have been informed by its accepted usage in determining whether a particular restriction on speech is necessary for the program's purposes and limitations. [Citing FCC v. League of Women Voters; Arkansas Educational Television Commission v. Forbes; and *Rosenberger*.]

"[Restricting] LSC attorneys in advising their clients and in presenting arguments and analyses to the courts distorts the legal system by altering the traditional role of the attorneys in much the same way broadcast systems or student publication networks were changed in the limited forum cases we have cited. Just as government in those cases could not elect to use a broadcasting network or a college publication structure in a regime which prohibits speech necessary to the proper functioning of those systems, it may not design a subsidy to effect this serious and fundamental restriction on advocacy of attorneys and the functioning of the judiciary. . . .

"Interpretation of the law and the Constitution is the primary mission of the judiciary when it acts within the sphere of its authority to resolve a case or controversy. Under [the challenged statute], however, cases would be presented by LSC attorneys who could not advise the courts of serious questions of statutory validity. The disability is inconsistent with the proposition that attorneys should present all the reasonable and well-grounded arguments necessary for proper resolution of the case. By seeking to prohibit the analysis of certain legal issues and to truncate presentation to the courts, the enactment under review prohibits speech and expression upon which courts must depend for the proper exercise of the judicial power. Congress cannot wrest the law from the Constitution which is its source. . . .

"It is no answer to say the restriction on speech is harmless because, under LSC's interpretation of the Act, its attorneys can withdraw. This misses the point. The statute is an attempt to draw lines around the LSC program to exclude from litigation those arguments and theories Congress finds unacceptable but which by their nature are within the province of the courts to consider.

"The restriction on speech is even more problematic because in cases where the attorney withdraws from a representation, the client is unlikely to find other counsel. [Thus], with respect to the litigation services Congress has funded, there is no alternative channel for expression of the advocacy Congress seeks to restrict. This is in stark contrast to *Rust*. There, a patient could receive the approved Title X family planning counseling funded by the Government and later could consult an affiliate or independent organization to receive abortion counseling. Unlike indigent clients who seek LSC representation, the patient in *Rust* was not required to forfeit the Government-funded advice when she also received abortion counseling through alternative channels. Because LSC attorneys must withdraw whenever a question of a welfare statute's validity arises, an individual could not obtain joint representation so that the constitutional challenge would be presented by a non-LSC attorney, and other, permitted, arguments advanced by LSC counsel.

"Finally, LSC and the Government maintain that [this restriction] is necessary to define the scope and contours of the federal program, a condition that ensures funds can be spent for those cases most immediate to congressional concern. [In the Government's] view, the restriction operates neither to maintain the current welfare system nor insulate it from attack; rather, it helps the current welfare system function in a more efficient and fair manner by removing from the program complex challenges to existing welfare laws.

"The effect of the restriction, however, is to prohibit advice or argumentation that existing welfare laws are unconstitutional or unlawful. Congress cannot recast a condition on funding as a mere definition of its program in every case, lest the First Amendment be reduced to a simple semantic exercise. Here, notwithstanding Congress' purpose to confine and limit its program, the restriction operates to insulate current welfare laws from constitutional scrutiny and certain other legal challenges, a condition implicating central First Amendment concerns. [There] can be little doubt that the LSC Act funds constitutionally protected expression; and in the context of this statute there is no programmatic message of the kind recognized in *Rust* and which sufficed there to allow the Government to specify the advice deemed necessary for its legitimate objectives. . . .

"Congress was not required to fund an LSC attorney to represent indigent clients; and when it did so, it was not required to fund the whole range of legal representations or relationships. The LSC and the United States, however, in effect ask us to permit Congress to define the scope of the litigation it funds to exclude certain vital theories and ideas. The attempted restriction is designed to insulate the Government's interpretation of the Constitution from judicial challenge. The Constitution does not permit the Government to confine litigants and their attorneys in this manner. We must be vigilant when Congress imposes rules and conditions which in effect insulate its own laws from legitimate judicial challenge."

Justice Scalia, joined by Chief Justice Rehnquist and Justices O'Connor and Justice Thomas, dissented: "The LSC Act is a federal subsidy program, not a federal regulatory program, and '[t]here is a basic difference between [the two].' Regulations directly restrict speech; subsidies do not. [In *Rust*, the Court upheld] a statutory scheme that is in all relevant respects indistinguishable from [the provision challenged in this case]. The LSC Act, like the scheme in *Rust*, does not [discriminate] on the basis of viewpoint, since it funds neither challenges to nor defenses of existing welfare law. The provision simply declines to subsidize a certain class of litigation, and under *Rust* that decision 'does not infringe the right' to bring such litigation. . . . The Court's repeated claims that [the act] 'restricts' and 'prohibits' speech, and 'insulates' laws from judicial review, are simply baseless. No litigant who, in the absence of LSC funding, would bring a suit challenging existing welfare law is deterred from doing so by [the act]. *Rust* thus controls [this case] and compels the conclusion that [the act] is constitutional.

"The Court contends that *Rust* is different because the program at issue subsidized government speech, while the LSC funds private speech. This is so unpersuasive it hardly needs response. If the private doctors' confidential advice to their patients at issue in *Rust* constituted 'government speech,' it is hard to imagine what subsidized speech would not be government speech. Moreover, the majority's contention that the subsidized speech in these cases is not government speech because the lawyers have a professional obligation to represent the interests of their clients founders on the reality that the doctors in *Rust* had a professional obligation to serve the interests of their patients. . . .

"The Court further asserts that these cases are different from *Rust* because the welfare funding restriction 'seeks to use an existing medium of expression and to control it . . . in ways which distort its usual functioning.' This is wrong on both the facts and the law. It is wrong on the law because there is utterly no precedent for the novel and facially implausible proposition that the First Amendment has anything to do with government funding that — though it does not actually abridge anyone's speech — 'distorts an existing medium of expression.' None of the three cases cited by the Court mentions such an odd principle. [The] Court's 'nondistortion' principle is also wrong on the facts, since there is no basis for believing that [the challenged provision], by causing 'cases [to] be presented by LSC attorneys who [can]not advise the courts of serious questions of statutory validity,' will distort the operation of the courts. It may well be that the bar of [the act] will cause LSC-funded attorneys to decline or to withdraw from cases that involve statutory validity. But that means at most that fewer statutory challenges to welfare laws will be presented to the courts because of the unavailability of free legal services for that purpose. So what? The same result would ensue from excluding LSC-funded lawyers from welfare litigation entirely. . . .

"Finally, the Court is troubled 'because in cases where the attorney withdraws from a representation, the client is unlikely to find other counsel.' That is surely irrelevant, since it leaves the welfare recipient in no worse condition than he would have been in had the LSC program never been enacted. [*Rust*] rejected a similar argument. . . . There is no legitimate basis for declaring [this law] unconstitutional."

### Note: *The Reach of Government Speech*

1. Rust *and* Velazquez. Is there a coherent distinction between *Rust* and *Velazquez*? If so, what is it? Note that Justice Kennedy was the only justice to vote differently in the two cases.

2. *Monuments in a public park*. Presumably, there is no first amendment right to erect monuments in a public park. But what if the government erects some monuments but not others? Pioneer Park, a public park in Pleasant Grove City, contains fifteen permanent displays, eleven of which were donated to the city by private groups. These include an historic granary, a wishing well, a September 11 monument, and a Ten Commandments monument donated by the Fraternal Order of Eagles in 1971. Summum is a religious organization founded in 1975 and headquartered in Salt Lake City. In 2003, Summum's president requested permission to erect a stone monument in Pioneer Park. The monument would contain the Seven Aphorisms of Summum, which according to Summum doctrine were inscribed on the original tablet handed down by God to Moses on Mount Sinai. The city denied the request, explaining that it permitted monuments to be displayed in the park only if they "directly related to the history of Pleasant Grove" or they "were donated by groups with longstanding ties to the Pleasant Grove community." The Court of Appeals for the Tenth Circuit held that because public parks have traditionally been regarded as public forums, the city could not constitutionally reject the Seven Aphorisms monument absent a compelling justification for doing so.

In a unanimous decision in Pleasant Grove City, Utah v. Summum, 555 U.S. 460 (2009), the Supreme Court reversed. Justice Alito delivered the to the receipt of federal assistance in order to further its policy objectives. But Congress may not 'induce' the recipient 'to engage in activities that would themselves be unconstitutional.' To determine whether libraries would violate the First Amendment by employing the filtering software that CIPA requires, we must [examine] the role of libraries in our society. Public libraries pursue the worthy missions of facilitating learning and cultural enrichment. [To] fulfill [these] missions, public libraries must have broad discretion to decide what material to provide to their patrons. Although they seek to provide a wide array of information, their goal has never been to provide 'universal coverage.' Instead, public libraries seek to provide materials 'that would be of the greatest direct benefit or interest to the community.' To this end, libraries collect only those materials deemed to have 'requisite and appropriate quality.' . . .

"We have held [in] analogous contexts that the government has broad discretion to make content-based judgments in deciding what private speech to make available to the public. [Citing *Finley*.] Just as forum analysis and heightened judicial scrutiny are incompatible with the role [of] the NEA, they are also incompatible with the discretion that public libraries must have to fulfill their traditional missions. [Most] libraries already exclude pornography from their print collections because they deem it inappropriate for inclusion. We do not subject these decisions to heightened scrutiny; it would make little sense to treat libraries' judgments to block online pornography any differently, when these judgments are made for just the same reason. . . .

"[The] dissents fault the tendency of filtering software to 'overblock' — that is, to erroneously block access to constitutionally protected speech that falls outside the categories that software users intend to block. [Assuming] that such erroneous blocking presents constitutional difficulties, any such concerns are dispelled by the ease with which patrons may have the filtering software disabled. When a patron encounters a blocked site, he need only ask a librarian to unblock it, [and CIPA] expressly authorizes library officials to 'disable' a filter altogether 'to enable access for bona fide research or other lawful purposes.' The Solicitor General confirmed that a [patron] would not 'have to explain . . . why he was asking a site to be unblocked or the filtering to be disabled.' The District Court viewed unblocking and disabling as inadequate because some patrons may be too embarrassed to request them. But the Constitution does not guarantee the right to acquire information at a public library without any risk of embarrassment.

"Appellees urge us to affirm the District Court's judgment on the alternative ground that CIPA imposes an unconstitutional condition on the receipt of federal assistance. Under this doctrine, 'the government may not deny a benefit to a person on a basis that infringes his constitutionally protected . . . freedom of speech even if he has no entitlement to that benefit.' Appellees argue that CIPA imposes an unconstitutional condition on libraries that receive [federal] subsidies by requiring them, as a condition on their receipt of federal funds, to surrender their First Amendment right to provide the public with access to constitutionally protected speech. . . .

"Within broad limits, 'when the Government appropriates public funds to establish a program it is entitled to define the limits of that program.'[Citing *Rust.*] The [Internet subsidy] programs were intended to help public libraries fulfill their traditional role of obtaining material of requisite and appropriate quality for educational and informational purposes. Congress may certainly insist that these 'public funds be spent for the purposes for which they were authorized.' Especially because public libraries have traditionally excluded pornographic material from their other collections, Congress could reasonably impose a parallel limitation on its Internet assistance programs. As the use of filtering software helps to carry out these programs, it is a permissible condition under *Rust.* [CIPA does not prohibit public libraries from providing computers to adult patrons that enable them to access material that is obscene for minors; it] simply reflects Congress' decision not to subsidize their doing so. ['A] refusal to fund protected activity, without more, cannot be equated with the imposition of a "penalty" on that activity.' [Quoting *Rust.*]" Justices Kennedy and Breyer filed concurring opinions.

Justice Stevens dissented: "Because the software [does] not have the capacity to exclude a precisely defined category of images, [it] necessarily results in the blocking of thousands of pages that 'contain content that is completely innocuous.' [A] statutory blunderbuss that mandates this vast amount of 'overblocking' abridges the freedom of speech. [Neither] the interest in suppressing unlawful speech nor the interest in protecting children from access to harmful materials justifies this overly broad restriction on adult access to protected speech. 'The Government may not suppress lawful speech as the means to suppress unlawful speech.' [Quoting Ashcroft v. Free Speech Coalition]. [Moreover, the] District Court expressly found that a variety of less restrictive alternatives are available. [The] plurality argues that [*Rust*] requires rejection of [the] unconstitutional conditions claim. But, as subsequent cases have explained, *Rust* only involved and only applies to instances of governmental speech — that is, situations in which the government seeks to communicate a specific message. The [subsidies] involved in this case do not subsidize any message favored by the Government. As Congress made clear, these programs were designed '[t]o help public libraries provide their patrons with Internet access' [to] a vast amount and wide variety of private speech. They are not designed to foster or transmit any particular governmental message. [This] Court should not permit federal funds to be used to enforce this kind of broad restriction of First Amendment rights. . . ."

Justice Souter, joined by Justice Ginsburg, also dissented: "[I]f the only First Amendment interests raised here were those of children, I would uphold application of the Act. [Nor] would I dissent if I agreed with the majority [that] an adult library patron could, consistently with the Act, obtain an unblocked terminal simply for the asking. [But] the District Court expressly from our cases is between conditions that define the limits of the government spending program — those that specify the activities Congress wants to subsidize — and conditions that seek to leverage funding to regulate speech outside the contours of the program itself. The line is hardly clear, in part because the definition of a particular program can always be manipulated to subsume the challenged condition. We have held, however, that 'Congress cannot recast a condition on funding as a mere definition of its program in every case, lest the First Amendment be reduced to a simple semantic exercise.' [*Velazquez.*]"

As an example, Chief Justices Roberts invoked FCC v. League of Women Voters, in which "the Court struck down a condition on federal financial assistance to noncommercial broadcast television and radio stations that prohibited all editorializing, including with private funds. Even a station receiving only one percent of its overall budget from the Federal Government, the Court explained, was 'barred absolutely from all editorializing.' [The] law provided no way for a station to limit its use of federal funds to noneditorializing activities, while using private funds 'to make known its views on matters of public importance.' The prohibition thus went beyond ensuring that federal funds not be used to subsidize 'public broadcasting station editorials,' and instead leveraged the federal funding to regulate the stations' speech outside the scope of the program.

"Our decision in *Rust* elaborated on the approach [in] *League of Women Voters*. In *Rust*, [the] organizations received funds from a variety of sources other than the Federal Government for a variety of purposes. The Act, however, prohibited the Title X federal funds from being 'used in programs where abortion is a method of family planning.' To enforce this provision, HHS regulations barred Title X projects from advocating abortion as a method of family planning, and required grantees to ensure that their Title X projects were 'physically and financially separate' from their other projects that engaged in the prohibited activities. . . .

"We explained that Congress can, without offending the Constitution, selectively fund certain programs to address an issue of public concern, without funding alternative ways of addressing the same problem. In Title X, Congress had defined the federal program to encourage only particular family planning methods. The challenged regulations were simply 'designed to ensure that the limits of the federal program are observed,' and 'that public funds [are] spent for the purposes for which they were authorized.' [The] regulations governed only the scope of the grantee's Title X projects, leaving it 'unfettered in its other activities.' [Title X grantees could continue to engage in abortion advocacy as long as they conducted] 'those activities through programs that are separate and independent from the project that receives Title X funds.' Because the regulations did not 'prohibit[ ] the recipient from engaging in the protected conduct outside the scope of the federally funded program,' they did not run afoul of the First Amendment. Here, however, [the] Policy Requirement falls on the unconstitutional side of the line. [By] demanding that funding recipients adopt — as their own — the Government's view on an issue of public concern, the condition by its very nature affects 'protected conduct outside the scope of the federally funded program.' [By] requiring recipients to profess a specific belief, the Policy Requirement goes beyond defining the limits of the federally funded program to defining the recipient. . . .

"The Government suggests that the Policy Requirement is necessary because, without it, the grant of federal funds could free a recipient's private funds 'to be used to promote prostitution.' [Citing Holder v. Humanitarian Law Project, section C, infra]. That argument assumes that federal funding will simply supplant private funding, rather than pay for new programs or expand existing ones. The Government offers no support for that assumption as a general matter, or any reason to believe it is true here. And if the Government's argument were correct, *League of Women Voters* would have come out differently, and much of the reasoning [of] *Rust* would have been beside the point.

"The Government cites but one case to support that argument, Holder v. Humanitarian Law Project. That case concerned the quite different context of a ban on providing material support to terrorist organizations, where the record indicated that support for those organizations' nonviolent operations was funneled to support their violent activities.

"Pressing its argument further, the Government contends that 'if organizations awarded federal funds to implement Leadership Act programs could at the same time promote or affirmatively condone prostitution or sex trafficking, whether using public *or private* funds, it would undermine the government's program and confuse its message opposing prostitution.' But the Policy Requirement goes beyond preventing recipients from using private funds in a way that would undermine the federal program. It requires them to pledge allegiance to the Government's policy of eradicating prostitution. As to that, we cannot improve upon what Justice Jackson wrote for the Court 70 years ago: 'If there is any fixed star in our constitutional constellation, it is that no official, high or petty, can prescribe what shall be orthodox in politics, nationalism, religion, or other matters of opinion or force citizens to confess by word or act their faith therein.' [Quoting West Virginia State Board of Education v. Barnette, section C, infra].

"The Policy Requirement compels as a condition of federal funding the affirmation of a belief that by its nature cannot be confined within the scope of the Government program. In so doing, it violates the First Amendment and cannot be sustained."

Justice Scalia, joined by Justice Thomas, dissented: "The First Amendment does not mandate a viewpoint neutral government. Government must choose between rival ideas and adopt some as its own: competition over cartels, solar energy over coal, weapon development over disarmament, and so forth. Moreover, the government may enlist the assistance of those who believe in its ideas to carry them to fruition; and it need not enlist for that purpose those who oppose or do not support the ideas. That seems to me a matter of the most common common sense. . . .

"The argument is that this commonsense principle will enable the government to discriminate against, and injure, points of view to which it is opposed. Of course the Constitution does not prohibit government spending that discriminates against, and injures, points of view to which the government is opposed; every government program which takes a position on a controversial issue does that. Anti-smoking programs injure cigar aficionados, programs encouraging sexual abstinence injure free-love advocates, etc. The constitutional prohibition at issue here is not a prohibition against discriminating against or injuring opposing points of view, but the First Amendment's prohibition against the coercing of speech. I am frankly dubious that a condition for eligibility to participate in a minor federal program such as this one runs afoul of that prohibition even when the condition is irrelevant to the goals of the program. Not every disadvantage is a coercion.

"But that is not the issue before us here. Here the views that the Government demands an applicant forswear — or that the Government insists an applicant favor — are relevant to the program in question. The program is valid only if the Government is entitled to disfavor the opposing view (here, advocacy of or toleration of prostitution). And if the program can disfavor it, so can the selection of those who are to administer the program. There is no risk that this principle will enable the Government to discriminate arbitrarily against positions it disfavors. It would not, for example, permit the Government to exclude from bidding on defense contracts anyone who refuses to abjure prostitution. But here a central part of the Government's HIV/AIDS strategy is the suppression of prostitution, by which HIV is transmitted. It is entirely reasonable to admit to participation in the program only those who believe in that goal. . . .

"Of course the most obvious manner in which the admission to a program of an ideological opponent can frustrate the purpose of the program is by freeing up the opponent's funds for use in its ideological opposition. [Money] is fungible. The economic reality is that when NGOs can conduct their AIDS work on the Government's dime, they can expend greater resources on policies that undercut the Leadership Act. The Government need not establish by record evidence that this will happen. To make it a valid consideration in determining participation in federal programs, it suffices that this is a real and obvious risk. [In] FCC v. League of Women Voters, the ban on editorializing [was] disallowed precisely because it did not further a relevant, permissible policy of the Federal Communications Act. . . .

"The majority cannot credibly say that this speech condition is coercive, so it does not. It pussyfoots around the lack of coercion by invalidating the Leadership Act for '*requiring* recipients to profess a specific belief' and "*demanding* that funding recipients adopt — as their own — the Government's view on an issue of public concern.' But like King Cnut's commanding of the tides, here the Government's 'requiring' and 'demanding' have no coercive effect. In the end, and in the circumstances of this case, [there] is no compulsion at all. It is the reasonable price of admission to a limited government-spending program that each organization remains free to accept or reject. . . ."

## C. SYMBOLIC CONDUCT

This section explores the use of nonverbal conduct — such as burning a draft card or mutilating a flag — as a means of "symbolic" expression. In what circumstances, if any, does such nonverbal conduct constitute protected "speech" within the meaning of the first amendment? Consider Henkin, Foreword: On Drawing Lines, 82 Harv. L. Rev. 63, 79–80 (1968): "A constitutional distinction between speech and conduct is specious. Speech *is* conduct, and actions speak. There is nothing intrinsically sacred about wagging the tongue or wielding a pen; there is nothing intrinsically more sacred about words than other symbols. [The] meaningful constitutional distinction is not between speech and conduct, but between conduct that speaks, communicates, and other kinds of conduct." In fact, the Court has long recognized that at least some forms of conduct may constitute "speech" within the meaning of the first amendment. In West Virginia State Board of Education v. Barnette, 319 U.S. 624 (1943), for example, Justice Jackson explained that "symbolism is a primitive but effective way of communicating ideas. [It] is a short cut from mind to mind." See also R.A.V. v. City of St. Paul, Chapter IV.H, supra (cross-burning); Tinker v. Des Moines Independent Community School District, 393 U.S. 503 (1969) (black armbands); Brown v. Louisiana, 383 U.S. 131 (1966) (sit-in); Stromberg v. California, 283 U.S. 359 (1931) (red flag).

If it is assumed that some forms of nonverbal conduct may constitute "speech," the question remains, how are we to determine what nonverbal conduct merits first amendment protection? At one level, it seems clear that "[everything] that one does, every action that one takes or fails to take, 'speaks' to anyone who is interested in looking for a message." That is, "all behavior is *capable of being understood* as communication." F. Haiman, Speech and Law in a Free Society 31 (1981). Surely, however, not all behavior that is "capable of being understood as communication" constitutes "speech," for that would bring all conduct within the ambit of the first amendment.

Consider Nimmer, The Meaning of Symbolic Speech under the First Amendment, 21 UCLA L. Rev. 29, 36 (1973):

A further element must be added to the mix before conduct may be considered to be speech. Whatever else may or may not be true of speech, as an irreducible minimum it must constitute a communication. That, in turn, implies both a communicator and a communicatee — a speaker and an audience. [Without] an actual or potential audience there can be no first amendment speech right. Nor may the first amendment be invoked if there is an audience but no actual or potential "speaker." [Unless] there is a human communicator intending to convey a meaning by his conduct, it would be odd to think of it as conduct constituting a communication protected by the first amendment.

Does all nonverbal conduct that is intended to communicate constitute "speech"? Note that such a doctrine might create a serious "imposter problem." That is, it would invite fraudulent claims by "criminals" that their actual intent was to communicate. Should courts be in the business of inquiring into the sincerity of individuals who claim to have exercised first amendment rights? Is there any way to avoid such inquiries? The issue of inquiry into sincerity in the religion context is examined in Part II, infra. Note also that, depending on the circumstances, nonverbal conduct that is intended to communicate may range across the entire spectrum of human behavior. It may include assassination, refusal to pay taxes, public nudity, flag burning, and urination on the steps of the state capitol. Does all such conduct constitute constitutionally protected "speech," so long as the actor intended to communicate?

## United States v. O'Brien

391 U.S. 367 (1968)

MR. CHIEF JUSTICE WARREN delivered the opinion of the Court.

On the morning of March 31, 1966, David Paul O'Brien and three companions burned their Selective Service registration certificates on the steps of the South Boston Courthouse. A sizable crowd, including several agents of the Federal Bureau of Investigation, witnessed the event. Immediately after the burning, [O'Brien] stated to FBI agents that he had burned his registration certificate because of his beliefs, knowing that he was violating federal law.

For this act, O'Brien was indicted, tried, convicted, and sentenced in the United States District Court for the District of Massachusetts. He did not contest the fact that he had burned the certificate. He stated in argument to the jury that he burned the certificate publicly to influence others to adopt his antiwar beliefs, as he put it, "so that other people would reevaluate their positions with Selective Service, with the armed forces, and reevaluate their place in the culture of today, to hopefully consider my position."

The indictment upon which he was tried charged that he "willfully and knowingly did mutilate, destroy, and change by burning [his] registration Certificate [in] violation of [§462(b)(3) of the Universal Military Training and Service Act of 1948]." Section 462(b)(3) [was] amended by Congress in 1965 (adding the words italicized below) so that at the time O'Brien burned his certificate an offense was committed by any person, "who forges, alters, *knowingly destroys, knowingly mutilates,* or in any manner changes any such certificate. . . ." (Italics supplied.) . . .

[The] Court of Appeals [held] the 1965 Amendment unconstitutional as a law abridging freedom of speech. At the time the Amendment was enacted, a regulation of the Selective Service System required registrants to keep their registration certificates in their "personal possession at all times." 32 C.F.R. §1617.1 (1962). [The] Court of Appeals [was] of the opinion that conduct punishable under the 1965 Amendment was already punishable under the nonpossession regulation, and consequently that the Amendment served no valid purpose; further, that in light of the prior regulation, the Amendment must have been "directed at public as distinguished from private destruction." On this basis, the court concluded that the 1965 Amendment ran afoul of the First Amendment by singling out persons engaged in protests for special treatment. [We] hold that the 1965 Amendment is constitutional both as enacted and as applied. . . .

[The] 1965 Amendment plainly does not abridge free speech on its face, and we do not understand O'Brien to argue otherwise. Amended §12(b)(3) on its face deals with conduct having no connection with speech. It prohibits the knowing destruction of certificates issued by the Selective Service System, and there is nothing necessarily expressive about such conduct. The Amendment does not distinguish between public and private destruction, and it does not punish only destruction engaged in for the purpose of expressing views. Compare Stromberg v. California, 283 U.S. 359 (1931). A law prohibiting destruction of Selective Service certificates no more abridges free speech on its face than a motor vehicle law prohibiting the destruction of drivers' licenses, or a tax law prohibiting the destruction of books and records.

O'Brien nonetheless argues that the 1965 Amendment is unconstitutional in its application to him, and is unconstitutional as enacted because what he calls the "purpose" of Congress was "to suppress freedom of speech." We consider these arguments separately.

## II

O'Brien first argues that the 1965 Amendment is unconstitutional as applied to him because his act of burning his registration certificate was protected "symbolic speech" within the First Amendment. His argument is that the freedom of expression which the First Amendment guarantees includes all modes of "communication of ideas by conduct," and that his conduct is within this definition because he did it in "demonstration against the war and against the draft."

We cannot accept the view that an apparently limitless variety of conduct can be labeled "speech" whenever the person engaging in the conduct intends thereby to express an idea. However, even on the assumption that the alleged communicative element in O'Brien's conduct is sufficient to bring into play the First Amendment, it does not necessarily follow that the destruction of a registration certificate is constitutionally protected activity. This Court has held that when "speech" and "nonspeech" elements are combined in the same course of conduct, a sufficiently important governmental interest in regulating the nonspeech element can justify incidental limitations on First Amendment freedoms. To characterize the quality of the governmental interest which must appear, the Court has employed a variety of descriptive terms: compelling; substantial; subordinating; paramount; cogent; strong. Whatever imprecision inheres in these terms, we think it clear that a government regulation is sufficiently justified if it is within the constitutional power of the Government; if it furthers an important or substantial governmental interest; if the governmental interest is unrelated to the suppression of free expression; and if the incidental restriction on alleged First Amendment freedoms is no greater than is essential to the furtherance of that interest. We find that the 1965 Amendment [meets] all of these requirements, and consequently that O'Brien can be constitutionally convicted for violating it.

The constitutional power of Congress to raise and support armies and to make all laws necessary and proper to that end is broad and sweeping. [Pursuant] to this power, Congress may establish a system of registration for individuals liable for training and service, and may require such individuals within reason to cooperate in the registration system. The issuance of certificates indicating the registration and eligibility classification of individuals is a legitimate and substantial administrative aid in the functioning of this system. And legislation to insure the continuing availability of issued certificates serves a legitimate and substantial purpose in the system's administration. . . .

1. The registration certificate serves as proof that the individual described thereon has registered for the draft. The classification certificate shows the eligibility classification of a named but undescribed individual. Voluntarily displaying the two certificates is an easy and painless way for a young man to dispel a question as to whether he might be delinquent in his Selective Service obligations. [Additionally,] in a time of national crisis, reasonable availability to each registrant of the two small cards assures a rapid and uncomplicated means for determining his fitness for immediate induction, no matter how distant in our mobile society he may be from his local board.

2. The information supplied on the certificates facilitates communication between registrants and local boards, simplifying the system and benefiting all concerned. To begin with, each certificate bears the address of the registrant's local board, an item unlikely to be committed to memory. Further, each card bears the registrant's Selective Service number, and a registrant who has his number readily available so that he can communicate it to his local board when he supplies or requests information can make simpler the board's task in locating his file. . . .

3. Both certificates carry continual reminders that the registrant must notify his local board of any change of address, and other specified changes in his status. . . .

The many functions performed by Selective Service certificates establish beyond doubt that Congress has a legitimate and substantial interest in preventing their wanton and unrestrained destruction and assuring their continuing availability by punishing people who knowingly and wilfully destroy or mutilate them. And we are unpersuaded that the pre-existence of the nonpossession regulations in any way negates this interest.

In the absence of a question as to multiple punishment, it has never been suggested that there is anything improper in Congress' providing alternative statutory avenues of prosecution to assure the effective protection of one and the same interest. [Here], the pre-existing avenue of prosecution was not even statutory. Regulations may be modified or revoked from time to time by administrative discretion. Certainly, the Congress may change or supplement a regulation.

Equally important, a comparison of the regulations with the 1965 Amendment indicates that they protect overlapping but not identical governmental interests, and that they reach somewhat different classes of wrongdoers. The gravamen of the offense defined by the statute is the deliberate rendering of certificates unavailable for the various purposes which they may serve. Whether registrants keep their certificates in their personal possession at all times, as required by the regulations, is of no particular concern under the 1965 Amendment, as long as they do not mutilate or destroy the certificates so as to render them unavailable. . . .

We think it apparent that the continuing availability to each registrant of his Selective Service certificates substantially furthers the smooth and proper functioning of the system that Congress has established to raise armies [and] that the 1965 Amendment specifically protects this substantial governmental interest. We perceive no alternative means that would more precisely and narrowly assure the continuing availability of issued Selective Service certificates than a law which prohibits their wilful mutilation or destruction.

[Moreover,] both the governmental interest and the operation of the 1965 Amendment are limited to the noncommunicative aspect of O'Brien's conduct. The governmental interest and the scope of the 1965 Amendment are limited to preventing harm to the smooth and efficient functioning of the Selective Service System. When O'Brien deliberately rendered unavailable his registration certificate, he wilfully frustrated this governmental interest. For this noncommunicative impact of his conduct, and for nothing else, he was convicted.

The case at bar is therefore unlike one where the alleged governmental interest in regulating conduct arises in some measure because the communication allegedly integral to the conduct is itself thought to be harmful. In Stromberg v. California, 283 U.S. 359 (1931), for example, this Court struck down a statutory phrase which punished people who expressed their "opposition to organized government" by displaying "any flag, badge, banner, or device." Since the statute there was aimed at suppressing communication it could not be sustained as a regulation of noncommunicative conduct. . . .

In conclusion, we find that because of the Government's substantial interest in assuring the continuing availability of issued Selective Service certificates, because amended §462(b) is an appropriately narrow means of protecting this interest and condemns only the independent noncommunicative impact of conduct within its reach, and because the noncommunicative impact of O'Brien's act of burning his registration certificate frustrated the Government's interest, a sufficient governmental interest has been shown to justify O'Brien's conviction.

## III

O'Brien finally argues that the 1965 Amendment is unconstitutional as enacted because what he calls the "purpose" of Congress was "to suppress freedom of speech." We reject this argument because under settled principles the purpose of Congress, as O'Brien uses that term, is not a basis for declaring this legislation unconstitutional.

It is a familiar principle of constitutional law that this Court will not strike down an otherwise constitutional statute on the basis of an alleged illicit legislative motive. . . .

Inquiries into congressional motives or purposes are a hazardous matter. When the issue is simply the interpretation of legislation, the Court will look to statements by legislators for guidance as to the purpose of the legislature, because the benefit to sound decision-making in this circumstance is thought sufficient to risk the possibility of misreading Congress' purpose. It is entirely a different matter when we are asked to void a statute that is, under well-settled criteria, constitutional on its face, on the basis of what fewer than a handful of Congressmen said about it. What motivates one legislator to make a speech about a statute is not necessarily what motivates scores of others to enact it, and the stakes are sufficiently high for us to eschew guesswork. We decline to void [legislation] which could be reenacted in its exact form if the same or another legislator made a "wiser" speech about it. . . .

We think it not amiss, in passing, to comment upon O'Brien's legislative-purpose argument. There was little floor debate on this legislation in either House. Only Senator Thurmond commented on its substantive features in the Senate. [After] his brief statement, and without any additional substantive comments, the [bill] passed the Senate. [In] the House debate only two Congressmen addressed themselves to the Amendment — Congressmen Rivers and Bray. [The] bill was passed after their statements without any further debate by a vote of 393 to 1. It is principally on the basis of the statements by these three Congressmen that O'Brien makes his congressional-"purpose" argument. We note that if we were to examine legislative purpose in the instant case, we would be obliged to consider not only these statements but also the more authoritative reports of the Senate and House Armed Services Committees. [While] both reports make clear a concern with the "defiant" destruction of so-called "draft cards" and with "open" encouragement to others to destroy their cards, both reports also indicate that this concern stemmed from an apprehension that unrestrained destruction of cards would disrupt the smooth functioning of the Selective Service System.

## IV

Since the 1965 Amendment to §12(b)(3) of the Universal Military Training and Service Act is constitutional as enacted and as applied, the Court of Appeals should have affirmed the judgment of conviction entered by the District Court. . . .

MR. JUSTICE MARSHALL took no part in the consideration or decision of these cases.

MR. JUSTICE HARLAN, concurring. . . .

I wish to make explicit my understanding that this [decision] does not foreclose consideration of First Amendment claims in those rare instances when an "incidental" restriction upon expression, imposed by a regulation which furthers an "important or substantial" governmental interest and satisfies the Court's other criteria, in practice has the effect of entirely preventing a "speaker" from reaching a significant audience with whom he could not otherwise lawfully communicate. This is not such a case, since O'Brien manifestly could have conveyed his message in many ways other than by burning his draft card.

MR. JUSTICE DOUGLAS, dissenting. . . .

[Justice Douglas maintained that the "underlying and basic [issue] in this case [is] whether conscription is permissible in the absence of a declaration of war." Justice Douglas therefore suggested that "this case should be put down for reargument" on that question. Justice Douglas briefly addressed the symbolic conduct issue in his concurring opinion the following term in Brandenburg v. Ohio, Chapter II.A, supra: "Action is often a method of expression and within the protection of the First Amendment. Suppose one tears up his own copy of the Constitution in eloquent protest to a decision of this Court. May he be indicted? Suppose one rips his own Bible to shreds to celebrate his departure from one 'faith' and his embrace of atheism. May he be indicted? [This] Court's affirmance of [O'Brien's conviction for burning the draft card] was not, with all respect, consistent with the First Amendment.]"

## Note: Draft Card Burning and the First Amendment

1. *Is draft card burning "speech"*? Did the Court decide that question? How would you decide it? Why was Chief Justice Warren reluctant in *O'Brien* to "accept the view that an apparently limitless variety of conduct can be labeled 'speech' whenever the person engaging in the conduct intends thereby to express an idea"? Consider the following propositions: (a) If nonverbal conduct that is intended "to express an idea" constitutes "speech," government may not restrict that conduct unless it poses a "clear and present danger" within the meaning of the Holmes/Brandeis formulation. (b) Even if nonverbal conduct that is intended to communicate constitutes "speech," the first amendment does not "afford the same kind of freedom to those who would communicate ideas by conduct [as it affords] to those who communicate by pure speech." Cox v. Louisiana, 379 U.S. 536, 555 (1965).

2. *Symbolic conduct and the content-based/content-neutral distinction.* Should a distinction be drawn between laws that restrict symbolic conduct because of its content and laws that restrict symbolic conduct for reasons unrelated to content? Compare, for example, a law prohibiting "any person to urinate in public" with a law prohibiting "any person to urinate on a public building as a symbolic act of opposition to government." Does the content-based/content-neutral distinction provide a useful framework for analyzing the constitutionality of such laws? Does *O'Brien* adopt such an analysis?

3. *Restrictions related "to the suppression of free expression"*: Stromberg, Tinker, *and* Schacht. In Stromberg v. California, discussed in *O'Brien,* the Court invalidated a statute prohibiting any person to display "a red flag [in] any public place [as] a [symbol] of opposition to organized government." The Court explained that the law might be construed to prohibit "peaceful and orderly opposition to government by legal means" and thus curtail "the opportunity for free political discussion."

In Tinker v. Des Moines Independent Community School District, 393 U.S. 503 (1969), decided a year after *O'Brien*, school officials, fearing possible disruption of school activities, suspended three public school students because they wore black armbands to school to protest the government's policy in Vietnam. In invalidating the suspensions, the Court observed that "the wearing of an armband for the purpose of expressing certain views is the type of symbolic act that is within [the] First Amendment" and is "closely akin to 'pure speech.'" The Court observed further that "the school authorities did not purport to prohibit the wearing of all symbols of political or controversial significance; [rather], a particular symbol — black armbands worn to exhibit opposition to this Nation's involvement in Vietnam — was singled out for prohibition." Consider Ely, Flag Desecration: A Case Study in the Roles of Categorization and Balancing in First Amendment Analysis, 88 Harv. L. Rev. 1482, 1498 & n.63 (1975): "[In] *Tinker* the state regulated [the armbands] because it feared the effect that the message those armbands conveyed would have on the other children. [*Tinker*] would have been quite a different case had it arisen [in] the context of a school regulation banning armbands in woodworking class along with all other sartorial embellishments liable to become safety hazards."

In Schacht v. United States, 398 U.S. 58 (1970), petitioner, who participated in a skit demonstrating opposition to American involvement in Vietnam, was convicted of violating 18 U.S.C. §702, which made criminal the unauthorized wearing of an American military uniform. The Court reversed the conviction. Citing *O'Brien*, the Court observed that section 702 "is, standing alone, a valid statute on its face." The Court noted, however, that another statute, 10 U.S.C. §772(f), authorized the wearing of an American military uniform in a theatrical production "if the portrayal does not tend to discredit [the armed forces]." Finding that petitioner's skit constituted a "theatrical production" within the meaning of section 772(f), the Court concluded: "[Petitioner's] conviction can be sustained only if he can be punished for speaking out against the role of our Army and our country in Vietnam. Clearly punishment for this reason would be an unconstitutional abridgement of freedom of speech. [Section 772(f)], which leaves Americans free to praise the war in Vietnam but can send persons like [petitioner] to prison for opposing it, cannot survive in a country which has the First Amendment."

4. *An intermediate case: Mitchell.* In Wisconsin v. Mitchell, Chapter IV.H, supra, which involved a racially motivated assault, the Court upheld a state statute enhancing the maximum penalty for an offense whenever the defendant "intentionally selects the person against whom the crime [is committed] because of the race, religion, color, disability, sexual orientation, national origin or ancestry of that person." The Court noted that "a physical assault is not by any stretch of the imagination expressive conduct protected by the First Amendment." But suppose X assaults Y to express his view that whites should not enter his neighborhood. This "message" is clearly understood by the "audience," and the relevant law authorizes enhanced punishment whenever an individual "physically assaults another as an expression of racial antagonism." Is it still clear that "a physical assault is not by any stretch of the imagination expressive conduct protected by the First Amendment"?

Note also that, in upholding the statute actually at issue in *Mitchell*, the Court observed that "the statute singles out for enhancement bias-inspired" crimes because such "crimes are more likely to provoke retaliatory crimes, inflict distinct emotional harms on their victims, and incite community unrest." Is this statute "related" or "unrelated" to the suppression of free expression? Note that the harms identified by the Court arise *only* if the victim or others know that the defendant committed a hate crime. In such circumstances, is the law "related" to the suppression of free expression because the harm sought to be prevented occurs only if the defendant has in some way communicated his motive?

5. *Restrictions "unrelated to the suppression of free expression."* O'Brien's analysis of restrictions that are "unrelated to the suppression of free expression"

applies the general principles of content-neutral balancing to the specific context of symbolic conduct. Is *O'Brien*'s application of those principles sufficiently speech-protective?

Consider Alfange, The Draft-Card Burning Case, 1968 Sup. Ct. Rev. 1, 23, 26:

> [As] the Court's own inventory of possible draft-card uses indicates, [the certificates] serve functions of dispensable convenience rather than urgent necessity. The Court's use of "substantial," therefore, is more appropriate if the term is understood in its sense of "having substance" or "not imaginary," rather than the sense of "considerable" or "large." [Moreover, the Court should have weighed] the importance of the government's interest against the impact of the draft law amendment on freedom of speech.

Should the Court have "balanced" the competing interests in *O'Brien*? How would you assess the importance of the draft law amendment's impact on free speech? Consider the following arguments:

a. "In view of the fact that the amendment does not punish dissent per se, but merely forbids one very specific means of conveying the expression of dissent, it cannot seriously be contended that the amendment's effect upon speech is anything but minor." Id. at 27.

b. "Burning a draft card [is] the ordinary person's way of attracting the attention of the national news media. [To] [prohibit] such an effective form of propagating one's views [is] to greatly diminish the effectiveness of the individual's right [to] make his dissent known." Velvel, Freedom of Speech and the Draft Card Burning Cases, 16 U. Kan. L. Rev. 149, 153 (1968).

c. "[Symbolic] conduct deserves a high degree of constitutional protection. [The] kind of stimulus necessary to activate the political conscience of [the] populace sometimes can be created only by transcending rationality and appealing to more primitive, more basic instincts. [The] communication achieved by the wave of draft-card burnings at the height of the United States involvement in Vietnam represents a paradigm example of the 'speech' with which the First Amendment is concerned." Blasi, The Checking Value in First Amendment Theory, 1977 Am. B. Found. Res. J. 521, 640.

d. "[Much] of the effectiveness of O'Brien's communication [derived] precisely from the fact that it was illegal. Had there been no law prohibiting draft card [burning], he might have attracted no more attention than he would have by swallowing a goldfish." Ely, supra, at 1489–1490. See G. Stone, Perilous Times: Free Speech in Wartime 471–472 (2004): "By 1965, the act of publicly burning one's draft card had become a potent means of protest. This was more than a clever way to express one's opposition to the war. Burning a copy of the Constitution is also a clever way to express opposition, but burning a copy of the Constitution (as distinct from burning the original) was not a crime. Burning a draft card was. Thus, this act represented not only symbolic dissent but direct resistance. Those who publicly burned their draft cards [crossed] the line between protest and civil disobedience."

e. "As applied to expression, the [*O'Brien*] statute had [a] disparate impact on those who opposed government policy, for who would destroy a draft card as an expression of *support* for government policy? [Indeed], in practical effect, the statute had essentially the same content-differential effect as a law prohibiting any person [to destroy] a draft card 'as a symbolic expression of protest against government policy.'" Stone, Content Regulation and the First Amendment, 25 Wm. & Mary L. Rev. 189, 222–223 (1983).

Is the Court's analysis of symbolic expression in *O'Brien* consistent with its analysis of content-neutral restrictions generally? Consider Ely, supra, at 1488–1489: "What was unconsciously going on in *O'Brien* [was] a reservation [of] serious balancing [for] relatively familiar [means] of expression, such as pamphlets, pickets, public speeches and rallies, [and a relegation of] other, less orthodox modes of communication to the [highly deferential approach] that sustained the draft card burning law."

6. *"Incidental" restrictions on free speech.* Note that, unlike most content-neutral restrictions, such as laws prohibiting leafleting, the law at issue in *O'Brien* was not expressly directed at speech. Its effect on speech was merely "incidental." Should it matter whether a content-neutral law expressly restricts speech or whether it restricts a broader range of activities but has only an incidental effect on speech? For analysis of incidental restrictions, see Kagan, Private Speech, Public Purpose: The Role of Governmental Motive in First Amendment Doctrine, 63 U. Chi. L. Rev. 415, 494–508 (1996) (the distinction between direct and incidental restrictions can be explained largely in terms of the concern with avoiding possible improper governmental motivation); Rubenfeld, The First Amendment's Purpose, 53 Stan. L. Rev. 767, 769 (2001) ("there is no such thing as a free speech immunity based on the claim that someone wants to break an otherwise constitutional law for expressive purposes"); Dorf, Incidental Burdens on Fundamental Rights, 109 Harv. L. Rev. 1175 (1996) ("sound reasons can be advanced for taking direct burdens more seriously than incidental burdens," but "*substantial* incidental burdens" raise "a bona fide constitutional problem"); Stone, Content-Neutral Restrictions, 54 U. Chi. L. Rev. 46, 114 (1987) (incidental restrictions may be unconstitutional if they have a highly disproportionate and significant impact on particular viewpoints).

For an example of a (relatively rare) decision in which the Court has invalidated an incidental restriction on expression, see NAACP v. Alabama, infra, in which the Court held at the height of the civil rights movement that an Alabama statute requiring all out-of-state corporations doing business in the state to disclose the names and addresses of all Alabama "members" was invalid as applied to the NAACP, because "on past occasions revelation of the identity of [the NAACP's] rank-and-file members has exposed these members to economic reprisal, loss of employment, threat of physical coercion, and other manifestations of public hostility." The Court concluded that, "under these circumstances, [compelled] disclosure of [the NAACP's] Alabama membership is likely to affect adversely the ability of [the NAACP] and its members to pursue their [constitutional rights]." For a more recent example, see Boy Scouts of America v. Dale, infra.

7. *When is an incidental restriction not "incidental"?* A paradigm example of an incidental restriction might be a law prohibiting any person to speed, as applied to an individual who speeds in order to express his opposition to speed limits. Note that two factors are present in this situation: (1) the law is not directed at speech and (2) it is not the expressive element of the act that causes the harm the state seeks to prevent. Both factors must be present for the incidental effect doctrine to apply. Consider, for example, a prosecution for breach of the peace based on an inflammatory speech given by an individual on a street corner that causes a fight. The breach of the peace statute is not directed at speech, as such. It applies to all sorts of nonspeech conduct, such as making loud noises late at night in a residential neighborhood or parking one's car on a sidewalk. In that sense, the statute has only an incidental effect on speakers. But because the speaker has breached the peace in light of the response of others to the message he has conveyed, the Court does not treat this as a mere incidental effect. Indeed, this is implicit in the World War I cases in which defendants were prosecuted for "obstructing the draft" and in the hostile audience cases in which they were prosecuted for breach of the peace. Put simply, where the relevant harm is caused by the message, the incidental effects doctrine is inapplicable.

Along these lines, consider Holder v. Humanitarian Law Project, 561 U.S. 1 (2010), which involved the constitutionality of a federal statute declaring it unlawful for any person knowingly to provide "material support" to a foreign terrorist organization, where the statute defined "material support" as including, among other things, property, money, lodging, safehouses, facilities, weapons, and expert advice. Plaintiffs, who wanted to advise foreign terrorist organizations how to further their ends through legal channels, challenged the constitutionality of the statute as applied to them. The government argued that the statute had only an incidental effect on speech and that *O'Brien* should govern. Although the Court upheld the statute on other grounds, it unanimously rejected the government's argument:

> *O'Brien* does not provide the applicable standard for reviewing a content-based regulation of speech, and [this statute] regulates speech on the basis of its content. [The government] argues that [the statute falls under *O'Brien*] because it *generally* functions as a regulation of conduct. That argument runs headlong into a number of our precedents, most prominently *Cohen v. California*, [which] involved a generally applicable regulation of conduct, barring breaches of the peace. But when Cohen was convicted for wearing a jacket bearing an epithet, we did not apply *O'Brien*. Instead, we recognized that the generally applicable

law was directed at Cohen because of what his speech communicated — he violated the breach of the peace statute because of the offensive content of his particular message. We accordingly applied more rigorous scrutiny and reversed his conviction. This suit falls into the same category.

8. *The problem of legislative motivation.* Should the Court in *O'Brien* have invalidated the 1965 amendment because "the 'purpose' of Congress was 'to suppress freedom of speech'"? As the Court noted, only two Representatives and one Senator commented directly on the legislation. Congressman Bray's comments are representative: "The need of this legislation is clear. Beatniks and so-called 'campus cults' have been publicly burning their draft cards to demonstrate their contempt for the United States and our resistance to Communist takeovers. [If] these 'revolutionaries' are permitted to deface and destroy their draft cards, our entire Selective Service System is dealt a serious blow."

Consider Alfange, supra, at 15, 16: "[What] emerges with indisputable clarity from an examination of the legislative history of the amendment is that the intent of its framers was purely and simply to put a stop to this particular form of antiwar protest, which they deemed extraordinarily contemptible and vicious — even treasonous — at a time when American troops were engaged in combat. [The Court's contrary conclusion blinked] the facts."

The Court has often inquired into the motivation underlying executive and administrative decisions. See, e.g., Cornelius v. NAACP Legal Defense & Educational Fund, 473 U.S. 788 (1985) ("the existence of reasonable grounds for limiting access to a nonpublic forum [will] not save a regulation that is in reality a facade for viewpoint-based discrimination"); Mt. Healthy City School District Board of Education v. Doyle, 429 U.S. 274 (1977) (although untenured teacher can be dismissed for "no reason whatever," he cannot be fired for exercise of first amendment rights); Keyes v. School District No. 1, 413 U.S. 189 (1973) (Denver schools held unlawfully segregated because school board decisions concerning the location of schools were motivated by racial considerations); Yick Wo v. Hopkins, 118 U.S. 356 (1886) (licensing law invalidated because of discriminatory administration).

The Court has also inquired into legislative motivation in cases where it is claimed that a facially neutral statute is motivated by racial animus. See, e.g., Hunter v. Underwood, 471 U.S. 222 (1985) (invalidating provision of the Alabama constitution disfranchising people convicted of misdemeanors of "moral turpitude" on the ground that it was motivated by racist ideology). Why should the Court be reluctant to investigate motive? Three explanations have usually been offered: the difficulty of ascertaining the "actual" motivation of a collective body; the futility of invalidating a law that could be reenacted with a show of "wiser" motives; and the inappropriateness of impugning the integrity of a coordinate branch of government. Are these explanations sufficiently weighty to justify the conclusion that "the purpose of Congress [is] not a basis for declaring [legislation] unconstitutional"? See Brest, Palmer v. Thompson: An Approach to the Problem of Unconstitutional Legislative Motive, 1971 Sup. Ct. Rev. 95; Ely, Legislative and Administrative Motivation in Constitutional Law, 79 Yale L.J. 1205 (1970).

### Note: Flag Desecration and Misuse

1. *Flag burning.* In Street v. New York, 394 U.S. 576 (1969), appellant, after hearing a news report that civil rights leader James Meredith had been shot, took his American flag out of a drawer, carried it to a nearby street corner, and lit it with a match. As it burned on the pavement, appellant said to a group of onlookers, "We don't need no damn flag. [If] they let that happen to Meredith we don't need an American flag." Appellant was convicted of violating a New York statute declaring it a misdemeanor "publicly [to] mutilate, deface, defile, trample upon, or cast contempt upon either by words or acts [any flag of the United States]." The Court, in a five-to-four decision, overturned appellant's conviction. The Court found it unnecessary, however, to address appellant's assertion "that New York may not constitutionally punish one who publicly destroys or damages an American flag as a means of protest," holding instead that the statute "was unconstitutionally applied in appellant's case because it permitted him to be punished merely for *speaking* defiant or contemptuous *words about* the American flag."

Chief Justice Warren and Justices Black, White, and Fortas dissented. Chief Justice Warren chastised the Court for ducking "the basic question presented" — "'whether the deliberate act of burning an American flag in public as a "protest" may be punished as a crime.'" On that question, Chief Justice Warren concluded that "the States and the Federal Government [have] the power to protect the flag from acts of desecration and disgrace." In a separate dissenting opinion, Justice Fortas elaborated:

> If a state statute provided that it is a misdemeanor to burn one's shirt [on] the public thoroughfare, it could hardly be asserted that the citizen's constitutional right is violated. [And if] the arsonist asserted that he was burning his shirt [as] a protest against the Government's fiscal policies, [it] is hardly possible that his claim to First Amendment shelter would prevail against the State's claim of a right to avert danger to the public and to avoid obstruction to traffic as a result of the fire. [If], as I submit, it is permissible to prohibit the burning of personal property on the public sidewalk, there is no basis for applying a different rule to flag burning. And the fact that the law is violated for purposes of protest does not immunize the violator. [Citing *O'Brien.*]

Suppose Street had been convicted of violating a law prohibiting any person to make any "open fire in public." Is the flag desecration statute distinguishable?

2. *Contemptuous treatment.* In Smith v. Goguen, 415 U.S. 566 (1974), appellee, who wore a small cloth replica of the United States flag sewn to the seat of his trousers, was convicted of violating a Massachusetts statute prohibiting any person to "publicly mutilate, trample upon, deface or treat contemptuously the flag of the United States." The Court, in an opinion by Justice Powell, overturned the conviction. The Court found it unnecessary to decide whether the statute was unconstitutionally overbroad, holding instead that it was "void for vagueness." The Court emphasized that appellee was charged not "with any act of physical desecration," but with "'publicly [treating] contemptuously the flag of the United States.'" Noting that "the flag has become 'an object of youth fashion and high camp,'" and that "casual treatment of the flag in many contexts has become a widespread contemporary phenomenon," the Court concluded that this aspect of the statute was "inherently vague" and hence violative of due process. Chief Justice Burger and Justices Blackmun and Rehnquist dissented.

3. *Flag misuse.* In Spence v. Washington, 418 U.S. 405 (1974), appellant, to protest the invasion of Cambodia and the killings at Kent State University, displayed a United States flag, which he owned, out of the window of his apartment. Affixed to the flag was a large peace symbol made of removable tape. Appellant was convicted under Washington's "flag misuse" statute, which prohibited the exhibition of a United States flag to which is attached or superimposed "any word, figure, mark, design, drawing, or advertisement." The Court held, in a per curiam opinion, that, "as applied to appellant's activity," which the Court described as "a pointed expression of anguish by appellant about [the] affairs of his government," the Washington statute "impermissibly infringed free expression":

> [The state maintains that it] has an interest in preserving the national flag as an unalloyed symbol of our country. [This] interest might be seen as an effort to prevent the appropriation of a revered national symbol by an individual, interest group, or enterprise where there was a risk that association of the symbol with a particular product or viewpoint might be taken erroneously as evidence of governmental endorsement. [Alternatively], the interest [may be understood as] based on the uniquely universal character of the national flag as a symbol. [If] it may be destroyed or permanently disfigured, it [could] lose its capability of mirroring the sentiments of all who view it.
>
> [We] need not decide in this case whether the interest advanced by the [state] is valid. We assume, arguendo, that it is. [But even if] it is valid, [it] is directly related to expression in the context of activity like that undertaken by appellant. For that reason [the] four-step analysis of [O'Brien] is inapplicable. [We hold that the statute is] unconstitutional as applied to appellant's activity. There was no risk that appellant's acts would mislead viewers into assuming that the Government endorsed his viewpoint. [Moreover, appellant] did [not] permanently disfigure the flag or destroy it. [And] his message was direct, likely to be understood, and within the contours of the First Amendment. [The] conviction must be reversed.

Justice Rehnquist, joined by Chief Justice Burger and Justice White, dissented:

> [The] Court's treatment [of the state's interest] lacks all substance. The suggestion that the State's interest somehow diminishes when the flag is decorated with *removable* tape trivializes something which is not trivial. The State [is] hardly seeking to protect the flag's resale value. [The] true nature of the State's interest in this case is [one] of preserving the flag as "an important symbol of nationhood and unity." [It] is the character, not the cloth, of the flag which the State seeks to protect. "[The] flag is a national property, and the Nation may regulate those who would make, imitate, sell, possess, or use it." . . .
>
> [That] the State has a valid interest in preserving the character of the flag does not mean, of course, that it can employ all conceivable means to enforce it. It certainly could not require all citizens to own the flag or compel citizens to salute one. [It] presumably cannot punish criticism of the flag, or the principles for which it stands, any more than it could punish criticism of this country's policies or ideas. But the statute in this case demands no such allegiance. Its operation does not depend upon whether [the] use of the flag is respectful or contemptuous. [It] simply withdraws a unique national symbol from the roster of materials that may be used as a background for communications. [The] Constitution [does not prohibit] Washington from making that decision.

Is *Spence* consistent with *O'Brien*? Do you agree with the Court that the interests underlying flag misuse statutes are "directly related to expression," and that the *O'Brien* standard thus should not govern? Consider Ely, Flag Desecration: A Case Study in the Roles of Categorization and Balancing in First Amendment Analysis, 88 Harv. L. Rev. 1482, 1503–1504, 1506–1508 (1975):

> [The flag misuse statute is] ideologically neutral on its face, and would proscribe the superimposition of "Buy Mother Fletcher's Ambulance Paint" [as] fully as it would the addition of a swastika. Such "improper use" provisions are [thus] more complicated constitutionally than the ideologically tilted "desecration" provisions. [In the flag misuse context], the state may assert an interest [similar] to that asserted in [defense of a content-neutral law prohibiting any person to interrupt a public speaker]. The state's interest in both of these cases might be characterized as an interest in preventing the [defendant] from interfering with the expression of others. [As with interruption of a public speaker, the] state does not care what message the defendant is conveying by altering the flag: all that matters is that he is interrupting the message conveyed by the flag. [There is, however, an answer to this argument, for] although improper use statutes do not single out certain messages for proscription, they *do* single out one set of messages, namely the set of messages conveyed by the American flag, for protection. That, of course, is not true of a law that generally prohibits the interruption of speakers. [In reality, then, an improper use statute] is, at best, analogous to a law prohibiting the interruption of patriotic speeches, and that is a law that is hardly "unrelated to the suppression of free expression."

4. *Flag desecration.* The Court directly confronted the issue of flag desecration in Texas v. Johnson, 491 U.S. 397 (1989). During the 1984 Republican National Convention, Johnson burned an American flag as part of a political demonstration protesting the policies of the Reagan administration. Johnson was arrested and convicted of violating a Texas flag desecration statute, which made it a crime for any person to "deface, damage or otherwise physically mistreat" the flag "in a way that the actor knows will seriously offend one or more persons likely to observe or discover his action." The Court, in a five-to-four decision, overturned the conviction.

In an opinion by Justice Brennan, the Court began by concluding that "Johnson's flag-burning was 'conduct' sufficiently imbued with elements of 'communication' to implicate the First Amendment." After rejecting the claim that the statute could be justified in terms of the state's interest in "preventing breaches of the peace," see Chapter II.B, supra, the Court turned to the heart of the issue:

The Government generally has a freer hand in restricting expressive conduct than it has in restricting the written or spoken word. It may not, however, proscribe particular conduct *because* it has expressive elements. [Thus], although we have recognized that where "'speech' and 'nonspeech' elements are combined in the same course of conduct, a sufficiently important governmental interest in regulating the nonspeech element can justify incidental limitations on First Amendment freedoms," [*O'Brien*], we have limited the applicability of *O'Brien*'s relatively lenient standard to those cases in which "the governmental interest is unrelated to the suppression of free expression." . . .

The State [asserts] an interest in preserving the flag as a symbol of nationhood and national unity. [We are] persuaded that this interest is related to expression in the case of Johnson's burning of the flag. The State, apparently, is concerned that such conduct will lead people to believe either that the flag does not stand for nationhood and national unity, but instead reflects other, less positive concepts, or that the concepts reflected in the flag do not in fact exist, that is, we do not enjoy unity as a Nation. These concerns blossom only when a person's treatment of the flag communicates some message, and thus are related "to the suppression of free expression" within the meaning of *O'Brien.* . . .

It remains to consider whether the State's interest in preserving the flag as a symbol of nationhood and national unity justifies Johnson's conviction. [Johnson] was prosecuted because he knew that his politically charged expression would cause "serious offense." [The] Texas law is thus not aimed at protecting the physical integrity of the flag in all circumstances, but is designed instead to protect it only against impairments that would cause serious offense to others. [Whether] Johnson's treatment of the flag violated Texas law thus depended on the likely communicative impact of his expressive conduct. [Because] this restriction [is] content-based, [we must] subject the State's asserted interest [to] "the most exacting scrutiny." . . .

If there is a bedrock principle underlying the First Amendment, it is that the Government may not prohibit the expression of an idea simply because society finds the idea itself offensive or disagreeable. We have not recognized an exception to this principle even where our flag is involved. [Citing *Street; Spence;* and *Goguen.*] [Nothing] in our precedents suggests that a State may foster its own view of the flag by prohibiting expressive conduct related to it. [If] we were to hold that a State may forbid flag-burning wherever it is likely to endanger the flag's symbolic role, but allow it wherever burning a flag promotes that role — as where, for example, a person ceremoniously burns a dirty flag — we would be saying that when it comes to impairing the flag's physical integrity, the flag itself may be used as a symbol [only] in one direction. We would be permitting a State to "prescribe what shall be orthodox" by saying that one may burn the flag to convey one's attitude toward it and its referents only if one does not endanger the flag's representation of nationhood and national unity.

    We never before have held that the Government may ensure that a symbol be used to express only one view of that symbol or its referents. [Citing *Schacht.*] To conclude that the Government may permit designated symbols to be used to communicate only a limited set of messages would be to enter territory having no discernible or defensible boundaries. Could the Government, on this theory, prohibit the burning of state flags? Of copies of the presidential seal? Of the Constitution? . . .

Chief Justice Rehnquist, joined by Justices White and O'Connor, dissented:

    The flag is not simply another "idea" or "point of view" competing for recognition in the marketplace of ideas. [Flag burning is] no essential part of any expression of ideas, [citing *Chaplinsky*], and [Johnson's] act [conveyed] nothing that could not have been conveyed [in] a dozen different ways. [Far] from being a case of "one picture being worth a thousand words," flag burning is the equivalent of an inarticulate grunt or roar that [is] most likely to be indulged in not to express any particular idea, but to antagonize others. [The] Texas statute deprived Johnson of only one rather inarticulate symbolic form of protest — a form of protest that was profoundly offensive to many — and left him with a full panoply of other symbols and every conceivable form of verbal expression to express his deep disapproval of national policy. Thus, in no way can it be said that Texas is punishing him because his hearers — or any other group of people — were profoundly opposed to the message that he sought to convey. [It] was Johnson's use of this particular symbol, and not the idea that he sought to convey by [it], for which he was punished.

Justice Stevens also dissented.

5. *Flag desecration revisited.* Almost immediately after the decision in *Johnson,* Congress enacted the Flag Protection Act of 1989, which made it a crime for any person knowingly to mutilate, deface, physically defile, burn, maintain on the floor or ground, or trample upon any flag of the United States. The government maintained that this act was constitutional because, unlike the statute addressed in *Johnson,* the act was designed to protect "the physical integrity of the flag under all circumstances," did "not target expressive

conduct on the basis of the content of its message," and proscribed "conduct (other than disposal) that damages or mistreats a flag, without regard to the actor's motive, his intended message, or the likely effects of his conduct on onlookers." In United States v. Eichman, 496 U.S. 310 (1990), the Court, in a five-to-four decision, invalidated this act.

Justice Brennan delivered the opinion:

> Although the [act] contains no explicit content-based limitation on the scope of prohibited conduct, it is nevertheless clear that the Government's asserted *interest* is "related to the suppression of free expression" and concerned with the content of such expression. The Government's interest in protecting the "physical integrity" of a privately owned flag rests upon a perceived need to preserve the flag's status as a symbol of our Nation and certain national ideals. But the mere destruction or disfigurement of a particular physical manifestation of the symbol, without more, does not diminish or otherwise affect the symbol itself in any way. For example, the secret destruction of a flag in one's own basement would not threaten the flag's recognized meaning. Rather, the Government's desire to preserve the flag as a symbol for certain national ideals is implicated "only when a person's treatment of the flag communicates [a] message" to others that is inconsistent with those ideals.
>
> Moreover, the precise language of the Act's prohibitions confirms Congress' interest in the communicative impact of flag destruction. The Act criminalizes the conduct of anyone who "knowingly mutilates, defaces, physically defiles, burns, maintains on the floor or ground, or tramples upon any flag." Each of the specified terms — with the possible exception of "burns" — unmistakably connotes disrespectful treatment. . . .
>
> Although Congress cast the [act] in somewhat broader terms than the Texas statute at issue in *Johnson*, the Act still suffers from the same fundamental flaw: it suppresses expression out of concern for its likely communicative impact. Despite the Act's wider scope, its restriction on expression cannot be "'justified without reference to the content of the regulated speech.'" The Act therefore must be subjected to "the most exacting scrutiny," and for the reasons stated in *Johnson*, the Government's interest cannot justify its infringement on First Amendment rights.

Justice Stevens, joined by Chief Justice Rehnquist and Justices White and O'Connor, dissented.

Central to the Court's reasoning in *Eichman* is its assertion that the Flag Protection Act was "related to the suppression of free expression" because "the Government's desire to preserve the flag as a symbol for certain national ideals" is implicated "only when a person's treatment of the flag 'communicates [a] message' to others that is inconsistent with those ideals." Is that assertion persuasive? Suppose Congress enacts the following statute: "No person may knowingly impair the physical integrity of the American flag." Do *Johnson* and *Eichman* require the invalidation of this law? See Stone, Flag Burning and the Constitution, 75 Iowa L. Rev. 111 (1989). Could government constitutionally protect the flag as a matter of copyright law? See Kmiec, In the Aftermath of *Johnson* and *Eichman*, 1990 B.Y.U. L. Rev. 577.

**BARNES v. GLEN THEATRE, INC., 501 U.S. 560 (1991).** Respondents, two Indiana establishments that present nude dancing as entertainment, brought suit to enjoin enforcement of Indiana's public indecency statute, which prohibits any person to appear "in a state of nudity" in any "public place." The state courts interpreted the statute as requiring nude dancers in such establishments to wear pasties and a G-string. The Court, in a five-to-four decision, rejected the claim that this statute, as applied to respondents, violates the first amendment.

Chief Justice Rehnquist, joined by Justices O'Connor and Kennedy, delivered the plurality opinion: "[Nude] dancing of the kind sought to be performed here is expressive conduct within the outer perimeters of the First Amendment, though we view it as only marginally so. [Indiana], of course, has not banned nude dancing as such, but has proscribed public nudity across the board. [Applying] the four-part *O'Brien* test, we find that Indiana's public indecency statute is justified despite its incidental limitations on some expressive activity. The public indecency statute is clearly within the constitutional power of the State and furthers substantial governmental interests. [Such statutes, which] are of ancient origin, and presently exist in at least 47 States, [reflect] moral disapproval of people appearing in the nude among strangers in public places. [The] traditional police power of the States is defined as the authority to provide for the public health, safety, and morals, and we have upheld such a basis for legislation. [Citing *Roth* and *Paris Adult Theatre*, section IV.E, supra.]

"This interest is unrelated to the suppression of free expression. [Respondents contend] that even though prohibiting nudity in public generally may not be related to suppressing expression, prohibiting the performance of nude dancing is related to expression because the state seeks to prevent its erotic message. [But] we do not think that when Indiana applies its statute to the nude dancing in these nightclubs it is proscribing nudity because of the erotic message conveyed by the dancers. Presumably numerous other erotic performances are presented at these establishments [without] any interference from the state, so long as the performers wear a scant amount of clothing. Likewise, the requirement that the dancers don pasties and a G-string does not deprive the dance of whatever erotic message it conveys; it simply makes the message slightly less graphic. The perceived evil that Indiana seeks to address is not erotic dancing, but public nudity. The appearance of people of all shapes and sizes in the nude at a beach, for example, would convey little if any erotic message, yet the state still seeks to prevent it. Public nudity is the evil the state seeks to prevent, whether or not it is combined with expressive activity. . . ."

Justice Scalia filed a separate concurring opinion: "[The] challenged regulation must be upheld [because], as a general law regulating conduct and not specifically directed at expression, it is not subject to First Amendment scrutiny at all. [Virtually] every law restricts conduct, and virtually any prohibited conduct can be performed for an expressive purpose — if only expressive of the fact that the actor disagrees with the prohibition. It cannot reasonably be demanded, therefore, that every restriction of expression incidentally produced by a general law regulating conduct pass normal First Amendment scrutiny, or even — as some of our cases have suggested, see, e.g., O'Brien — that it be justified by an 'important or substantial' government interest. . . .

"This is not to say that the first amendment affords no protection to expressive conduct. Where the government prohibits conduct precisely because of its communicative attributes, we hold the regulation unconstitutional. See, e.g., Eichman; Johnson; Spence. [In] each of the foregoing cases, we explicitly found that suppressing communication was the object of the regulation of conduct. Where that has not been the case, however — where suppression of communicative use of the conduct was merely the incidental effect of forbidding the conduct for other reasons — we have allowed the regulation to stand. [All] our holdings (though admittedly not some of our discussion) support the conclusion that 'the only First Amendment analysis applicable to laws that do not directly or indirectly impede speech is the threshold inquiry of whether the purpose of the law is to suppress communication. If not, that is the end of the [matter].' We have explicitly adopted such a regime in another First Amendment context: that of Free Exercise. [Citing Employment Division, Department of Human Resources v. Smith, Chapter IX.B, infra.] I think we should avoid wherever possible [a] mode of analysis that requires judicial assessment of the 'importance' of government interests — and especially of government interests in various aspects of morality."

Justice Souter also filed a concurring opinion: "[I] agree with the plurality that the appropriate analysis to determine the actual protection required by the First Amendment is the four-part enquiry described in O'Brien. [I rest my concurrence, however,] not on the possible sufficiency of society's moral views [but] on the State's substantial interest in combating the secondary effects of adult establishments of the sort typified by respondents' establishments. [In] my view, the interest [in] preventing prostitution, sexual assault, and other criminal activity, although presumably not a justification for all applications of the statute, is sufficient under O'Brien to justify the State's enforcement of the statute against the type of adult entertainment at issue here. [Citing Renton and Young, Chapter IV.G, supra.] [This] justification of the statute may not be ignored merely because it is unclear to what extent this purpose motivated the Indiana Legislature in enacting the statute. Our appropriate focus is not an empirical enquiry into the actual intent of the enacting legislature, but rather the existence [of a] governmental interest in the service of which the challenged application of the statute may be constitutional. [The] secondary effects rationale on which I rely would be

*Renton*

open to question if the State were to seek to enforce the statute by barring expressive nudity in classes of productions that could not readily be analogized to the adult films at issue in *Renton*. It is difficult to see, for example, how the enforcement of Indiana's statute against nudity in a production of 'Hair' or 'Equus' somewhere other than in an 'adult' theater would further the State's interest in avoiding harmful secondary effects. . . ."

Justice White, joined by Justices Marshall, Blackmun, and Stevens, dissented: "The purpose of forbidding people from appearing nude in parks, beaches, hot dog stands, and like public places is to protect others from offense. But that could not possibly be the purpose of preventing nude dancing in theaters and barrooms since the viewers are exclusively consenting adults who pay money to see these dances. The purpose of the proscription in these contexts is to protect the viewers from what the State believes is the harmful message that nude dancing communicates. [This] being the case, it cannot be that the statutory prohibition is unrelated to expressive conduct. [It] is only because nude dancing performances may generate emotions and feelings of eroticism and sensuality among the spectators that the State seeks to regulate such expressive activity, apparently on the assumption that creating or emphasizing such thoughts and ideas in the minds of the spectators may lead to increased prostitution and the degradation of women. But generating thoughts, ideas, and emotions is the essence of communication. The nudity element of nude dancing performances cannot be neatly pigeonholed as mere 'conduct' independent of any expressive component of the dance. That fact dictates the level of First Amendment protection to be accorded the performances at issue here. [Content] based restrictions 'will be upheld only if narrowly drawn to accomplish a compelling governmental interest.' [Neither] the Court nor the State suggests that the statute could withstand scrutiny under that standard."

---

Consider Justice Scalia's response to Justice White's dissent: "The dissent confidently asserts that the purpose of restricting nudity in public places in general is to protect nonconsenting parties from offense; and argues that since only consenting, admission-paying patrons see respondents dance, that purpose cannot apply and the only remaining purpose must relate to the communicative elements of the performance. Perhaps the dissenters believe that 'offense to others' ought to be the only reason for restricting nudity in public places generally, but there is no basis for thinking that our society has ever shared that Thoreauvian 'you-may-do-what-you-like-so-long-as-it-does-not-injure-someone-else' beau ideal — much less for thinking that it was written into the Constitution. The purpose of Indiana's nudity law would be violated, I think, if 60,000 fully consenting adults crowded into the Hoosier-dome to display their genitals to one another, even if there were not an offended innocent in the crowd. Our society prohibits, and all human societies have prohibited, certain activities not because they harm others but because they are considered in the traditional phrase, 'contra bonos mores,' i.e., immoral. [The] purpose of the Indiana statute [is] to enforce the traditional moral belief that people should not expose their private parts indiscriminately, regardless of whether those who see them are disedified. Since that is so, the dissent has no basis for positing that, where only thoroughly edified adults are present, the purpose must be repression of communication."

Consider the constitutionality, after *Barnes*, of the application of Indiana's public nudity statute to movies, art exhibits, and television productions depicting nudity. For the argument that "the outcome in *Barnes* would have been different" had Indiana attempted to apply its "statute to accepted media for the communication of ideas, as for example by attempting to prohibit nudity in movies or in the theater," see Post, Recuperating First Amendment Doctrine, 47 Stan. L. Rev. 1249, 1255–1259 (1995).

**CITY OF ERIE v. PAP's A.M., 529 U.S. 277 (2000).** Erie, Pennsylvania, enacted an ordinance banning public nudity. The preamble stated that the "purpose" of the ordinance was to respond to "a recent increase in nude live entertainment within the City, which activity adversely impacts . . . the public health, safety and welfare by providing an atmosphere conducive to violence, sexual harassment, public intoxication, prostitution, the spread of sexually transmitted diseases and other deleterious effects." The ordinance was challenged by the owner of Kandyland, a nude dancing establishment. Does the existence of this preamble distinguish this case from *Barnes*? The Court, in a six-to-three decision, upheld the ordinance.

Justice O'Connor delivered a plurality opinion, joined by Chief Justice Rehnquist and Justices Kennedy and Breyer: "The ordinance here, like the statute in *Barnes*, is on its face a general prohibition on public nudity. [It] bans all public nudity, regardless of whether that nudity is accompanied by expressive activity. [Moreover, the] State's interest in preventing harmful secondary effects is not related to the suppression of expression. In trying to control the secondary effects of nude dancing, the ordinance seeks to deter crime and the other deleterious effects caused by the presence of such an establishment in the neighborhood. [Citing *Renton*.]

"[Even] if Erie's public nudity ban has some minimal effect on the erotic message by muting that portion of the expression that occurs when the last stitch is dropped, [erotic dancers] are free to perform wearing pasties and G-strings. Any effect on the overall expression is *de minimis*. . . .

"[This] case is, in fact, similar to [*O'Brien*]. The justification for the government regulation in each case prevents harmful 'secondary' effects that are unrelated to the suppression of expression. [While] the doctrinal theories behind 'incidental burdens' and 'secondary effects' are, of course, not identical, there is nothing objectionable about a city passing a general ordinance to ban public nudity (even though such a ban may place incidental burdens on some protected speech) and at the same time recognizing that one specific occurrence of public nudity — nude erotic dancing — is particularly problematic because it produces harmful secondary effects. . . .

"We conclude that Erie's asserted interest in combating the negative secondary effects associated with adult entertainment establishments [is] unrelated to the suppression of the erotic message conveyed by nude dancing. The ordinance [is] therefore valid if it satisfies the four-factor test from *O'Brien* for evaluating restrictions on symbolic speech." Justice O'Connor then went on to find that the ordinance did, indeed, satisfy the *O'Brien* test.

Justice Scalia, joined by Justice Thomas, concurred in the judgment, reaffirming his position in *Barnes* that because the public nudity ordinance is "a general law regulating conduct and not specifically directed at expression, it is not subject to First Amendment scrutiny at all." Justice Scalia argued further that the existence of the preamble is irrelevant to the constitutionality of the ordinance because it neither "make[s] the law any less general in its reach nor demonstrate[s] that what the municipal authorities *really* find objectionable is expression rather than public nakedness."

Justice Stevens, joined by Justice Ginsburg, dissented: "The censorial purpose of Erie's ordinance precludes reliance on [*Barnes*]. As its preamble forthrightly admits, the ordinance's 'purpose' is to 'limit' a protected form of speech. [Moreover,] Erie's ordinance differs from the statute in *Barnes* in another respect, [for in] an earlier proceeding in this case, [the city stipulated that it had] permitted a production of [the play] Equus to proceed without prosecution [even though it included public nudity]. [Thus, unlike the statute in *Barnes*, the Erie] ordinance is deliberately targeted at Kandyland's type of nude dancing (to the exclusion of plays like Equus)."

In her plurality opinion, Justice O'Connor offered the following response to Justice Stevens's argument about the purpose of the ordinance: "The argument that the ordinance is 'aimed' at suppressing expression through a ban on nude dancing — an argument [supported] by pointing to statements [that] the public nudity ban was not intended to apply to 'legitimate' theater productions — is really an argument that the city council [had] an illicit motive in enacting the ordinance. [But] this Court will not strike down an otherwise constitutional statute on the basis of an alleged illicit motive. [Citing *O'Brien*.]" Justice Souter also dissented.

## Note: Other Forms of Symbolic Speech

1. *Political boycotts.* Suppose an antiabortion group boycotts all manufacturers who sell supplies to abortion clinics. Is such a concerted refusal to deal "speech"? May the group constitutionally be punished under a statute that prohibits "two or more persons, acting in concert, to refuse to deal with any

merchant in an effort to induce such merchant to adopt a policy it would not otherwise choose to adopt"? See NAACP v. Claiborne Hardware Co., 458 U.S. 886 (1982), in which the Court invalidated a civil judgment against the NAACP for instituting a boycott of white merchants designed to induce business and civic leaders to adopt a number of reforms, including the desegregation of public facilities. The Court explained that "speech does not lose its protected character . . . simply because it may . . . coerce [others] into action." And while "States have broad powers to regulate economic activity, we do not find a comparable right to prohibit peaceful political activity such as that found in the boycott in this case."

2. *Banning military recruiters.* Suppose law schools exclude from their placement facilities any employer, including the military, who discriminates against gays and lesbians. Suppose also that the government makes it a crime for any institution of higher education to discriminate against the military in the use of its placement facilities. Is the exclusion of military recruiters "speech" within the meaning of the first amendment? Is the constitutionality of the statute governed by O'Brien?

In Rumsfeld v. FAIR, 547 U.S. 47 (2006), the Court, in an opinion by Chief Justice Roberts, declared that "we have extended First Amendment protection only to conduct that is *inherently* expressive." Unlike burning a draft card, the exclusion by law schools of military recruiters "is not inherently expressive," because such conduct has meaning only if the law schools accompany "their conduct with speech explaining it." Indeed, "an observer who sees military recruiters interviewing away from the law school has no way of knowing whether the law school is expressing its disapproval of the military, all the law school's interview rooms are full, or the military recruiters decided for reasons of their own that they would rather interview someplace else." The Court concluded that the fact that "explanatory speech is necessary" to give content to the act "is strong evidence that the conduct [is] not so inherently expressive that it warrants protection under O'Brien." In any event, the Court held that even if the law were regarded as incidentally burdening speech it would satisfy O'Brien because it serves the government's legitimate interest in facilitating military recruitment.

3. *Are signatures on a referendum petition "speech" within the meaning of the First Amendment?* In Doe v. Reed, 561 U.S. 186 (2010), the Court considered the constitutionality of a Washington state public records statute, which authorizes the public disclosure of the names of individuals who sign referendum petitions. The plaintiffs argued that public disclosure would chill the willingness of individuals to sign such petitions. Although upholding the statute on its face, the Court rejected the argument that such signatures are not "speech" because "signing a petition is a legally operative legislative act and therefore 'does not involve any significant expressive element.'" The Court concluded that "[p]etition signing remains expressive even when it has legal effect in the electoral process." Although concurring in the result, Justice

Scalia expressed "doubt whether signing a petition" that has legal effect "fits within 'the freedom of speech' at all." He explained: "When [a] voter signs a referendum [petition], he is acting as a legislator. [A] voter who signs a referendum petition [is] exercising legislative power because his signature, somewhat like a vote for or against a bill in the legislature, seeks to affect the legal force of the measure at issue. [There] is no precedent from this Court holding that legislating is protected by the First Amendment."

4. *Are legislative votes "speech" within the meaning of the First Amendment?* In Nevada Commission on Ethics v. Carrigan, 131 S. Ct. 2343 (2011), Carrigan, a state legislator, voted to approve a casino project that had used his longtime friend and campaign manager as a paid consultant. The commission held that, by so doing, Carrigan had violated a state ethics rule prohibiting public officials from voting on legislative matters with respect to which they have a conflict of interest. Carrigan claimed that this finding violated his rights under the First Amendment. The key issue was whether the casting of a vote by a state legislator is constitutionally protected speech. In a unanimous decision, the Court rejected Carrigan's claim.

Justice Scalia delivered the opinion of the Court: "Laws punishing libel and obscenity are not thought to violate 'the freedom of speech' [because] such laws existed in 1791 and have been in place ever since. The same is true of legislative recusal rules. [Such] rules have been commonplace for over 200 years. '[E]arly congressional enactments "provid[e] contemporaneous and weighty evidence of the Constitution's meaning,"' [and that] evidence is dispositive here. Within 15 years of the founding, both the House of Representatives and the Senate adopted recusal rules. [Moreover, today,] virtually every State has enacted some type of recusal law. . . .

"But how can it be that restrictions upon legislators' voting are not restrictions upon legislators' protected speech? The answer is that a legislator's vote is the commitment of his apportioned share of the legislature's power to the passage or defeat of a particular proposal. The legislative power thus committed is not personal to the legislator but belongs to the people; the legislator has no personal right to it. [In] this respect, voting by a legislator is different from voting by a citizen. . . .

"There are, to be sure, instances where action conveys a symbolic meaning — such as the burning of a flag to convey disagreement with a country's policies. But the act of voting symbolizes nothing. It *discloses*, to be sure, that the legislator wishes (for whatever reason) that the proposition on the floor be adopted, just as a physical assault discloses that the attacker dislikes the victim. But neither the one nor the other is an act of communication. Moreover, the fact that a nonsymbolic act is the product of deeply held personal belief — even if the actor would like it to *convey* his deeply held personal belief — does not transform action into First Amendment speech. . . .

"Carrigan and Justice Alito [cite] Doe v. Reed as establishing 'the expressive character of voting.' But *Reed* did no such thing. That case held only that a citizen's signing of a petition — "'core political speech'" — was not deprived of its protected status simply because, under state law, a petition that garnered a sufficient number of signatures would suspend the state law to which it pertained, pending a referendum. It is one thing to say that an inherently expressive act remains so despite its having governmental effect, but it is altogether another thing to say that a governmental act becomes expressive simply because the governmental actor wishes it to be so." Justice Alito filed a concurring opinion rejecting the Court's distinction of Doe v. Reed, but agreeing with the result because "legislative recusal rules were not regarded during the founding era as *impermissible* restrictions on freedom of speech." Justice Kennedy also filed a concurring opinion.

Are you persuaded by the Court's distinction of Doe v. Reed? What do you think of the Court's "originalist" argument? Note that Justice Scalia was wrong about obscenity laws. In fact, there were no antiobscenity laws in the United States until the nineteenth century. See Stone, Sex, Violence, and the First Amendment, 74 U. Chi. L. Rev. 1857, 1861–1863 (2007). What does this tell you about the dangers of "originalism" as a method of constitutional interpretation? Does *Carrigan* suggest that New York Times v. Sullivan was wrong and that a modern Sedition Act based on the Sedition Act of 1798 would be constitutional?

## D.   REGULATION OF POLITICAL SOLICITATION, CONTRIBUTION, EXPENDITURE, AND ACTIVITY

It has been suggested that the "critical problem for contemporary First Amendment theory is the unequal access that wealth can buy." Carter, Technology, Democracy, and the Manipulation of Consent, 93 Yale L.J. 581 (1984). This section explores that "problem." To what extent is the solicitation, contribution, or expenditure of money "speech" within the meaning of the first amendment? To what extent may government regulate or restrict such activities in order to "enhance" the quality of public debate?

### Buckley v. Valeo

424 U.S. 1 (1976)

PER CURIAM.

These appeals present constitutional challenges to the key provisions of the Federal Election Campaign Act of 1971 (Act), and related provisions of the Internal Revenue Code of 1954, all as amended in 1974. . . .

[The] statutes at issue [contain] the following provisions: (a) individual political contributions [and expenditures] "relative to a clearly identified candidate" are limited, [and] campaign spending by candidates for various federal offices [is] subject to prescribed limits; (b) contributions and expenditures above certain threshold levels must be reported and publicly disclosed; (c) a system for public funding of Presidential campaign activities is established; [and] (d) a Federal Election Commission is established to administer and enforce the legislation. . . .

[The Court upheld the constitutionality of the individual contribution limits, the disclosure and reporting provisions, and the public financing scheme. The Court invalidated the composition of the Federal Election Commission and the limitations on expenditures. The following excerpts relate to the contribution and expenditure limitations.]

## I. CONTRIBUTION AND EXPENDITURE LIMITATION

The intricate statutory scheme adopted by Congress to regulate federal election campaigns includes restrictions on political contributions and expenditures that apply broadly to all phases of and all participants in the election process. The major contribution and expenditure limitations in the Act prohibit individuals from contributing more than $25,000 in a single year or more than $1,000 to any single candidate for an election campaign and from spending more than $1,000 a year "relative to a clearly identified candidate." Other provisions restrict a candidate's use of personal and family resources in his campaign and limit the overall amount that can be spent by a candidate in campaigning for federal office. . . .

### A. GENERAL PRINCIPLES

The Act's contribution and expenditure limitations operate in an area of the most fundamental First Amendment activities. Discussion of public issues and debate on the qualifications of candidates are integral to the operation of the system of government established by our Constitution. . . .

In upholding the constitutional validity of the Act's contribution and expenditure provisions on the ground that those provisions should be viewed as regulating conduct, not speech, the Court of Appeals relied upon [O'Brien].

We cannot share the view that the present Act's contribution and expenditure limitations are comparable to the restrictions on conduct upheld in O'Brien. The expenditure of money simply cannot be equated with such conduct as destruction of a draft card. Some forms of communication made possible by the giving and spending of money involve speech alone, some involve conduct primarily, and some involve a combination of the two. Yet this Court has never suggested that the dependence of a communication on the expenditure of money operates itself to introduce a nonspeech element or to reduce the exacting scrutiny required by the First Amendment. . . .

Even if the categorization of the expenditure of money as conduct were accepted, the limitations challenged here would not meet the *O'Brien* test because the governmental interests advanced in support of the Act involve "suppressing communication." The interests served by the Act include restricting the voices of people and interest groups who have money to spend and reducing the overall scope of federal election campaigns. Although the Act does not focus on the ideas expressed by persons or groups subject to its regulations, it is aimed in part at equalizing the relative ability of all voters to affect electoral outcomes by placing a ceiling on expenditures for political expression by citizens and groups. Unlike *O'Brien*, where the Selective Service System's administrative interest in the preservation of draft cards was wholly unrelated to their use as a means of communication, it is beyond dispute that the interest in regulating the alleged "conduct" of giving or spending money "arises in some measure because the communication allegedly integral to the conduct is itself thought to be harmful." . . .

Nor can the Act's contribution and expenditure limitations be sustained, as some of the parties suggest, by reference to the constitutional principles reflected in such decisions as [Adderley v. Florida and Kovacs v. Cooper, supra]. Those cases stand for the proposition that the government may adopt reasonable time, place, and manner regulations, which do not discriminate among speakers or ideas, in order to further an important governmental interest unrelated to the restriction of communication. [In] contrast to *O'Brien*, where the method of expression was held to be subject to prohibition, [*Adderley*] and *Kovacs* involved place or manner restrictions on legitimate modes of expression — picketing, parading, demonstrating, and using a sound-truck. The critical difference between this case and those time, place, and manner cases is that the present Act's contribution and expenditure limitations impose direct quantity restrictions on political communication and association by persons, groups, candidates, and political parties in addition to any reasonable time, place, and manner regulations otherwise imposed.[17]

A restriction on the amount of money a person or group can spend on political communication during a campaign necessarily reduces the quantity of expression by restricting the number of issues discussed, the depth of their exploration, and the size of the audience reached.[18] This is because virtually

---

17. The nongovernmental appellees argue that just as the decibels emitted by a sound truck can be regulated consistently with the First Amendment, [*Kovacs*,] the Act may restrict the volume of dollars in political campaigns without impermissibly restricting freedom of speech. [This] comparison underscores a fundamental misconception. The decibel restriction upheld in *Kovacs* limited the *manner* of operating a soundtruck, but not the *extent* of its proper use. By contrast, the Act's dollar ceilings restrict the extent of the reasonable use of virtually every means of communicating information. . . .

18. Being free to engage in unlimited political expression subject to a ceiling on expenditures is like being free to drive an automobile as far and as often as one desires on a single tank of gasoline.

every means of communicating ideas in today's mass society requires the expenditure of money. . . .

The expenditure limitations contained in the Act represent substantial rather than merely theoretical restraints on the quantity and diversity of political speech. The $1,000 ceiling on spending "relative to a clearly identified candidate," [for example,] would appear to exclude all citizens and groups except candidates, political parties, and the institutional press from any significant use of the most effective modes of communication.[20] . . .

By contrast with a limitation upon expenditures for political expression, a limitation upon the amount that any one person or group may contribute to a candidate or political committee entails only a marginal restriction upon the contributor's ability to engage in free communication, [for] it permits the symbolic expression of support evidenced by a contribution but does not in any way infringe the contributor's freedom to discuss candidates and issues. While contributions may result in political expression if spent by a candidate or an association to present views to the voters, the transformation of contributions into political debate involves speech by someone other than the contributor.

Given the important role of contributions in financing political campaigns, contribution restrictions could have a severe impact on political dialogue if the limitations prevented candidates and political committees from amassing the resources necessary for effective advocacy. There is no indication, however, that the contribution limitations imposed by the Act would have any dramatic adverse effect on the funding of campaigns and political associations.[23] The overall effect of the Act's contribution ceilings is merely to require candidates and political committees to raise funds from a greater number of persons and to compel people who would otherwise contribute amounts greater than the statutory limits to expend such funds on direct political expression, rather than to reduce the total amount of money potentially available to promote political expression. . . .

In sum, although the Act's contribution and expenditure limitations both implicate fundamental First Amendment interests, its expenditure ceilings impose significantly more severe restrictions on protected freedoms of political expression and association than do its limitations on financial contributions.

---

20. The record indicates that, as of January 1, 1975, one full-page advertisement in a daily edition of a certain metropolitan newspaper cost $6,971.04 — almost seven times the annual limit on expenditures "relative to" a particular candidate imposed on the vast majority of individual citizens and associations by [the act].

23. Statistical findings agreed to by the parties reveal that approximately 5.1% of the $73,483,613 raised by the 1,161 candidates for Congress in 1974 was obtained in amounts in excess of $1,000. . . .

## B. CONTRIBUTION LIMITATIONS

Section 608(b) provides, with certain limited exceptions, that "no person shall make contributions to any candidate with respect to any election for Federal office which, in the aggregate, exceed $1,000." . . .

[The] primary First Amendment problem raised by the Act's contribution limitations is their restriction of one aspect of the contributor's freedom of political association. The Court's decisions involving associational freedoms establish that the right of association is a "basic constitutional freedom," [and that] governmental "action which may have the effect of curtailing the freedom to associate is subject to the closest scrutiny." Yet, it is clear that "Neither the right to associate nor the right to participate in political activities is absolute." [Even] a "'significant interference' with protected rights of political association" may be sustained if the State demonstrates a sufficiently important interest and employs means closely drawn to avoid unnecessary abridgment of associational freedoms. . . .

It is unnecessary to look beyond the Act's primary purpose — to limit the actuality and appearance of corruption resulting from large individual financial contributions — in order to find a constitutionally sufficient justification for the $1,000 contribution limitation. [The] increasing importance of the communications media and sophisticated mass-mailing and polling operations to effective campaigning make the raising of large sums of money an ever more essential ingredient of an effective candidacy. To the extent that large contributions are given to secure a political quid pro quo from current and potential office holders, the integrity of our system of representative democracy is undermined. . . .

Of almost equal concern [is] the appearance of corruption stemming from [the] opportunities for abuse inherent in a regime of large individual financial contributions. [Congress] could legitimately conclude that the avoidance of the appearance of improper influence [is] "critical [if] confidence in the system of representative Government is not to be [eroded]." . . .

Appellants contend that the contribution limitations must be invalidated because bribery laws and narrowly drawn disclosure requirements constitute a less restrictive means of dealing with "proven and suspected quid pro quo arrangements." But laws making criminal the giving and taking of bribes deal with only the most blatant and specific attempts of those with money to influence governmental action. And while disclosure requirements serve [many salutary purposes] Congress was surely entitled to conclude that disclosure was only a partial measure, and that contribution ceilings were a necessary legislative concomitant to deal with the reality or appearance of corruption. . . .

We find that, under the rigorous standard of review established by our prior decisions, the weighty interests served by restricting the size of financial contributions to political candidates are sufficient to justify the limited effect upon First Amendment freedoms caused by the $1,000 contribution ceiling.

[Appellants argue further, however,] that the contribution limitations work [an] invidious discrimination between incumbents and [challengers].[33] [But] there is [no] evidence [that] contribution limitations [discriminate] against major-party challengers to incumbents, [and although] the charge of discrimination against minor-party and independent candidates is more troubling, [the] record provides no basis for concluding that the Act invidiously disadvantages such candidates. [Indeed, in some circumstances] the restriction would appear to benefit minor-party and independent candidates relative to their major-party opponents because major-party candidates receive far more money in large contributions. . . .

In view of these considerations, we conclude that the impact of the Act's $1,000 contribution limitation on major-party challengers and on minor-party candidates does not render the provision unconstitutional on its face.

[For similar reasons, the Court also upheld the $5,000 limit on contributions by "political committees," the limits on volunteers' incidental expenses, and the $25,000 limit on total political contributions by an individual during a single calendar year.]

## C. EXPENDITURE LIMITATIONS

The Act's expenditure ceilings impose direct and substantial restraints [on] the quantity of campaign speech by individuals, groups, and candidates. The restrictions, while neutral as to the ideas expressed, limit political expression "at the core of our electoral process and of the First Amendment freedoms." . . .

### 1.   The $1,000 Limitation on Expenditures "Relative to a Clearly Identified Candidate"

Section 608(e)(1) provides that "[n]o person may make any expenditure . . . relative to a clearly identified candidate during a calendar year [which] exceeds $1,000." [Appellants maintain] that the provision is

33. In this discussion, we address only the argument that the contribution limitations alone impermissibly discriminate against nonincumbents. We do not address the more serious argument that these limitations, in combination with the limitation on expenditures [invidiously] discriminate against major-party challengers and minor-party candidates.

Since an incumbent is subject to these limitations to the same degree as his opponent, the Act, on its face, appears to be evenhanded. The appearance of fairness, however, may not reflect political reality. Although some incumbents are defeated in every congressional election, it is axiomatic that an incumbent usually begins the race with significant advantages. [In some circumstances] the overall effect of the contribution and expenditure limitations enacted by Congress could foreclose any fair opportunity of a successful challenge.

However, since we decide in Part I-C, infra, that the ceilings on [expenditures] are unconstitutional under the First Amendment, we need not express any opinion with regard to the alleged invidious discrimination resulting from the full sweep of the legislation as enacted.

unconstitutionally vague. [The] use of so indefinite a phrase as "relative to" a candidate fails to clearly mark the boundary between permissible and impermissible [speech]. "Such a distinction offers no security for free [discussion]." [To] preserve the provision against invalidation on vagueness grounds, §608(e)(1) must be construed to apply only to expenditures for communications that in express terms advocate the election or defeat of a clearly identified candidate for federal office.

We turn then to the basic First Amendment question — whether §608(e)(1), even as thus narrowly and explicitly construed, impermissibly burdens the constitutional right of free expression. . . .

The discussion in Part I-A, supra, explains why the Act's expenditure limitations impose far greater restraints on the freedom of speech and association than do its contribution limitations. . . .

We find that the governmental interest in preventing corruption and the appearance of corruption is inadequate to justify §608(e)(1)'s ceiling on independent expenditures. [First], §608(e)(1) prevents only some large expenditures. So long as persons and groups eschew expenditures that in express terms advocate the election or defeat of a clearly identified candidate, they are free to spend as much as they want to promote the candidate and his views. The exacting interpretation of the statutory language necessary to avoid unconstitutional vagueness thus undermines the limitation's effectiveness. . . .

Second, [although the] parties defending §608(e)(1) contend that it is necessary to prevent would-be contributors from avoiding the contribution limitations [by] paying directly for media advertisements or for other portions of the candidate's campaign activities, [such] coordinated expenditures are treated as contributions rather than expenditures under the Act [and are thus limited by the] contribution ceilings. [Thus], §608(e)(1) limits [only] expenditures [made] totally independently of the candidate and his campaign. [But the] absence of [coordination with respect to such expenditures] undermines the value of the expenditure to the candidate [and] alleviates the danger that expenditures will be given as a quid pro quo for improper commitments. [Thus,] §608(e)(1) severely [restricts] independent advocacy despite its substantially diminished potential for abuse. . . .

It is argued [further, however, that the] governmental interest in equalizing the relative ability of individuals [to] influence the outcome of elections [justifies the] expenditure ceiling. But the concept that government may restrict the speech of some [in] order to enhance the relative voice of others is wholly foreign to the First Amendment, which was designed "to secure 'the widest possible dissemination of information from diverse and antagonistic sources.'" [The] First Amendment's protection against governmental abridgment of free expression cannot properly be made to depend on a person's financial ability to engage in public discussion. [Section] 608(e)(1)'s [expenditure] limitation is unconstitutional under the First Amendment.

### 2.   *Limitation on Expenditures by Candidates from Personal or Family Resources*

The Act also [limits] expenditures by a candidate "from his personal funds, or the personal funds of his immediate family, in connection with his campaigns during any calendar year." . . .

The ceiling on personal expenditures by candidates on their own [behalf] imposes a substantial restraint on the ability of persons to engage in protected First Amendment expression. The candidate, no less than any other person, has a First Amendment right to engage in the discussion of public issues and [to] advocate his own election. . . .

The [interest] in equalizing the relative financial resources of candidates competing for elective office is clearly not sufficient to justify the provision's infringement of fundamental First Amendment rights. . . .

### 3.   *Limitations on Campaign Expenditures*

Section 608(c) places limitations on overall campaign expenditures by candidates seeking nomination for election and election to federal office. [For example, the] Act imposes blanket $70,000 limitations on both primary campaigns and general election campaigns for the House of Representatives. . . .

No governmental interest that has been suggested is sufficient to justify the restriction on the quantity of political expression imposed by §608(c)'s campaign expenditure limitations. [The] interest in alleviating the corrupting influence of large contributions is served by the Act's contribution limitations and disclosure provisions, [and the] interest in equalizing the financial resources of candidates [is not a] convincing justification for restricting the scope of federal election campaigns. [The] campaign expenditure ceilings appear to be designed primarily to [reduce] the allegedly skyrocketing costs of political campaigns. [But the] First Amendment denies government the power to determine that spending to promote one's political views is wasteful, excessive, or unwise. In the free society ordained by our Constitution it is not the government, but the people — individually as citizens and candidates and collectively as associations and political committees — who must retain control over the quantity and range of debate on public issues in a political campaign.

For these reasons we hold that §608(c) is constitutionally invalid.

In sum, the provisions of the Act that impose a $1,000 [limitation on contributions] are constitutionally valid. These limitations [serve] the basic governmental interest in safeguarding the integrity of the electoral process without directly impinging upon the rights of individual citizens and candidates to engage in political debate and discussion. By contrast, the First Amendment requires the invalidation of the Act's independent expenditure [ceilings]. These provisions place substantial and direct restrictions on the ability of candidates, citizens, and associations to engage in protected political expression, restrictions that the First Amendment cannot tolerate. . . .

[Affirmed] in part and reversed in part.

MR. CHIEF JUSTICE BURGER, concurring in part and dissenting in part. . . .

[The contribution limitations are unconstitutional. Contributions] and expenditures are two sides of the same First Amendment coin. [Limiting] contributions, as a practical matter, will limit expenditures and will put an effective ceiling on the amount of political activity [that] the Government will permit to take place. . . .

The Court's attempt to distinguish the communication inherent in political *contributions* from the speech aspects of political *expenditures* simply "will not wash." We do little but engage in word games unless we recognize that people — candidates and contributors — spend money on political activity because they wish to communicate ideas, and their constitutional interest in doing so is precisely the same whether they or someone else utters the words. [Moreover, the contribution] restrictions are hardly incidental in their effect upon particular campaigns. [Such restrictions] will foreclose some candidacies,[9] [and] alter the nature of some electoral contests drastically.[10]

At any rate, the contribution limits are a far more severe restriction on First Amendment activity than the sort of "chilling" legislation for which the Court has shown such extraordinary concern in the past. See, e.g., [Cohen v. California, Chapter IV.G, supra]. If such restraints can be justified at all, they must be justified by the very strongest of state interests. . . .

MR. JUSTICE WHITE, concurring in part and dissenting in part. . . .

I dissent [from] the Court's view that the expenditure limitations [violate] the First Amendment. . . .

The congressional judgment [was that expenditure limitations are necessary] to counter the corrosive effects of money in federal election campaigns. [The] Court strikes down [§608(e)], strangely enough claiming more [knowledge] as to what may improperly influence candidates than is possessed by the majority of Congress that passed this bill and the President who signed it. [I] would take the word of those who know — that limiting independent expenditures is essential to prevent transparent and widespread evasion of the contribution limits. . . .

The Court also rejects Congress' judgment manifested in §608(c) that the federal interest in limiting total campaign expenditures by individual candidates justifies the incidental effect on their opportunity for effective political speech. I disagree. . . .

9. Candidates who must raise large initial contributions in order to appeal for more funds to a broader audience will be handicapped. . . .

10. Under the Court's holding, candidates with personal fortunes will be free to contribute to their own campaigns as much as they like, since the Court chooses to view the Act's provisions in this regard as unconstitutional "expenditure" limitations rather than "contribution" limitations. . . .

[The] argument that money is speech and that limiting the flow of money to the speaker violates the First Amendment proves entirely too much. Compulsory bargaining [has] increased the labor costs of those who publish newspapers, [and] taxation directly removes from company coffers large amounts of money that might be spent on larger and better newspapers. [But] it has not been suggested [that] these laws, and many others, are invalid because they siphon [off] large sums that would otherwise be available for communicative activities.

[The] judgment of Congress was that reasonably effective campaigns could be conducted within the limits established by the Act. [There] is no sound basis for invalidating the expenditure limitations, so long as the purposes they serve are legitimate and sufficiently substantial, which in my view they are.

[Expenditure] ceilings reinforce the contribution limits and help eradicate the hazard of corruption. [Without] limits on total expenditures, campaign costs will [inevitably] escalate, [creating an incentive to accept unlawful contributions. Moreover,] the corrupt use of money by candidates is as much to be feared as the corrosive influence of large contributions. There are many illegal ways of spending money to influence elections. [The] expenditure limits could play a substantial role in preventing unethical practices. There just would not be enough of "that kind of money" to go around. . . .

It is also important to [restore] public confidence in federal elections. It is critical to obviate [the] impression that federal elections are purely and simply a function of money. [The] ceiling on candidate expenditures represents the considered judgment of Congress that elections are to be decided among candidates none of whom has overpowering advantage by reason of a huge campaign war chest. [This] seems an acceptable purpose and the means chosen a common-sense way to achieve it. . . .

I also disagree with the Court's judgment that §608(a), which limits the amount of money that a candidate or his family may spend on his campaign, violates the Constitution. [By] limiting the importance of personal wealth, §608(a) helps to assure that only individuals with a modicum of support from others will be viable candidates. [This] would tend to discourage any notion that the outcome of elections is primarily a function of money. Similarly, §608(a) tends to equalize access to the political arena, encouraging the less wealthy [to] run for political office. [Congress] was entitled to determine that personal wealth ought to play a less important role in political campaigns than it has in the past. Nothing in the First Amendment stands in the way of that determination. . . .

MR. JUSTICE MARSHALL, concurring in part and dissenting in part.

[The] Court invalidates §608(a), [which limits the amount a candidate may spend from personal or family funds], as violative of the candidate's First Amendment Rights. [I] disagree.

[The] perception that personal wealth wins elections may not only discourage potential candidates without significant personal wealth from entering the political arena, but also undermine public confidence in the integrity of the electoral process.[1]

The concern that candidacy for public office not become, or appear to become, the exclusive province of the wealthy assumes heightened significance when one considers the impact of §608(b), which the Court today upholds. That provision prohibits contributions from individuals and groups to candidates in excess of $1,000, and contributions from political committees in excess of $5,000. While the limitations on contributions are neutral there can be no question that large contributions generally mean more to the candidate without a substantial personal fortune to spend on his campaign. Large contributions are the less wealthy candidate's only hope of countering the wealthy candidate's immediate access to substantial sums of money. [Section 608(a) thus provides] some symmetry to a regulatory scheme that otherwise enhances the natural advantage of the wealthy. . . .

MR. JUSTICE BLACKMUN, concurring in part and dissenting in part.

I am not persuaded that the Court makes [a] principled constitutional distinction between the contribution limitations [and] the expenditure limitations. [I] therefore do not join Part I-B of the Court's opinion or those portions of Part I-A that are consistent with Part I-B. As to those, I dissent. . . .

## Note: Buckley *and the Problem of Abridging Speech to* "Enhance" *the Electoral Process*

1. *The problem of unequal resources.* In upholding the expenditure and contribution limitations in *Buckley*, the court of appeals explained:

[The] statute taken as a whole affirmatively enhances First Amendment values. By reducing in good measure disparity due to wealth, the Act tends to equalize both the relative ability of all voters to affect electoral outcomes, and the opportunity of all interested citizens to become candidates for elective federal office. This broadens the choice of candidates and the opportunity to hear a variety of views.

519 F.2d 817, 841 (D.C. Cir. 1975). Do you agree that, if the purpose and "net effect of the legislation [are] to enhance freedom of speech, the exacting review reserved for abridgements of free speech is inapposite"? L. Tribe, American Constitutional Law 1135 (2d ed. 1988). Do you agree with the Court that "the concept that government may restrict the speech of some elements of our

1. "In the Nation's seven largest States in 1970, 11 of the 15 major senatorial candidates were millionaires. The four who were not millionaires lost their bid for election." . . .

society in order to enhance the relative voice of others is wholly foreign to the First Amendment"?

Note that *Buckley* posed a conflict between two conceptions of a properly functioning system of free expression, and between two conceptions of the role of the state. Under one view, government should take the "private" status quo for granted and all persons, no matter their resources, are free to press their interests on the political process. If some people have more money than others, and if their greater resources permit more speech, that result is something for which government is not itself responsible and which cannot be "remedied" consistent with the first amendment. The role of government is to remain "neutral" as people in the private sphere compete in the political marketplace.

Under the competing view, a system of free expression is one in which there is fair deliberation on what the public good requires, and inequality of resources, which can seriously distort that deliberation, is understood to be at least in part the product of governmental choices. If government permits the process of political deliberation to become distorted by this inequality of resources, the result is inconsistent with first amendment aspirations. Under this view, government efforts to equalize resources are permitted (and perhaps even required) in order to promote a more fair public debate. See Balkin, Some Realism about Pluralism: Legal Realist Approaches to the First Amendment, 1990 Duke L.J. 375.

2. *Competing views.* Consider the following:

a. Wright, Politics and the Constitution: Is Money Speech?, 85 Yale L.J. 1001, 1005, 1015–1019 (1976):

> Nothing in the First Amendment prevents us, as a political community, from [choosing] to move closer to the kind of community process that lies at the heart of the First Amendment conception — a process wherein ideas and candidates prevail because of their inherent worth, not because [one] side puts on a more elaborate show of support. [The] picture of the political process that emerges from [*Buckley*] corresponds [to the] pluralist model. [To] the pluralist, the political process consists [of] the pulling and hauling of various competing interest groups. [Force] collides with counterforce, [and] the strongest force [determines] the outcome of [the] process. [This model] gives undeserved weight [to] highly organized and wealthy groups [and drains] politics of its moral and intellectual content.

b. Kagan, Private Speech, Public Purpose: The Role of Governmental Motive in First Amendment Doctrine, 63 U. Chi. L. Rev. 415, 467–475 (1996):

> In what has become one of the most castigated passages in modern First Amendment case law, the Court pronounced in *Buckley* that "the concept that government may restrict the speech of some elements of our society in order to enhance the relative voice of others is wholly foreign to the First Amendment. . . ." [The]

*Buckley* principle emerges not from the view that redistribution of speech opportunities is itself an illegitimate end, but from the view that governmental actions justified as redistributive devices often (though not always) stem partly from hostility or sympathy toward ideas — or, even more commonly, from self-interest. [The] nature of [such] regulations, as compared with other content-neutral regulations, creates [a special problem]: that governmental officials (here, legislators) more often will take account of improper factors. [This] increased probability of taint arises [from] the very design of laws directed at equalizing the realm of public expression. Unlike most content-neutral regulations, these laws not only have, but are supposed to have, content-based effects. . . . In considering such a law, a legislator's own views of the ideas (or speakers) that the equalization effort means to suppress or promote may well intrude, consciously or not, on her decisionmaking process. [Thus,] there may be good reason to distrust the motives of politicians when they apply themselves to reconstructing the realm of expression.

c. Strauss, Corruption, Equality, and Campaign Finance, 94 Colum. L. Rev. 1369, 1383–1386 (1994):

[The principle] "one person, one vote" is [the] decisive counterexample to the suggestion [in *Buckley*] that the aspiration [of equalizing "speech"] is foreign to the First Amendment. We do not think of "one person, one vote" as an example of reducing the speech of some to enhance the relative speech of others, but that is only because the principle seems so natural. When legislatures were malapportioned, rural voters had a more effective voice than urban voters. Reapportionment reduced their influence in order to enhance the relative influence of others. We might unreflectively say that the rural voters were deprived of voting power that was not rightfully theirs, while my ability to make a campaign contribution is rightfully [mine]. But this formulation begs the question. We have to explain why superior spending power is rightfully mine but superior voting power is not. . . .

The problem with promoting equality in campaign finance occurs not at the level of aspiration, as [*Buckley*] suggests, but at the level of institutional specifics. [If] "one person, one vote" shows why *Buckley*'s dictum about equality is incorrect, then a different analogy to voting rights — gerrymandering — shows why *Buckley*'s conclusion is not so easily rejected. Reapportionment [has] apparently been a success story, in the sense that there are no longer any grossly malapportioned legislatures. [But the] experience with gerrymandering has been the opposite. It is notoriously difficult to define administrable standards to control gerrymandering. The result has been [a] system in which incumbent protection is the order of the day. Unless campaign finance reform reflects a clear and plausible conception of equality, we may well end up with the gerrymandering experience, rather than the reapportionment experience. That is, simply turning Congress loose to promote "equality" [could] just lead to measures that give even more protection to political incumbents or other favored interests. In fact it would be surprising if it did not lead to such a result.

3. *A comparative perspective.* The Canada Elections Act of 2000 set limits for third-party spending in elections. Specifically, the act provides that a third party (i.e., a group or individual who is not a candidate) "shall not incur election advertising expenses of a total amount of more than $150,000 during an election period in relation to a general election" and "not more than $3,000 [to] promote or oppose the election of one or more candidates in a given electoral district." The act defines "election advertising expenses" as including any paid message that names candidates, shows their likeness, or takes a position on an issue "with which they are particularly associated." Stephen Harper, the head of a conservative political group, brought suit claiming that the act violated the Canadian Charter of Rights and Freedoms, which guarantees to every person the fundamental "freedom of thought, belief, opinion and expression." The charter provides that fundamental freedoms may be subjected "only to such reasonable limits [as] can be demonstrably justified in a free and democratic society." In Harper v. Canada, 1 S.C.R. 827 (2004), excerpted in Hasen, Regulation of Campaign Finance, in V. Amar and M. Tushnet eds., Global Perspectives on Constitutional Law 198 (2009), the Supreme Court of Canada upheld these provisions of the act, therefore reaching a different result than the Supreme Court of the United States did in *Buckley.*

Justice Bastarache delivered the opinion of the court: "Third party advertising is political expression. [As such, it] lies at the core of the expression guaranteed by the Charter and warrants a high degree of constitutional protection. [In] some circumstances, however, third party advertising will be less deserving of constitutional protection. Indeed, it is possible that third parties who have access to significant financial resources can manipulate political discourse to their advantage through political advertising. [Advertising] expense limits may restrict free expression to ensure that participants are able to meaningfully participate in the electoral process. For candidates, political parties and third parties, meaningful participation means the ability to inform voters of their position. For voters, meaningful participation means the ability to hear and weigh many points of view. The difficulties of striking this balance are evident. . . .

"The question, then, is what promotes an informed voter? For voters to be able to hear all points of view, the information disseminated by third parties, candidates, and political parties cannot be unlimited. In the absence of spending limits, it is possible for the affluent or a number of persons or groups pooling their resources and acting in concert to dominate the political discourse. [If] a few groups are able to flood the electoral discourse with their message, it is possible, indeed likely, that the voices of some will be drowned out. Where those having access to the most resources monopolize the election discourse, their opponents will be deprived of a reasonable opportunity to speak and be heard. This unequal dissemination of points of view undermines the voter's ability to be adequately informed of all views. In this way, equality in the political discourse is necessary for meaningful participation in the electoral process and ultimately enhances the right to vote."

## Note: Subsidy and Disclosure

1. *Public financing of campaigns.* <u>Buckley</u> concluded that, absent extraordinary circumstances, government cannot constitutionally *restrict* speech in order to eliminate imbalance in the marketplace. What other means, if any, might government employ to achieve this objective? Consider Powe, Mass Speech and the Newer First Amendment, 1982 Sup. Ct. Rev. 243, 268–269, 282–283:

> [To] attempt to tone down a debate [in] the interests of enhancing the marketplace [is] wildly at odds with the normal First Amendment belief that more speech is better. [If the problem is that] the wealthy are too powerful, [we should provide] significant additional public funding [for] electoral campaigns, so that the advantages of wealth can [be] minimized.

2. *Subtitle H.* In *Buckley*, the Court considered the constitutionality of subtitle H of the Internal Revenue Code, which established a scheme of campaign "subsidies" to equalize the financial resources of political candidates. Under subtitle H, major political parties (those that had received more than 25 percent of the vote in the preceding presidential election) qualified for subsidies of up to $20 million for their candidates' presidential campaigns. Minor parties (those that had received between 5 and 25 percent of the vote in the preceding presidential election) qualified for subsidies proportional to their share of the vote in the preceding or current election, whichever was higher. All other political parties qualified for subsidies only if they received more than 5 percent of the vote in the current election. Subtitle H provided for public financing of primaries and party nominating conventions on similar terms. All subsidies were indexed to inflation. Major party candidates were eligible for public funding only if they agreed to forgo all private contributions and to limit their expenditures to the amount of the subsidy. Other candidates who accepted subsidies were permitted to supplement their public funding with private contributions as long as they agreed to limit their total expenditures to the amount of the major party subsidy.

The Court upheld the public financing provisions: "Subtitle H is a congressional effort, not to abridge, restrict, or censor speech, but rather to use public money to facilitate and enlarge public discussion and participation in the electoral process, goals vital to a self-governing people. Thus, Subtitle H furthers, not abridges, pertinent First Amendment values." Is this consistent with the Court's analysis in other parts of the opinion?

The Court held further that subtitle H's requirement that a candidate who accepts public financing agree to limit total campaign expenditures to the amount of the major party subsidy did not independently violate the first amendment: "Congress [may] condition acceptance of public funds on an agreement by the candidate to abide by specified expenditure limitations.

Just as a candidate may voluntarily limit the size of the contributions he chooses to accept, he may decide to forgo private fundraising and accept public funding." Consider Polsby, Buckley v. Valeo: The Nature of Political Speech, 1976 Sup. Ct. Rev. 1, 26: "[No] sooner does the Court resolve a most fundamental First Amendment question [concerning the constitutionality of expenditure limitations] in a manner highly favorable to the interest in personal liberty, then it takes it all back again, letting expenditure ceilings in the back door by allowing them as a condition to the candidate's accepting public financing. [The] clash of the holdings is startling."

3. *Equality and the first amendment.* Another issue posed in *Buckley* was whether "as constructed public financing invidiously discriminates [against non-major party candidates]." In *Buckley*, the Court rejected the equal protection challenge:

> Subtitle H does not prevent any candidate from getting on the ballot or any voter from casting a vote for the candidate of his choice; the inability, if any, of minor-party candidates to wage effective campaigns will derive not from lack of public funding but from their inability to raise private contributions. [Third parties have historically been] incapable of matching the major parties' ability to raise money and win elections. Congress was [thus] justified in providing both major parties full funding and all other parties only a percentage of the major-party entitlement. Identical treatment of all [parties] would [make] it easy to raid the United States Treasury [and] artificially foster the proliferation of splinter parties. [Finally, there has been no showing] that the election funding plan disadvantages nonmajor parties by operating to reduce their strength below that attained without any public financing. [We thus] conclude that the general election funding system does not work an invidious discrimination against candidates of nonmajor parties.

Other aspects of the intersection of equal protection and free expression are explored in Chapter II, supra.

4. *Subsidizing individuals rather than parties.* Consider the following proposal: "The principle of equal-dollars-per-voter means that each eligible voter should receive the same amount of financial resources for the purpose of participating in electoral politics. [The] only money that voters would be permitted to [spend or contribute] would be the money they receive from the government." Foley, Equal-Dollars-Per-Voter: A Constitutional Principle of Campaign Finance, 94 Colum. L. Rev. 1204, 1206–1207 (1994). For a variant of this proposal, consider B. Ackerman and I. Ayres, Voting with Dollars 4–8, 156–157 (2002):

> [The] American citizen should [be] given a more equal say in [campaign] funding decisions. Just as he receives a ballot on election day, he should also receive a special credit card to finance his favorite candidate. [Suppose] that Congress seeded every voter's account with fifty [dollars, which each voter could then allocate among the candidates for federal office as he sees fit. Additional

private contributions should be permitted, but contributors should] be barred from giving money directly to candidates. They [should] instead pass their checks through a blind trust [so candidates] won't be able to identify who provided the funds. [There] are lots of reasons for contributing to campaigns, and this [approach] undercuts only one of them — the desire to obtain a quid pro quo from a victorious candidate. [This two-pronged approach] promises an effective increase in both political equality *and* political expression.

See Karlan, Elections and Change Under "Voting with Dollars," 91 Cal. L. Rev. 706 (2003) (suggesting some contradictions between first amendment theory and the proposal's reliance on anonymous donation).

5. *Disclosure*. To what extent is disclosure of the identity of contributors an effective and constitutional means of preventing undue influence? The Federal Election Campaign Act of 1971 requires every political candidate and "political committee" to maintain records of the names and addresses of all persons who contribute more than $10 in a calendar year and to make such records available for inspection by the commission. Moreover, the act provides that such reports are to be available "for public inspection and copying." In *Buckley*, the Court upheld these provisions:

> The governmental interests sought to be vindicated by the disclosure require-ments [fall] into three categories. First, disclosure provides the electorate with information "as to where political campaign money comes [from]" in order to aid the voters in evaluating those who seek federal office. [Second,] disclosure requirements deter actual corruption and avoid the appearance of corruption by exposing [contributions] to the light of publicity. [Third, such] requirements are an essential means of gathering the data necessary to detect violations of the contribution limitations. [Thus, the] disclosure requirements [directly] serve substantial governmental interests. . . .
>
> Appellants contend that the Act's requirements are [nonetheless unconstitutional] insofar as they apply to contributions to minor parties [because] the governmental interest in this information is minimal and the danger of significant infringement on First Amendment rights is greatly increased. [It is true that the] Government's interest in deterring the "buying" of elections and the undue influence of large contributors on officeholders [may] be reduced where contributions to a minor party [are] concerned, for it is less likely that the candidate will be victorious. [Moreover, these] movements are less likely to have a sound financial base and thus are more vulnerable to falloffs in contributions. In some instances fears of reprisal may deter contributions to the point where the movement cannot survive. [Thus, there] could well be a case [where] the threat to the exercise of First Amendment rights is so serious and the state interest furthered by disclosure so insubstantial that the Act's requirements cannot be constitutionally applied. But no appellant in this case has tendered record evidence of [that] sort. . . .

In Brown v. Socialist Workers '74 Campaign Committee, 459 U.S. 87 (1982), the Court held that the disclosure provisions of the Ohio campaign

3. *Political parties.* After *Buckley*, can the government constitutionally limit the amount a political party can spend in support of its own candidates? Are such expenditures "contributions" or "expenditures" within the meaning of *Buckley?* See Colorado Republican Federal Campaign Committee v. Federal Election Commission, 518 U.S. 604 (1996), in which the Court held that the first amendment prohibits the application of a provision of the Federal Election Campaign Act that imposes dollar limits on political party "expenditures in connection with the general election campaign of a [congressional] candidate." In a plurality opinion, Justice Breyer, joined by Justices O'Connor and Souter, held that, under *Buckley*, the first amendment prohibits the application of this provision to expenditures that the political party makes "independently, without coordination with a candidate."

In Federal Election Commission v. Colorado Republican Federal Campaign Committee, 533 U.S. 431 (2001) (*Colorado II*), the Court rejected the claim that a political party's *coordinated* expenditures on behalf of its electoral candidates should be treated as expenditures rather than contributions. The Court explained that "a party's right to make unlimited expenditures coordinated with a candidate would induce individual and other nonparty contributors to give to the party in order to finance coordinated spending for a favored candidate beyond the contribution limits, [and thus bypass the very limits] that *Buckley* upheld." Chief Justice Rehnquist and Justices Scalia, Kennedy, and Thomas dissented.

**McCONNELL v. FEDERAL ELECTION COMMISSION, 540 U.S. 93 (2003).** The Bipartisan Campaign Reform Act of 2002 (BCRA), which amended the Federal Election Campaign Act of 1971 (FECA), sought to address several important developments in the years since *Buckley*, including the increased importance of "soft money" and the disturbing findings of a Senate investigation into campaign practices related to the 1996 federal elections.

Prior to BCRA, FECA's contribution limitations extended only to so-called "hard money" contributions made for the purpose of influencing an election for federal office. Political parties and candidates were able to contribute "soft money" — money unregulated under FECA — to support activities intended to influence state or local elections, to support get-out-the-vote (GOTV) drives and generic party advertising, and to pay for legislative advocacy advertisements, even if they mentioned a federal candidate's name, as long as the ads did not expressly advocate the candidate's election or defeat. In BCRA, Congress sought to close these soft-money "loopholes" on the premise that they facilitated widespread circumvention of FECA's requirements.

Justices Stevens and O'Connor, joined by Justices Souter, Ginsburg, and Breyer, delivered the opinion of the Court: "The solicitation, transfer, and use of soft money [has] enabled parties and candidates to circumvent FECA's limitations on the source and amount of contributions in connection with federal elections.

"In 1998 the Senate Committee on Governmental Affairs issued a six-volume report summarizing the results of an extensive investigation into the campaign practices in the 1996 federal elections. The report gave particular attention to the effect of soft money on the American political system, including elected officials' practice of granting special access in return for political contributions. [The report concluded] that both parties promised and provided special access to candidates and senior Government officials in exchange for large soft-money contributions. . . .

"The cornerstone of Title I [of the BCRA is] §323(a), which prohibits national party committees and their agents from soliciting, receiving, directing, or spending any soft money. . . .

"[In] *Buckley*, [we] recognized that contribution limits, unlike limits on expenditures, 'entai[l] only a marginal restriction upon the contributor's ability to engage in free communication.' [The] less rigorous standard of review we have applied to contribution limits [shows] proper deference to Congress' ability to weigh competing constitutional interests in an area in which it enjoys particular expertise. [Like] the contribution limits we upheld in *Buckley*, §323's restrictions have only a marginal impact on the ability of contributors, candidates, officeholders, and parties to engage in effective political speech. Complex as its provisions may be, §323, in the main, does little more than regulate the ability of wealthy individuals, corporations, and unions to contribute large sums of money to influence federal elections, federal candidates, and federal officeholders. . . .

"[Section 323(a)] provides that 'national committee[s] of a political party . . . may not solicit, receive, or direct to another person a contribution, donation, or transfer of funds or any other thing of value, or spend any funds, that are not subject to the limitations, prohibitions, and reporting requirements of this Act.' [Before the enactment of this provision], national parties were able to use vast amounts of soft money in their efforts to elect federal candidates. Consequently, as long as they directed the money to the political parties, donors could contribute large amounts of soft money for use in activities designed to influence federal elections. New §323(a) is designed to put a stop to that practice.

"The Government defends §323(a)'s ban on national parties' involvement with soft money as necessary to prevent the actual and apparent corruption of federal candidates and officeholders. Our cases have made clear that the prevention of corruption or its appearance constitutes a sufficiently important interest to justify political contribution limits. [The] idea that large contributions to a national party can corrupt or, at the very least, create the appearance of corruption of federal candidates and officeholders is neither novel nor implausible. . . .

"The question for present purposes is whether large *soft-money* contributions to national party committees have a corrupting influence or give rise to the appearance of corruption. Both common sense and the ample record in these cases confirm Congress' belief that they do. [The] evidence in the record shows that candidates and donors alike [have] exploited the soft-money loophole, the former to increase their prospects of election and the latter to create debt on the part of officeholders, with the national parties serving as willing intermediaries. . . .

"The core of §323(b) is a straightforward contribution regulation: It prevents donors from contributing [soft money] to state and local party committees to help finance 'Federal election activity.' The term 'Federal election activity' encompasses four distinct categories of electioneering: (1) voter registration activity during the 120 days preceding a regularly scheduled federal election; (2) voter identification, get-out-the-vote (GOTV), and generic campaign activity that is 'conducted in connection with an election in which a candidate for Federal office appears on the ballot'; (3) any 'public communication' that 'refers to a clearly identified candidate for Federal office' and 'promotes,' 'supports,' 'attacks,' or 'opposes' a candidate for that office; and (4) the services provided by a state committee employee who dedicates more than 25% of his or her time to 'activities in connection with a Federal election.' . . .

"[In] addressing the problem of soft-money contributions to state committees, Congress both drew a conclusion and made a prediction. Its conclusion, based on the evidence before it, was that the corrupting influence of soft money does not insinuate itself into the political process solely through national party committees. Rather, state committees function as an alternate avenue for precisely the same corrupting forces. [Congress] also made a prediction. Having been taught the hard lesson of circumvention by the entire history of campaign finance regulation, Congress knew that soft-money donors would react to §323(a) by scrambling to find another way to purchase influence. [We] 'must accord substantial deference to the predictive judgments of Congress.' [Preventing] corrupting activity from shifting wholesale to state committees and thereby eviscerating FECA clearly qualifies as an important governmental interest. [Because] voter registration, voter identification, GOTV, and generic campaign activity all confer substantial benefits on federal candidates, the funding of such activities creates a significant risk of actual and apparent corruption. Section 323(b) is a reasonable response to that risk."

Justice Scalia concurred in part and dissented in part: "We are governed by Congress, and this legislation prohibits the criticism of Members of Congress by those entities most capable of giving such criticism loud voice: national political parties. [To] be sure, the legislation is evenhanded: It similarly prohibits criticism of the candidates who oppose Members of Congress in their reelection bids. But as everyone knows, this is an area in which evenhandedness is not fairness. [If] incumbents and challengers are limited to the same quantity of electioneering, incumbents are favored. [Beyond] that, however, the present legislation *targets* for prohibition certain categories of campaign speech that are particularly harmful to incumbents. Is it accidental, do you think, that incumbents raise about three times as much 'hard money' — the sort of funding generally *not* restricted by this legislation — as do their challengers? Or that lobbyists [give] 92 percent of their money in 'hard' contributions? [Is] it mere happenstance [that] national-party funding, which is severely limited by the Act, is more likely to assist cash-strapped challengers than flush-with-hard-money incumbents?"

Justice Kennedy, joined in part by Chief Justice Rehnquist and Justices Scalia and Thomas, filed an opinion concurring in part and dissenting in part: "Today's decision [replaces] respected First Amendment principles with new, amorphous, and unsound rules, rules which dismantle basic protections for speech. [Our] precedents teach, above all, that Government cannot be trusted to moderate its own rules for suppression of speech. The dangers posed by speech regulations have led the Court to insist upon principled constitutional lines and a rigorous standard of review. The majority now abandons these distinctions and limitations. . . .

"In *Buckley*, the Court held that one, and only one, interest justified the significant burden on the right of association involved there: eliminating, or preventing, actual corruption or the appearance of corruption stemming from contributions to candidates. [The] Court [today] ignores these constitutional bounds and in effect interprets the anticorruption rationale to allow regulation not just of 'actual or apparent *quid pro quo* arrangements,' but of any conduct that wins goodwill from or influences a Member of Congress. [The] very aim of *Buckley*'s standard [was] to define undue influence by reference to the presence of *quid pro quo* involving the officeholder. The Court, in contrast, concludes that access, without more, proves influence is undue. [This] new definition of corruption sweeps away all protections for speech that lie in its path."

Justice Thomas, joined in part by Justice Scalia, also concurred in part and dissented in part.

**DAVIS v. FEDERAL ELECTION COMMISSION**, 554 U.S. 724 (2008). Section 319(a) of the Bipartisan Campaign Reform Act of 2002, the so-called Millionaire's Amendment, provides that if a candidate for Congress spends $350,000 or more of his own money in order to secure his own election, the opposing candidate is then permitted to accept individual campaign contributions up to three times larger than would otherwise be allowed. (The opposing candidate cannot accept additional contributions under this provision that would in total exceed the "millionaire" candidate's personal expenditures.) The Court, in a five-to-four decision, held the provision unconstitutional.

Justice Alito delivered the opinion of the Court: "In *Buckley*, we soundly rejected a cap on a candidate's expenditure of personal funds to finance campaign speech. [We] rejected the argument that [such] an expenditure cap could be justified on that ground that it served [the] 'interest in equalizing making contributions or expenditures "for the purpose [of] influencing or affecting the vote on any question submitted to the voters, other than one materially affecting any of the property, business or assets of the corporation." The statute specified further that "[n]o question submitted to the voters solely concerning the taxation of the income, property or transactions of individuals shall be deemed materially to affect the property, business or assets of the corporation." The state court, in upholding the statute, held that the first amendment rights of a corporation are limited to issues that materially affect its business, property, or assets.

The Court, in a five-to-four decision, reversed. In an opinion by Justice Powell, the Court explained that the state court had "posed the wrong question." The proper question "is not whether corporations 'have' First Amendment rights and, if so, whether they are coextensive with those of natural persons, [but] whether [the statute] abridges expression that the First Amendment was meant to protect." The statute is directed against speech that is "indispensable to decisionmaking in a democracy," and that lies "at the heart of the First Amendment's protection." Moreover, the Court could "find no support in the First [Amendment], or in the decisions of this Court, for the proposition that speech that otherwise would be within the protection of the First Amendment loses that protection simply because its source is a corporation that cannot prove, to the satisfaction of a court, a material effect on its business or property."

The state maintained that the statute was necessary to preserve "the integrity of the electoral process." The participation of corporations in the electoral process, the state argued, "would exert an undue influence [and] destroy the confidence of the people in the democratic process and the integrity of government." Corporations, the state explained, "are wealthy and powerful and their views may drown out other points of view."

The Court gave this argument short shrift: "To be sure, corporate advertising may influence the outcome of the vote; this would be its purpose. But the fact that advocacy may persuade the electorate is hardly a reason to suppress it. [As we noted in *Buckley*,] 'the concept that government may restrict the speech of some elements of our society in order to enhance the relative voice of others is wholly foreign to the First [Amendment].' [Moreover,] the people in our democracy are entrusted with the responsibility for judging and evaluating the relative merits of conflicting arguments. They may consider, in making their judgment, the source and credibility of the advocate. But if there be any danger that the people cannot evaluate the information and arguments advanced by [corporations], it is a danger contemplated by the Framers of the First Amendment."

Justice White, joined by Justices Brennan and Marshall, dissented: "[The] special status of corporations has placed them in a position to control vast amounts of economic power which may, if not regulated, dominate not only the economy but also the very heart of our democracy, the electoral process. Although [*Buckley*] provides support for the position that the desire to equalize the financial resources available to candidates does not justify the limitation upon the expression of support which a restriction upon individual contributions entails, the interest of Massachusetts [is] quite different. It is not one of equalizing the resources of opposing candidates or opposing positions, but rather of preventing institutions which have been permitted to amass wealth as a result of special advantages extended by the State for certain economic purposes from using that wealth to acquire an unfair advantage in the political process. [The] State need not permit its own creation to consume it." Justice Rehnquist also dissented.

2. *Corporate treasury funds.* In Austin v. Michigan Chamber of Commerce, 494 U.S. 652 (1990), the Court, in a six-to-three decision, upheld section 54(1) of the Michigan Campaign Finance Act, which prohibited corporations from using corporate treasury funds for independent expenditures in support of or in opposition to any candidate for state office. In an opinion by Justice Marshall, the Court observed that "the unique legal and economic characteristics of corporations" — such as "limited liability, perpetual life, and favorable treatment of the accumulation and distribution of assets" — enable corporations "to use 'resources amassed in the economic marketplace' to obtain 'an unfair advantage in the political marketplace.'" Noting that section 54(1) was designed to deal with "the corrosive and distorting effects of immense aggregations of wealth that are accumulated with the help of the corporate form and that have little or no correlation to the public's support for the corporation's political ideas," the Court held that "the State has articulated a sufficiently compelling rationale to support its restriction on independent expenditures by corporations."

Justice Scalia dissented: "[Corporations] are, to be sure, given special advantages, [but] so are other associations and private individuals, [ranging] from tax breaks to contract awards to public employment to outright cash subsidies. It is rudimentary that the State cannot exact as the price of those special advantages the forfeiture of First Amendment rights. [Moreover], the fact that corporations 'amas[s] large treasuries' [is] not sufficient justification for the suppression of political speech, unless one thinks it would be lawful to prohibit men and women whose net worth is above a certain figure from endorsing political candidates. [The] object of the law we have approved today is not to prevent wrongdoing but to prevent speech. Since those private associations known as corporations have so much money, they will speak so much more, and their views will be given inordinate prominence in election campaigns. This is not an argument that our democratic traditions allow."

3. *Advocacy corporations.* North Carolina Right to Life, a nonprofit advocacy corporation that counsels pregnant women how to deal with unwanted pregnancies without resorting to abortion, challenged the constitutionality of 2 U.S.C. §441, which prohibits corporations from making political contributions directly to candidates for federal office, but permits them to establish,

regulated under *McConnell*, or whether they were "genuine" issue ads, which, he maintained, could not be regulated consistent with the first amendment:

"In drawing that line, the First Amendment requires us to err of the side of protecting political speech rather than suppressing it. We conclude that the speech at issue in this as-applied challenge is not the 'functional equivalent' of express campaign speech. We further conclude that the interests held to justify restricting corporate campaign speech or its functional equivalent do not justify restricting issue advocacy, and accordingly we hold that BCRA §203 is unconstitutional as applied to the advertisements at issue. . . .

"[The] proper standard for an as-applied challenge to [§203] must [focus] on the substance of the communication rather than amorphous considerations of intent and effect. [A] court should find that an ad is the functional equivalent of express advocacy only if the ad is susceptible of no reasonable interpretation other than as an appeal to vote for or against a specific candidate. Under this test, WRTL's [ads] are plainly not the functional equivalent of express advocacy. [Section 203] can be constitutionally applied to WRTL's ads only if it is narrowly tailored to further a compelling interest. This Court has never recognized a compelling interest in regulating ads, like WRTL's, that are neither express advocacy nor its functional equivalent."

Justice Scalia, joined by Justices Kennedy and Thomas, concurred in the result: "[It] was adventurous for *McConnell* to extend *Austin* beyond corporate speech constituting express advocacy. Today's cases make it apparent that the adventure is a flop. [Which] brings me to the question of *stare decisis*. [*Stare decisis* carries] little weight when an erroneous 'governing decision[n]' has created an 'unworkable' regime. [The] *McConnell* regime is unworkable because of the inability of any acceptable as-applied standard to validate the facial constitutionality of §203. [Neither] do any of the other considerations relevant to *stare decisis* suggest adherence to *McConnell*. These cases do not involve property or contract rights, where reliance interests are involved. And *McConnell*'s §203 holding has assuredly not become 'embedded' in our 'national culture.' [I] would overrule that part of the Court's decision in *McConnell* upholding §203(a) of the BCRA."

Justice Souter, joined by Justices Stevens, Ginsburg, and Breyer, dissented: "[In] *McConnell*, we found [§203] to be 'easily understood and objective[e]' [and] we held that the [line] separating regulated election speech from general political discourse does not, on its face, violate the First Amendment. [We] found '[l]ittle difference . . . between an ad that urged viewers to "vote against Jane Doe" and one that condemned Jane Doe's record on a particular issue before exhorting viewers to "call Jane Doe and tell her what you think"'. . . .

"*McConnell*'s holding that §203 is facially constitutional is overruled. [It] is hard to imagine the Chief Justice would ever find an ad to be 'susceptible of reasonable interpretation other than as an appeal to vote for or against a specific candidate' unless it contained words of express advocacy. [The] price of *McConnell*'s demise [seems] to me a high one. The Court (and I think the country) loses when important precedent is overruled without good reason, and there is no justification for departing from our usual rule of *stare decisis* here."

## Citizens United v. Federal Election Commission

558 U.S. 310 (2010)

JUSTICE KENNEDY delivered the opinion of the Court.

Federal law prohibits corporations and unions from using their general treasury funds to make independent expenditures for speech defined as an "electioneering communication," or for speech expressly advocating the election or defeat of a candidate. Limits on electioneering communications were upheld in [*McConnell*]. The holding of *McConnell* rested to a large extent on [*Austin*, which] had held that political speech may be banned based on the speaker's corporate identity.

In this case we are asked to reconsider *Austin* and, in effect, *McConnell*. [We] hold that *stare decisis* does not compel the continued acceptance of *Austin*. . . .

### I

Citizens United is a nonprofit corporation. [In] January 2008 Citizens United released a film entitled *Hillary: The Movie*. [It] is a 90-minute documentary about then-Senator Hillary Clinton, who was a candidate in the Democratic Party's 2008 Presidential primary elections. . . .

Before the Bipartisan Campaign Reform Act of 2002 (BCRA), federal law prohibited — and still does prohibit — corporations and unions from using general treasury funds [to] make independent expenditures that expressly advocate the election or defeat of a candidate. 2 U.S.C. §441b. [BCRA §203 prohibited] any "electioneering communication" as well. [The Federal Elections Commission held that *Hillary* was an "electioneering communication" within the meaning of BCRA §203.] . . .

### III

. . . The law before us is an outright ban [on speech], backed by criminal sanctions. Section 441b makes it a felony for all corporations [either] to expressly advocate the election or defeat of candidates or to broadcast electioneering communications within 30 days of a primary election and 60 days of a general election. [If] §441b applied to individuals, [it would clearly be

*Must be Narrowly tailored*

*☆* unconstitutional under *Buckley*]. Laws that burden political speech are "subject to strict scrutiny," which requires the Government to prove that the restriction "furthers a compelling interest and is narrowly tailored to achieve that interest." [*WRTL*]. . . .

Premised on mistrust of governmental power, the First Amendment stands against attempts to disfavor certain subjects or viewpoints. Prohibited, too, are restrictions distinguishing among different speakers, allowing speech by some but not others. [Citing *Bellotti*.] As instruments to censor, these categories are interrelated: Speech restrictions based on the identity of the speaker are all too often simply a means to control content. [By] taking the right to speak from some and giving it to others, the Government deprives the disadvantaged person or class of the right to use speech to strive to establish worth, standing, and respect for the speaker's voice. The Government may not by these means deprive the public of the right and privilege to determine for itself what speech *★* and speakers are worthy of consideration. The First Amendment protects speech and speaker, and the ideas that flow from each. [We] find no basis for the proposition that, in the context of political speech, the Government may impose restrictions on certain disfavored speakers. . . .

*( ) corporation)*

**A**

The Court has recognized that First Amendment protection extends to corporations. [Citing *Bellotti*; *Cox Broadcasting*; New York Times v. United States; New York Times v. Sullivan.] Under the rationale of these precedents, political speech does not lose First Amendment protection "simply because its source is a corporation." [*Bellotti*]. The Court [has] rejected the argument that political speech of corporations or other associations should be treated differently under the First Amendment simply because such associations are not "natural persons." [*Bellotti*.] . . .

*Austin included*

*Austin* "uph[eld] a direct restriction on the independent expenditure of funds for political speech for the first time in [this Court's] history." [To] bypass *Buckley* and *Bellotti*, the *Austin* Court identified a new governmental interest in limiting political speech: an antidistortion interest. *Austin* found a compelling governmental interest in preventing "the corrosive and distorting effects of immense aggregations of wealth that are accumulated with the help of the corporate form and that have little or no correlation to the public's support for the corporation's ideas."

**B**

This Court is thus confronted with conflicting lines of precedent: a pre-*Austin* line that forbids restrictions on political speech based on the speaker's corporate identity and a post-*Austin* line that permits them. [In] its defense of the corporate-speech restrictions in §441b, the Government notes the antidistortion rationale. . . . [This] rationale cannot support §441b. If the First Amendment has any force, it prohibits Congress from fining or jailing citizens, or associations of citizens, for simply engaging in political speech. If the antidistortion rationale were to be accepted, however, it would permit Government to ban political speech simply because the speaker is an association that has taken on the corporate form. [*Austin*] sought to defend the antidistortion rationale as a means to prevent corporations from obtaining "an unfair advantage in the political marketplace" by using "resources amassed in the economic marketplace." But *Buckley* rejected the premise that the Government has an interest "in equalizing the relative ability of individuals and groups to influence the outcome of elections."

[T]he *Austin* majority undertook to distinguish wealthy individuals from corporations on the ground that "[s]tate law grants corporations special advantages — such as limited liability, perpetual life, and favorable treatment of the accumulation and distribution of assets." This does not suffice, however, to allow laws prohibiting speech. "It is rudimentary that the State cannot exact as the price of those special advantages the forfeiture of First Amendment rights." . . .

The censorship we now confront is vast in its reach. The Government has "muffle[d] the voices that best represent the most significant segments of the economy." The purpose and effect of this law is to prevent corporations [from] presenting both facts and opinions to the public. [The] speech that §441b forbids [is] public, and all can judge its content and purpose. References to massive corporate treasuries should not mask the real operation of this law. Rhetoric ought not obscure reality. [When] Government seeks to use its full power, including the criminal law, to command where a person may get his or her information or what distrusted source he or she may not hear, it uses censorship to control thought. This is unlawful. The First Amendment confirms the freedom to think for ourselves. . . .

What we have said also shows the invalidity of other arguments made by the Government. [The] Government falls back on the argument that corporate political speech can be banned in order to prevent corruption or its appearance. In *Buckley*, the Court found this interest "sufficiently important" to allow limits on contributions but did not extend that reasoning to expenditure limits. [Indeed], 26 States do not restrict independent expenditures by for-profit corporations. The Government does not claim that these expenditures have corrupted the political process in those States. [The] appearance of influence or access, furthermore, will not cause the electorate to lose faith in our democracy. [The] fact that a corporation, or any other speaker, is willing to spend money to try to persuade voters presupposes that the people have the ultimate influence over elected officials. . . .

When Congress finds that a problem exists, we must give that finding due deference; but Congress may not choose an unconstitutional remedy. If elected officials succumb to improper influences from independent expenditures; if they surrender their best judgment; and if they put expediency before principle, then surely there is cause for concern. [The] remedies enacted by law, however, must comply with the First Amendment; and, it is our law and our tradition that more speech, not less, is the governing rule. An outright ban on corporate political speech is not a permissible remedy. . . .

The Government contends further that corporate political expenditures can be limited because of its interest in protecting dissenting shareholders from being compelled to fund corporate political speech. This asserted interest, like *Austin*'s antidistortion rationale, would allow the Government to ban the political speech even of media corporations. [In any event], the remedy is not to restrict speech but to consider and explore other regulatory mechanisms. . . .

C

. . . For the reasons above, it must be concluded that *Austin* was not well reasoned. [Due] consideration leads to this conclusion: *Austin* should be and now is overruled. We return to the principle established [in] *Bellotti* that the Government may not suppress political speech on the basis of the speaker's corporate identity. No sufficient governmental interest justifies limits on the political speech [of] corporations. [Given] our conclusion we are further required to overrule the part of *McConnell* that upheld BCRA §203's extension of §441b's restrictions on corporate independent expenditures.

CHIEF JUSTICE ROBERTS, with whom JUSTICE ALITO joins, concurring.

. . . The text and purpose of the First Amendment point in the same direction: Congress may not prohibit political speech, even if the speaker is a corporation or union. What makes this case difficult is the need to confront our prior decision in *Austin*. [Fidelity] to precedent — the policy of *stare decisis* — is vital to the proper exercise of the judicial function. "*Stare decisis* is the preferred course because it promotes the evenhanded, predictable, and consistent development of legal principles, fosters reliance on judicial decisions, and contributes to the actual and perceived integrity of the judicial process." For these reasons, we have long recognized that departures from precedent are inappropriate in the absence of a "special justification." [But] *stare decisis* is neither an "inexorable command," nor "a mechanical formula of adherence to the latest decision," especially in constitutional cases. If it were, segregation would be legal, minimum wage laws would be unconstitutional, and the Government could wiretap ordinary criminal suspects without first obtaining warrants. . . . *Stare decisis* is instead a "principle of policy." When considering whether to reexamine a prior erroneous holding, we must balance the importance of having constitutional questions *decided* against the importance of having them *decided right*. . . .

[Several] considerations weigh against retaining our decision in *Austin*. First, [that] decision was an "aberration" insofar as it departed from the robust protections we had granted political speech in our earlier cases. *Austin* undermined the careful line that *Buckley* drew to distinguish limits on contributions to candidates from limits on independent expenditures on speech. *Buckley* rejected the asserted government interest in regulating independent expenditures, concluding that "restrict[ing] the speech of some elements of our society in order to enhance the relative voice of others is wholly foreign to the First Amendment." *Austin*, however, allowed the Government to prohibit these same expenditures out of concern for "the corrosive and distorting effects of immense aggregations of wealth" in the marketplace of ideas. *Austin's* reasoning was — and remains — inconsistent with *Buckley's* explicit repudiation of any government interest in "equalizing the relative ability of individuals and groups to influence the outcome of elections." *Austin* was also inconsistent with *Bellotti's* clear rejection of the idea that "speech that otherwise would be within the protection of the First Amendment loses that protection simply because its source is a corporation." . . .

Second, the validity of *Austin's* rationale [has] proved to be the consistent subject of dispute among Members of this Court ever since. [Citing *WRTL* and *McConnell*]. The simple fact that one of our decisions remains controversial is, of course, insufficient to justify overruling it. But it does undermine the precedent's ability to contribute to the stable and orderly development of the law. In such circumstances, it is entirely appropriate for the Court [to] address the matter with a greater willingness to consider new approaches capable of restoring our doctrine to sounder footing. [Because] continued adherence to *Austin* threatens to subvert the "principled and intelligible" development of our First Amendment jurisprudence, I support the Court's determination to overrule that decision.

JUSTICE SCALIA, with whom JUSTICE ALITO joins, and with whom JUSTICE THOMAS joins in part, concurring.

I join the opinion of the Court. I write separately to address Justice Stevens' discussion of "*Original Understandings*." This section of the dissent purports to show that today's decision is not supported by the original understanding of the First Amendment. The dissent attempts this demonstration, however, in splendid isolation from the text of the First Amendment. It never shows why "the freedom of speech" that was the right of Englishmen did not include the freedom to speak in association with other individuals, including association in the corporate form. To be sure, in 1791 (as now) corporations could pursue only the objectives set forth in their charters; but the dissent provides no evidence that their speech in the pursuit of those objectives could be censored.

Instead of taking this straightforward approach to determining the Amendment's meaning, the dissent embarks on a detailed exploration of the Framers' views about the "role of corporations in society." The Framers didn't like corporations, the dissent concludes, and therefore it follows (as night the day) that corporations had no rights of free speech. Of course the Framers' personal affection or disaffection for corporations is relevant only insofar as it can be thought to be reflected in the understood meaning of the text they enacted — not, as the dissent suggests, as a freestanding substitute for that text. [Even] if we thought it proper to apply the dissent's approach of excluding from First Amendment coverage what the Founders disliked, and even if we agreed that the Founders disliked founding-era corporations; modern corporations might not qualify for exclusion. Most of the Founders' resentment towards corporations was directed at the state-granted monopoly privileges that individually chartered corporations enjoyed. Modern corporations do not have such privileges, and would probably have been favored by most of our enterprising Founders. . . .

But to return to, and summarize, my principal point, which is the conformity of today's opinion with the original meaning of the First Amendment. [Its] text offers no foothold for excluding any category of speaker, from single individuals to partnerships of individuals, to unincorporated associations of individuals, to incorporated associations of individuals — and the dissent offers no evidence about the original meaning of the text to support any such exclusion. We are therefore simply left with the question whether the speech at issue in this case is "speech" covered by the First Amendment. No one says otherwise. A documentary film critical of a potential Presidential candidate is core political speech, and its nature as such does not change simply because it was funded by a corporation. [To] exclude or impede corporate speech is to muzzle the principal agents of the modern free economy. We should celebrate rather than condemn the addition of this speech to the public debate.

JUSTICE STEVENS, with whom JUSTICE GINSBURG, JUSTICE BREYER, and JUSTICE SOTOMAYOR join, concurring in part and dissenting in part.

. . . The basic premise underlying the Court's ruling is its iteration, and constant reiteration, of the proposition that the First Amendment bars regulatory distinctions based on a speaker's identity, including its "identity" as a corporation. While that glittering generality has rhetorical appeal, it is not a correct statement of the law. [In] the context of election to public office, the distinction between corporate and human speakers is significant. Although they make enormous contributions to our society, corporations are not actually members of it. They cannot vote or run for office. [The] financial resources, legal structure, and instrumental orientation of corporations raise legitimate concerns about their role in the electoral process. Our lawmakers have a compelling constitutional basis, if not also a democratic duty, to take measures designed to guard against the potentially deleterious effects of corporate spending in local and national races.

The majority's approach to corporate electioneering marks a dramatic break from our past. Congress has placed special limitations on campaign spending by corporations ever since the passage of the Tillman Act in 1907. [The] Court today rejects a century of history when it treats the distinction between corporate and individual campaign spending as an invidious novelty born of *Austin*. Relying largely on individual dissenting opinions, the majority blazes through our precedents, overruling or disavowing a body of case law including *WRTL* [and] *McConnell*. . . .

## II

. . . I am not an absolutist when it comes to *stare decisis*, [but] if this principle is to do any meaningful work in supporting the rule of law, it must at least demand a significant justification, beyond the preferences of five Justices, for overturning settled doctrine. [No] such justification exists in this case, and to the contrary there are powerful prudential reasons to keep faith with our precedents. The Court's central argument for why *stare decisis* ought to be trumped is that it does not like *Austin*. [I] am perfectly willing to concede that if one of our precedents were dead wrong in its reasoning or irreconcilable with the rest of our doctrine, there would be a compelling basis for revisiting it. But neither is true of *Austin*. [The] Court proclaims that "*Austin* is undermined by experience since its announcement." [But it] has no empirical evidence with which to substantiate [this claim.] Nor does the majority bother to specify in what sense *Austin* has been "undermined." . . .

In the end, the Court's rejection of *Austin* and *McConnell* comes down to nothing more than its disagreement with their results. Virtually every one of its arguments was made and rejected in those cases, and the majority opinion is essentially an amalgamation of resuscitated dissents. The only relevant thing that has changed since *Austin* and *McConnell* is the composition of this Court. Today's ruling thus strikes at the vitals of *stare decisis*, "the means by which we ensure that the law will not merely change erratically, but will develop in a principled and intelligible fashion" that "permits society to presume that bedrock principles are founded in the law rather than in the proclivities of individuals."

## III

The novelty of the Court's [approach] to *stare decisis* is matched by the novelty of its ruling on the merits. The ruling rests on several premises. First, the Court claims [that] the First Amendment precludes regulatory distinctions based on speaker identity, including the speaker's identity as a corporation. [Second], it claims that *Austin* and *McConnell* were radical outliers in our First Amendment tradition. . . . Each of these claims is wrong. . . .

### IDENTITY-BASED DISTINCTIONS

The second pillar of the Court's opinion is its assertion that "the Government cannot restrict political speech based on the speaker's . . . identity." The case on which it relies for this proposition is *Bellotti*, [but] the holding in that case was far narrower than the Court implies. [In] a variety of contexts, we have held that speech can be regulated differentially on account of the speaker's identity, when identity is understood in categorical or institutional terms. The Government routinely places special restrictions on the speech rights of students, prisoners, members of the Armed Forces, foreigners, and its own employees. [In] contrast to the blanket rule that the majority espouses, our cases recognize that the Government's interests may be more or less compelling with respect to different classes of speakers. . . .

The election context is distinctive in many ways, and the Court, of course, is right that the First Amendment closely guards political speech. But in this context, too, the authority of legislatures to enact viewpoint-neutral regulations based on content and identity is well settled. We have, for example, allowed state-run broadcasters to exclude independent candidates from televised debates. [Citing *Forbes*. Recall also *Perry* and *Regan*]. The same logic applies to this case with additional force because it is the identity of corporations, rather than individuals, that the Legislature has taken into account. [Not] only has the distinctive potential of corporations to corrupt the electoral process long been recognized, but [campaign] finance distinctions based on corporate identity tend to be less worrisome [because] the "speakers" are not natural persons, much less members of our political [community]. . . .

In short, the Court dramatically overstates its critique of identity-based distinctions, without ever explaining why corporate identity demands the same treatment as individual identity. Only the most wooden approach to the First Amendment could justify the unprecedented line it seeks to draw.

OUR FIRST AMENDMENT TRADITION

A third fulcrum of the Court's opinion is the idea that *Austin* and *McConnell* are radical outliers [in] our First Amendment tradition. The Court has it exactly backwards. It is today's holding that is the radical departure from what had been settled First Amendment law. To see why, it is useful to take a long view.

### 1.   Original Understandings

[T]here is not a scintilla of evidence to support the notion that anyone believed [the First Amendment] would preclude regulatory distinctions based on the corporate form. To the extent that the Framers' views are discernible and relevant to the disposition of this case, they would appear to cut strongly against the majority's position.

[T]he Framers [held] very different views [than the majority does today] about the nature of the First Amendment right and the role of corporations in society. Those few corporations that existed at the founding were authorized by grant of a special legislative charter. [Corporations] were created, supervised, and conceptualized as quasi-public entities, "designed to serve a social function for the state." It was "assumed that [they] were legally privileged organizations that had to be closely scrutinized by the legislature because their purposes had to be made consistent with public welfare." [The] Framers thus took it as a given that corporations could be comprehensively regulated in the service of the public welfare. Unlike our colleagues, [the Framers] had little trouble distinguishing corporations from human beings, and when they constitutionalized the right to free speech in the First Amendment, it was the free speech of individual Americans that they had in mind. . . .

Justice Scalia criticizes the foregoing discussion for failing to adduce statements from the founding era showing that corporations were understood to be excluded from the First Amendment's free speech guarantee. Of course, Justice Scalia adduces no statements to suggest the contrary proposition. . . . Nothing in his account dislodges my basic point that members of the founding generation held a cautious view of corporate power and a narrow view of corporate rights (not that they "despised" corporations), and that they conceptualized speech in individualistic terms. If no prominent Framer bothered to articulate that corporate speech would have lesser status than individual speech, that may well be because the contrary proposition — if not also the very notion of "corporate speech" — was inconceivable. . . .

### 2.   Legislative and Judicial Interpretation

A century of more recent history puts to rest any notion that today's ruling is faithful to our First Amendment tradition. At the federal level, the express distinction between corporate and individual political spending on elections stretches back to 1907, when Congress passed the Tillman Act, banning all corporate contributions to candidates. [By] the time Congress passed FECA in 1971, the bar on corporate contributions and expenditures had become such an accepted part of federal campaign finance regulation that [in *Buckley*] no one even bothered to argue that the bar as such was unconstitutional. [Thus], it was unremarkable, that [in FEC v. National Right to Work Committee, 459 U.S. 197 (1982)] then-Justice Rehnquist wrote for a unanimous Court that [the] governmental interest in preventing both actual corruption and the appearance of corruption of elected representatives has long been recognized" [and that] "there is no reason why it may not . . . be accomplished by treating . . . corporations . . . differently from individuals." [Several] years later, in *Austin*, we [held that] corporations [could] be barred from using general treasury funds to make independent expenditures in support of, or in opposition to, candidates. In the 20 years since *Austin*, we have reaffirmed its holding and rationale a number of times, most importantly in *McConnell*, where we upheld the provision challenged here. . . .

### 3.   Buckley and Bellotti

Against [the] extensive background of congressional regulation of corporate campaign spending, and our repeated affirmation of this regulation as

constitutionally sound, the majority dismisses *Austin* as "a significant departure from ancient First Amendment principles." How does the majority
attempt to justify this claim? Selected passages from two cases, *Buckley* and
*Bellotti*, do all of the work. [The] case on which the majority places [its primary
emphasis] is *Bellotti*, claiming it "could not have been clearer" that *Bellotti's*
holding forbade distinctions between corporate and individual [expenditures].
The Court's reliance is odd. The only thing about *Bellotti* that could not be
clearer is that it declined to adopt the majority's position. *Bellotti* ruled, in an
explicit limitation on the scope of its holding, that "our consideration of a
corporation's right to speak on issues of general public interest implies no
comparable right in the quite different context of participation in a political
campaign for election to public office." *Bellotti*, in other words, did not touch
the question presented in *Austin* and *McConnell*, and the opinion squarely
disavowed the proposition for which the majority cites it. [The] basis for this
distinction is perfectly coherent: The anticorruption interests that animate
regulations of corporate participation in candidate elections, the "importance"
of which "has never been doubted," do not apply equally to regulations of
corporate participation in referenda. A referendum cannot owe a political debt
to a corporation, seek to curry favor with a corporation, or fear the corporation's
retaliation. . . .

   *Austin* and *McConnell*, then, sit perfectly well with *Bellotti*. Indeed, all six
Members of the *Austin* majority had been on the Court at the time of *Bellotti*, and
none so much as hinted in *Austin* that they saw any tension between the decisions.
The difference between the cases is not that *Austin* and *McConnell* rejected First
Amendment protection for corporations whereas *Bellotti* accepted it. The
difference is that [the] State has a greater interest in regulating independent
corporate expenditures on candidate elections than on referenda, because in a
functioning democracy the public must have faith that its representatives owe
their positions to the people, not to the corporations with the deepest pockets. . . .


## IV

Having explained [why] *Austin* and *McConnell* [sit] perfectly well with "First
Amendment principles," I come at last to the interests that are at stake. . . .

### THE ANTICORRUPTION INTEREST

. . . On numerous occasions we have recognized Congress' legitimate interest
in preventing the money that is spent on elections from exerting an "'undue
influence on an officeholder's judgment'" and from creating "'the appearance
of such influence,'" beyond the sphere of *quid pro quo* relationships. [Our]
"undue influence" cases [have recognized that when] private interests are seen
to exert outsized control over officeholders solely on account of the money

spent on (or withheld from) their campaigns, the result can depart so thoroughly "from what is pure or correct" in the conduct of Government that it amounts to a "subversion . . . of the electoral process." [This] understanding of corruption has deep roots in the Nation's history. . . .

Rather than show any deference to a coordinate branch of Government, the majority [rejects] the anticorruption rationale without serious analysis. Today's opinion provides no clear rationale for being so dismissive of Congress, but the prior individual opinions on which it relies have offered one: the incentives of the legislators who passed BCRA. Section 203, our colleagues have suggested, may be little more than "an incumbency protection plan," a disreputable attempt at legislative self-dealing rather than an earnest effort to facilitate First Amendment values and safeguard the legitimacy of our political system. This possibility, the Court apparently believes, licenses it to run roughshod over Congress' handiwork.

In my view, we should instead start by acknowledging that "Congress surely has both wisdom and experience in these matters that is far superior to ours." [This] is not to say that deference would be appropriate if there were a solid basis for believing that a legislative action was motivated by the desire to protect incumbents or that it will degrade the competitiveness of the electoral process. [But] it is the height of recklessness to dismiss Congress' years of bipartisan deliberation and its reasoned judgment on this basis, without first confirming that the statute in question was intended to be, or will function as, a restraint on electoral competition. . . .

We have no record evidence from which to conclude that BCRA §203, or any of the dozens of state laws that the Court today calls into question, reflects or fosters such invidious discrimination. Our colleagues have opined that "'*any* restriction upon a type of campaign speech that is equally available to challengers and incumbents tends to favor incumbents.'" [*McConnell* (opinion of Scalia, J.)]. This kind of airy speculation could easily be turned on its head. The electioneering prohibited by §203 might well tend to *favor* incumbents, because incumbents have pre-existing relationships with corporations and unions, and groups that wish to procure legislative benefits may tend to support the candidate who, as a sitting officeholder, is already in a position to dispense benefits and is statistically likely to retain office. If a corporation's goal is to induce officeholders to do its bidding, the corporation would do well to cultivate stable, long-term relationships of dependency. [We] do not have a solid theoretical basis for condemning §203 as a front for incumbent self-protection, and it seems equally if not more plausible that restrictions on corporate electioneering will be self-denying.

### *AUSTIN* AND CORPORATE EXPENDITURES

Just as the majority gives short shrift to the general societal interests at stake in campaign finance regulation, it also overlooks the distinctive considerations raised by the regulation of *corporate* expenditures. The majority fails to appreciate that *Austin*'s antidistortion rationale is itself an anticorruption rationale, tied to the special concerns raised by corporations. Understood properly, "antidistortion" is simply a variant on the classic governmental interest in protecting against improper influences on officeholders that debilitate the democratic process. It is manifestly not just an "'equalizing'" ideal in disguise. . . .

### 1. Antidistortion

The fact that corporations are different from human beings might seem to need no elaboration, except that the majority opinion almost completely elides it. *Austin* set forth some of the basic differences. Unlike natural persons, corporations have "limited liability" for their owners and managers, "perpetual life," separation of ownership and control, "and favorable treatment of the accumulation and distribution of assets . . . that enhance their ability to attract capital and to deploy their resources in ways that maximize the return on their shareholders' investments." '[T]he resources in the treasury of a business corporation [are] not an indication of popular support for the corporation's political ideas.'" "'They reflect instead the economically motivated decisions of investors and customers. The availability of these resources may make a corporation a formidable political presence, even though the power of the corporation may be no reflection of the power of its ideas.'" [Corporations] help structure and facilitate the activities of human beings, to be sure, and their "personhood" often serves as a useful legal fiction. But they are not themselves members of "We the People" by whom and for whom our Constitution was established.

These basic points help explain why corporate electioneering is not only more likely to impair compelling governmental interests, but also why restrictions on that electioneering are less likely to encroach upon First Amendment freedoms. One fundamental concern of the First Amendment is to "protec[t] the individual's interest in self-expression." [A] regulation such as BCRA §203 may affect the way in which individuals disseminate certain messages through the corporate form, but it does not prevent anyone from speaking in his or her own voice. [Take] away the ability to use general treasury funds for some of those ads, and no one's autonomy, dignity, or political equality has been impinged upon in the least. . . .

Recognizing the weakness of a speaker-based critique of *Austin*, the Court places primary emphasis not on the corporation's right to electioneer, but rather on the listener's interest in hearing what every possible speaker may have to say. [There] are many flaws in this argument. [*Austin*] recognized that there are substantial reasons why a legislature might conclude that unregulated general treasury expenditures will give corporations "unfai[r] influence" in the electoral process and distort public debate in ways that undermine rather than advance the interests of listeners. [In] addition to [the] drowning out of noncorporate voices, [corporate] "domination" of electioneering can generate the impression that corporations dominate our democracy. [Citizens] may lose faith in their capacity, as citizens, to influence public policy. [The] predictable result is cynicism and disenchantment. . . .

The Court's facile depiction of corporate electioneering assumes away all of these complexities. Our colleagues ridicule the idea of regulating expenditures based on "nothing more" than a fear that corporations have a special "ability to persuade," as if corporations were our society's ablest debaters and viewpoint-neutral laws such as §203 were created to suppress their best arguments. [Our] colleagues simply ignore the fundamental concerns of the *Austin* Court and the legislatures that have passed laws like §203: to safeguard the integrity, competitiveness, and democratic responsiveness of the electoral process. All of the majority's theoretical arguments turn on a proposition with undeniable surface appeal but little grounding in evidence or experience, "that there is no such thing as too much speech." If individuals in our society had infinite free time to listen to and contemplate every last bit of speech uttered by anyone, anywhere; and if broadcast advertisements had no special ability to influence elections apart from the merits of their arguments (to the extent they make any); and if legislators always operated with nothing less than perfect virtue; then I suppose the majority's premise would be sound. In the real world, we have seen, corporate domination of the airwaves prior to an election may decrease the average listener's exposure to relevant viewpoints, and it may diminish citizens' willingness and capacity to participate in the democratic process. . . .

### 2.  *Shareholder Protection*

There is yet another way in which laws such as §203 can serve First Amendment values. Interwoven with *Austin*'s concern to protect the integrity of the electoral process is a concern to protect the rights of shareholders from a kind of coerced [speech]. When corporations use general treasury funds to praise or attack a particular candidate for office, it is the shareholders [who] are effectively footing the bill. Those shareholders who disagree with the corporation's electoral message may find their financial investments being used to undermine their political convictions. [*Austin*'s] acceptance of restrictions on general treasury spending "simply allows people who have invested in the business corporation for purely economic reasons" — the vast majority of investors, one assumes — "to avoid being taken advantage of, without sacrificing their economic objectives."

The concern to protect dissenting shareholders and union members has a long history in campaign finance reform. [Indeed], we have unanimously recognized the governmental interest in "protect[ing] the individuals who have paid money into a corporation or union for purposes other than the support of candidates from having that money used to support political candidates to whom they may be opposed"

and bias, and the public distrust that such an approach engenders. As the Court continues to push the United States away from more modest attempts at campaign finance regulation, then, it is increasingly pushing public policy toward the one alternative that many conservatives most abhor: full public financing of all federal elections. . . .

d. Sachs, Unions, Corporations, and Political Opt-Out Rights After Citizens United, 112 Colum. L. Rev. 800, 801–803, 861–862 (2012):

For more than half a century, federal campaign finance law has bound unions and corporations to symmetrical restrictions on their ability to spend money in politics. [In] 1971, the Federal Election Campaign Act forbad "any corporation, whatever, or any labor organization," to fund with general treasury monies expenditures that expressly advocated the election or defeat of a candidate. [On its face, *Citizens United*] leaves unions and corporations equally unconstrained and free to use their general treasuries to fund federal electoral expenditures. [In fact, however, after *Citizens United*] the law treats union and corporate political spending differently. [This is so because federal law] prohibits unions from spending any individual employees' dues on politics if those employees object to such use. [Corporations, however,] are free to spend [general treasury funds] generated from shareholders' capital contributions . . . on politics even if individual shareholders object. [Unlike union members, shareholders] enjoy no right to opt out of financial corporate political activity. . . .

The asymmetric rule of political opt-out rights [imposes] on unions substantive and administrative burdens that corporations [do] not bear, [even though there is] no "special characteristic" of unions [that] justifies treating unions and corporations differently in this respect. [This is especially problematic, because] asymmetric opt-out rules will have a predictable effect on viewpoint. [By] imposing restrictions on unions that corporations [do not] face, the asmmetric opt-out rules will have the effect of favoring the corporate viewpoint over the union one when those viewpoints conflict.

Is such asymmetric treatment of corporations and unions unconstitutional?
e. Hellman, Money Talks but It Isn't Speech, 95 Minn. L. Rev. 953, 953–955 (2011):

*Buckley* [and *Citizens United* rest] on the claim that restrictions on both giving and spending money are tantamount to restrictions on speech. [The] justification for this claim [is] this: money facilitates speech; money incentivizes speech; and giving and spending money are themselves expressive activities. [Missing] from this analysis is the recognition that money facilitates and incentivizes the exercise of many other constitutionally protected rights. It does so because money is useful. Moreover, it is not at all obvious that restrictions on the ability to give or spend money to exercise these other rights are constitutionally impermissible. One has the right to vote, but not to buy or sell votes. One has the right to private sexual intimacy, but not to spend money to facilitate the exercise of that right — outlawing prostitution is constitutionally permissible. [When] do constitutionally protected rights include a right to give or spend money to effectuate them?

Would it be constitutional for a state to prohibit individuals to spend money for an abortion or a newspaper? Are those situations distinguishable from a law prohibiting individuals to spend money to help elect a political candidate? To buy votes?

f. Kang, The End of Campaign Finance Law, 98 Va. L. Rev. 1, 63–65 (2012):

> [*Buckley*] split the difference between political contributions and expenditures and [offered] "a solomonic solution to an intractable analogical crisis." [As] a practical matter, though, the holding that expenditures received greater constitutional protection meant only that outright expenditure limits on individuals were unconstitutional. The three pillars of campaign finance regulation — source restrictions, contribution limits, and disclosure requirements — applied to different forms of expenditures even if independent expenditures themselves could not be limited in the aggregate. *Citizens United*, however, fully realized the promise in *Buckley* that independent expenditures do not "appear to pose dangers of real or apparent corruption by fully deregulating them as had not been the case following *Buckley*. This is *Citizens United*'s profound impact on campaign finance law far beyond its limited extension of corporate electioneering.
>
> Already this meant in the 2010 elections that money shifted away from candidates and parties to independent expenditures by outside groups that operate almost entirely beyond the ambit of campaign finance regulation. The 2010 elections were only a glimpse of what will be an accelerating trend toward independent expenditures by outside groups. Since those 2010 elections, the FEC has further conceded that even groups that make contributions can still collect unrestricted funds for independent expenditures provided those unrestricted funds are placed into a segregated account. In short, outside groups now can make independent expenditures on a virtually unregulated basis whether or not they separately make contributions. The 2010 elections thus were only a glimpse ahead of what will be an accelerating trend toward independent expenditures by outside groups.
>
> With independent expenditures now fully deregulated, a new question looms over the campaign finance regulation that remains: To what degree will the Court declare the government regulation of contributions unconstitutional as well? Although the Court has always deferred to legislatures on the regulation of contributions, [the] logic of *Citizens United* may inevitably eat away at the constitutional underpinnings of that longstanding deference. *Citizens United* defined the government interest in prevention of corruption so narrowly that courts may not be able to find the regulation of contributions sufficiently connected with that compelling government interest to uphold its constitutionality in many of its forms. [When] the government interest in the prevention of corruption is so viciously limited, there is simply little ground for campaign finance regulation of any sort.

g. In Western Tradition Partnership, Inc. v. Attorney General of Montana, 271 P.3d 1 (Mont. 2010), the Montana Supreme Court distinguished *Citizens United* and upheld a Montana law providing that "a corporation may not make . . . an expenditure in connection with a candidate or a political party." The Montana court explained that in *Citizens United* the Court "found that the Government did not claim that corporate expenditures had actually corrupted the political process and concluded that 'independent expenditures, including those made by corporations, do not give rise to corruption or the appearance of corruption.'" Thus, the Court in *Citizens United* "determined that the government had not provided a compelling interest to justify the speech restriction at issue." In *Western Tradition Partnership*, however, the Montana court found that the state had presented sufficient evidence to satisfy the strict scrutiny standard of *Citizens United*.

Specifically, the Montana court observed that Montana had had a long and bitter history in which its political elections had been dominated by "mining and industrial enterprises controlled by foreign trusts or corporations." Indeed, it was precisely that history that had led the state to enact the challenged law in the first place. Moreover, the Montana court pointed to recent studies that showed that prior to *Citizens United* the "percentage of campaign contributions from individual voters drops sharply from 48% in states with restrictions on corporate spending to 23% in states without." Thus, the court concluded that the challenged statute furthered "the compelling interest of the people of Montana in strong voter participation in the process."

In Western Tradition Partnership, Inc. v. Bullock, 132 S. Ct. 2490 (2012), the Supreme Court summarily reversed in a per curiam opinion, declaring that "Montana's arguments . . . either were already rejected in *Citizens United*, or fail to meaningfully distinguish that case."

Justice Breyer, joined by Justices Ginsburg, Sotomayor, and Kagan, dissented: "[E]ven if I were to accept *Citizens United*, this Court's legal conclusion should not bar the Montana Supreme Court's finding, made on the record before it, that independent expenditures by corporations did in fact lead to corruption or the appearance of corruption in Montana," contrary to the Court's assertion in *Citizens United* that "independent expenditures, including those made by corporations, do not give rise to corruption or the appearance of corruption." In light of "the history and political landscape in Montana, that court concluded that the State had a compelling interest in limiting independent expenditures by corporations. Thus, Montana's experience, like considerable experience elsewhere since the Court's decision in *Citizens United*, casts grave doubt on the Court's supposition that independent expenditures do not corrupt or appear to do so."

2. *Super PACs*. What is the connection between *Citizens United* and the sudden emergence since 2010 of so-called Super PACs, which now raise and spend unlimited amounts of money in the electoral process? Political organizations known as 527s (a reference to a provision of the Internal Revenue

Code) raise money from contributions and then make independent expenditures (i.e., expenditures that are not coordinated with any candidate) to support or oppose the election of federal candidates. Prior to *Citizens United*, 527s were governed by provisions of the Federal Elections Campaign Act. Those provisions prohibited individuals from contributing more than $5,000 in any calendar year to any 527 and from contributing more than $69,900 in total to 527s over the course of two years. Thus, although 527s could spend as much as they wished to support or oppose the election of federal candidates, they could not receive large contributions. Until *Citizens United*, no one questioned the constitutionality of this scheme.

In SpeechNow.org v. Federal Election Commission, 599 F.3d 686 (D.C. Cir. 2010), however, the District of Columbia Circuit Court held that, in light of *Citizens United*, those limitations on 527s were unconstitutional. The court explained:

> [The] Supreme Court has recognized only one interest as sufficiently important to outweigh the First Amendment interests implicated by contributions for political speech: preventing corruption or the appearance of corruption. [In] *Citizens United*, [the] Court held that the government has *no* anti-corruption interest in limiting independent expenditures. [The] Court stated, "[W]e now conclude that independent expenditures, including those made by corporations, do not give rise to corruption or the appearance of corruption." [The Court justified this conclusion by rejecting the logic of *McConnell* and other prior decisions, and narrowly construing the concept of corruption as limited *only* to the interest in preventing the reality or appearance of *quid pro quo* corruption].
>
> In light of the Court's holding as a matter of law that independent expenditures do not corrupt or create the appearance of *quid pro quo* corruption, contributions to groups that make only independent expenditures also cannot corrupt or create the appearance of corruption. The Court has effectively held that there is no corrupting "quid" for which a candidate might in exchange offer a corrupt "quo."
>
> Given this analysis from *Citizens United*, we must conclude that the government has no anti-corruption interest in limiting contributions to an independent expenditure group such as SpeechNow. This simplifies the task of weighing the First Amendment interests implicated by contributions to SpeechNow against the government's interest in limiting such contributions. [After all], "something . . . outweighs nothing every time." . . .

**McCUTCHEON v. FEDERAL ELECTION COMMISSION, 134 S. Ct. 1434 (2014).** The federal Bipartisan Campaign Reform Act imposes two types of limits on campaign contributions. The first, called base limits, restricts how much money a donor may contribute to a particular candidate or committee. The second, called aggregate limits, restricts how much money a donor may contribute in total to all candidates or committees. In *Buckley*, the Court upheld the constitutionality of the base contribution limits. This case concerned the constitutionality of the aggregate contribution limits.

For the 2013–2014 election cycle, the aggregate limits permitted an individual to contribute a total of $48,600 to federal candidates and a total of $74,600 to other political committees. In the 2011–2012 election cycle, Shaun McCutcheon contributed a total of $33,088 to sixteen different federal candidates, in compliance with the then-applicable base limits applicable. McCutcheon wanted to contribute $1,776 to each of twelve additional candidates, but was prevented from doing so by the aggregate limit on contributions to candidates. He also wanted to contribute to several additional political committees, including $25,000 to each of the three Republican national party committees, but again was prevented from doing so by the aggregate limit on contributions to political committees. The Republican National Committee wanted to receive the contributions that McCutcheon and other potential contributors wanted to make to it — contributions otherwise permissible under the base limits for national party committees, but foreclosed by the aggregate limit on contributions to political committees.

The Supreme Court, in a five-to-four decision, held the aggregate contribution limits unconstitutional. Chief Justice Roberts announced the judgment of the Court and delivered an opinion, in which Justices Scalia, Kennedy, and Alito joined:

"The right to participate in democracy through political contributions is protected by the First Amendment, but that right is not absolute. Our cases have held that Congress may regulate campaign contributions to protect against corruption or the appearance of corruption. [Citing *Buckley*.] At the same time, we have made clear that Congress may not regulate contributions simply to reduce the amount of money in politics, or to restrict the political participation of some in order to enhance the relative influence of others. [Citing *Bennett*.] Many people might find those latter objectives attractive. [Money] in politics may at times seem repugnant to some, but so too does much of what the First Amendment vigorously protects. If the First Amendment protects flag burning, funeral protests, and Nazi parades — despite the profound offense such spectacles cause — it surely protects political campaign speech despite popular opposition. . . .

"In a series of cases over the past 40 years, we have spelled out how to draw the constitutional line between the permissible goal of avoiding corruption in the political process and the impermissible desire simply to limit political speech. We have said that government regulation may not target the general gratitude a candidate may feel toward those who support him or his allies, or the political access such support may afford. [Any] regulation must instead target what we have called 'quid pro quo' corruption or its appearance. That Latin phrase captures the notion of a direct exchange of an official act for money. [Campaign] finance restrictions that pursue other objectives . . . impermissibly inject the Government 'into the debate over who should govern.' [Quoting *Bennett*.]

"The statute at issue in this case [restricts] how much money a donor may contribute in total to all candidates or committees. This case does not involve any challenge to the base limits, which we have previously upheld as serving the permissible objective of combatting corruption. The Government contends that the aggregate limits also serve that objective, by preventing circumvention of the base limits. We conclude, however, that the aggregate limits do little, if anything, to address that concern, while seriously restricting participation in the democratic process. The aggregate limits are therefore invalid under the First Amendment. . . .

"To put it in the simplest terms, the aggregate limits prohibit an individual from fully contributing to the campaigns of [all the candidates he wants to support], even if all contributions fall within the base limits Congress views as adequate to protect against corruption. [It] is no answer to say that the individual can simply contribute less money to more people. To require one person to contribute at lower levels than others because he wants to support more candidates or causes is to impose a special burden on broader participation in the democratic process. [The] First Amendment burden is especially great for individuals who do not have ready access to alternative avenues for supporting their preferred politicians and policies. In the context of base contribution limits, *Buckley* observed that a supporter could vindicate his associational interests by personally volunteering his time and energy on behalf of a candidate. Such personal volunteering is not a realistic alternative for those who wish to support a wide variety of candidates or causes. . . .

"With the significant First Amendment costs for individual citizens in mind, we turn to the governmental interests asserted in this case. This Court has identified only one legitimate governmental interest for restricting campaign finances: preventing corruption or the appearance of corruption. We have consistently rejected attempts to suppress campaign speech based on other legislative objectives. No matter how desirable it may seem, it is not an acceptable governmental objective to 'level the playing field,' or to 'level electoral opportunities,' or to 'equaliz[e] the financial resources of candidates.' . . .

"Moreover, while preventing corruption or its appearance is a legitimate objective, Congress may target only a specific type of corruption — 'quid pro quo' corruption. [Spending] large sums of money in connection with elections, but not in connection with an effort to control the exercise of an officeholder's official duties, does not give rise to such quid pro quo corruption. Nor does the possibility that an individual who spends large sums may garner 'influence over or access to' elected officials or political parties. [The] line between quid pro quo corruption and general influence may seem vague at times, but the distinction must be respected in order to safeguard basic First Amendment rights. . . .

"'When the Government restricts speech, the Government bears the burden of proving the constitutionality of its actions.' Here, the Government seeks to carry that burden by arguing that the aggregate limits further the permissible objective of preventing quid pro quo corruption. The difficulty is that once the aggregate limits kick in, they ban all contributions of any amount. But

Congress's selection of a $5,200 base limit indicates its belief that contributions of that amount or less do not create a cognizable risk of corruption. If there is no corruption concern in giving nine candidates up to $5,200 each, it is difficult to understand how a tenth candidate can be regarded as corruptible if given $1,801, and all others corruptible if given a dime. And if there is no risk that additional candidates will be corrupted by donations of up to $5,200, then the Government must defend the aggregate limits by demonstrating that they prevent circumvention of the base limits.

"The problem is that they do not serve that function in any meaningful way. In light of the various statutes and regulations currently in effect, [the] fear that an individual might 'contribute massive amounts of money to a particular candidate through the use of unearmarked contributions' to entities likely to support the candidate, is far too speculative. We 'have never accepted mere conjecture as adequate to carry a First Amendment burden.' [The] primary example of circumvention, in one form or another, envisions an individual donor who contributes the maximum amount under the base limits to a particular candidate, say, Representative Smith. Then the donor also channels 'massive amounts of money' to Smith through a series of contributions to PACs that have stated their intention to support Smith. Various earmarking and antiproliferation rules disarm this example. Importantly, the donor may not contribute to the most obvious PACs: those that support only Smith. Nor may the donor contribute to the slightly less obvious PACs that he knows will route 'a substantial portion' of his contribution to Smith. [Any scheme to funnel huge amounts of money to Smith by indirection, given the restraints already built into the system,] is highly implausible [and] either illegal under current campaign finance laws or divorced from reality. [The] dissent [maintains] that, even with the aggregate limits in place, individuals 'have transferred large sums of money to specific candidates' in excess of the base limits. But the cited sources do not provide any real-world examples of circumvention. . . .

"[Moreover], there are multiple alternatives available to Congress that would serve the Government's anticircumvention interest, while avoiding 'unnecessary abridgment' of First Amendment rights. The most obvious might involve targeted restrictions on transfers among candidates and political committees. There are currently no such limits on transfers among party committees and from candidates to party committees. Perhaps for that reason, a central concern of the District Court [and] the dissent has been the ability of party committees to transfer money freely. If Congress agrees that this is problematic, it might tighten its permissive transfer rules. Doing so would impose a lesser burden on First Amendment rights, as compared to aggregate limits that flatly ban contributions beyond certain levels. [Indeed], Congress has adopted transfer restrictions, and the Court has upheld them, in the context of state party spending. [In addition,] disclosure of contributions minimizes the potential for abuse of the campaign finance system. Disclosure requirements [burden] speech, but — unlike the aggregate limits — they do not impose a ceiling on speech. For that reason, disclosure often represents a less restrictive alternative to flat bans on certain types or quantities of speech. [We] do not mean to opine on the validity of any particular proposal. The point is that there are numerous alternative approaches available to Congress to prevent circumvention of the base limits. . . .

"For the past 40 years, our campaign finance jurisprudence has focused on the need to preserve authority for the Government to combat corruption, without at the same time compromising the political responsiveness at the heart of the democratic process, or allowing the Government to favor some participants in that process over others. [Constituents] have the right to support candidates who share their views and concerns. Representatives are not to follow constituent orders, but can be expected to be cognizant of and responsive to those concerns. Such responsiveness is key to the very concept of self-governance through elected officials. The Government has a strong interest, no less critical to our democratic system, in combatting corruption and its appearance. We have, however, held that this interest must be limited to a specific kind of corruption — quid pro quo corruption — in order to ensure that the Government's efforts do not have the effect of restricting the First Amendment right of citizens to choose who shall govern them. [We] conclude that the aggregate limits on contributions do not further the only governmental interest this Court accepted as legitimate in Buckley. They instead intrude without justification on a citizen's ability to exercise 'the most fundamental First Amendment activities.'"

Justice Thomas concurred in the judgment: "I adhere to the view that this Court's decision in *Buckley* denigrates core First Amendment speech and should be overruled. [Contributions] to political campaigns, no less than direct expenditures, 'generate essential political speech' by fostering discussion of public issues and candidate qualifications."

Justice Breyer, joined by Justices Ginsburg, Sotomayor, and Kagan, dissented: "Taken together with *Citizens United*, today's decision eviscerates our Nation's campaign finance laws, leaving a remnant incapable of dealing with the grave problems of democratic legitimacy that those laws were intended to resolve. [The] plurality's conclusion rests upon three separate but related claims. Each is fatally flawed. First, the plurality says that given the base limits on contributions to candidates and political committees, aggregate limits do not further any independent governmental objective worthy of protection. And that is because, given the base limits, '[s]pending large sums of money in connection with elections' does not 'give rise to . . . corruption.' In making this argument, the plurality relies heavily upon a narrow definition of 'corruption' that excludes efforts to obtain 'influence over or access to' elected officials or political parties.' Second, the plurality assesses the instrumental objective of the aggregate limits, namely, safeguarding the base limits. It finds that they 'do not serve that function in any meaningful way.' That is because, even without the aggregate limits, the possibilities for circumventing the base limits are 'implausible' and 'divorced from reality.' Third, the plurality says the aggregate limits are 'poorly tailored to the Government's interest in preventing circumvention of the base limits.' The plurality imagines several alternative regulations that it says might just as effectively thwart circumvention. Accordingly, it finds, the aggregate caps are out of 'proportion to the [anticorruption] interest served.' . . .

"The plurality's first claim — that large aggregate contributions do not 'give rise' to 'corruption' — is plausible only because the plurality defines 'corruption' too narrowly. [Its] definition of 'corruption' is inconsistent with the Court's prior case law (with the possible exception of *Citizens United*) [and] it misunderstands the constitutional importance of the interests at stake. [T]he history of campaign finance reform shows [that] the anticorruption interest that drives Congress to regulate campaign contributions is a far broader, more important interest than the plurality acknowledges. It is an interest in maintaining the integrity of our public governmental institutions. And it is an interest rooted in the Constitution and in the First Amendment itself. [Speech] does not exist in a vacuum. Rather, political communication seeks to secure government action. A politically oriented 'marketplace of ideas' seeks to form a public opinion that can and will influence elected representatives. This is not a new idea. [Citing Whitney v. California, (Brandeis, J., concurring).] [Accordingly], the First Amendment advances not only the individual's right to engage in political speech, but also the public's interest in preserving a democratic order in which collective speech matters.

"What has this to do with corruption? It has everything to do with corruption. Corruption breaks the constitutionally necessary 'chain of communication' between the people and their representatives. [Where] enough money calls the tune, the general public will not be heard. Insofar as corruption cuts the link between political thought and political action, a free marketplace of political ideas loses its point. [The] 'appearance of corruption' can make matters worse. It can lead the public to believe that its efforts to communicate with its representatives or to help sway public opinion have little purpose. And a cynical public can lose interest in political participation altogether. The upshot is that the interests the Court has long described as preventing 'corruption' or the 'appearance of corruption' are more than ordinary factors to be weighed against the constitutional right to political speech. Rather, they are interests rooted in the First Amendment itself. They are rooted in the constitutional effort to create a democracy responsive to the people — a government where laws reflect the very thoughts, views, ideas, and sentiments, the expression of which the First Amendment protects. Given that end, we can and should understand campaign finance laws as resting upon a broader and more significant constitutional rationale than the plurality's limited definition of 'corruption' suggests. We should see these laws as seeking in significant part to strengthen, rather than weaken, the First Amendment. To say this is not to deny the potential for conflict between (1) the need to permit contributions that pay for the diffusion of ideas, and (2) the need to limit payments in order to help maintain the integrity of the electoral process. But that conflict takes place within, not outside, the First Amendment 's boundaries. . . .

"The plurality invalidates the aggregate contribution limits for a second reason. It believes they are no longer needed to prevent contributors from circumventing federal limits on direct contributions to individuals, political parties, and political action committees. [The] plurality is wrong. Here, as in *Buckley,* in the absence of limits on aggregate political contributions, donors can and likely will find ways to channel millions of dollars to parties and to individual candidates, [producing] 'corruption' or 'appearance of corruption.' The methods for using today's opinion to evade the law's individual contribution limits are complex, but they are well known, or will become well known, to party fundraisers. [Justice Breyer then described three such methods in detail.] The plurality believes that the three scenarios I have just depicted either pose no threat, or cannot or will not take place. Not so. [Justice Breyer then explained in detail why, in his view, the absence of aggregate contribution limits will, in fact, enable substantial circumvention of the base contribution limits.] . . .

"The plurality [substitutes its limited understanding] of how the political process works for the understanding of Congress, [and in so doing it] creates huge loopholes in the law [and] undermines, perhaps devastates, what remains of campaign finance reform."

Consider the following views:

a. Hellman, Defining Corruption and Constitutionalizing Democracy, 111 Mich. L. Rev. 1385 (2013):

> The main front in the battle over the constitutionality of campaign finance laws has long focused on defining corruption. [But] corruption is a derivative concept, meaning it depends on a theory of the institution or official involved. [What] constitutes corruption in a democracy depends on a theory of democracy. To put the point in a more grounded fashion, what constitutes corruption of legislators depends on a view of the proper basis for decisionmaking by elected officials. [Our] campaign finance case law contains at least three distinct conceptions of legislative corruption. I call these 'corruption as the deformation of judgment,' 'corruption as the distortion of influence,' and 'corruption as the sale of favors.' . . .
>
> On one view, a legislator ought to exercise his own independent judgment about each decision he faces. [The] legislator, according to this view, should consider only the merits-based reasons that bear on the decision at hand. [Corruption as the "deformation of judgment"] occurs when non-merits-based factors influence the legislator's judgment. . . .
>
> Corruption as the distortion of influence sees the legislator as properly attentive to the desires and preferences of those he represents. In a well-functioning democracy, the legislator responds to these desires and preferences. [On this

view,] corruption occurs when a legislator weighs the preferences of some too heavily, especially when the legislator considers the wishes of wealthy contributors more than others. . . .

A third view of proper legislative conduct [requires] only that the legislator not actually exchange votes or favors for money. [Corruption], on this view, is narrowly defined as quid pro quo corruption — that is, the sale of some public favor. . . .

[W]hen the Court defines corruption [in its campaign finance case law], it inescapably puts forward a conception of the proper role of a legislator in a democracy. That is a task that the Court should be cautious to take up. [Because there] are many reasonable ways to instantiate representative democracy, [we] should eschew judicial actions that adopt one view of representative democracy [over another]. Because judicial pronouncements about what constitutes corruption entail commitments to contested conceptions of democracy, there are strong reasons for courts to avoid defining corruption.

b. R. Post, Citizens Divided: Campaign Finance Reform and the Constitution 4, 60–65 (2014):

[P]roponents of campaign finance reform have failed to advance justifications for regulation that can be inosculated with basic First Amendment principles. They have instead promoted justifications like "distortion" or "equality," which are inconsistent with essential premises of First Amendment doctrine. . . .

[F]irst Amendment rights presuppose that elections must be structured to select for persons who possess the "communion of interests and sympathy of sentiments" to remain responsive to public opinion. [The concept of "electoral integrity" denominates] elections that have the property of choosing candidates whom the people trust to possess this sympathy and connection. Without electoral integrity, First Amendment rights necessarily fail to achieve their constitutional purpose. If the people do not believe that elected officials listen to public opinion, participation in public discourse, no matter how free, cannot create the experience of self-government. . . .

The democratic structure and legitimacy of our government depend on electoral integrity. Yet the Court in its campaign finance opinions has not considered the state's interest in promoting the electoral integrity required by the First Amendment. The Court has instead been preoccupied by the attempt to balance First Amendment rights against the need to prevent [quid pro quo] corruption. . . .

If [we] reformulate our campaign finance jurisprudence upon the principle of electoral integrity, [we] may create a more enduring foundation for the contested area of campaign finance reform. [This] formulation of the issue [requires] us merely to affirm [that] Americans cannot maintain the blessings of self-government unless they believe that elections produce representatives who are responsive to public opinion. [Electoral] integrity is a compelling government interest because without it Americans have no reason to exercise the communicative rights guaranteed by the First Amendment.

[There] are good reasons to worry that electoral integrity is today under threat. Americans' trust and confidence in their representative institutions has fallen to record lows; we are [experiencing] what most regard as a crisis of representation. In such circumstances it is especially disappointing that the Court seems unwilling to recognize even the existence of the constitutional principle of electoral integrity. . . .

### c. Lessig, What an Originalist Would Understand "Corruption" to Mean, 102 Cal. L. Rev. 1, 3–11 (2014):

The United States [effectively] has two distinct elections. One election is discete — call it the "voting election." [All] "voters" are permitted to participate in that election. [The] other election is continuous — call it the "money election." It happens throughout the election cycle. Any citizen [is] permitted to participate in that money election. [To] be allowed to run in the voting election [one] has to do extremely well in the money election. [In] the 2012 election cycle, 84 percent of the House candidates and 67 percent of the Senate candidates with more money than their opponents won. [The] money election produces a subtle, perhaps camouflaged bending [of the process] to keep the funders of the money election happy. [Importantly,] the relevant number of funders is [small]. [In] the 2012 presidential election 0.000032 percent [of Americans] — or 99 Americans — provided 60 percent of the individual Super PAC money spent. . . .

[The] way we fund elections has created a dependency that conflicts with the dependency intended by the Constitution. That conflict is a corruption. [In] the Framers' language, [the concept of "corruption"] included a collective sense — the corruption of an institution, or a people, and not just a person. [Congress] was intended to be "dependent on the people alone." It has become dependent upon an additional dependence, "the funders" of campaigns. Because of who "the funders" are, this additional dependence is a conflicting dependence, and that conflict constitutes "corruption."

This sense of corruption, as constituted by "improper dependence," was perfectly familiar to the Framers. It is with this sense of "corruption" in mind that we can see why our current Congress is "corrupt." For the Framers, Congress was [to] have an intended dependence. That dependence was to be, as James Madison wrote in The Federalist No. 52, "on the people." [For the Framers,] the anti-corruption challenge was not how to ensure that criminals stayed away from Congress; the challenge was how to secure the influences most likely to align the institution to its proper ends by protecting it from improper dependence. [It] is this fact that makes the current Supreme Court's jurisprudence about "corruption" so weird. [Only] a non-originalist could embrace [the Court's] position.

### d. L. Tribe and J. Matz, Uncertain Justice: The Roberts Court and the Constitution 100–101, 104–105, 108–109, 112–113 (2014):

*Citizens United* decisively rejected the anti-distortion justification for campaign finance laws. . . . To be sure, money can powerfully advantage a speaker in the marketplace of ideas [and] concentrated wealth, left unregulated, can create a risk that most headlines and TV ads will be controlled by a small group. . . . Still, it would be a mistake to leave judgments about the "proper" distribution of speech to politicians. Arming them with a roving license to level the playing field by silencing or adjusting the volume of disfavored speakers is an invitation to self-serving behavior and, ultimately, tyranny. The anti-distortion argument can too easily lead down this dangerous path, and [the Court] rightly discarded it. . . .

[Another argument made against the Court's approach in these cases focuses on a broad conception of "corruption."] "Corruption," in this view, occurs when politicians become dependent on a wealthy clique and government is no longer responsive to the public interest. [The justices in the majority in these cases] are unreservedly hostile to such arguments. They worry that noble-sounding rationales for campaign finance laws can too easily conceal efforts by incumbents to protect themselves and punish their enemies. [The Court has not adopted] a narrow definition of corruption because it is naïve or apathetic. It has done so because it doubts that the Court [can] create workable First Amendment law that adequately guards against abuse by politicians. Embracing a broader view of the anti-corruption interest risked creating an exception that swallowed the rule. . . .

In an age of political dysfunction, the extraordinary sums of money that candidates avidly pursue present hard questions about how to reconcile competing national values. [The Court's decisions in these cases will likely affect] policy outcomes by causing an across-the-board realignment of government priorities toward interests backed by big money. Every capable politician has an eye on the next election and a keen sense of who provided support last time, who didn't, who might be persuaded to shift their opinions, and how that might be achieved. [The Court's decisions are] therefore likely to trigger a self-reinforcing cycle. [As] the group of victorious candidates comes to consist mainly of politicians who can successfully navigate these structures and depend on them for reelection, the impetus for change among officeholders will fade. [Perhaps the best solution would be the enactment of new disclosure requirements.] In the post-*Citizens United* era, transparency would provide at least a measure of reassurance. . . .

e. In Six Amendments: How and Why We Should Change the Constitution (2014), former Justice John Paul Stevens proposed the following amendment to the Constitution:

Neither the First Amendment nor any other provision of this Constitution shall be construed to prohibit the Congress or any state from imposing reasonable limits on the amount of money that candidates for public office, or their supporters, may spend in election campaigns.

## Note: Additional Regulation of the Electoral Process

1. *Prohibiting paid petitioners.* In Meyer v. Grant, 486 U.S. 414 (1988), the Court invalidated a Colorado statute prohibiting the use of paid circulators to

obtain signatures for petitions to qualify proposed state constitutional amendments for inclusion on the general election ballot:

> The refusal to permit appellees to pay petition circulators restricts political expression in two ways: First, it limits the number of voices who will convey appellees' message and the hours they can speak and, therefore, limits the size of the audience they can reach. Second, it makes it less likely that appellees will garner the number of signatures necessary to place the matter on the ballot, thus limiting their ability to make the matter the focus of statewide attention. [Colorado's] prohibition of paid petition circulators restricts access to the most effective, fundamental, and perhaps economical avenue of political discourse, direct one-on-one communication.

See also Buckley v. American Constitutional Law Foundation, 525 U.S. 182 (1999), in which the Court, relying upon *Meyer*, invalidated a state law providing that (a) only registered voters may circulate ballot-initiative petitions; (b) petition circulators must wear a badge identifying them by name; and (c) ballot-initiative proponents must file a report listing each petition circulator by name and stating the amount paid to each circulator.

2. *Regulating campaign promises.* In Brown v. Hartlage, 456 U.S. 46 (1982), petitioner, a candidate for local office in Kentucky, promised the voters that, if elected, he would reduce the salary of the office "to a more realistic level." Petitioner was elected, but a state court declared the election void on the ground that petitioner had violated Kentucky's Corrupt Practices Act. The Court reversed:

> The [act] prohibits a political candidate from giving, or promising to give, anything of value to a voter in exchange for his vote or support. In many of its possible applications, this provision would appear to present little constitutional difficulty, for a State may surely prohibit a candidate from buying votes. [But here, petitioner's promise] was made openly, subject to the comment and criticism of his political opponent and to the scrutiny of the voters. [His] was a declaration of intention to exercise the fiscal powers of government office within what he believed [to] be the recognized framework of office. [Petitioner's] promise to reduce his salary cannot be considered as inviting the kind of corrupt arrangement the appearance of which a State may have a compelling interest in avoiding.

3. *Regulating the speech of judicial candidates.* Minnesota elects its judges. It prohibits candidates for judicial office from announcing their views of any disputed legal issues that might come before them as judges. In Republican Party of Minnesota v. White, 536 U.S. 735 (2002), the Court, in a five-to-four decision, held that this prohibition (known as the "announce clause") violated the first amendment.

§7324(a)(2), which prohibits federal employees from taking "an active part in political management or in political campaigns." Specifically, the act prohibits federal employees from soliciting contributions for a partisan political purpose, taking an active part in a political campaign, soliciting votes for any candidate, or endorsing any candidate. The Court, in an opinion by Justice White, expressly reaffirmed United Public Workers v. Mitchell, 330 U.S. 75 (1947), and upheld the act:

> [Until] after the Civil War, the spoils system under which federal employees came and went depending upon party service and changing administrations, was the prevalent basis for governmental employment and advancement. [That] system did not survive. [[It is now] the judgment of Congress, the Executive, and the country [that] partisan political activities by federal employees must be limited if the Government is to operate effectively and fairly, elections are to play their proper part in representative government, and employees themselves are to be sufficiently free from improper influences. The restrictions [imposed] on federal employees are not aimed at particular parties, groups, or points of view, but apply equally to all partisan activities of the type described. . . .
>
> [The] problem in any case is to arrive at a balance between the interests of the [employee] and the [interests] of the [government]. Although Congress is free to strike a different balance than it has, [we] think the balance it [has] struck is sustainable by the obviously important interests sought to be served by [the] Hatch Act.
>
> It seems fundamental [that] employees [of] the Government [should] administer the law in accordance with the will of Congress, rather than in accordance with [the] will of a political party. [Moreover,] it is not only important that [Government] employees in fact avoid practicing political justice, but [also] that they appear to the public to be avoiding it, if confidence in the system of representative Government is not to be eroded. [Another] major concern [is] the conviction that the rapidly expanding Government work force should not be employed to build a powerful, invincible, and perhaps corrupt political machine. [A] related concern [is] to make sure that Government employees [are] free from pressure [to] vote in a certain way or perform political chores in order to curry favor with their superiors rather than to act out of their own beliefs.

Justices Douglas, joined by Justices Brennan and Marshall, dissented: "The Hatch Act [prohibits] federal employees from taking 'an active part in political management or in political campaigns.' [No] one could object if employees were barred from using office time to engage in outside activities whether political or otherwise. But it is of no concern of Government what an employee does in his spare time, [unless] what he does impairs efficiency or other facets of the merits of his job. Some [activities may] affect the employee's job performance. But his political creed, like his religion, is irrelevant. In the areas of speech, like religion, it is of no concern what the employee says in private to his wife or to the public in Constitution Hall."

In Broadrick v. Oklahoma, 413 U.S. 601 (1973), decided on the same day as *Letter Carriers*, the Court upheld Oklahoma's Merit System of Personnel Administration Act, which "serves roughly the same function as the analogous provisions of the other 49 States, and is patterned on §9(a) of the Hatch Act." Appellants, several state employees charged with violating the Oklahoma act, maintained that the act was unconstitutionally overbroad because it had been construed to prohibit public employees from wearing political buttons and displaying political bumper stickers. Finding that appellants' own activities could clearly be proscribed, and that the act was not "substantially" overbroad, the Court found it unnecessary to decide the overbreadth issue. See Chapter III.A, supra. Can Oklahoma constitutionally prohibit its public employees from wearing political buttons and displaying political bumper stickers? For an interesting variation, see United States v. National Treasury Employees Union, 513 U.S. 454 (1995) (invalidating a provision of the Ethics in Government Act that prohibited a broad class of government employees from accepting any compensation for making speeches or writing articles without regard to whether the subject of the speech or article or the person or group paying the honorarium had any connection with the employee's official duties).

2. *Criticizing government policy.* In Pickering v. Board of Education, 391 U.S. 563 (1968), a teacher was dismissed from his position by the Board of Education for sending a letter to a local newspaper in connection with a recently proposed tax increase that was critical of the way in which the board and the district superintendent of schools had handled past proposals to raise new revenue for the schools. The teacher's dismissal resulted from a determination by the board, after a full hearing, that the publication of the letter was "detrimental to the efficient operation and administration of the schools of the district." The Court, in an opinion by Justice Marshall, held that the teacher's right to freedom of speech had been violated:

> The problem in any case is to arrive at a balance between the interests of the teacher, as a citizen, in commenting upon matters of public concern and the interest of the State, as an employer, in promoting the efficiency of the public services it performs through its employees. . . .
>
> An examination of the statements in appellant's letter objected to by the Board reveals that [they] consist essentially of criticism of the Board's allocation of school funds between educational and athletic programs. [The] statements are in no way directed towards any person with whom appellant would normally be in contact in the course of his daily work as a teacher. Thus no question of maintaining either discipline by immediate superiors or harmony among cow-orkers is presented here. Appellant's employment relationships with the Board and, to a somewhat lesser extent, with the superintendent are not the kind of close working relationships for which it can persuasively be claimed that personal loyalty and confidence are necessary to their proper functioning. Accordingly, to the extent that the Board's position here can be taken to suggest

## Note: Litigation and the First Amendment

1. Button *in context.* Consider H. Kalven, The Negro and the First Amendment 66–69, 75–79 (1965):

> One of the most distinctive features of the Negro revolution [of the 1950s and 1960s was] its almost military assault on the Constitution via the strategy of systematic litigation. [Chapter 33 was designed] to slow down [NAACP litigation]. Unless the NAACP [could go] out and sign up the client, pay for the case, and deliver the client to one of its expert lawyers, it [would have been] unable to recruit the needed flow of litigation. Unless it [could] control the timing and line of attack in the litigation once it was begun, its grand strategy of war by lawsuit [would have been] frustrated. [The] case thus raised a profound question for our scheme of constitutional adjudication.

2. *Litigation as "speech."* Why does *Button* pose a first amendment issue? Because the law might be discriminatorily applied against persons espousing a particular view? Because association for the purpose of litigation is "speech"? Because litigation is "speech"? Because litigation is "speech" when it attempts to enforce constitutional rights? In Borough of Duryea, Pennsylvania v. Guarnieri, 131 S. Ct. 2438 (2011), the Court held that "the Petition Clause protects the right of individuals to appeal to courts [for] the resolution of legal disputes." In a dissenting opinion, Justice Scalia concluded that "the proposition that a lawsuit is a constitutionally protected 'Petition'" is "quite doubtful." Scalia reasoned that "[t]here is abundant historical evidence that 'Petitions' were directed to the executive and legislative branches of government, not to the courts." Nonetheless, recognizing that some "scholars have made detailed historical arguments to the contrary," and because the parties had not litigated the issue, he agreed to "leave its resolution to another day." If litigation is not "Petition," can it still be "Speech"?

3. *The reach of* Button: Primus. In In re Primus, 436 U.S. 412 (1978), an ACLU "cooperating lawyer" wrote a letter to a woman who had been sterilized, informing her of the ACLU's willingness to provide free legal representation to women in her position in a proposed lawsuit challenging the constitutionality of an alleged program of sterilizing pregnant mothers as a condition of their continued receipt of Medicaid benefits. The Disciplinary Board of the South Carolina Supreme Court reprimanded the ACLU lawyer for violating a disciplinary rule prohibiting any "lawyer who has given unsolicited advice to a layman that he should [take] legal action [to] accept employment resulting from that advice."

The Court held the reprimand unconstitutional. The Court emphasized that "for the ACLU, as for the NAACP, 'litigation is not a technique of resolving private differences'; it is 'a form of political expression' and 'political association.'" To justify a restriction on such "'core First Amendment rights,'" the state must demonstrate that the attorney's "activity in fact involved the type of misconduct at which South Carolina's [prohibition on solicitation] is said to be directed." Since the record did "not support [the state's] contention that undue influence, overreaching, misrepresentation, or invasion of privacy [had] actually occurred," the reprimand violated the first amendment.

See also United Transportation Union v. State Bar of Michigan, 401 U.S. 576 (1971) (invalidating an injunction prohibiting the union from recommending attorneys to its members only if the attorneys agreed that their fees would not exceed 25 percent of the recovery); United Mine Workers v. Illinois Bar Association, 389 U.S. 217 (1967) (invalidating an injunction prohibiting the union from employing a salaried attorney to assist its members with workers' compensation claims); Brotherhood of Railroad Trainmen v. Virginia State Bar, 377 U.S. 1 (1964) (invalidating an injunction prohibiting a union from recommending lawyers to its members to represent them in railroad personal injury litigation).

4. *The reach of* Button: Ohralik. In Ohralik v. Ohio State Bar Association, 436 U.S. 447 (1978), decided on the same day as *Primus*, appellant, an attorney, after learning about an automobile accident, personally contacted two young women who had been injured in the accident and arranged to represent them in subsequent litigation. As a result of this "ambulance chasing," Ohralik was suspended by the Ohio State Bar for violation of a disciplinary rule prohibiting any "lawyer who has given unsolicited advice to a layman that he should obtain counsel" to accept "employment resulting from that advice."

The Court upheld the suspension. The Court explained that *Ohralik* was not governed by *Button* and *Primus*, for appellant's "approaches to the young women [did not involve] political expression or an exercise of associational freedom '[to] secure constitutionally guaranteed civil rights.'" Moreover, *Ohralik* was not governed by the union cases, for "[appellant cannot] compare his solicitation to the mutual assistance in asserting legal rights that was at issue [in those cases]." Indeed, a "lawyer's procurement of remunerative employment is a subject only marginally affected with First Amendment concerns. It falls within the State's proper sphere of economic and professional regulation." Appellant's conduct, the Court added, was analogous to commercial expression, which occupies only a "subordinate position in the scale of First Amendment values."

**NAACP v. ALABAMA, 357 U.S. 449 (1958).** Alabama has a statute, similar to those of many other states, that requires out-of-state corporations to qualify before doing business in the state. For membership organizations, this requirement includes disclosure of the names and addresses of all Alabama members of the organization. In an opinion by Justice Harlan, the Court held at the height of the civil rights movement in the South that this otherwise valid requirement could not constitutionally be applied to the NAACP:

"It is hardly a novel perception that compelled disclosure of affiliation with groups engaged in advocacy may constitute [an effective] restraint on freedom ambit, a group must engage in some form of expression, whether it be public or private. . . .

"The Boy Scouts is a private, nonprofit organization. According to its 'mission statement,' [the] general mission of the Boy Scouts is '[t]o instill values in young people.' The Boy Scouts seeks to instill these values by having its adult leaders spend time with the youth members, instructing and engaging them in activities like camping, archery, and fishing. During the time spent with the youth members, the scoutmasters and assistant scoutmasters inculcate them with the Boy Scouts' values — both expressly and by example. It seems indisputable that an association that seeks to transmit such a system of values engages in expressive activity. . . .

"Given that the Boy Scouts engages in expressive activity, we must determine whether the forced inclusion of Dale as an assistant scoutmaster would significantly affect the Boy Scouts' ability to advocate public or private viewpoints. This inquiry necessarily requires us first to explore, to a limited extent, the nature of the Boy Scouts' view of homosexuality. [Although the] Boy Scout Oath and Law do not expressly mention sexuality or sexual orientation, [the] Boy Scouts asserts that it 'teach[es] that homosexual conduct is not morally straight' [and] that it does 'not want to promote homosexual conduct as a legitimate form of behavior.' [We] accept the Boy Scouts' assertion. . . .

"We must then determine whether Dale's presence as an assistant scoutmaster would significantly burden the Boy Scouts' desire to not 'promote homosexual conduct as a legitimate form of behavior.' As we give deference to an association's assertions regarding the nature of its expression, we must also give deference to an association's view of what would impair its expression. [That] is not to say that an expressive association can erect a shield against antidiscrimination laws simply by asserting that mere acceptance of a member from a particular group would impair its message. But here Dale, by his own admission, is one of a group of gay Scouts who have 'become leaders in their community and are open and honest about their sexual orientation.' Dale was the co-president of a gay and lesbian organization at college and remains a gay rights activist. Dale's presence in the Boy Scouts would, at the very least, force the organization to send a message, both to the youth members and the world, that the Boy Scouts accepts homosexual conduct as a legitimate form of behavior.

"The New Jersey Supreme Court determined that the Boy Scouts' ability to disseminate its message was not significantly affected by the forced inclusion of Dale as an assistant scoutmaster because 'Boy Scout members do not associate for the purpose of disseminating the belief that homosexuality is immoral.' [We] disagree with the New Jersey Supreme Court's [reasoning]. First, associations do not have to associate for the 'purpose' of disseminating a certain message in order to be entitled to the protections of the First Amendment. An association must merely engage in expressive activity that could be impaired in order to be entitled to protection. Second, [the] First Amendment simply does not require that every member of a group agree on every issue in order for the group's policy to be 'expressive association.' The Boy Scouts takes an official position with respect to homosexual conduct, and that is sufficient for First Amendment purposes. . . .

"Having determined that the Boy Scouts is an expressive association and that the forced inclusion of Dale would significantly affect its expression, we inquire whether the application of New Jersey's public accommodations law to require that the Boy Scouts accept Dale as an assistant scoutmaster runs afoul of the Scouts' freedom of expressive association. We conclude that it does. . . .

"We recognized in cases such as *Roberts* [that] States have a compelling interest in eliminating discrimination against women in public accommodations. But in each of these cases we went on to conclude that the enforcement of these statutes would not materially interfere with the ideas that the organization sought to express. In *Roberts*, we said '[i]ndeed, the Jaycees has failed to demonstrate [any] serious burden on the male members' freedom of expressive association.' We thereupon concluded in each of these cases that the organizations' First Amendment rights were not violated by the application of the States' public accommodations laws.

"[We] have already concluded that a state requirement that the Boy Scouts retain Dale as an assistant scoutmaster would significantly burden the organization's right to oppose or disfavor homosexual conduct. The state interests embodied in New Jersey's public accommodations law do not justify such a severe intrusion on the Boy Scouts' rights to freedom of expressive association. That being the case, we hold that the First Amendment prohibits the State from imposing such a requirement through the application of its public accommodations law."

Justice Stevens, joined by Justices Souter, Ginsburg, and Breyer, dissented: "[Until] today, we have never once found a claimed right to associate in the selection of members to prevail in the face of a State's antidiscrimination law. To the contrary, we have squarely held that a State's antidiscrimination law does not violate a group's right to associate simply because the law conflicts with that group's exclusionary membership policy. [Citing *Roberts*.]

"Surely there are instances in which an organization that truly aims to foster a belief at odds with the purposes of a State's antidiscrimination laws will have a First Amendment right to association that precludes forced compliance with those laws. But that right is not a freedom to discriminate at will, nor is it a right to maintain an exclusionary membership policy simply out of fear of what the public reaction would be if the group's membership were opened up. It is an implicit right designed to protect the enumerated rights of the First Amendment, not a license to act on any discriminatory impulse. To prevail in asserting a right of expressive association as a defense to a charge of violating an antidiscrimination law, the organization must at least show it has adopted and advocated an unequivocal position inconsistent with a position advocated or epitomized by the person whom the organization seeks to exclude. . . .

featuring the Confederate battle flag on the ground that the plate consisted of government, rather than private, speech:

> Our determination that Texas's specialty license plate designs are government speech does not mean that the designs do not also implicate the free speech rights of private persons. We have acknowledged that drivers who display a State's selected license plate designs convey the messages communicated through those designs. [*Wooley*]. And we have recognized that the First Amendment stringently limits a State's authority to compel a private party to express a view with which the private party disagrees. But here, compelled private speech is not at issue. And just as Texas cannot require [The Sons of Confederate Veterans] to convey "the State's ideological message," [*Wooley*], [The Sons of Confederate Veterans] cannot force Texas to include a Confederate battle flag on its specialty license plates.

4. *A St. Patrick's Day parade.* The City of Boston authorized the South Boston Allied War Veterans Council to organize the annual St. Patrick's Day Parade. The council refused a place in the parade to GLIB, an organization formed for the purpose of expressing its members' pride in their Irish heritage as openly gay, lesbian, and bisexual individuals. GLIB filed suit claiming that this refusal violated a Massachusetts law prohibiting discrimination on account of sexual orientation in places of public accommodation. In Hurley v. Irish-American Gay, Lesbian and Bisexual Group of Boston, 515 U.S. 557 (1995), the Court, in a unanimous opinion by Justice Souter, held that application of the statute in this context violated the first amendment rights of the council.

The Court explained that, because "every participating unit affects the message conveyed by the private organizers," application of the statute in this context effectively required the council "to alter the expressive content" of its parade. The Court declared that "this use of the State's power violates the fundamental rule" that "a speaker has the autonomy to choose the content of his own message." Thus, if the council "objects," for example, to GLIB's implicit assertion that homosexuals and bisexuals are entitled to full and equal "social acceptance," it has a right "not to propound" this message.

The Court held that *PruneYard* was distinguishable because (1) the proprietors of the shopping center "were running 'a business establishment that [was] open to the public,'" (2) they "could 'expressly disavow any connection with the message by simply posting signs in the areas where the speakers or hand-billers stand,'" and (3) the shopping center owners' own right to speak was not implicated because they "did not even allege that [they] objected to the content" of the speech. On the disclaimer issue, the Court observed that disclaimers would not be sufficient to protect the interests of the council because "such disclaimers would be quite curious in a moving parade."

5. *Military recruiting in law schools.* Most law schools do not permit employers who discriminate on the basis of race, religion, gender, national origin, or

sexual orientation to use their placement facilities. In the 1980s, most law schools extended this policy to the U.S. military, because it discriminated on the basis of sexual orientation. In response, Congress enacted the Solomon Amendment, which provides that if any part of an institution of higher education denies military recruiters access equal to that provided other recruiters, the entire institution will lose access to federal funds. Because most universities are heavily dependent on federal support for research and financial aid, most law schools waived their nondiscrimination policy as applied to the military. The Forum for Academic and Institutional Rights (FAIR), an association of law schools and law faculties, filed suit to enjoin the application of the Solomon Amendment on the ground that it violates the first amendment.

In a unanimous decision, the Court rejected this argument in Rumsfeld v. FAIR, 547 U.S. 47 (2006). In his opinion for the Court, Chief Justice Roberts observed that the Solomon Amendment "gives universities a choice: Either allow military recruiters the same [access] afforded any other recruiter or forgo certain federal funds." Roberts distinguished *Hurley* on the ground that in that case "the complaining speaker's own message was affected by the speech it was forced to accommodate." Indeed, he explained, the "expressive nature of a parade was central" to the result in *Hurley*. In this case, however, "accommodating the military's message does not affect the law schools' speech, because the schools are not speaking when they host interviews and recruiting receptions. Unlike a parade organizer's choice of parade contingents, a law school's decision to allow recruiters on campus is not inherently expressive." Roberts concluded that, in this respect, the case was governed by *PruneYard*.

6. *Conditions on recipients of public funds.* See Agency for International Development v. Alliance for Open Society International, 133 S. Ct. 2321 (2013), supra.

7. *Union dues.* May a state compel government employees to pay union dues? See Abood v. Detroit Board of Education, 431 U.S. 209 (1977) (upholding a state statute authorizing unions representing government employees to charge members dues insofar as the dues are used to support collective bargaining and related activities, but invalidating the statute insofar as the union uses the dues "to contribute to political candidates and to express political views unrelated to its duties as exclusive bargaining representative"); Ellis v. Brotherhood of Railway, Airline & Steamship Clerks, 466 U.S. 85 (1984) (compelled contributions may constitutionally be used to pay for union conventions, social activities, and publications); Keller v. State Bar of California, 496 U.S. 1 (1990) (an integrated state bar association may not use compulsory dues to finance political and ideological activities with which particular members disagree when such expenditures are not "necessarily or reasonably incurred for the purpose of regulating the legal profession or improving the quality of legal services"); Lehnert v. Ferris Faculty Association, 500 U.S. 507 (1991) (a union may constitutionally charge dissenting employees only for those activities that are (1) "germane" to collective bargaining; (2) justified

by the government's interests in labor peace and avoiding free riders; and (3) not significantly burdening of speech); Davenport v. Washington Education Association, 551 U.S. 177 (2007) (a state may constitutionally require public-sector unions to receive affirmative authorization from nonmembers before spending their agency fees for election-related purposes); Knox v. Service Employees International Union, 132 S. Ct. 2277 (2012) (when a public-sector union imposes a special assessment or midyear dues increase, the union cannot constitutionally require nonmembers to pay the increased amount unless they choose to opt in by affirmatively consenting).

In Harris v. Quinn, 134 S. Ct. 2618 (2014), the Court considered the constitutionality of an Illinois law that allowed Medicaid recipients who normally would need institutional care to hire a "personal assistant" (PA) to provide homecare services. Under the law, the Medicaid homecare recipients and the state both play a role in the employment relationship with the PAs.

Pursuant to this program, the Service Employees International Union (SEIU) was designated the exclusive union representative for the PAs. SEIU entered into collective-bargaining agreements with the state that included an agency fee provision, which requires PAs who do not wish to join the union to pay the union a fee for the cost of collective-bargaining expenses but not for the cost of any political activities of the union unrelated to collective bargaining. A group of PAs who have not joined the union and do not want to pay any union fees brought this suit claiming that the law violated their first amendment right not to be compelled to support the union. Pursuant to *Abood*, the lower courts rejected this challenge and upheld the law.

In a five-to-four decision, the Supreme Court reversed. In an opinion by Justice Alito, the Court cast serious doubt on *Abood*, insofar as it permitted the state to compel nonunion members to pay union fees even for the costs of collective-bargaining activities that benefit them. Ultimately, though, the Court invalidated the law without overruling *Abood*, by distinguishing the specific factual situation in the context of PAs from the situations in other public union arrangements. Justice Kagan, joined by Justices Ginsburg, Breyer, and Sotomayor, dissented. Kagan insisted that *Abood* reflected sound first amendment principles and that the situation in this case was not in any principled way distinguishable from the Court's prior decisions.

8. *Student activity fees.* Board of Regents of the University of Wisconsin System v. Southworth, 529 U.S. 217 (2000), concerned the constitutionality of the University of Wisconsin's requirement that all full-time students pay an annual activities fee, part of which is allocated by the student government to support registered student organizations that engage in a broad range of expressive and other activities. Examples of the more than six hundred registered student organizations at the University of Wisconsin are the College Democrats, the College Republicans, the International Socialist Organization, and the Future Financial Gurus of America. Citing *Abood*, respondents challenged the constitutionality of this program on the ground that by compelling

them financially to support political and ideological expression with which they disagree, the program violates their first amendment right "not to speak."

In a unanimous decision, the Court rejected this challenge. Justice Kennedy authored the opinion of the Court:

> In *Abood* [the] constitutional rule took the form of limiting the required subsidy to speech germane to the purposes of the [union]. The standard of germane speech as applied to student speech at a university is [unworkable]. The speech the University seeks to encourage in the program before us is distinguished not by discernable limits but by its vast, unexplored bounds. To insist upon asking what speech is germane would be contrary to the very goal the University seeks to pursue. It is not for the Court to say what is or is not germane to the ideas to be pursued in an institution of higher learning. . . .

9. *The right not to publish or broadcast.* In what circumstances, if any, may government constitutionally compel a broadcaster or publisher to broadcast or publish material? See Denver Area Education Telecommunications Consortium, Inc. v. FCC, 518 U.S. 727 (1996) (considering the constitutionality of several provisions of the Cable Television Consumer Protection and Competition Act of 1992 concerning the broadcasting of "indecent" programming on public access and leased access channels); Turner Broadcasting System Inc. v. FCC, 512 U.S. 622 (1994) (upholding "must carry" provisions for cable television); Columbia Broadcasting System v. FCC, 453 U.S. 367 (1981) (upholding an FCC rule requiring broadcasters "to allow reasonable access [by] a legally qualified candidate for Federal elective office on behalf of his candidacy"); Miami Herald Publishing Co. v. Tornillo, 418 U.S. 241 (1974) (invalidating a "right of reply" statute requiring any newspaper that "assails" the character of a political candidate to print the candidate's reply); Red Lion Broadcasting Co. v. FCC, 395 U.S. 367 (1969) (upholding the FCC's "fairness doctrine").

10. *Compelled abortion counseling.* Do statutes that require women seeking an abortion to undergo counseling violate the First Amendment? For an argument that they do, see Corbin, Compelled Disclosures, 54 Ala. L. Rev. 1277 (2014). At least one lower court has upheld mandatory counseling against a free speech attack. See Texas Medical Providers Performing Abortion Services v. Lakey, 667 F. 3d 570 (5th Cir. 2012). On the other hand, as Corbin points out, some lower courts have invalidated statutes requiring "crisis pregnancy centers" to disclose the fact that they do not make referrals for abortions or birth control services. Are the two situations distinguishable?

11. *Is there a right not to speak?* Consider Massaro, Tread on Me!, 17 U. Pa. J. Const. L. 365, 368 (2014):

> Contrary to Justice Robert Jackson's rhetorically arresting "no fixed star" celebration of individual freedom from compulsory pledges of allegiance,

government often demands private expression, crafts it, or silences it altogether. Constitutionally mandated oaths of office, occupation-specific codes of conduct, audience and context-specific regulation of the content of information disclosures, many employment and civil rights statutes, student conduct codes, conditions on government benefits, anti-fraud laws, and many other forms of government speech regulation demonstrate that there is no across-the-board constitutional mandate against government-compelled expression.

## Note: Content-Neutral Restrictions — Final Thoughts

Consider the following evaluation: The Court has long recognized that by limiting the availability of particular means of communication, content-neutral restrictions can significantly impair the ability of individuals to communicate their views to others. This is a central first amendment concern. The Court generally tests content-neutral restrictions with an implicit balancing approach: The greater the interference with the opportunities for free expression, the greater the burden on government to justify the restriction. When the challenged restriction has a relatively severe effect, the Court invokes strict scrutiny. See, e.g., *Button*; *Buckley* (expenditure limitations); *Roberts*. When the challenged restriction has a significant, but not severe, effect, the Court employs intermediate scrutiny. See, e.g., *Schneider*; *Buckley* (contribution limitations); *Martin*. And when the restriction has a relatively modest effect, the Court applies deferential scrutiny. See, e.g., *O'Brien*; *Heffron*, Chapter IV, supra; *Clark*, supra. There are exceptions to this pattern, and the exceptions are often quite revealing, for they suggest the impact of additional factors, such as "public property" or "incidental effect," that may trump the central concern of content-neutral analysis. But the general pattern is clear: As the restrictive effect increases, the standard of review increases as well. Is this an accurate description of the Court's analysis? If so, does it reflect a satisfactory approach? See Stone, Content-Neutral Restrictions, 54 U. Chi. L. Rev. 46 (1987).

For critical analyses of the Court's content-based/content-neutral distinction, see Bhagwat, Purpose Scrutiny in Constitutional Analysis, 85 Cal. L. Rev. 297 (1997); McDonald, Speech and Distrust: Rethinking the Content Approach to Protecting the Freedom of Expression, 81 Notre Dame L. Rev. 1347 (2006); Huhn, Assessing the Constitutionality of Laws That Are Both Content-Based and Content-Neutral: The Emerging Constitutional Calculus, 79 Ind. L.J. 801 (2004).

Consider Kendrick, Content Discrimination Revisited, 98 Va. L. Rev. 231, 235–242, 299–300 (2012):

At a high level of generality, content discrimination is, as a doctrinal matter, fairly straightforward. In application, however, critics argue that it is inconsistent and confused. [The] two basic ideas behind the content-discrimination principle are that it is usually wrong for the government to regulate speech

## E.  Other Means of Expression

because of what it is saying and that it is usually acceptable, as a First Amendment matter, for the government to regulate speech for reasons other than what
is saying. . . .

[Some] critics contend that, even if the content-discrimination principle
normatively acceptable, the doctrine implementing this principle has been
utter failure. Content analysis is unpredictable and imposes little, if any, restraint
on judicial decision-making. [The] upshot [they say] is that the doctrinal rules
are so unclear that the Court picks and chooses among its own pronouncements
to suit its own ends. . . . .

There may be many reasons to reconsider the content-discrimination
principle, but incoherence is not a good one. Tracing the contours of the
principle [illustrates] that the Court's conception of content discrimination
[has] proved surprisingly coherent in both aim and approach. Overhauling it
would risk upending this coherence. . . .

# VI

## Freedom of the Press

This chapter examines the first amendment's guarantee of "freedom [of] the press." The focus is on four questions. First, in what circumstances, if any, is the press, because of its constitutionally protected status, exempt from laws of otherwise general application? Second, to what extent, if any, does the first amendment guarantee a right to "gather" news? Third, in what circumstances, if any, may government treat the press differently from other institutions? Fourth, in what circumstances, if any, may government regulate the press in order to improve the "marketplace of ideas"?

## A. A "PREFERRED" STATUS FOR THE PRESS?

The first amendment prohibits any law "abridging the freedom of speech, or of the press." Does the press clause confer any rights that would not be conferred by the speech clause alone? Consider the views of Justice Stewart and Chief Justice Burger:

a. Stewart, "Or of the Press," 26 Hastings L.J. 631, 633–634 (1975):

The publishing business is the only organized private business that is given explicit constitutional protection. [If] the Free Press guarantee meant no more than freedom of expression, it would be a constitutional redundancy. [By] including both [the speech and press] guarantees in the First Amendment, the Founders quite clearly recognized the distinction between the two. [In] setting up the three branches of the Federal Government, the Founders deliberately created an internally competitive system. [The] primary purpose of the constitutional guarantee of a free press was [to] create a fourth institution outside the Government as an additional check on the three official branches. [The] relevant metaphor [is that] of the Fourth Estate. [The first amendment thus protects] the institutional autonomy of the press.

b. First National Bank of Boston v. Bellotti, 435 U.S. 765, 797–801 (1978)
(Burger, C.J., concurring):

> [There are those] who view the Press Clause as somehow conferring special and
> extraordinary privileges or status on the "institutional press." [I] perceive two
> fundamental difficulties with [such a] reading of the Press Clause. First,
> although certainty on this point is not possible, the history of the Clause does
> not suggest that the authors contemplated a "special" or "institutional" privilege.
> [Most] pre-First Amendment commentators "who employed the term 'freedom
> of speech' [used] it synonymously with freedom of the press." [The] second
> fundamental difficulty with interpreting the Press Clause as conferring special
> status on a limited group is one of definition. [The] very task of including some
> entities within the "institutional press" while excluding others [is] reminiscent of
> the abhorred licensing system [that] the First Amendment was intended to ban.
> [In my view,] the First Amendment does not "belong" to any definable category
> of persons or entities: It belongs to all who exercise its freedoms.

Consider also Associated Press v. NLRB, 301 U.S. 103 (1937). The Associated Press is a cooperative organization whose members in 1937 included
approximately 1,350 newspapers. It collects, compiles, and distributes news
to its members. The NLRB found that the Associated Press discharged an
employee in violation of section 7 of the National Labor Relations Act,
which confers on employees the right to organize and to bargain collectively.
The Court, in a five-to-four decision, held that application of section 7 to the
Associated Press did not violate the first amendment:

> The business of the Associated Press is not immune from regulation because it is
> an agency of the press. The publisher of a newspaper has no special immunity
> from the application of general laws. He has no special privilege to invade the
> rights and liberties of others. He must answer for libel. He may be punished for
> contempt of court. He is subject to the anti-trust laws. Like others he must pay
> equitable and nondiscriminatory taxes on his business. The regulation here in
> question has no relation whatever to the impartial distribution of news.

See also Dun & Bradstreet v. Greenmoss Builders, Chapter IV.A, supra (the
media are not entitled to any greater protection against actions for libel than
other speakers); Citizen Publishing Co. v. United States, 394 U.S. 131 (1969)
(Sherman Antitrust Act); Oklahoma Press Publishing Co. v. Walling, 327 U.S.
186 (1946) (Fair Labor Standards Act); cf. Grosjean v. American Press Co.,
297 U.S. 233 (1936) (taxation). Are these decisions consistent with Justice
Stewart's contention that the "publishing business is the only organized private
business that is given explicit constitutional protection"? Are there *some* circumstances in which the first amendment exempts the press from tax, labor,
antitrust, or other laws of general application?

# B.   A RIGHT TO "GATHER" NEWS?

## Branzburg v. Hayes

408 U.S. 665 (1972)

Opinion of the Court by MR. JUSTICE WHITE. . . .

[Branzburg, a newspaper reporter, published several articles describing unlawful drug activities in Frankfort, Kentucky. He refused, on first amendment grounds, to disclose to a state grand jury the identities of the persons whose activities he had described.]

The issue in these cases is whether requiring newsmen to appear and testify before state or federal grand juries abridges the freedom of speech and press guaranteed by the First Amendment. We hold that it does not.

Petitioners [press] First Amendment claims that may be simply put: that to gather news it is often necessary to agree either not to identify the source of information published or to publish only part of the facts revealed, or both; that if the reporter is nevertheless forced to reveal these confidences to a grand jury, the source so identified and other confidential sources of other reporters will be measurably deterred from furnishing publishable information, all to the detriment of the free flow of information protected by the First Amendment. Although the newsmen [do] not claim an absolute privilege against official interrogation in all circumstances, they assert that the reporter should not be forced either to appear or to testify before a grand jury or at trial until and unless sufficient grounds are shown for believing that the reporter possesses information relevant to a crime the grand jury is investigating, that the information the reporter has is unavailable from other sources, and that the need for the information is sufficiently compelling to override the claimed invasion of First Amendment interests occasioned by the disclosure. [The] heart of the claim is that the burden on news gathering resulting from compelling reporters to disclose confidential information outweighs any public interest in obtaining the information.

We do not question the significance of free speech, press, or assembly to the country's welfare. Nor is it suggested that news gathering does not qualify for First Amendment protection; without some protection for seeking out the news, freedom of the press could be eviscerated. But these cases involve no [restriction] on what the press may publish, and no express or implied command that the press publish what it prefers to withhold. [The] use of confidential sources by the press is not forbidden or restricted. [The] sole issue before us is the obligation of reporters to respond to grand jury subpoenas as other citizens do and to answer questions relevant to an investigation into the commission of crime. . . .

[The] First Amendment does not invalidate every incidental burdening of the press that may result from the enforcement of civil or criminal statutes of general applicability. [Citing Associated Press v. NLRB; Oklahoma Press Publishing Co. v. Walling.] . . .

It has generally been held that the First Amendment does not guarantee the press a constitutional right of special access to information not available to the public generally. [In Zemel v. Rusk, 381 U.S. 1 (1965)], for example, the Court sustained the Government's refusal to validate passports to Cuba even though that restriction "render[ed] less than wholly free the flow of information concerning that country." The ban on travel was held constitutional, for "[t]he right to speak and publish does not carry with it the unrestrained right to gather information."

Despite the fact that news gathering may be hampered, the press is regularly excluded from grand jury proceedings, our own conferences, the meetings of other official bodies gathered in executive session, and the meetings of private organizations. Newsmen have no constitutional right of access to the scenes of crime or disaster when the general public is excluded, and they may be prohibited from [attending] trials if such restrictions are necessary to assure a defendant a fair trial before an impartial tribunal. . . .

It is thus not surprising that the great weight of authority is that newsmen are not exempt from the normal duty of appearing before a grand jury and answering questions relevant to a criminal investigation. [The] prevailing constitutional view of the newsman's privilege is very much rooted in the ancient role of the grand jury. [Because] its task is to inquire into the existence of possible criminal conduct and to return only well-founded indictments, its investigative powers are necessarily broad. [On] the records now before us, we perceive no basis for holding that the public interest in law enforcement and in ensuring effective grand jury proceedings is insufficient to override the consequential, but uncertain, burden on news gathering that is said to result from insisting that reporters, like other citizens, respond to relevant questions put to them in the course of a valid grand jury investigation or criminal trial.

This conclusion [does not] threaten the vast bulk of confidential relationships between reporters and their sources. [Only] where news sources themselves are implicated in crime or possess information relevant to the grand jury's task need they or the reporter be concerned about grand jury subpoenas. Nothing before us indicates that a large number or percentage of all confidential news sources falls into either category and would in any way be deterred by our holding. . . .

[Moreover, although the] argument that the flow of news will be diminished by compelling reporters to aid the grand jury in a criminal investigation is not [irrational, we] remain unclear how often and to what extent informers are actually deterred from furnishing information when newsmen are forced to testify before a grand jury. [The] evidence fails to demonstrate that there would be a significant constriction of the flow of news to the public if this Court

reaffirms the prior common-law and constitutional rule regarding the
testimonial obligations of newsmen.[33]

[Furthermore, the] administration of a constitutional newsman's privilege
would present practical and conceptual difficulties of a high order. Sooner or
later, it would be necessary to define those categories of newsmen who qualified for the privilege, a questionable procedure in light of the traditional
doctrine that liberty of the press is the right of the lonely pamphleteer [just]
as much as of the large metropolitan publisher. [Almost] any author may
[assert] that he is contributing to the flow of information to the public, that
he relies on confidential sources of information, and that these sources will be
silenced if he is forced to make disclosures before a grand jury.

In each instance where a reporter is subpoenaed to testify, the courts would
also be embroiled in preliminary factual and legal determinations with respect
to whether the proper predicate had been laid for the reporter's appearance: Is
there probable cause to believe a crime has been committed? Is it likely that
the reporter has useful information gained in confidence? Could the grand
jury obtain the information elsewhere? Is the official interest sufficient to
outweigh the claimed privilege? . . .

Finally, as we have earlier indicated, news gathering is not without its First
Amendment protections, and grand jury investigations if instituted or conducted other than in good faith, would pose wholly different issues for resolution under the First Amendment. Official harassment of the press
undertaken not for purposes of law enforcement but to disrupt a reporter's
relationship with his news sources would have no justification. Grand juries
are subject to judicial control and subpoenas to motions to quash. We do not
expect courts will forget that grand juries must operate within the limits of the
First Amendment. . . .

MR. JUSTICE POWELL, concurring.

I add this brief statement to emphasize what seems to me to be the limited
nature of the Court's holding. The Court does not hold that newsmen, subpoenaed to testify before a grand jury, are without constitutional rights with
respect to the gathering of news or in safeguarding their sources. . . .

As indicated in the concluding portion of the opinion, the Court states that
no harassment of newsmen will be tolerated. If a newsman believes that the
grand jury investigation is not being conducted in good faith he is not without
remedy. Indeed, if the newsman is called upon to give information bearing

33.  In his Press Subpoenas: An Empirical and Legal Analysis, Study Report of the Reporters'
Committee on Freedom of the Press 6–12, Prof. Vince Blasi [found] that slightly more than half
of the 975 reporters questioned said that they relied on regular confidential sources for at least
10% of their stories. Of this group of reporters, only 8% were able to say with some certainty that
their professional functioning had been adversely affected by the threat of subpoena; another
11% were not certain whether or not they had been adversely affected. [Relocated footnote.
— EDS.]

only a remote and tenuous relationship to the subject of the investigation, or if he has some other reason to believe that his testimony implicates confidential source relationships without a legitimate need of law enforcement, he will have access to the court on a motion to quash and an appropriate protective order may be entered. The asserted claim to privilege should be judged on its facts by the striking of a proper balance between freedom of the press and the obligation of all citizens to give relevant testimony with respect to criminal conduct. The balance of these vital constitutional and societal interests on a case-by-case basis accords with the tried and traditional way of adjudicating such questions.

In short, the courts will be available to newsmen under circumstances where legitimate First Amendment interests require protection.

Mr. Justice Douglas, dissenting. . . .

Today's decision will impede the wide-open and robust dissemination of ideas and counterthought which a free press both fosters and protects and which is essential to the success of intelligent self-government. . . .

I see no way of making mandatory the disclosure of a reporter's confidential source of the information on which he bases his news story. . . .

Mr. Justice Stewart, with whom Mr. Justice Brennan and Mr. Justice Marshall join, dissenting.

The Court's crabbed view of the First Amendment reflects a disturbing insensitivity to the critical role of an independent press in our society. [While] Mr. Justice Powell's enigmatic concurring opinion gives some hope of a more flexible view in the future, the Court in these cases holds that a newsman has no First Amendment right to protect his sources when called before a grand jury. The Court thus invites state and federal authorities to undermine the historic independence of the press by attempting to annex the journalistic profession as an investigative arm of government. . . .

A corollary of the right to publish must be the right to gather news. [The] right to gather news implies, in turn, a right to a confidential relationship between a reporter and his source. [Informants] are necessary to the news-gathering process as we know it today. [And] the promise of confidentiality may be a necessary prerequisite to a productive relationship between a newsman and his informants. . . .

The impairment of the flow of news cannot, of course, be proved with scientific precision, as the Court seems to demand. [But] we have never before demanded that First Amendment rights rest on elaborate empirical studies demonstrating beyond any conceivable doubt that deterrent effects exist. . . .

Rather, on the basis of common sense and available information, we have asked, often implicitly, (1) whether there was a rational connection between the cause (the governmental action) and the effect (the deterrence or impairment of First Amendment activity), and (2) whether the effect would occur with some regularity, i.e., would not be de minimis. [Citing, e.g., NAACP v. Alabama; New York Times v. Sullivan.] Once this threshold inquiry has been satisfied, we have then examined the competing interests in determining whether there is an unconstitutional infringement of First Amendment freedoms. . . .

Surely [the] claim of deterrence here is as securely grounded in evidence and common sense as the claims in the cases cited above. [To] require any greater burden of proof is to shirk our duty to protect values securely embedded in the Constitution. . . .

Posed against the First Amendment's protection of the newsman's confidential relationships in these cases is society's interest in the use of the grand jury to administer justice fairly and effectively. [To] perform these functions the grand jury must have available to it every man's relevant evidence. [But] the longstanding rule making every person's evidence available to the grand jury is not absolute. The rule has been limited by the Fifth Amendment, the Fourth Amendment, and the evidentiary privileges of the common law. . . .

In striking the proper balance between the public interest in the efficient administration of justice and the First Amendment guarantee of the fullest flow of information, we must begin with the basic proposition [that] First Amendment rights require special safeguards. . . .

Accordingly, when a reporter is asked to appear before a grand jury and reveal confidences, I would hold that the government must (1) show that there is probable cause to believe that the newsman has information that is clearly relevant to a specific probable violation of law; (2) demonstrate that the information sought cannot be obtained by alternative means less destructive of First Amendment rights; and (3) demonstrate a compelling and overriding interest in the information. . . .

No doubt the courts would be required to make some delicate judgments in working out this accommodation. But that, after all, is the function of courts of law. Better such judgments, however difficult, than the simplistic and stultifying absolutism adopted by the Court in denying any force to the First Amendment in these cases. . . .

## Note: A Right to Gather News?

1. *Newsgathering.* Does the first amendment guarantee the press a right to gather as well as to publish the news? Has the press a first amendment right to gather news through such practices as deception, burglary, wiretapping, and the bribing of sources? Suppose a reporter breaks into a government official's home to uncover evidence of corruption. Can the reporter be prosecuted? Note that this issue implicates the incidental effects doctrine. Recall *O'Brien.* If fraud, burglary, wiretapping, and bribery are generally unlawful, does the first amendment create a special exemption for the press? If the

reporter can constitutionally be prosecuted for the break-in, the wiretap, or the bribery, does it follow that her newspaper can be punished for publishing the information? Recall *Pentagon Papers, Bartnicki,* and *Ferber.* See Stone, Government Secrecy v. Freedom of the Press, 1 Harv. L. & Pol'y. Rev. 185 (2007).

2. *Journalist's privilege.* In light of Justice Powell's concurring opinion, is it fair to say that the Court divided "by a vote of four and a half to four and a half"? Stewart, "Or of the Press," 26 Hastings L. Rev. 631, 635 (1975). Note that Justice Powell joined the majority opinion in *Branzburg.* Suppose he had filed his concurring opinion without joining Justice White's opinion. Would that have affected the meaning of the decision?

Forty-nine states and the District of Columbia have adopted some form of journalist-source privilege, but the federal government has no such privilege. If you were a member of Congress and thought that the press required some protection, how would you draft legislation that provided it? Three questions are especially vexing: (1) Should the privilege be absolute or qualified? That is, should the government be able to overcome the privilege with a sufficient showing of need? (2) Should the privilege protect the confidentiality of a source whose disclosure is *unlawful*? If the purpose of the privilege is to encourage a source to communicate, does it make any sense to extend the privilege to unlawful communications? Note that this query has particular relevance to unlawful leaks of classified information. (3) Who should be able to assert the privilege? Presumably, the privilege would cover disclosures to a reporter for the Washington Post or CNN, but what about disclosures to a professor who is writing a book, to bloggers, or to the editor of a high school newspaper? See Papandrea, Citizen Journalism and the Reporter's Privilege, 91 Minn. L. Rev. 515 (2007); Stone, Why We Need a Federal Reporter's Privilege, 34 Hofstra L. Rev. 39 (2005).

3. *Protecting the anonymity of the source.* Instead of focusing on the First Amendment right of the reporter to keep sources confidential, would it make more sense to focus on the First Amendment right of the source to engage in anonymous speech? After all, in a series of decisions, including Talley v. California, McIntyre v. Ohio Elections Commission, NAACP v. Alabama and Brown v. Socialists Workers, the Court has protected a right to anonymous speech, noting that anonymous speech has "played an important role in the progress of mankind" and that "persecuted groups" throughout history "have been able to criticize oppressive practices either anonymously or not at all." Consider Jones, Re-Thinking Reporter's Privilege, 111 Mich. L. Rev. 1221 (2013):

> A confidential source who does not wish to have her name revealed is analytically indistinguishable from any other author, writer, or speaker who wishes to convey information anonymously. Like the leafleteer in Talley . . . and the concerned taxpayer in McIntyre, . . . a confidential source offers information that she wishes to make public without attribution . . . for any number of reasons

that the Court has acknowledged as valid. [The] source should be entitled to protection under the anonymous speech doctrine for statements made to a reporter in confidence.

4. *Investigative journalism or criminal solicitation?* Suppose a reporter persuades a public employee unlawfully to leak classified information. Can the reporter constitutionally be convicted of the crime of criminal solicitation? Recall O'Brien. Suppose a journalist conducts an illegal wiretap in order to prove that a congressman took a bribe. Would her conduct be protected by the First Amendment? If not, is criminal solicitation any different? See G. Stone, Top Secret: When Government Keeps Us in the Dark 29–38 (2007) (arguing that because prosecution of journalists for the crime of solicitation would interject "government into the very heart of the journalist-source relationship" and thus "have a serious chilling effect" on legimate and important journalist-source exchanges, the government should not be able to punish journalists for encouraging public employees to disclose classified information unless the journalist (a) expressly incites the leak and (b) knows that publication of the information would likely cause imminent and grave harm to the national security.)

5. *Newsroom searches.* In Zurcher v. Stanford Daily, 436 U.S. 547 (1978), the Daily, a student newspaper, published articles and photographs concerning a violent clash on campus between demonstrators and police. Thereafter, the police obtained a warrant for an immediate search of the newspaper's offices for negatives, films, and pictures that might enable them to identify some of the demonstrators. The Daily's photographic laboratories, filing cabinets, desks, and wastepaper baskets were searched, but the police found only those photographs that had already been published. The Daily brought this civil action on the theory that the decision of the police to conduct a search, rather than to proceed by subpoena duces tecum, violated the first amendment. The Daily maintained that, unlike subpoenas, "searches of newspaper offices for evidence of [crime] seriously threaten the ability of the press to gather, analyze, and disseminate news." In a five-to-three decision, the Court, in an opinion by Justice White, rejected this argument:

> Properly administered, the preconditions for a warrant — probable cause, specificity with respect to the place to be searched and the things to be seized, and overall reasonableness — should afford sufficient protection against the harms that are assertedly threatened by warrants for searching newspaper offices. [Nor] are we convinced, any more than we were in [Branzburg], that confidential sources will disappear. [Whatever] incremental effect there may be in this regard [does] not make a constitutional difference.

In the Privacy Protection Act of 1980, 42 U.S.C. §2000aa, Congress prohibited any government officer to search for work product or other

documents of any "person reasonably believed to have a purpose to disseminate to the public a newspaper, book, broadcast, or other similar form of
public communication," unless there is either probable cause to believe that
the person is involved in the crime being investigated or there is otherwise
reason to believe that giving notice by subpoena would result in the loss of
the evidence.

6. *Breach of promise.* In Cohen v. Cowles Media Co., 501 U.S. 663 (1991),
petitioner, who was associated with one party's campaign during the 1982
Minnesota gubernatorial race, gave court records disclosing derogatory information about another party's candidate to respondent newspapers after receiving a promise of confidentiality from the reporters. Despite this promise, the
newspapers identified him in their stories, and petitioner was thereafter fired
from his job. In a five-to-four decision, the Court held that the first amendment
did not bar petitioner's state law action for damages for breach of promise.
Justice White delivered the opinion of the Court:

> Generally applicable laws do not offend the First Amendment simply because
> their enforcement against the press has incidental effects on its ability to gather
> and report the news. [There] can be little doubt that the Minnesota doctrine of
> promissory estoppel is a law of general applicability. It does not target or single
> out the press. [The] First Amendment does not forbid its application to the press.

Justices Souter, Marshall, Blackmun, and O'Connor dissented.

7. *Does the press have a right to publish someone else's "property"?* Consider
Zacchini v. Scripps-Howard Broadcasting Co., 433 U.S. 562 (1977), in which
petitioner's fifteen-second "human cannonball" act, in which he is shot from a
cannon into a net some two hundred feet away, was, without his consent,
filmed in its entirety at a county fair and shown on a television news program
later the same day. Petitioner filed a damage action alleging an "unlawful
appropriation" of his "professional property." The Court held that the first
amendment did not bar petitioner's action: "[The first amendment does not
give the media a right to] broadcast a performer's entire act without his consent. The Constitution no more prevents a State from requiring respondent to
compensate petitioner for broadcasting his act on television than it would
privilege respondent to film and broadcast a copyrighted dramatic work
without liability to the copyright owner."

8. *The first amendment and copyright.* Is copyright protection consistent with
the first amendment? See Harper & Row, Publishers v. Nation Enterprises,
471 U.S. 539 (1985) (a magazine's unauthorized publication of verbatim
quotes from President Ford's unpublished memoirs constituted an actionable
copyright infringement); Eldred v. Ashcroft, 537 U.S. 186 (2003) (upholding
the 1998 Copyright Extension Act, which extended the duration of existing
copyrights by an additional twenty years).

Does an artist have a first amendment right to use a famous movie star's image in one of her paintings? Does the first amendment protect an individual who produces and sells T-shirts that mock well-known politicians or products? See R. Tushnet, Copy This Essay: How the Fair Use Doctrine Harms Free Speech and How Copying Serves It, 114 Yale L.J. 535 (2004).

For an interesting twist on this problem, see Simon & Schuster, Inc. v. Members of the New York State Crime Victims Board, 502 U.S. 428 (1991) (invalidating New York's Son of Sam law, which required any entity contracting with a person convicted of a crime to publish any depiction of the crime to turn over any income under the contract to the Crime Victims Board, which was then required to deposit the payments in an escrow account for the benefit of any victims).

## Note: A Press Right of Access to Information?

1. A *right of access?* To what extent, if any, does the press have a first amendment right of access to information from the government? For example, do members of the press ever have a constitutional right to be present during military operations, to interview prisoners, to demand information from government officials, or to attend criminal trials? If the right of the press to *publish* information about the activities of government is central to the first amendment, isn't the right of the press to *obtain* such information equally central? Consider BeVier, An Informed Public, An Informing Press: The Search for a Constitutional Principle, 68 Cal. L. Rev. 482, 498–499 (1980):

> The effect on the flow of information [of] government denials of access to information [is] similar to the [effect of such direct restrictions on publication as punishment and censorship. [But] the failure of government to [grant] access cannot be credibly argued to be the constitutional equivalent of [such direct restrictions. Punishment and censorship] interfere quite directly with the freedom to publish. When the government denies access to information, however, it poses no threat to freedom, at least if that word is given its ordinary legal meaning. [Punishment and] censorship directly undermine the value of *free* speech, while the denial of access to information undermines [only] the value of *well-informed* speech.

If there is a first amendment right of press access to government information, what are its limits? Is government under a constitutional obligation to make public all information that might enhance "the ability of our people through free and open debate to consider and resolve their own destiny"? Is it "impossible to conceive of a court making case-by-case determinations of the 'necessity' of nondisclosure in any way that would bear even the faintest resemblance [to] 'reasoned elaboration'"? BeVier, supra, at 510.

2. *Access to prisons*. In Pell v. Procunier, 417 U.S. 817 (1974), the Court held that professional journalists had no first amendment right to conduct face-to-face interviews of prison inmates:

> The First and Fourteenth Amendments bar government from interfering in any way with a free press. The Constitution does not, however, require government to accord the press special access to information not shared by members of the public generally. It is one thing to say that a journalist is free to seek out sources of information not available to members of the general public, that he is entitled to some constitutional protection of the confidentiality of such sources, cf. [*Branzburg*], and that government cannot restrain the publication of news emanating from such sources. Cf. [*Pentagon Papers*, Chapter II.C, supra]. It is quite another thing to suggest that the Constitution imposes upon government the affirmative duty to make available to journalists sources of information not available to members of the public generally. That proposition finds no support in the words of the Constitution or in any decision of this Court.

Justices Douglas, Brennan, Marshall, and Powell dissented.

3. *Access to the military*. Consider Anderson, Freedom of the Press in Wartime, 77 U. Colo. L. Rev. 49, 66, 95–98 (2006): "So far as existing case law is concerned, there appears to be nothing to prevent the Pentagon from eliminating on-scene coverage of military operations, detention facilities, military hospitals, and other auxiliaries of war. [A] judicial response that leaves news about the conduct of war at the sufferance of the military is an abdication of constitutional responsibility."

4. *Are there potential dangers in recognizing a "preferred" status for the press?* Consider Van Alstyne, The First Amendment and the Free Press: A Comment on Some New Trends and Some Old Theories, 9 Hofstra L. Rev. 1, 19–23 (1980):

> [If] journalists may assert access to certain public facilities [in] "first amendment preference" to laypersons, [it] may follow symmetrically that the ensuing published story must meet a standard of professionalism commensurate with the privileged standing of the reporter. [The press operates] most effectively and most legitimately precisely because it forms no part of government. [The] security of the [press] from the encumbrance of public regulation [may] be at risk if one's accent is not on the freedom of the press but is, rather, on the public's right to know. [We] have already imposed upon radio and television substantial "public" obligations — in exchange for exclusive, cost-free licensing privileges. [There] is no reason to suppose that the matter will be different for newspapers should they, too, "succeed" in securing particular rights [that others] cannot claim under a single and indivisible amendment.

5. *Access to judicial proceedings*. In Gannett v. DePasquale, 443 U.S. 368 (1979), the defendants in a murder prosecution requested that the public and the press be excluded from a pretrial hearing on a motion to suppress allegedly

involuntary confessions. The district attorney did not oppose the request, and the trial judge, finding that the adverse publicity might jeopardize the defendants' right to a fair trial, granted the closure motion. In upholding this order, the Court focused primarily on the claim that the order violated the sixth amendment's guarantee that "[in] all criminal prosecutions, the accused shall enjoy the right to a [public] trial." Although conceding that "there is a strong societal interest in public trials," the Court concluded that the sixth amendment guarantee "is personal to the accused," and that "members of the public" thus "have no constitutional right under the Sixth [Amendment] to attend criminal trials."

**RICHMOND NEWSPAPERS v. VIRGINIA, 448 U.S. 555 (1980):** In 1976, Stevenson was convicted of murder. The conviction was reversed, however, and two subsequent trials ended in mistrials. At the outset of his fourth trial, Stevenson moved that the proceeding be closed to the public. Neither the prosecutor nor anyone else present, including two of appellant's reporters, objected to the motion. The trial judge, acting pursuant to a Virginia statute authorizing the court, "in its discretion," to "exclude from the trial any persons whose presence would impair the conduct of a fair trial," ordered "that the Courtroom be kept clear of all parties except the witnesses when they testify." Later that day appellant moved to vacate the closure order. In defense of the order, Stevenson argued that he "didn't want information to leak out," be published by the media, perhaps inaccurately, and then be seen by the jurors. The trial judge, noting also that "having people in the Courtroom is distracting to the jury," denied the motion to vacate and ordered the trial to continue "with the press and public excluded." The following day the trial judge excused the jury and found Stevenson "not guilty." As soon as the trial ended, tapes of the proceeding were made available to the public.

In a divided set of opinions, the Court held that the order closing the trial to the press and the public was unconstitutional. Chief Justice Burger, joined by Justices White and Stevens, authored a plurality opinion: "The narrow question presented in this case is whether the right of the public and press to attend criminal trials is guaranteed under the United States Constitution. [The] origins of [the] modern criminal trial in Anglo-American justice can be traced back beyond reliable historical records. [Throughout] its evolution, the trial has been open to all who cared to observe. [This] is no quirk of history; rather, it has long been recognized as an indispensable attribute of an Anglo-American trial. [Such openness gives] assurance that the proceedings [are] conducted fairly to all concerned, and it [discourages] perjury, the misconduct of participants, and decisions based on secret bias or partiality. [Moreover,] public trials [have] significant community therapeutic value. [When] a shocking crime occurs, a community reaction of outrage and public protest often follows. Thereafter the open processes of justice serve an important prophylactic purpose, providing an outlet for community concern, hostility, and emotion. . . .

"The Bill of Rights was enacted against the backdrop of the long history of trials being presumptively open. [In] guaranteeing freedoms such as those of speech and press, the First Amendment can be read as protecting the right of everyone to attend trials so as to give meaning to those explicit guarantees. [The] First Amendment goes beyond protection of the press and the self-expression of individuals to prohibit government from limiting the stock of information from which members of the public may draw. Free speech carries with it some freedom to listen. In a variety of contexts this Court has referred to a First Amendment right to 'receive information and ideas.' What this means in the context of trials is that the First Amendment guarantees of speech and press, standing alone, prohibit the government from summarily closing courtroom doors which had long been open to the public at the time that Amendment was adopted. . . .

"It is not crucial whether we describe this right to attend criminal trials to hear, see, and communicate observations concerning them as a 'right of access,'[11] or a 'right to gather information,' for we have recognized that 'without some protection for seeking out the news, freedom of the press could be eviscerated.'[Branzburg.] The explicit, guaranteed rights to speak and to publish concerning what takes place at a trial would lose much meaning if access to observe the trial could, as it was here, be foreclosed arbitrarily. [We] hold that the right to attend criminal trials[17] is implicit in the guarantees of the First Amendment; without the freedom to attend such trials, which people have exercised for centuries, important aspects of freedom of speech and 'of the press could be eviscerated.'

"Having concluded there was a guaranteed right of the public under the First and Fourteenth Amendments to attend the trial of Stevenson's case, we return to the closure order challenged by appellants. [The] trial judge made no findings to support closure; no inquiry was made as to whether alternative solutions would have met the need to ensure fairness; there was no recognition of any right under the Constitution for the public or press to attend the trial. [Absent] an overriding interest articulated in findings, the trial of a criminal case must be open to the public."[18]

11. *Procunier* and *Saxbe* are distinguishable in the sense that they were concerned with penal institutions which, by definition, are not "open" or public places. Penal institutions do not share the long tradition of openness. . . .

17. Whether the public has a right to attend trials of civil cases is a question not raised by this case, but we note that historically both civil and criminal trials have been presumptively open.

18. We have no occasion here to define the circumstances in which all or parts of a criminal trial may be closed to the public, but our holding today does not mean that the First Amendment rights of the public and representatives of the press are absolute. Just as a government may impose reasonable time, place, and manner restrictions upon the use of its streets in the interest of such objectives as the free flow of traffic, see, e.g., Cox v. New Hampshire, [chapter V supra], so may a trial judge, in the interest of the fair administration of justice, impose reasonable limitations on access to a trial. [Moreover], since courtrooms have limited capacity, there may be occasions when not every person who wishes to attend can be accommodated. In such

Justice Brennan, joined by Justice Marshall, filed a concurring opinion: "Customarily, First Amendment guarantees are interposed to protect communication between speaker and listener. [But] the First Amendment embodies more than a commitment to free expression and communicative interchange for their own sakes; it has a *structural* role to play in securing and fostering our republican system of self-government. Implicit in this structural role is not only 'the principle that debate on public issues should be uninhibited, robust, and wide-open,' but the antecedent assumption that valuable public debate [must] be informed. The structural model links the First Amendment to that process of communication necessary for a democracy to survive, and thus entails solicitude not only for communication itself, but also for the indispensable conditions of meaningful communication.

"However, because 'the stretch of this protection is theoretically endless,' it must be invoked with discrimination and temperance. [At] least two helpful principles may be sketched. First, the case for a right of access has special force when drawn from an enduring and vital tradition of public entree to particular proceedings or information. Such a tradition commands respect in part because the Constitution carries the gloss of history. More importantly, a tradition of accessibility implies the favorable judgment of experience. Second, the value of access must be measured in specifics. Analysis is not advanced by rhetorical statements that all information bears upon public issues; what is crucial in individual cases is whether access to a particular government process is important in terms of that very process. [Our] ingrained tradition of public trials and the importance of public access to the broader purposes of the trial process tip the balance strongly toward the rule that trials be open. What countervailing interests might be sufficiently compelling to reverse this presumption of openness need not concern us now,[24] for the statute at stake here authorizes trial closures at the unfettered discretion of the judge and parties."

Justice Stewart concurred in the judgment: "It has for centuries been a basic presupposition of the Anglo-American legal system that trials shall be public trials. [With] us, a trial is by very definition a proceeding open to the press and to the public. In conspicuous contrast to a military base, Greer v. Spock, [Chapter V.B, supra]; a jail, Adderley v. Florida, [Chapter V.B, supra]; or a prison, [*Pell*], a trial courtroom is a public place. Even more than city streets, sidewalks, and parks as areas of First Amendment activity, a trial courtroom is a place where representatives of the press and of the public are not only free to be, but where their presence serves to assure the integrity of what goes on. But this does not mean that the First Amendment right of members of the public and

---

situations, reasonable restrictions on general access are traditionally imposed, including preferential seating for media representatives. . . .

24. For example, national security concerns about confidentiality may sometimes warrant closures during sensitive portions of trial proceedings, such as testimony about state secrets. Cf. United States v. Nixon, 418 U.S. 683, 714–716 (1974).

representatives of the press to attend [criminal] trials is absolute. Just as a legislature may impose reasonable time, place, and manner restrictions upon the exercise of First Amendment freedoms, so may a trial judge impose reasonable limitations upon the unrestricted occupation of a courtroom by representatives of the press and members of the public." Justice Rehnquist dissented.

**GLOBE NEWSPAPER CO. v. SUPERIOR COURT, 457 U.S. 596 (1982):** To protect the minor victims of sex crimes from further trauma and embarrassment and to encourage such victims to come forward and testify in a truthful and credible manner, section 16A of chapter 278 of Massachusetts General Laws requires trial judges, at trials for specified sexual offenses involving a victim under age eighteen, to exclude the press and general public from the courtroom during the testimony of the victim. The Court, in a six-to-three decision, held section 16A unconstitutional. Justice Brennan delivered the opinion of the Court:

"*Richmond Newspapers* firmly established for the first time that the press and general public have a constitutional right of access to criminal trials. [Where], as in the present case, the State attempts to deny the right of access in order to inhibit the disclosure of sensitive information, it must be shown that the denial is necessitated by a compelling governmental interest, and is narrowly tailored to serve that interest.] . . .

"We agree [that the Commonwealth's interest in] safeguarding the physical and psychological well-being of a minor [is] a compelling one. But as compelling as that interest is, it does not justify a *mandatory*-closure rule, for it is clear that the circumstances of the particular case may affect the significance of the interest. A trial court can determine on a case-by-case basis whether closure is necessary to protect the welfare of a minor victim. Among the factors to be weighed are the minor victim's age, psychological maturity and understanding, the nature of the crime, the desires of the victim, and the interests of parents and relatives. [Section] 16A cannot be viewed as a narrowly tailored means of accommodating the State's asserted interest. . . .

"Nor can §16A be justified on the basis of the Commonwealth's [interest in] the encouragement of minor victims of sex crimes to come forward and provide accurate testimony. The Commonwealth has offered no empirical support for the claim that the rule of automatic closure [will] lead to an increase in the number of minor sex victims coming forward and cooperating with state authorities. . . ." Chief Justice Burger, joined by Justice Rehnquist, dissented.

### Note: Variations on the Press Right of Access

1. *Voir dire hearings.* In Press-Enterprise Co. v. Superior Court, 464 U.S. 501 (1984), the Court held that a state court order closing the voir dire examination of prospective jurors in a criminal trial violated the first amendment.

The Court explained that the "presumption of openness may be overcome only by an overriding interest based on findings that closure is essential to preserve higher values and is narrowly tailored to serve that interest." Although conceding that the "jury selection process may, in some circumstances, give rise to a compelling [privacy] interest of a prospective juror when interrogation touches on deeply personal matters," the Court concluded that the trial court in this case had not adequately considered the alternatives to closure. See also Press-Enterprise Co. v. Superior Court, 478 U.S. 1 (1986) (holding that a newspaper has a first amendment right of access to the transcript of a preliminary hearing).

In what circumstances, if any, does the first amendment guarantee the media a right to attend civil trials? Deportation hearings? Congressional hearings? To what extent, if any, does the first amendment give the media a right to televise criminal trials?

2. *Conditioned access to information.* Despite *Richmond Newspapers*, government is under no general constitutional obligation to disclose information to the press or public and indeed may ordinarily prohibit its employees from disclosing "confidential" information. To what extent, then, may government condition its voluntary disclosure of information on the press's agreement not to publish?

Consider Seattle Times Co. v. Rhinehart, 467 U.S. 20 (1984). In a defamation action against the Seattle Times, a state court ordered the plaintiff to disclose certain information in discovery. The state court entered a protective order prohibiting the newspaper from using the disclosed information, which included the names of contributors to a controversial religious group, for any purpose other than trial of the case. The Supreme Court unanimously rejected the newspaper's claim that the order violated the first amendment:

> [The newspaper] gained the information [only] by virtue of the trial court's discovery processes. [It had] no First Amendment right of access to [the information]. [Moreover, the] protective order prevents [the dissemination only of] information obtained through [discovery. The newspaper is free to] disseminate the identical information [if it obtains it] through means independent of the court's processes. [Thus], continued court control over the discovered information does not raise the same spectre of government censorship that such control might suggest in other situations. [We] therefore hold that where [a] protective order is entered on a showing of good cause, [is] limited to the context of pretrial civil discovery, and does not restrict the dissemination of the information if gained from other sources, it does not offend the First Amendment.

## C.   DIFFERENTIAL TREATMENT OF THE PRESS

Consider the constitutionality of the following laws: (1) A sales tax of 4 percent on all sales of goods. This is challenged by a newspaper publisher who argues that, as applied to his sales, the tax constitutes an impermissible "tax on the

Minnesota legislature decided to provide newspapers with an exemption from the sales tax and impose a use tax on ink and paper. [The] problem the Court finds too difficult to deal with is whether this difference in treatment results in a significant burden on newspapers. The record reveals that in 1974 [appellant had total sales of] $46,498,738. Had a 4% sales tax been imposed, [appellant] would have been liable for $1,859,950. [The] record further indicates that [appellant] paid $608,634 in use taxes in 1974. We need no expert testimony [to] determine that the [use tax] is significantly less burdensome than the [sales tax]. Ignoring these calculations, the Court concludes that 'differential treatment' alone [requires] that the [tax] be found 'presumptively unconstitutional' and declared invalid 'unless the State asserts a [compelling justification].' The 'differential treatment' standard [is] unprecedented and unwarranted. [No] First Amendment issue is raised unless First Amendment rights have been infringed. . . .

"[The] Court also says that even if the resultant burden on the press is lighter than on others '[t]he very selection of the press for special treatment threatens the press [with] the possibility of subsequent differentially *more burdensome* [treatment].' Surely the Court does not mean what it seems to say. [This] Court is quite capable of dealing with changes in state taxing laws which are intended to penalize newspapers. [Furthermore], the Court itself intimates [in footnote 13 that certain forms of differential treatment are permissible, even though they too have the] potential for 'the threat of sanctions,' because the legislature could at any time raise the taxes to the higher rate. . . .

"[In my view, the] State [in this case] is required to show [only] that its taxing scheme is rational. [In] this case that showing can be made easily. [There] must be few such inexpensive items sold in Minnesota in the volume of newspaper sales. [The] legislature could have concluded that paper boys, corner newsstands, and vending machines provide an unreliable and unsuitable means for collection of a sales tax. [The] reasonable alternative Minnesota chose to impose [was] the use tax on ink and paper. [The Court also] finds [that] the exemption newspapers receive for the first $100,000 of ink and paper [used] violates the First Amendment because the result is that only a few of the newspapers actually pay a use tax. I cannot agree. [Absent] any improper motive on the part of the Minnesota legislature in drawing the lines of this exemption, it cannot be construed as violating the First Amendment. [There] is no reason to conclude that the State [acted] other than reasonably and rationally to fit its sales and use tax scheme to its own local needs and usages."

Justice White concurred in part and dissented in part.


### Note: Differential Treatment

1. *Preserving press neutrality.* Consider Bezanson, Political Agnosticism, Editorial Freedom, and Government Neutrality toward the Press, 72 Iowa

L. Rev. 1359, 1371 (1987): "[A sound] reason for making constitutionally suspect any formal singling out of the press [is] to protect the political neutrality of the press [and to] prevent the government from undermining the [neutrality of the press] by forcing [it] to engage actively in the political process [to] protect its own self-interest." Does this mean that even a law expressly benefiting the press, such as an exemption from a state's sales tax, should be invalid? Consider footnote 13 in *Minneapolis Star*.

2. *Content-based differentiation.* The Court relied on *Minneapolis Star* in Arkansas Writers' Project, Inc. v. Ragland, 481 U.S. 221 (1987), to invalidate an Arkansas statute that imposed a state sales tax on general interest magazines but exempted religious, professional, trade, and sports journals. In an opinion by Justice Marshall, the Court invalidated the law because the discrimination was "content-based." Justice Scalia, joined by Chief Justice Rehnquist, dissented.

3. *Intermedia differentiation:* Leathers. In Leathers v. Medlock, 499 U.S. 439 (1991), the Court considered the constitutionality of the Arkansas Gross Receipts Act, which imposes a 4 percent tax. The act expressly exempts receipts from subscription and over-the-counter newspapers and magazine sales but imposes the tax on cable television. The Court, in an opinion by Justice O'Connor, rejected petitioners' argument that such "intermedia discrimination" violates the first amendment. The Court explained that such a tax is "suspect" only if it "threatens to suppress the expression of particular ideas or viewpoints," "singles out the press," "targets a small group of speakers," or "discriminates on the basis [of] content." Because the "Arkansas tax [presents] none of these types of discrimination," the Court concluded that Arkansas's "extension of its generally applicable sales tax to [cable television], while exempting the print media, does not violate the First Amendment." Justice Marshall, joined by Justice Brennan, dissented.

4. *Intermedia discrimination:* Turner. In Turner Broadcasting Inc. v. FCC, 512 U.S. 622 (1994), the Court upheld "must carry" provisions for cable television that favored broadcast over cable programmers. The Court observed:

> Regulations that discriminate among media, or among different speakers within a single medium, often present serious First Amendment concerns. [Citing *Minneapolis Star* and *Arkansas Writers' Project*.] It would be error to conclude, however, that the First Amendment mandates strict scrutiny for any speech regulation that applied to one medium (or a subset thereof) but not others. [The] taxes invalidated in *Minneapolis Star* and *Arkansas Writers' Project* [targeted] a small number of speakers [and] were structured in a manner that raised suspicions that their objective [was] the suppression of certain ideas.
>
> But such heightened scrutiny is unwarranted [where, as here,] the differential treatment [is] not structured in a manner that carries the inherent risk of undermining First Amendment interests. The ["must carry"] regulations [apply] to almost all cable systems in the country, rather than just a select few. As a result, [they] do not pose the same dangers of suppression and manipulation that were

posed by the more narrowly targeted regulations in *Minneapolis Star* and *Arkansas Writers' Project*.

5. *Intermedia discrimination: shield laws*. Suppose a journalist-shield law allows reporters for mainstream newspapers and television and radio stations to invoke the journalist-source privilege, but does not extend to bloggers. Does such intermedia discrimination violate the first amendment? Consider Stone, Why We Need a Federal Reporter's Privilege, 34 Hofstra L. Rev. 39, 48 (2005):

> [Although the issue of "who is a member of the press"] was a serious constraint on the Court in *Branzburg*, it poses a much more manageable issue in the context of legislation. Government often treats different speakers and publishers differently from one another. Which reporters are allowed to attend a White House briefing? Which are eligible to be embedded with the military? Broadcasting is regulated, but print journalism is not. Legislation treats the cable medium differently from both broadcasting and print journalism. These categories need not conform perfectly to the undefined phrase "the press" in the First Amendment. Differentiation among different elements of the media is constitutional, as long as it is not based on viewpoint or any other invidious consideration, and as long as the differential is reasonable.

## D.   REGULATING THE PRESS TO "IMPROVE" THE MARKETPLACE OF IDEAS

In what circumstances, if any, is it appropriate for government to regulate the media in order to "improve" the system of free expression? Recall the discussion of this issue in the electoral context in Chapter V supra.

**MIAMI HERALD PUBLISHING CO. v. TORNILLO**, 418 U.S. 241 (1974): In *Tornillo*, the Court considered the constitutionality of a Florida "'right of reply' statute which [provided] that if a candidate for [political office] is assailed regarding his personal character or official record by any newspaper, the candidate has the right to demand that the newspaper print, free of cost to the candidate, any reply the candidate may make to the newspaper's charges. The reply must appear in as conspicuous a place and in the same kind of type as the charges which prompted the reply, provided it does not take up more space than the charges." The Court, in a unanimous decision, held the statute invalid. Chief Justice Burger delivered the opinion of the Court:

"[Advocates] of an enforceable right of access to the press [urge] that at the time the First Amendment [was ratified] the press was broadly representative of the people it was serving. [Entry] into publishing was inexpensive [and a] true marketplace of ideas existed in which there was relatively easy access to the channels of communication. Access advocates submit that [the press of today is] very different. [Newspapers] have become big business and [the press] has become noncompetitive and enormously powerful and influential in its capacity to manipulate popular opinion. [The] result of these vast changes has been to place in a few hands the power to inform the American people and shape public opinion. [There] tends to be a homogeneity of editorial opinion, commentary, and interpretative analysis. [The] obvious solution [would] be to have additional newspapers. But [economic factors] have made entry into the marketplace of ideas served by the print media almost impossible. [The] First Amendment interest of the public in being informed is said to be in peril. . . .

"However much validity may be found in these arguments, [the] implementation of a remedy such as an enforceable right of access necessarily [brings] about a confrontation with the express provisions of the First Amendment. [The] argument that the Florida statute does not amount to a restriction of [the newspaper's] right to speak because 'the statute in question here has not prevented [the newspaper] from saying anything it wished' begs the core question. Compelling editors or publishers to publish that which "'reason' tells them should not be published" is what is at issue in this case. The Florida statute operates as a command in the same sense as a statute or regulation forbidding [the newspaper] to publish specified matter. [The] Florida statute exacts a penalty on the basis of the content of a newspaper. The first phase of the penalty [is] exacted in terms of the cost in printing [and] in taking up space that could be devoted to other material the newspaper may have preferred to print. [Faced with such a penalty,] editors might well conclude that the safe course is to avoid controversy. [Thus, the government-enforced] right of access inescapably 'dampens the vigor and limits the variety of public debate.' . . .

"[Moreover, even] if a newspaper would face no additional costs to comply with a compulsory access law and would not be forced to forgo publication of news or opinion by the inclusion of a reply, the Florida statute fails to clear the barriers of the First Amendment because of its intrusion into the function of editors. A newspaper is more than a passive receptacle or conduit for news, comment, and advertising. The choice of material to go into a newspaper [constitutes] the exercise of editorial control and judgment. It has yet to be demonstrated how governmental regulation of this crucial process can be exercised consistent with First Amendment guarantees of a free press as they have evolved to this time."

Consider the possibility that the law in *Tornillo* was a kind of "candidate protection act," and illegitimate because its purpose and effect were to insulate political figures from criticism. In a concurring opinion in *Tornillo*, Justice Brennan asserted that "the Court's opinion [implies] no view upon the constitutionality of 'retraction' statutes affording plaintiffs able to prove defamatory falsehoods a statutory action to require publication of a retraction." Do you agree? Suppose, instead of a "right-of-reply" law, Florida adopted a "right-of-access" law, requiring every newspaper to set aside one page each issue for letters to the editor, not to exceed five hundred words, to be selected for publication without regard to content. Would such a law be invalid under *Tornillo*? Recall *PruneYard*, Chapter V.E, supra.

**RED LION BROADCASTING CO. V. FCC, 395 U.S. 367 (1960):** In *Red Lion*, the Court upheld the constitutionality of the Federal Communication Commission's fairness doctrine and its component regulations governing personal attacks and political editorializing. The fairness doctrine, which originated "very early in the history of broadcasting," imposes "on radio and television broadcasters the requirement that discussion of public issues be presented on broadcast stations, and that each side of those issues must be given fair coverage." The personal attack rule requires that when, "during the presentation of views on a controversial issue of public importance, an attack is made upon the honesty, character, integrity or like personal qualities of an identified person or group," the attacked person or group must be given notice, a transcript, and a reasonable opportunity to respond. The political editorializing rule requires that when, in an editorial, a broadcaster endorses or opposes a political candidate, the broadcaster must notify the opposed candidate or the opponents of the endorsed candidate and give them a "reasonable opportunity" to reply.

Justice White delivered the opinion of the Court: "The broadcasters [allege] that the [challenged] rules abridge their freedom of speech and press. Their contention is that the First Amendment protects their desire to use their allotted frequencies continuously to broadcast whatever they choose, and to exclude whomever they choose from ever using that frequency. [Although] broadcasting is clearly a medium affected by a First Amendment interest, differences in the characteristics of new media justify differences in the First Amendment standards applied to them. [Where] there are substantially more individuals who want to broadcast than there are frequencies to allocate, it is idle to posit an unabridgeable First Amendment right to broadcast comparable to the right of every individual to speak, write, or publish. If 100 persons want broadcast licenses but there are only 10 frequencies to allocate, all of them may have the same "right" to a license; but if there is to be any effective communication by radio, only a few can be licensed and the rest must be barred from the airwaves. It would be strange if the First Amendment, aimed at protecting and furthering communications, prevented the Government from making radio communication possible by requiring licenses to broadcast and by limiting the number of licenses so as not to overcrowd the spectrum. . . .

"By the same token, as far as the First Amendment is concerned those who are licensed stand no better than those to whom licenses are refused. A license permits broadcasting, but the licensee has no constitutional right to be the one who holds the license or to monopolize a radio frequency to the exclusion of his fellow citizens. There is nothing in the First Amendment which prevents the Government from requiring a licensee to share his frequency with others and to conduct himself as a proxy or fiduciary with obligations to present those views and voices which are representative of his community and which would otherwise, by necessity, be barred from the airwaves. [The] people as a whole retain their interest in free speech by radio and their collective right to have the medium function consistently with the ends and purposes of the First Amendment. It is the right of the viewers and listeners, not the right of the broadcasters, which is paramount. [It] is the right of the public to receive suitable access to social, political, esthetic, moral, and other ideas and experiences which is crucial here. . . .

"[We cannot] say that it is inconsistent with the First Amendment goal of producing an informed public capable of conducting its own affairs to require a broadcaster to permit answers to personal attacks occurring in the course of discussing controversial issues, or to require that the political opponents of those endorsed by the station be given a chance to communicate with the public. Otherwise, station owners and a few networks would have unfettered power to make time available only to the highest bidders, to communicate only their own views on public issues, people and candidates, and to permit on the air only those with whom they agreed. There is no sanctuary in the First Amendment for unlimited private censorship operating in a medium not open to all. . . .

"It is strenuously argued, however, that if political editorials or personal attacks will trigger an obligation in broadcasters to afford the opportunity for expression to speakers who need not pay for time and whose views are unpalatable to the licensees, then broadcasters will be irresistibly forced to self-censorship and their coverage of controversial public issues will be eliminated or at least rendered wholly ineffective. Such a result would indeed be a serious matter, for should licensees actually eliminate their coverage of controversial issues, the purposes of the doctrine would be stifled. [At] this point, however, as the Federal Communications Commission has indicated, that possibility is at best speculative. [And] if experience with the administration of these doctrines indicates that they have the net effect of reducing rather than enhancing the volume and quality of coverage, there will be time enough to reconsider the constitutional implications. . . .

"It is argued that even if at one time the lack of available frequencies for all who wished to use them justified the Government's choice of those who would best serve the public interest by acting as proxy for those who would present differing views, or by giving the latter access directly to broadcast facilities, this condition no longer prevails so that continuing control is not justified. To this there are several answers. Scarcity is not entirely a thing of the past. Advances in technology, such as microwave transmission, have led to more efficient utilization of the frequency spectrum, but uses for that spectrum have also grown apace. [Nothing] in this record, or in our own researches, convinces us that the resource is no longer one for which there are more immediate and potential uses than can be accommodated. . . .

"[Moreover], the fact remains that existing broadcasters have often attained their present position because of their initial government selection in competition with others before new technological advances opened new opportunities for further uses. Long experience in broadcasting, confirmed habits of listeners and viewers, network affiliation, and other advantages in program procurement give existing broadcasters a substantial advantage over new entrants, even where new entry is technologically possible. These advantages are the fruit of a preferred position conferred by the Government. Some present possibility for new entry by competing stations is not enough, in itself, to render unconstitutional the Government's effort to assure that a broadcaster's programming ranges widely enough to serve the public interest.

"In view of the scarcity of broadcast frequencies, the Government's role in allocating those frequencies, and the legitimate claims of those unable without governmental assistance to gain access to those frequencies for expression of their views, we hold the [regulations] constitutional."[28]

## Note: *Regulating the Airwaves*

1. Buckley *and* Red Lion. Note that *Red Lion*, like Buckley v. Valeo, Chapter V.D, supra, involves a conflict between competing theories of the role of government and of the appropriate conception of a system of freedom of expression. Under one view, government is permitted and may even have an obligation to intervene in order to prevent the distorting effects on deliberative processes that are created by the operation of the "private" sphere. Under the competing view, government should accept the private sphere "as is" and may not consider inequalities that derive therefrom as "distortions" at all. Why do *Buckley* and *Red Lion* resolve what is in many respects the same dispute in such different ways? See C. Sunstein, Democracy and the Problem of Free Speech (1993) (approving *Red Lion*, criticizing *Buckley*, and calling for greater regulation of the media to promote free expression).

2. *Licensing the airwaves.* In the Communications Act of 1934, the government, "to maintain the control of the United States over [the channels of] radio transmission; and to provide for the use of such channels, but not the ownership thereof, by persons for limited periods of time," established the FCC and granted it broad power to license and regulate the broadcast spectrum "as public convenience, interest, or necessity requires." In National Broadcasting

---

28. We need not deal with the argument that even if there is no longer a technological scarcity of frequencies limiting the number of broadcasters, there nevertheless is an economic scarcity in the sense that the Commission could or does limit entry to the broadcasting market on economic grounds and license no more stations than the market will support. Hence, it is said, the fairness doctrine or its equivalent is essential to satisfy the claims of those excluded and of the public generally. A related argument, which we also put aside, is that quite apart from scarcity of frequencies, technological or economic, Congress does not abridge freedom of speech or press by legislation directly or indirectly multiplying the voices and views presented to the public through time sharing, fairness doctrines, or other devices which limit or dissipate the power of those who sit astride the channels of communication with the general public. . . .

Co. v. United States, 319 U.S. 190 (1943), the Court held that such government licensing did not violate the first amendment because, "[unlike] other modes of expression, radio inherently is not available to all." Consider the following arguments:

a. Powe, "Or of the [Broadcast] Press," 55 Tex. L. Rev. 39, 55–56 (1976):

> As a theory, scarcity begins with the premise [that] information sources do not compete effectively with each other. This premise is not successfully explained, and seems contradictory to the normal first amendment assumption. [Moreover,] if one looks to actual numbers [there are more radio and television stations in the United States than daily newspapers].

b. Coase, The Federal Communications Commission, 2 J.L. & Econ. 1, 14–18 (1959):

> [The Court] seems to believe that federal regulation is needed because radio frequencies are limited in number and people want to use more of them than are available. But it is a commonplace of economics that almost all resources used in the economic system (and not simply radio and television frequencies) are limited in amount and scarce, in that people would like to use more than exists. [It] is true that some mechanism has to be employed to decide who [should] be allowed to use the scarce resource. But the way this is usually done [is] to employ the price mechanism, and this allocates resources to users without the need for government regulation. [An] administrative agency which attempts to perform the function normally carried out by the pricing mechanism [cannot], by the nature of things, be [fully aware] of the preferences of consumers. [Allocation by means of the pricing mechanism is thus more likely than allocation by administrative action to serve the "public convenience, interest, or necessity."]

c. Van Alstyne, The Mobius Strip of the First Amendment: Perspectives on *Red Lion*, 29 S.C. L. Rev. 539, 562 (1978):

> The [Coase] argument is appealing, but it is based on a fatal myopia in its failure to see how clearly freedom of speech [is] abridged by a government policy that adheres only to a private property system and a market-pricing mechanism in determining who shall be able to speak. [Allocation by means of the pricing mechanism would winnow] the field of otherwise eligible applicants strictly according to their ability to pay; it [would eliminate] from the licensing competition those who lack dollars to put in an effective bid.

d. In FCC v. Fox Television Stations, 556 U.S. 502 (2009), Chapter IV.G, supra, Justice Thomas called *Red Lion* into question in a separate concurring opinion:

> *Red Lion* [was] unconvincing when [it was] issued, and the passage of time has only increased doubt regarding [its] continued validity. [*Red Lion*] relied heavily

on the scarcity of available broadcast frequencies. [Dramatic] technological advances have eviscerated the factual assumptions underlying [that decision]. Broadcast spectrum is significantly less scarce than it was 40 years ago. [And] the trend should continue. [Moreover], traditional broadcast television and radio are no longer the "uniquely pervasive" media forms they once were. For most consumers, traditional broadcast media programming is now bundled with cable or satellite services. Broadcast and other video programming is also widely available over the Internet. [The] extant facts that drove this Court to subject broadcasters to unique disfavor under the First Amendment simply do not exist today.

e. Bollinger, Freedom of the Press and Public Access: Toward a Theory of Partial Regulation of the Mass Media, 75 Mich. L. Rev. 1, 26–36 (1976):

The] Court's decisions on the question of access [to the print and broadcast media] exhibit fundamental good sense. The good sense, however, derives not from the Court's treatment of broadcasting as being somehow special, but rather from its apparent desire to limit the over-all reach of access regulation. [There] are good first amendment reasons for being both receptive to and wary of access regulation. [Only under a partial regulatory scheme,] with a major branch of the press remaining free of regulation, will the costs and risks of regulation be held at an acceptable level. [By] permitting different treatment of the two institutions, the Court can facilitate realization of the benefits of two distinct constitutional values, both of which ought to be fostered: access in a highly concentrated press and minimal governmental intrusion. [The] Court has imposed a compromise — a compromise, however, not based on notions of expediency, but rather on a reasoned, and principled, accommodation of competing first amendment values.

f. Logan, Getting Beyond Scarcity: A New Paradigm for Assessing the Constitutionality of Broadcast Regulation, 85 Cal. L. Rev. 1687, 1709–1714 (1997):

If the Supreme Court were to reject the scarcity rationale, the public forum doctrine could provide an alternative basis for upholding broadcast content regulation. [The] central premise of this argument is that broadcasters have been granted the exclusive use of a valuable resource — the electromagnetic spectrum — which Congress has deemed to be public property. [Because] access to the spectrum [has traditionally been] limited to those broadcasters who have received a license to use the airwaves, and they [have traditionally been allowed to] program their channels as they see fit as long as they abide by their public interest obligations, [the] broadcast spectrum is best characterized as a limited designated public forum, [in which the] government may impose content-based restrictions [provided] they are "reasonable in light of the purpose served by the forum" and do not "discriminate against speech on the basis of its viewpoint."

Suppose a city builds an auditorium and licenses X to manage it. Can the city constitutionally instruct X that he must give priority to political events and must be evenhanded when he permits the auditorium to be used for such events? Is broadcasting any different?

3. *Regulating the airwaves.* Assuming licensing of the airwaves is not itself unconstitutional, what factors may the FCC consider in its allocation of licenses?

a. May the FCC compel an applicant for a broadcast license to ascertain the problems, needs, and interests of his community and to provide programming to meet those needs? See Ascertainment of Community Problems by Broadcast Applicants Primer, 57 F.C.C.2d 418 (1976). May the FCC, for example, deny a license to an applicant for a radio station in a community with a significant minority population unless the applicant agrees to devote a significant portion of her programming to information and entertainment designed specifically for the minority community?

b. May the FCC prohibit broadcasters from airing programs that contain profanity? May it prohibit programs that incite to crime? That are sexually explicit? That depict a racial or religious group in a degrading manner? Recall FCC v. Pacifica Foundation, Chapter IV.G, supra.

c. Consider the following proposal made by Reed Hundt, then-chair of the FCC, in Hundt, The Public's Airwaves: What Does the Public Interest Require of Television Broadcasters?, 45 Duke L.J. 1089, 1099–1100, 1105–1106 (1996):

> In the aggregate, political candidates at all levels spent [$500 million in 1996] on media advertising. [The] cost of television advertising makes fundraising an enormous entry barrier for candidates seeking public office, an oppressive burden for incumbents seeking reelection, a continuous threat to the integrity of our political institutions, and a principal cause of the erosion of public respect for public service. [To address this problem,] broadcasters should be required, [as] a condition of their licenses, to provide free airtime for political candidates. . . .
>
> [This could be accomplished by requiring] broadcasters [to] donate [$500 million worth of] airtime to [a time] bank and [authorizing] candidates [to] draw airtime from the bank during their campaigns. [How] would we divide the time contributed to a time bank? One approach would be to grant each eligible candidate a right to a specific dollar amount of free time. Candidates would then negotiate with broadcasters for advertising time, just as they currently do, but would pay with time bank credits rather than actual dollars. Why would broadcasters accept credits? Because they would be required to provide free time worth, say, 2 percent of their annual advertising revenues as a condition of using the public airwaves for free. Indeed, it would be important for broadcasters to provide time to candidates lest they lose their licenses.

4. *Related issues.* See FCC v. League of Women Voters, 468 U.S. 364 (1984) (invalidating section 399 of the Public Broadcasting Act of 1967, which prohibited any noncommercial educational station that receives a grant from the

Corporation for Public Broadcasting to "engage in editorializing"); CBS v. FCC, 453 U.S. 367 (1981) (upholding the constitutionality of FCC rules interpreting section 312(a)(7) of the Communications Act, which requires broadcasters to permit "a legally qualified candidate for Federal elective office" to purchase "reasonable amounts of time" on "behalf of his candidacy"); FCC v. Midwest Video Corp., 440 U.S. 689 (1979) (FCC rules requiring cable systems to hold out dedicated channels for all users on a first-come, nondiscriminatory basis violate section 3(h) of the Communications Act, which provides that "a person engaged [in] broadcasting shall not [be] deemed a common carrier"); Columbia Broadcasting System v. Democratic National Committee, 412 U.S. 94 (1973) (the first amendment does not itself require broadcast licensees to sell advertising time to groups or individuals wishing to express their views on controversial issues of public importance).

5. *Repeal of the fairness doctrine.* In 1987, the FCC repealed the fairness doctrine, asserting that the doctrine was unconstitutional because it "chilled" the first amendment rights of broadcasters.

6. *Regulating the media to achieve a "more advanced democratic society."* Consider L. Bollinger, Images of a Free Press 133–145 (1991):

> [Under the image of freedom of the press established in New York Times v. Sullivan], the goal of press freedom [was] viewed as the creation of a vast space for "uninhibited, robust, and wide-open" public discussion [and it was] assumed that the role of the Supreme Court is to stand guard against government intervention. [This approach is] insensitive to problems affecting the quality of public discussion that are posed by a laissez-faire system of modern mass media. [What is needed is a] more fundamental understanding [of press freedom].
>
> [To achieve this more fundamental understanding, we] must address the nature of our own behavior in the discussion of public questions. [A] democratic society, like an individual, should strive to remain conscious of the biases that skew, distort, and corrupt its own thinking about public issues. [Even] in a world in which the press is entirely free and open to all voices, with a perfect market in that sense, human nature would still see to it that quality public debate and decisionmaking would not rise naturally to the surface but would [need] the buoyant support of some form of collective action [involving] public institutions.
>
> [Although the mass media may] give viewers and readers what they "want" [through] the expression of their preferences in the marketplace, [it is nonetheless imaginable] that we — the same "we" that issue our marketplace votes for what we get — might be very concerned about [what] choices we are making in that system. [Accordingly, we may] decide together, through public regulation, that we would like to alter [the] demands we find ourselves making in that market context, [for we may] recognize that if we are left to choose on our own whether and how to inform ourselves, too many will neglect to undertake the burdens of self-education, choosing instead to pursue more pleasant things. [It] would be a more [advanced] democratic society that could act to correct deficiencies arising out of [the] citizens themselves.

**TURNER BROADCASTING SYSTEM INC. v. FCC, 512 U.S. 622 (1994):** The "must carry" provisions of the Cable Television Consumer Protection and Competition Act of 1992 require cable television systems to devote a portion of their channels, free of charge, to the transmission of local broadcast television stations. The rationale of these provisions was explained by the Court:

"Cable technology affords two principal benefits over broadcast. First, it eliminates the signal interference sometimes encountered in over-the-air [broadcasting]. Second, it is capable of transmitting many more channels than are available through broadcasting. [Congress] enacted the 1992 Cable Act after conducting three years of [hearings]. Congress concluded that [the] overwhelming majority of cable operators exercise a monopoly over cable service [and that] this market position gives cable operators the power and the incentive to harm broadcast competitors. The power derives from the cable operator's ability [to refuse to transmit broadcast signals]. The incentive derives from the economic reality that '[c]able television systems and broadcast systems increasingly compete for television advertising revenues.' By refusing carriage of broadcasters' signals, cable operators [can] reduce the number of households that have access to the broadcasters' programming, and thereby capture advertising dollars that would otherwise go to broadcast stations. [In such circumstances], Congress concluded that unless cable operators are required to carry local broadcast stations, '[t]here is a substantial likelihood [that] the economic viability of free local broadcast television [will] be seriously jeopardized.' [Congress] sought to avoid the elimination of broadcast television [because]' '[s]uch programming is . . . free to those who own television sets and does not require cable transmission to receive broadcast signals.' [The] provisions are designed to [ensure] that every individual with a television set can obtain access to free television programming."

Although the Court divided sharply on the constitutionality of the "must carry" provisions, it was unanimous in holding that the regulation of cable television should not be governed by the same constitutional standards as broadcast regulation. Justice Kennedy delivered the opinion of the Court:

"[The] rationale for applying a less rigorous standard of First Amendment scrutiny to broadcast regulation [does] not apply in the context of cable regulation. The justification for our distinct approach to broadcast regulation rests upon the unique physical limitations of the broadcast medium. As a general matter, there are more would-be broadcasters than frequencies available in the electromagnetic spectrum. And if two broadcasters were to attempt to transmit over the same frequency in the same locale, they would interfere with one another's signals, so that neither could be heard at all. The scarcity of broadcast frequencies thus required the establishment of some regulatory mechanism to divide the electromagnetic spectrum and assign specific frequencies to particular broadcasters. [The] broadcast cases are inapposite in the present context because cable television does not suffer from the inherent limitations that characterize the broadcast medium. Indeed, given the rapid advances in fiber optics and digital compression technology, soon there may be no practical limitation on the number of speakers who may use the cable medium. Nor is there any danger of physical interference between two cable speakers attempting to share the same channel. In light of these fundamental technological differences between broadcast and cable transmission, application of the more relaxed standard of scrutiny adopted in *Red Lion* [is] inapt when determining the First Amendment validity of cable regulation. . . .

"Although the Government acknowledges the substantial technological differences between broadcast and cable, it advances a second argument for application of the *Red Lion* framework to cable regulation. It asserts that the foundation of our broadcast jurisprudence is not the physical limitations of the electromagnetic spectrum, but rather the 'market dysfunction' that characterizes the broadcast market. Because the cable market is beset by a similar dysfunction, the Government maintains, the *Red Lion* standard of review should also apply to cable. While we agree that the cable market suffers certain structural impediments, the Government's argument is flawed in two respects. First, as discussed above, the special physical characteristics of broadcast transmission, not the economic characteristics of the broadcast market, are what underlies our broadcast jurisprudence. Second, the mere assertion of a dysfunction or failure in a speech market, without more, is not enough to shield a speech regulation from the First Amendment standards applicable to nonbroadcast media."

In his opinion for the Court, Justice Kennedy conceded that the "must carry" "provisions interfere with cable operators' editorial discretion by compelling them to offer carriage [to] broadcast stations," but emphasized that "the extent of the interference does not depend upon the content of the cable operators' programming." Justice Kennedy therefore concluded that "the appropriate standard by which to evaluate the constitutionality of [the 'must carry' provisions] is [not 'the most exacting level' of first amendment scrutiny, but] the intermediate level of scrutiny applicable to content-neutral restrictions that impose an incidental burden on speech," invoking the standard set forth in United States v. O'Brien, Chapter V.C, supra.

Applying this standard, Justice Kennedy, writing at this point only for himself and three other justices, remanded for further fact-finding on whether the "must carry" rules are in fact "necessary to protect the viability of broadcast television." Justice Kennedy explained that the government "must demonstrate that the recited harms are real, not merely conjectural, and that the regulation will in fact alleviate these harms in a direct and material way." Although agreeing that "courts must accord substantial deference to the predictive judgments of Congress," Justice Kennedy nonetheless concluded that the courts have an "obligation to exercise independent judgment when First Amendment rights are implicated [to] assure that, in formulating its judgments, Congress has drawn reasonable inferences based on substantial evidence." In this case, without "a more substantial elaboration [of] the predictive or historical evidence upon which Congress relied, or the introduction of some additional evidence to establish [that] broadcasters would be at serious [risk], we cannot determine whether the threat to broadcast television is real enough to overcome the challenge to the provisions. . . ."

In a concurring opinion, Justice Stevens agreed "with most of Justice Kennedy's reasoning," but concluded that the "must carry" provisions should be upheld without a remand: "[The] question for us is merely whether Congress could fairly conclude that cable operators' monopoly position threatens the continued viability of broadcast television and that must carry is an appropriate means of minimizing that risk. [Accorded] proper deference, the [congressional] findings [are] sufficient to sustain the must carry [provisions]. An industry need not be in its death throes before Congress may act to protect it from economic harm. . . ."

Justice O'Connor, joined by Justices Scalia, Thomas, and Ginsburg, dissented in part. At the outset, Justice O'Connor observed that the act "implicates the First Amendment rights of two classes of speakers": "First, it tells cable operators which programmers they must [carry]. Second, [it] deprives [cable programmers] of access to over one-third of an entire medium. Cable programmers may compete only for those channels that are not set aside by the must carry provisions. [It] is as if the government ordered all movie theaters to reserve at least one-third of their screening for films made by American production companies, or required all bookstores to devote one-third of their shelf space to nonprofit publishers."

Justice O'Connor argued further that the "must carry" provisions are content-based, rather than content-neutral, because various congressional findings supporting the legislation expressed "[preferences] for diversity of viewpoints, for localism, for educational programming, and for news and public affairs." Although the Court concluded that such findings showed "nothing more than the recognition that the services provided by broadcast television have some intrinsic value and, thus, are worth preserving against the threats posed by cable," Justice O'Connor argued that the "controversial judgment at the heart of the statute is not that broadcast television has some value, [but] that broadcasters should be preferred over cable programmers" because of the content of broadcast programming. In Justice O'Connor's view, the government's "interest in ensuring access to a multiplicity of diverse and antagonistic sources of information [is] directly tied to the content of what the speakers will likely say." Justice O'Connor therefore reasoned that the "must carry" provisions must be tested by "exacting" standards of content-based analysis and must be "narrowly tailored to a compelling state interest."

Applying this standard, Justice O'Connor concluded that the provisions could not withstand constitutional scrutiny.

### Note: Turner *and the Regulation of Cable*

1. Turner *and the problem of content.* Consider Justice O'Connor's argument that the "must carry" regulations are content-based because they were designed in part to promote "access to a multiplicity of diverse and antagonistic sources of information." Is a city council's decision to permit individuals to display messages in the interior of city-owned buses "content-based" because the city council's goal is to promote "access to a multiplicity of diverse and antagonistic sources of information"? Should it make a difference whether the challenged provision attempts to achieve this goal (a) by expanding opportunities for free expression in a facially content-neutral manner or (b) by providing expanded speech opportunities for particular, otherwise underrepresented, viewpoints in an explicitly content-based manner?

2. Turner *revisited.* In Turner Broadcasting System Inc. v. FCC, 520 U.S. 180 (1997) (*Turner II*), the Court, in a five-to-four decision, upheld under "intermediate scrutiny" the constitutionality of the must-carry provisions at issue in *Turner I,* affirming the district court's decision that the expanded record presented to it on remand from *Turner I* contained substantial evidence supporting Congress's predictive judgment that the "must carry" provisions further important governmental interests in preserving cable carriage of local broadcast stations, and that the provisions are narrowly tailored to promote those interests. In reaching this conclusion, the Court, in an opinion by Justice Kennedy, emphasized that "we owe Congress' findings deference [because Congress] 'is far better equipped than the judiciary to "amass and evaluate the vast amounts of data" bearing upon' legislative questions." Thus, "we need not put our imprimatur on Congress' economic theory in order to validate the reasonableness of its judgment," nor should we "re-weigh the evidence de novo" or "replace Congress' factual predictions with our own."

In a concurring opinion, Justice Stevens emphasized that "if this statute regulated the content of speech, rather than the structure of the market, our task would be quite different." Justice O'Connor, joined by Justices Scalia, Thomas, and Ginsburg, dissented. Justice O'Connor maintained that "the principal opinion" exhibits "an extraordinary and unwarranted deference for congressional judgments, a profound fear of delving into complex economic matters, and a willingness to substitute untested assumptions for evidence." As a consequence, the principal opinion "trivializes the First Amendment issue at stake in this case."

The bottom line seems to be that, in at least most respects, the Court will treat cable television as more analogous to the traditional print media for first amendment purposes than to the broadcast media. Is that a sensible conclusion?

## Note: The First Amendment in Cyberspace

1. *New technologies and the first amendment.* As new technologies revolutionize communication, questions inevitably arise about how the first amendment should apply. *Red Lion* struggled with the novel challenges posed by broadcasting, and *Denver Area* wrestled with how to assess the special issues posed by cable. The Court encountered similar difficulties when it first considered motion pictures and sound trucks. Recall Kovacs v. Cooper, Chapter V.A, supra. What, then, of cyberspace? Consider the following views:

a. Berman and Weitzner, Abundance and User Control: Renewing the Democratic Heart of the First Amendment in the Age of Interactive Media, 104 Yale L.J. 1619, 1624 (1995):

> Unlike the channelized networks of today's mass media, open-access networks are decentralized: No single point is designated for the origination of content. A single user can send information to [millions] of other users on the networks, without any advance negotiation or special arrangement with the network operator. [With no] centralized distribution point on the network, it is much harder for a network operator — or any other entity — to stifle independent information sources. [The] abundance generated by such an open-access network eliminates one of the key First Amendment diversity difficulties found in mass media. Instead of network operators or government regulators allocating a small number of channels among a large number of information sources, all information providers [will] have the opportunity to speak. . . .

b. Fiss, In Search of a New Paradigm, 104 Yale L.J. 1613, 1614–1615 (1995):

> [Much of current First Amendment analysis is premised] on an outmoded paradigm: the street corner speaker. [A] body of doctrine that did no more than protect the street corner speaker from the menacing reach of the police would leave the values served by the First Amendment vulnerable [and] largely unfulfilled. [But we are now in the midst] of a new technological revolution. [What] is happening is nothing less than a redefinition of the way we read and write, the way we talk to and correspond with one another [and] how we perform our roles as citizens. [We must begin the process of thinking] through the implications for the First Amendment of the technological revolution through which we are now living.

c. Krattenmaker and Powe, Converging First Amendment Principles for Converging Communications Media, 104 Yale L.J. 1719, 1721, 1725, 1726, 1740 (1995):

> No matter how often one repeats the statement, it cannot be true that "[d]ifferent communications media [should be] treated differently for First Amendment purposes." Should everything we knew about regulation of books have been discarded once talking motion pictures were invented? Did discovery of the

personal computer [render] obsolete everything the courts said about the First Amendment and broadcasting, or cable, or telephones? [Past] complaints will be prologue for future complaints about what creators place on, and users receive from, [cyberspace]. Some will complain that an insufficient amount of the appropriate type or quality of information is available. Others [will] complain that users may be accessing information they ought not have. [In responding to these familiar issues,] only a unitary First Amendment for all media will do. [The] general principles underlying regulation of the [traditional print] media should apply fully to the new as well as the old electronic communications media.

*2. The first amendment in cyberspace — some specific issues.*
a. Lessig, The Path of Cyberlaw, 104 Yale L.J. 1743, 1750, 1752 (1995):

[We] can see many good reasons why someone would want to remain anonymous. [One] wants to contribute to a political discussion without suffering the costs of unpopular views; one wants to find information without revealing that one needs that information; one wants to assume a role in certain discussion groups to explore an alternative identity. [Not] all anonymity, however, is so benign. Perfect anonymity makes perfect crime possible. The ability to appear invisibly on the network [certainly] will increase the incidence of those on the network who slander, or harass or assault. [A careful] balance will have to be drawn. [Already] the extremes are well staked, with some arguing that no regulation [of anonymity] should be permitted, and others arguing that only with regulation should [anonymity] be allowed.

b. Kreimer, Technologies of Protest: Insurgent Social Movements and the First Amendment in the Era of the Internet, 150 U. Pa. L. Rev. 119, 122–124 (2001):

Given the structure of twentieth-century communications media, established or well-financed contenders in the public arena [had] a built-in advantage: the cost of disseminating arguments or information to a broad audience threatened effectively to exclude outsiders from public debate. [The Internet] has changed this dynamic, for [almost] any social movement can put up a website. [From] neo-Nazism and Christian Identity to gay liberation and disability rights, [the Internet] facilitates challenges to the status quo. . . .

c. C. Sunstein, republic.com 8–9, 16, 54, 65, 71, 86 (2001):

[A] well-functioning system of free expression must meet two distinctive requirements. First, people should be exposed to materials that they would not have chosen in advance. Unplanned [encounters] are central to democracy [and people should] often come across views and topics that they have not specifically selected. Second, [citizens] should have a range of common experiences. Without shared experiences, [people may] find it hard to understand one another. [There] are serious dangers in a system in which individuals [restrict] themselves to opinions and topics of their own choosing. . . .

The specialization of Websites [and discussion groups] is obviously important here. [For example], there are hundreds of Websites created [by] hate groups and extremist organizations [which] provide links to one another. [Such Websites] are being used [to] reinforce existing convictions. [They are] permitting people [to] spread rumors, many of them paranoid and hateful. [This is an example of group polarization, which] refers to something very simple: After deliberation, people are likely to move toward a more extreme point in the direction to which the group's members were originally inclined. . . .

With respect to the Internet, [the] implication is that groups of like-minded people, engaged in discussion with one another, will end up thinking the same thing that they thought before — but in more extreme form. [Group] polarization is unquestionably occurring on the Internet, [which] is serving as a breeding ground for extremism. [For] citizens of a heterogeneous democracy, a fragmented communications market creates considerable dangers.

d. Leiter, Cleaning Cyber-Cesspools: Google and Free Speech, in S. Levmore and M. Nussbaum, eds., The Offensive Internet 155 (2010):

I shall use the term "cyber-cesspool" to refer to those places in cyberspace — chat rooms, websites, blogs, and often the comment sections of blogs — which are devoted in whole or in part to demeaning, harassing, and humiliating individuals. [The] Internet is currently full of cyber-cesspools. [Since] cyber-cesspools are in large part beyond the reach of regulation [because] of constitutional protections, a number of commentators have suggested enhancing private remedies by, for example, making intermediaries — those who host blogs or perhaps even service providers — liable for tortious harms on their sites. This would require repeal of Section 250 of the Communications Decency Act (47 U.S.C. §230), which provides that "No provider or user of an interactive computer service shall be treated as the publisher or speaker of any information provided by another information content provider." The effect of that simple provision has been to treat cyber-cesspools wholly differently from, for example, newspapers that decide to publish similar material. Whereas publishers of the latter are liable for the tortious letters or advertisements they publish [recall New York Times v. Sullivan, Chapter IV.A, supra], owners of cyber-cesspools are held legally unaccountable for even the most noxious material on their sites, even when put on notice as to its potentially tortious nature. But why should blogs, whose circulation sometimes dwarfs that of many newspapers, be insulated from liability for actionable material they permit on their site?

3. *Indecency on the Internet.* In Reno v. American Civil Liberties Union, Chapter IV.G, supra, the Court invalidated provisions of the Communications Decency Act of 1996 (CDA) that prohibited any person from sending over the Internet in a way that would be available to a person under eighteen years of age any "indecent" material or any material that "depicts or describes, in terms patently offensive as measured by contemporary community standards, sexual

or excretory activities or organs." In distinguishing the Internet from broadcasting, the Court explained:

> [We have] observed that "[e]ach medium of expression . . . may present its own problems." Thus, some of our cases have recognized special justifications for regulation of the broadcast media that are not applicable to other speakers [citing, e.g., *Red Lion; Pacifica*]. In these cases, the Court relied on the history of extensive government regulation of the broadcast medium, the scarcity of available frequencies at its inception, and its "invasive" nature.
>
> Those factors are not present in cyberspace. Neither before nor after the enactment of the CDA have the vast democratic fora of the Internet been subject to the type of government supervision and regulation that has attended the broadcast industry. Moreover, the Internet is not as "invasive" as radio or television. The District Court specifically found that "[c]ommunications over the Internet do not 'invade' an individual's home or appear on one's computer screen unbidden. Users seldom encounter content 'by accident.'" [Finally], unlike the conditions that prevailed when Congress first authorized regulation of the broadcast spectrum, the Internet can hardly be considered a "scarce" expressive commodity. It provides relatively unlimited, low cost capacity for communication of all kinds. [Our] cases provide no basis for qualifying the level of First Amendment scrutiny that should be applied to this medium.

Should local community standards apply in deciding whether sexually explicit material posted on the Internet is "obscene"? See Ashcroft v. American Civil Liberties Union, Chapter IV.E, supra.

4. *The liability of cable and Internet carriers for the speech of users.* In what circumstances, if any, should cable or Internet carriers be liable for the libelous, obscene, or otherwise actionable speech they carry? Consider the liability of (a) a store that sells typewriters for the messages typed by purchasers; (b) a telephone company for the speech of callers; (c) a bookstore for the contents of the books it sells; (d) a news vendor for the contents of the newspapers it sells; (e) a newspaper or magazine for the statements made by guest columnists; (f) a cable operator for the programs it carries; and (g) an email service provider for the messages it transmits. Should the standards of liability differ across these different situations? Should it matter whether the defendant exercises "editorial" control? Should the defendants in all or some of these cases be liable only "if they have actual notice that the speech has previously been adjudicated illegal or unprotected"? Myerson, Authors, Editors, and Uncommon Carriers: Identifying the "Speaker" within the New Media, 71 Notre Dame L. Rev. 79, 122 (1995).

5. *Freedom of the press in a global society.* Consider L. Bollinger, Uninhibited, Robust, and Wide-Open: A Free Press for a New Century 105–106, 116–117 (2010):

> [We] are facing the emergence of a global society, with the technological capacity to provide a free and independent press to a world in desperate need

of such an institution, but there is also a myriad of laws, policies, practices, and conditions that inhibit and impede that from happening. Without a central, overriding system of constitutional protections, there is a risk of a collapse to the bottom, where jurisdictions that have the least degree of freedom will undermine the freedom of those that value it the most. . . .

This situation poses a significant challenge to the United States and the world. For a society uniquely committed to unconstrained public debate and for which knowledge of the entire world is increasingly vital, we must now see how we can achieve this goal — to make it a shared principle as well as a working reality — in a world that is not in full agreement with the American conception of a free press. [To help achieve this, the Supreme Court must] begin the process of making the shift from the constitutional paradigm of a national public forum to a global one.

## Note: Free Expression — Final Thoughts

Consider Post, Recuperating First Amendment Doctrine, 47 Stan. L. Rev. 1249, 1249–1250 (1995):

Contemporary First Amendment doctrine [is] striking chiefly for its superficiality, its internal incoherence, its distressing failure to facilitate constructive judicial engagement with significant contemporary social issues connected with freedom of speech. . . . [It] has become increasingly a doctrine of words merely, and not of things.

Consider also Nagel, How Useful Is Judicial Review in Free Speech Cases?, 69 Cornell L. Rev. 302, 303, 335–338 (1984):

The dominant consensus that has prevailed for the last [seventy] years holds that the adjudication of individual cases can promote the level and quality of public debate. [The] assumptions upon which this [consensus] rests are largely unproven and often doubtful. [Indeed, a] general assessment of free speech cases is not reassuring. [Since 1919], much of the admiration for judges as protectors of free speech is predicated upon eloquent [dissents]. There are numerous major decisions in which the Court has subordinated free speech values to other social [interests]. Even in the cases that ultimately protect free speech, the Court often achieves the protection by [indirection]. In the relatively few decisions resting directly on free speech considerations, the Court often hedges its rulings with enough cautions and limitations to put into question the scope of the Court's commitment to free speech. [Moreover, judicial] efforts — such as those to protect corporate expenditures, nude dancing, and advertising — erode popular support by breeding resentment and bringing into question the utility of free speech. [Indeed,] the Court's program, taken as a whole, has done great damage to the public's understanding and appreciation of free speech by making it seem trivial, foreign, and unnecessarily costly.

On the other hand, consider S. Shiffrin, The First Amendment, Democracy, and Romance 159 (1990):

> American citizens not only feel a deep emotional attachment to the country, but also [a] sense of pride about the first amendment. The first amendment speaks to the kind of people we are and the kind of people we aspire to be. [It] plays an important role in the construction of an appealing story, a story about a nation that promotes independent people, a nation that affords a place of refuge for peoples all over the globe, a nation that welcomes the iconoclast, a nation that respects, tolerates, and even sponsors dissent. [The] image called up by this national picture [encourages] us to picture Walt Whitman's citizenry — vibrant, diverse, vital, stubborn, and independent. It encourages us to believe with Emerson that "America is the idea of emancipation."

Finally, consider D. Strauss, The Living Constitution 52–53 (2010):

> [The] First Amendment — that is, the principles protecting free speech — has been a tremendous success story in American constitutional law. But where did these successful principles come from? They did not come from the text of the Constitution. The First Amendment was part of the Constitution for a century and a half before the central principles of the American regime of free speech [became] established in the law. Nor did those principles come from the original understandings. [To] the extent that we can determine the views of [the Framers], they did not think they were establishing a system of freedom of expression resembling what we have today.
>
> The central principles of the American system of freedom of expression, in other words, are not the product of a moment of inspired constitutional genius 200-plus years ago. We owe those principles, instead, to the living, common law Constitution. The central features of First Amendment law were hammered out in fits and starts, in a series of judicial decisions and extrajudicial developments, over the course of the twentieth century. The story of the emergence of the American constitutional law of free speech is a story of evolution and precedent, trial and error — a demonstration of how the living Constitution works.

# PART II

## The Constitution and Religion

# VII

## Historical and Analytical Overview

The first amendment bars Congress from making laws "respecting an establishment of religion, or prohibiting the free exercise thereof." In addition to discussing doctrinal approaches to church/state issues, this chapter examines whether the relative clarity of the constitutional text, or its history, eases the task of constitutional adjudication or reduces the necessity for other theoretical underpinnings to the constitutional law of religion.

This Part has four chapters. The first provides historical background and outlines the general approaches that courts and commentators have taken to the religion clauses. The second examines problems of establishment, highlighting the tension between the idea that the establishment clause requires some degree of separation between church and state and a history that includes substantial state support of religious activities. The third chapter deals with problems of free exercise, focusing on the degree to which government must or may adjust its programs to claims that the programs burden the free exercise of religion. The fourth deals with the constitutional status of legislative efforts to accommodate religion through laws that arguably relieve burdens on the free exercise of religion.

**EVERSON v. BOARD OF EDUCATION, 330 U.S. 1 (1947).** New Jersey authorized its local school boards to repay parents with children in private schools for the cost of bus transportation to the schools. Most of the private schools were Roman Catholic parochial institutions. By a five-to-four vote, the Court upheld the statute against an establishment clause challenge, concluding that the state could pay the fares "as part of a general program under which it pays the fares of pupils attending public and other schools." This satisfied the first amendment's requirement that "the state [be] neutral in its relations with groups of religious believers and non-believers." Justice Black's opinion for the Court "[reviewed] the background and environment of" the first amendment:

"A large proportion of the early settlers of this country came here from Europe to escape the bondage of laws which compelled them to support

539

The dissenters agreed with Justice Black's description of the relevant history but argued that the New Jersey statute breached the "wall" of separation. Questions regarding state aid to nonpublic education are discussed in more detail in Chapter VIII.D infra.

## Note: *The History of the Religion Clauses*

1. *Two views of the Memorial and Remonstrance.* In Rosenberger v. Rectors & Visitors of the University of Virginia, 515 U.S. 819 (1995), Justices Thomas (concurring) and Souter (in dissent) offered competing interpretations of the establishment clause's history.

Summarizing the view of legal commentators, Justice Thomas wrote, "For some, the experience in Virginia is consistent with the view that the Framers saw the Establishment Clause simply as a prohibition on governmental pre-ferences for some religious faiths over others. Other commentators have rejected this view, concluding that the Establishment Clause forbids not only government preferences for some religious sects over others, but also government preferences for religion over irreligion." Justice Thomas found "much to commend the former view. [The] funding provided by the Virginia assessment was to be extended only to Christian sects, and the Remonstrance seized on this defect: 'Who does not see that the same authority which can establish Christianity, in exclusion of all other Religions, may establish with the same ease any particular sect of Christians, in exclusion of all other Sects.'" He continued:

> [Even] if Madison believed that the principle of non-establishment of religion precluded government financial support for religion per se (in the sense of government benefits specifically targeting religion), there is no indication that at the time of the framing he took the [extreme] view that the government must discriminate against religious adherents by excluding them from more generally available financial subsidies.

Justice Thomas pointed to "historical examples of funding that date back to the time of the founding. [Both] Houses of the First Congress elected cha-plains." There were "other, less familiar examples of what amount to direct funding [in] early Acts of Congress. See, e.g., Act of Feb. 20, 1833 (authorizing the State of Ohio to sell 'all or any part of the lands heretofore reserved and appropriated by Congress for the support of religion within the Ohio Com-pany's . . . purchases . . . and to invest the money arising from the sale thereof, in some productive fund; the proceeds of which shall be for ever annually applied . . . for the support of religion within the several townships for which said lands were originally reserved and set apart, and for no other use or purpose whatsoever')."

Justice Souter offered a different interpretation of Madison's position. "[The] bill [to which the Remonstrance was directed would] have allowed a taxpayer to refuse to appropriate his levy to any religious society, in which case the legislature was to use these unappropriated sums to fund 'seminaries of learning.' While some of these seminaries undoubtedly would have been religious in character, others would not have been, as a seminary was generally understood at the time to be 'any school, academy, college or [university].' N. Webster, An American Dictionary of the English Language (1st ed. 1828). [The] fact that the bill, if passed, would have funded secular as well as religious instruction did nothing to soften Madison's opposition to it."

Justice Souter continued, "Nor is it fair to argue that Madison opposed the bill only because it treated religious groups unequally. [Madison] strongly inveighed against the proposed aid for religion for a host of reasons [and] many of those reasons would have applied whether or not the state aid was being distributed equally among sects, and whether or not the aid was going to those sects in the context of an evenhanded government program. See, e.g., ¶ 1 ('In matters of Religion, no man's right is abridged by the institution of Civil Society, and . . . Religion is wholly exempt from its cognizance'); ¶ 7 ('Experience witnesseth that ecclesiastical establishments, instead of maintaining the purity and efficacy of Religion, have had a contrary operation'). [Madison's] Remonstrance did not argue for a bill distributing aid to all sects and religions on an equal basis, and the outgrowth of the Remonstrance and the defeat of the Virginia assessment was not such a bill; rather, it was the Virginia Bill for Establishing Religious Freedom, which [proscribed] the use of tax dollars for religious purposes."

2. *Some historical detail.* Justice Souter's concurring opinion in Lee v. Weisman, 505 U.S. 577 (1992), offered this view of the first amendment's background and early history:

> When James Madison arrived at the First Congress with a series of proposals to amend the National Constitution, one of the provisions read that "the civil rights of none shall be abridged on account of religious belief or worship, nor shall any national religion be established, nor shall the full and equal rights of conscience be in any manner, or on any pretext, infringed." Madison's language [was] sent to a Select Committee of the House, which, without explanation, changed it to read that "no religion shall be established by law, nor shall the equal rights of conscience be infringed." Thence the proposal went to the Committee of the Whole, which was in turn dissatisfied with the Select Committee's language and adopted an alternative proposed by Samuel Livermore of New Hampshire: "Congress shall make no laws touching religion, or infringing the rights of conscience." . . .
>
>   The House rewrote the amendment once more before sending it to the Senate, this time adopting, without recorded debate, language derived from a proposal by Fisher Ames of Massachusetts: "Congress shall make no law establishing Religion, or prohibiting the free exercise thereof, nor shall the rights

During his first three years in office, James Madison also refused to call for days of thanksgiving and prayer, though later, amid the political turmoil of the War of 1812, he did so on four separate occasions. Upon retirement, in an essay condemning as an unconstitutional "establishment" the use of public money to support congressional and military chaplains, he concluded that "religious proclamations by the Executive recommending thanksgivings & fasts are shoots from the same root with the legislative acts reviewed. Altho' recommendations only, they imply a religious agency, making no part of the trust delegated to political rulers." . . .

Madison's failure to keep pace with his principles in the face of congressional pressure cannot erase the principles. He admitted to backsliding, and explained that he had made the content of his wartime proclamations inconsequential enough to mitigate much of their impropriety. . . .

To be sure, the leaders of the young Republic engaged in some of the practices that separationists like Jefferson and Madison criticized. The First Congress did hire institutional chaplains, and Presidents Washington and Adams unapologetically marked days of "public thanksgiving and prayer." Yet in the face of the separationist dissent, those practices prove, at best, that the Framers simply did not share a common understanding of the Establishment Clause, and, at worst, that they, like other politicians, could raise constitutional ideals one day and turn their backs on them the next. . . .

3. *A challenge to originalist approaches.* What are the implications of the observation (if correct) that the historical materials "prove [that] the Framers [did] not share a common understanding"? Consider these observations by Justice Brennan, concurring in Abington School District v. Schempp, 374 U.S. 203 (1963), which held unconstitutional the practice of devotional Bible-reading in public schools:

> [An] awareness of history and an appreciation of the aims of the Founding Fathers do not always resolve concrete problems. [A] more fruitful inquiry [is] whether the practices [threaten] those consequences which the Framers deeply feared; whether, in short, they tend to promote that type of interdependence between religion and state which the First Amendment was designed to prevent. . . .
>
> [Our] religious composition makes us a vastly more diverse people than were our forefathers. They knew differences chiefly among Protestant sects. Today the Nation is far more heterogeneous religiously. [In] the face of such profound changes, practices which may have been objectionable to no one in the time of Jefferson and Madison may today be highly offensive to many persons, the deeply devout and the nonbelievers alike.

Consider the proposition that social change, such as the expansion of government, ought to affect the interpretation of both religion clauses: When government was confined to the enforcement of the common law and relatively little else, its potential for adversely affecting religious exercises was small, and a regime of government neutrality with respect to religion might have allowed religious liberty to flourish; an expansive government means that neutral government rules may interfere substantially with religious liberty. To what extent do current controversies arise in circumstances threatening the kinds of public disorder with which the framers were familiar? Consider as well the general arguments originalists make against interpretation predicated on the (imputed) general purposes of constitutional provisions.

4. *Other traditions.* L. Tribe, American Constitutional Law 1158–1160 (2d ed. 1988), describes another tradition:

> [The] evangelical view (associated primarily with Roger Williams) [was] that "worldly corruptions [might] consume the churches if sturdy fences against the wilderness were not maintained." . . . Roger Williams saw separation largely as a vehicle for protecting churches against the state. To the extent that it was possible to accept state aid without state control, he urged cooperation; indeed, he argued that the state must "countenance, encourage, and supply" those in religious service. Thus, his view has been called one of positive toleration, imposing on the state the burden of fostering a climate conducive to all religion.
>
> Thomas Jefferson, in contrast, saw separation as a means of protecting the state from the church. [It] was Jefferson's conviction that only the complete separation of religion from politics would eliminate the formal influence of religious institutions and provide for a free choice among political views; he therefore urged the strictest "wall of separation between church and state."
>
> James Madison believed that both religion and government could best achieve their high purposes if each were left free from the other within its respective sphere; he thus urged that the "tendency to a usurpation on one side or the other, or to a corrupting coalition or alliance between them, will be best guarded against by an entire abstinance [sic] of the Government from interference in any way whatever, beyond the necessity of preserving public order, & protecting each sect against trespass on its legal rights by others.'

For an analysis of Williams's views, see Hall, Roger Williams and the Foundations of Religious Liberty, 71 B.U. L. Rev. 455 (1991).

In Zelman v. Simmons-Harris, 536 U.S. 639 (2002), criticizing the Court's decision upholding a school voucher program that allowed vouchers to be used at religiously affiliated schools, Justice Souter discussed how, in his view, the risk that religion would be corrupted by government aid was "already being realized." He pointed to statutory provisions meaning that "the school may not give admission preferences to children who are members of the patron faith," suggesting that "a participating religious school may [be] forbidden to choose a member of its own clergy to serve as teacher or principal over a layperson of a different religion claiming equal qualification for the job," and suggesting that participating schools might not be allowed to "[teach] traditionally legitimate articles of faith as to the error, sinfulness, or ignorance of others, if they want government money for their schools." What basis is there of Christianity," citing, among other sources, Justice Joseph Story's Commentaries on the Constitution. "The original understanding of the type of 'religion' that qualified for constitutional protection under the Establishment Clause likely did not include [followers] of Judaism and Islam. . . . The inclusion of Jews and Muslims inside the category of constitutionally favored religions surely would have shocked [Justice] Story. [The] history of the Establishment Clause's original meaning just as strongly supports a preference for Christianity as it does a preference for monotheism."

In his opinion in *McCreary County*, Justice Scalia replied, "Since most thought the Clause permitted government invocation of monotheism, and some others thought it permitted government invocation of Christianity, [Justice Stevens] proposes that it be construed not to permit any government invocation of religion at all. [Those] narrower views of the Establishment Clause were as clearly rejected as the more expansive ones."

The majority opinion written by Justice Souter in *McCreary County* took the position that Justice Scalia's argument "[failed] to consider the full range of evidence showing what the Framers believed."

> The dissent is certainly correct in putting forward evidence that some of the Framers thought some endorsement of religion was compatible with the establishment ban. [But there] is also evidence supporting the proposition that the Framers intended the Establishment Clause to require government neutrality in matters of religion. . . . [The] fair inference is that there was no common understanding about the limits of the establishment prohibition. . . . What the evidence does show is a group of statesmen [who] proposed a guarantee with contours not wholly worked out, leaving the Establishment Clause with edges still to be determined. And none the worse for that.
>
> [Historical] evidence thus supports no solid argument for changing course. . . . [The] divisiveness of religion in current public life is inescapable. This is no time to deny the prudence of understanding the Establishment Clause to require the Government to stay neutral on religious belief, which is reserved for the conscience of the individual.

Balkin asks, "[W]hy did Jews and Muslims get thrown in the mix of first class religious citizens? After all, if you exclude them you still have about 91% of the population. So why couldn't the government offer prayers to Jesus Christ, our Lord and Savior?" Blog entry for June 27, 2005, available at http://balkin.blogspot.com. Is Justice Scalia's response, read in light of the observations of Justices Stevens and Souter, adequate?

Consider Garnett, A Hands-Off Approach to Religious Doctrine, 84 Notre Dame L. Rev. 837, 850–851, 853, 854 (2009):

> What does it mean, really, for a court [to] take a "hands-off approach to religious doctrine"? [It] is certainly not the case that government officials and courts may not render decisions that touch upon, affect, motivate, or even regulate religious

believers and religiously motivated individuals. ["Religion"] and law are (almost) everywhere, and so there is no avoiding contact between them. [It] also seems misguided to see the rule simply as the specification of a general "neutrality" requirement. [It] is [a] rule that state actors should not render [decisions] involving the resolution of religious questions.

5. *Voluntarism and separatism.* L. Tribe, supra, at 1160–1161, argues that the religion clauses rest on "a pair of fundamental [principles:] voluntarism and separatism." As to voluntarism,

> [the] free exercise clause was at the very least designed to guarantee freedom of conscience by preventing any degree of compulsion in matters of belief. It prohibited not only direct compulsion but also any indirect coercion which might result from subtle discrimination; hence it was offended by any burden based specifically on one's religion. So viewed, the free exercise clause is a mandate of religious voluntarism. The establishment clause [can] be understood as designed in part to assure that the advancement of a church would come only from the voluntary support of its followers and not from the political support of the state. Religious groups, it was believed, should prosper or perish on the intrinsic merit of their beliefs and practices. . . .
>
> Separatism [calls] for much more than the institutional separation of church and state; it means that the state should not become involved in religious affairs or derive its claim to authority from religious sources, that religious bodies should not be granted governmental powers, and — perhaps — that sectarian differences should not be allowed unduly to fragment the body politic. Implicit in this ideal of mutual abstinence was the principle that under no circumstance should religion be financially supported by public taxation: "for the men who wrote the Religion Clauses [the] 'establishment' of a religion connoted sponsorship, financial support, and active involvement of the sovereign in religious activity."

Is the result in *Everson* consistent with these principles? When might the principles conflict with each other? Consider whether nondiscriminatory aid involves "indirect coercion" or "political support" of "a church" that might displace voluntary support by its members.

6. *"Equal Liberty."* Eisgruber and Sager, Religious Freedom and the Constitution (2007), offer a general theory they call Equal Liberty, which contains two principles: "In the name of equality [no one] ought to be devalued on account of the spiritual foundations of their important commitments and projects." Aside from attention to discrimination and "hostility and neglect," religion should not be treated "as deserving special benefits or as subject to special disabilities." In addition, a broad understanding of general constitutional liberties, such as rights of free speech and association "will allow religious practice to flourish." Id. at 52–53. For a collection of commentaries (raising questions about how to identify "hostility and neglect," and about the difference between this approach and others), see Book Review Colloquium, 85 Tex. L. Rev. 1185–1287 (2007).

7. *Religious pluralism and the political process.* Consider whether a justification for allowing governments some leeway in dealing with religion lies in the contemporary political process: The United States is a religiously pluralist society in which most religious groups are tolerant of views that diverge from their own. As proposals work their way through the political process, religiously based interest groups will affect their contours. It might be unlikely that programs threatening the values with which the religion clauses are concerned will emerge from that process. Is this pluralist sketch of the political process accurate? Are there programs on which substantial majorities can agree that disregard intense views of religious minorities, and that have substantial religious components?

In Zelman v. Simmons-Harris, 536 U.S. 639 (2002), Justice Souter's dissenting opinion argued that "[religious] teaching at taxpayer expense simply cannot be cordoned from taxpayer politics, and every major religion currently espouses social positions that provoke intense opposition. Not all taxpaying Protestant citizens [will] be content to underwrite the teaching of the Roman Catholic Church condemning the death penalty. Nor will all of America's Muslims acquiesce in paying for the endorsement of the religious Zionism taught in many religious Jewish schools, which combines 'a nationalistic sentiment' in support of Israel with a 'deeply religious' element. Nor will every secular taxpayer be content to support Muslim views on differential treatment of the sexes, or, for that matter, to fund the espousal of a wife's obligation of obedience to her husband, presumably taught in any schools adopting the articles of faith of the Southern Baptist Convention. Views like these, and innumerable others, have been safe in the sectarian pulpits and classrooms of this Nation not only because the Free Exercise Clause protects them directly, but because the ban on supporting religious establishment has protected free exercise, by keeping it relatively private. With the arrival of vouchers in religious schools, that privacy will go, and along with it will go confidence that religious disagreement will stay moderate."

In connection with those observations, consider whether religious and political pluralism might combine to moderate disagreement, either through compromises that allow each religious institution to receive public assistance while maintaining its own views or through compromises that restrict all religious institutions. (Would the latter compromises violate the free speech clause?)

Consider in this connection the range of programs the Court has examined: state-supported nativity scenes, devotional prayer in public schools, tax support to nonpublic education, tax exemptions for churches.

8. *Baselines.* Douglas Laycock, The Underlying Unity of Separation and Neutrality, 46 Emory L.J. 43, 49, 69–71 (1997), discusses the "no aid" and "equal access" theories, similar to strict separation and nonpreferentialism:

> In the no-aid theory, the baseline is government inactivity, because doing nothing neither helps nor hurts religion. Any government aid to a religion is

a departure from that baseline, and thus a departure from neutrality. In the nondiscrimination theory, the baseline is the government's treatment of analogous secular activities; a government that pays for medical care should pay equally whether the care is provided in a religious or a secular hospital.

Laycock argues for a standard of "minimizing government influence":

[The] underlying criterion for choosing among baselines depends on the incentives that government creates. If government says that it will pay for your soup kitchen if and only if you secularize it, that is a powerful incentive to secularize. [In] this context, the baseline of analogous secular activity is substantively neutral: if government will pay both religious and secular providers, it creates no incentive for either to change. [In] the regulatory context, substantive neutrality generally requires the baseline of government inactivity. If government says it will send you to jail if you consume peyote in a worship service, that is a powerful disincentive to religious behavior. But an exemption for religious behavior rarely encourages people to join the exempted church. [When] the claim to religious exemption is not contaminated by secular self-interest, exemption minimizes government influence on religion. [If] government were free to praise or condemn religion, celebrate religious holidays, or lead prayers or worship services, government could potentially have enormous influence on religious belief and liturgy. Government is large and highly visible; for better or worse, it would model one form of religious speech or observance as compared to others.

Is Justice Souter's concern in *Zelman-Harris* that the availability of a subsidy — or exemption? — might subtly influence religious doctrine relevant to Laycock's argument?

9. *Why protect religion?* Is the constitutional text alone sufficient to justify giving religion special protection? Must we also have reasons for thinking that religion ought to be specially protected? Consider these observations: (a) Laycock, Religious Liberty as Liberty, 7 J. Contemp. Legal Issues 313, 317 (1996): "First, in history that was recent to the American founders, government attempts to suppress disapproved religious views had caused vast human suffering. [Second], beliefs about religion are often of extraordinary importance to the individual — important enough to die for, to suffer for, to rebel for, to emigrate for, to fight to control the government for. [Third], beliefs at the heart of religion [are] of little importance to the civil government." Are the first and second reasons distinctive to religion? Is the third reason true? (b) Garvey, An Anti-Liberal Argument for Religious Freedom, 7 J. Contemp. Legal Issues 275 (1996): "We protect it because religion is important."

For recent discussions of this question, see Leiter, Why Tolerate Religion? (2012), offering a perspective from moral and political theory, and Koppelman, Defending American Religious Neutrality (2013), offering a perspective from political theory and law. For a review of these works, see Greene, Religion and Theistic Faith: On Koppelman, Leiter, Secular Purpose, and Accommodations, 49 Tulsa L. Rev. 441 (2013). See also Schwartzman, What If Religion Is Not Special?, 79 U. Chi. L. Rev. 1351 (2012):

> [Many] of the most widely held normative justifications for favoring (or disfavoring) religion are prone to predictable forms of internal incoherence [and] accounts [that] manage to avoid such incoherence succeed only at the cost of committing other serious errors, especially in allowing various types of unfairness toward religious believers, nonbelievers, or both. The upshot of all this is that principles of disestablishment and free exercise ought to be conceived in terms that go beyond the category of religion. Instead of disabling or protecting only religious beliefs and practices, the law ought to provide similar treatment for comparable secular ethical, moral, and philosophical views.

### Note: Defining Religion

The religion clauses require the courts to determine whether a form of belief is a "religion" within their meaning. If the free exercise clause requires the state to accommodate its secular programs to religious, but not to nonreligious (e.g., political), belief, courts must decide whether an objector's belief is religious. The courts may be asked to decide whether the teaching of evolution or of creationism is an establishment of religion. What general considerations might guide the definitional effort?

1. *Unitary or variable definitions?* Justice Rutledge, dissenting in *Everson*, supra:

> "Religion" appears only once in the [First] Amendment. But the word governs two prohibitions and governs them alike. It does not have two meanings, one narrow to forbid "an establishment" and another, much broader, for securing "the free exercise thereof." "Thereof" brings down "religion" with its entire and exact content, no more and no less, from the first into the second guaranty, so that Congress and now the states are as broadly restricted concerning the one as they are regarding the other.

L. Tribe, American Constitutional Law 826–828 (1st ed. 1978):

> At least through the nineteenth century, religion was given the same fairly narrow reading in the two clauses: "religion" referred to theistic notions respecting divinity, morality, and worship, and was recognized as legitimate and protected only insofar as it was generally accepted as "civilized" by Western standards. . . .
>
> [But religion] in America, always pluralistic, has become radically so in the latter part of the twentieth century. [There] are, of course, many traditionally theistic American theologians, but for many others there has been a shift in religious thought from a theocentric, transcendental perspective to forms of

religious consciousness that stress the immanence of meaning in the natural order. . . .

[Clearly,] the notion of religion in the free exercise clause must be expanded beyond the closely bounded limits of theism to account for the multiplying forms of recognizably legitimate religious exercise. It is equally clear, however, that in the age of the affirmative and increasingly pervasive state, a less expansive notion of religion was required for establishment clause purposes lest all "humane" programs of government be deemed constitutionally suspect. Such a twofold definition of religion — expansive for the free exercise clause, less so for the establishment clause — may be necessary to avoid confronting the state with increasingly difficult choices that the theory of permissible accommodations [could] not indefinitely resolve. . . .

Is Tribe's approach consistent with the language of the Constitution? In the second edition of his treatise, Tribe calls this proposal "a dubious solution to a problem that [may] not exist at all" because courts can and should focus on the more important ideas of tolerance and establishment. L. Tribe, American Constitutional Law 1186–1187 (2d ed. 1988).

2. *An expansive definition by the Supreme Court: the conscientious objector cases.* The Court's most extended consideration of the definition of religion occurred in a series of cases interpreting a federal statute granting an exemption from compulsory military service to any person "who, by reason of religious training and belief, is conscientiously opposed to participation in war in any form" and defining "religious training and belief" as "an individual's belief in relation to a Supreme Being involving duties superior to those arising from any human relation, but [not] any essentially political, sociological, or philosophical views or a merely personal moral code." (The reference to a "Supreme Being" was deleted in 1967.)

The Court interpreted these provisions in United States v. Seeger, 380 U.S.163 (1965). Seeger stated on his draft form that he "preferred to leave the question as to his belief in a Supreme Being open," and that he had a "belief in and devotion to goodness and virtue for their own sakes, and a religious faith in a purely ethical creed [without] belief in God, except in the remotest sense." The Court unanimously found that Seeger qualified for the statutory exemption. The test was "whether a given belief that is sincere and meaningful occupies a place in the life of its possessor parallel to that filled by the orthodox belief in God of one who clearly qualifies for the exemption. Where such beliefs have parallel positions in the lives of their respective holders we cannot say that one is 'in relation to a Supreme Being' and the other is not." The Court mentioned "the richness and variety of spiritual life in our country."

Justice Douglas, concurring in *Seeger*, thought that a broadly defined exemption was required by the free exercise clause and by concepts of equal protection. The plurality in Welsh v. United States, 398 U.S. 333 (1970), applied the Seeger test to grant an exemption to someone who crossed off the word "religious" on the draft form. Justice Harlan concurred only in the result. He argued that *Seeger* had stretched the statutory language to its limit. "Congress [could eliminate] all exemptions for conscientious objectors. Such a course would be wholly 'neutral.' [However,] having chosen to exempt, it cannot draw the line between theistic or nontheistic religious beliefs on the one hand and secular beliefs on the other." To do so would violate the establishment clause.

In Gillette v. United States, 401 U.S. 437 (1971), the Court held that the statutory exemption was unavailable to those who had religious objections "relating to a particular conflict." It rejected the claim that the free exercise clause required that the exemption be available to such "selective" objectors and concluded that an exemption limited to objectors to all wars was sufficiently neutral to avoid establishment clause problems. The "de facto discrimination among religions" was not an establishment of religion because the discrimination "serves a number of purposes having nothing to do with a design to foster or favor any sect, religion, or cluster of religions [such] as the hopelessness of converting a sincere conscientious objector into an effective fighting man." The "interest in maintaining a fair system" might be defeated by requiring the draft system to inquire into the "enormous number of variables" that make selective objection "ultimately subjective." "There is a danger that as between two would-be objectors, both having the same complaint against a war, that objector would succeed who is more articulate, better educated, or better counseled." This danger was greater "the more discriminating and complicated the basis of classification." Justice Douglas dissented.

For an argument that protection should be extended to claims based on conscience as well as religion, see Smith, Converting the Religious Equality Amendment into a Statute with a Little "Conscience," 1996 BYU L. Rev. 645.

3. *The futility of definition?* Commentators, drawing on modern theology, have suggested that religion must involve "ultimate concern" or belief in "extratemporal consequences" or in a "transcendent reality." See, e.g., Note, Toward a Constitutional Definition of Religion, 91 Harv. L. Rev. 1056 (1978); Choper, Defining "Religion" in the First Amendment, 1982 U. Ill. L. Rev. 579. Are the following belief systems religions? Does it matter whether the issue is free exercise or establishment? (a) Transcendental meditation (see Malnak v. Yogi, 592 F.2d 197 (3d Cir. 1979), finding that a school board established religion when it authorized the teaching of TM in the public schools); (b) pantheism (see Africa v. Pennsylvania, 662 F.2d 1025 (3d Cir. 1981), finding a system strongly resembling pantheism not a religion when its adherent sought to require prison officials to provide him with a diet of raw foods only); (c) secular humanism (see Grove v. Mead School District, 753 F.2d 1528 (9th Cir. 1985), finding no establishment clause violation in allowing public school students to satisfy requirements by reading a book said to advance secular humanism).

Consider Freeman, The Misguided Search for the Constitutional Definition of "Religion," 71 Geo. L.J. 1519, 1553, 1556 (1983): A "religious belief
system" has some of the following "relevant features": belief in a supreme
being, belief in a transcendent reality, a moral code, a worldview accounting
for people's role in the universe, sacred rituals, worship and prayer, a sacred
text, membership in a social organization. But "there is no single feature or set
of features that constitutes the essence of religion." Rather, "a belief system
[may] be more or less religious depending on how closely it resembles [the]
paradigm" having all eight features.

How can the religion clauses be interpreted unless there is a definition of
religion? Consider whether it would be possible to develop doctrines by
accepting all sincerely proffered claims that a belief is religious and then
determining whether the state's secular goals justify imposing a burden
on that belief or whether the state's secular goals justify its adopting the
program at issue. Freeman suggests that such doctrines might be unacceptable
because the courts would be unable to distinguish between belief systems at
the core of the concept of religion and those at its periphery; distaste for
granting a free exercise exemption to the peripheral religion might distort
the doctrines dealing with the balance between secular goals and burdens
on religion.

4. *Determining sincerity.* In United States v. Ballard, 322 U.S. 78 (1944), the
leaders of the "I Am" religion were indicted for mail fraud. The religion, an
offshoot of the theosophy movement, was centered in the western states. Its
founder, Guy Ballard, was said to have met a Master Saint Germain, who used
Ballard as a messenger. Ballard's widow and son were charged with making
representations that they knew were false regarding their power to cure diseases. The Supreme Court held that the jury could not be allowed to determine the truth or falsity of the representations about the Ballards' ability to
cure. It could determine only whether the Ballards believed the representations they made. "Men may believe what they cannot prove. [Religious] experiences which are as real as life to some may be incomprehensible to others. [If]
one could be sent to jail because a jury in a hostile environment found [his]
teachings false, little indeed would be left of religious freedom." Justice
Jackson would have gone further:

> I do not see how we can separate an issue as to what is believed from considera-
> tions as to what is believable. [Any] inquiry into intellectual honesty in religion
> raises profound psychological problems. [It] seems to me an impossible task for
> juries to separate fancied [religious experiences] from real ones, dreams from
> happenings, and hallucinations from true clairvoyance. [Further,] I do not know
> what degree of skepticism or disbelief in a religious representation amounts to an
> actionable fraud. [Religious] symbolism is even used by some with the same
> mental reservations one has in teaching of Santa Claus or Uncle Sam or Easter
> bunnies or dispassionate judges.

Chief Justice Stone, whose dissent was joined by Justices Roberts and Frankfurter, countered, "[If] it were shown that a defendant [had] asserted [that] he had physically shaken hands with St. Germain in San Francisco on a day named, or that [by] the exertion of his spiritual power he 'had in fact cured [hundreds] of persons . . . ,' it would be open to the Government to submit to the jury proof that he had never been in San Francisco and that no such cures had ever been effected." Justice Jackson agreed that a church leader could be prosecuted for fraud if he or she "represents that funds are being used to build a church when in fact they are being used for personal purposes." How does that differ from what the Ballards were charged with?

Note that inquiries into sincerity may be a disguised attempt to question whether the underlying belief is religious at all. Would that justify or cast doubt on the propriety of inquiries into sincerity?

# VIII

---

## The Establishment Clause

---

In Lemon v. Kurtzman, 403 U.S. 602 (1971), the Court identified three "tests" for determining whether a statute violates the establishment clause: "First, the statute must have a secular legislative purpose; second, its principal or primary effect must be one that neither advances nor inhibits religion; finally, the statute must not foster 'an excessive government entanglement with religion.'" The so-called *Lemon* test has not been formally repudiated by the Supreme Court. A majority of the justices sitting in 2011 have criticized it, and it has not been relied on by a majority to invalidate any practice since 1985. For an overview of developments, see Lupu, The Lingering Death of Separationism, 62 Geo. Wash. L. Rev. 230 (1994). In a concurring opinion in Lamb's Chapel v. Center Moriches Union Free School District, 508 U.S. 384 (1993), Justice Scalia criticized the *Lemon* test by analogizing it to "a ghoul in a late-night horror movie that repeatedly sits up in its grave and shuffles abroad, after being repeatedly killed and buried. [It] is there to scare us [when] we wish it to do so, but we can command it to return to the tomb at will. When we wish to strike down a practice it forbids, we invoke it; when we wish to uphold a practice it forbids, we ignore it entirely. [Such] a docile and useful monster is worth keeping around, at least in a somnolent state; one never knows when one might need him."

The materials that follow are organized around some more particularized themes that can be connected to the components of the *Lemon* test. Sections A and B deal with two ways — coercion and endorsement — in which government practices might be said to "advance" (or inhibit) religion. Section C deals with issues that arise in connection with identifying whether a government practice has a religious or a secular purpose. Section D discusses cases and problems in which the effects, principal or otherwise, of a government program might be said to advance (or inhibit) religion.

L.J. 1237 (1986). If common ground can be defined which permits once conflicting faiths to express the shared conviction that there is an ethic and a morality which transcend human invention, the sense of community and purpose sought by all decent societies might be advanced. But though the First Amendment does not allow the government to stifle prayers which aspire to these ends, neither does it permit the government to undertake that task for itself.

The First Amendment's Religion Clauses mean that religious beliefs and religious expression are too precious to be either proscribed or prescribed by the State. The design of the Constitution is that preservation and transmission of religious beliefs and worship is a responsibility and a choice committed to the private sphere, which itself is promised freedom to pursue that mission. It must not be forgotten then, that while concern must be given to define the protection granted to an objector or a dissenting non-believer, these same Clauses exist to protect religion from government interference. . . .

These concerns have particular application in the case of school officials, whose effort to monitor prayer will be perceived by the students as inducing a participation they might otherwise reject. [Our precedents] caution us to measure the idea of a civic religion against the central meaning of the Religion Clauses of the First Amendment, which is that all creeds must be tolerated and none favored. The suggestion that government may establish an official or civic religion as a means of avoiding the establishment of a religion with more specific creeds strikes us as a contradiction that cannot be accepted.

The degree of school involvement here made it clear that the graduation prayers bore the imprint of the State and thus put school-age children who objected in an untenable position. . . .

[It] is argued that [high] school students no doubt have been required to attend classes and assemblies and to complete assignments exposing them to ideas they find distasteful or immoral or absurd or all of these. Against this background, students may consider it an odd measure of justice to be subjected during the course of their educations to ideas deemed offensive and irreligious, but to be denied a brief, formal prayer ceremony that the school offers in return. This argument [overlooks] a fundamental dynamic of the Constitution.

The First Amendment protects speech and religion by quite different mechanisms. Speech is protected by insuring its full expression even when the government participates, for the very object of some of our most important speech is to persuade the government to adopt an idea as its own. The method for protecting freedom of worship and freedom of conscience in religious matters is quite the reverse. In religious debate or expression the government is not a prime participant, for the Framers deemed religious establishment antithetical to the freedom of all. The Free Exercise Clause embraces a freedom of conscience and worship that has close parallels in the speech provisions of the First Amendment, but the Establishment Clause is a specific prohibition on forms of state intervention in religious affairs with no precise counterpart in the speech provisions. The explanation lies in the lesson of history that was and is the inspiration for the Establishment Clause, the lesson that in the hands of government what might begin as a tolerant expression of religious views may end in a policy to indoctrinate and coerce. A state-created orthodoxy puts at grave risk that freedom of belief and conscience which are the sole assurance that religious faith is real, not imposed.

The lessons of the First Amendment are as urgent in the modern world as in the 18th Century when it was written. One timeless lesson is that if citizens are subjected to state-sponsored religious exercises, the State disavows its own duty to guard and respect that sphere of inviolable conscience and belief which is the mark of a free people. To compromise that principle today would be to deny our own tradition and forfeit our standing to urge others to secure the protections of that tradition for themselves.

[There] are heightened concerns with protecting freedom of conscience from subtle coercive pressure in the elementary and secondary public schools. [What] to most believers may seem nothing more than a reasonable request that the nonbeliever respect their religious practices, in a school context may appear to the nonbeliever or dissenter to be an attempt to employ the machinery of the State to enforce a religious orthodoxy.

[The] school district's supervision and control of a high school graduation ceremony places public pressure, as well as peer pressure, on attending students to stand as a group or, at least, maintain respectful silence during the Invocation and Benediction. This pressure, though subtle and indirect, can be as real as any overt compulsion. Of course, in our culture standing or remaining silent can signify adherence to a view or simple respect for the views of others. And no doubt some persons who have no desire to join a prayer have little objection to standing as a sign of respect for those who do. But for the dissenter of high school age, who has a reasonable perception that she is being forced by the State to pray in a manner her conscience will not allow, the injury is no less real. [For] many, if not most, of the students at the graduation, the act of standing or remaining silent was an expression of participation in the Rabbi's prayer. That was the very point of the religious exercise. It is of little comfort to a dissenter, then, to be told that for her the act of standing or remaining in silence signifies mere respect, rather than participation. What matters is that given our social conventions, a reasonable dissenter in this milieu could believe that the group exercise signified her own participation or approval of it.

Finding no violation under these circumstances would place objectors in the dilemma of participating, with all that implies, or protesting. [We] think the State may not, consistent with the Establishment Clause, place primary and secondary school children in this position. Research in psychology supports the common assumption that adolescents are often susceptible to pressure from their peers towards conformity, and that the influence is strongest in matters of social convention. To recognize that the choice imposed by the State constitutes an unacceptable constraint only acknowledges that the

Our decisions have gone beyond prohibiting coercion, [because] the Court has recognized that "the fullest possible scope of religious liberty," *Schempp* (Goldberg, J., concurring) [Chapter VII, supra], entails more than freedom from coercion. The Establishment Clause protects religious liberty on a grand scale; it is a social compact that guarantees for generations a democracy and a strong religious community — both essential to safeguarding religious liberty. "Our fathers seem to have been perfectly sincere in their belief that the members of the Church would be more patriotic, and the citizens of the State more religious, by keeping their respective functions entirely separate." Religious Liberty, in Essays and Speeches of Jeremiah S. Black 53 (C. Black ed. 1885) (Chief Justice of the Commonwealth of Pennsylvania). . . .

[A concurring opinion by Justice Souter, joined by Justices Stevens and O'Connor, is omitted.]

JUSTICE SCALIA, with whom THE CHIEF JUSTICE, JUSTICE WHITE, and JUSTICE THOMAS join, dissenting. . . .
[In] holding that the Establishment Clause prohibits invocations and benedictions at public-school graduation ceremonies, the Court [lays] waste a tradition [that] is a component of an even more longstanding American tradition of nonsectarian prayer to God at public celebrations generally. . . .

# I . . .

From our Nation's origin, prayer has been a prominent part of governmental ceremonies and proclamations. The Declaration of Independence "[appealed] to the Supreme Judge of the world for the rectitude of our intentions" and avowed "a firm reliance on the protection of divine Providence." In his first inaugural address, after swearing his oath of office on a Bible, George Washington deliberately made a prayer a part of his first official act as President:

> it would be peculiarly improper to omit in this first official act my fervent supplications to that Almighty Being who rules over the universe, who presides in the councils of nations, and whose providential aids can supply every human defect, that His benediction may consecrate to the liberties and happiness of the people of the United States a Government instituted by themselves for these essential purposes.

Such supplications have been a characteristic feature of inaugural addresses ever since. . . .
Our national celebration of Thanksgiving likewise dates back to President Washington. [This] tradition of Thanksgiving Proclamations — with their religious theme of prayerful gratitude to God — has been adhered to by almost every President. . . .

## II

The Court presumably would separate graduation invocations and benedictions from other instances of public "preservation and transmission of religious beliefs" on the ground that they involve "psychological coercion." [A] few citations of "research in psychology" that have no particular bearing upon the precise issue here cannot disguise the fact that the Court has gone beyond the realm where judges know what they are doing. The Court's argument that state officials have "coerced" students to take part in the invocation and benediction at graduation ceremonies is, not to put too fine a point on it, incoherent.

A

[According] to the Court, students at graduation who want "to avoid the fact or appearance of participation," in the invocation and benediction are psychologically obligated "[to] stand as a group or, at least, maintain respectful silence" during those prayers. This assertion [does] not say [that] students are psychologically coerced to bow their heads, place their hands in a Dürer-like prayer position, pay attention to the prayers, utter "Amen," or in fact pray. [It] claims only that students are psychologically coerced "to stand . . . or, at least, maintain respectful silence." Both halves of this disjunctive [merit] particular attention.

[The] Court's notion that a student who simply sits in "respectful silence" during the invocation and benediction [has] somehow joined — or would somehow be perceived as having joined — in the prayers is nothing short of ludicrous. We indeed live in a vulgar age. But surely "our social conventions" have not coarsened to the point that anyone who does not stand on his chair and shout obscenities can reasonably be deemed to have assented to everything said in his presence. Since the Court does not dispute that students exposed to prayer at graduation ceremonies retain [the] free will to sit, there is absolutely no basis for the Court's decision. . . .

But let us assume the very worst, that the nonparticipating graduate is "subtly coerced" . . . to stand! Even that half of the disjunctive does not remotely establish a "participation" (or an "appearance of participation") in a religious exercise. [If] it is a permissible inference that one who is standing is doing so simply out of respect for the prayers of others that are in progress, then how can it possibly be said that a "reasonable dissenter . . . could believe that the group exercise signified her own participation or approval"? [Maintaining] respect for the religious observances of others is a fundamental civic virtue that government [can] and should cultivate — so that even if [the] displaying of such respect might be mistaken for taking part in the prayer, I would deny that the dissenter's interest in avoiding even the false appearance of participation constitutionally trumps the government's interest in fostering respect for religion generally.

[The] Court itself has not given careful consideration to its test of psychological coercion. For if it had, how could it observe [that] students stood for the

[was] the central value invoked by the states that proposed constitutional amendments on the question of religion, and the purpose that underlay the Establishment Clause when it was enacted," and that "the Constitution [protects] liberty of conscience [only] in the sphere of government action that relates specifically to religion." What does the establishment clause understood in this way add to the free exercise and free speech clauses?

4. *Prayers at football games.* Santa Fe Independent School District v. Doe, 530 U.S. 290 (2000), held unconstitutional a district's policy that authorized students to vote, first, whether to allow "invocations" at high school football games, and then to choose a person to deliver them. Relying on Board of Regents v. Southworth, Chapter V.E, supra, Justice Stevens, writing for six justices, concluded that the speech the selected student gave would not be private speech because of the policy authorizing an election in which a majority would determine whether to have invocations. The Court then held that an invocation at a high school football game violated the principle established in *Lee.* The establishment clause was designed "to remove debate over this kind of issue from governmental supervision or control." Some students, such as cheerleaders and team members, were compelled to attend the games, and other students would feel "immense social pressure" and "truly genuine desire" to attend the games. The delivery of a religious invocation would therefore coerce them in the way condemned in *Lee.* Chief Justice Rehnquist and Justices Scalia and Thomas dissented.

Does the distinction between permissible private speech and arguably impermissible government speech make sense in the contexts of *Lee* and *Santa Fe?* Consider the suggestion in Brady, The Push to Private Religious Expression: Are We Missing Something?, 70 Fordham L. Rev. 1147, 1199 (2002), that "the most promising approach is for students of all perspectives to 'opt in' to the educational process by voicing and defending differing views" in these contexts. Would school authorities have to develop guidelines setting out the limits beyond which student speech could not go in these contexts? If so, would those guidelines convert private into government speech? Would school authorities be barred from developing such guidelines by free speech principles?

## B.   THE NONENDORSEMENT PRINCIPLE AND DE FACTO ESTABLISHMENTS

## Lynch v. Donnelly
465 U.S. 668 (1984)

THE CHIEF JUSTICE [BURGER] delivered the opinion of the Court. . . .

Each year, in cooperation with the downtown retail merchants' association, the City of Pawtucket, Rhode Island, erects a Christmas display as part of its observance of the Christmas holiday season. The display is situated in a park owned by a nonprofit organization and located in the heart of the shopping district. The display is essentially like those to be found in hundreds of towns or cities across the Nation — often on public grounds — during the Christmas season. The Pawtucket display comprises many of the figures and decorations traditionally associated with Christmas, including, among other things, a Santa Claus house, reindeer pulling Santa's sleigh, candy-striped poles, a Christmas tree, carolers, cutout figures representing such characters as a clown, an elephant, and a teddy bear, hundreds of colored lights, a large banner that reads "SEASONS GREETINGS," and the crèche at issue here. All components of this display are owned by the City. . . .

[The court of appeals held that maintaining the crèche violated the establishment clause.] [Rather] than mechanically invalidating all governmental conduct or statutes that confer benefits or give special recognition to religion in general or to one faith — as an absolutist approach would dictate — the Court has scrutinized challenged legislation or official conduct to determine whether, in reality, it establishes a religion or religious faith, or tends to do so. . . .

In each case, the inquiry calls for line drawing; no fixed, per se rule can be framed. . . .

In the line-drawing process we have often found it useful to inquire whether the challenged law or conduct has a secular purpose, whether its principal or primary effect is to advance or inhibit religion, and whether it creates an excessive entanglement of government with religion. [*Lemon.*] But, we have repeatedly emphasized our unwillingness to be confined to any single test or criterion in this sensitive area. . . .

[In] this case, the focus of our inquiry must be on the crèche in the context of the Christmas season. . . .[12]

[When] viewed in the proper context of the Christmas Holiday season, it is apparent that, on this record, there is insufficient evidence to establish that the inclusion of the crèche is a purposeful or surreptitious effort to express some kind of subtle governmental advocacy of a particular religious message. In a pluralistic society a variety of motives and purposes are implicated. The City, like the Congresses and Presidents, however, has principally taken note of a significant historical religious event long celebrated in the Western World. . . .

The narrow question is whether there is a secular purpose for Pawtucket's display of the crèche. The display is sponsored by the City to celebrate the Holiday and to depict the origins of that Holiday. These are legitimate secular purposes. . . .

12. Justice Brennan states that "by focusing on the holiday 'context' in which the crèche appear[s]," the Court seeks to "explain away the clear religious import of the crèche," and that it has equated the crèche with a Santa's house or a talking wishing well. Of course this is not true. [Relocated footnote. — EDS.]

authority in the service of a particular faith. [Unlike] such secular figures as Santa Claus, reindeer and carolers, a nativity scene represents far more than a mere "traditional" symbol of Christmas. The essence of the crèche's symbolic purpose and effect is to prompt the observer to experience a sense of simple awe and wonder appropriate to the contemplation of one of the central elements of Christian dogma — that God sent His son into the world to be a Messiah. [The] crèche is far from a mere representation of a "particular historic religious event." It is, instead, best understood as a mystical re-creation of an event that lies at the heart of Christian faith. To suggest, as the Court does, that such a symbol is merely "traditional" and therefore no different from Santa's house or reindeer is not only offensive to those for whom the crèche has profound significance, but insulting to those who insist for religious or personal reasons that the story of Christ is in no sense a part of "history" nor an unavoidable element of our national "heritage." . . .

## II . . .

Intuition tells us that some official "acknowledgment" is inevitable in a religious society if government is not to adopt a stilted indifference to the religious life of the people. It is equally true, however, that if government is to remain scrupulously neutral in matters of religious conscience, as our Constitution requires, then it must avoid those overly broad acknowledgments of religious practices that may imply governmental favoritism toward one set of religious beliefs. This does not mean, of course, that public officials may not take account, when necessary, of the separate existence and significance of the religious institutions and practices in the society they govern. . . .

[At] least three principles — tracing the narrow channels which government acknowledgments must follow to satisfy the Establishment Clause — may be identified. First, although the government may not be compelled to do so by the Free Exercise Clause, it may, consistently with the Establishment Clause, act to accommodate to some extent the opportunities of individuals to practice their religion. [That] principle would justify government's decision to declare December 25th a public holiday.

Second, [while] a particular governmental practice may have derived from religious motivations and retain certain religious connotations, it is nonetheless permissible for the government to pursue the practice when it is continued today solely for secular reasons. [The] mere fact that a governmental practice coincides to some extent with certain religious beliefs does not render it unconstitutional. Thanksgiving Day, in my view, fits easily within this principle, for despite its religious antecedents, the current practice of celebrating Thanksgiving is unquestionably secular and patriotic. . . .

Finally, we have noted that government cannot be completely prohibited from recognizing in its public actions the religious beliefs and practices of the

American people as an aspect of our national history and culture. While I remain uncertain about these questions, I would suggest that such practices as the designation of "In God We Trust" as our national motto, or the references to God contained in the Pledge of Allegiance can best be understood [as] a form of "ceremonial deism," protected from Establishment Clause scrutiny chiefly because they have lost through rote repetition any significant religious content. Moreover, these references are uniquely suited to serve such wholly secular purposes as solemnizing public occasions, or inspiring commitment to meet some national challenge in a manner that simply could not be fully served in our culture if government were limited to purely non-religious phrases. . . .

The crèche fits none of these categories. . . .

## III . . .

The intent of the Framers with respect to the public display of nativity scenes is virtually impossible to discern primarily because the widespread celebration of Christmas did not emerge in its present form until well into the nineteenth century. Carrying a well-defined Puritan hostility to the celebration of Christ's birth with them to the New World, the founders of the Massachusetts Bay Colony pursued a vigilant policy of opposition to any public celebration of the holiday. To the Puritans, the celebration of Christmas represented a "Popish" practice lacking any foundation in Scripture. . . .

During the eighteenth century, sectarian division over the celebration of the holiday continued. As increasing numbers of members of the Anglican and the Dutch and German Reformed churches arrived, the practice of celebrating Christmas as a purely religious holiday grew. But denominational differences continued to dictate differences in attitude toward the holiday. [Many] non-conforming Protestant groups, including the Presbyterians, Congregationalists, Baptists, and Methodists, continued to regard the holiday with suspicion and antagonism well into the nineteenth century. This pattern of sectarian division concerning the holiday suggests that for the Framers of the Establishment Clause, who were acutely sensitive to such sectarian controversies, no single view of how government should approach the celebration of Christmas would be possible. . . .

Furthermore [the] public display of nativity scenes as part of governmental celebrations of Christmas does not come to us supported by an unbroken history of widespread acceptance. It was not until 1836 that a State first granted legal recognition to Christmas as a public holiday. [Congress] did not follow the States' lead until 1870 when it established December 25th, along with the Fourth of July, New Year's Day, and Thanksgiving, as a legal holiday in the District of Columbia. . . .

[The] City's action should be recognized for what it is: a coercive, though perhaps small, step toward establishing the sectarian preferences of the

For a full discussion of the cases discussing divisiveness, see Garnett, Religion, Division, and the First Amendment, 94 Geo. L.J. 1667 (2006). Garnett concludes that the "divisiveness" argument "has rarely been outcome-determinative or done much real work," and that none of the versions of the argument he describes are convincing: "That concerns about 'political division along religious lines' are real and reasonable does not mean that they can or should supply the enforceable content of the First Amendment's prohibition on establishments of religion." Id. at 1670.

5. *De facto establishments.* Consider M. Howe, The Garden and the Wilderness 11–12 (1965):

> [Roger Williams's] principle of separation endorsed a host of favoring tributes to faith [so] substantial that they have produced in the aggregate what may fairly be described as a de facto establishment of religion [in which] the religious institution as a whole is maintained and activated by forces not kindled directly by government. [Some] elements of our religious establishment are, of course, reinforced by law. Whenever that situation prevails, as it does, for instance, when the law secures the sanctity of Sunday, the courts are apt to seek out a secular justification for the favoring enactment and, by this evasive tactic, meet the charge that an establishment de jure exists. [Yet] the Supreme Court, by pretending that the American principle of separation is predominantly Jeffersonian and by purporting to outlaw even those aids in religion which do not affect religious liberties, seems to have endorsed a governmental policy aimed at the elimination of de facto establishments.

For an argument that most aspects of "ceremonial deism" violate the Court's establishment clause doctrine, see Epstein, Rethinking the Constitutionality of Ceremonial Deism, 96 Colum. L. Rev. 2083 (1996). In McGowan v. Maryland, 366 U.S. 420 (1961), the Court rejected an establishment clause challenge to laws requiring that most large-scale commercial enterprises remain closed on Sundays. The Court's review of history demonstrated that Sunday closing laws were originally efforts to promote church attendance. "But, despite the strongly religious origin of these laws, nonreligious arguments for Sunday closing began to be heard more distinctly." The Court said that the Constitution "does not ban federal or state regulation of conduct whose reason or effect merely happens to coincide with the tenets of some or all religions." It concluded that, "as presently written and administered, most [Sunday closing laws] are of a secular rather than of a religious character." They "provide a uniform day of rest for all citizens. [To] say that the States cannot prescribe Sunday as a day of rest for these purposes solely because centuries ago such laws had their genesis in religion would give a constitutional interpretation of hostility to the public welfare rather than one of mere separation of church and State." As of 1961, was Howe's characterization of Sunday closing laws more accurate than the Court's? As of the present?

6. *History as a guide.* In Walz v. Tax Commission, section A, supra, the Court noted that every state had a property tax exemption for churches, and that the federal income tax has since its inception exempted religious organizations. It found "significant" that Congress exempted churches from real estate taxes in 1802. "[An] unbroken practice of according the exemption to churches, openly and by affirmative state action, not covertly or by state inaction, is not something to be lightly cast aside." Justice Brennan, concurring, agreed that "the existence from the beginning of the Nation's life of a practice [is] a fact of considerable import in the interpretation of abstract constitutional language. [The] more longstanding and widely accepted a practice, the greater its impact upon constitutional interpretation." He found two "secular purposes" for the exemption: Churches, like other exempt groups, "contribute to the well-being of the community in a variety of nonreligious ways," and they "uniquely contribute to the pluralism of American society."

Marsh v. Chambers, 463 U.S. 783 (1983), relied on a "unique history" to uphold the constitutionality of opening legislative sessions with prayers led by a state-employed chaplain. The history ran from colonial times to the present and included the first Congress's hiring a chaplain in 1789, only three days before it reached final agreement on the language of the first amendment:

> [Historical] evidence sheds light not only on what the draftsmen intended the Establishment Clause to mean, but also on how they thought that Clause applied to the practice authorized by the First Congress — their actions reveal their intent. [In] light of the unambiguous and unbroken history of more than 200 years, there can be no doubt that the practice of opening legislative sessions with prayer has become part of the fabric of our society.

Justice Brennan, joined by Justice Marshall, dissented. He argued that "legislative prayer [intrudes] on the right to conscience by forcing some legislators either to participate in a 'prayer opportunity' with which they are in basic disagreement, or to make their disagreement a matter of public comment by declining to participate. [It] has the potential for degrading religion by allowing a religious call to worship to be intermeshed with a secular call to order." He criticized the Court's reliance on the actions of the first Congress: "Legislators, influenced by the passions and exigencies of the moment, the pressure of constituents and colleagues, and the press of business, do not always pass sober constitutional judgment on every piece of legislation they enact." James Madison, who voted for the bill in the first Congress, later said that the practice was unconstitutional. This "may not have represented so much a change of mind as a change of role, from a member of Congress engaged in the hurly-burly of legislative activity to a detached observer engaged in unpressured reflection." For a discussion of the early history of the congressional chaplaincy, see Lund, The Congressional Chaplaincies, 17 Wm. & Mary Bill Rts. J. 1171 (2009), which describes antebellum controversies adjudicatory hearings, they request the Board to grant [applications] for various permits."

"Let's say that a Muslim citizen of Greece goes before the Board to [request] some permit. [Just] before she gets to speak her piece, a minister deputized by the Town asks her to pray 'in the name of God's only son Jesus Christ.' She must think [that] Christian worship has become entwined with local governance. And now she faces a choice — to pray alongside the majority [or] somehow to register her deeply felt difference. [That] is no easy call — especially given that the room is small and her every action [will] be noticed. She does not wish to be rude to her neighbors, nor does she wish to aggravate the Board members whom she will soon be trying to persuade. And yet she does not want to acknowledge Christ's divinity. [So] assume she declines to participate with the others in the first act of the meeting — or even [stands] up and leaves the room. [She] becomes a different kind of citizen. [And] she thus stands at a remove, based solely on religion, from her fellow citizens and her elected representatives. Everything about that situation [infringes] the First Amendment.

Justice Kagan would allow some prayer activities. "What the circumstances here demand is the recognition that we are a pluralistic people. [If] the Town Board had let its chaplains know that they should speak in nonsectarian terms, [then] no one would have valid grounds for complaint. [Or] it might have invited clergy of many faiths to serve as chaplains. [But] Greece could not do what it did: infuse a participatory government body with one (and only one) faith." For her, "[when] a citizen stands before her government, [her] religious beliefs do not enter into the picture. The government she faces favors no particular religion, either by word or by deed. And that government [imposes] no religious tests on its citizens, sorts none of them by faith, and permits no exclusion based on belief. When a person goes to court, a polling place, or an immigration proceeding, [government] officials do not engage in sectarian worship, nor do they ask her to do likewise. They all participate in the business of government not as Christians, Jews, Muslims (and more), but only as Americans — none of them different from any other for that civic purpose."

Justice Alito, joined by Justice Scalia, responded to Justice Kagan in a concurring opinion, calling "the narrow aspect" of her dissent's objections to the holding "really quite niggling." He argued that "there [is] no historical support for the proposition that only generic prayer is allowed," and observed that "as our country has become more diverse, composing a prayer that is acceptable to all members of the community who hold religious beliefs has become [harder.]" Further, "if a town attempts to go beyond simply recommending that a guest chaplain deliver a prayer that is broadly acceptable, [the] town will [encounter] sensitive problems," including possible prescreening or reviewing prayers. The alternative of compiling a list of clergy from numerous traditions to serve as guest chaplains meant that Justice Kagan's objection was only the "[the] town's clerical employees did a bad job in compiling the list" they used.

8. *The Pledge of Allegiance, history, and ceremonial deism.* In Elk Grove Unified School District v. Newdow, 542 U.S. 1 (2004), the Court refused, on standing grounds, to consider the merits of a challenge to the constitutionality of the inclusion of the words "under God" in the Pledge of Allegiance. Chief Justice Rehnquist and Justices O'Connor and Thomas disagreed with that holding and wrote opinions explaining why they believed that the constitutional challenge should be rejected on the merits. Chief Justice Rehnquist relied on history to show that "our national culture allows public recognition of our Nation's religious history and character." He wrote, "I do not believe that the phrase 'under God' in the Pledge converts its recital into a 'religious exercise.' . . . Instead, it is a declaration of belief in allegiance and loyalty to the United States flag and the Republic. . . . The phrase [is] in no sense a prayer, nor an endorsement of any religion. . . . Reciting the Pledge, or listening to others recite it, is a patriotic exercise, not a religious one; participants promise fidelity to our flag and our Nation, not to any particular God, faith, or church."

Justice Thomas wrote, "It is difficult to see how [the phrase] does not entail an affirmation that God exists." For him, "as a matter of our precedent, the Pledge policy is unconstitutional." He would overrule Lee v. Weisman and eliminate its test of "coercion," replacing it with a test of "legal compulsion."

Justice O'Connor relied on the endorsement test, and characterized the phrase in the Pledge as an example of permissible "ceremonial deism," although she called it a "close question." Ceremonial deism, which involved "solemnizing an event and recognizing a shared religious history," included expressions that had "legitimate nonreligious purposes." Those purposes were revealed "when a given practice has been in place for a significant portion of the Nation's history, and when it is observed by enough persons that it can fairly be called ubiquitous." Further, ceremonial deism was characterized by the "absence of worship or prayer" and by a "highly circumscribed reference to God." Brief references tend "to confirm that the reference is being used to acknowledge religion or to solemnize an event rather than to endorse religion in any way," and "it makes it easier for those participants who wish to 'opt out' [to] do so without having to reject the ceremony entirely [and] tends to limit the ability of government to express a preference for one religious sect over another." Also, "no religious acknowledgement could claim to be an instance of ceremonial deism if it explicitly favored one particular religious belief system over another." She also observed that "[a]ny coercion that persuades an onlooker to participate in an act of ceremonial deism is inconsequential, as an Establishment Clause matter, because such acts are simply not religious in character."

9. *A cross as a war memorial?* Salazar v. Buono, 559 U.S. 700 (2010), considered but did not definitively resolve an establishment clause challenge to the 2004 transfer to private ownership of federal land on which a Latin cross had been erected in 1934. The cross was located in a remote area of the Mojave

purpose": The commandments were "undeniably a sacred text in the Jewish and Christian faiths," and "if the posted copies [are] to have any effect at all, it will be to induce the school children to read, meditate upon, perhaps to venerate and obey, the Commandments. However desirable this might be as a matter of private devotion, it is not a permissible state objective under the Establishment Clause." Justice Rehnquist's dissent relied on a statement in the statute that its purpose was secular and argued that the requirement had a secular purpose because "the Ten Commandments have had a significant secular impact on the development of secular legal codes of the Western World."

*Stone* relied heavily on the school prayer cases. In Engel v. Vitale, 370 U.S. 421 (1962), the New York Board of Regents drafted and recommended that school districts have classes recite aloud the following prayer: "Almighty God, we acknowledge our dependence upon Thee, and beg Thy blessings upon us, our parents, our teachers and our Country." Justice Black, writing for the Court, stated that "in this country it is no part of the business of government to compose official prayers for any group of the American people to recite as a part of a religious program carried on by government."

In Abington School District v. Schempp, 374 U.S. 203 (1963), the Court held unconstitutional a state law requiring that ten verses from the Bible be read aloud at the opening of each public school day. Justice Clark's opinion for the Court stated that Bible-reading had a religious character and found the state's policy of permitting nonattendance was not "consistent with the contention that the Bible is here used either as an instrument for nonreligious moral inspiration or as a reference for the teaching of secular subjects." Justice Stewart dissented, finding "a substantial free exercise claim" that "a compulsory state educational system so structures a child's life that if religious exercises are held to be an impermissible activity in schools, religion is placed at an artificial and state-created disadvantage."

Wallace v. Jaffree, 472 U.S. 38 (1985), held unconstitutional an Alabama statute authorizing schools to set aside one minute at the start of the school day "for meditation or voluntary prayer." The statute amended an earlier one authorizing a moment of silence "for meditation." The Court drew on Madison and Everson to conclude that "the individual freedom of conscience [embraces] the right to select any religious faith or none at all" because "religious beliefs worthy of respect are the product of free and voluntary choice by the faithful." The bill's sponsor stated that it was "an 'effort to return voluntary prayer' to the public schools." The Court said that the statute served "no secular purpose" not already served by the "meditation" statute. It noted that the statute could not be a permissible accommodation of religion because, prior to its enactment, "there was no governmental practice impeding students from silently praying for one minute at the beginning of the school day. [What] was missing [was] the State's endorsement and promotion of religion and a particular religious practice."

Justice O'Connor concurred in the judgment on the ground that the statute's "purpose and likely effect [were] to endorse and sponsor voluntary prayer in the public schools." She argued that simple "moment of silence" statutes were constitutional because "a moment of silence is not inherently religious [and because] a pupil who participates in a moment of silence need not compromise his or her belief." Thus, the "State does not necessarily endorse any activity that might occur during the period. Even if a statute specifies that a student may choose to pray silently during a quiet moment, the State has not thereby encouraged prayer over other specified alternatives. [The] crucial question is whether the state has conveyed or attempted to convey the message that children should use the moment of silence for prayer." She also wrote, "[A] legislature [might] enunciate a sham secular [purpose, but] our courts are capable of distinguishing a sham secular purpose from a real one."

Chief Justice Burger dissented, noting that the bill's sponsor testified that "one of his purposes [was] to clear up a widespread misunderstanding that a schoolchild is legally prohibited from [praying] once he steps inside a public school building."

Is it accurate to say that each of these statutes had no purpose other than the promotion of religion? Alternatively, do the statutes have no substantial secular purposes? Consider whether the purposes discussed in Lynch v. Donnelly are substantial.

2. *Determining legislative purpose: nondiscrimination and gerrymandering.* Larson v. Valente, 456 U.S. 228 (1982), involved a Minnesota statute imposing reporting requirements on religious organizations that solicit more than 50 percent of their funds from nonmembers. The legislative history included one legislator's statement that "what you're trying to get at here is the people who are running around streets and soliciting people" and another's that he was "not sure why we're so hot to regulate the Moonies anyway." Five members of the Court, in an opinion by Justice Brennan, held that the statute violated "the clearest command of the Establishment Clause[ — that] one religious denomination cannot be officially preferred over another." Such "denominational preferences" must be "justified by a compelling governmental interest, and [be] closely fitted to further that interest." The state's "interest in protecting its citizens from abusive practices" might be compelling, but the 50 percent rule was not closely fitted to preventing abuse. The distinctions in the statute "engender a risk of politicizing religion" and "led the Minnesota legislature to discuss the characteristics of various sects with a view towards 'religious gerrymandering.'" Justice White, joined by Justice Rehnquist, dissented on the ground that the statute was not "a deliberate and explicit preference for some religious denominations over others" because it "names no churches or denominations. [Some] religions will qualify and some will not, but this depends on the source of their contributions, not on their brand of religion."

McCreary County v. ACLU of Kentucky, 545 U.S. 844 (2005), revisited the issue of government posting of the Ten Commandments, and applied the "academic freedom." The Court stated that the statute would not promote academic freedom in the sense of "enhancing the freedom of teachers to teach what they will" or even "teaching all the evidence" in part because it required that curriculum guides be developed for creation science but not for evolution. The Court also stressed that the case presented "[the] same historic and contemporaneous antagonisms between the teachings of certain religious denominations and the teaching of evolution" that it had found in Epperson. "The preeminent purpose of the Louisiana legislature was clearly to advance the religious viewpoint that a supernatural being created humankind."

The Court's analysis concluded:

> We do not imply that a legislature could never require that scientific critiques of prevailing scientific theories be taught. [Teaching] a variant of scientific theories about the origins of humankind to school children might be validly done with the clear secular intent of enhancing the effectiveness of science instruction. But because the primary purpose of the [Louisiana] Act is to endorse a particular religious doctrine, the Act furthers religion in violation of the Establishment Clause.

Justice Powell's concurring opinion, in which Justice O'Connor joined, agreed that the statute had no secular purpose. Justice Scalia wrote a long dissent, in which Chief Justice Rehnquist joined. His examination of the legislative history led him to conclude that one purpose of the statute was to advance academic freedom, as it stated, in the sense of enhancing "students' freedom from indoctrination," which the legislature believed was occurring in biology courses that presented only the theory of evolution.

Could a legislature prohibit the teaching of evolution because it was a scientifically questionable theory whose acceptance by many scientists resulted from their antireligious biases? What sort of legislative hearings or findings would be required? Could a judge reassess the legislature's evaluation of the scientific status of the theory of evolution? In the absence of an illicit motivation of the sort found in Aguillard, does the Constitution require states to teach only the truth in matters of science? Political theory?

## D.  FACIALLY NEUTRAL STATUTES THAT INCIDENTALLY AID RELIGION: PERMISSIBLE AND IMPERMISSIBLE EFFECTS

### Note: The Problem and Its Background

1. *The basic problem.* The school prayer cases indicate that, de facto establishments aside, legislation with the sole (or predominant?) purpose of aiding religion is unconstitutional. Sometimes the Court will treat legislation that

does not use religion as a basis for classification as a religious gerrymander, inferring an impermissible purpose from the statute's structure and history. More complex problems arise when the Court is unwilling to infer an impermissible purpose for a statute that does not use religion as a basis for classification, yet the legislation substantially aids religious institutions.

The Court has examined this problem most extensively in cases questioning legislative efforts to support nonpublic education. Below the college level, nearly all such education occurs in schools affiliated with churches, so that usually 75 percent or more of the aid goes to church-related schools. The Court's first substantial decision was *Everson*. The Court said that the first amendment

"requires the state to be a neutral in its relations with groups of religious believers and non-believers; it does not require the state to be their adversary." It should not be interpreted "to prohibit [the state] from extending its general state law benefits to all its citizens without regard to their religious belief." The bus transportation statute "does no more than provide a general program to help parents get their children, regardless of their religion, safely and expeditiously to and from accredited schools."

Justice Rutledge's dissent was joined by Justices Frankfurter, Jackson, and Burton. He contended that the first amendment "broadly forbids state support, financial or other, of religion in any guise, form or degree. It outlaws all use of public funds for religious purposes." In this case, "parents pay money to send their children to parochial schools and funds raised by taxation are used to reimburse them. This not only helps the children to get to school and the parents to send them. It aids them in a substantial way to get [religious] training and teaching" in part because "transportation [is] as essential to education as any other element." He argued that it was impossible to apportion the expenditures between the parochial schools' religious instruction and their instruction in secular subjects.

The transportation subsidy makes it less expensive for parents to provide their children with a comprehensive religious education. In this sense, the subsidy "supports" or "aids" religion. But if the legislation is truly neutral, should this kind of support violate the Constitution? Is it distinguishable from the provision of general police and fire protection to churches and parochial schools, which could purchase private security services to provide those protections? In Rosenberger v. Rectors & Visitors of the University of Virginia, 515 U.S. 819 (1995), Justice Souter, for four dissenters, argued that these forms of aid should be limited to "essential public benefits." Justice Thomas, in a separate concurring opinion, responded that to do so would be inconsistent with "[our] Nation's tradition of allowing religious adherents to participate in evenhanded government programs."

2. *Subsequent developments.* Since 1968, the Court has decided over a dozen cases involving public aid to nonpublic education. For earlier decisions, see McCollum v. Board of Education, 333 U.S. 203 (1948) (invalidating a

the Minnesota tax laws. [The] Minnesota legislature's judgment that a deduction for educational expenses fairly equalizes the tax burden of its citizens and encourages desirable expenditures for educational purposes is entitled to substantial deference.[6]

Other characteristics of §290.09, subd. 22, argue equally strongly for the provision's constitutionality. Most importantly, the deduction is available for educational expenses incurred by all parents, including those whose children attend public schools and those whose children attend nonsectarian private schools or sectarian private [schools:] "the provision of benefits to so broad a spectrum of groups is an important index of secular effect."

In this respect, as well as others, this case is vitally different from the scheme struck down in *Nyquist*. There, public assistance amounting to tuition grants was provided only to parents of children in nonpublic schools. [Unlike] the assistance at issue in *Nyquist*, §290.09, subd. 22, permits all parents — whether their children attend public school or private — to deduct their childrens' educational expenses. [A] program, like §290.09, subd. 22, that neutrally provides state assistance to a broad spectrum of citizens is not readily subject to challenge under the Establishment Clause.

We also agree [that,] by channeling whatever assistance it may provide to parochial schools through individual parents, Minnesota has reduced the Establishment Clause objections to which its action is subject. It is true, of course, that financial assistance provided to parents ultimately has an economic effect comparable to that of aid given directly to the schools attended by their children. It is also true, however, that under Minnesota's arrangement public funds become available only as a result of numerous, private choices of individual parents of school-age children. [It] is noteworthy that all but one of our recent cases invalidating state aid to parochial schools have involved the direct transmission of assistance from the state to the schools themselves. The exception [was] *Nyquist*, which [is] distinguishable from this case on other grounds. Where, as here, aid to parochial schools is available only as a result of decisions of individual parents no "imprimatur of State approval" [*Widmar*, Chapter V. B3, supra] can be deemed to have been conferred on any particular religion, or on religion generally.

---

6. Our decision in [*Nyquist*] is not to the contrary on this point. [The] outright grants to low-income parents did not take the form of ordinary tax benefits. As to the benefits provided to middle-income parents, the Court said:

> The amount of the deduction [is] apparently the product of a legislative attempt to assure that each family would receive a carefully estimated net benefit, [comparable] to, and compatible with, the tuition grant for lower income families.

[While] the economic consequences of the program in *Nyquist* and that in this case may be difficult to distinguish, we have recognized on other occasions that "the form of the [State's assistance to parochial schools must be examined] for the light that it casts on the substance." [*Lemon*.] The fact that the Minnesota plan embodies a "genuine tax deduction" is thus of some relevance. . . .

We find it useful [to] compare the attenuated financial benefits flowing to parochial schools from the section to the evils against which the Establishment Clause was designed to protect. These dangers are well-described by our statement that "[w]hat is at stake as a matter of policy [in Establishment Clause cases] is preventing that kind and degree of government involvement in religious life that, as history teaches us, is apt to lead to strife and frequently strain a political system to the breaking point." [*Nyquist.*] It is important, however, to "keep these issues in perspective":

> At this point in the 20th century we are quite far removed from the dangers that prompted the Framers to include the Establishment Clause in the Bill of Rights. The risk of significant religious or denominational control over our democratic processes — or even a deep political division along religious lines — is remote, and when viewed against the positive contributions of sectarian schools, any such risk seems entirely tolerable in light of the continuing oversight of this Court.

[*Wolman*] (Powell, J., concurring in part, concurring in the judgment in part, and dissenting in part). The Establishment Clause of course extends beyond prohibition of a state church or payment of state funds to one or more churches. We do not think, however, that its prohibition extends to the type of tax deduction established by Minnesota. The historic purposes of the clause simply do not encompass the sort of attenuated financial benefit, ultimately controlled by the private choices of individual parents, that eventually flows to parochial schools from the neutrally available tax benefit at issue in this case.

Petitioners argue that, notwithstanding the facial neutrality of §290.09, subd. 22, in application the statute primarily benefits religious institutions. Petitioners rely [on] a statistical analysis of the type of persons claiming the tax deduction. They contend that most parents of public school children incur no tuition expenses and that other expenses deductible under §290.09, subd. 22, are negligible in value; moreover, they claim that 96% of the children in private schools in 1978–1979 attended religiously-affiliated institutions. Because of all this, they reason, the bulk of deductions taken under §290.09, subd. 22, will be claimed by parents of children in sectarian schools. . . .

[We] would be loath to adopt a rule grounding the constitutionality of a facially neutral law on annual reports reciting the extent to which various classes of private citizens claimed benefits under the law. [The] fact that private persons fail in a particular year to claim the tax relief to which they are entitled — under a facially neutral statute — should be of little importance in determining the constitutionality of the statute permitting such relief.

Finally, [if] parents of children in private schools choose to take especial advantage of the relief provided by §290.09, subd. 22, it is no doubt due to the fact that they bear a particularly great financial burden in educating their

Responding to concerns expressed by four dissenters, Justice Kennedy's opinion said that the decision "cannot be read as addressing an expenditure from a general tax fund. [This] is a far cry from a general public assessment designed and effected to provide financial support for a church." Further, the case did not involve "direct money payments to an institution or group that is engaged in religious activity" because the payments were made to the printer.

Justice Souter's dissent, joined by Justices Stevens, Ginsburg, and Breyer, argued that it was not enough that the student activities fees were "available on an evenhanded basis to secular and sectarian applicants alike." Rather, "whenever affirmative government aid ultimately benefits religion, the Establishment Clause requires some justification beyond evenhandedness on the government's part; [direct] public funding of core sectarian activities, even if accomplished pursuant to an evenhanded program, would be entirely inconsistent with the Establishment Clause and would strike at the very heart of the Clause's protection. [In] the doubtful cases (those not involving direct public funding), [even-handedness] serves to weed out those laws that impermissibly advance religion by channeling aid to it exclusively. Evenhandedness is therefore a prerequisite to further enquiry into the constitutionality of a doubtful law, but evenhandedness [does] not guarantee success under Establishment Clause scrutiny." He distinguished *Mueller* on the ground that it involved only indirect public funding.

5. *Agostini*. *Agostini v. Felton*, 521 U.S. 203 (1997), overruled *Aguilar*. Justice O'Connor, writing for the Court, said that the Court would not presume "that the placement of public employees on parochial school grounds inevitably results in the impermissible effect of state-sponsored indoctrination or constitutes a symbolic union between government and religion." Nor would it assume "that the presence of a public employee on private school property creates an impermissible 'symbolic link' between government and religion." In addition, the Court said, not "all government aid that directly aids the educational function of religious schools is invalid [*Witters*]."

> First, there is no reason to presume that, simply because she enters a parochial school classroom, a full-time public employee such as a Title I teacher will depart from her assigned duties and instructions and embark on religious indoctrination, any more than there was a reason in *Zobrest* to think an interpreter would inculcate religion by altering her translation of classroom lectures. Certainly, no evidence has ever shown that any New York City Title I instructor teaching on parochial school premises attempted to inculcate religion in students. Thus, both our precedent and our experience require us to reject respondents' remarkable argument that we must presume Title I instructors to be "uncontrollable and sometimes very unprofessional." . . . *Zobrest* also repudiates [the] assumption that the presence of Title I teachers in parochial school classrooms will, without more, create the impression of a "symbolic union" between church and state. [Title] I services may be provided to sectarian school students in off-campus locations, even though that notion necessarily presupposes that

the danger of "symbolic union" evaporates once the services are provided off-campus. Taking this view, the only difference between a constitutional program and an unconstitutional one is the location of the class room. [We] do not see any perceptible (let alone dispositive) difference in the degree of symbolic union between a student receiving remedial instruction in a classroom on his sectarian school's campus and one receiving instruction in a van parked just at the school's curbside . . .

The Court then addressed "the criteria by which an aid program identifies its beneficiaries":

[The] criteria might themselves have the effect of advancing religion by creating a financial incentive to undertake religious indoctrination. This incentive is not present, however, where the aid is allocated on the basis of neutral, secular criteria that neither favor nor disfavor religion, and is made available to both religious and secular beneficiaries on a nondiscriminatory basis. Under such circumstances, the aid is less likely to have the effect of advancing religion. See Widmar v. Vincent, 454 U.S. 263, 274 (1981) ("The provision of benefits to so broad a spectrum of groups is an important index of secular effect"). [Title] I services are allocated on the basis of criteria that neither favor nor disfavor religion. The services are available to all children who meet the Act's eligibility requirements, no matter what their religious beliefs or where they go to school. The Board's program does not, therefore, give aid recipients any incentive to modify their religious beliefs or practices in order to obtain those services.

Finally, the Court addressed the argument "that New York City's Title I program resulted in an excessive entanglement between church and state. [The] factors we use to assess whether an entanglement is 'excessive' are similar to the factors we use to examine 'effect.'" The Court concluded that it should treat entanglement as "an aspect of the inquiry into a statute's effect." The opinion continued: "Not all entanglements [have] the effect of advancing or inhibiting religion. Interaction between church and state is inevitable, and we have always tolerated some level of involvement between the two. Entanglement must be 'excessive' before it runs afoul of the Establishment Clause." Neither "administrative cooperation" nor the danger of political divisiveness created excessive entanglement, particularly in light of the fact that they would be present even if the title I services were offered off-campus. And, given the Court's refusal to assume that public school teachers working in parochial schools "would be tempted to inculcate religion," there was no need for "pervasive monitoring." The unannounced monthly visits were not excessive entanglement.

Justice Souter, joined by Justices Stevens and Ginsburg and in part by Justice Breyer, dissented. In the portion of the dissent that Justice Breyer did not join, Justice Souter said that the Court's decision "authorize[d] direct state aid to religious institutions on an unparalleled scale, in violation of the school boards and receive twice the per-student funding as participating private schools, or magnet schools, which are public schools emphasizing a particular subject area, teaching method, or service, and for which the school district receives the same amount per student as it does for a student enrolled at a traditional public school."

Finding "no dispute that the program [was] enacted for the valid secular purpose of providing educational assistance to poor children in a demonstrably failing public school system," the Court said that "[the] question presented is whether the Ohio program [has] the forbidden 'effect' of advancing or inhibiting religion." Relying on *Mueller*, *Witters*, and *Zobrest*, it concluded that the program did not have such an effect. Those cases, the Court said, "make clear that where a government aid program is neutral with respect to religion, and provides assistance directly to a broad class of citizens who, in turn, direct government aid to religious schools wholly as a result of their own genuine and independent private choice, the program is not readily subject to challenge under the Establishment Clause. A program that shares these features permits government aid to reach religious institutions only by way of the deliberate choices of numerous individual recipients. The incidental advancement of a religious mission, or the perceived endorsement of a religious message, is reasonably attributable to the individual recipient, not to the government, whose role ends with the disbursement of benefits."

It continued, "[the] Ohio program is neutral in all respects toward religion. It is part of a general and multifaceted undertaking by the State of Ohio to provide educational opportunities to the children of a failed school district. It confers educational assistance directly to a broad class of individuals defined without reference to religion, i.e., any parent of a school-age child who resides in the Cleveland City School District. The program permits the participation of all schools within the district, religious or nonreligious. Adjacent public schools also may participate and have a financial incentive to do so. Program benefits are available to participating families on neutral terms, with no reference to religion. The only preference stated anywhere in the program is a preference for low-income families, who receive greater assistance and are given priority for admission at participating schools.

"There are no 'financial incentives' that 'skew' the program toward religious schools. [*Witters*.] Such incentives '[are] not present . . . where the aid is allocated on the basis of neutral, secular criteria that neither favor nor disfavor religion, and is made available to both religious and secular beneficiaries on a nondiscriminatory basis.' [*Agostini*.] The program here in fact creates financial disincentives for religious schools, with private schools receiving only half the government assistance given to community schools and one-third the assistance given to magnet schools. Adjacent public schools, should any choose to accept program students, are also eligible to receive two to three times the state funding of a private religious school. Families too have a financial disincentive to choose a private religious school over other schools. Parents that choose to participate in the scholarship program and then to enroll their children in a private school (religious or nonreligious) must copay a portion of the school's tuition. Families that choose a community school, magnet school, or traditional public school pay nothing. Although such features of the program are not necessary to its constitutionality, they clearly dispel the claim that the program 'creates . . . financial incentives for parents to choose a sectarian school.' [*Zobrest*.]"

On whether the program gave "genuine opportunities for Cleveland parents to select secular educational options for their school-age children," the Court argued that "Cleveland schoolchildren enjoy a range of educational choices: They may remain in public school as before, remain in public school with publicly funded tutoring aid, obtain a scholarship and choose a religious school, obtain a scholarship and choose a nonreligious private school, enroll in a community school, or enroll in a magnet school. That 46 of the 56 private schools now participating in the program are religious schools does not condemn it as a violation of the Establishment Clause. The Establishment Clause question is whether Ohio is coercing parents into sending their children to religious schools, and that question must be answered by evaluating all options Ohio provides Cleveland schoolchildren, only one of which is to obtain a program scholarship and then choose a religious school."

Relying on *Mueller*, the Court rejected the argument that "we should attach constitutional significance to the fact that 96% of scholarship recipients have enrolled in religious schools. They claim that this alone proves parents lack genuine choice, even if no parent has ever said so. We need not consider this argument in detail, since it was flatly rejected in *Mueller*, where we found it irrelevant that 96% of parents taking deductions for tuition expenses paid tuition at religious schools." Explaining why it rejected the argument, the Court pointed out that "[the] 96% figure [discounts] entirely (1) the more than 1,900 Cleveland children enrolled in alternative community schools, (2) the more than 13,000 children enrolled in alternative magnet schools, and (3) the more than 1,400 children enrolled in traditional public schools with tutorial assistance. Including some or all of these children in the denominator of children enrolled in nontraditional schools during the 1999–2000 school year drops the percentage enrolled in religious schools from 96% to under 20%. The 96% figure also represents but a snapshot of one particular school year. In the 1997–1998 school year, by contrast, only 78% of scholarship recipients attended religious schools."

Justices O'Connor and Thomas wrote concurring opinions. Justices Stevens, Souter, Ginsburg, and Breyer dissented. Justice Souter's dissent asserted that "the espoused criteria of neutrality in offering aid, and private choice in directing it, [are] nothing but examples of verbal formalism." To apply the neutrality test, he argued, "it makes sense to focus on a category of aid that may be directed to religious as well as secular schools, and ask whether the scheme favors a religious direction. Here, one would ask whether the voucher

4. *The meaning of neutrality.* Will a requirement of neutrality increase the cost of providing aid to nonpublic schools and thereby alter the political dimensions of the issue? Consider this justification for upholding direct appropriations to private schools: Public schools are subsidized through ordinary appropriations; neutrality is achieved by the separate appropriations to private schools. Finding the latter to violate neutrality artificially divides a unitary system of state-supported education that, taken as a whole, is neutral. Consider the proposal in Choper, The Establishment Clause and Aid to Parochial Schools, 56 Cal. L. Rev. 260, 266 (1968), that aid should be allowed "so long as such aid does not exceed the value of the secular educational service rendered by the school." How likely is it that a legislature, constrained by pluralist politics and tax limitations, would enact a program that violated this test? Does it simply restate the requirement of neutrality? Berg, Religion Clause Anti-Theories, 72 Notre Dame L. Rev. 693, 703–704 (1997), argues that "[government] should, as much as possible, minimize the effect it has on the voluntary, independent religious decisions of the people as individuals and in voluntary groups. The baseline against which effects on religion should be compared is a situation in which religious beliefs and practices succeed or fail solely on their merits — as those merits are presented and judged by individuals and groups, not by government." Consider the assumptions implicit in the term "the merits" in this formulation.

For a discussion of the problem of identifying an appropriate baseline, see Gedicks, The Rhetoric of Church and State: A Critical Analysis of Religion Clause Jurisprudence 57–58, 60 (1995): "How does one identify the baseline measure of religious neutrality? [In] the modern welfare state, [government] aid to both individuals and organizations is widespread and pervasive. Since in the United States most persons and entities are entitled to some kind of government aid, religious neutrality would generally seem to require that this aid not be denied to otherwise qualified recipients simply because they are religious. Indeed, to deny aid to such persons and entities constitutes a tax on religious exercise which skews private choice away from religion. [If] one were to imagine a world of minimalist government in which secular public schools did not exist, then government action mandating religious instruction [would] violate neutrality." Berg discusses some implications of Gedicks' position: "[If] a system of subsidized secular public schools does, in fact, discourage religiously informed education, why can't government include religious teaching in the public school curriculum? [Any] statement the government makes is bound to favor one faith over another." Berg, supra, at 743.

Consider the implications of the argument that voucher and similar programs have a disparate impact on different religious denominations because of their positions on the propriety of accepting government aid even in the form of vouchers. Should the fact that the disparate impact results from religiously motivated choices be sufficient to dispel concerns about sect preference? Consider these observations:

> All institutions [have] an intense interest in their own survival. Programs distributing aid under the neutrality principle offer financial inducements for religious groups to participate in certain programs that "government" desires for the nation and that may [conflict] with certain tenets of the nation's faith communities. These programs easily can [tempt] religious groups to go against their basic principles in order to secure government funding and receive the same benefits [as] other faith traditions. [It] will be those programs that center on social issues more "in the gray" respecting a faith community's belief system that will begin the [assimilation] of our nation's religious traditions. [If a group] buckles to [the] government-supplied financial incentive and chooses to participate, after many years [will] the members of the community even remember the original position of their [tradition?] [One] might easily predict the homogenization of America's diverse faith traditions into a form of civil religion that encourages a malleability of doctrine shaped by the designs of government programs.

Davis, A Commentary on the Supreme Court's "Equal Treatment" Doctrine as the New Constitutional Paradigm for Protecting Religious Liberty, 46 J. Church & St. 717, 733–734 (2004).

5. *Indirect versus direct aid.* Do the cases support a distinction between direct aid — payments or donations of goods and services made to religiously affiliated schools — and indirect aid — payments made to parents who then use the funds to pay such schools? Would it be constitutional for a state to pay a portion of the salary of mathematics teachers in nonpublic schools as part of a "general program" of paying the salaries of all mathematics teachers? In *Rosenberger,* Justice Souter argued that the Court's approach "would permit a State to pay all the bills of any religious institution." Justice Kennedy's opinion for the Court responded that the student publication involved was "not a religious institution, at least in the usual sense of that term." After Rosenberger, must a state include religiously affiliated schools in any voucher program it adopts? What is the basis for the proposition that direct aid to religious institutions is impermissible?

6. *Monetary versus nonmonetary aid.* Justice Thomas's opinion in *Mitchell* noted that prior cases had found 'special Establishment Clause dangers' when money is given to religious schools or entities directly rather than [indirectly]. But [we] refuse to allow a 'special' case to create a rule for all cases." Justice O'Connor wrote, "If [a] per-capita-aid program is identical in relevant constitutional respects to a true private-choice program, then there is no reason that [the] government should be precluded from providing direct money payments to religious organizations [based] on the number of persons belonging to each organization." If the distinction between direct and indirect aid is

Until 1963, the Supreme Court had not squarely held that the free exercise clause protects religious beliefs differently, or more extensively, than the free speech clause protects political beliefs. Reynolds v. United States, 98 U.S. 145 (1879), upheld a conviction of a Mormon for bigamy, rejecting a free exercise defense. The Court said that under the first amendment "Congress was deprived of all legislative power over mere opinion, but was left free to reach actions which were in violation of social duties or subversive of good order. [Laws] are made for the government of actions, and while they cannot interfere with mere religious belief and actions, they may with practices." In Cantwell v. Connecticut, 310 U.S. 296 (1940), the Court said that the free exercise clause "embraces two concepts, — freedom to believe and freedom to act. The first is absolute, but in the nature of things, the second cannot be. Conduct remains subject to regulation for the protection of society. [*Reynolds.*] [In] every case the power to regulate must be so exercised as not [unduly] to infringe the protected freedom."

**BRAUNFELD v. BROWN, 366 U.S. 599 (1961).** Pennsylvania's law requiring that businesses be closed on Sundays was challenged on free exercise grounds by Orthodox Jews, whose religion required that they close their stores on Saturdays. They alleged that the Sunday closing laws placed them at a competitive disadvantage so severe as to force them out of business. Chief Justice Warren's plurality opinion rejected the free exercise claim. Citing *Reynolds*, it said, "[The] statute [does] not make criminal the holding of any religious belief or opinion, nor does it force anyone to embrace any religious belief. [It simply] make[s] the practice of their religious beliefs more expensive. [To] strike down [legislation] which imposes only an indirect burden on the exercise of religion [would] radically restrict the operating latitude of the legislature. [We] are a cosmopolitan nation made up of people of almost every conceivable religious preference. [Consequently,] it cannot be expected, much less required, that legislators enact no law regulating conduct that may in some way result in an economic disadvantage to some religious sects and not to others because of the special practices of the various religions. [If] the State regulates conduct by enacting a general law within its power, the purpose and effect of which is to advance the State's secular goals, the statute is valid despite its indirect burden on religious observance unless the State may accomplish its purposes by means which do not impose such a burden." An exemption for Saturday-observers was not required because it "might well undermine the State's goal of providing a day that, as best possible, eliminates the atmosphere of commercial noise and activity. [Enforcement] problems would be more difficult [and Saturday-observers] might well [receive] an economic advantage over their competitors who must close on that day."

Justice Brennan, in dissent, described the state's interest as "the mere convenience of having everyone rest on the same day" and called the plurality's concern about a system allowing exemptions "fanciful." This "[exalts] administrative convenience to a constitutional level high enough to justify making one religion economically disadvantageous." Justice Stewart's dissent said that the law "compels an Orthodox Jew to choose between his religious faith and his economic survival. That is a cruel choice. It is a choice which I think no State can constitutionally demand. For me this is not something that can be swept under the rug and forgotten in the interest of enforced Sunday togetherness."

**SHERBERT v. VERNER, 374 U.S. 398 (1963).** Mrs. Sherbert, a Seventh-Day Adventist, was fired by her employer because she would not work on Saturday, her church's Sabbath. She was unable to find other employment in her town that would allow her to observe her Sabbath. She sought unemployment compensation, which was denied because she had lacked good cause to refuse suitable work. (The unemployment systems in most states, but not Sherbert's, treated inability to find work that would allow observance of the worker's Sabbath to be "good cause" for refusing to accept job offers.)

The Supreme Court, in an opinion by Justice Brennan, held that the denial of unemployment compensation violated the free exercise clause. The denial "imposes [a] burden on the free exercise" of religion. "Here not only is it apparent that appellant's declared ineligibility for benefits derives solely from the practice of her religion, but the pressure upon her to forego that practice is unmistakable. The ruling forces her to choose between following the precepts of her religion and forfeiting benefits, on the one hand, and abandoning one of the precepts of her religion in order to accept work, on the other hand. Governmental imposition of such a choice puts the same kind of burden upon the free exercise of religion as would a fine imposed against appellant for her Saturday worship."

The Court then considered "whether some compelling state interest [justifies] the substantial infringement of appellant's First Amendment right." The only interest asserted was prevention of the filing of fraudulent claims, but, according to the Court, the Constitution required that the state demonstrate that "no alternative forms of regulations would combat such abuses without infringing First Amendment rights." Unlike Braunfeld, where allowing exemptions would necessarily impair the interest in preserving a uniform day of rest, here exemptions could be administered without undermining the unemployment compensation system.

Justice Stewart concurred in the result. "The guarantee of religious liberty embodied in the Free Exercise Clause affirmatively requires government to create an atmosphere of hospitality and accommodation to individual belief or disbelief. [Our] Constitution commands the positive protection by government of religious freedom [for] each of us."

Justice Harlan, joined by Justice White, dissented. The Court's holding, he said, meant that "the State [must] single out for financial assistance those whose behavior is religiously motivated, even though it denies such assistance granting these requests would noticeably impair the overall image of the service."

b. *Prisons.* O'Lone v. Estate of Shabazz, 482 U.S. 342 (1987), concerned a challenge by Muslim prisoners to a prison policy that prevented them from attending Jumu'ah, a weekly Muslim congregational service mandated by the Koran. Prison regulations, adopted for security reasons, prevented prisoners with respondents' classification from being inside the building where the service was held. The Court held that in a prison context alleged infringements on free exercise interests "are judged under a 'reasonableness' test less restrictive than that ordinarily applied to [infringements] of fundamental constitutional rights." Applying this reasonableness test to the facts before it, the Court concluded that the restriction was justified by security concerns.

4. *The concept of burdens: internal government operations.* Is there a constitutionally cognizable burden in the following cases?

Bowen v. Roy, 476 U.S. 693 (1986), rejected religion-based objections to a federal statute requiring applicants for certain welfare benefits to provide the states with their Social Security numbers and requiring the states to use the numbers in administering the program. Appellees had applied for such benefits, including food stamps. They contended that providing a Social Security number for their two-year-old daughter and use of that number by the government would violate their religious beliefs.

Writing for eight justices, Chief Justice Burger rejected appellees' claim that the free exercise clause was infringed when the government used the number. "Never to our knowledge has the Court interpreted the First Amendment to require the Government itself to behave in ways that the individual believes will further his or her spiritual development. [The] Free Exercise Clause affords an individual protection from certain forms of governmental compulsion; it does not afford an individual a right to dictate the conduct of the Government's internal procedures." The Court did not definitively rule on the claim that appellees could not be required to apply for Social Security numbers, although a majority of the justices indicated that, were the Court to reach the issue, they would hold that free exercise required that appellees could not be so required.

Lyng v. Northwest Indian Cemetery Protective Association, 485 U.S. 439 (1988), rejected a free exercise challenge to the Forest Service's plan to permit timber harvesting and road construction in part of a national forest that was traditionally used by various Indian tribes as sacred areas for religious rituals. The Court held, in an opinion by Justice O'Connor, that the government did not have to show a compelling need to engage in the relevant projects:

> In both [*Roy* and *Lyng*] the challenged governmental action would interfere significantly with private persons' ability to pursue spiritual fulfillment according to their own religious beliefs. In neither case, however, could the affected

individuals be coerced by the Government's action into violating their religious beliefs; nor would either governmental action penalize religious activity by denying any person an equal share of the rights, benefits, and privileges enjoyed by other citizens.

The Court acknowledged that

indirect coercion or penalties on the free exercise of religion; not just outright prohibitions, are subject to scrutiny under the First Amendment. [But] this [cannot] imply that incidental effects of government programs, which may make it more difficult to practice certain religions but which have no tendency to coerce individuals into acting contrary to their religious beliefs, require government to bring forward a compelling justification for its otherwise lawful actions. The crucial word in the constitutional text is "prohibit."

The Court noted that the projects at issue "could have devastating effects on traditional Indian religious practices . . . intimately and inextricably bound up with the unique features" of the area, but it concluded that "government simply could not operate if it were required to satisfy every citizen's religious needs and desires."

In a dissenting opinion joined by Justices Marshall and Blackmun, Justice Brennan criticized the Court's conception of "coercion":

Ultimately, the Court's coercion test turns on a distinction between governmental actions that compel affirmative conduct inconsistent with religious belief, and those governmental actions that prevent conduct consistent with religious belief. [The] crucial word in the constitutional text, as the Court itself acknowledges, is "prohibit," a comprehensive term that in no way suggests that the intended protection is aimed only at governmental actions that coerce affirmative conduct. [Religious] freedom is threatened no less by governmental action that makes the practice of one's chosen faith impossible than by governmental programs that pressure one to engage in conduct inconsistent with religious belief.

In what sense is the land in *Lyng* more "the government's" than was the money in *Sherbert*? Note that in *Lyng* there was even greater coercion than in *Sherbert* — an across-the-board foreclosure rather than a financial inducement to abandon religious practice.

# Employment Division, Department of Human Resources v. Smith

494 U.S. 872 (1990)

JUSTICE SCALIA delivered the opinion of the Court.

This case requires us to decide whether the Free Exercise Clause of the First Amendment permits the State of Oregon to include religiously inspired peyote press by the First Amendment is likely to enact laws that affirmatively foster the dissemination of the printed word, so also a society that believes in the negative protection accorded to religious belief can be expected to be solicitous of that value in its legislation as well. It is therefore not surprising that a number of States have made an exception to their drug laws for sacramental peyote use. But to say that a nondiscriminatory religious-practice exemption is permitted, or even that it is desirable, is not to say that it is constitutionally required, and that the appropriate occasions for its creation can be discerned by the courts. It may fairly be said that leaving accommodation to the political process will place at a relative disadvantage those religious practices that are not widely engaged in; but that unavoidable consequence of democratic government must be preferred to a system in which each conscience is a law unto itself or in which judges weight the social importance of all laws against the centrality of all religious beliefs.

[Reversed.]

JUSTICE O'CONNOR, with whom JUSTICE BRENNAN, JUSTICE MARSHALL, and JUSTICE BLACKMUN join as to [Part] II, concurring in the judgment. . . .

## II . . .

### A

[Because] the First Amendment does not distinguish between religious belief and religious conduct, conduct motivated by sincere religious belief, like the belief itself, must therefore be at least presumptively protected by the Free Exercise Clause.

[A] law that prohibits [conduct] that happens to be an act of worship for someone [manifestly] does prohibit that person's free exercise of his religion. A person who is barred from engaging in religiously motivated conduct is barred from freely exercising his religion. Moreover, that person is barred from freely exercising his religion regardless of whether the law prohibits the conduct only when engaged in for religious reasons, only by members of that religion, or by all persons. It is difficult to deny that a law that prohibits religiously motivated conduct, even if the law is generally applicable, does not at least implicate First Amendment concerns.

The Court responds that generally applicable laws are "one large step" removed from laws aimed at specific religious practices. The First Amendment, however, does not distinguish between laws that are generally applicable and laws that target particular religious practices. Indeed, few States would be so naive as to enact a law directly prohibiting or burdening a religious practice as such. Our free exercise cases have all concerned generally applicable laws that had the effect of significantly burdening a religious practice. If the First Amendment is to have any vitality, it ought not be construed to cover only the extreme and hypothetical situation in which a State directly targets a religious practice. . . .

To say that a person's right to free exercise has been burdened, of course, does not mean that he has an absolute right to engage in the conduct. Under our established First Amendment jurisprudence, we have recognized that the freedom to act, unlike the freedom to believe, cannot be absolute. Instead, we have respected both the First Amendment's express textual mandate and the governmental interest in regulation of conduct by requiring the Government to justify any substantial burden on religiously motivated conduct by a compelling state interest and by means narrowly tailored to achieve that interest. The compelling interest test effectuates the First Amendment's command that religious liberty is an independent liberty, that it occupies a preferred position, and that the Court will not permit encroachments upon this liberty, whether direct or indirect, unless required by clear and compelling governmental interests "of the highest order" [*Yoder*]. . . .

[In] each of the [cases] cited by the Court to support its categorical rule, we rejected the particular constitutional claims before us only after carefully weighing the competing interests. That we rejected the free exercise claims in those cases hardly calls into question the applicability of First Amendment doctrine in the first place. Indeed, it is surely unusual to judge the vitality of a constitutional doctrine by looking to the win-loss record of the plaintiffs who happen to come before us.

B . . .

[The] essence of a free exercise claim is relief from a burden imposed by government on religious practices or beliefs, whether the burden is imposed directly through laws that prohibit or compel specific religious practices, or indirectly through laws that, in effect, make abandonment of one's own religion or conformity to the religious beliefs of others the price of an equal place in the civil community. . . .

Legislatures, of course, have always been "left free to reach actions which were in violation of social duties or subversive of good order." [*Reynolds.*] Yet because of the close relationship between conduct and religious belief, "[i]n every case the power to regulate must be so exercised as not, in attaining a permissible end, unduly to infringe the protected freedom." [*Cantwell.*] Once it has been shown that a government regulation or criminal prohibition burdens the free exercise of religion, we have consistently asked the Government to demonstrate that unbending application of its regulation to the religious objector "is essential to accomplish an overriding governmental interest" [*Lee*], or represents "the least restrictive means of achieving some compelling state interest" [*Thomas*]. To me, [the] approach more consistent with our role as judges to decide each case on its individual merits [is] to apply this test in each case to determine whether the burden on the specific plaintiffs before us controlling the use of dangerous drugs compatible with an exemption for religious use of peyote.

The carefully circumscribed ritual context in which respondents used peyote is far removed from the irresponsible and unrestricted recreational use of unlawful drugs.[6] The Native American Church's internal restrictions on, and supervision of, its members' use of peyote substantially obviate the State's health and safety concerns. . . .[7]

The State's apprehension of a flood of other religious claims is purely speculative. Almost half the States and the Federal Government have maintained an exemption for religious peyote use for many years, and apparently have not found themselves overwhelmed by claims to other religious exemptions.[8] Allowing an exemption for religious peyote use would not necessarily oblige the State to grant a similar exemption to other religious groups. The unusual circumstances that make the religious use of peyote compatible with the State's interests in health and safety and in preventing drug trafficking would not apply to other religious claims. Some religions, for example, might not restrict drug use to a limited ceremonial context, as does the Native American Church. Some religious claims involve drugs such as marijuana and heroin, in which there is significant illegal traffic, with its attendant greed and violence, so that it would be difficult to grant a religious exemption without seriously compromising law enforcement efforts. . . .

### Note: Should Accommodation Be Required?

1. *Free exercise and free speech.* United States v. O'Brien, Chapter V.C, supra, held that facially neutral statutes serving important purposes unrelated to suppression of speech are constitutional if the incidental impact on speech is no greater than necessary. Is the Court correct in stating that *Smith* transfers the *O'Brien* approach to the free exercise area? Gedicks, The Normalized Free Exercise Clause, 75 Ind. L.J. 77 (2000), argues that *Smith* adopts a "rational basis" standard of review and thereby "contradicts the Court's Speech Clause doctrine governing [incidental] burdens on speech occurring as the result of otherwise legitimate government regulations of conduct or the time, place, or

6. [Respondents'] use of peyote seems closely analogous to the sacramental use of wine by the Roman Catholic Church. During Prohibition, the Federal Government exempted such use of wine from its general ban on possession and use of alcohol. However compelling the Government's then general interest in prohibiting the use of alcohol may have been, it could not plausibly have asserted an interest sufficiently compelling to outweigh Catholics' right to take communion.

7. The use of peyote is, to some degree, self-limiting. The peyote plant is extremely bitter, and eating it is an unpleasant experience, which would tend to discourage casual or recreational use.

8. Over the past years, various sects have raised free exercise claims regarding drug use. In no reported case, except those involving claims of religious peyote use, has the claimant prevailed.

manner of expression," which requires that such regulations satisfy an intermediate standard of review. Is Gedicks's description of free speech doctrine accurate?

2. *The scope of* Smith. How broadly does *Smith* undermine a doctrine of mandatory accommodation?

a. *Individualized determinations.* Was the unemployment commission in *Sherbert* in a position to balance the impairment of free exercise against the prevention of fraudulent claims? Consider Brownstein, Protecting Religious Liberty: The False Messiahs of Free Speech Doctrine and Formal Neutrality, 18 J.L. & Pol. 119, 191–192 (2002): Under the "individualized determination" exception, "[religion] is granted something like most favored nation status. If any secular interest can justify an exemption from a law, then the state must recognize that religious interests also deserve to be exempt from the law. [But an] extraordinary range of laws contain[s] exemptions to their application, including most civil rights laws [and] even homicide statutes. [This] militates against such an understanding." See also Duncan, Free Exercise Is Dead, Long Live Free Exercise: Smith, Lukumi, and the General Applicability Requirement, 3 U. Pa. J. Const. L. 850, 868 (2001): "[A] law burdening religious conduct is under-inclusive, with respect to any particular government interest, if the law fails to pursue that interest uniformly against other conduct that causes similar damage to that government interest." Does this meet Brownstein's concerns?

b. *Hybrid claims.* Is the Court's explanation of Yoder persuasive? Consider the proposition that, because there is no substantive due process right, independent of a religious claim, to keep children out of school, and there is no religious claim, independent of a due process claim, to do so, the two inadequate arguments taken together cannot add up to a valid claim. Consider Brownstein, Protecting Religious Liberty: The False Messiahs of Free Speech Doctrine and Formal Neutrality, 18 J.L. & Pol. 119, 191–192 (2002): "A hybrid rights situation involves a neutral law of general applicability that substantially burdens the exercise of religion and sufficiently burdens some other constitutionally protected interest to invoke the application of the requisite standard of review [short] of strict scrutiny." Brownstein argues that this idea is coherent but inconsistent with "basic constitutional intuitions." "Hybrid rights analysis suggests that religious people should be treated preferentially with regard to the exercise of fundamental rights when their religious beliefs influence the way they exercise their rights. [That] cannot be right. There is an equality dimension to liberty rights. [Religious] people do not get special treatment with respect to these basic freedoms. No one does."

Suppose a state adopts an antidiscrimination statute prohibiting discrimination on the basis of sexual orientation, applicable to businesses that offer services to the general public. Does a photographer who has religious objections to assisting in the public acknowledgement of weddings of same-sex couples have a hybrid claim (on the ground that commercial photography is an expressive activity within the general ambit of the free speech clause)?

the political process over marginal religions and over nonreligion. Legislation is likely to enhance the positions of mainstream religions. In the long run, religious minorities will be better off under a regime of strict separation, even though the application of neutral regulations may sometimes affect them adversely.

5. There need be no tension. If states are barred from using religion as a basis for either conferring benefits or imposing burdens, legislators will be required to use neutral rules to accomplish their goals, and the legislation resulting from a political process constrained by a requirement of neutrality will threaten neither free exercise nor nonestablishment values.

## Corporation of Presiding Bishop of the Church of Jesus Christ of Latter-Day Saints v. Amos

483 U.S. 327 (1987)

JUSTICE WHITE delivered the opinion of the Court.

Section 702 of the Civil Rights Act of 1964 exempts religious organizations from Title VII's prohibition against discrimination in employment on the basis of religion. The question presented is whether applying the §702 exemption to the secular nonprofit activities of religious organizations violates the Establishment Clause of the First Amendment. The District Court held that it does. . . .

[The appellee was a janitor at the Deseret Gymnasium, a nonprofit facility, open to the public, run by the Mormon church. He was fired after he failed to qualify for a certificate stating that he was a member of the church eligible to attend its temples because he observed the church's standards involving church attendance, tithing, and abstinence from coffee, tea, alcohol, and tobacco.]

"This Court has long recognized that the government may (and sometimes must) accommodate religious practices and that it may do so without violating the Establishment Clause." [*Hobbie*, Chapter IX, supra] It is well established, too, that "[t]he limits of permissible state accommodation to religion are by no means co-extensive with the noninterference mandated by the Free Exercise Clause." [*Walz*, Chapter VIII, supra.] There is ample room under the Establishment Clause for "benevolent neutrality which will permit religious exercise to exist without sponsorship and without interference." At some point, accommodation may devolve into "an unlawful fostering of religion" [*Hobbie*], but these are not such cases, in our view. . . .

*Lemon* requires first that the law at issue serve a "secular legislative purpose." This does not mean that the law's purpose must be unrelated to religion — that would amount to a requirement "that the government show a callous indifference to religious groups," Zorach v. Clauson, 343 U.S. 306, 314 (1952), and the Establishment Clause has never been so interpreted. Rather, *Lemon*'s "purpose" requirement aims at preventing the relevant governmental decisionmaker — in this case, Congress — from abandoning neutrality and acting with the intent of promoting a particular point of view in religious matters.

Under the *Lemon* analysis, it is a permissible legislative purpose to alleviate significant governmental interference with the ability of religious organizations to define and carry out their religious missions. Appellees argue that there is no such purpose here because §702 provided adequate protection for religious employers [when] it exempted only the religious activities of such employers from the statutory ban on religious discrimination. We may assume for the sake of argument that [that] exemption was adequate in the sense that the Free Exercise Clause required no more. Nonetheless, it is a significant burden on a religious organization to require it, on pain of substantial liability, to predict which of its activities a secular court will consider religious. The line is hardly a bright one, and an organization might understandably be concerned that a judge would not understand its religious tenets and sense of mission. Fear of potential liability might affect the way an organization carried out what it understood to be its religious mission. [Congress's] purpose was to minimize governmental "interfer[ence] with the decision-making process in religions." [This] purpose does not violate the Establishment Clause.

The second requirement under *Lemon* is that the law in question have "a principal or primary effect . . . that neither advances nor inhibits religion." Undoubtedly, religious organizations are better able now to advance their purposes than they were prior to the 1972 amendment to §702. [A] law is not unconstitutional simply because it allows churches to advance religion, which is their very purpose. For a law to have forbidden "effects" under *Lemon*, it must be fair to say that the government itself has advanced religion through its own activities and influence. . . .

The District Court appeared to fear that sustaining the exemption would permit churches with financial resources impermissibly to extend their influence and propagate their faith by entering the commercial, profit-making world. The cases before us [involve] a nonprofit activity instituted over 75 years ago. [Moreover], we find no persuasive evidence in the record before us that the Church's ability to propagate its religious doctrine through the Gymnasium is any greater now than it was prior to the passage of the Civil Rights Act in 1964. In such circumstances, we do not see how any advancement of religion achieved by the Gymnasium can be fairly attributed to the Government, as opposed to the Church.[15]

We find unpersuasive the District Court's reliance on the fact that §702 singles out religious entities for a benefit. Although the Court has given weight

---

15. Undoubtedly, [appellee's] freedom of choice in religious matters was impinged upon, but it was the Church[, and] not the Government, who put him to the choice of changing his religious practices or losing his job. This is a very different case than Estate of Thornton v. Caldor, Inc., 472 U.S. 703 (1985). In *Caldor*, the Court struck down a Connecticut statute prohibiting an employer from requiring an employee to work on a day designated by the employee as his Sabbath. In effect, Connecticut had given the force of law to the employee's designation of a Sabbath day and required accommodation by the employer regardless of the burden which that constituted for the employer or other employees. . . .

of religion is the justification, by definition religion is being singled out." Although "it is not always easy to determine when accommodation slides over into promotion, and neutrality into favoritism," the tax exemption was an easy case because imposing a general sales tax on the sale of religious publications was at least arguably unconstitutional as a burden on religion. (Does this argument survive *Smith*, Chapter IX, supra?) Justice Brennan's opinion rejected this argument on the ground that it was obviously not unconstitutional to impose a general sales tax on religious publications. For Justice Brennan, accommodations must not "impose substantial burdens on nonbeneficiaries [or must be] designed to alleviate government intrusions that might significantly deter adherents of a particular faith from conduct protected by the Free Exercise Clause." The tax exemption did burden nonbeneficiaries by increasing their tax bills and did not alleviate a "demonstrated and possibly grave imposition on religious activity sheltered by the Free Exercise Clause."

Justice Blackmun, whose opinion concurring in the result was joined by Justice O'Connor, expressed more sympathy with the accommodation argument. He argued that the tax exemption was unconstitutional because it was "limited to the sale of religious literature by a religious organization." (Justice White also concurred in the result, relying on Arkansas Writers' Project v. Ragland, Chapter VI.D, supra.)

**BOARD OF EDUCATION OF KIRYAS JOEL VILLAGE SCHOOL DISTRICT v. GRUMET, 512 U.S. 687 (1994).** The village of Kiryas Joel in New York is a religious enclave of Satmar Hasidim, a group of Orthodox Jews "who make few concessions to the modern world and go to great lengths to avoid assimilation." Most children in the village are educated in private religious schools. Educating handicapped children in such schools is quite expensive, and the village residents arranged to have a public school system provide education for their handicapped children in an annex to one of the religious schools. That arrangement ended after the Court's decision in Aguilar v. Felton, Chapter VIII, supra. The children were then sent to schools in the neighboring public school system. The village residents found the education there unsatisfactory in part because the children suffered "panic, fear and trauma" from "leaving their own community and being with people whose ways were so different." In 1989, the New York legislature enacted a statute designating the village of Kiryas Joel as a separate school district. The Supreme Court held the statute unconstitutional.

Justice Souter's opinion for the Court stated, "The fact that this school district was created by a special and unusual Act of the legislature [gives] reason for concern whether the benefit received by the Satmar community is one that the legislature will provide equally to other religious (and nonreligious) groups." For the Court, "[the] fundamental source of constitutional concern [is] that the legislature itself may fail to exercise governmental authority in a religiously neutral way. The anomalously case-specific nature of the legislature's exercise of state authority in creating this district for a religious community leaves the Court without any direct way to review such state action for the purpose of safeguarding a principle at the heart of the Establishment Clause, that government should not prefer one religion to another, or religion to irreligion." The difficulty was that Kiryas Joel had not received its authority "simply as one of many communities eligible for equal treatment under a general law," so the Court could not be sure "that the next similarly situated group seeking a school district of its own will receive one; [a] legislature's failure to enact a special law is itself unreviewable." The Court agreed that the state could "accommodate religious needs by alleviating special burdens," but creating a separate district "singles out a particular religious sect for special treatment" and thereby violated the principle that "neutrality as among religions must be honored."

Justice Stevens, joined by Justices Blackmun and Ginsburg, added that, to meet the concerns about "panic, fear and trauma," the state "could have taken steps to alleviate the children's fear by teaching their schoolmates to be tolerant and respectful of Satmar customs. Action of that kind would raise no constitutional concerns and would further the strong public interest in promoting diversity and understanding in the public schools." But the state's response, "a solution that affirmatively supports a religious sect's interest in segregating itself and preventing its children from associating with their neighbors," was unconstitutional. It "increased the likelihood that they would remain within the fold, faithful adherents of their parents' religious faith," and thereby "provided official support to cement the attachment of young adherents to a particular faith."

Justice Kennedy, concurring, argued that "[the] real vice of the school district [is] that New York created it by drawing political boundaries on the basis of religion." He criticized the Court's broader analysis. "[By] creating the district, New York did not impose or increase any burden on non-Satmars, compared to the burden it lifted from the Satmars, that might disqualify the District as a genuine accommodation." There was no evidence "that the legislature has denied another religious community like the Satmars its own school district under analogous circumstances. The legislature, like the judiciary, is sworn to uphold the Constitution, and we have no reason to presume that the New York Legislature would not grant the same accommodation in a similar future case. The fact that New York singled out the Satmars for this special treatment indicates nothing other than the uniqueness of the handicapped Satmar children's plight. It is normal for legislatures to respond to problems as they arise — no less so when the issue is religious accommodation."

Justice O'Connor argued that "[the] Satmars' living arrangements were accommodated by their right — a right shared with all other communities, religious or not, throughout New York — to incorporate themselves as a village." In her view, "one's religion ought not affect one's legal rights or duties or quoted legislative history indicating that "[l]awmakers supporting [the act] were mindful of the urgency of discipline, order, safety, and security in penal institutions" and "anticipated that courts would apply the Act's standard with 'due deference'" to the judgment of prison administrators. "Should inmate requests for religious accommodations become excessive, impose unjustified burdens on other institutionalized persons, or jeopardize the effective functioning of an institution, the facility would be free to resist the imposition. In that event, adjudication in as-applied challenges would be in order."

The Court found a prison regulation of beard length to violate RLUIPA in Holt v. Hobbs, 135 S. Ct. 853 (2015).

### Note: Free Exercise, Free Speech, and the Right of Expressive Association

**HOSANNA-TABOR EVANGELICAL LUTHERAN CHURCH & SCHOOL v. EEOC, 132 S. Ct. 694 (2012).** Cheryl Perich was a "called" teacher at a school operated by the Lutheran Church. "Called" teachers completed special training, including theological study. Most of Perich's classes were in secular subjects, but she did teach a religion class. After Perich took disability leave for narcolepsy, her employer asked that she resign. She refused and informed the school that she had consulted a lawyer. The school then fired her, citing among other things her threats to take legal action. Perich filed a complaint with the Equal Employment Opportunity Commission, which after an investigation sued the school for retaliating against Perich for threatening to file her lawsuit under the Americans with Disabilities Act. The school sought dismissal of the EEOC lawsuit, invoking the "ministerial exemption." That exemption, written into some nondiscrimination statutes but not into the ADA's anti-retaliation provision, is available to religious institutions in connection with the employment of "ministers."

Chief Justice Roberts, writing for a unanimous Court, held that both the establishment and free exercise clauses required that religious institutions be able to invoke a ministerial exemption, and that Perich was a minister within the constitutionally required exemption. "The members of a religious group put their faith in the hands of their ministers. Requiring a church to accept or retain an unwanted minister, or punishing a church for failing to do so, intrudes upon more than a mere employment decision. Such action interferes with the internal governance of the church, depriving the church of control over the selection of those who will personify its beliefs. [This] infringes the Free Exercise Clause, which protects a religious group's right to shape its own faith and mission through its appointments. According the state the power to determine which individuals will minister to the faithful also violates the Establishment Clause, which prohibits government involvement in such ecclesiastical decisions."

The Court found "untenable" the position that church interests were adequately protected by the right of expressive association implicit in the first amendment. That position would lead to the conclusion that "the First Amendment analysis should be the same, whether the association in question is the Lutheran Church, a labor union, or a social club. That result is hard to square with the text of the First Amendment itself, which gives special solicitude to the rights of religious organizations." Although the ADA's antiretaliation provision was "a valid and neutral law of general applicability," Employment Division v. Smith was inapposite because it "involved government regulation of only outward physical acts. The present case [concerns] government interference with an internal church decision that affects the faith and mission of the church itself." The Court refused "to adopt a rigid formula for deciding when an employee qualifies as a minister. It is enough for us to conclude [that] the exception covers Perich. [Hosanna-Tabor] held Perich out as a minister, with a role distinct from that of most of its members. [Her] title as a minister reflected a significant degree of religious training followed by a formal process of commissioning. [Her] job duties reflected a role in conveying the Church's message and carrying out its mission."

Concurring, Justice Thomas wrote that "the Religion Clauses require civil courts [to] defer to a religious organization's good-faith understanding of who qualifies as a minister. [The] question of whether an employee is a minister is itself religious in nature, and the answer will vary widely. Judicial attempts to fashion a civil definition of 'minister' through a bright-line test or multi-factor analysis risk disadvantaging those religious groups whose beliefs, practices, and membership are outside of the 'mainstream' or unpalatable to some." Also concurring, Justice Alito, joined by Justice Kagan, wrote that defining who was a minister "should focus on the function performed by persons who work for religious bodies," and "[should] apply to any 'employee' who leads a religious organization, conducts worship services or important religious ceremonies or rituals, or serves as a messenger or teacher of its faith."

### Note: The Relation between the Religion Clauses and Other Protections of Expression

1. *Free exercise versus other protected first amendment rights?* Many activities associated with religion are forms of expression, either expressly (prayer) or as action that can be described as symbolic speech (some or all religious rituals). Would the analysis of the restriction on the use of peyote in *Smith* differ were that use characterized as symbolic speech? Conversely, why is a decision to hire or fire an employee not an "outward physical act"? Could the restriction on ritual sacrifice invalidated in *Hialeah* be characterized as discrimination against expressive activity based on its content? Epps, What We Talk about When We Talk about Free Exercise, 30 Ariz. St. L.J. 563, 577–578 (1998),

wish to conduct a meeting within that limited open forum on the basis of the religious, political, philosophical, or other content of the speech at such meetings." A limited open forum is created when the school allows "noncurriculum related student groups to meet on school premises during noninstructional time." The Court upheld the constitutionality of the Equal Access Act in Board of Education of Westside Community Schools v. Mergens, 496 U.S. 226 (1990). Justice O'Connor's plurality opinion on the constitutional question concluded that "the logic of *Widmar* applies" to the Equal Access Act. Prohibiting discrimination on the basis of political as well as religious speech was a secular purpose under *Lemon*. Equal access would not have the effect of conveying a message of government endorsement of religion. "We think that secondary school students are mature enough and are likely to understand that a school does not endorse or support student speech that it merely permits on a nondiscriminatory basis." Congress had made a similar determination, and Justice O'Connor said that the Court should not "lightly second-guess [legislative] judgments, particularly where the judgments are based in part on empirical determinations," as this one was. She noted that "the broad spectrum of officially recognized student groups [counteracts] any possible message of official endorsement of or preference for religion or a particular religion. [To] the extent that a religious club is merely one of many different student-initiated voluntary clubs, students should perceive no message of government endorsement of religion."

4. *Religion in politics.*

a. *Church members as political actors.* Torcaso v. Watkins, 367 U.S. 488 (1961), invalidated a provision in the Maryland Constitution requiring state officials to declare their belief in the existence of God. "[Neither] a State nor the Federal Government can constitutionally force a person 'to profess a belief or disbelief in any religion' [and] neither can aid those religions based on a belief in the existence of God as against those religions founded on different beliefs."

In McDaniel v. Paty, 435 U.S. 618 (1978), the Court invalidated, without dissent, a provision of the Tennessee Constitution barring ministers from serving as legislators or as delegates to the state's constitutional convention. Chief Justice Burger's plurality opinion reviewed the history of such disqualifications, which were in effect in seven of the original states and which were adopted by six states later admitted to the Union. Disqualification was designed "to assure the success of a new political experiment, the separation of church and state." But "as the value of the disestablishment experiment was perceived, 11 of the 13 States [gradually] abandoned that limitation," until by 1900 only Maryland and Tennessee retained it. The opinion continued, "[The] right to the free exercise of religion unquestionably encompasses the right to preach [and] to be a minister." If the disqualification "were viewed as depriving the clergy of a civil right solely because of their religious beliefs," *Torcaso* would control. But the disqualification was triggered by the minister's status, defined "in terms of conduct and activity rather than in terms of belief."

Thus, the relevant precedent was *Yoder*, which required an "interest of the highest order." But the state had "failed to demonstrate that [the] dangers of clergy participation in the political process have not lost whatever validity they may once have enjoyed. [The] American experience provides no persuasive support for the fear that clergymen in public office will be less careful of anti-establishment interests or less faithful to their oaths of civil office than their unordained counterparts."

Justice Brennan, joined by Justice Marshall and Justice Stewart, submitted separate concurring opinions arguing that *Torcaso* controlled. Justice Brennan wrote, "[Freedom] of belief [embraces] freedom to profess or practice that belief, even including doing so to earn a livelihood." Tennessee's rule was therefore "absolutely prohibited," and no balancing of interests was required. Justice Brennan argued that

> public debate of religious ideas [may] arouse emotion, [but] the mere fact that a purpose of the Establishment Clause is to reduce or eliminate religious divisiveness or strife, does not place religious discussion, association, or political participation in a status less preferred than rights of [political] participation generally. [Religionists] no less than members of any other group enjoy the full measure of protection afforded speech. [The] antidote which the Constitution provides against zealots who would inject sectarianism into the political process is to subject their ideas to refutation in the market-place of ideas and their platforms to rejection at the polls. With these safeguards [and] with judicial enforcement of the Establishment Clause, any measure of success they achieve must be short-lived, at best.

Justice White concurred in the judgment, relying on the equal protection clause rather than the free exercise clause, because he did not see how the minister "has been deterred in the observance of his religious beliefs."

What result in *McDaniel* under the free speech clause? Is the confidence expressed by Chief Justice Burger and Justice Brennan in the political process warranted? Should a state be precluded from taking a more jaundiced view of the efficacy of the political process in matters of religion?

b. *Churches as political actors.* Larkin v. Grendel's Den, 459 U.S. 116 (1982), held unconstitutional a statute granting churches and schools the power to veto the issuance of liquor licenses to restaurants within five hundred feet of the church or school buildings. The Court acknowledged the "interest in being insulated from certain kinds of commercial establishments," but found that delegating the veto power to churches had the effect of advancing religion and "provides a significant symbolic benefit to religion in the minds of some." Further, the statute "enmeshes churches in the exercise of substantial governmental powers." Note that delegation of similar authority to other private organizations is unlikely to raise federal constitutional questions.

Justice Souter, writing only for a plurality in *Kiryas Joel*, regarded the New York statute as a delegation of state power to a religious institution, barred by *Larkin*. Justice Scalia's dissent called "breathtaking" this "steamrolling of the difference between civil authority held by a church, and civil authority held by members of a church." It "boils down to the quite novel proposition that any group of citizens (say, the residents of Kiryas Joel) can be invested with political power, but not if they all belong to the same religion. Of course such disfavoring of religion is positively antagonistic to the purposes of the Religion Clauses."

## Note: *Concluding Observations*

Do the preceding materials demonstrate that contemporary religion clause doctrine is hostile to religion in the name of neutrality? In a religiously pluralist nation with an expansive government, is neutrality toward religion possible? Are the two religion clauses incompatible in such a nation? The establishment clause requires (some sort of) neutrality, while the free exercise clause requires (some sort of) preference to religion and may permit other preferences. Does the concept of benevolent neutrality reconcile the clauses? When does a permissible benevolence become a prohibited encouragement? Consider whether the religion clauses are incompatible because of religious pluralism: Any purported benevolent encouragement of some or many religions will discourage others; given the range of actions required by some religions and prohibited by others, no regulation can be neutral in its effects as between some religions and others or between religion and nonreligion.

# Table of Cases

# Table of Authorities